Supporting institutions and services

A variety of institutions and activities including the training of teachers, research and development, and educational television services are discussed in this volume. It describes in detail the creation and growth of the Ontario Institute for Studies in Education and its research activities, and gives an account of the educational activities of institutions such as the Royal Ontario Museum, the CBC, and the provincial libraries.

W.G. FLEMING studied at Queen's University and the University of Toronto (MEd, Ed D). He has taught elementary (1941–3) and high school (1948–54) and was principal of an intermediate school in the province of Quebec (1943–5). He joined the faculty of the University of Toronto in 1954 and since that time has been a researcher and instructor in the graduate school. He was assistant director of the Department of Educational Research from 1962 to 1966 and was the first coordinator of research and assistant director of the Ontario Institute for Studies in Education. At present he is professor of education at the University of Toronto and at OISE. He has travelled widely, studying and making recommendations on educational planning, and other matters.

ONTARIO'S EDUCATIVE SOCIETY / V

Supporting institutions and services

W.G. FLEMING

UNIVERSITY OF TORONTO PRESS

Toronto and Buffalo
Reprinted in paperback 2017

Volume v

ISBN 978-0-8020-3271-3 (cloth)
ISBN 978-1-4875-9864-8 (paper)

Volumes I–V (set)
ISBN 0-8020-3258-3
Microfiche ISBN 0-8020-0079-7
LC 77-166928

Preface

The series entitled ONTARIO'S EDUCATIVE SOCIETY, of which this volume is the fifth, deals with many formal and informal aspects of education as they have developed in Ontario in recent years. The province of Ontario is particularly suitable for a study of this kind. Its population of approximately 7.5 million, the largest of any Canadian province, demonstrates a rich and varied mosaic of cultures and traditions. Its extended territory includes a wide range of topographical and climatic features shaping the lives of its people in many different ways. During the post-war period it has surged with unprecedented life and vitality, striding ahead in population, in resource development, in technology, and in culture. As both a highly developed and a rapidly developing society, it offers examples of many of the problems and difficulties involved in meeting the challenges of the modern world.

Recent educational progress in Ontario has been impressive in both quantity and quality. Such a judgment has been made by numerous observers from other provinces and from abroad. This does not mean, of course, that the province has become the universal model; in some respects it is in the process of catching up with developments already completed elsewhere. It is perhaps not unreasonable to suggest, however, that many of its achievements are at least worthy of attention, if not of emulation, in other parts of the world.

Education is defined in a broad sense to include training activities of many kinds, even those with very limited goals. Such treatment does not imply that there is no value in distinguishing between education and training as concepts. The danger in dwelling excessively on such distinctions is that it becomes difficult to discern the larger pattern in which both types of activity have a part. They are often in practice so inextricably intertwined that any effort at separate treatment becomes highly artificial.

The reader will be conscious of two somewhat different approaches, one for the great majority of events and developments, where I have been largely or exclusively a bystander, and the other for situations where I have had some significant personal involvement. Examples of the latter are the operation of the departmental grade 13 examination system and the origin and early expansion of the Ontario Institute for Studies in Education. No matter what the topic, I have attempted to present an objective factual account. However, where direct experience has seemed to justify it, I have been much freer about offering opinions and assessments than where my material has been obtained at second hand. I trust that I have been successful in keeping fact separated from opinion. A second feature distinguishing the two types of material is that I have presented a relatively large amount of information about the developments in which I have had a substantial role. As a result, my attempt to present a fairly complete overview of education in Ontario has perhaps been somewhat distorted. I can only hope that there is value in the more thorough treatment which I have felt particularly qualified to provide.

For the whole series I have used the title ONTARIO'S EDUCATIVE SOCIETY. In doing so, I have deliberately obscured a valid distinction between the ideal and the actual. Imperfect human society will not soon be truly educative in the sense that education in all its manifestations is universally accepted as the central activity to which all others are subordinated. Yet if modern civilization, and even humanity itself, is to survive, I firmly believe that there will have to be a strong and consistent move in that direction. Future generations, if any, will have to ask themselves first of any activity: "Is it educative?" Only when they have answered affirmatively will they then be justified in asking: "Is it productive of material goods?" "Is it entertaining?"

If Ontario does not yet, strictly speaking, have an educative society, a study of the record of recent years suggests that remarkable strides have been made toward that objective. The extension of formal opportunities for learning has been impressive enough in itself. When one also considers the multiplicity of informal influences that are actually or potentially educative, the over-all effect is awesome. It is possible to feel in moments of optimism that the ultimate ideal is not completely unattainable.

Volume I, *The expansion of the educational system*, provides an introduction to the whole series, in which some of the major contemporary issues and problems in education are discussed briefly, followed by seven chapters containing most of the quantitative information in compact form. For many readers it may serve chiefly for reference purposes. Volume II, *The administrative structure*, deals with the development and functions of the Department of Education and of local school systems, the financing of education, and the educational activities of the provincial and federal governments. Volume III, *Schools, pupils, and teachers*, covers the evolution of the school structure and curriculum, and attempts to show how the process of education has operated up to the end of secondary school. Volume IV, *Post-Secondary and adult education*, deals with the development and activities of universities, colleges of applied arts and technology, and other institutions of post-secondary education, as well as with public and private training activities in business and industry. Volume V, *Supporting institutions and services*, relates to a variety of institutions and activities such as teacher preparation, research and development, educational television services, and externally administered examinations. Volume VI, *Significant developments in local school systems*, indicates some of the educational contributions arising chiefly from local initiative. Volume VII, *Educational contributions of associations*, attempts to demonstrate the extent to which educative activities in Ontario are initiated and conducted through voluntary effort as a supplement to formal and official services. A companion volume to the series, *Education: Ontario's preoccupation*, contains a review of the main highlights of educational development in Ontario, with less emphasis on fact and more on interpretation.

The main focus of the series is on the recent period. An attempt was made to record developments of major importance up to early 1970, just before the first five volumes were delivered to the publisher. Volumes VI and VII, which were written during the latter part of the same year, contain a certain amount of more recent material. Very few additions or changes were made during the editorial stage. The result is that a number of the speculations about future developments have already lost some of the value they might have had earlier.

The treatment of the topic is essentially descriptive. As a means of conveying a reasonable understanding of recent developments, it was thought desirable to trace the origins of many current institutions and practices back into the nineteenth century. For the relevant material in the earlier period, I have relied almost exclusively on secondary sources. Treatment of the last four decades, particularly the period since the Second World War, involved increasing use of primary data.

Acknowledgments

I am deeply indebted to the Honourable William G. Davis, Minister of Education and of University Affairs at the time of writing, for providing me the full co-operation of his departments in the production of the series of volumes constituting ONTARIO'S EDUCATIVE SOCIETY. In this task I was given access to all pertinent material in the two departments under his direction. His officials at the time of writing, headed by Dr J.R. McCarthy, Deputy Minister of Education, and Dr E.E. Stewart, Deputy Minister of University Affairs, were also extraordinarily co-operative and helpful. I am particularly grateful to these officials for enabling me to pursue the work in a way that most appeals to a member of the university community: that is, I was completely free to choose, present, and interpret the facts according to my own best judgment. I did not feel the slightest pressure to adapt or modify the material in any way so as to present an "official" version of educational developments in Ontario. As a consequence, I am completely responsible for any opinions or interpretations of the facts that the work contains. The generous assistance for the project provided by the Ontario government, without which publication would have been impossible, does not involve any responsibility for the contents.

I would like to express my particular gratitude to those who assisted me so devotedly in the project: Miss L. McGuire, my loyal secretary, who served from the time the work began in the spring of 1968, Mrs E. West, who also served with extraordinary devotion and competence during most of the same period, and Mrs S. Constable, Miss D. McDowell, and Mrs G.J. Moore, each of whom participated during an extended period. Mr C.H. Westcott, who served as Executive Assistant to the Minister of Education and University Affairs, gave me continuous encouragement and helped to deal with practical problems relating to production and publication. Particularly helpful advice and information were given by Dr C.A. Brown, Professor E.B. Rideout, and Dr J.A. Keddy. Arrangements by Dr G.E. Flower to relieve me of the majority of my other professional obligations during most of a three-year period are also greatly appreciated. In addition, I would like to acknowledge my general indebtedness to the hundreds of people who supplied information so willingly in a variety of forms. That I am unable to name them all individually does not mean that I am any the less grateful for their contributions.

W.G. FLEMING
June 1971

Contents

ONTARIO'S EDUCATIVE SOCIETY / V

Supporting institutions and services

ONE

The development of facilities and certification requirements for the preparation of elementary school teachers

THE BACKGROUND

Ontario has never been noted for the importance it has placed on the formal preparation of its elementary school teachers. In fact, it has lagged conspicuously behind some other Canadian provinces, to say nothing of advanced countries in other parts of the world. The slowness with which early provisions were made and the lengthy period required before the majority of schools were staffed with certificated teachers established a trend that had not yet been decisively reversed even in 1970.

First provision for formal training

The Common School Act of 1843 authorized counties to establish and maintain county model schools to improve the qualifications of teachers of common schools. This provision constituted the first recognition on the part of the Ontario government of the need to prepare teachers for their work. The government did not, at this stage, go so far as to provide any financial support. The model schools were basically designed to give prospective teachers an opportunity to observe what were intended to be examples of worthy practice.[1] The plan did not arouse general interest and was soon superseded by other arrangements.

Establishment of the Toronto Normal School

The next major step was taken in 1847 on the initiative of Egerton Ryerson, when a normal school was opened in Toronto. The word "normal" in this context meant that the program was offered "according to rule."[2] For many years a five-month course was given twice each year for students with or without previous teaching experience. In 1850–2, a nine-month course was provided; it was dropped partly for the ostensible reason that it was too arduous and adversely affected the health of the students, but the lack of enrolment probably carried more weight. Graduates of the five-month course received Second Class Certificates. Separate model schools for males and females, established in 1848, were Separate model schools for males and females, established in 1848, were attached to the Toronto Normal School to allow for observation and practice teaching, despite the fact that the program was more academic than professional.

Township model schools

Provision was made in 1850 for a system of township model schools. These were simply specially designated elementary schools where teachers or potential teachers could observe existing practice under some kind of supervision. Those who attended ordinarily had only an elementary school education. Their attendance was not related to the process of certification.

After 1847 certificates were granted by county boards to those who had attended at least one session of the normal school and received its recommendation. In 1850 the Chief Superintendent of Education undertook the granting of the Certificate of Qualification under the same conditions.[3] Certificate-holders were of course a select group, since the great majority of practising teachers lacked formal qualifications. A further step was taken toward the tightening of central control in 1875 with the prescription of courses leading to First and Second Class Certificates.

County model schools

Ryerson hoped that the system of teacher education would evolve toward an adequate network of normal schools that would soon supersede other provisions. In 1874 he proposed the addition of three more normal schools in London, Kingston, and Ottawa. For the time being, the only one established was the Ottawa Normal School, with an attendant model school. In 1877 the province committed itself to a system of county model schools, of which there were forty-seven by 1880.[4]

As C.E. Phillips describes the situation, the principal of the model school held a First Class Certificate and three assistant teachers had Second Class or higher certificates. The student teachers underwent a brief apprenticeship and a little instruction, reinforced by lectures from the local inspector.[5] The final examination was conducted by the county board of examiners, which was appointed by the county council, and consisted of the inspector or inspectors having jurisdiction within the county, together with two other persons with qualifications prescribed by the Department of Education. The successful candidate, who was supposed to show academic proficiency, was awarded a Third Class Certificate valid for three years. Renewal depended on evidence of efficiency and aptitude, as well as of improved academic standing.[6]

Those attending county model schools were supposed to have the Third Class non-professional Certificate, awarded after at least two years of high school, as an admission requirement. After a year or two more of teaching, those who had serious professional aspirations attended high school for another year, unless they already had more than the minimum academic qualifications, and then took the normal school course. They might further upgrade their qualifications by attaining academic standing equivalent to senior matriculation or higher and, after further normal school training, obtain a First Class Certificate. A disappointingly small number, however, proceeded this far. In 1893 the Junior Leaving Certificate, requiring at least three years of attendance at high school, replaced the Third Class non-professional Certificate as a requirement for admission to the model schools. Later the high school academic course required for admission was extended to four years.

McCutcheon offers the following assessment of the weaknesses of the model schools.

> Their sessions were too short; the professional training afforded was little more than introductory to a proper course; the opportunities for observation and practice-teaching were too limited; and they lacked facilities to incorporate such new subjects as nature study, manual training, and household science, and were thus unable to keep abreast of the times. In addition, they had the effect of supplying the schools with too large a percentage of teachers possessing the lowest grade of professional certificate, a condition which required many years to remedy.[7]

A majority of teachers had no better than a Third Class Certificate at the end of the century. Furthermore, only a small proportion of model school graduates continued on to take the normal school course. Harris notes the argument that practical necessity leads to practical results, but questions whether the results really deserved that description.[8] J.G. Althouse, Chief Director of Education from 1944 to 1956, referred to the devastating effect of the model schools on the status of the profession and declared that they succeeded only in handing over the vast majority of the schools to the half-trained and immature.[9]

A better appraisal of the situation might be to say that nothing more satisfactory than the county model schools was politically feasible for some time. It is, of course, always a question of the extent to which political and educational leaders can be expected to mould public opinion as compared with the extent to which they are controlled by it. That there were difficult problems is indicated by the reaction to the abolition of these schools. Since many rural school boards were unable or unwilling to pay the salaries demanded by normal school graduates, the Department of Education was forced to supplement the seven normal schools with a number of provincial model schools. These increased in number from seven in 1908 to thirteen in 1911 and were not finally abolished until 1924. The model school idea was not completely abandoned in all its forms until the schools associated with the normal schools at Ottawa and Toronto were discontinued in 1940 and 1941 respectively.

Early development of normal schools

In 1877 an applicant for admission to normal school was expected to have an academic Second Class Certificate, one session's experience at a county model school, and one year's successful teaching experience. There were only slight changes for approximately thirty years, when the county model schools were abolished. After that, teaching experience was not demanded, and the requirements were a Normal School Entrance or higher academic certificate, a certificate of moral character, and a physician's certificate. Candidates had to be at least eighteen years of age and, if successful, had to teach in Ontario for at least one year.[10] In 1904 the normal school course was extended to a full year but with little apparent change in the nature of the program. An optional second-year course was added in 1930. Although McCutcheon declares that it was a success, it was discontinued in 1934 after being made compulsory only the year before.[11] Financial considerations apparently had a good deal to do with this decision.

The Provincial School of Pedagogy was established in 1890 to assume the responsibility for preparing candidates for the First Class Certificate. The normal schools at Toronto and Ottawa were left with the program for the Second Class Certificate, supplemented after 1885 with a special course for the preparation of kindergarten teachers in Toronto. The London Normal School, established in 1900, those opened at Hamilton, Peterborough, and Stratford in 1908, and that at North Bay in 1909 prepared candidates only for the Second Class Certificate, with the addition, in the latter, of a model school course. A candidate for a Second Class Certificate who passed in practice teaching and failed by only a small margin in the academic work might receive a Limited Third Class Certificate valid for five years in schools unable to secure the services of a teacher with higher qualifications. In 1920 a program for the First Class Certificate was reinstated in the normal schools, and in 1936 that for the Second Class Certificate was discontinued except in the University of Ottawa Normal School.[12]

Unlike the practice in the county model schools, the normal schools originally granted permanent certificates to successful graduates. After 1908 the initial certificates were permanent only for graduates twenty-one years of age and over; younger candidates attained the same status on reaching that age. The introduction of the second-year normal school course in 1930 involved an important change in that attendance in this course, after not less than two or more than four years of teaching experience, was required in order to obtain a permanent certificate. After 1934 further study at a university or through departmental summer courses replaced this requirement. In 1951 under pressure of the serious shortage of teachers, there was a further relaxation of standards; it became possible for an interim teaching certificate to be made permanent on submission of evidence of two years' successful teaching experience.

Special provisions for teachers for bilingual schools

As a response to the needs of the bilingual schools in certain parts of Ontario, the first English-French training school, really a type of model school, was opened at Ottawa in 1907, and a second at Sturgeon Falls three years later. More of these followed in subsequent years, but the establishment of the University of Ottawa Normal School in 1927 made a superior form of preparation available for bilingual teachers, and by 1935 the last of the bilingual model schools were discontinued.

The Royal Commission on Education in Ontario, which reported in 1950, made recommendations that were never acted upon to accommodate the training of bilingual teachers in other institutions. Hinging on the proposal to establish provincial junior colleges of education, they read as follows:

(a) that the agreement between the Minister of Education and the Corporation of the University of Ottawa for the establishment and operation of the University of Ottawa Normal School be cancelled, in accordance with Section 12 of the said agreement;

(b) that the professional preparation of prospective teachers for publicly supported elementary schools in which French is a subject of study and language of instruction and communication with the permission of the Minister be afforded as a part of a two-year programme ... for training prospective teachers for publicly supported elementary schools, through the provision of additional special courses in one or more, as may be necessary, of the provincial junior colleges of education.[13]

DECLINING STANDARDS IN THE 1940S AND 1950S

Although the Second Class Certificate was offered for a time after 1935 only in the University of Ottawa Normal School, it made a comeback between 1944 and 1953, when it was awarded after the successful completion of two six-week summer courses. In 1940 the entrance requirement for the course for the First Class Certificate specified credit for eight grade 13 papers, as compared with the nine that had been required after 1935. In 1944 this requirement was reduced to seven credits and in 1945 to five, but students holding fewer than eight were granted only Deferred Interim First Class Certificates upon completion of their course. The certificate was upgraded to Interim First Class when the candidate had met the academic deficiency. In 1948 the Interim Certificate was granted without deferment to successful students who had been admitted with credit for a minimum of five papers. In 1953 the requirement was restored to eight papers. The fact that only one of these need be in English caused a good deal of criticism.

Along with this raising of the requirement for the regular one-year course leading to the Interim First Class Certificate, two other routes to certification were provided. One was a two-year course offered in all normal schools, subsequently called teachers' colleges, except the one at the University of Ottawa. The admission requirement was the Ontario Secondary School Graduation, or grade 12, Diploma of the General course. It was hoped that the program would attract a reasonable number of capable students. It was also intended to, and did, appeal to a group who had poor prospects of success in grade 13. One teachers' college master has suggested that about half those enrolled in the course had good potential and about half were very poor. The capacity of the group as a whole would have formed almost a bimodal curve. Those in the first group, whose work was considered to be on a par with that of grade 13 students, were inclined to be of an outgoing type.

According to people involved at the time, the new course was introduced without consultation with teachers' college principals or staffs and with little advance warning. Rather than planning a sequential program involving an adequate balance between academic and professional work, the teachers' colleges initially offered much the same professional program to the same students for two years in succession. At least the students may be assumed to have had the benefits of observation and practice in a reasonably wide range of circumstances. After the program was properly organized, the subject offerings were complementary, with the introduction of some subjects delayed until the second year.

An even more controversial program was the so-called Pre-Teachers' College summer course offered for the first time in the summer of 1952 to applicants with the same qualifications as those admissible to the two-year course. After a successful summer course of six weeks' duration, student teachers received temporary certificates valid for one year in the elementary schools of the province. Holders of these certificates were expected to return for a second course the following summer to qualify for a one-year renewal of the certificates. After the completion of the two summer courses, they would be eligible for admission to the one-year course at a teachers' college leading to an Interim First Class Certificate.

It was claimed that this particular combination of formal preparation and practical experience produced some very seasoned and competent teachers, and no doubt it did. But the fact was that the attrition rate was very great, and large numbers of pupils were taught by teachers with no more than the first six-week instalment of preparation. According to inspectors who were in service at the time, some of the teaching by such individuals was execrable. One area superintendent on the point of retirement in 1968 made a comparison between the graduates of the emergency program for the Second Class Certificates begun in 1944 and this group. In the former case, there was an effective selective process operating to separate those who were capable of securing higher academic qualifications from those who were not. In the latter, the situation was not nearly so clear-cut, and a much smaller proportion of really effective teachers emerged.

By comparison with developments in Alberta during this period, Ontario's progress, if it can be called that, was extremely limited in concept and practice. In 1945 Alberta abandoned its normal schools and turned over the responsibility for teacher preparation to the University of Alberta. A four-year program was instituted for teachers at all levels, leading to the Bachelor of Education degree. The hope was that all teachers would ultimately enter the profession through this route. During the initial stages, elementary school teachers were expected to attend university for two years before beginning to teach and to complete the degree requirements in summer sessions. For a time an emergency one-year course was offered as a pre-service alternative because of the teacher shortage. The machinery for successive improvements in the program had, however, been established. Phillips lists several creditable outcomes from the new plan: 1 / it gave prospective teachers the opportunity to associate with those preparing for other professions; 2 / it provided for university levels of instruction; 3 / it helped to raise the status of elementary school teaching; 4 / it brought elementary and secondary school teachers into closer association; 5 / it encouraged teachers to improve their qualifications, since all further education during service counted toward a degree.[14]

W.J. Dunlop, at this time Ontario Minister of Education, was in a very difficult position. No matter what the critics might say, political realities demanded a body in every classroom. The unusual disproportion between the age-group born in the years of the depression of the 1930s and the school population, which was beginning to reflect the post-war fertility explosion, meant that levels of capacity and preparation considerably below the ideal had to be drawn on if the emergency was to be met. One group of critics expounded the theory that higher salaries for teachers would provide the answer and cited the paradox that, in some institutions where admission requirements had been raised, the number of available candidates had risen, apparently because of the increased prestige of the course. But, although there are circumstances in which this argument may be valid, a little population arithmetic reveals that the problem in Ontario at the time could not have been solved by such an approach. There were too many professions and occupations pursuing too small a group.

A more valid criticism was advanced by the teachers' federations. While recognizing the need for additional recruits to the profession, they complained that the First Class Certificate was being cheapened in being granted for an inferior course. The revival of the Second Class Certificate, as had been done for the 1944–53 emergency program, seemed a much more satisfactory arrangement.

Dunlop did his case little good by the kind of defence he mounted for his course of action. He refused persistently to acknowledge the extent of the teacher shortage, except to proclaim from time to time that it was over. One official was required to deliver an address denying that the shortage existed while he had hundreds of letters on his desk from school board representatives complaining that they could not find enough teachers. In 1955 Dunlop proclaimed in the Legislature:

... everyone has heard of the shortage of teachers. I am pleased to say, that the shortage of elementary teachers has now been averted, and we have enough elementary teachers for the public and separate schools, under present conditions ... the shortage of elementary teachers has been definitely, explicitly and emphatically, averted for the present at least.[15]

Speaking on the same occasion of the emergency summer course program, he said: "In effect that was an adjustment of standards and not lessening them ... We did not reduce standards at all. We readjusted them slightly to give the training in another way." As to the graduates of the emergency program, Dunlop consistently proclaimed their virtues. In 1956 he asserted that "the inspectors have told me that these young teachers are doing well. The principals of the teachers' colleges tell me that they are among their best students, and the whole thing has been a complete success."[16] He tended to answer criticisms of the program with praise of the character and devotion of the young people so inadequately trained. The logic of his position seemed at times to be that, with enough of these qualities, no formal training would be needed at all. The assertion that Ontario had the finest young people in the world might rest on doubtful foundations, but it was not easy for political opponents to challenge. Donald MacDonald continually tried to make the point that, however fine these people were, they would have been better teachers had they had more adequate preparation.

There were times when Dunlop came closer to the real point. For example, during the presentation of the Department of Education estimates in 1958 he argued that "a condition that has grown up for more than 20 years can scarcely be cured under 10 years anywhere. We began these courses in 1952, and we shall have to carry them on, I think, because we have the few to teach the many."[17] He referred with satisfaction to a discussion that was reputed to have taken place at the Canadian Conference on Education, where someone suggested that each member of the group declare what he himself would have done under the emergency conditions of 1952. "They discussed it from that angle for quite a while, and then they came to the conclusion that each of them, in that group, would have done exactly what I have done to solve the situation."[18] Apparently no one asked the unthinkable question. Would not some of the pupils who spent their school days in subjection to the worst of these teachers have been better off out of school altogether, where they at least would have had the opportunity of benefiting from life's experiences? The rapid progress of the communications media certainly would have given them opportunities for educative experiences unknown to previous generations.

ADMISSION AND CERTIFICATION IN THE 1950S AND 1960S

Courses for basic certificates

The Royal Commission on Education reviewed the requirements for admission to the normal schools as laid down in 1950. Candidates had to be British subjects, of good character, and able to pass the required medical examination. The distinction between a British subject and a Canadian citizen was still rather indefinite at this time, since the concept of the latter had been established only after the Second World War. A certificate of character represented a recognition of the importance of traditional virtues, but it is doubtful that many candidates who were otherwise qualified were ever stopped by failure to secure one. The medical examination was established at the insistence of the Superannuation Commission in order to reduce the number of claimants of early pensions on grounds of physical disability. It was apparently quite strict during the period of teacher surplus in the late 1930s, since a considerable number of applicants were rejected. This number declined substantially during the next decade. In terms of academic requirements for the First Class course, the minimum standing in five subjects had to include either English literature or English composition. For admission to the University of Ottawa Normal School, in addition to the English requirement, one paper had to be either French literature or French composition. Candidates for the Second Class Certificate in the same institution had to have standing in grades 11 and 12 in English, Special French, mathematics, and social studies. Those wishing to attend the emergency summer course for the Second Class Certificate offered at that time in other normal schools required similar academic qualifications, along with at least five months of experience on a Letter of Permission.

The First Class Certificate was replaced by the Elementary School Teacher's Certificate in 1956. For admission to the one-year course for that certificate in the 1957–8 session the candidate had to have standing in eight grade 13 papers, one of which was to be in English literature or English composition or, alternatively, a degree approved by the minister from a university in the British Commonwealth. In lieu of the indicated grade 13 standing, however, successful completion of any one of the following courses was acceptable: 1 / the first year at Assumption College; 2 / the first year at Carleton College; 3 / the preliminary year at McMaster University; 4 / the first year at the University of Ottawa; 5 / the first year at the University of Western Ontario; 6 / the two-year course in Childhood Management at the Ryerson Institute of Technology; 7 / the two-year course in Home Economics at the Ryerson Institute of Technology; 8 / the two-year course in Art Education for Prospective Teachers at the Ontario College of Art. The last two qualifications were acceptable only at the Toronto Teachers' College.[19] In 1958 the first year at the University of Sudbury, with a prescribed course in English, was added to the list of grade 13 alternatives. By 1962, the preliminary year at McMaster and the University of Western Ontario and the Ontario College of Art courses were dropped and the preliminary year at Waterloo University College added.

The academic requirement for the two-year course and for the completing course that succeeded the Pre-Teachers' College summer courses was the Secondary School Graduation Diploma of the General course with at least three options. At this time, most recipients of the three-option diploma were regarded as inferior to those receiving the four-option diploma in ability, application, or both. Those entering the completing course had to have, in addition, two years of successful teaching on a temporary certificate.

Three regular programs were available at the University of Ottawa Teachers' College at that time. 1 / There was a one-year course leading to the Interim Elementary School Teacher's Certificate, which differed from that for the other colleges in that one of the eight papers had to be in French literature or French composition. If the first year at the University of Ottawa was offered instead of grade 13, the courses had to include certain prescriptions in English and Français. 2 / Admission to the one-year course leading to the Deferred Interim Elementary School Teacher's Certificate, to which there was at this time no counterpart in the other colleges, required standing in five grade 13 papers, of which one was to be a paper in English and another in French. The 'deferred' qualification would be removed on completion of the eight papers required for the course leading to the Interim Elementary School Teacher's Certificate. 3 / For admission to the one-year course leading to the Interim Second Class Certificate, the requirement was a Secondary School Graduation Diploma of the General course with at least three options, one of which was to be French literature or French composition.

The University of Ottawa Teachers' College offered a series of three summer sessions as compared with two in the other colleges. Success in the first of these led to the award of a Deferred Interim Second Class Certificate valid for one year in the public and separate schools in which the minister had approved the use of French as the language of instruction. Success in the second summer school led to a renewal of this one-year certificate and, in the third summer school, to the award of an Interim Second Class Certificate, valid for five years in the same schools. Admission requirements to the first of these sessions were similar to those in the other teachers' colleges except for the special qualification in French. The three-option diploma, however, continued to be accepted after a four-option diploma was specified for the others.

According to a policy established in 1950, each teachers' college candidate was interviewed by a representative of a Teachers' College Committee of Selection. The principal of each college acted as chairman of the committee, and the members were drawn from the staff of the college, elementary school inspectors, and members of the Ontario Teachers' Federation. Members of the committee went around to secondary schools, where they interviewed prospective applicants. Opportunities were provided at the same time for interviewing "mature persons" in the community who held the academic qualifications required for admission and were interested in entering the teaching profession. Those with experience on this committee comment that it was not an effective screening device. In the absence of well-defined criteria other than the possession of necessary academic qualifications, few candidates failed to get the benefit of any doubt about their promise. In 1969 a senior department official dismissed the whole selection procedure as "window-dressing."

In 1959 the requirement for admission to the two-year course and to the Pre-Teachers' College summer course, offered in Toronto and Port Arthur, was raised to a four-option Grade 12 Diploma obtained before September 1 of the year of admission. The increased supply of teachers with higher qualifications was offered as the justification for the change.[20] The program was phased out after the last second-year course was provided in 1961. It was possible at this time also to discontinue the summer courses at the University of Ottawa Teachers' College leading to the Second Class Certificate. Meanwhile, what was described as a raising of standards of admission to teachers' colleges involved the requirement of credit in both English literature and English composition rather than one of the two.

Although quantitative growth of the supply of teachers has been dealt with primarily in volume I, it may be noted here that the number in the in-service summer and follow-up courses had been declining rapidly. The number entering them fell from 1,120 in 1958 to 734 in 1959, and to 562 in 1960. Approximately 5,100 students, of whom 3,336 were in the one-year course, graduated in 1961. According to the *Report of the Minister, 1961*, this number slightly exceeded the requirements of the elementary schools.

The ultimate end of the two-year course was foreshadowed by two aspects of departmental policy: 1 / prospective candidates were warned that admissions might have to be limited, and that those with the minimum qualifications could be given no assurance that they would be accepted, and 2 / students planning to enter the profession were advised to obtain the grade 13 standing required for admission to the one-year course. In 1965 and 1966, the first and second years respectively of the two-year course were discontinued.

In a retrospective assessment of the emergency courses offered as alternatives to the one-year course during the period of teacher shortage, Davis commented in 1966: "I think that without these emergency courses, there would have been in this province hundreds of classrooms staffed by personnel who had not had the benefit of any professional training."[21] In theory, the two-year course need not have been an inferior alternative to grade 13 plus a one-year program of professional preparation. A number of advantages might have been cited in its favour. A combination of a rigorous academic program comparable to that offered in grade 13 with a professional program extending over two years might have provided a more adequate professional orientation and a better opportunity to see relationships between the academic and professional elements. The weakness from the beginning was that the course had the reputation of being intended for candidates of inferior academic promise. This factor practically compelled the colleges to tolerate an inferior academic standard. Of course, the offering of a real counterpart to grade 13 programs would have demanded teachers with a different background from that of most college masters, whose teaching experience naturally tended to be in elementary schools.

An important new certification plan, announced in 1962, was designed to formalize recognition of in-service credits for university work and for departmental summer or equivalent winter courses. According to the new scheme, the basic requirement for all four standards of the Elementary School Teacher's Certificate was successful completion of the one-year course at a teachers' college. Additional requirements for higher standards were as follows: Standard 2 – credit for five university courses beyond the grade 13 level, for which the candidate might substitute the same number of departmental summer or equivalent winter sessions; Standard 3 – ten university credits, for which the candidate might substitute no more than five departmental summer or equivalent winter sessions; Standard 4 – a Bachelor of Arts degree from an Ontario university or a degree judged by the minister to be equivalent. The Interim Certificate was henceforth to be valid for five years. Regardless of which standard applied, it could be made permanent on the recommendation of an inspector after two years of successful teaching. This series of standards was seen as a convenient means whereby minimum teachers' qualifications might be upgraded step by step. It might be possible simply to drop successive steps until a degree was eventually required of all teachers.

At the same time that the two-year course was ended in most of the colleges, a new two-year program with comparable admission requirements was introduced at the University of Ottawa Teachers' College in 1966, and in the Sudbury Teachers' College the following year. This program led to the Interim Elementary School Teacher's Certificate, Standard 1 and marked the end of courses in the two colleges leading to the Second Class Certificate.

Certain changes in requirements for admission to the one-year course followed adjustments in the grade 13 examination system and in the procedures for university admission. As of September 1965 the following three-hour papers, if written successfully, counted as two for purposes of making up the prescribed total of eight: English, Français, French,

German, Greek, Italian, Latin, Russian, and Spanish. An applicant could not claim credit for more than two papers for his standing in any one language. More important was the result of the recommendation of the Grade 13 Study Committee of 1964 to the effect that the number of credits required for entrance to universities be reduced from nine to seven in order to permit greater concentration of effort at the end of secondary school. When this recommendation was implemented in 1967, the teachers' colleges decided to follow suit. But the reduction of their requirements by only one credit now left them in a position of equality in this respect with the universities. Some people chose to regard the change in both types of institutions as a reduction in standards, a view which discounted the hope that more intensive and higher quality work would result from the new policy. In 1969–70 the teachers' colleges moved to a position of full equality with the universities in terms of their standard admission requirements for general courses by demanding a minimum average of 60 per cent. It was practical to take this step because of the plentiful supply of candidates and because of the substantial rise in the mark distribution following the abolition of the departmental examination system after 1967.

The change to the 60 per cent requirement for admission to teachers' colleges was made more quickly than originally intended, for as recently as 1968, it was considered reasonable to hope that the objective could be attained by 1971. In the Legislature Walter Pitman traced some of the implications of the sudden change and voiced some of his misgivings:

> ... the meaning of 60 per cent no longer holds really the same kind of meaning as it did before. What I am asking is: Will those who are being brought into the universities for elementary school training have the same qualifications? We may very well find that with the change in the system in grade 13, we will have many more people with 60 per cent and possibly the whole university system will have to put up its admission requirement and that the universities and the department will feel that 65 per cent under the new system would be a more accurate configuration in terms of deciding who should be best at a university and that 55 per cent and 60 per cent at a college of applied arts and technology. I do not know.[22]

A further step toward higher admission requirements was taken in 1970 with the announcement that the minimum qualification in 1971–2 would be one year of university work. Again, the move was made possible by evidence that numbers of graduates from the teachers' colleges were unable to find positions. There were predictions that teachers' college enrolment in 1970–1 would be comparable to that in 1968–9, with numbers of candidates taking advantage of the last opportunity to gain admission on the basis of the grade 13 qualification.

In 1968 recognition was extended to the work of the colleges of applied arts and technology and to a wider range of courses taken at Ryerson Polytechnical Institute. A student could qualify for admission to a teachers' college by successfully completing a two-year course, or the first two years of a three-year course in any of these institutions with a minimum average of 60 per cent in the second year. Also, beginning in 1968, standing as an associate at the Ontario College of Art was accepted in lieu of the grade 13 requirement. Successful applicants who subsequently obtained an Elementary School Teacher's Certificate might be admitted to a summer course in art leading to a Supervisor's Certificate.[23]

The recent citizenship requirement has meant that an applicant for admission to an Ontario college of education or an Ontario teachers' college, or an applicant for a Letter of Standing, must submit evidence that he is a British subject with "landed immigrant" status, or a Canadian citizen, or has filed a Declaration of Intention to become a Canadian citizen. As of January 1, 1966, the same requirements applied to applicants for admission to the teaching profession. Over the years, there has been a relaxation in the technicalities, but not in the intention of having Ontario children taught by people who are presumed to give first priority to Canadian interests.

Courses for special certificates

Kindergarten and Primary Specialists

A special course for the training of kindergarten teachers was established at the Toronto and Ottawa Normal Schools in 1885. Direct entry into this course was possible until 1914. After that time, it was first necessary to obtain a Second Class Certificate by attending a normal school. The Kindergarten-Primary course set up under such conditions lasted until 1939, when it was replaced by the Primary School Specialist course. The establishment of the latter resulted from the efforts of a special committee appointed by the Minister of Education which recommended the recognition of a primary school unit consisting of the work of the nursery school, kindergarten, and grades 1 and 2. The program for teaching at this level included a first year, coinciding largely with the regular normal school course, and a second year, affording specialized training in the work of the primary school.[24]

The Primary School Specialist course was extended to the Hamilton and Ottawa Teachers' Colleges in 1966. The newly stated alternatives for admission as of 1968 were 1 / an Interim or Permanent Ontario Elementary School Teacher's Certificate, an Interim or Permanent Ontario First Class Certificate, or an equivalent Letter of Standing, or 2 / a certificate that the applicant held a degree from an accredited university approved as to standard and content of courses by the Minister of Education. The three colleges offering this course in 1966 had an enrolment of fifty.

Teachers of French in English-speaking schools

The move to extend the teaching of French into English-speaking schools began to gain momentum in the early 1960s. Particularly in view of the emphasis placed on oral instruction, the inadequacy of the average teachers' college graduate to handle the subject was glaringly evident. Some effort to deal with the problem was made by encouraging the entry of teachers from Quebec and from French-speaking nations abroad. There were, however, certain problems regarding certification, and, for this and other reasons, the number so obtained was not large. The main reliance had to be placed on programs developed in Ontario.

The first summer course for teachers of French in English-speaking elementary schools was offered in Ottawa in 1964 and extended to the Toronto, Lakeshore, and Windsor Colleges in 1965.[25] The limited number of applicants admitted did not require basic teaching certificates but had to have academic qualifications in French equivalent to Ontario grade 13 standing. They had also to demonstrate to a committee appointed by the minister a high degree of fluency in the French language. In common with those admitted to other courses at this time, each applicant had to be a British subject or a Canadian citizen, or to have signed a certificate of intention to become a Canadian citizen. There was also a minimum age requirement of twenty-five years, intended to ensure a high degree of maturity. Course content included a study of current methods, teaching aids, and class organization and objectives. Special emphasis was given to methods of teaching French as a second language. Success in the course led to the award of a temporary certificate as Teacher of French to English-speaking Pupils in Elementary Schools, renewable annually on the recommendation of the inspector.

Another course with somewhat similar objectives was the Intensive French course offered at Elliot Lake in the summer of 1966 and again in 1967. Held under departmental auspices, it was attended by elementary and secondary school teachers desirous of improving their fluency and methodology. Course content included a study of the customs of French Canada and of France and, in 1967, of linguistics. The program was continued at Sainte-Thérèse-de-Blainville, Quebec, in the summer of 1968, and at Compton, Quebec, in 1969.

As of 1968 there were two alternatives to this special course for those wishing to teach French in an English-speaking elementary school. They could, if qualified, take the French option in the regular course at a teachers' college or they could obtain an approved university degree and attend a college of education, where they must include French and the Elementary School option in their program.

Teachers of the deaf

Differing from other full-year courses in that it was offered outside the teachers' colleges was that for the Specialist Certificate as Teacher of the Deaf provided from 1967 on at the Ontario School for the Deaf in Belleville. It was introduced as a result of the increasing need for trained staff in the provincial schools and in regular day school classes for children with impaired hearing. To qualify for admission, a candidate had to have a Letter of Standing to teach in an elementary or secondary school and had to show that he would be employed to teach children with a hearing impairment.

Elementary Music Certificate

Somewhat similar to the special French program was one that provided extra qualifications in music. It was offered to one-year students along with their regular program. They took two hours a week of music along with special practice. If successful, they were awarded an Elementary Music Certificate, Type B.

Teachers for special education

From time to time the Department of Education was urged to improve its provisions for the preparation of teachers for special education. It was often suggested that the one-year course in the teachers' colleges might be adapted to meet this need. The response was to introduce as much course content as possible into the areas of differences in learning ability, factors influencing the efficient use of ability, the nature and needs of exceptional children, and community resources for teacher assistance. Some college programs included a limited amount of supervised observation in opportunity classes. The general objective was to provide all college students with an orientation toward special education. But it was not considered desirable to offer a special program in the one-year course. It was thought that their first year was too soon to give teachers responsibility for classes of exceptional children. Also, the length of the basic program provided serious limitations on what could be covered. Preparation for working with exceptional children required more than the introduction of additional subject matter offered in the form of an option. These considerations did not, of course, explain why preparation of teachers of special groups could not be provided in a second year in the teachers' colleges, rather than being offered exclusively in summer courses.

In the winter issue of the *Toronto Education Quarterly* for 1964–5, R.E. Jones, Assistant Superintendent of Public Schools in Toronto, deplored the lack of adequate facilities for the preparation of teachers for special education.

> The summer courses in Auxiliary Education, excellent in content and in standards of instruction, are of only five weeks' duration and simply cannot cope with the need. In my view, at least a full year's training is needed for teachers

to master the complexities of philosophical background, medical and psychological understandings, and their educational application, required for special education teaching. Perhaps such a course of training could be offered by our teacher training institutions, so that it will not be necessary to send teachers out of the country to obtain adequate qualification. It is of interest that at present the only special class teachers in the province required to have this full year's additional training are teachers of the deaf.[26]

The development of programs of teacher education in the universities is expected to provide an opportunity to devise adequate measures for the preparation of special education teachers. At the time of writing, there was a definite indication that York University would enter this particular field. How many other universities would ultimately participate was still an unsettled question.

Preparation of teachers of pre-school children

There has been no public assumption of responsibility for the preparation of teachers of nursery school or pre-kindergarten children, but assistance at this level has been provided occasionally by certain institutions. McMaster University's Department of Extension, for example, has offered a summer school course in three parts. Following the successful completion of the first two of these, a letter of standing has been issued by the Nursery Education Association, recommending the holder as a student assistant. Completion of the third part has led to certification as a pre-school teacher. The most important recent developments in this field have been the programs established at Ryerson Polytechnical Institute and at a number of the colleges of applied arts and technology. The courses have attracted considerable numbers of candidates and promise to transform the supply situation within a relatively short period of time.

THE EXTENSION OF THE TEACHERS' COLLEGE SYSTEM

The establishment of the first normal school in Toronto was regarded as something of an experiment, or perhaps a hope on the part of Ryerson that a high level of formal teacher preparation would soon emerge. The decision to rely first on township model schools and later on a somewhat superior counterpart established by the counties represented the acceptance of a much more limited objective. The Toronto Normal School remained a kind of elite institute for the minority who were prepared to seek a special level of professional preparation. For many years, Ryerson informally urged the extension of the normal school system to other parts of the province. In a letter to Alexander Mackenzie, then Provincial Treasurer, on October 12, 1872, he mentioned in support of this objective that very few students from the eastern part of the province had been registered at the Toronto Normal School, and that the latter was, in reality, only a local institution serving the community in which it was located. Two years later, at Mackenzie's request for more specific information, he recommended additional schools at Ottawa, Kingston, and London. This recommendation was not definitely rejected, but there was insufficient determination to overcome obstacles at London and Kingston, and decisive action was taken only at Ottawa. The City Council moved to obtain the site on which the institution established in 1875 still stands and conveyed it to the government. Ryerson declared the founding of the Ottawa Normal School his final act on behalf of education for the province.

A further extension of the normal school system occurred with the establishment of an institution in London in 1900. This step was only a very tentative one in terms of the adoption of a new policy. The real change came with the appearance of schools at Hamilton, Peterborough, and Stratford in 1908 and one in North Bay in 1909. They signified an abandonment of the county model school system, a policy change which was not as clearcut as it might have been, since a number of provincial model schools had to be maintained during the transitional period. The establishment of the North Bay Teachers' College in particular seemed a questionable venture. A pamphlet providing a historical sketch of the institution between 1909 and 1959 declares: "It seemed a bold venture to place a large training school some hundreds of miles from any city and in a region so [sparsely] populated." Although the number in attendance for the first few years was small, a total of 7,402 attended during the fifty years after the school was established.

The establishment of the University of Ottawa Normal School was an isolated incident in the expansion of the system of provincial normal schools. It was significant because it corresponded with a change of the official policy toward the bilingual schools from one of relative disfavour and repression to one of cautious positive measures to improve the quality of the program offered. The account of changing conditions for admission and of the succession of certificates offered demonstrates that special efforts have been required up to the present time to secure enough teacher candidates with minimum qualifications to supply the schools in question.

Before the move from the late 1950s to establish new teachers' colleges, the inadequacies of some of the existing institutions had to be faced. In 1955 a step was taken in this direction by the provision of a new building for the Toronto Teachers' College. The decision to locate it in what was then regarded as the outskirts of Metropolitan Toronto was widely criticized. In the Legislature, J.B. Salsberg claimed that the government had ignored appeals and requests made to it by almost every educational institution, by the teachers, and by the students themselves. In "the extreme northeast of the city," where there were zoning regulations in force, the students would find it difficult to obtain accommodation. More important, however, was the fact that the college was being moved too far from the centre of other educational facilities in the city. Students would be unable to use the library of the University of Toronto, the public libraries, and other institutions located within the central area.[27] The minister's answer was that there would soon be a need for another teachers' college in the Toronto area, and he hoped to have one at each end. As far as the university library was concerned, the university did not allow outsiders to use it anyway. In what was probably a serious remark, but today sounds more like an attempt at humour, he said: "I was informed that some people wanted the Teachers' College located in the centre of the city so that students could hear the best preachers on Sunday. I said to them: 'Do you suppose the students are going to go to church from the college or from their boarding houses?' They had not thought of that." The location of the college was later cited as a serious obstacle to the integration of its program with that of the University of Toronto. The alternatives, apart from making no move in this direction at all, were, on the one hand, to try to dispose of a spacious and fairly modern building and, on the other, to forego the intimate association with other university activities that were supposed to do so much for the improvement of teacher preparation.

In the program of new construction, the Hamilton Teachers' College got a modern new building in association with the campus of McMaster University, and London Teachers' College with that of the University of Western Ontario. Much less fortunate were the colleges at Ottawa, Peterborough, Stratford, and North Bay, all left with antique structures, ennobled by tradition and completely inadequate for a modern program of teacher preparation, to say nothing of student enrolments that, particularly in 1968–9, were much larger than they had ever been intended to accommodate. Consisting of little but classrooms, an auditorium, and a couple of offices for the principal and a minimum of supporting clerical staff, these buildings constitute a tangible appeal for a speedy solution of the problem of integrating teacher preparation into the universities. The building of the University of Ottawa Teachers' College was comparable in 1968–9, but the pressure of student enrolment was not as great.

Criticism of the lack of facilities in some of these colleges has been voiced from time to time. In 1962 Leo Troy commented in the Legislature during the discussion of the education estimates:

> In regard to the hon. Prime Minister's physical fitness programme and the recommendations that were made by the committee. It seems to me that those teachers' colleges should be expanded at least to have some facilities for training teachers to put into effect a fitness programme. There are not any facilities to speak of at these teachers' colleges.[28]

Robarts, as Minister of Education, responded that there was no plan to build gymnasiums. There was a large building program to project into the future, and new construction had to take priority over renovations of old buildings.

Dunlop's promise of a new institution for the Metropolitan Toronto area was implemented with the opening of the Lakeshore Teacher's College in 1959. It was followed by additional colleges at the Lakehead in 1960, Windsor in 1962, Sudbury in 1963, and St Catharines in 1965. The Lakehead, Sudbury, and St Catharines Colleges were located so as to facilitate association with neighbouring universities. The Lakeshore and Windsor Colleges were not so conveniently placed. The site factor did not, however, prevent the University of Windsor from reaching an agreement to take over the Windsor Teachers' College program in 1970.

There was special significance in the establishment of the Sudbury Teachers' College. It was designed to extend the facilities for the preparation of teachers for French-speaking pupils, which up to this time had been provided only by the University of Ottawa Teachers' College. A year after the establishment of the Sudbury college, the enrolment in the two institutions rose by 26 per cent. The new college was first housed in temporary quarters in a secondary school and later in a building owned by Laurentian University. In 1968–9 it was still awaiting a permanent building.

TWO

The development of the educational process in institutions for the preparation of elementary school teachers

EARLY PROGRAMS

Before the middle of the nineteenth century, there was little to break the traditional pattern of teaching. There was no formal training program whatever before 1843, and for long after that only a minority of teachers availed themselves of the opportunities that were offered. The first county model schools, and the township model schools established from 1850 on, offered an opportunity for observation of what were considered desirable models. Whether this experience proved particularly beneficial is open to question. For some time after its establishment in 1847, the Toronto Normal School concentrated on academic work paralleling that of the secondary schools. As time went on, it became customary for those admitted to normal school to have one or two years of high school education, the quality of which was at the same time showing substantial improvement. Thus the normal schools began to shift their emphasis to professional preparation, which in those days no one hesitated to call "training."

An informally produced history of the Ottawa Normal School written by T.A. Brown and Miss L.E. Monaghan on the institution's seventy-fifth anniversary gives some idea of the program offered during the first few years. In the single session extending from September 15 to July 15, the classes were divided into two groups known as the First and Second Divisions. The latter was divided in turn into the Junior and Senior Sections. Successful candidates in the First Division received First Class Certificates, and in the respective sections of the Second Division, Second Class A and Second Class B Certificates respectively. The subjects, which were the same for all students, were almost entirely academic, including reading, spelling, writing, grammar, etymology, composition, geography, arithmetic, mensuration, algebra, natural philosophy, physiology, Euclid, education, drawing, music, botany, school law, bookkeeping, and chemistry. Those in the higher division took work at the more advanced level. After the first three years, two sessions were held each year until the full-year sessions were restored in 1908.

J.M. McCutcheon dates the transition of the normal school program from academic to mainly professional training from about 1885.[1]

Preparation for actual practice has continued to be the keynote right up to the present time. The whole procedure was very rigidly controlled by the department, particularly after 1916 when manuals were introduced prescribing in detail how the subjects were to be taught. These stayed in service until 1937. It was not until after 1951 that the responsibility for setting and marking final examinations was delegated to the staffs of the normal schools.

THE BOWERS COMMITTEE

A significant appraisal of the normal school programs appeared in 1950 in a report prepared by a committee of the Ontario Normal School Teachers' Association under the chairmanship of H. Bowers, Principal of the Stratford Normal School.[2] As an explanation for the actions of the association, the preface referred to an impression that the prestige of the normal schools had undergone erosion; that, "instead of mingling their current with the main stream of educational thought and action in the province, [they had] become tranquil pools along its course"; and that a sense of frustration among a number of normal school teachers had arisen from "the maintenance of classification lines so taut as to suggest a rigid caste system."

The Bowers Committee recommended the requirement of a longer period of preparation for teaching as soon as the supply of student-teachers warranted it. It suggested a period of two successive years of training for those who entered with grade 13 standing. The two-year course would be planned carefully to make the second year a definite advance on the first, and to include a good course in psychology. It was thought highly desirable to make the possession of a university degree a definite asset in elementary school teaching. For those who had such a qualification, a higher certificate should be available. The committee foresaw a one-year training course for students with a university degree paralleling a two-year course for those who entered with grade 13 standing.[3] Rather than suggesting integration of the program with that of the universities, the committee recommended that affiliation of the normal schools with the universities be sought, and that consideration be given to the granting of credit for normal school work and departmental summer school courses towards a bachelor's degree.[4]

Considerable dissatisfaction was expressed with the quality of some of the candidates who had been admitted to the existing course. The committee recommended that for a trial period of three years normal school staff should interview prospective students. The value of the practice should be considered at the end of that time, and a decision made as to whether or not to continue it. The committee also recommended that every student be interviewed by a psychologist during the first week of attendance, and that doubtful cases be referred to a panel consisting of at least two psychologists.[5]

With respect to the content of the normal school course of study, the committee asserted that child study should be the central theme: "Every Ontario Normal School student should enter the teaching profession equipped with a knowledge of the child and the learning process as complete as modern investigation and the ability of the student will allow."[6] A large proportion of the student's time must therefore be spent on educational psychology, including child study and mental hygiene. The committee observed that, as a result of the emphasis placed on subject matter in the school of the late nineteenth and early twentieth centuries, elaborate methods for teaching each subject of the curriculum had developed, and specific methods had received increased attention in the normal schools. Although it was agreed that students required assistance in applying general principles of method to particular subjects, the modern trend was toward flexibility of method. The time spent in studying the application of methods to particular subjects might well be reduced. Also, while no staff member had been compelled to follow the details of the prescribed course, as far as the members of the committee knew, except to the extent that the final examination papers involved compulsion, greater autonomy was recommended for each normal school to experiment in the organization and content of the curriculum.

Strong emphasis was placed on the importance of observation and practice teaching. The two main functions of practice teaching were identified as follows: 1 / to provide preliminary experience in teaching, in dealing with atypical pupils, and in coping with managerial situations, and 2 / to provide means by which student-teachers who were poor risks might be identified, and to supply data to justify their elimination. The committee reported considerable disagreement over the effects of a regulation that students should teach at least twenty lessons in urban schools or for at least twenty hours in rural schools during their year of normal school attendance. Those who opposed this regulation claimed that it placed emphasis upon individual blocks of subject matter rather than on the whole topic in its relation to children's needs. Others declared that the units did not have to be assigned in isolation, and suitable co-operation between practice teacher and students could ensure that any bad effects would be avoided.[7]

At that time, some special training was given to practice teachers, but the committee considered it quite inadequate. In one normal school, at least, preliminary practice was given such teachers in marking three lessons before the students began to teach. But even the combination of this practice and guidance throughout the year by weekly bulletins, or staff meetings, or by a combination of bulletins and staff meetings, apparently failed to eliminate "gross variations in standards of marking."[8] The committee recommended that time be allowed at the beginning of the year for practice teachers to receive training in the marking and discussion of not fewer than ten lessons taught by students.

In view of the strongly expressed desire for greater autonomy for the normal schools, it might be supposed that the committee would have recommended the abolition of the centralized examination system. In fact, it did not do so. Not only was it considered desirable to attempt to ensure common standards, but value was also seen in bringing members of the normal school staffs together where they would have opportunities for conference and discussion.[9]

The committee treated its superiors in the department with appropriate deference. Senior officials were said to have a perfect record of granting interviews to members of normal school staffs who had sought them, and to have conducted such interviews with graciousness, consideration, and sincerity. But there were one or two matters that had caused "embarrassment and even chagrin." For instance, there had been considerable variation in the department's practice in consulting the principal when a new appointment was made. It was suggested that the principal at least be informed through official channels of the identity of his future colleagues. Occasionally the department requested and received expressions of opinion from staffs and staff members. Sometimes these had been submitted voluntarily. In some cases they had been accepted with evidence of appreciation, and sometimes completely ignored.[10]

THE BEGINNING OF RELAXATION OF CONTROLS

It is difficult to tell at this stage how much influence the Bowers Committee had on subsequent developments. However, the calendar of the normal schools was revised in 1951 to provide for a further relaxation of the rigid central control imposed on the program up to this time. The courses of study were outlined in more general terms, and the normal schools were given somewhat more responsibility for determining how they would be interpreted. The *Report of the Minister, 1951* declared that principals and staffs assumed a greater share in the planning and presentation of their courses. By present-day standards, however, there was still a great deal of rigidity in the system. The students still had a long list of subjects in which they had to write examinations, and the number of areas of prescribed study tended to counteract any tendency toward flexibility of treatment.

The same report declared that the emphasis in practice teaching shifted from the single lesson to more extended periods of observation and practice. An informal paper reviewing the development of the North Bay Normal School from 1909 to 1959 dated this transition from 1936–7, when students began to go to the practice schools for a full week under the supervision of one teacher in addition to teaching single lessons. Later this period was increased to two weeks in a school near the student's home, following the Christmas and Easter vacations.

The relaxation of controls in the early 1950s was in part a result of the victory of views held by F.S. Rivers, who became Director of Teacher

Education in 1948. His successor, H.E. Elborn, believed that rigid prescription was the way to ensure excellence in the program. His examination procedure involved obtaining submissions from the various colleges from which he distilled a set of questions. The policy of progressive relaxation of controls initiated by Rivers was carried on by Elborn's successors, C.A. Mustard, G.L. Duffin, and G.L. Woodruff. Their main problem lay not in anyone's personal opposition but in traditional methods of operation and established bureaucratic practices.

Over the years the term used to describe the teacher who supervised the student's practice work shifted from "critic" to "practice" to "associate" teacher. The term "practice teacher" is still, however, in general use. The assignment of student teachers was often a relatively mechanical process, and the role of the normal school master or, after 1953, the teachers' college master, was largely one of appraisal rather than of assisting with the student's development.

The limited nature of these reforms was emphasized by the expression of views across Canada. At the meeting of the Canadian Education Association in September 1952 almost unanimous agreement was expressed that a one-year program of initial preparation was insufficient. Leading educators felt that at least an extra year was needed, and that it should be devoted in large measure to subjects of culture, with professional subjects such as educational psychology being explored more fully than in the first year. Canada was said to be the only major nation in the world where a one-year training program was widely used. Nevertheless, it was to be a long time before Ontario demanded anything better.

CONTENT OF EMERGENCY COURSES

The two-year course introduced in 1953 was a combination of academic and professional study, although the range of academic offerings was limited. The subjects included English, geography, history, child psychology, and educational psychology. There were also supplementary subjects such as history of education, the school and the community, audio-visual education, and children's literature.

Students enrolled in the Pre-Teachers' College summer course were expected to attend regularly throughout the session from 8:00 am to 1:00 pm. The principal was empowered to dismiss at any time a student who, in his judgment or that of the staff, seemed to lack the scholarship, personality, or other qualities desirable in a teacher, or for unsatisfactory conduct, progress, or attendance. Regular records were kept on the written and practical work of the students, and those who obtained 66 per cent or higher on such records in any subject might be recommended for exemption from the final examination in that subject. Final examinations were offered in school management, principles of teaching, English, arithmetic, social studies, and primary reading. The minimum pass mark was 60 per cent on each paper.

CONTENT OF ONE-YEAR COURSE

In the teachers' college programs in the regular sessions in the early 1960s, the formal studies included academic and professional subjects such as English, mathematics, science, social studies, art, music, physical and health education, industrial arts, home economics, library methods, religious instruction, methods in religious education, educational psychology, mental health, child study, school management, classroom management, the teacher, the teaching position, and the Ontario school system. It is no wonder that some people feared that the student teachers were in danger of getting mental indigestion.

Between November and April the students spent a total of eight weeks observing and teaching in different schools. Going out in pairs, they observed on Mondays and then alternated teaching assignments for the rest of the week. One taught for the first and fourth quarters and the other for the second and third quarters of the day. The observation and practice teaching schedule gave the students different supervising teachers, partners, schools, grades, and locations each time, so that each one visited twelve different classrooms during the year. At least twice during the year, each student met with the staff to discuss his practice teaching progress. In addition to their own personal observations, the staff took into account the reports of the supervising teachers in the schools where the students had taught.

The final examinations were held in educational psychology, school management, English Part I (methods, grades 1–3), English Part II (methods, grades 4–8), mathematics, social studies, science, art and music, physical education and health, and history and philosophy of education.

STAFF CONFERENCE AT TORONTO TEACHERS' COLLEGE, 1964

A conference of the Ontario Teachers' College Association held in April 1964 during the presidency of D.C.D. Sifton produced a report entitled "Suggested Changes in the One Year Course at the Ontario Teachers' Colleges," edited by J.D. Londerville. This report contained a large number of recommendations about various aspects of the teachers' college program which had varying degrees of influence on later developments. The interest aroused in the possibility of changes was said to have played a part in the establishment of the Minister's Committee on the Training of Elementary School Teachers.

The discussion group which dealt with the selection of student teachers recommended that entrance requirements to the colleges be equated with those for admission from grade 13 to an Ontario university; that candidates for admission to the English-speaking teachers' colleges be expected to have an average of more than 60 per cent on their grade 13 English papers; that candidates for admission to the bilingual teachers' colleges have an average of more than 60 per cent on their English or French papers; that those considering entrance to teachers' colleges be required to take grade 13 history and encouraged to take geography and biological sciences and to supplement these subjects by an adequate knowledge of art and music. The group was opposed to the lowering of standards for admission for candidates with incomplete qualifications.

Various groups made recommendations on the treatment of certain subjects on the college curriculum, such as English, sociology, philosophy and history of education, and psychology. In general, the suggestions reflected a search for greater relevance to the needs of the student teachers. The group dealing with general methodology was concerned in particular about existing overlapping and unnecessary repetition and sought means of co-ordinating the work of masters teaching general methodology and theory and those teaching the methodology of specific subjects. One of its recommendations was the establishment of a course entitled Principles and Practices, which would consist of some of the topics listed under General Methodology as well as some under School Management. General principles would then be exemplified by the masters in charge of the specific methodologies. A co-ordinating committee would ensure concentration on essential principles and on an appropriate distribution of effort. The group advocated greater use of new instructional media, the elimination of one set of examinations, and the establishment of a separate class for university graduates.

A group concerned with specialization criticized the existing arrangement whereby all students were subjected to the same treatment on the grounds that it resulted in a superficial treatment of course content and failed to take account of individual differences in ability and interest. While a remedy might be sought in some degree of specialization, shortage of time would place obvious limitations on this process. The group recommended that students be encouraged to concentrate on the primary and junior levels or the junior and intermediate levels and that provision be made for concentration in particular subject areas. Concentration would be delayed until after Christmas so that students might become familiar with the whole range of the elementary school curriculum and have an opportunity to discover the divisions and subjects in which they were particularly interested. Specialization would be achieved not by dropping one or more subjects but by more intensive study of the subject or subjects of special interest. This process would be facilitated by grouping by interest and ability.

Some of the recommendations of the group discussing practice teaching were that demonstration lessons normally given during September be spread over a greater portion of the school year; that topical outlines of lessons for continuous weeks be forwarded to students by practice teachers one week in advance; that the practice teacher direct students' observation step by step, e.g., by pointing out in advance the steps of the intended lesson, the type of questioning to be used, and the proposed method in each case; that practice teachers be encouraged to give a written as well as an oral evaluation of each day's work during a continuous week; that students with a special interest or with special qualifications in a particular subject such as science, physical education, or music be allowed the option of spending the last week of practice teaching with a teacher of rotary classes in this subject; that during the last week of practice teaching, kindergarten be available as a practice class for those with a particular interest in that level. Measures were proposed for ensuring that competent practice teachers be selected, and that they be given more guidance.

A group discussing university credits for college courses agreed that the existing course was academically limited and inadequate, mainly because of a shortage of time. It was thus recommended that the program be extended to two and eventually three years beyond grade 13. Attempts would be made to get university recognition for particular courses. University staff members might be persuaded to instruct in such courses, thus serving as supplementary members of the college staffs. The establishment of a working relationship with universities might ultimately lead to total integration with them. A less desirable alternative was to develop programs leading to the award of degrees in education by the colleges.

The same group recommended the following emphases in the comprehensive course of the future: 1 / understanding the child, the learning process, the adjustment process, the social setting of the school; 2 / the aims, purposes, and history of education and the existing curriculum; 3 / understanding of the aims, structure, and techniques of particular subjects or disciplines at various levels; 4 / opportunities to practise in a variety of classrooms; 5 / the development of aesthetic tastes and sensitivities and personal development; 6 / the development of an ability to communicate effectively; 7 / the opportunity for partial specialization in some field or at some academic level.

Some of the most significant contributions came from the group which discussed "the college and local autonomy." This group observed that there had been a definite move toward increased local autonomy during the previous decade and speculated that such a trend might eventually lead to the abandonment of control by the department in favour of commission, university, professional, or local control or to independent status similar to that of the universities. Its recommendations were limited, however, by the assumption that the existing framework would be maintained. Among the most important were the following. 1 / The colleges should be responsible for admission, subject to departmental regulations. 2 / There should be a fee for teachers' college students. 3 / The colleges should be given control of their travel and maintenance budgets within the framework of the amounts budgeted per month, subject to monthly accounting. 4 / Instructional staff should be selected from a wider geographical area and from a broader academic and professional base. 5 / The principal and appropriate staff committees should have a greater responsibility in determining staff requirements and in selecting new staff members. 6 / The department should indicate the broad subject areas of the curriculum while the principal and staff should be responsible for the details of each course, the methods of instruction, period allotments, textbooks, and the amount and type of specialization. 7 / The role of the department should be to provide educational leadership; that of the principal, to supervise and co-ordinate the instructional program; that of subject department heads, to co-ordinate subject areas; and that of staff members, to be responsible for the quality of the teaching. 8 / The colleges should be responsible for the timetabling of their final examinations within the examination period set by the department. 9 / The colleges should be fully responsible for their final results. 10 / The department should, at least for the time being, retain the right of certification.

RECENT PROGRAMS IN THE TEACHERS' COLLEGES

General set-up in 1966

In *Ontario Education News*, Principal S.J. Rogers of the Ottawa Teachers' College described the teachers' college program as it was conducted in 1966.[11] An orientation period, beginning two weeks after school opened and lasting for five weeks, was designed to ease the transition from grade 13 to the new status. In the orientation period, each student did preliminary practice teaching. Once a week he observed an elementary school classroom teacher for half a day and two days later returned to teach a single lesson to the same class. The schools he visited during this period were varied to give him as much experience as possible in different subjects and grades. When he was not engaged in practice teaching at the orientation stage, a student attended classes at the college and took part in a special program called a "demonstration half day," which was designed to familiarize him with teaching methods. Its first phase involved discussion of such matters as the art of questioning, the need to develop rapport between teachers and pupils, and the use of teaching aids. Then the masters demonstrated the application of general methods using a class of children brought in from a local school. In the final phase, the students visited masters to ask questions about teaching in general.

Program and examination reforms in 1968

At the 1967 fall meeting of the principals of Ontario teachers' colleges, a Teachers' College Final Examination Committee was established under the chairmanship of S.J. Rogers. Its terms of reference were considerably broader than its title suggests:

(1) To examine the emergency curricula of the professional One-Year Course in Teachers' Colleges, to consider the pertinent recommendations of the

Report of the Minister's Committee on the training of elementary school teachers, and to consider the recent restructuring of the Curriculum Branch into: a) Humanities, b) Pure Sciences, c) Social Sciences, and d) General, and, in consequence, to make recommendations to the Director, Teacher Education Branch, reducing the number of Teachers' College final examinations.

(2) To make recommendations to the Director, Teacher Education Branch, relative to any consequently desirable changes in the system of exemptions from final examinations.

(3) To consider and, if necessary, comment upon the implications for future curriculum development of the professional One-year Course at Teachers' Colleges.[12]

The committee offered what it called "self-established guidelines," which were in the nature of principles upon which examination procedures were to be based. The most relevant of these were 1 / that final examinations were a court of appeal for a final judgment and should not be dispensed with completely; 2 / that they should be broad enough in scope to permit course experimentation and expansion, including the possibility of options; 3 / that final examinations which were broad in scope would have to be compulsory, but those testing specific subject matter might permit exemptions; and 4 / that it was not necessary to examine students in the methods of teaching all elementary school subjects and, in any case, a reduction in the number of examinations made this impossible. The acceptance of the second and fourth of these principles in particular freed the curriculum from many of its former rigidities and placed a new type of responsibility on the college staffs. The recommendation that some examinations be compulsory was the only important part of the committee's recommendations that was not accepted by the department.

The committee recommended that, in the teachers' college session of 1968–9, final examinations be reduced from ten to five. Those in Group I, foundations of education, would be in educational psychology and philosophy of education; those in Group II, curriculum and instruction, would be in administration, teaching methods, and curriculum construction and content. Examinations in the last two would be compulsory, while those in the other three would be subject to current regulations regarding exemptions. The committee commented that there was nothing in the recommendations to conflict with the recent division of the Curriculum Branch of the department into four sections. But to apply such a division to teachers' college final examinations would, in the committee's view, require expansion or subdivision of two of the Group II examinations, which would make it impossible to reduce the number of final examinations. The committee declared that the broad scope of Group II examinations would recognize and encourage flexibility and variety in college programs. In particular, the plan should encourage the introduction and extension of team teaching approaches to the presentation of general methods, thus helping to avoid overlapping and duplication.

Some explanation was offered regarding the material to be covered in each of the examinable subject areas. Educational psychology was largely equated with earlier course designations. So also was philosophy of education, but the committee recommended greater emphasis on current theories and philosophies and on historical development as the record of human experience to explain the emergence of these theories and philosophies. Administration was to cover former courses on school management, school law and administration, and school and community of the defunct two-year course, with up-to-date topics such as "problems of the ungraded school" and "other plans for the continuous progress of children." The new teaching methods would include general techniques and method, lesson types, principles of lesson planning, co-operative learning processes, team teaching, and the discovery approach. Curriculum construction and content would include the aims, scope, content, sequence, and construction of specific curricula, curriculum building, principles and practices exclusive to specific subjects, and unit planning. The five-part division of examinations was said to imply an expansion of the time allotted to educational psychology, philosophy of education, and administration, but it was not suggested that the time spent on all five programs should be equal. Teaching methods and curriculum construction and content each were to get more than one-fifth of the time.

Recent approaches to internal organization and instruction

The staffs of the colleges were consulted to a considerable extent when the committee was preparing its recommendations, and for the most part they welcomed the new freedom and responsibility. The greatest challenge was apparently in teaching methods, where those who had previously taught individual subjects were expected, not simply to rest on their reputation for competence in a specific area, but to consider broader issues. At Peterborough Teachers' College, they plunged right into an experiment in an unstructured approach during the five-week orientation period by abandoning timetables and most of the formalities. The staff, acting as a team, gave large group presentations and conducted small group discussions as the need arose. Because the staff-student ratio was approximately 1 to 30, the staff found the experiment very tiring, although rewarding. Many of the students found the transition to regular timetables a distinct let-down, although others were relieved at the security they felt in clearly defined procedures and identifiable supporting structure.

Staff planning in 1968–9 at Lakeshore Teachers' College centred around an attempt to define the institution's objectives in behavioural terms. Out of this examination of objectives, the staff hoped to identify the common elements in different subjects as a basic for integration. This procedure was seen as paralleling what the teachers were increasingly expected to do in the schools. Such planning activities were seen by the principal, W.C. McClure, as a fundamental step in developing a co-ordinated, team approach to instruction.

Some of the colleges moved much more slowly in the attempt to modify the older approach. Instructors continued to present their own particular subjects, with only an occasional combined presentation involving the co-operation of several instructors. The former examination practices were retained during the year, with the five-examination approach used only for the finals. A real integration of methodological studies appeared to be a long-term challenge.

Some of the colleges tried to deal with the problem of humanizing instruction in the face of rapidly rising enrolments by organizing panels, sometimes called "houses" or "sections." In 1968–9 Hamilton Teachers' College, for example, had twenty-three classes grouped in three panels, two consisting of eight and one of seven classes. This system was considered particularly desirable in a very large institution like Toronto Teachers' College. There, where an instructor formerly taught a single subject, he might have to get to know the names of as many as seven hundred different students. Each time he went to observe practice teaching, he saw a different student. It was thus usually impossible to get to know any student well enough to give him effective assistance in developing his full potential. Under the panel system a small team of instructors worked with a limited number of students. An instructor might teach three different subjects instead of one. Each panel produced its own timetable and modified it constantly to meet the students' desires and needs. Class periods might be combined into blocks in order to facilitate larger units of study and to make team presentations possible. Planning was of course costly in terms of staff time required. There was also some loss in that there was little opportunity for consultation among those teaching the same subject in different panels. But there seemed no doubt that the panel system represented a very constructive development.

The panel system was in operation at London Teachers' College for several years before 1968–9. Each panel included a co-ordinator and eleven or twelve masters, who planned and supervised both the intramural program and practice teaching. A staff counsellor worked with two panels, travelling with the members as they went around for practice teaching. Seminars were organized in intervening weeks to discuss issues that had been raised during practice teaching.

Colleges where there were students with university degrees, or at least some university experience, commonly provided a special program for them. But certain problems arose over the wide variety of subjects these students had had. For example, some had taken several courses in philosophy or psychology, and others none. Some of them might also be three years away from any study of mathematics. A number had been strongly impressed by the use of the lecture method and had an extra problem in adapting to the types of teaching needed in the elementary school. R.H. Brayford, Principal of Hamilton Teachers' College, commented on the edge the university graduate had in the ability to express himself on paper and explained that the college staff tried to capitalize on this facility. A master in another college found this group somewhat less creative than the grade 13 graduates.

Particular advances were made at Hamilton Teachers' College in the use of television. Work began on a closed-circuit system in 1968. A television tower was installed, a television studio was constructed, and at least one set was placed in every classroom. Educational television programs from outside networks were recorded on video tape for later display. Children were brought into the studio from neighbouring schools, where their performance was shown live or taped for subsequent use. Student teachers were enabled to analyse, dissect, and comment on a particular instructional approach, or compare different approaches, at their leisure. Those who had an opportunity to observe their own recorded performance in a classroom had one of the most effective kinds of criticism available to them. An example of this procedure was reported from St Catharines Teachers' College, where, with the help of the Educational Television Branch of the Department of Education, recordings were made of ten-minute sessions conducted by student-teachers with about seven pupils. The student teacher was then given about half an hour to revise his presentation and try it on a different group of pupils.[18] Comparable techniques were tried in the London Teachers' College.

Teachers' colleges once had the reputation of treating their students like children. There was a great deal of awareness in 1969 among principals and staffs of the current student demands for freedom from restrictions. The response varied considerably. Some colleges insisted on neatness in dress and appearance and imposed certain limits on what might be worn on the grounds that these restrictions were in line with what was expected in the schools. Others left it entirely up to the schools to say whether or not a student-teacher was properly attired. Some colleges checked attendance, not so much because regimentation was considered desirable, but more because some of the complex scheduled activities would be severely hampered by unnecessary absence. In other cases, it was claimed that the student was completely free to attend college classes or not as he saw fit. If he missed term work, of course, he had to pay the penalty of writing the final examination. Keeping appointments for practice teaching assignments was regarded as essential. The colleges for French-speaking students seemed to place their students under greater restrictions than did most of the others.

Evaluation of practice teaching

Practice teaching was at one time conducted almost as a completely separate operation. The teachers were selected on the recommendation of the local school inspector without any reference to the college. Students were assigned mechanically to practice schools, originally to teach one lesson at a time and later, as has been noted, for a full week.

There had been several major moves by 1969 to bring the two aspects of the teacher preparation program into closer association and to improve practice teaching as an experience for the student. The selection of practice teachers was still mainly the responsibility of the local administration, with some reported use of advisory committees. Typically the principal of the school made the original nomination, which was confirmed by the director or superintendent. The creation of the county school board units promised to ensure a more uniformly satisfactory level of appointment.

So many practice teachers, scattered over a wide area, were required that it was unrealistic to think that the teachers' college staff could play an active part in their selection. But it was becoming easier to have an obviously unsatisfactory practice teacher removed. There was a very great turnover of practice teachers in some areas, partly because of the mobility of the teaching force and partly, no doubt, because they received only a token $2.50 a day for the extra burden of supervision that the task required.

There were greatly increased opportunities for consultation between college staff members and practice teachers. On occasion, the latter were assembled in groups at the college for discussions and planning. Local school boards were showing a greater willingness to release them during school time for this purpose. There were also more individual meetings and discussions between teachers' college staffs and practice teachers.

Most of the colleges were moving toward the two-week block of practice teaching time in the same school. In some cases this arrangement was provided only once during the year, but the practice showed prospects of being extended. There was also some discussion of the possibility of providing for even longer blocks. While the "open classroom" approach emphasizes the potential advantages of such a practice, as explained later, there was hesitation at going too far for at least three main reasons: 1 / a practice teacher and class might find that three or four weeks constituted an excessive period to be subjected to a really poor student; 2 / the quality of the practice teaching force was not yet such that it could be considered safe to place students under the supervision of certain teachers for long periods of time; 3 / the students would lose some of the advantages of breadth of experience.

By 1969 there had been a major improvement in the way students were assigned to practice classrooms. Former mechanical procedures had given way to attempts to study the characteristics and needs of individuals. The practice teacher was looked upon less as a critic and an evaluator than as a helper and guide. The student was encouraged to think of himself as a teacher's aide and to provide assistance with various tasks as the opportunity arose. Increasing efforts were made to discuss, analyse, and benefit from practice teaching experiences after the students returned to the college.

One teachers' college used a ten-point rating scale for practice teaching in 1968–9. The points were related to descriptive terms as follows: excellent, 8–10 points; very good, 7 or 8 points; satisfactory, 6 or 7 points; less than satisfactory, 5 or 6 points; poor, 1–4 points. Ten aspects of the student's performance were rated: 1 / *preparation and planning* (adequate knowledge of subject matter; content thoroughly prepared, logical, and clearcut; evidence of resourcefulness, originality, initiative; lesson plan or day book carefully completed in advance; chalkboard work, visual aids, seatwork prepared); 2 / *guidance of learning* (teacher recognizes difficulties and helps children to solve them; adjusts his teaching to the abilities of the class; keeps lesson moving at a good pace; never loses sight of the aim of the lesson); 3 / *questioning* (questions clear, challenging, correct form, good distribution; proper acceptance of answers; good use made of answers; little or no repetition of questions or answers); 4 / *illustrative material* (effective use of chalkboard; format; legibility; summaries, visual aids; objective material); 5 / *degree of participation by the pupils* (mental activity stimulated; children actively responding and participating in the lesson orally and, if desirable, manually and physically; 6 / *consolidation of the lesson* (thoroughness in the application step or expression step; recapitulation of main points and, where necessary, drill, review, useful and well-supervised seatwork); 7 / *teacher-pupil relationship* (cooperation between teacher and pupils; pleasant rapport; pupils not under tension but relaxed, busy, and happy); 8 / *personality and grooming* (alert, cheerful, businesslike, enthusiastic, appealing, natural, colourful; professional appearance and grooming); 9 / *language and voice* (language – correct, clear, fluent; good enunciation, proper pronunciation; voice – audible, pleasant, well modulated); 10 / *management and discipline* (teacher in control at all times; sensitive to inattention and eliminates the cause quickly; handles breaches of discipline objectively and calmly). The teacher doing the rating also had a substantial amount of space on the back of the form to comment on the student's strong and weak points.

It is impossible to pass judgment on a rating form of this kind without knowing how it is actually used. But the large amount of detail provided by way of explanation presents some dangers. In the first place, it is very easy to sum up many individual points in such a way that the total fails to correspond to a more valid over-all impression. For any particular individual, a few overwhelmingly strong points may more than compensate for a number of weak ones, and vice versa, but the scale makes it impossible to do justice to such a person. It rather tends to set up a single, uniform stereotype of perfection. A second danger is that when students find out about how they are rated, and they usually do arrive at some approximation of the situation, they may busy themselves attempting to satisfy a multitude of minute criteria instead of concentrating on a few fundamentals.

Rating of teacher performance in Ontario, as in many other places, has been plagued by the fallacy of the "good lesson." This particular bit of showmanship can be a model of organization and smooth presentation, with a stimulating beginning, an effective climax, and a neat ending. The teacher performs vigorously and the pupils respond with the right answers at the right time. The whole procedure is under complete but unobtrusive control. On a detailed rating scale, each desirable trait or requirement could be given a top mark, and the whole thing would add up to perfection. The only problem is that the good lesson is a single unit that may or may not fit into the fabric of a good education. It is coming to be realized that the best learning may be a ragged, noisy, and apparently disorganized process where the teacher may be standing at the side in seeming inactivity.

Children may be doing different things, employing different media, interacting with one another, or sitting in apparent idleness "just thinking." Although there is a very definite underlying order in such a situation, it may not be recognizable at a glance. And certainly a detailed rating scale such as the one referred to is entirely inappropriate for appraising the teacher who is guiding the process. It is possible that circumstances under which practice teaching is done cannot provide adequate opportunities for the demonstration of this kind of teaching. If not, however, it is still reasonable to urge that nothing be done to reinforce the traditional stereotypes of teachers or lessons.

From the practice teacher's point of view, it is sometimes difficult to free the student teacher's mind from some of the traditional stereotypes. At the annual convention of the Ontario Educational Association in March 1969, Elizabeth Thorn dealt with this problem in recounting some of the difficulties in arranging for practice teaching in classes where the language experience program had been introduced.[14] She agreed that the student teachers were carefully prepared and understood and accepted the idea at an intellectual level. They saw the need for more meaningful instruction in language and for greater involvement of the pupils in the school program. Nevertheless, the informal atmosphere often had a shock effect because it differed so much from their own prior experience. For a time, also, they clung to the dream of becoming a teacher whose every word was law, until they realized that working closely with the children was more rewarding than performing at the front of the classroom. Miss Thorn emphasized how important it was that they recognize what was being gained by the children. If not, they tended to opt for teaching in a closely structured classroom, which was easier and fitted better into the pattern of elementary school experiences that they remembered.

Miss Thorn mentioned that questions are raised about the role in this program of the formal lesson, with its introduction, presentation, summary, and conclusion. She expressed the view that such a lesson is extremely important in the unstructured situation, and that the students possibly need an even more thorough understanding of the essential steps of a lesson so that they can recognize them in a learning situation that arises out of the pupils' interests. "For example the student who understands the introductory step of a lesson as a procedure to prepare the child for the new learning rather than a gimmick to attract attention, will recognize that a lesson which grows directly out of a child's problem or question, has already been introduced ..."

There are special problems for student teachers during a period when drastically new approaches are being introduced in some schools while traditional practices flourish in others. Miss Thorn commented on this point that

> ... students moving from school to school have difficulty deciding on the teacher's role. In one instance they are expected to assume a strong, dominating position, to be able to catch and hold children's attention on the ideas they are presenting. "Forceful presentation"; "enthusiastic"; and so on, are the sought after comments. In the language experience classroom, the teacher fades into the background, and the limelight belongs to the children ... The student teachers who make a name by being showmen have difficulty in adjusting to this.

There is also likely to be a problem with practice teachers who disapprove of the new method and are determined to do their bit to prevent the virus from spreading. Although their adverse comments may not have any serious influence on the success of a candidate who fails to identify and conform to their point of view, an encounter with one of them may make an unfortunate impression on the candidate's feelings about the teaching profession.

The period at the end of the 1960s was one of considerable difficulty for many elementary school teachers. The old landmarks were falling away, and traditional approaches and practices were being condemned. Yet for many of them it was difficult to see what they were expected to do. To many, the ungraded school, the open classroom, the language experience program, and individualized instruction were practically synonymous with chaos, as well they might be unless the underlying concept was understood thoroughly and handled with skill. Much of this atmosphere was felt by the student teacher. If he was self-confident and secure, he might welcome the opportunity to work out some of his idealism, but if he lacked these qualities, the challenge of being a teacher could seem quite forbidding.

The language experience program, as Miss Thorn explained it, called for an intensified evolution away from the "fragmentary" approach to practice teaching. This program was built not only on an understanding of child growth and development, but also on the experiences and needs of individual children within the group. "This presupposes that the teacher has a thorough knowledge of the children in her group, knows their academic standing in each subject, knows them as people, knows their strengths and their weaknesses, knows their levels of development, their interests and their needs." Student teachers do not have an opportunity to acquire this knowledge and thus have a tendency to impose lessons rather than let them grow out of class needs. Such a problem points to the desirability of providing for longer periods of practice in a single classroom, despite the disadvantages previously noted.

Miss Thorn's list of items to be observed with respect to a student teacher's performance in the language experience program would make quite a different rating scale from the one commented on earlier. She asked the following questions: 1 / Does the student make sure that every pupil knows *what* to do? 2 / Does the student organize activities to use space to good advantage? 3 / Does the student appear to be firm and consistent in handling classroom procedures? 4 / Has the student chosen an appropriate method for the topic? 5 / Has the student himself adequate knowledge of the topic so that he can direct and focus the pupil's efforts, and question to give greater depth to the pupil's thinking? 6 / Is the student aware of further resources pupils might call on? 7 / Has the student planned to ensure maximum benefit from the group process? 8 / Has the student planned a balance between group and individual activities? 9 / Is the student sufficiently sensitive to the pupils' knowledge and experience to recognize when the teacher takes over and when the pupils can carry the ball? 10 / Is the student aware of the present level of pupil achievement and attempting to raise that level? 11 / Is the student making some provision for pupil evaluation? Rather than centring attention on the student teacher as a person and as a performer, this set of questions deals with his effectiveness in furthering a constructive learning process.

Appraisal of the program

Administrators and staff of Ontario teachers' colleges have not been hesitant about soliciting the opinions of their students regarding the quality and appropriateness of the programs they offer. In the spring of 1969, a short list of questions and items was submitted to each of two groups in a certain college: those who had entered from grade 13 and those who had previously had some university experience. The following sets of comments, taken directly from their unsigned answer sheets, are designed to show the full range of responses, although not the frequency of each type of response. The grade 13 group consisted of a casually selected sample of thirty-four, and the university group, a sample of ten. The first question, asked only of the grade 13 group, was: "What are the chief differences between attending high school and attending Teachers' College?"

Responses: classes more open to discussion at teachers' college; we don't learn fact as much as we do how to apply it in the classroom; more responsibility; more freedom of movement; interested teachers instead of paid ones; more unity in teachers' college because of common goal; greater challenge in teachers' college; must relive elementary school days in projects – cutting out pictures, reading nursery rhymes, etc.; more varied activity in teachers' college; less stress on texts and notes at teachers' college; same approach, although some difference in content; treated as adults in teachers' college; you work more seriously at teachers' college because your career is at stake; allowed to use A–V facilities on own; better lunch facilities; very little difference; less written work but more reading in teachers' college.

These responses give the impression of a reasonable transition from the restrictions imposed in high school to a recognition of a higher level of maturity and responsibility. The evidence of greater motivation is evident, and there is little sign of impatience with activities designed to produce familiarity with the elementary school program. The group seemed to feel that they were getting a better quality of instruction than that offered in high school.

The students with university degrees were asked a different, although parallel, question: "What are the chief differences between attending University and attending Teachers' College?"

Responses: university more stimulating, more discussion, more room for dissent; university provides 24-hour way of life, more room to meet informally, library for study; university does not require attendance; university has active students' council; university requires more active participation for learning; university offers choice of subjects; university has better library; university requires less "in-class" time; university classes have a greater variety of classes – stimulating; teachers' college wastes time on mechanics of teaching; students have no feeling of responsibility, not treated as adults at teachers' college; little chance to follow individual interests at teachers' college; teachers' college lacks the stimulation of a variety of programs; better knowledge of teaching methods at the teachers' college than at the university.

These comments, as might be expected, established some clear differences between the groups. The greater maturity of the university had made the students much more critical and questioning. In terms of freedom and responsibility, the teachers' college obviously stood between the high school and the university. Some of the practices criticized – for example, the lack of variety in the programs – were clearly not subject to change under existing circumstances.

Some extra insights were provided by the responses to a request for "recommendations for consideration in improving our professional program."

Responses from grade 13 group: allow selection of specialized courses; more practice teaching and fewer weeks at college; should have at least three weeks of practice teaching in succession; treat students as adults – rather degrading to be reminded of gum chewing or being late in class, but may be necessary; orientation should be kept up; not enough time now in attendance at college; more help for students in preparing practice lessons; period of preparation should be increased; classes not always stimulating – perhaps because of subject matter; more work on the setting up of a programme for a year for your classroom, more work on the art of questioning, less emphasis on philosophy; associate teachers should be checked carefully, as to ability and standards, before they are allowed to be associates; too much philosophy which is of no use for teaching children.

It is interesting to observe certain contradictory demands, with one student, for example, wanting more time in the college and another less. There seems to have been a desire to get as much practice as possible. In view of the generally accepted idea that student teachers would benefit from a stronger cultural background, the impatience with philosophy should be noted.

Many of the suggestions made by the university group were similar. There was also evidence of more imagination in the proposals for improvement.

Responses from university group: more time in classroom; would like to help teacher rather than just teach and be criticized; some practice teachers have bad attitude, are unprofessional; specialization in teaching subjects or grades; more practical audio-visual experiences; better evaluation; fewer subjects; more time for study and research; apprenticeship basis would be better with team teaching the means of instruction; more field trips to see educational innovations; associate (practice) teachers should be trained for their role; deal with contradictory attitudes among practice teachers – what some regard as good, others regard as bad; longer periods of time (one month) for practice teaching.

The students were asked their opinions about the proposal to establish a teachers' college on the university campus. The specific question was: "What advantages do you see in this plan?"

Responses from grade 13 group: advantage of getting a degree at the same time; information sources more readily available; more room and equipment; more social events in university, more boys; mingling with more people with more varied interests would create broad-mindedness; teachers-in-training would be less looked down on by university students; better chance of relating teacher preparation courses to university work, which under present circumstances they must arrange to take later; those unsuited to teaching may be attracted to some other field, and thus "weeded out"; more people may be encouraged to become teachers since there will be more prestige attached to the job.

Responses from university group: more professional attitude coming from association with mature and professional people; teacher will feel closer to heart or hub of the education system which is university or the educated people; greater maturity of teachers; better philosophy of life; better academic preparation; association; methodology courses can be spread over four years; at teachers' college, too many important points are put forward too quickly and are forgotten because they are not reinforced by actual experience; better opportunity for research; discourage people who do not really want to be teachers, but take the course because it lasts only one year; longer period of time to be sure that teaching is right for you; will improve college *esprit de corps*; a more standardized program of instruction; a more highly qualified teaching staff from the point of subject matter and teaching methods employed.

Many of the responses from both groups corresponded to the official reasons for transferring the teachers' colleges to the universities. Quite a few of the improvements suggested did not, however, depend on such a transfer but could have been made with no fundamental change in the status of the colleges.

The final question, again relating to the proposed transfer of the colleges to the universities, was: "Are there some disadvantages?"

Responses from grade 13 group: all this education before they go into training will create a barrier between them and the pupils they teach; possibility of practice teaching beginning too late; expect fee for course; may be less practice teaching at University; unfavourable influences such as drugs, excessive drinking; more years to get diploma; the atmosphere at university is charged with laziness; bad influence on students' reliability; dress affected.

It is not clear from these responses whether the students who felt that the university had a bad influence on character were apprehensive for themselves or for their colleagues. Some of the points, such as the amount of practice teaching and the imposition of fees, are not an inherent part of the institutional structure. The university group were less inclined to identify disadvantages.

Responses from university group: expense; none whatsoever; young student may fall into carefree attitude of some students on campus – but better weed them out at that stage than in the classroom; fewer teachers will be produced; some will be unable to cope with university freedom. They should not be teachers anyway; discipline may be challenged; a few well-qualified staff may be lost because they do not meet university standards.

During brief visits to most of the teachers' colleges in the early months of 1969, the writer formed certain opinions about the quality of the program being offered and of the efforts being made by the staffs. It hardly seems necessary to reiterate the point that the students tended to be immature and naïve and that, despite the substantial progress that many of them made at the college, these deficiencies could not be adequately remedied during a single year. The staff were quite aware of the desirability of their having a sounder grasp of subject matter and a broader cultural background in order to deal with pupils nurtured on television and exposed to an unprecedented range of direct experiences in an increasingly sophisticated society. The objective of requiring a university degree of all prospective teachers was apparently universally welcomed.

Teachers' college staffs tended to feel on the defensive. Although many presentations on the future of teacher education began with a nod in their direction and a comment on the fine work they were doing, what followed was usually an outline of a scheme so different from anything that existed at the time that they could not help but sense an implied condemnation of themselves and all their works. It seemed most unfair that they should be put in this position. Within the serious limitations under which they had operated, including utterly unreasonable enrolments, inadequate buildings and facilities, and a period of extended uncertainty about their future, they had generally performed in a creditable fashion.

There was a good deal of uncertainty among college staffs about what would happen under agreements with the universities. Inevitably some of this concern had to do with their own personal occupational security, pensions, and other benefits. But they were also concerned about the kind of program that would emerge. Some genuinely feared that university interests were unsympathetic to the very idea of professional preparation and would press for the complete dominance of academic studies. There was apprehension lest these studies might be directed toward advanced scholarship rather than toward the provision of an optimum background for elementary school teaching. A great many hopes were being pinned on the advisory committees which were intended to be an essential part of the scheme. These were seen as providing opportunities for threshing out differences in points of view and reaching a reasonable compromise. Generally speaking, teachers' college staffs favoured the concurrent plan proposed by the Minister's Committee, but felt that they could accept the consecutive plan as long as the year of professional training retained the orientation they had worked out.

THREE

Issues in teacher education, with particular application to the elementary school level

BASIC CONCEPTS

It is impossible to say what kind of professional preparation teachers should have without raising and, in some tentative way at least, answering the most fundamental questions in education. One set of these questions centres on values. What are the aims and goals of the educational process? What kind of people do we wish to see emerge from it? What importance do we place on different facets of the human personality, such as the intellectual and the emotional? What do we expect of those with different levels of intellectual potential, different inclinations, and different temperaments?

A second set of questions has to do with ways and means. How do individuals proceed toward the different goals of learning? What can and should be done to encourage or assist them along the way? If, through unproductive personal associations and undesirable environmental influences, their impulse toward healthy development is reduced or destroyed, to what extent and how can the damage be repaired? What place in the teaching process should be assigned to effective communication, to personal inspiration, to the creation of a stimulating environment? What is the role of coercion?

A third group of questions concerns the kind of treatment that is appropriate for different groups of individuals categorized by age, sex, intelligence, interests, and attitudes. How should we handle the pre-school child? the early adolescent? the student who is intellectually capable of but not temperamentally inclined toward graduate work in a university? Under what restrictions, including the kind of buildings and facilities we provide, must learning take place at each level and among each category of learner?

The number and complexity of these factors rules out any notion that there is a single model of the ideal teacher. The qualities sought must correspond to the needs defined. That does not, of course, invalidate the search for some underlying and unifying trait or combination of traits that good teachers, regardless of the specifics of their task, have in common. This matter has received some attention in volume III. Of particular appeal is the "productive" personality type defined by Erich Fromm. Such a person is capable of truly fruitful relationships with others because he has learned to value his own being in the best and highest sense. Confident, secure, and serene, he can reach out to help another without manifesting a pernicious desire to dominate and control.

Practical circumstances have often made the question of the characteristics of the ideal teacher a matter almost of idle speculation. The number required and the relative unattractiveness of the task have made it necessary to accept all candidates who have met what has been generally recognized to be a very inadequate criterion. In a sense, of course, the problem can be remedied only in varying degrees. There is no pool of ideal prospective teachers any more than there is such a pool from which we can fill any other role in society. The concept of the ideal can help only in making the best possible selection from available resources.

Several questions about appropriate structures and programs for teacher preparation have concerned Ontario educators in recent years. These may be summarized briefly before the most important of them are discussed in detail. Some of these concerning institutional arrangements are as follows. 1 / What should be the essential characteristics of institutions for the preparation of teachers for the different levels of the system? 2 / What should be their relationship to other educational institutions? 3 / Should teachers be prepared in the same or different institutions for service at different levels of the system? 4 / How much variety in institutional arrangements is possible or desirable?

The chief questions relating to program have been as follows. 1 / What should be the role, if any, of general academic study? of professional study? of observation and practice? 2 / Assuming that there is a place for all three, what should be the balance of attention among them? 3 / By whom should each be presented? 4 / In what relationship to one another should they be presented? 5 / How long should the program be? 6 / What should be the criteria for admission? 7 / What kind of formal recognition should be given for successful completion of the program?

THE QUESTION OF UNIVERSITY PREPARATION

The fundamental historical facts concerning the establishment and growth of the normal school system have been presented in chapter 1. By 1950 Canada was confronted with the well-advanced policy in the United States of requiring degrees for elementary school teachers. An adoption of approaches developed in that country might have involved the conversion of the normal schools, or teachers' colleges as they were renamed in 1953, into degree-granting institutions. As has been noted in chapter 2, this possibility was considered by a study group of the Ontario Teachers' College Association in 1964. Such a move might have met some of the demands for a more extended program involving any or all of the basic elements of teacher preparation. It would also have provided for greater maturity on the part of beginning teachers. The alternative method of offering a degree program, involving a transfer of the function of teacher preparation to the universities, had been adopted by Alberta in 1945. It was to be a long time before the average elementary teacher was to enter service in that province with a degree, but at least the foundations had been laid, and future lines of development were clear.

In Ontario the possibility of increasing the required period of preparation would have been remote during the 1950s, regardless of what the attitudes of leading educators had been. There was an unusual combination of a disproportionately small age group from which the teachers must be drawn and an unusually large school population, resulting from a birth rate almost uniquely high among industrialized countries, plus the largest rate of immigration in Canada. While in theory it might seem that, given the necessary incentives, a longer period of preparation need not have reduced the number available for teaching and might well have improved the retention rate in the teaching force, an extension of the period of preparation was prohibited by two decisive factors. 1 / It seemed impossible to afford the loss of service entailed by the addition of successive years to the period of preparation. 2 / There was at least a temporary need for recruits whose intellectual limitations would have given them only a slight chance of meeting degree requirements in line with traditional Ontario standards.

But Ontario educators were by no means convinced that the course of action chosen in Alberta was necessary or desirable. The Royal Commission reported in 1950: "We are unable to concur in the view that the training of all prospective teachers for the publicly supported schools of the province should be provided by the universities."[1] It agreed that more extended preparation was desirable but suggested that the addition of one year would be sufficient. The organization of the appropriate facilities depended on the implementation of some of its other proposals:

> For the training of teachers for the proposed elementary schools: a two-year course to be taken in consecutive years; candidates to hold a junior college graduation diploma (equivalent, under our proposed reorganization, to the present Secondary School Honour Graduation Diploma – grade XIII or upper school); the course to lead to an Interim Elementary School Teaching Certificate.[2]

The commission further recommended

> ... that the Minister of Education be empowered to provide for the operation, administration, supervision, and financing of a number of institutions, to be designated junior colleges of education, for the professional education of teachers for publicly supported elementary schools.[3]

It was of course the minister's political duty to defend the reduction of formal teacher preparation involved in his introduction of emergency summer courses, however regrettable such a reduction might have seemed. But he did not in fact seem to place very high value on formal preparation. He said of his critics: "They seem to maintain that, if one year's preparation makes a good teacher, 10 years' training would make a better one. Teaching is an art. The rudiments are learned in the period of preparation; mastery comes only with work in the classroom."[4]

The *Report of the Royal Commission on Education in Manitoba*, released in 1959, was not regarded among educators as a very progressive document. Yet it recommended that, as soon as possible, the length of the course at the Manitoba Teachers' College be increased to two years, one academic and one professional. Believing that this type of program involved a closer integration of the Teachers' College with the University of Manitoba, the commission recommended that it be made an affiliated college or, failing that, that it be transferred to the Faculty of Pedagogy of the university. Under such a transfer, the Senate of the university would exercise the same control over the curriculum and examinations as it did with respect to other affiliated colleges.[5]

In *The Politics of Education*, published in 1960, Frank MacKinnon came out strongly for the handling of all teacher preparation in universities and junior colleges of recognized standing whose standards were acceptable to the teaching profession. He advocated the abolition of separate normal schools and control by political officials. Under the university arrangement, teacher trainees would no longer be a group apart, "screened off from other students by political auspices and confined to a narrow programme encouraging methodological inbreeding and with special low standards all its own."[6] They would have access to courses on the same terms as other students and would enjoy the influences and associations that only a university could give.

MacKinnon would make sure that teacher preparation was really integrated into the university program. He advocated control by an educational council of the faculty of arts and science. This would be a radical change from existing practice because it would mean a much closer contact between university departments and school teaching. He felt that the lack of such contact was one of the reasons for the current playing-down of academic attainment as a requirement for teacher preparation. "The authorities who license teachers have hitherto dealt almost exclusively with faculties of 'education'; and professors in the arts and science subjects have largely ignored school teaching because there has been no incentive to develop an interest on their own part and no consultation of them by authorities."[7]

The major recommendation of the Minister's Committee on the Training of Elementary School Teachers in 1966, reviewed more fully in chapter 4, was, of course, the transfer of elementary school teacher preparation to the universities. While recognizing the excellent work being done by the teachers' colleges in the field of methodology, it declared that there were fundamental weaknesses in teacher education in Ontario that could not be resolved under the existing system. The major deficiencies it identified had to do with inadequate academic education and insufficient maturity on the part of the student teacher.[8]

The committee did not see fit to recommend the structural integration advocated by MacKinnon. It expressed the view that teacher education should be offered within its own college or faculty so that facilities and materials required by the program might be made readily available, and so that the students pursuing a common purpose might exchange ideas and develop a professional spirit. It was nevertheless considered desirable that the students should form an integral part of the university community and that they should study the liberal arts subjects with students in other faculties.[9] It is possible that the hope of establishing an active dual loyalty is unrealistic, especially in the light of what has happened in some other places.

RELATIONSHIPS AMONG PROGRAMS OF TEACHER PREPARATION FOR DIFFERENT LEVELS

Programs for the professional preparation of elementary and secondary school teachers in Ontario have developed along different lines. To a large extent, the division has reflected the sharp line of demarcation between the two levels in the school system. Despite a series of steps taken in the 1950s and 1960s to bridge the gap, the division remained fairly clear. The processes of teacher education were considered among the main influences contributing to its perpetuation.

Bascom St John commented in 1963 on the deep split between teacher training at the two levels. He observed that it was possible to attend the Ontario College of Education and take the public school option, which gave the potential secondary school teacher training in elementary school methods. But, except for public school teachers who had acquired a degree to qualify for teaching in secondary schools, very few secondary teachers had any idea of how to teach a young child. And of course few graduates of teachers' colleges were qualified to teach in secondary schools. He contrasted this situation with that in Russia, where the program covered the whole gamut of teaching. The teacher was reputed to learn not only how to teach the conventional groupings of elementary and secondary school children, but also how to run youth groups, summer camps, and adult education classes. In comparing this approach to that of Ontario, to the latter's disadvantage, he wrote: "What our teachers' associations and our Government do not recognize is that a teacher who can teach only one part of the program is a fractional teacher. To be truly professional, he should be a whole teacher."[10] He was not advocating that a single person attempt to spread his teaching efforts over all levels, but rather that he have a broad framework of understanding within which he could appraise his own role.

The establishment of the Minister's Committee on the Training of Secondary School Teachers, which reported in 1962, was criticized in some quarters because it was asked to devote its efforts only to the secondary level. It commented on the wide difference between teacher preparation at the two levels and suggested that there might be an advantage in considering a rapprochement provided that certain conditions were met. The committee declared that it could see advantages in a joint program involving the bringing of teachers' colleges into closer contact with the universities, the mingling of all teachers at all levels, and the growing concept of education as one continuous process. Joint training would be possible, however, only when a first degree was required of all prospective teachers at all levels of the educational system.[11]

The Minister's Committee on the Training of Elementary School Teachers recommended that, where feasible, elementary and secondary school teacher education be offered within the same university faculty or college.

> A well-articulated program of cumulative education from kindergarten through graduate school should be our ultimate goal. Since much of the psychology, sociology, and philosophy of education offered in teacher-education courses is relevant to the teaching of young people at any grade level, the committee feels that integration of the training program for teachers should be encouraged. Beyond these areas of study the students would pursue courses particularly adapted to their needs.[12]

Robert M. Stamp, as a member of the faculty at Althouse College of Education, recently made the case for a program dealing with the needs of prospective teachers for all groups from pre-school children to adult learners.[13] He suggested that economic considerations alone might well dictate some form of common or shared training. Schools of education must be well equipped with television, data processing, and other electronic facilities which are too expensive to duplicate in colleges that prepare teachers for just one level of the school system. If this means that the institutions must be very large because of such factors, this writer's view is that there are sure to be some undesirable concomitants.

Stamp went on to say that in the long run educational considerations would be of even greater importance. The elementary school teacher must know the approaches used in the nursery school, and the secondary school teacher must be familiar with elementary school techniques. It would be advantageous to have these shared experiences begin in the period before teachers entered their classrooms. Combined training would give all prospective teachers an over-view of the educational process, which would be increasingly important in the future as the concept of continuous progress took hold and grade divisions gradually disappeared.

Many of those who have been active in programs for secondary school teacher preparation have had reservations about relating the two. V.S. Ready, Dean of McArthur College of Education at Queen's University, has expressed the firm belief that few, if any, of the universities of Ontario should become involved in preparing the whole range of teachers from kindergarten to grade 13.

> Wherever I have visited in Faculties of Education, which train the whole range of teachers, I have observed that the secondary area seems to be a peripheral one in the total effort. Certainly no integrated faculty seems to produce the same staff strength in curriculum and instruction at the secondary level which our Colleges of Education have.[14]

As new faculties were being established and planned by various universities at the end of the 1960s and the beginning of the 1970s, the question of how much ground each university's program should cover was a cause of considerable concern. The possible range was not simply from kindergarten to grade 13, but from pre-school to adult education, with the additional dimension of education for those with special needs. There was a particular desire among forward-looking educators to blur the traditional distinction between the elementary and secondary levels. One suggestion was that every faculty or college of education offer an undifferentiated basic certificate, and that individual teachers seek additional specialized qualifications for any one of a large number of areas in which they might wish to concentrate their teaching efforts.

VIEWS ABOUT APPROPRIATE PROGRAM CONTENT

A major question that must be considered with respect to the program of elementary teacher preparation is the ideal balance between professional and academic studies. The earliest efforts at formal preparation were largely devoted to academic work, mainly because the applicants were extremely deficient in this area. As the high school programs improved and additional high school experience was demanded of the applicants, the emphasis shifted to professional preparation, and there it has remained ever since. With the basic program of a single year's duration, it would be unreasonable to expect anything else. This is not to say that there are not some straight presentations of academic subject matter in the teachers' colleges. The writer observed such a lesson taught in the spring of 1969 in typical high school fashion. Judging by the amount of knowledge displayed by the students, the approach did not seem by any means inappropriate.

In the discussions about the integration of the programs with those of the university, the prevailing view seemed to be that all of the extra three years to be added eventually to teacher training would consist of academic studies and that, whether the consecutive or the concurrent plan was adopted, the remainder of the program, including both professional study and practice, would amount to a single year. The Minister's Committee on the Training of Elementary School Teachers strongly supported this view, which it declared to be widely held.[15] There have certainly been expressions of opinion along such lines for many years.

The Ontario Conference on Education gave strong support for an extension of academic studies in programs for initial preparation and in-service training. Looking to the time when a degree would be required for elementary school teachers, it made the following recommendation.

> The opinion of the majority of our group is that the future course for elementary teachers should be a year of professional study following a degree in liberal arts rather than a degree in education as a result of a composite of academic and professional courses. We feel that the greatest need on the part of our present graduates is intellectual and cultural maturity rather than more professional training.[16]

Looking at the existing situation, the same group felt that it was desirable and feasible to restore the in-service training requirements that existed up to 1951 for making an interim certificate permanent. This would be a practicable way of moving toward a full arts degree for elementary school teachers.

The committees whose work was reported in *Design for Learning* had some suggestions for the improvement of the teachers' college program, mainly in the direction of stronger emphasis on academic work. The English Study Committee observed that the limited period of time spent in the colleges encouraged an emphasis on methods rather than on content. It suggested, however, that the college could do much by its presentation to make young teachers realize the importance of knowing their subject matter, of constantly adding to their knowledge, and of understanding that they should know more than they could teach. They should be acquainted with ways in which they could enrich their background of reading and improve their powers of expression. The teachers' college libraries should be libraries of good reading and not merely of pedagogical reference. "Library assignments, lectures on books and book selection, and the provision of book lists should be part of the general curriculum."[17]

The parallel Social Sciences Study Committee favoured more drastic changes. It recommended that the teachers' college course be reorganized to give some part of the time to training in subjects. Although there was some question as to whether this course of action was possible in a one-year program, the committee felt that it should be tried. Under the proposed scheme, a student teacher would have to choose, some time in the first term, whether he wanted to be prepared for teaching in the primary, junior, or intermediate division of the school system, and which subjects he wanted to teach. For the latter part of the year, he should devote something like two hours a day to the study of his chosen subject. There was a case for an extra year of preparation in subject matter for those who chose to teach in intermediate and senior divisions.[18] The idea of extending subject specialists into the elementary school shows the contrast between ideas promoted at that time and the attitudes of the Hall-Dennis Committee and its supporters such a short time later.

A report of the senate committee, set up after the release of the report of the Minister's Committee to study McMaster University's responsibilities for the preparation of elementary school teachers, recommended the adoption of the consecutive plan, in part because it was feared that the concurrent plan would lead to pressure to expand the professional part of the program beyond the share originally allotted to it.[19] This apprehension was undoubtedly well founded, but it is legitimate to ask whether the desire to keep the professional studies in a strictly subordinate role is designed to give elementary teachers the best possible preparation for their future role or to ensure that any degree awarded to them fit exactly into the traditional university mould. Serious consideration should be given to the possibility that professional studies might be made at least as rigorous and intellectually demanding as those in the traditional disciplines. If this could be done, the apparently conflicting interests of the academically and professionally oriented groups might be reconciled.

Professional studies in education have had an almost universally bad reputation in scholarly circles. This kind of reputation could hardly have been acquired without being at least in part deserved. There have been innumerable candidates for the teaching profession who have complained of courses consisting of the presentation of trivial and boring details. Educators do themselves little good by defending such practices on the grounds that someone needs to show a beginning teacher how to fill out a register and perform other similar housekeeping chores. A teacher who cannot learn how to handle these matters on his own, or with help provided within the school, might well have his credentials questioned. It might be better to let him flounder a bit during his first few weeks in the classroom if the time he might have spent learning mechanical tasks were employed instead in absorbing some of the fundamentals of human behaviour or in improving his intellectual competence.

Professional educational programs have got themselves into trouble in universities by offering their own versions of traditional disciplines such as history of education and philosophy of education. While there is little argument that these disciplines have important implications for teachers, serious scholars have been irritated at the assumption that they can be adequately taught by instructors with a superficial background of formal study in the discipline, or even none at all.

One of the reasons why professional courses have so often been unworthy of respect is that the instructors have attained their position essentially through demonstrated skill in practice rather than because of intellectual attainments. A stimulating environment for learning and high standards of achievement have also been difficult to maintain in the traditional isolation of the teachers' college. Furthermore, as long as applicants did not have to meet the same admission standards as those entering university, they could not be expected to demand or meet as rigorous an intellectual challenge as that encountered in the university. But most of the universities have insisted on three conditions for accepting the program of teacher preparation: 1 / that the instructors secure satisfactory academic qualifications, 2 / that the integration of the program with that of the rest of the university be genuine, and 3 / that the students meet the same admission requirements as all other applicants (a condition met in 1969–70). Under such conditions, it might be thought that university authorities would welcome the opportunity to influence the professional aspects of the program to suit their concept of what is fitting. The desire to ensure that professional studies continue to be confined to their fraction of the compound should thus diminish or disappear.

The need for professional studies can and should be based on an analysis of the requirements of the teaching task itself. A good teacher of elementary school children must know an enormous amount about how children function, grow, and learn, about how to communicate with them, about how to motivate and inspire them. He must understand how social and other environmental factors influence and shape them. He must not only know a great deal about many subject fields, and this is where more advanced academic studies will help, but he must also know how to select, organize, and present content to meet the child's developing needs. He must understand how to measure and appraise pupil progress and how to diagnose the causes if unusual difficulties are encountered. He must be able to recognize the full range of talents, capacities, and interests of normal children and also to identify those aberrations that should be referred to specialists for treatment. These skills are in part learned and to a great degree perfected on the job, but to say that only one year of a four-year program should be devoted to the initial steps in acquiring them is hardly an excessive tribute to their importance.

There are some in the university community who will say in effect: "Yes, we accept the validity of this case, and agree that an elementary school teacher needs a very great range of skills. But we do not feel that they result from the kind of study that should count toward a good, sound academic degree. By all means provide for them, but do so outside the degree framework." There are others who believe that most of the skills in question are acquired intuitively through perceptive observation and sensitively analysed experience. Such a view has been reflected by Frank MacKinnon, who stated the case for scholarship as the necessary and sufficient condition for good teaching.

Most good scholars do become good teachers for the simple reason that they know their subjects, they may have studied under able teachers, they know from first-hand experience what the learning process is about, and they have enough common sense to pick up techniques in a relatively short time. Certainly they would seem to be better prospects, especially for high school teaching, than weak students who have only teacher training and lack other qualifications. Because the opportunities for scholars who have not had teacher training are few in the school system and numerous outside, general comparisons are difficult to make. I have watched both types at work in my own and in other institutions. The teacher training graduates are usually better prepared for teaching during the first month or two in the classroom because they have been taught some schoolroom procedure. But they find, or rather their pupils later find, that adeptness at procedure is no substitute for knowledge; and in too many cases superficial entertaining and emphasis on textbooks and projects become the established routine. Too often analysis of methods is neglected in favour of slavishly following *the* method which was learned in teacher training; discussion in class is often confined to the posing and answering of stereotyped, standardized questions; and the kindling of the imagination of the pupils is abandoned in favour of prepared stimuli and the expected response.

On the other hand, most of the scholars who have been employed without teacher training soon overcome an initial awkwardness, learn from experience, catch on to the details of procedure quickly, or seek the advice of colleagues, as everyone else must do in any job. They teach on the basis of their substantial knowledge and abilities, and their judgment and imagination is rarely hampered by excess routine. Unquestionably the best high school teaching I have seen has been done by able honour graduates in regular academic subjects who have never been near a teacher training college yet who know what they are doing because they know what they are saying.[20]

Harold J. Uhlman has taken the contrary position in asserting that any given individual, regardless of the excellence of his academic background, will be a better teacher if he has had preparatory training which places some emphasis on the imparting of knowledge.

The acquisition of knowledge for personal consumption does not carry with it a guarantee that the possessor will be able to pass along that knowledge to a captive audience in a school classroom, the members of which vary greatly in ability, interest, attitudes, and background knowledge; and this is true, up to a point, even when homogeneous grouping of students is practiced.[21]

Both MacKinnon and Uhlman reflect views of the teacher as an imparter of information rather than as a stimulator of learning, to refer to the current concept of the teacher. This change in views does not so much throw the argument in one direction or another as reduce the relevance of both claims.

The case for the strong emphasis on academic studies in teacher preparation rests on two main propositions: 1 / that teachers should have a sound cultural and intellectual background in order to be suitable bearers of the traditions, knowledge, and attitudes of Western civilization in its Canadian manifestations, and 2 / that they should know enough about the subject content dealt with in elementary schools to ensure that children obtain accurate information and a reasonable concept of the significance of various areas of study. These propositions are indisputably sound. It is as distressing to see a teacher whose attitudes and actions display an ignorance of his cultural heritage as it is to see inaccurate facts being imparted. But it cannot be assumed that all battles have been won and all problems solved merely by requiring prospective teachers to have three years of university study. The university program itself bears careful examination.

Henry Johnson observed that, if courses in the liberal arts and sciences were, in their design, appropriate for the future elementary or secondary school teacher, then all was well. But he complained that, as departments expanded, courses in a discipline were reorganized and fragmented to produce not only the broadly educated graduate, but also the specialist. It became increasingly difficult to plan programs to produce the liberally educated man. Too frequently the universities' service to liberal education ended at the sophomore year. This condition would not be so regrettable if the courses in the first two years could be taught by men selected for the breadth and liberality of their scholarship, and if such qualities in a scholar were prized and rewarded by the universities. But Johnson pointed out that this was rarely the case.[22] The move toward the restructuring of courses in the University of Toronto in 1969 appeared advantageous in terms of the needs of elementary school teachers. Some of the smaller universities in Ontario provided the kinds of instruction and guidance that also seemed promising.

It can hardly be doubted that the arts and science faculties in universities would shrink from offering courses in "English for the Elementary School Teacher" or "Science as the Child Sees It." Discussions since the release of the *Report of the Minister's Committee on the Training of Elementary School Teachers, 1966* have emphasized that the university courses taken by the prospective teachers must be the same as those taken by other students. But the desire to maintain standards and to guarantee the status of teacher candidates among other students should not end consideration of what kind of preparation will be in the best interests of the children who will eventually be taught.

All the foregoing discussion has been based on the assumption that raising the educational level of the teachers will improve the educational process and thus the achievement level of the pupils. Seymour Metzner cited a long series of research studies to show that this claim could not be substantiated. He said, with reference to these studies, that they "are indicative of the strong research trend showing a weak or nonexistent relationship between teacher academic attainment and pupil achievement at all levels."[23] Much the same conclusion resulted from attempts to see whether additional professional preparation resulted in greater pupil gains. It did not matter whether the preparation was measured by degrees earned, time spent in training, or recency of training. Metzner put his conclusion in the bluntest terms: "The plain fact is that there is not a single study that, after equating for pupil intelligence and socio-economic status, has found the length of teacher preparation variable to be even peripherally related to pupil gain, let alone being of major importance in this educational outcome." One can react to this conclusion in several ways: 1 / by asserting that the studies must have been defective, 2 / by claiming that the benefits from a higher level of teacher education are to be found in the "intangibles," or 3 / by ignoring it. It is probable that Canadian educators will respond with a combination of the last two reactions. If so, there may well be a certain amount of disappointment in a few years over the degree of educational improvement traceable to the new programs of teacher preparation.

FOUR

The report of the Minister's Committee on the Training of Elementary School Teachers

THE COMMITTEE AND ITS RECOMMENDATIONS

As mentioned in chapter 3, the Minister's Committee on the Training of Secondary School Teachers reported its findings in 1962. One of the chief criticisms leveled against it was that it had considered the preparation of secondary school teachers in isolation. Nevertheless, the separate pattern was continued, and Education Minister Davis set up a corresponding committee, chaired by C.R. MacLeod, Director of Education for Windsor, to consider the problems involved in preparing elementary school teachers. In reviewing his reasons later, he commented as follows.

> After studying the forecast for secondary school and university enrolments and in view of the changing demands of society, I felt that the time had come to reassess the role of the elementary school teacher and to reappraise the effectiveness of the present programme of teacher education.[1]

The conference of the Ontario Teachers' College Association in 1964, reference to which was made in chapter 2, produced some proposals that anticipated those of the MacLeod Committee. Discussion group 18, which dealt with the future of elementary school education, urged a longer period of preparation and affiliation with the universities. It outlined a four-year teacher education program after grade 13 consisting of three main parts: a broad education in the liberal arts and sciences, to which the first two years of university would be devoted; scholarly competence in a major field of learning related to teaching, the study of which would begin early in the student's college career, but would be concentrated in the third and fourth years; and professional competence in education, which would comprise approximately one-half the program in the third and fourth years. The group felt that elementary and secondary school teachers should be prepared in the same multi-purpose colleges of education within the universities. It recommended that all teachers have similar preparation in the liberal arts and sciences and in the foundations of education. Secondary school teachers would have more specialized study in a major field of learning. It was recommended that a one-year professional preparation course, involving internship, be offered for university graduates.

In a brief to the conference the group recommended a series of steps that might lead to the establishment of its "ideal" program.

(a) The One-year Course should be kept to balance the supply with the demand for teachers. Special courses within selected Teachers' Colleges should be drawn up for university graduates.
(b) Introduce an optional Two-year Course which would include a one-year university programme and a one-year teacher education programme to run concurrently or consecutively. This could incorporate the suggestions of the ideal programme for the third and fourth years, especially with respect to teaching practice. Graduates would get a Standard Two certificate. This Two-year Course could be offered initially by Teachers' Colleges in university centres.
(c) As soon as possible, multi-purpose Colleges of Education should be organized within universities to educate elementary and secondary school teachers. Three main types of organization should be available: (i) Professional preparation concurrent with liberal arts and sciences in third and fourth year (ii) Professional preparation concurrent with honours arts and sciences in the fourth and fifth years (iii) Professional preparation after a Pass B.A. or an Honour B.A.
(d) These Colleges of Education should develop graduate studies and research facilities.
(e) A Commission on Teacher Education could be organized to facilitate this transfer of Teacher Education to the Colleges of Education within the universities. The Minister of Education would appoint the nominees of the Teachers' Federation, Trustees Association, and Universities as members of this commission. He would also appoint officials of the Department of Education and Department of University Affairs to the Commission. This Commission would advise the Ministers of Education and University Affairs regarding the Colleges of Education – construction, curriculum, and certification.

After a certain organizational period the Colleges of Education within the universities would be allowed local autonomy for their curriculum and certification. The Commission on Teacher Education would then advise the Minister of Education regarding the accreditation of the programmes of the Colleges of Education and the licensing of their graduates.

As the supply of potential teachers increases, the length of training required should be gradually increased to the level of the ideal programme.

The minister's committee consisted of eighteen members representing school trustees, universities, school superintendents, directors of education, inspectors, teachers' colleges, the Elementary and Secondary Branches of the Department of Education, and each of the five affiliates of the Ontario Teachers' Federation. It is evident from this list that the widest possible range of points of view was sought. Their specific terms of reference were as follows:

1. to examine the teacher-training program now being followed at the Ontario Teachers' Colleges;
2. to examine other selected teacher-training programs;
3. to recommend changes that might be made immediately to improve the present One-year Course;
4. to develop, in some detail, what the committee considers to be an ideal program for the training of teachers for the elementary schools of Ontario;
5. to suggest the successive steps that might be taken, over a period of time, to achieve the implementation of this ideal program.[2]

Although there was no specific commission to deal with secondary school teacher preparation, the minister made it clear that consideration might be given to the co-ordination and integration of programs at the two levels.

The committee began nearly two years of intensive activity with its first meetings in September 1964. During the remainder of that year and in 1965 it met on forty-nine occasions and studied briefs from ninety-nine individuals and organizations. The members visited institutions for the preparation of teachers in all the Canadian provinces, in several of the American states, in Great Britain, and in continental Europe. Their work was thus based on the results of very comprehensive study.

The report, published in 1966, recommended three plans for the professional preparation of elementary school teachers: 1 / a four-year concurrent plan in which university work and professional preparation would be taken together; 2 / a consecutive plan in which a one-year course of teacher preparation followed university graduation; and 3 / an internship plan implemented co-operatively by school boards and the Department of Education.[3] In each case, a teacher would require a university degree before entering the teaching profession. The report recognized that it would take time to establish the full program and outlined a series of steps for the achievement of this objective.

It was recommended that the programs for teacher education be provided by the universities, but that responsibility for certification continue to rest with the minister. This kind of arrangement needs careful definition before it is possible to say exactly what it means. Obviously if the requirements for the certificate were laid down in great detail, not only with reference to the courses to be included, but also in terms of topics to be covered in each course, the universities would have little room for initiative except to select an instructor to go through the prescribed motions. It is hardly to be expected that a university would, except under compulsion, accept such a role. The only possible basis for co-operation would seem to be to state the certificate requirements only in the most general terms. There would seem to be no way in which the department could use its certificate-granting powers to enforce any kind of uniformity of standards, or even any minimum standard, without getting involved in a detailed examination of each university's program. Again, such action would involve an intolerable interference in the university's traditional freedom to manage its own affairs. The inevitable status of certificate-granting power appears to be reduction to a formality, with decision-making powers to be called into play only in the most unusual circumstances. It is true, of course, that the University of Toronto long tolerated an arrangement whereby the affairs of the College of Education were supervised in some detail by the department. But the penalty was that the college was regarded as a kind of unwelcome boarder, to be tolerated in view of certain accompanying benefits and implied threats, but never for a moment to be treated as one of the family.

Whichever plan was adopted, the committee advised that the candidates for teacher education comply with regular university admission requirements, and that they share the privileges and responsibilities of the students in other faculties. Professors in liberal arts and in education would cooperate in providing the program. Approximately 75 per cent of the four-year program would be devoted to academic studies and the remainder to professional preparation. The four main components of teacher education would be a liberal or academic education, foundations of education, curriculum and instruction, and practice teaching. The committee recommended that candidates select liberal arts courses providing a broad and sound background of scholarship and that these be as relevant as possible to teaching. The disciplines should be as challenging as those chosen by candidates for other degrees. There should also be an opportunity for teachers to develop competence in special subject areas. Preparation in special education might take two forms: a basic degree and professional preparation followed by specialist preparation in a special field, and the provision of options within the regular professional program. The first of these was viewed with more favour in the department.

More specific recommendations concerning the professional program involved the inclusion in foundations of education of at least one course in each of psychology, philosophy, and sociology. Curriculum and instruction should include instructional techniques, management and administration, and religious knowledge, with an opportunity to select an area of concentration and specialization.

The committee recommended that the minister enter into separate agreements with the governing bodies of the universities for the establishment of teacher education programs, which would preferably involve elementary and secondary school teacher education within the same faculty or college. An advisory board appointed at the same time as the agreement was reached would make recommendations to the university and to the minister concerning the planning of the physical plant, admission requirements, curriculum, examinations, and matters affecting the faculty. Although the government would establish, equip, operate, and maintain the colleges of education, each college would be administered as an integral part of its own university. The dean of the college would be appointed by the university "with the concurrence and approval of the Minister" and the instructional staff of the college "by the university in consultation with the Minister."

The implementation of the plan might be undertaken in three phases. The teachers' colleges already located on university campuses might be incorporated as quickly as possible into their respective universities, while the remaining colleges, during the transitional period, offered an improved one-year professional course. In the first phase, prospective elementary school teachers would be required to qualify for university admission. The program would consist either of a two-year course in the colleges operated within the university or a year of academic study and a year of professional preparation, depending on whether a concurrent or a consecutive program was desired. In the second phase, the same pattern would be extended to add another year, and in the third phase, the complete four-year program would be attained. An implementation committee, with representation from the universities, was to be established by the minister to study and implement the committee's proposals.

A single professional certificate was to be the basic qualification for all teachers. It would indicate that a teacher was qualified to teach from kindergarten to grade 10 or from grade 7 to grade 13, and would also show, through endorsements or validations, the grade division and subject area of major concentration. The existing certification system, with its Standards II and III, would serve for the transitional period, but instead of a Standard I Certificate a temporary licence would be awarded, valid for perhaps five years.

Davis commented enthusiastically on the work of the committee and welcomed its recommendations. "The department and the Minister are in complete agreement with the general programme suggested and it will be the policy of my department to implement plans to this end as quickly as possible."[4] He felt it necessary, however, to reassure all elementary school teachers that they would be allowed to complete the requirements for a permanent basic certificate under the regulations in effect when they began their teacher education program. Although the majority of teachers were expected to continue to improve their academic and professional qualifications, no teacher who had received a certificate would be forced to undertake further education.

The Hall-Dennis Committee in its turn found the recommendations of the MacLeod Committee very much to its liking. Its approval was given in these terms: "As a result of its studies, the committee gives whole-hearted support to the major recommendations of the MacLeod Committee and also supports most of the proposals concerning the details and plans for implementation of these recommendations."[5] Thus the work of the two committees appears to have been on the same philosophical path.

CHANGES ACCOMPANYING THE REPORT

Teachers' college programs for university graduates

The general direction of the MacLeod committee's recommendations had been anticipated by the teachers' colleges, and some changes were already under way as indicated in earlier chapters. One of these entailed a special elementary teachers' course for university graduates with acceptable degrees. It involved a recognition of the rather obvious fact that such candidates should have an opportunity to take academic work at a higher level than those entering with the minimum grade 13 standing. Their greater maturity and wider variety of experience might also be expected to be taken into account. This course was begun in the Toronto Teachers' College in 1965 and was extended to the colleges at Hamilton, Lakeshore, and Ottawa the following year. In a somewhat similar category, but reflecting also the recommendation to integrate the preparation of elementary and secondary school teachers, was an experiment with a course operated on a co-operative basis between the London Teachers' College and Althouse College of Education. This experiment was, however, ended in 1967 when the University of Western Ontario decided to offer a full Elementary School option at Althouse College.

The Internship Plan

The basic objective of the Internship Plan was to permit the larger school boards to enable people of mature years with adequate qualifications, including a university degree, to acquire professional experience under supervision within the school system. Direct experience was supplemented by two summer courses. The program was expected to appeal to housewives who found themselves in a position to undertake a professional career but who would be unlikely to attend a regular teachers' college session largely in the company of younger people.

The privilege of accepting candidates was restricted to school boards where the elementary school enrolment totalled three thousand pupils or more. They might handle one internship trainee for every three thousand pupils or additional fractions of this number. A board wishing to accept candidates under the plan had to secure the approval of the director of the Teacher Education Branch of the Department of Education. The registrar of the department was to rule on the acceptability of each candidate. The customary requirements of citizenship and good character were expected to be met. Although the basic academic qualification was an acceptable university degree, candidates were admissible under the age of twenty-five only if they had credit for at least one year of graduate study, as evidenced by a degree such as that of Bachelor of Library Science, or a diploma from the Institute of Child Study at the University of Toronto (formerly awarded after one year of graduate study).[6]

For at least twenty consecutive days during May and June of the year of admission, the candidate was expected to serve in elementary school classrooms under the supervision of the inspector and the school principal. It was suggested that at least one full week be spent in each of the primary, junior, and intermediate divisions of the school. During this period, the candidate was to participate in routine duties such as assembly programs, dismissals, supervision of halls and classrooms, yard duty, and recording attendance. These responsibilities were to be increased as he gained in experience and confidence. One would hope that a mature university graduate would rise to the necessary level of competence in a reasonably short period of time. For the first two or three days, he was also expected to observe the teacher in action. The latter was supposed to exemplify in his work the basic principles of teaching and discuss these with the candidate. After a short interval, the candidate, with the help of the practice teacher, began to plan and teach lessons, beginning with one or two a day and increasing in number during subsequent weeks. Practice teacher and candidate were to discuss these lessons at the end of the day.

If the early period of practice was considered satisfactory by the director, superintendent, or inspector and by the school principal, the candidate might attend a six-week summer course offered at the Lakeshore Teachers' College. The course consisted of classes in educational psychology, school management, general methodology (social studies, science, and mathematics), Part I or Part II, and English, Part I or Part II. Term tests were given to each candidate, and final examinations to those who failed to obtain at least 66 per cent on these tests.

During the fall term, each trainee who had successfully completed the summer course worked with several classroom teachers under the supervision of a school principal. He spent at least two consecutive weeks in a classroom of each division of the elementary school. During the second week of each two-week period, he was expected to teach for approximately half his time. Discussion of observation and practice lessons and seminar discussions with officials of the board or with supervisory teachers and, where desirable, with the staff of the teachers' college in the area were supposed to form a major part of the work during this period. For the rest of the fall term, he was assigned to classrooms at the discretion of the school principal on the advice of the inspector. It was intended that the grade level to which he was best suited would be established, and that he would be given some experience in elementary school subjects such as art, music, and physical and health education where he showed particular aptitude and interest. At least once during the fall term, a member of the district teachers' college staff was to visit him while he taught in the classroom, counsel him on the work observed, and submit a written report to the principal of the district teachers' college and to the school board concerned. At the close of the fall term, the school principal discussed the candidate's work with him in detail "with particular attention to the improvement of teaching and professional conduct."

During the remainder of the year, the candidate might be given regular teaching assignments or supply teacher work in any school under the board's jurisdiction. Similar methods of evaluation were continued, with the teachers' college staff member reporting in writing to the principal of the college on the candidate's teaching ability. By May 1 the inspectors involved with internship candidates and the principal of the district teachers' college were to assess the candidate's suitability to attend the second summer course. This course involved classes in history and philosophy of education, whichever of English Part I and Part II had not been taken during the first summer, whichever of general methodology Part I and Part II had not been taken during the first summer, and methods in special subjects such as art, music, and physical and health education. Candidates judged successful by the same standards as those in the first summer course were given an Interim Elementary School Teacher's Certificate.

Most of the program remained as it was originally planned up to 1969–70, except for the content of the summer courses. The first year now consisted of psychology in education, Part I; administration; teaching methods; and communications media. That of the second year consisted of psychology in education, Part II; philosophy in education; curriculum construction and content (primary and junior or junior and intermediate); and teaching methods in art, music, and physical education.

This plan might well get close attention from those who feel that the important thing in learning to be a good teacher, assuming one has an adequate general education and has achieved reasonable personal as well as chronological maturity, is to get right down to the practical work of teaching. A certain amount of methodological study can then be introduced when the need for it is felt. Others claim that such an approach is the most effective way to ensure that traditional practices, many of them inevitably bad, will be perpetuated. They advocate doing everything possible to encourage an imaginative and critical examination of the fundamental nature of education before there has been a hardening of mental and behavioural patterns. A stimulating undergraduate program in the university is seen as an important step toward this goal. Thought-provoking studies about education itself, whether combined with or separated from general studies, are considered an essential element in the process. Of course, if professional preparation is to consist merely of the demonstration of a set of methods and techniques that can be applied more or less mechanically, the main argument in favour of having the function performed in a special institution is that the demonstration may be better than that likely to be encountered in field practice, an assumption that can by no means always be made with safety.

Dean Ready of McArthur College of Education has commented rather unenthusiastically about internship.

There is no doubt that if a student teacher is fortunate in the school and teacher to whom he is assigned he can gain a very valuable experience from a long internship under supervision in such a school. But I feel that it tends to put too large a percentage of the student's time devoted to professional training into the hands of teachers who have neither the time nor the special background necessary to train teachers. If we think of teacher training as the time when the student's mind should be directed towards innovation in teaching, then an internship programme relies too heavily on current practices.[7]

After the Internship Plan got established, it produced about fifty teachers a year. A senior department official appraised these as very good people, to a considerable degree because they have been carefully selected by the school boards before entering the program.

Departmental response to the MacLeod report

The minister's unequivocal declaration of approval of course determined the policy of the Department of Education. But the implementation of the large number of recommendations depended on how soon certain courses of action could be devised and certain obstacles overcome. In part, especially where the improvement of the existing one-year course at the teachers' colleges was concerned, some immediate steps were possible. In others, notably where university co-operation was essential, changes might await the results of cautious negotiations.

By 1968 it could in a sense be said that all three of the committee's plans were in operation in Ontario. The existing concurrent program was the two-year course offered at the University of Ottawa and the Sudbury Teachers' Colleges, involving a combination of university academic and professional instruction. This scheme, of course, was hardly what the committee had in mind, but it could be said to represent the kind of foundation on which a full-blown concurrent program, leading to a university degree, could be developed.

Reasonable priority was given to the recommendation that each principal should have greater responsibility for the operation of his college so that the program might be more flexible, and so that each college might develop an individuality of its own. It was also recommended that the principal should assume responsibility for co-ordination of the instructional program and for supervision within the college. There had, of course, always been some room for individuality resulting from such factors as differences in the period of origin and geographical location of different colleges. But the similarity of the buildings constructed in the same periods was visible evidence of central authority. The observer in 1969 could still identify many aspects of the operation of the colleges, seemingly of no great importance, that were being referred to the central office for decision. The approval of the director of the Teacher Education Branch was requested, for example, before outside speakers were invited to visit certain of the colleges. The explanation offered was that official authorization had to be given for the budgetary expenditure involved, but that the college principal's judgment of the suitability of the proposed speaker's credentials was not questioned. Department officials exercised more authority than they in fact seemed to desire, partly because traditions were difficult to break, and partly because the incumbents were constantly available to assist with whatever difficulties might arise.

Under the heading "decentralization of authority," the MacLeod Committee recommended that, when a student's practice teaching, academic results, or personal attitudes were unsatisfactory, the college should have greater authority to require him to withdraw from the course. It was suggested that the colleges should be responsible for their final results, subject to an appeal by the student to a board of revision. The problem that had existed and, to a considerable degree, still did in 1969, was that dissatisfied candidates did not hesitate to appeal to their local member of the Legislature or to some other political figure. The member assumed that he owed it to his constituent to conduct inquiries, which, even if made in the friendliest manner, as they usually were, tended to embarrass the college. Although the hope of the incumbent director might to some extent be realized, and unsatisfactory candidates might increasingly make their own decision to withdraw in recognition of their inadequacies, there was an obvious need to remove even the vaguest threat of a political appeal against an adverse decision.

Under the heading "administration," the committee recommended that the staff-student ratio be reduced. Practically every educational institution can be counted on to make a case for this particular proposition, but that of the teachers' colleges had become overwhelming. The increase in enrolment from 6,853 in 1967–8 to about 9,300 in 1968–9 was apparently largely unforeseen, and no particular increase in staff was provided to deal with it. The result was that staff-student ratios at their worst came close to 1 to 40. The figures were mostly very far from the ideal of 1 to 12 recommended by the committee. Under such circumstances, severe criticism of the achievement of the colleges within the existing framework should be regarded as unfair. Of course the solution was not easy. While the colleges remained in a kind of limbo, it was extremely difficult to attract competent staff or to retain those already in service. And the worse conditions of service became, the less attractive were the positions on the college staff. If there were villains in the drama, they were those on either side who failed to press the negotiations for the integration of the colleges into the universities.

Another administrative recommendation involved the strengthening of the powers of selection committees which, as has been observed, have generally been regarded as ineffective. The department showed no great enthusiasm for this idea, perhaps regarding the committee arrangement as inadequate for the expressed purpose in any case. As to the recommendation that deadlines for admission should be more rigidly enforced, this is the kind of improvement that usually appeals more to the outsider than to the person expected to carry it out.

The recommendation that the teacher training program should be scheduled to permit large group instruction and seminar discussion was welcomed. But the limitations of the older buildings, and even of the newer ones, in the light of enrolment increases, made such arrangements difficult. It was easier to respond favourably to the suggestion that outstanding school officials, inspectors, and curriculum specialists should be brought in from time to time as guest speakers and "resource persons." How to integrate the contribution of such individuals to the regular program is an ever-present problem. In the same "program" category was the recommendation that the foundations of education program should provide an opportunity for students to study various types of children such as slow learners, those with superior ability, or the culturally disadvantaged. It seems rather unrealistic to expect that arrangements of this kind could be made in the shadow of the drastic changes expected with integration into the universities. Also, important as these children were, the one-year program could be extended only so far.

In the spirit of the Hall-Dennis Committee, even before its report appeared, there was a warm official reception for the idea of increasing emphasis on problem solving, creativity, discovery, and evaluation as they applied to learning and instruction. There was also a positive response to the proposal that there be greater integration between the foundations of education courses and those dealing with methods in the subject areas so that the relationship between theory and practice could be established and undue repetition in methodology courses avoided. Provision for more individual study was regarded as desirable, but crowded conditions and meagre facilities delayed progress in this direction. Lack of funds made it difficult or impossible to provide clinics to correct deficiencies in speech, language, writing, and reading.

The requirement of a post-graduate degree as a qualification for appointment to a college staff has been regarded as desirable. Those already on the staff have been encouraged to secure more advanced qualifications through attendance at summer school. Many have enrolled in the University of Toronto program for the degrees of Master of Education and Master of Arts in Education. In some universities contemplating the integration of a teachers' college, the preponderance of degrees in education and the relative scarcity of degrees in the traditional disciplines have been regarded with disapproval, mainly on the assumption that the former do not provide evidence of the attainment of high intellectual standards. In a sense, this view is confirmed by the decision, made essentially in the

Ontario Institute for Studies in Education, that the Toronto M Ed was to be regarded mainly as a terminal "practitioners' " degree, and that the MA is to be considered the normal route to the Ph D. In actual circumstances, a teachers' college master found it difficult to meet the requirement of full-time attendance needed to obtain the degrees regarded as "respectable" in more traditional university circles.

In principle, the recommendation that library facilities should be increased was received with approval. But practical circumstances made some of the further suggestions, at least as interim measures, appear rather unrealistic, although in the long run their implementation might be highly desirable. Among these were the following:

17. The library should become the educational centre of the college, should provide additional services, and should remain open in the evenings and on Saturdays.
18. The services of the library should be extended to the practising teachers in the area served by the college.
19. The professional librarians and clerical assistants should be employed on the scale recommended by the Canadian Library Association Committee on University and College Libraries.
20. The chief librarian of each college should hold a teaching certificate as well as the B.L.S. degree and should be paid in accordance with these qualifications.[8]

The committee's recommendations with respect to practice teaching were, in considerable measure, implemented, as indicated in chapter 2. More adequate measures were taken to co-ordinate practice teaching activities and to improve liaison with local authorities. Better arrangements were made for staff counselling of small groups of students, for seminar discussions, and for special supervisory attention during the practice teaching periods. But again the effect of great increases in enrolment, and the consequent deterioration of staff-student ratios, must be noted. Although full advantage was not taken of the opportunities offered, students were, in accordance with the recommendations, encouraged to visit elementary schools during the opening weeks to observe the problems encountered during the beginning of the school year. The period of practice teaching in a single school was extended, although the possible disadvantages of too narrow a range of experience were also considered. Cognizance was generally taken of the recommendation that there be more frequent sessions for discussion and planning between the colleges and the practice teachers, although not all the suggested contacts were possible.

Attitude of the universities

The universities were, on the whole, favourably disposed toward the assumption of responsibility for teacher education, provided that it could be done on terms they regarded as acceptable. In this respect, the recommendations of the MacLeod Committee were considered generally satisfactory. The most important points seemed to be that candidates be admitted on the same basis as other students, that the program of general or liberal studies be essentially the same in content and quality as that offered to other students, that the attention given to professional studies be a controlled and limited proportion of the total program, and that the university have and retain the essential elements of control over the program. What the universities wanted to be sure of avoiding was a caretaker role in which their reputation for scholarly excellence would be extended over a set of activities designed and controlled in detail by the department, particularly if, in response to the need for teachers, it meant lower standards of admission and achievement than those demanded of other students. Fortunately, the department's unequivocal acceptance of the committee's recommendations ensured that such conditions would not be proposed. The universities, however, wished to make certain that this was the case.

Negotiations for the integration of the colleges with the universities

The negotiations took a good deal longer than the minister apparently originally intended. In reviewing the situation in detail in the Legislature on May 25, 1967, he mentioned that departmental staff were planning for the implementation of the major recommendations of the report, and that they were visiting each of the campuses involved and holding discussions with university representatives. Each institution had been requested to set up a committee to consider the possibility of implementing the scheme. Among various areas requiring study, he mentioned the problem of transferring staff. In what sounded like an unequivocally reassuring statement, he said: "The interests of these employees regarding their salaries, pensions, sick leave credits and the like will be guaranteed in the transfer to the university staffs."[9]

Davis's optimism was shown in his statement that the first transfer of a program to a university was expected to be completed by July 1, 1968. It seemed conceivable that two institutions might be ready to make the transfer at that time. He proceeded to outline the teacher education situation as he saw it developing. 1 / A modern teachers' college had been erected a few years earlier on a site adjacent to the campus of Lakehead University. The university had agreed to undertake teacher education, and discussions were under way on the details. 2 / Since the opening of the teachers' college at St Catharines in September 1965, classes had been provided in the Brock University buildings. Additional facilities had been made available to the university to house the teachers' college students. The university had provided a site for a new college in the central core of its campus adjacent to the main tower, plans for the building had been completed, and construction was to begin in the near future. 3 / The Senate and Board of Governors of the University of Ottawa had approved the establishment of a new college on a site that the university would make available. The plan called for the preparation of teachers for bilingual classes at both elementary and secondary levels. 4 / Carleton University had agreed to consider the establishment of a new college on its campus, but details remained to be worked out. 5 / The London Teachers' College was adequately housed and favourably located. Davis felt that it would be a relatively simple matter to complete the integration of the whole program within one institution providing for both elementary and secondary school teacher preparation. Useful lessons had been learned from the experimental program of the previous two years, involving the sharing of responsibility between the staffs of the London Teachers' College and Althouse College of Education for the preparation of a group of teachers for qualifications at both levels. 6 / The Hamilton Teachers' College was on a site adjacent to the campus of McMaster University. There was a possibility that, with the expansion of the science buildings in that direction, the college building might be exchanged for a new location within the arts complex. 7 / The arrangement at Sudbury was very similar to that at Brock University, with the teachers' college students accommodated in the buildings of Laurentian University and a new building in prospect. 8 / The Peterborough Teachers' College was housed in a structure built in 1908. Preliminary discussions had been held with Trent University about the possibility of establishing facilities for teacher education on campus, and the prospects looked good. 9 / The teachers' college at North Bay was in an unusual position, since there was a unique opportunity there to integrate a number of institutions in one educational complex. These included the North Bay branch of the Cambrian College of Applied Arts and Technology; Nipissing College, an affiliate of the Laurentian University, which was to offer first year arts courses beginning in September 1967; and the local school of nursing. If all these institutions could be established on a single site, it would be possible to provide ancillary services such as a central library, a gymnasium, residences, and a cafeteria, which none of the institutions could afford individually. 10 / The University of Windsor had expressed interest in providing for teacher education and was prepared to supply a suitable site. The relatively new college building, which was located some distance away, could be utilized appropriately to meet pressing needs for educational facilities in the Windsor area. 11 / The Stratford Teachers' College, housed in one of the older structures, would obviously need a new building on a new site. Existing plans called for a college that it was hoped might be operated under the aegis of a neighbouring university. It may be mentioned here as an aside that Robarts, at an earlier stage in his career, is said to have promised the people of Stratford that they would not lose their teachers' college. The writer heard the view expressed, in a visit in 1969, that Stratford was too small and isolated to justify any large investment in educational facilities at the post-secondary level, and that the college would probably go elsewhere eventually. 12 / In Toronto, moves were being made to assemble land adjacent to the College of Education on Bloor Street. Funds had been allocated for a large addition to, and a refurbishing of, the existing structure so that there would be sufficient space for the new program. 13 / It was hoped also that York University would proceed with the establishment of facilities for teacher education.[10]

At McMaster University the "Report to the Senate by the Senate Committee on the Training of Elementary School Teachers," which appeared in mimeographed form on September 19, 1967, provided an example of the series of exploratory studies conducted in response to the adoption of the new policy. A brief review of some of its concepts may help to provide an insight into university attitudes. The committee had quickly come to the unanimous conclusion that McMaster University should assume some responsibility for implementing the recommendations contained in the report prepared by the MacLeod Committee. It shared the view that the time had come for a new concept of, and new programs for, teacher education. It hoped that such programs would produce elementary school teachers with deeper scholarship and greater maturity. The implications of the report of the MacLeod Committee had been examined on the premise that each university must evolve the program that best fitted its own traditions and circumstances.

The essential point underlying a number of the Senate Committee's decisions was that the consecutive plan be adopted, as opposed to the concurrent plan, and that a bachelor's degree, normally resulting from three years' work in one of the Faculties of Humanities, Social Sciences, and Science, be required for admission to it. Graduates would receive the Diploma of Teacher Education. The professional year would be taken in a Department of Teacher Education in the Faculty of Social Sciences. It was recommended that a Senate Committee on Objectives and Long-term Planning be set up to assist the Chairman of the Department of Teacher Education and the Dean of the Faculty of Social Sciences with the organization of the new department and with its integration into the university as a whole. This committee might consider whether it was desirable for McMaster University to undertake the professional preparation of secondary school teachers, and the role the existing staff of the Hamilton Teachers' College might play in providing faculty for the new department. This last suggestion foreshadowed the later tension resulting from the determination of the Department of Education to provide several years of security for teachers' college staff. Another controversial proposal was that the Hamilton Teachers' College continue to provide teacher education programs until the completion of a four-year program became the minimum requirement for the certification of new teachers. That is, the Senate Committee felt that the university should not be involved in the transitional stages proposed by the MacLeod Committee. There were elements of an impasse in that official policy did not leave room for two different programs conducted in neighbouring buildings.

The Senate Committee's reasons for favouring the consecutive plan were as follows. 1 / It was the simplest possible way of maintaining a ratio of 75 per cent academic work and 25 per cent professional training in a four-year program, as recommended by the MacLeod Committee. Under a concurrent plan, there could be great pressure to increase professional work at the expense of academic work. Also, the professional year could be of a higher calibre, since all entrants would have extensive academic experience, an advantage that would facilitate the recruitment of competent staff. 2 / A consecutive plan would give the students the maximum possible flexibility in career choice. 3 / Practice teaching would be confined to a purely professional year, thus avoiding interruptions in academic course work. 4 / The consecutive plan was currently working well for the preparation of secondary school teachers. A further point that the Senate Committee did not see fit to record was the apprehension that, under the concurrent plan, lower standards in the professional work might erode those in the academic courses. Experience in the combined Arts and Physical Education course had been unfavourable in that the students involved nearly always passed in physical education, and tension was set up when they failed in arts subjects.

The Presidents' Subcommittee on Teacher Education, under the chairmanship of President J.A. Gibson of Brock University, met in September 1967 with the Deputy Minister of Education, the director of the Teacher Education Branch of the Department of Education, and the chairman of the Committee on University Affairs. The participants undertook to explore the common principles that should underlie each agreement for the integration of a program of teacher education into a university. The decision was made to set up a drafting committee "to prepare a statement of the essential conditions under which the universities would be prepared to assume responsibility for teacher-education programmes."[11] The committee concerned itself with the following matters: the transfer of buildings and facilities, enrolment projections, capital and operating grants, the establishment of advisory committees, policies and standards for the admission of students, the appointment of staff, curriculum and certification, termination of the agreements, and filing of agreements.

The drafting committee prepared a statement for circulation to members of the Committee of Presidents in January 1968. Comments received from various universities led to the production of a revised draft, which was endorsed by the Committee of Presidents at the beginning of March, and copies of which were sent to the minister and to officials in the Departments of Education and University Affairs. Discussions continued during the next two months, leading to broad agreement on the principles that were to guide the working out of agreements with individual universities. There were, however, certain points which caused a delay in the formal acceptance of the guidelines.

One source of difficulty was that the deputy minister stood firm on the principle that provision for teacher education in a university had to be made in a college, faculty, school, or other autonomous division. A department within a faculty of arts, arts and science, social science, or other such division was not acceptable. This stand was in accord with a promise made by the minister to the teachers' federations. A more serious source of difficulty centred on the conditions under which teachers' college staff would be accepted into the universities. There had been certain problems inherent in the situation from the beginning. One was that the staff had been selected to a large extent on the basis of their reputed excellence as practitioners rather than for their scholarly attainments. In an address to the Teacher Education Section of the Ontario Educational Association on March 24, 1970, J.T. Angus, who assumed the deanship of the Lakehead Faculty of Education on September 1, 1969, elaborated on the reasons for their poor reputation among the university community.

There has been no compulsion on Teachers' College Masters as there is on Professors in Faculties of Education in other jurisdictions to take advanced degrees, conduct research, publish, assume leadership positions in professional organizations, serve on academic committees, deliver scholarly papers or engage in any of the other forms of competitive professional activity on which promotion, tenure or merit increases in salary are normally based. This is not to suggest that some Teachers' College Masters have not done these things. Rather the point is being made that there has been no endemic need to do them.

Angus explained the position of the university community in this manner.

Most University Professors adopt the position that the vast majority of Teachers' College masters should be denied University appointments at the time of a Teachers' College transfer for two simple reasons, (a) most are not qualified for University teaching and (b) if they are given appointments on a probationary basis it would be almost impossible to get rid of them if they turned out to be incompetent. Let us examine the second reason first. It relates to the political character of a University Faculty Association. If a Teachers' College staff was transferred to the University with the expectation that say no more than half of the persons involved would attain permanent appointment then the Faculty Association would be placed in an untenable position. The Faculty Association would find it difficult to accept the termination of many probationary appointments in a short period of time. As a result, tenure would be accorded in a large number of cases and, it is argued, the whole purpose of the transfer of teacher education to the University, i.e. reform in teacher training, would be undermined.

The kind of qualifications needed for teaching in a university faculty of education was a question that would have to be decided in terms of the kind of program that would be developed. Again, Angus indicated the prevalent attitude in the universities.

> Generally, most University personnel do not have a benevolent attitude towards the Department of Education and the whole system of public education in Ontario. Most see the present system as a hide-bound, dictatorial structure incapable of changing from within. The present Teachers' Colleges are perceived as part of that structure. Some claim that only a revolution in pedagogy and a complete overthrow of the present system can bring about the implementation of new ideas such as those proposed by the Hall-Dennis Report. Many argue that this revolution can not be brought about by most of the current practitioners or their neophytes, but only by teachers who have been educated outside the present system and who, hopefully, have assimilated a sympathetic attitude toward reform.

Departmental officials took the attitude that the onus would be placed on the teachers' college masters to upgrade their qualifications during the interval in which their positions would be guaranteed. The Director of Teacher Education, G.L. Woodruff, expressed the view that any who were not capable of obtaining graduate degrees should not be given responsibility in the teacher education program. The department was prepared to facilitate the upgrading process by making generous provision for study leave.

University faculty members have felt that teachers' college staff have been paid more than their academic qualifications have merited. The universities will face a continuing dilemma in this respect. If they expect to place the professional aspects of their teacher education programs in the hands of the most competent people with experience in the educational system, they will have to compete in the public market by offering salaries based on something other than purely academic qualifications. If they rely completely on those who have risen through the university ranks without such experience, they will risk producing programs that are less relevant to the needs of a modern school system than the worst ever maintained in the teachers' colleges. It may be, of course, that some of the attractions of working in a university atmosphere, such as the stimulating intellectual climate, the more adequate facilities, the wider range of associations, the better staff-student ratio, and the prestige of a university title will compensate to some extent for existing salary rewards in the teachers' colleges, and that salary levels can be brought somewhat more into line.

A stalemate in the negotiations with the universities lasted for several months, and the prospects of an agreement looked poor. In the meantime, at least two universities were anxious to conclude agreements with the department, and it seemed possible that they might break ranks. In November 1968 the Committee of Presidents set up a new committee under the chairmanship of J.J. Deutsch to attempt to reach an understanding. In essence, the department had its way on the disputed points. An agreement on the guidelines was announced jointly by the minister and A.D. Dunton, Chairman of the Committee of Presidents, in March 1969. The principles enunciated in the report of the MacLeod Committee were declared to be the basis for the agreement. Conditions dealt with in the guidelines included procedures to be followed with respect to buildings and facilities, capital and operating grants, the admission of students, the structure of the teacher education set-up and of advisory committees, staffing, certification, and curriculum.

Land, buildings, and facilities of an existing teachers' college adjacent to a university would be transferred to the latter. The planning and construction of additional buildings would be carried out as a regular part of the university's building program. The cost would be met in full by the provincial government. It was considered likely that ancillary services such as general libraries, cafeterias, gymnasiums, and residences should be part of the university's over-all provision of such facilities. It was intended that operating costs would eventually be paid on a formula basis, in line with the system established in 1967 for operating grants to universities. At the beginning, however, the full cost of each program would be met by special grants.

The recommendation of the committee on the establishment of advisory committees was accepted. Each of these committees would consist of members named by the minister, the university, and any other bodies specified in the agreement. Its functions, including such matters as staffing policy and curriculum, would be similarly specified. Admission to the program was to be open to students satisfying the normal academic admission requirements of the university. There might be a variety of organizational structures, including a college of education or a faculty. The guidelines preserved the minister's right to grant certificates and to prescribe the conditions for certification.

Although staff members transferred from the teachers' college to the university were to have their positions guaranteed for four years, they were to be encouraged to take study leave to improve their qualifications. The department promised to provide funds for this purpose. It would also undertake to discover alternative openings for those who did not join the university staff, or who failed to secure tenure after four years. All new staff appointments were to be made in accordance with established university procedures.

The question of payment of fees was raised from time to time. Prospective student teachers were unlikely to look forward to the prospect of losing the existing privilege of free attendance at teachers' college. To a question asked by Walter Pitman in the Legislature, the minister replied:

> ... that has not been determined; we have not reached this point yet.
>
> I am just speaking, again, of my own initial reaction, and it is that probably ... they should be treated the same as other students at the institution. They can be charged fees, and then receive some sort of additional bursary, or something from the department, if they are going into teacher education. But, as the hon. member just remarked, we do not want them treated as different students on campus.[12]

The first agreement under the new guidelines was one which transferred control and operation of the Lakehead Teachers' College to Lakehead University as of July 1, 1969. The announcement by the minister and W.G. Tamblyn, President of the University, indicated that a further agreement would soon be reached to provide for the establishment in 1970 of facilities at Lakehead University to prepare secondary school teachers. The new faculty would include the existing Lakehead Teachers' College, which disappeared with the implementation of the agreement.

As described by J.T. Angus in his address to the Teacher Education Section of the OEA, the principles on which the new program was based were as follows.

1. The programme should provide both secondary and elementary teachers with a general education in breadth;
2. The programme should provide some academic specialization for both elementary and secondary teachers;
3. Education students should be required to show evidence of academic and scholarship abilities;
4. Prospective elementary and secondary teachers should have an adequate grounding in teaching principles and methods;
5. The academic education and, wherever practicable, the professional training of elementary and secondary teachers should be integrated;
6. The study of academic and professional education should normally take place concurrently;
7. The professional aspect of the teacher education programme should maintain a balance among education theory, methods and practice;
8. The Faculty of Education should not try to duplicate courses and services already provided by some other Faculty, School or administrative department in the University;
9. The Faculty of Education should recognize the right and responsibility of members of the teaching profession to participate as partners with Profes-

sors in the Faculty of Education in the preparation of teachers, especially in determining whether a student should be recommended for certification on the basis of his performance in a practice school;

10. Specialist training for teachers in professional courses should not be provided in the undergraduate programme, but should be made available through summer courses or graduate study.

The Lakehead plans involved the granting of two degrees to be awarded simultaneously at the end of four or five years in a concurrent program. These would consist of any of the following combinations: BA, B Ed; B Sc, B Ed; BPHE, B Ed. The candidate for a double degree would be required to major in some area of study in arts or science and to satisfy all other university requirements for a BA or B Sc, in addition to which he would take thirty units, the equivalent of one year, in education courses. He would also have to demonstrate competence in practice teaching and submit a major paper on some topic in education.

The programs for elementary and secondary school teachers were to be similar, and it would be possible to qualify for certification at both levels at the same time. The same foundation courses would be provided for both levels, while the methodology courses would be directed toward either the elementary or the secondary school. The first year of the program would be mainly academic; the second year would involve one education course; the third year would be divided about equally between academic and professional courses, with the introduction of practice teaching; and the fourth year would involve completion of the work for both degrees, with more practice teaching and the submission of the major paper. In addition to the concurrent program, there would be a consecutive program for those already holding a university degree.

During 1969–70 the one-year program leading to elementary school certification was maintained. There were plans to continue it along with a new two-year concurrent program leading to an Elementary School Teacher's Certificate, Standard 2. Students with two years of arts or science from any Ontario university were to be admitted to the secondary program in September 1970. After two further years of study, they might obtain the two degrees and the appropriate certification.

By the end of the 1969–70 academic year, Lakehead University had been joined by the University of Ottawa and the University of Windsor in providing programs which involved the absorption of teachers' colleges. At the time of writing, it did not appear likely that the University of Windsor would have time to work out a degree program for 1970–1. The expectations were that the one-year program hitherto offered by the Windsor Teachers' College would continue. It was assumed that negotiations between the minister and the University of Western Ontario would have produced an agreement leading to the establishment of a program for the preparation of elementary teachers in the Althouse

College of Education, and the consequent termination of the independent existence of the London Teachers' College, by 1971–2. Carleton and McMaster were prepared to establish a program, but were showing continued reluctance to absorb the teachers' colleges in their respective areas. With the appointment of a new president, York's plans were expected to be brought to a point where they could be implemented.

At the time of writing, serious discussions were taking place over the system of formula grants by which the programs for teacher preparation would be financed through the university grants formula. There appeared to be substantial differences of opinion between the Committee on University Affairs and the universities over the amounts the latter would need to finance the programs. The whole situation contained the seeds of future problems, which might grow intense if the portfolios of Education and University Affairs were held by different ministers. Would the appraisal of need by the Committee of University Affairs, which had the responsibility of recommending the appropriate level of financial support, correspond with that of the Department of Education, which had the responsibility of carrying out policies designed to ensure that the schools were adequately staffed?

The problems of negotiating with the universities, both collectively and individually, may have seemed a long and, in some respects, a difficult process. But the critical period is yet to come, as certain comments by A.B. Hodgetts indicate.

> We were particularly discouraged by the relationships that exist on many campuses between the academic community and faculties of education or teachers' colleges. The lack of any real communication, the failure to understand each other, the petty jealousies and rivalries – there is no other word for them – are elements that should not exist at any level of education. Both sides, we suggest, are equally guilty of making serious mistakes so far as our special area of interest is concerned. The academicians have slighted the special needs of the teaching profession, while the faculties of education have become ingrown, frequently oblivious to the wider society, overconcerned with methods divorced from a philosophical approach to subject matter, and therefore prone to swing uncritically on the pendulum of change. The teachers themselves are inclined to be much less critical of their academic than of their professional training. There is an almost universal feeling across Canada that a great deal of the course work in faculties of education and teachers' colleges is a sheer waste of time, something to be passively endured because it is the only way to enter the profession. The main values are derived from practice teaching and even in this area the criticisms and disillusionment of teachers would fill a separate volume.[13]

In the address referred to earlier, J.T. Angus foresaw other possible dangers.

With Universities largely autonomous over their own programmes and with budgets supervised by the Department of University Affairs, teacher education policies and programme definition may well develop independently of other education policies for the Province. This situation may be further complicated by the fact that the Department of Education and not the Department of University Affairs controls certification. There is the possibility that teacher education programmes developed in the Universities may lose congruence with certification requirements prescribed by the Department of Education. There is the further possibility that both may get out of line with the ever-changing expectations of the school system for the role of the teacher. If the Department of Education's certification regulations is [*sic*] the only co-ordinating force we could have developing in Ontario a confusing jumble of teacher education programmes and facilities ...

Another unanticipated consequence of teacher education in the University is the fact that those who are vitally concerned with teacher education may find it increasingly difficult to have a voice in its development. I am speaking of the Teachers' Federations, the Trustees' Council, the Association of School Education Officials, the Home and School Association, etc. The old channels of communication and influence through the Department of Education will be closed.

Angus urged the formation of a provincial board similar to that in the province of Alberta to serve as an advisory body on matters pertaining to teacher education and certification. The Alberta board consisted of a chairman appointed by the Minister of Education and eighteen others, including representatives of the teachers' and trustees' associations, and the Department of Education. It made recommendations with respect to standards of teacher education, types of certificates, regulations and principles governing certification in all acceptable institutions, and the establishment of criteria for granting charters to institutions proposing to offer programs of teacher education. It also conducted studies in all matters relating to teacher education and certification.

FIVE

The development of the colleges of education

THE BACKGROUND

First attempts to initiate formal preparation

When provision was made in 1797 for the establishment of grammar schools in Upper Canada, no qualifications were specified for their staffs. By 1819 trustees were required to examine candidates for appointment, and one of the duties of the Board of Education established in 1823 was to review and confirm these appointments. The Common School Act of 1841 required a standing committee to examine candidates for headmasterships, and headmasters were supposed to consult the Council of King's College before appointing assistants.[1]

Graduates of the Toronto Normal School, established in 1847, who held First Class Certificates were eligible to teach in the grammar schools. The course did not, however, give them any specific professional preparation for such a task. In order to remedy this deficiency, Egerton Ryerson advocated the establishment of a model grammar school in 1853. Delayed by lack of funds, such a school was finally opened in Toronto five years later. It did not, however, awaken general public interest, and was closed in 1863.[2] The grammar schools continued to be staffed largely with untrained teachers having very limited academic qualifications. There were, however, exceptions and some grammar schools were widely known for the excellence of their instruction.[3]

Provisions before 1920

The need for good teachers was substantially increased with the establishment of a system of public secondary education by the High Schools Act of 1871. It was not until later, however, that any definite step was taken to provide for their professional preparation. In 1885 the Minister of Education was authorized to enter into agreements with five collegiate institutes by which they would undertake to set up training institutes. Four were actually selected: those at Hamilton, Kingston, Guelph, and Kitchener. The fourteen-week course consisted of two weeks of instruction by the principal in general theory, including school organization and management, six weeks of observation and instruction with department heads acting as tutors, and six weeks in teaching practice.[4] There were no lectures in pedagogy, methods, or philosophy of education. The plan was ineffective because of lack of enthusiasm on the part of educational leaders, the absence of professional training on the part of the instructors, interference with the work of regular classes, the extra strain on the teachers, and the small number attending the course.[5] The training institutes were therefore discontinued in 1890, and a provincial School of Pedagogy established instead.

The School of Pedagogy, located in the Toronto Normal School building, offered a course similar to that of the normal school, but on a more advanced level. The students attended lectures for six weeks and then spent six weeks at training schools. After the first year, there was no provision for practice teaching, and the students were reduced to practising on each other. The fact that the program was voluntary also constituted a serious handicap. The universities were said to have accelerated the failure of the program by openly opposing professional training for teachers. In 1897 the school was transferred to Hamilton under the name of the Ontario Normal College. It occupied space in the new collegiate institute, where facilities were provided for observation and practice teaching. The principal of the collegiate was also principal of the normal college, and the heads of collegiate departments served as lecturers for the student teachers. The program flourished and by 1907 a substantial number were preparing for First Class, High School Assistant's, and Specialist's Certificates. During the interval, the university professors had become converted to the idea of having the program in Toronto, and exerted considerable pressure to achieve this end.[6] In 1907 the functions of the normal college were transferred to newly established Faculties of Education at Queen's University and the University of Toronto.

The faculties offered programs leading to the same three certificates as had the Ontario Normal College, the first of which was available to non-graduates and the latter two to graduates. They also conducted courses leading to the certificate of Public or Separate School Inspector and to the degrees of Bachelor and Doctor of Paedagogy. By 1919–20 the enrolment in the faculty at Queen's amounted to little more than one-tenth that at Toronto. In 1920 both faculties were discontinued, and the Ontario College of Education was established in their place.

The agreement between the minister and the University of Toronto, 1920

The memorandum of agreement between the Minister of Education and the governors of the University of Toronto on June 30, 1920, was subsequently criticized widely on the grounds that the association with the university was merely a matter of departmental convenience and left the university no real influence over the program. Of the ten clauses, the first and last were only matters of form. The others were as follows:

2. The Ontario College of Education shall provide for (1) graduate courses of instruction in education; (2) courses for certificates as High School Assistants and Specialists; and (3) such other courses for certificates of the Department of Education as may be required by the Minister of Education and agreed to by the Governors. It shall also co-operate, so far as may be deemed practicable by both parties to this agreement, both in instruction and in practice-teaching, with other Provincial training schools in the training of teachers for Provincial certificates.
3. The courses of study for students in training for certificates of the Department of Education and all proposed regulations affecting the training, conduct, and health of such students shall be approved by the Lieutenant-Governor-in-Council on the report of the Minister.
4. The names of all persons to be appointed to the College staff of instructors in courses for certificates of the Department shall be submitted to the Minister for approval and the appointments shall be subject to the approval of the Lieutenant-Governor-in-Council.
5. By arrangement between the Minister and the President of the University, the work done in the College, and in the observation and practice schools in connection therewith, shall be open at any time to the visitation and inspection of the Provincial Director of Professional Training Schools, or such other person or persons as may be designated by the Minister of Education.
6. The Governors shall submit to the Minister of Education before the 31st of December of each year detailed estimates of the proposed expenditure upon the College upon capital account and for maintenance for the following academic year, and, if approved by the Minister of Education, these shall be submitted to the Legislative Assembly as a part of the Estimates of the Department of Education.
7. All tuition, examination, graduation, or other fees imposed upon students in training for certificates of the Department shall be subject to the approval of the Minister of Education.
8. The certificates of the Department of Education shall be awarded to students in training upon the report of the Dean of the College and the Provincial Director of Professional Training Schools, approved by the Minister, in whose name the certificates shall be issued.
9. This agreement shall remain in force from year to year subject to cancellation by notice in writing from either party to the other at least one year before the cancellation becomes effective.

The most significant elements in this agreement were the minister's right not only to grant certificates, but also to approve the courses and regulations applying to the students; to approve all instructors in certificate courses; to inspect the work of the college; and to control the budget in detail. The omission of any indication of how the dean was to be appointed was to cause serious difficulties later. The university's right to terminate the agreement on a year's notice was of doubtful value, especially when the institution became dependent to a substantial degree on government funds.

Beginning of preparation of technical and vocational teachers
The first steps were taken in 1917–18 to provide professional preparation for shop instructors and teachers in technical schools with the provision of a course of extension lectures in methods of teaching and class management at Toronto, Hamilton, and London. In 1921 these evening classes were supplemented by summer courses designed mainly to train teachers who were already on the staffs of technical schools but who lacked professional qualifications. These two types of courses were weak in their failure to provide proper facilities for practice teaching. For some time the provincial government hoped for federal-provincial co-operation in providing a central institution for the preparation of technical school teachers, but finally moved to establish the Ontario Training College for Technical Teachers. This institution was transferred to a site close to the Hamilton Technical Institute.

At first the standard course was one of twenty weeks' duration, with provision for summer sessions for untrained teachers already serving in the technical schools. Entrance requirements were gradually raised as supply and demand came into balance, and the winter course was extended to twenty-five weeks. Special courses were offered from time to time to meet particular needs: for example, extension courses for teachers without technical training who were conducting evening courses in vocational subjects, and a course in general education in 1934 for skilled craftsmen who wished to become shop instructors but had not completed high school. Provision was made in 1928 for both Ordinary and Specialist's Certificates, and in 1934 for a High School Principal's Certificate.

As of September 1, 1946, the Ontario Training College for Technical Teachers was reorganized as a department of the Ontario College of Education. It offered courses for the Ordinary Vocational Certificate and for the Intermediate and Specialist Certificates in industrial arts and crafts.

Establishment of the Vocational Guidance Centre
In 1945 what was at first known as the Vocational Guidance Centre, and later simply as the Guidance Centre, was established as a division of the college. Its function was to develop, produce, and distribute materials for school guidance programs, and to take part in the training of school guidance workers. A kind of partnership was worked out with the Department of Educational Research for the sale of testing materials produced by the latter agency. The centre also acted as the agent for a number of publishers of educational materials in the United States.

Recommendations of the Royal Commission

The Royal Commission's report in 1950 suggested an end to the monopoly of the Ontario College of Education in the preparation of secondary school teachers. It also favoured an arrangement between the Department of Education and certain universities, giving the latter more control over the program than was enjoyed by the University of Toronto by the terms of the agreement of 1920. The commission indicated the extent to which the minister would control the process and the way in which he would exercise his control by recommending

> that the Minister of Education retain the power of licensing teachers and issue such licenses upon recommendation of a licensing board, appointed by him, based either upon the results of written and oral examinations conducted by it or, in lieu thereof, on the results of examinations conducted by Faculties of Education accredited by it for this purpose.[7]

The Appointment of B.C. Diltz as Dean of the Ontario College of Education

There was particular significance in the appointment of B.C. Diltz as Dean of the Ontario College of Education in 1958. In that year, A.C. Lewis, who had guided the destinies of the college in a benevolent if rather despotic manner for many years, was at an age when retirement on full pension was possible but not mandatory. Lewis and Education Minister Dunlop had apparently had some disagreements, and the latter was not reluctant to see a new dean appointed. When word of Lewis's decision to retire at the end of the year reached him, M. St A. Woodside, who was Acting President of the University of Toronto for the year, took steps to form a committee to nominate a successor. Dunlop dismissed his efforts and initiated independent action.

Dunlop proceeded to have his own nominee, Diltz, appointed to the deanship by government order-in-council. Diltz had long been known for his powerful personality and his outstanding brilliance as a teacher of English. He was also a very controversial figure who was fond of denouncing guidance and psychology in particular. His colleagues were by no means all enthusiastic about his elevation; in fact, some were extremely apprehensive. By the time his five-year term of office was over, however, he had shown himself to be a humane and tolerant administrator, and he left in the midst of genuine expressions of affection. He appealed to Dunlop, apparently, because he stood for the sound traditional virtues as opposed to the ephemeral fads of modern education.

In making the appointment, Dunlop apparently saw fit to cast aspersions on Woodside's integrity, although the university authorities were firmly behind him. But the attorney-general of the province declared that there was nothing they could do under the terms of the agreement of 1920, which had said nothing about the procedure of appointing the dean. The atmosphere from that time on was naturally extremely chilly, and the college was pushed further into isolation. For some time, the Board of Governors declined to approve recommendations for professorial appointments in the usual way, but merely "noted" that they had been made.

C.T. Bissell, President of the University from 1958, recognized an unsatisfactory situation and at the same time foresaw the possibility of future improvement in his report for 1960–1.

> The problem is primarily one of finding a method of preparing for a teaching career that is attractive and intellectually stimulating in its own right. I doubt whether even the most enthusiastic defender of the present system of teacher training for secondary schools would say that these conditions obtained today. The present system suffers from its undue isolation from the university, and from a conspicuous absence of the usual academic procedures by which vigorous and salty democracy is maintained within a university faculty ... The current expansion of teacher training facilities gives us an opportunity to improve our method of procedure in teacher education. This may well be the key to our whole educational enterprise. I express the hope that the opportunity will be seized with vigour and imagination.[8]

Despite his differences with the University of Toronto, Diltz placed a great deal of value on academic achievement. He established a staff honours list to single out certain students for their scholarly acumen, mature tastes, and teaching power. In the same report in which Bissell criticized the existing program, Diltz deplored the withdrawal of 23 per cent of the candidates admitted to both winter and summer courses and wondered why some of them were ever awarded university degrees in the first place. He wrote: "The great need of the teaching profession is for candidates with better degrees."[9]

As dean, Diltz concentrated his efforts on the programs for the High School Assistant's Certificates, Types A and B, and delegated a great deal of power to the heads of other departments such as the Department of Vocational Education, the School of Library Science, the Department of Graduate Studies, the Department of Educational Research, and the Guidance Centre. Even the tenuous links that had previously existed among them were loosened, and by the time of his retirement, the college was ready to disintegrate. The School of Library Science was the first to go, followed by graduate studies and research.

The Minister's Committee on the Training of Secondary School Teachers

In February 1961 the Minister of Education, Robarts, set up a committee to study the following subjects:

1. Admission requirements of colleges of education and the courses at universities leading thereto.
2. The curriculum in special subjects and summer courses therein.
3. Practice teaching in all its aspects.
4. Diplomas, certificates, and degrees.
5. The relationship of the colleges to the universities and to the Department of Education in matters both academic and non-academic.
6. The relationship of the academic and the professional education of teachers, in both time and arrangement.[10]

Dean Diltz exerted effective pressure to have this committee set up. Reflecting his antagonism toward the university, it was at first to consist exclusively of educational practitioners, with a heavy weighting of administrators. Later a single university representative, M. St A. Woodside, was added. He is said to have exerted a very strong influence on the deliberations of the committee.

Members of the committee travelled widely and observed schemes for the preparation of secondary school teachers in operation in various provinces and in other countries. They recognized four accepted methods: 1 / the independent teacher training college, fairly prevalent in the United States; 2 / the institution operated directly by the Department of Education, as were the teachers' colleges in Ontario; 3 / provision for a program within the university; and 4 / an arrangement for shared authority between the Department of Education and the university. The committee reviewed the favourable and unfavourable arguments advanced for each of these schemes and rejected all but the last, which led Bascom St John to comment: "Ontario is therefore destined to retain a secondary teacher training system of a type which exists almost nowhere else. In other words, in this particular we are right and all the rest of the world is wrong. And, of course, perhaps it is."[11]

The committee took a strong stand against the idea of a concurrent program of combined academic and professional studies. The members were persuaded that there was a kind of inevitability about such a program becoming watered down with weak and trivial education courses. They were impressed by surveys in the United States showing that education students typically ranked at or near the bottom of the list in terms of scholastic aptitude and various measures of academic achievement. They saw political pressures, particularly in times of teacher shortage, forcing a lowering of admission and graduation standards for this particular group. Their attitude was perhaps best exemplified by the following passage:

> It is noteworthy that undergraduate courses in colleges and faculties of education, as a result of the serious weakening of their intellectual content and the inclusion of a multiplicity of "education" courses, too frequently of a

fragmentary kind, inevitably become "soft" courses to which are attracted a great many students who wish to acquire a university degree by the easiest means. There is ample evidence that education faculties offering undergraduate courses have attracted students of low general ability, as compared with the ability of students in other faculties.[12]

There was an apparent assumption that a program managed within a university faculty must necessarily be of the concurrent type. But there was really no reason why a consecutive program could not have been managed under the same auspices. St John called attention to the committee's failure to give full consideration to this possibility, which he found especially strange because Ontario's secondary school teachers had been prepared in the Faculties of Education at Toronto and Queen's before 1920. He observed that virtually all the members of the committee must have been taught by graduates of those faculties, with no apparent harm. He was resigned to the fact that the Department of Education would almost certainly accept the committee's recommendation to continue with the existing type of post-graduate training college, with modifications in its structure and program. His own preference came out strongly in his comments. "Thus, the chance to create a really vital university-sponsored faculty or institute of education, paralleling the faculties of medicine, law and engineering, is being lost. The continuance of departmental control of teacher training will delay indefinitely the teachers' goal of a self-governing profession."[13]

The committee was quite dissatisfied with the existing agreement between the minister and the University of Toronto and offered detailed suggestions for a new arrangement. Its main effect would be to associate the college more closely with the university, in part by enlisting the support of professors from other faculties, as well as of secondary school teachers, in the conduct of college affairs. The report advocated that two bodies be established: 1 / an advisory board, consisting of the dean, and nominees of the minister, the president, and the Ontario Teachers' Federation, to advise the president on all matters affecting the college; and 2 / a college council, consisting of college staff, members of other departments, and associate teachers, which would be modeled on other such councils. Dean Dadson commented in his contribution to the president's report for 1962–3 that at first sight it might appear that the independence of the college would be lost in a maze of committees. But he felt that "the counsel of an experienced and outstanding staff would carry enough weight to ensure the essential margin of autonomy without which a college is unworthy of the name."[14] The Minister's Committee recommended such procedures for appointing a dean as would ensure against a repetition of the events surrounding Diltz's assumption of the office. He would be appointed by the university with the approval of the minister. The essence of the existing method of financing would continue, with the government supplying the university with the amount needed for the operation of the college which the university would then hand over to the latter.

In order to integrate some aspects of the college program with university work, the committee recommended interchanges of faculty. Professors from the Faculty of Arts might, for example, lecture in such subjects as psychology and sociology, with adaptations to suit the specific needs of the student teachers. Bascom St John's view on this recommendation was that it would be a miracle if the scheme worked. It was a widely held assumption that a professor did nothing to advance his own scholarly career, and might even do it considerable harm, if he immersed himself to any great degree in lecturing to student teachers. The College of Education staff also tended to hold reservations about the competence of other professors, based particularly on their concept of good teaching.

The committee recommended the establishment of at least two new colleges of education in different parts of the province. This development was practically implied by the extension of the special summer course to London and Kingston in 1960. By the time the report appeared, active plans were under way for the founding of Althouse College of Education as an affiliate of the University of Western Ontario.

William Davis had become Minister of Education by the time the report appeared, and his method of handling it was in accordance with his policy of maximum consultation. It was announced that the government had not finally adopted the report except in one or two details, and that it hoped that comment and discussion would arise that would clarify understanding of its principles and possibly uncover weaknesses.[15] By the middle of 1968, a department official was able to state that, of the 148 recommendations contained in the report, well over 100 had already been implemented.

EARLY DEVELOPMENT OF ALTHOUSE COLLEGE OF EDUCATION

Establishment

On March 28, 1960, Education Minister Robarts commented on the establishment for the first time of a summer course for the preparation of secondary school teachers to be given at London and Kingston. He said that, if these courses proved to be successful, and there was every indication that they would be, the next step would be to establish permanent colleges of education in each of these centres.[16] When the Minister's Committee reported in 1962, with its recommendation of such a development, it was really only giving approval to established policy.

An agreement between the minister and the University of Western Ontario was reached on April 16, 1963. In several respects, it was the least favourable to the university of the first three such agreements drawn up in the 1960s. Its first clause provided as follows:

The Minister shall establish, on land and in a building or buildings provided by the Province of Ontario, equip, maintain and provide all costs of the operation and maintenance of a college in the City of London to be known as the Althouse College of Education, University of Western Ontario, London ... and all land, buildings and equipment so provided for shall be and remain the property of the Province of Ontario.

The fact that all of an institution's physical assets were under government ownership did not help to create the impression that it was an integral part of a university.

The next clause provided that the college would offer courses leading to the High School Assistant's Certificate, Types A and B, possibly including as an option a course leading to certification of candidates as elementary school teachers; courses leading to the Interim Vocational Certificate, Types A and B; and "such other courses leading to certification of candidates as secondary school teachers as may be determined jointly by the Minister and the University." The content of these courses would also be decided jointly. The university might establish courses in the college leading to post-graduate degrees, and the content of such courses was to be determined by the university. As compared with arrangements made with the University of Toronto three years later, these prescriptions, except for the ones dealing with post-graduate degrees, were clearly much more definite.

An Advisory Committee was established consisting of the dean *ex officio* and the following additional members: four appointed by the minister; four appointed by the university; three appointed by the Ontario Teachers' Federation, one of whom was to be a principal recommended by the Ontario Secondary School Headmasters' Association; and one appointed by the Ontario Secondary School Superintendents' Association. The Advisory Committee was to "make recommendations in matters concerning admission requirements, curriculum, examinations and other matters affecting the College."

The dean of the college was to be appointed "by the University with the concurrence and approval of the Minister." The university was also to make all appointments to the teaching staff of the college subject to the approval of the minister. This provision, however, came under a clause worded as follows: "Save with respect to post-graduate courses, the University shall act in pursuance of this agreement only as agent for and on behalf of the Minister and as such agent shall undertake the administration and operation of the College on the following terms." This clause did not appear in the later agreements with Queen's and the University of Toronto.

The government was to maintain fairly specific controls over the budget, for which it was to provide the funds in their entirety, apart from receipts from students' fees. The university was to "submit to the Minister estimates of its proposed expenditures for the College on capital account and for operating and maintenance costs ... in such detail as the Minister shall require, and if approved by the Minister such estimates shall be submitted to the Legislative Assembly as part of the estimates of the Department of Education." The university was to submit annually to the minister an audited statement showing the manner in which legislative grants for the college were expended, and showing any surplus or deficit; it was also required to "allow the auditors of the Department of Education access at all reasonable times to all financial records of the University maintained on behalf of the College."

One contribution to the concept of the college as a distinct entity apart from the university was the provision that mutual agreement between the minister and the university was required, not only for exchanges of accommodations and equipment, but also for exchanges of teaching staff. Such a clause could certainly operate as a distinct barrier to any attempt at real integration.

There was considerable dissatisfaction with the terms of the agreement. Some university critics believed that it was not the government's original intention of giving the university real control over the program. They felt that the terms might well have been different had the Board of Governors given the matter full consideration. A subcommitte of the college Advisory Committee proceeded to work on a revision of the agreement after successively less restrictive conditions were agreed upon in comparable situations by Queen's University and the University of Toronto.

Agreements of this type are perhaps less important for their exact wording than for the spirit in which they are applied. Serious differences are usually well developed before important decisions hinge on the legalistic interpretation of a single clause. W.S. Turner, the distinguished educational administrator whose services the college was fortunate enough to secure during the period immediately preceding its opening and for the first four years of its operation, was determined that the association with the university would be a meaningful one. He therefore consistently interpreted the agreement as much as possible in that light. It is said that the pursuit of this objective did not always have the enthusiastic support of departmental officials. In general, however, it was obviously in line with sentiments expressed by Davis on frequent occasons over the years. There has apparently, at least in recent years, been no fundamental conflict in approach but rather an occasional difference about the significance of a specific event or decision. It has nonetheless been important that such matters be handled perceptively, since significant patterns are established as the sum of many small precedents.

On the basis of his convictions and experience, Turner believed that there were two acceptable forms of agreement between the minister and a university. 1 / There might be no formal document at all but simply a gentleman's agreement, with the university left to run things completely, as it does with respect to such faculties as dentistry and medicine. 2 / There might be a very simple document, including a statement of objectives and assurances of financial support on the part of the government. The university would be left free to plan the kind of program it wanted. Such arrangements would allow for a wide variety of programs in different universities. The minister would retain the responsibility only for certification, which would involve the right to subject the program to a general appraisal.

Facilities

The college had to begin its first regular session in September 1965 in temporary quarters in the London Teachers' College and the Ontario Vocational Centre. Shortage of space necessitated operating on a shift system. It was not until January 1966 that occupation of the new building, constructed in close proximity to the main campus of the university, was possible. The building was carefully designed to suit the nature of the program envisaged, with particular emphasis on provision for seminar rooms. In his report for the first year, however, Dean Turner was already indicating the need, when the enrolment justified an addition, for accommodation for a program in television arts, for more adequate space for courses in business and commerce, particularly data processing, for additional lecture rooms, and for a suitably designed area for school librarianship, including sufficient accommodation for demonstration libraries.[17] During the first few years, enrolments rose more quickly than originally anticipated, and complaints about overcrowding were being heard. Other institutions, however, were higher on the priority list for new or extended accommodation, and the prospects were that Althouse would have to suffer for a time before full relief came.

Relationships with the university

Relationships between the college and the rest of the university were said to be harmonious on the administrative level. There were also some exchanges of faculty, although no more than five or six of the approximately fifty college staff members were lecturing in other departments in 1968–9. The policy of the college was to employ instructors with academic qualifications acceptable to the university in the foundation subjects such as history, philosophy, and psychology, and to work toward joint appointments with the regular university departments in these areas. Most of the program was carried on by staff members whose reputation was largely based on successful practice.

Program

During its first regular winter session, the courses and certificates offered were as follows: 1 / Interim High School Assistant's Certificate, Type A (in academic and supplementary subjects); 2 / Interim High School Assistant's Certificate, Type B; 3 / Interim Occupational Certificate, Type B; 4 / Interim Vocational Certificate, Types A and B; 5 / Part I of the Intermediate Certificate in Art, Commercial (accountancy, data processing, marketing and merchandising, or secretarial), Home Economics, Music (either instrumental or vocal music or both), Physical Education, and School Librarianship; 6 / Intermediate Certificate (accountancy, data processing, marketing and merchandising, or secretarial); 7 / Specialist Certificate, Commercial (accountancy, data processing, marketing and merchandising, or secretarial); 8 / Elementary Certificate in Guidance; 9 / Certificate in Theatre Arts.[18]

Space does not permit a detailed description of the program. Certain features of special interest may, however, be noted. 1 / Students were permitted to substitute a subject in another academic department of the university for a third methodology option. This arrangement was made both because it emphasized the importance of advanced study and because it was seen as a means of fostering a good relationship with the rest of the univeristy. 2 / Small group instruction and tutorials were emphasized. 3 / The foundation subjects, including psychology and sociology, history of education, and philosophy were offered at different levels in keeping with the varying academic backgrounds of the students. 4 / Quite distinct programs were offered at the A and B levels.

Between 1965 and 1967, Althouse College and the London Teachers' College operated an experimental combined program for university graduates registered at the latter institution. These students attended Althouse for courses in philosophy, psychology and sociology, and history of education, as well as one methodology option at the secondary school level leading to certification for teaching in grades 9 to 12. In 1967 this program gave way to the elementary school option offered exclusively by Althouse College.

MCARTHUR COLLEGE OF EDUCATION

Establishment

Agreement was reached with Queen's University in 1965 for the establishment of an institution to be known as McArthur College of Education. This college was named in honour of Duncan McArthur, who served successively as Head of the History Department at Queen's University, as Chief Director and Deputy Minister of Education, and as Minister of Education from 1940–3.

The agreement by which the college was established owed a great deal to the influence of J.A. Corry, then Principal of Queen's University. A few clauses at the beginning established the general tone.

... WHEREAS the Minister considers it of prime importance

1) that the College should have the benefits of close association with the University in all matters relating to the operation of the College.
2) that both staff and students of the College should have full participation in the life of the University, and desires, therefore, that the University should administer the College and treat it as an integral part of the University,

AND WHEREAS the University considers and the Minister agrees that the acceptance by the University of full responsibility for operation of the College must carry assurance of as wide a range of discretion in the said operation as is compatible with the final responsibility of the Minister for policy and for adequate preparation of teachers,

The insertion of these clauses provided a conspicuous contrast in tone to the agreement between the minister and the University of Western Ontario with respect to Althouse College.

The rights and obligations of the minister and the university were then specified in some detail. As in the Althouse agreement, the government (the minister) would provide the necessary building and meet all the operating costs. The college would offer, as and when required, 1 / courses leading to teaching certificates valid in secondary schools which might include an option leading to certification of candidates as elementary school teachers, and 2 / "such courses leading to certification as teachers as may be determined jointly by the Minister and the University." Somewhat different from the Althouse wording was the provision that the content of all such courses was to be determined by the university after consultation with the minister. The university and the minister were to be jointly responsible for establishing conditions for admission to the courses offered. The university might establish courses in the college leading to post-graduate degrees in education, and would have complete control over these programs.

The dean, like his counterpart at Althouse, was to be appointed with the prior concurrence and approval of the minister. The dean was to report to the principal through the normal university channels. There was to be an Advisory Committee consisting of the dean of the college *ex officio* and five members appointed by the minister, five appointed by the university, two elected by the Faculty Board of the College of Education, and two appointed by the Ontario Teachers' Federation, one by the Ontario Secondary School Headmasters' Council, one by the Ontario Secondary School Superintendents' Association, and one by the Ontario Association of Directors of Education. The functions of this committee were the same as those set down for the corresponding committee at the University of Western Ontario with respect to Althouse College. The university, like the University of Western Ontario with respect to Althouse College, was to make all appointments to the teaching staff after prior consultation with the minister. In practice, it became established procedure for the dean merely to inform the department of decisions to appoint certain individuals.

In budgetary matters, the agreement differed only in minor respects from that affecting Althouse College. The university was required to "set forth the estimated revenues and expenditures for the cost of operation of the College in such detail and according to such form as the Minister may require." In the preparation of the estimates, the minister and the Advisory Committee were to be consulted. A further financial restriction was stated in the following terms: "The University shall furnish annually to the Minister a statement audited by the University auditors, showing the manner in which legislative grants for the College were expended, and showing any surplus or deficit, and shall allow the auditors of the Department of Education access at all reasonable times to all financial records of the University maintained for the College." When the formula for university operating grants was developed, the hope was expressed that it might also eventually apply to the college.

Internal organization

It was an organizational objective of the college to have as little formal structure as possible. The Faculty Board, which included student representatives, played a key role, with its numerous committees. Rather than organizing among departments or disciplines, an attempt was made to co-ordinate functions or programs such as the B Ed program, graduate studies, and educational media. This kind of arrangement promised to guarantee maximum flexibility rather than allowing the organization to harden along traditional lines.

Relationship with the university

McArthur's relationship with Queen's University in the early years appears to have been a harmonious one, particularly in terms of planning and control. The actual working out of the program, however, seems to have been left largely in the hands of the professional educators. The composition of the Advisory Committee appeared to guarantee that such would remain the case. The primary criterion for selection of staff, like that in other colleges, was successful practical experience. University department heads were, however, given the opportunity of saying whether or not they would wish to have prospective appointees working actively with them. Not only was there some encouragement for this kind of activity, but there was also a suggestion that college courses in psychology and sociology might be recognized in the corresponding departments. Whatever the attitude of Queen's professors, there were some expressions of irritation on the part of university people in various parts of the province at the perpetuation of the practice of equating school administrative and teaching experience with scholarly achievement in assigning academic ranks. They felt that those engaged in teacher preparation must be prepared to lose something in their efforts to come to terms with the university community if they insist on creating "instant professors" in terms of their own unique criteria.

Facilities

The original plans for the new college building provided for a maximum enrolment of six hundred students, but later estimates of provincial need by the Department of Education indicated that more than this number might have to be accommodated. A satisfactory extension of the structure by the addition of classrooms, offices, and seminar rooms appeared feasible, and the plans were revised accordingly. The principal, the dean, and the Advisory Committee felt, however, that nine hundred should be considered the maximum enrolment for the college in view of the limitations of the site and the secondary school resources in the area needed to accommodate the practice teaching program. Indications from the department were that the nine hundred figure would not be exceeded. The intention was that, when the need arose, additional institutions in other centres would be made available for the preparation of secondary school teachers.

The addition of even as few as two hundred students to the total enrolment of Queen's University, along with normal increases in other departments, created serious problems of accommodation in 1968–9. The city of Kingston was considered to be strained to the limit to provide rooms and apartments in private homes. The college was forced to arrange for the use of space in hotels and motels and faced difficulties in providing transportation. The university held some hope that the Department of Education would offer special financial assistance in the light of its commitment to defray all the costs incurred on account of the college. Since a departure from the regular policy would have established precedents entailing very substantial expenditures in various parts of the province, the departmental decision was that the students themselves would have to assume responsibility for extra costs.

Program

The course leading to the High School Assistant's Certificate, Type A or B, earned a B Ed degree at Queen's University. A candidate for either certificate chose two of the following list of options: biology, chemistry, elementary education, English, Français, French, geography, guidance and counselling, history, Latin, mathematics, physical education, physics, psychology and sociology, and school librarianship. No related university background was required for elementary education, school librarianship, and physical education.

The program of studies was divided into five major areas: educational foundations, curriculum and instruction, observation and practice teaching, clinical or field studies, and supporting or related studies. The candidate was required to complete a program totalling 135 points, with forty, thirty, forty, ten, and fifteen in each of the respective areas. A point corresponded roughly to one-fifth of an hour per week. The point system was designed to provide for individualized study plans and at the same time to ensure that students' selections satisfied graduation and certification requirements.

RECENT DEVELOPMENTS AT THE COLLEGE OF EDUCATION, UNIVERSITY OF TORONTO

Status of the college

What was formerly the Ontario College of Education has, since the establishment of other colleges with similar purposes, been referred to as the College of Education, University of Toronto, and the old term is applied to all of the colleges as a group. Dean Dadson took up his appointment in 1963 under conditions quite different from those of 1958. The minister and the president had engaged in civilized discussion and come to a mutual agreement. Dadson's first objective was to get an agreement signed and implemented to replace that of 1920. Although he had the support of the recommendations of the Minister's Committee, he found the subsequent period very frustrating. Since the affairs of the college tended to be matters of minor concern to the university, there was no great pressure for action from the latter. The department officials were for a time concerned with working out a satisfactory arrangement with the University of Western Ontario with respect to Althouse College and were not excessively eager to settle the issue with the University of Toronto until that task was completed. Thus it was not until July 1966 that the agreement was finally signed. There was also a long delay in getting university members appointed to the College Council and the Advisory Board, as well as ministerial representatives to the latter.

"The College of Education, University of Toronto" was recognized in the agreement as the official name of the college. Early clauses in the agreement conceded to the university, subject to cancellation of the agreement, ownership of the existing building, of the land on which it was situated, and of existing furnishings, furniture, accessories, and equipment originally provided by the minister, i.e., the government, for use in connection with the maintenance and operation of the college. All costs for additional land, buildings, and equipment and all costs of operation and maintenance were to be provided by the minister. On cancellation of the agreement, the ownership of everything paid for by the minister would revert to him. This arrangement gave the university the dignity of formal ownership, but ensured that, in the unlikely event that the university withdrew from the agreement, the Department of Education would have the means of continuing the program.

The college was definitely committed to providing

(1) courses leading to certification of candidates as secondary school teachers and of candidates as elementary school teachers, one requirement for admission to such courses being a first degree acceptable to the Senate of the University;
(2) courses leading to certification of candidates as vocational teachers.

It also had the option of providing for courses leading to post-graduate degrees in education, such other courses as the college might consider appropriate, and research.

There was to be an Advisory Board of the college consisting of the dean, five members appointed by the president of the university, five members appointed by the minister, two members elected by the Council of the College from the staff of the college, two members appointed by the Ontario Teachers' Federation, one member appointed by the Ontario Secondary School Headmasters' Council, one member appointed by the Ontario Secondary School Superintendents' Association, and one member appointed by the Ontario Association of Directors of Education. The rather meagre representation from the Council of the College perhaps reflected conditions in the days before the Duff-Berdahl report began to influence developments. The function of the Advisory Board was "to advise the President on all matters affecting the College."

The dean was to be appointed by the university on the recommendation of the president. Prior steps were prescribed whereby the Advisory Board would have the exclusive right to submit one or more nominations to the president and would do so only after ensuring that the nominations were acceptable both to the minister and to the president. All other academic and non-academic appointments to the staff of the college were to be made by the university on recommendation by the dean. The academic appointments might be recommended "after discussion where deemed appropriate with the Minister."

There was to be a Council of the College under the chairmanship of the president or his delegate, and made up as follows:

(a) the Dean and all full-time members of the teaching staff of the College;
(b) five members of the academic staff of other divisions of the University appointed annually by the University on the recommendation of the President;
(c) five members of the staff of the school engaged in supervising practice-teaching appointed annually by the University on the recommendation of the President.

Among the most important functions of this council were, subject to the approval of the Senate of the university, "to prescribe the courses of study in the College and the arrangements for conducting the same" and "to appoint the examiners for and to conduct the examinations in the courses in the College and to determine the results of such examinations." Also, subject to an appeal to the Revising Board of the Ontario Colleges of Education, it was "to deal with and decide upon all applications and memorials by students with respect to examinations and to admission to courses leading to teaching certificates valid in Ontario."

The estimates were to be prepared by the dean on the advice of the Advisory Board, and were to be submitted to the minister by the university. Some of the most important specifications with respect to the estimates were that they would

(c) set forth the estimated revenues and expenditures for the cost of operation of the College in such detail and in such form as the Minister may require;
(d) provide for expenditures for permanent improvements;
(e) set forth under separate sections the revenues and expenditures applicable to,
  (i) the winter session of the College;
  (ii) the summer session of the College;
  (iii) the Guidance Centre;
  (iv) the University of Toronto Schools and
  (v) such other sections as may from time to time be established.

The university was to keep separate accounts for college funds and submit an audited annual statement to the minister with respect to these accounts.

Dadson regarded the departure of the Departments of Graduate Studies and Educational Research to form the nucleus of the Ontario Institute for Studies in Education as a severe blow to his hopes for the future development of the college. He described the loss of graduate studies as "decapitation," and felt that the college was in a very difficult position in having no direct avenue to such programs. He declared that it would be difficult for the institution to thrive alongside its sisters in London and Kingston as long as it was relegated to the task of preparing teachers for a departmental certificate and denied its own resources for graduate study, research, and the continuing education of teachers in appropriate areas.[19] There was some hope that the development of a Master of Arts in Teaching program might give some of the staff an involvement in further education, but progress in this area was slow.

The staff applauded the prospect of a new agreement with the university. There was a stronger feeling than had been manifested in earlier years that they must become an integral part of the academic community. At their Geneva Park conference in 1966, the desire for more active interchange of staff was expressed thus: "While we must involve academics directly in the whole process of teacher education, this involvement must not be a one-way street. Appropriate members of the College staff should teach in other faculties of the University."[20] They hoped that they might co-operate with other faculty members in drafting and presenting courses for undergraduates who intended to enter teaching. Progress along this line during the next two or three years was not, however, impressive. Apart from the tradition of isolation that had to be broken, it would have required the strongest initiative on both sides to establish and maintain a meaningful staff interchange on any large scale. By 1969 evidence that the necessary impulse was being generated in other parts of the university was not yet very obvious. Ultimately, the question would be decided in terms of the attitude of individual professors.

Administration

Dadson took action to delegate powers in order to leave himself freer to represent and oversee the whole institution. He arranged for the appointment of an assistant dean to exercise the same kind of general responsibility for the High School Assistants' program as did other department heads for their divisions in the college. He also established the policy of taking no action on matters of importance without full staff consultation. Recognizing the importance of student opinion, he set up a Dean's Committee of staff and student representatives with the right to discuss any matter concerning the students' welfare or program and to make recommendations to the dean.

Procedural changes in 1964 included an attempt to dispel some of the secondary school atmosphere that characterized the college. "The secondary school type of time-table which [had] regulated college life for so long, activated by bells and geared to 40-minute periods and to classes formed by students taking the same combination of options"[21] gave way to a schedule more characteristic of the university, with fifty-minute periods starting on the hour. Also, classes were formed with reference to academic background as well as to combinations of options to allow for adaptation of instruction.

In the February 1970 issue of the *Bulletin* of the Ontario Secondary School Teachers' Federation, H.O. Barrett, the assistant dean, mentioned some of the administrative changes that had followed the signing of the new agreement. The Advisory Board was functioning according to expectations. The College Council had a series of committees as follows: the Executive Committee, the Programme Committee, the Application and Petitions Committee, the Salary, Tenure, and Personnel Committee, the Student Relations Commitee (one-half students and one-half faculty), the Educational Research Committee, the Building Committee, the Advisory Faculty Recruitment and Appointments Committee, the Publications and Lectures Committee, and the Public Relations Committee. During the previous year, there were student representatives on most of these committees with the important exceptions of the Salary, Tenure, and Personnel Committee and the Advisory Faculty Recruitment and Appointments Committee. The contributions of the students were considered to have been valuable. Since there had been no legal provision made for student membership on the College Council, students had been able to attend its meetings only as observers. While Barrett thought the agreement should be revised to provide for full membership, he was not hopeful that the change could be made immediately.

The dean and the assistant dean were responsible for carrying out the policy determined by the council through its various committees. The functions of the dean had changed considerably from pre-council days. Barrett made comparisons with the situation in the secondary schools, where there were no legally constituted entities to relieve the principal of full responsibility for running the school. In comparison with the dean of the college, a principal still had opportunities for acting as a despot, benevolent or otherwise.

Facilities

The inadequacy of the facilities at the college has long been a cause for lament. Dadson said in 1963: "I don't think since the building was built in 1911 that the college has had the facilities equal to those that would be found in an ordinary good Ontario secondary school." He pointed out the need for extensive renovations and additions not only for seminars, but also for staff and administrative offices. He gave first priority to a respectable library, followed by laboratories for science, geography, and languages, as well as specially-equipped rooms for commercial and vocational subjects. In assessing the general effect of the material inadequacies, he declared:

> I know that at the present time a student that comes to the Ontario College of Education after leaving a campus like Queen's, McMaster, or Western, feels let down when he compares his facilities to those which he has left ... Good facilities at the college would make an improved programme possible and would do a great deal to attract students to the winter course. I'm beginning to feel that the provision of these facilities is becoming essential for the maintenance of standards, perhaps even of the keenest staff morale.[22]

While the need for fundamental improvements remained, the dean was able to report a certain amount of progress during 1966–7. Renovation was going ahead as fast as possible in a building that was being used ten months in the year. Funds had been provided for a linguistics laboratory, a centre for data processing and business machines, a centre for audio-visual aids and educational television, modernization of some classrooms, and the conversion of others into offices. The library area had been reorganized in order to expand reference services and bring about other improvements.[23]

Program

Provision was made in 1964–5 for a more varied program in practice teaching for students in the regular course. More than half of the 560 who enrolled spent a week or so in neighbourhood schools observing classroom procedures. Also, practice teaching was extended from the Metropolitan Toronto area to include ninety-three rural and urban secondary schools of all types, mostly in the area from Niagara Falls to Peterborough. This step met a long-standing complaint that experience was confined to one particular type of environment.

Program developments at the college at the end of the decade and at the beginning of the 1970s were characterized by increasing flexibility and a widening range of course choices in certain areas. As described in the calendar for 1970–1, the work for the B Ed degree fell into four parts: teaching subjects, educational theory, professional practice, and additional courses. The student took at least one of the seven subjects in the first group of teaching subjects and a second either from the same list or from a second list consisting of twenty items, some of which involved prerequisites or other limiting conditions. Educational theory included as a compulsory course Structural and Legal Bases of the Ontario School System and offered lists of courses under the headings Administrative and Program Development, Educational Psychology, and History, Philosophy, and Sociology of Education, of which the student had to take three, including one from each of at least two areas. Additional related courses came under the headings Administration and Program Development; Computer Studies; Educational Media; Educational Psychology; Elementary School; English; Geography; History, Philosophy, Sociology of Education; Modern Languages; Physical and Health Education; Science; Technical and Industrial Arts. The student took a course from one of these areas, or a third teaching subject, or a graduate or undergraduate course in another part of the university which was relevant to one of his teaching subjects.

THE FACULTY OF EDUCATION OF THE UNIVERSITY OF OTTAWA

Formal arrangements for teacher preparation by the University of Ottawa, completed finally in 1969, have been to a considerable extent a matter of provincial recognition of existing programs. From as far back as 1943 the Faculty of Psychology and Education offered courses in education leading to the B Ed, M Ed, MA, and Ph D degrees. The prerequisite for the B Ed was a BA meeting acceptable standards for admission to the Ontario College of Education. As of 1967 the program included practice teaching, methodology, and the foundation subjects.

Theoretically, a B Ed student was to get between eight and ten weeks of practice teaching. In actual fact, this period was restricted to two or three weeks because of lack of funds. The methodology courses were related to the students' university work at the undergraduate level, and were largely handled by teachers in the local secondary schools.

Graduates with the B Ed from the University of Ottawa were recognized for certification in a number of Canadian provinces but not in Ontario, where there had long been an unfavourable opinion of the quality of the program. Strangely enough, however, the holder of an Ottawa B Ed could receive a certificate in another province and return to teach in Ontario on a Letter of Standing. Thus Ontario sometimes ended up by granting certification for training that it originally refused to accept.

Maurice Chagnon, Vice-Rector of the University of Ottawa, made a reasoned case for the recognition of the Ottawa program in a letter to G.L. Woodruff in January 1967. He also dwelt on the advantages of the bilingual approach:

> Because of the bilingual and bicultural character of this University, we feel that we occupy a unique position in that we can supply the secondary schools of Ontario with teachers qualified to teach Français and French as well as to teach in French, Latin, Geography and History when and where this would be required.
>
> The teaching of these subjects in French is increasing in the Province and it is strongly felt that specialized teacher preparation must be provided in order to cope with the situation and to maintain quality education for the pupils of Ontario's high schools.[24]

Chagnon pointed out that recognition of the university's teacher education program by the Department of Education might well be expressed in an agreement between the Board of Governors and the department. He declared that the university was prepared to negotiate such an agreement.

On April 7, 1967, the Senate of the university recommended to the board of governors the immediate establishment of a separate Faculty of Education with two divisions: a Graduate Division and a Teacher-Education Division. On April 10 the board gave the recommendation unanimous approval, authorizing the rector to proceed with the establishment of a selection committee for the appointment of the officers of the new faculty and to initiate negotiations with the Department of Education to produce the necessary agreement. The appointment of staff for the teacher preparation section of course had to await the agreement, but the new faculty was forthwith created as a result of the division of the former Faculty of Psychology and Education. Lionel Desjarlais, long prominent in Ontario educational circles, was named dean. The new College of Education facilities for secondary education were opened in September 1969 with J.M. Tessier as associate dean of the faculty.

STEPS TOWARD THE ESTABLISHMENT OF FACILITIES IN NORTHWESTERN AND NORTHERN ONTARIO

Support for the establishment of a college of education at Lakehead University developed over a number of years. President W.G. Tamblyn wrote to the minister in December 1966 observing that the *Report of the Minister's Committee on the Training of Elementary School Teachers* had urged that teacher education eventually be conducted wholly within the universities and that, as part of phase 1 of the plan, those teachers' colleges that were on university campuses should be incorporated as soon as possible within their respective universities. Since the Lakehead Teachers' College adjoined the campus of Lakehead University, it seemed appropriate that the latter be associated with this development from the beginning. He also noted that the report envisioned that ultimately the education of secondary teachers should be conducted together with that of elementary teachers. He reported the view of the Senate that such a scheme should be implemented at the Lakehead.[25]

In November 1968 a "Brief in Support of the Establishment of a Faculty of Education at Lakehead University and the Provision of an Emergency Teacher Training Program for the Secondary Schools of Northern Ontario," prepared by the Northwestern Ontario Headmasters' Association, was sent to J.R. McCarthy, Deputy Minister of Education.[26] The case for a faculty of education at the university for the preparation of both elementary and secondary teachers was put in terms of the needs of the area. The brief suggested that the current enrolment of some 257 at the teachers' college would be augmented by the 150 or so needed to staff secondary schools in the area. Anticipating that the Lakehead faculty would also meet the needs of the rest of northern Ontario, and implying that there would be no other such faculty in the north, it estimated that an enrolment of five to six hundred might be expected immediately, and that the number would increase in subsequent years.

Among the advantages would be the likelihood that a large proportion of the graduates would continue to work in the north. Training in this area would provide them with the kind of background necessary to adjust to its peculiar conditions of isolation. The brief saw a great need to foster curriculum and other studies indigenous to the area. It was claimed that the development of the north required that the leadership of the educational community be centred there so as to be responsive to local growth needs.

The brief also contained a proposal to establish a special summer course at Lakehead University in the summer of 1969 to meet the needs of the 1969–70 school year in all of the secondary schools in northern Ontario. The students admitted to this course would agree before registration to teach for two years in northern Ontario. Some details were supplied about how this course might be conducted. It was to begin in May with instruction combined with observation and practice teaching during the last few weeks of the school year. The school boards would co-operate in making the schools available for the practical aspects of the program.

McCarthy's response was that plans for the proposed development would be contingent on the completion of an agreement by Lakehead University to incorporate the Lakehead Teachers' College. As things turned out, desires of the group were met with respect to both of their main proposals. The announcement in May by the minister and the university president paved the way for the development of a regular program of secondary school teacher preparation. The particular needs of the area were also recognized in the conduct of a special type of summer course in 1969.

This special course, announced jointly by the minister and the President of Lakehead University on March 28, 1969, was in the spirit of the brief's recommendations, but did not follow them to the letter. It was to begin at the end of the school year, and thus did not permit the suggested period of first-hand experience in the schools. Eligibility for the course required the possession of an approved university degree and a contract with a school board to teach in a secondary school in a territorial district during 1969–70. The initial eight-week session was to be followed by a second session of similar length the following year. Before a candidate received an Interim High School Assistant's Certificate, Type B, he must teach for a year in a territorial district after completing the second summer session. The program was organized and conducted by Lakehead University. The misgivings of the Ontario Teachers' Federation and the Ontario Secondary School Teachers' Federation over the adoption of another form of the detested summer course were allayed in the light of the obvious special needs of the area. Strong hopes were expressed, however, that the measure would be only a temporary expedient.

Naturally the rest of what is sometimes called in sweeping terms "northern Ontario" was not entirely ready to let the Lakehead be the source of trained secondary teachers for the whole area. In December 1968 E.W. Martel, member of the Legislature for Sudbury, pointed out the advantages of his own constituency.[27] He declared that Sudbury was the most centrally located for the three major areas of North Bay, Timmins, and Sault Ste Marie. He purposely excluded Fort William and Port Arthur because they were so far away that it would be more convenient for students in northeastern Ontario to go to Toronto or Kingston, thus defeating the purpose of having the development in the north. As a second point, he added that Laurentian offered honours courses and a variety of subjects in the arts, with a prospect of similar developments in the sciences. Furthermore, the new teachers' college that was under construction on the Laurentian campus had a number of seminar rooms, a closed-circuit television room, a cafeteria, an auditorium, a gymnasium, a library, and offices. Martel thought a complex for the preparation of teachers at both levels could well be built around the structures that were already being erected.

Martel kept up the pressure the following year. On November 25, 1969, he deplored the fact that plans for a college of education at Laurentian were not developing as he thought they should. He called attention to the large proportion of unqualified teachers in the secondary schools and predicted that the number would increase because the emergency courses, except that at the Lakehead, had ended. He noted the reluctance of graduates from programs conducted in southern Ontario to go north. Even those who had originated in that part of the province were not eager to return. While Davis did not demonstrate quite the same sense of urgency that Martel expressed, his response was not entirely discouraging.

I can only say to the hon. member that we recognize the new college that is being built at Laurentian which will be integrated, of course, with that institution, that one should always broaden one's horizons and anticipate the possibility of extending it into the secondary school field as well.[28]

SIX

Requirements for admission to colleges of education and courses and certificates offered

ACADEMIC COURSES, 1950

In 1950–1, a candidate wishing to teach in the academic secondary school program enrolled in the course for the Interim High School Assistant's Certificate, Type B, at a regular session at the Ontario College of Education. To gain admission, he had to demonstrate that he would be at least twenty years of age before October 1 of the date of admission, and had also to provide 1 / a certificate from a clergyman or other competent authority that he was of good moral character, 2 / a certificate of successful vaccination, 3 / a certificate that he was a British subject, and 4 / a certificate of graduation as Bachelor or Master of Arts, Bachelor or Master of Science, Bachelor of Commerce, Bachelor of Science in Agriculture, Bachelor of Applied Science, Bachelor of Household Science, Bachelor of Music, or Bachelor of Physical and Health Education from a British university after a university course approved by the Minister of Education with respect to admission requirements and course content. He must also submit a certificate of physical fitness signed by a medical examiner appointed by the minister. Before final acceptance, he also had to be approved by a selection committee consisting of at least three members of the college staff and a member of the Ontario Secondary School Teachers' Federation.

The course consisted of two main parts: Part I, professional studies, and Part II, observation and practice teaching. The first part was subdivided into 1 / general professional courses, including an introduction to education, educational psychology, and school management and law, and 2 / courses in methods of teaching any two of English, geography and history, mathematics, science, Latin, French, German, Greek, Spanish, and Italian. Special permission was required by Type B candidates to take one of the last four, unless they were also Type A candidates in the same subject area. A short course in diction and voice production was also offered in the early part of the session. Observation began in the third week of the session, and practice teaching in the fifth week. Exclusive of introductory work, these two activities took a minimum of twenty-five full days during the session.

Final standing was based on the combined results of the year's work and marks obtained on the final examinations, and on success in observation and practice teaching. Exemption from the final examinations was, however, granted to those whose progress during the year was regarded as satisfactory. In order to be recommended for a certificate, the candidate had to obtain at least 50 per cent on each of the required subjects of Part I and 60 per cent of the aggregate of marks in Part II. If he failed in not more than one subject in Part I and was successful in Part II, he was exempted from further attendance, and might rewrite the subject he missed at a subsequent regular examination. All others who failed to secure the required final standing had to attend the part of a subsequent session beginning after the Christmas vacation. After teaching successfully in Ontario in a secondary school, or in grade 9 or 10 of a public or separate school, the holder of an Interim High School Assistant's Certificate, Type B, might apply for a Permanent High School Assistant's Certificate.

Extramural candidates for the Interim High School Assistant's Certificate, Type B, included others in addition to those rewriting examinations in courses in which they had failed to secure standing in a regular session. There were candidates exempted from attendance in recognition of equivalent training in other provinces or countries, or because they held Permanent First Class Certificates obtained under certain conditions and had met other specified requirements. These people wrote the prescribed final examinations in the subjects of Part I, and also satisfied the examiners that they were competent to teach the subjects of the high school courses, either by undergoing practical tests or by securing appropriate statements from their inspectors.

Another group who had fulfilled the requirements for admission to the High School Assistant's course, Type B, and held Ontario First Class Certificates, Permanent Second Class Certificates, or Interim Vocational Certificates, as well as meeting other conditions, particularly experience requirements, were also exempted from attendance at a regular session. They attended a summer course at the College of Education, and then wrote the final examinations in the prescribed subjects of Part I. They also had to satisfy the examiners with respect to their teaching competence in one of the two ways open to candidates who were not required to attend either a regular or a summer course. There were provisions for an additional attempt by those who failed in any part of their initial effort.

Applicants for admission to a course leading to the award of an Interim High School Assistant's Certificate, Type A, had also to be applicants for the course for the Interim High School Assistant's Certificate, Type B. In addition to meeting all the admission requirements for the latter, they had to have a minimum of 66 per cent in the final or graduation courses in a degree program approved by the minister. Courses for the Type A Certificate were awarded in the following areas: agriculture, classics, English and French, English and Latin, English, geography, history, French and German, French and Italian, French and Spanish, Latin and French,

Latin and Greek, mathematics, mathematics and physics, science, physics and chemistry, physics and biology, chemistry and biology, and home economics. In addition to these "academic" Type A courses, there were also Type A courses in physical education, art and crafts, instrumental music, and vocational music, for entrance to which there were certain special degree requirements. Type A courses consisted of at least the equivalent of two seminar periods a week throughout the session, as well as observation and practice teaching in the subjects of specialization.

Standing leading to the award of the Interim High School Assistant's Certificate, Type A, required a minimum of 66 per cent of the aggregate of marks obtained during the session and on the final examinations and 66 per cent of the marks obtained in practice teaching. Holders of the High School Assistant's Certificate who acquired the qualifications for admission to the Type A course could obtain the certificate by writing the examinations with the required degree of success, without attending a regular session. After two years of successful teaching, including classes at the grade 11 level or higher, the holder of a High School Assistant's Certificate, Type A, might apply for a Permanent High School Specialist's Certificate.

Students in the High School Assistant's course, Type B, whether or not they were also doing Type A work, also had the privilege of taking a supplementary course leading to one of the following: 1 / the Elementary Physical Education Certificate, Type A; 2 / the Elementary Art and Crafts Certificate; 3 / the Elementary Vocal Music Certificate, Type A; 4 / the Elementary Instrumental Music Certificate; 5 / the Elementary Commercial Certificate; 6 / the Elementary Industrial Arts and Crafts Certificate, Type A; 7 / the Intermediate Home Economics Certificate; and 8 / the First Class Public School Certificate. In some cases, the requirements could not be met completely in a single regular session: for example, a subsequent summer session was required for the First Class Public School Certificate, and two subsequent summer sessions for the Elementary Industrial Arts and Crafts Certificate, Type A. There were particular undergraduate requirements for applicants for admission to the Intermediate Home Economics course.

VOCATIONAL COURSES, 1950

An applicant for admission to the Ordinary Vocational course had to be between twenty-three and thirty-five years of age if a male and between twenty-three and thirty-two if a female. For the Intermediate Industrial Arts and Crafts course, there was a minimum age requirement of twenty and no maximum. For the Specialist Industrial Arts and Crafts course, the minimum was twenty-three and the maximum thirty-five for both sexes. Other non-academic requirements were similar to those for the Type B course. The educational requirements for the Ordinary Vocational course were secondary school graduation or equivalent, or success in examinations in English, mathematics, and science held at the college on the first day of the session. The candidate also had to have a substantial amount of trade training and experience, varying according to the nature of the trade. He had to demonstrate in an examination, part written and part practical, that he was competent in terms of fundamental principles, operations, processes, and skills of the trade.

The course for the Interim Ordinary Vocational Certificate consisted of two parts. Part I included educational psychology, school law and regulations, English, history of vocational education, principles of teaching and classroom management, and technical subjects. As in the academic courses, Part II involved observation and practice teaching. An effort was made to send student teachers first to vocational departments in the smaller composite schools and later to technical schools in the larger centres. An Interim Vocational Certificate qualified the holder to teach a shop subject for two years in a vocational school. A Specialist's Vocational Certificate qualified the holder to act as shop director in the same type of school.

The course for the Intermediate Certificate in Industrial Arts and Crafts lasted two years and was designed for those desiring to teach the subject in public, separate, continuation, and high schools. Admission requirements included evidence of graduation from a four-year industrial course in a vocational school and at least one year of approved industrial wage-earning experience. Applicants were excused from the first year of the course if they held a Second Class or more advanced Ontario teaching certificate and either the Elementary Manual Training Certificate or a statement indicating successful completion of the work of Part I of the Elementary Industrial Arts and Crafts course, Type A or Type B. Part I of the Intermediate Arts and Crafts course consisted of activity analysis and course of study, shop work, history of industrial arts and crafts education, and guidance. Part II was, as in other courses, observation and practice teaching.

The course for the Specialist Certificate in Industrial Arts and Crafts was designed for those contemplating teaching the subject in a collegiate institute. The admission requirement was a Permanent Intermediate Industrial Arts and Crafts Certificate. Part I of the course consisted of activity analysis, course of study and shop management, and advanced shop work.

CHANGES IN THE EARLY 1950S

For several years, admission requirements, courses of study, and certificates remained much the same. Possible areas of study for the Type A Certificate were extended somewhat by the addition of some new combinations of languages: for example, English and German, and English and Spanish. In 1954–5 the Ordinary Vocational Certificate gave way to the

Interim Vocational Certificates, Types A and B. For the second of these, admission requirements were much the same as for the earlier certificate. Graduates in applied science could also be admitted with at least two years of experience after graduation in the major subject area. For the Type A Certificate, the minimum educational requirement was a degree in applied science with at least 66 per cent in the final and one other year, and at least two years' experience in the major subject area. During the college session, the candidate had to secure at least 66 per cent on all the courses for the Type B Certificate and to take additional courses in the organization, administration, and supervision of vocational schools, with special reference to the duties and responsibilities of technical or industrial directors, assistant principals, and principals.

Provision was made in 1954 for the Letter of Standing, which was granted to those who had fulfilled the requirements for admission to the course leading to the Interim High School Assistant's Certificate, Type B, and who were exempted by the minister from attendance at the college in recognition of equivalent training in other provinces or other commonwealth countries. The Letter of Standing was good for one year, after which the recipient might be recommended for an Interim Type B Certificate by his inspector on the basis of successful performance.

The major innovation in 1955 was the introduction of the special summer course, which played a major role until nearly the end of the next decade. While its existence exerted an extremely important influence on the regular winter session, it was not directly responsible for any substantial changes in admission or course requirements for the latter or in the nature of the certificates offered.

CHANGES IN THE LATE 1950s

In 1957 a new plan was introduced to encourage holders of the Permanent High School Assistant's Certificate, or the Type B Certificate, to upgrade their academic qualifications by attending summer or evening courses in order to qualify for the Type A Certificate. The actual academic requirements were not, however, relaxed. In order to obtain the equivalent of a four-year honours degree or equivalent, it was still necessary to take the equivalent of at least an additional year's work, and often more. In February 1958 a kind of intermediate stage was recognized when the system of "endorsement" was introduced. A Permanent High School Assistant's or a Type B Certificate might be endorsed for teaching a certain subject if the candidate's undergraduate degree showed concentration in that subject amounting, generally speaking, to about half the credits necessary for a Type A Certificate, that is, five full-course credits. Endorsement was strictly by individual subject, and not by broader subject areas, as in the case of certain Type A Certificates. Endorsement could, however, be secured in two subjects if the candidate had the equivalent of four full university courses in each, or five in one and three in the other. Credits secured after January 1, 1958, had to be at the second class level or better to be counted toward endorsement.

In 1958–9 a Type A course in Applied Science was offered for the first time. This change put an end to long-standing complaints by engineering graduates that they were eligible only for the Type B Certificate, despite the high qualifications many of them had in mathematics and science. Teaching thus offered more appeal to a whole new group of potential candidates. The same year saw the introduction of a combined Type A course in English and history.

In 1959 the citizenship requirement was changed to allow for the admission of a candidate who made a declaration of intention to become a Canadian citizen. A major change was made in the course requirements for the Type B Certificate in that a student had to take methods of any three academic subjects instead of the two that had been required during the previous decade. This change was defended by Dean Diltz on the ground that it represented a raising of standards, although many felt that it was more likely to encourage superficiality. It also seemed to go against the trend in high school teaching, where the increasing size of schools enabled most teachers to concentrate their efforts in restricted areas.

Certain changes appeared in the list of options available to candidates for the Type B Certificate. Some of these paralleled the addition of new courses in the secondary schools accompanying the introduction of the Reorganized Program. The calendar for 1964–5 showed professional courses in history and philosophy of education, educational psychology, and school management and law. The three methods options could be chosen from the following list: English, history, geography, mathematics, science, Latin, French, Français, German, Greek, Spanish, Italian, Russian, one of political science, economics, geology, and psychology and sociology, and one of a list of supplementary courses, including Part I of intermediate art, intermediate physical education, intermediate vocal music, intermediate instrumental music, intermediate vocal and instrumental music, intermediate commercial accountancy or secretarial, intermediate industrial arts, intermediate school librarianship, and elementary school teachers', as well as intermediate home economics and theatre arts. The academic courses offered for the Interim High School Assistant's Certificate Type A, were as follows: agriculture, classics, English, English and French, English and German, English and Latin, English and Spanish, English and history, geography, geology and geography, history, political science, economics, political science and economics, French language and literature, French and German, French and Italian, French and Spanish, French and Russian, Latin and French, Latin and Greek, Latin and Italian, mathematics, mathematics and physics, science, physics and chemistry, physics and biology, chemistry and biology, chemistry, biology, physics, and home economics.

The appearance of the Occupations course in the secondary schools led to provision for the Interim Occupational Certificate, Type B. Admission requirements were similar to those for the more specialized vocational certificates except that more diversified work experience was required. Graduation from a three-year course in a provincial institute of technology reduced the amount of work experience required for all courses in the vocational area.

The extended scope of activities in the Department of Vocational Education was recorded in the report of the Dean of the College of Education in the University of Toronto president's report for 1964–5.

Vocational programmes are becoming more diversified and flexible in order to train teachers in special trades for a growing number of educational institutions and secondary school courses. As well as for secondary schools, the Department now trains instructors for adult training programmes, Ontario vocational centres, institutes of trade and occupations and reform institutions. From secondary schools the demand is growing most rapidly for teachers in the new two-year Occupations Course, in which training for 60 different occupations may be offered.[1]

CHANGES IN REQUIREMENTS FOR ACADEMIC COURSES

It was provided in 1964 that the candidate for the Type B course must have taken a minimum of twenty-one credits, that is, the equivalent of at least seven full courses, in at least two academic subjects providing background for secondary school teaching. A maximum of six credits was allowed for courses in geology, political science, economics, psychology, and sociology. Although fifteen credits in the subject were required for a candidate to choose one of these subjects (psychology and sociology counted as one) as an option, no more than six credits in the whole group could be counted for admission. However, candidates who possessed the academic requirements for the Type A Certificate in geology, geology and geography, political science and economics, or psychology and sociology were considered to have met the requirements.

Changes introduced at the College of Education of the University of Toronto in 1965–6 included the acceptance of guidance as one of the three methods options in the Type B program. Certain candidates were also allowed to count Parts I and II of the intermediate commercial course as two of their three options. Provision was also made for selected students to substitute for one of the three methods options a course in the appropriate faculty or school in the University of Toronto in a subject related to their other two options.

As of July 1, 1966, the requirement of two methods options was restored. In announcing the change, the Department of Education pointed out that few teachers in secondary schools instructed in more than two subjects. It was suggested that the reduction would permit more intensive preparation for teaching the selected subjects in grades 9 to 13 and also allow for some preparation for teaching grades 7 and 8 in certain fields.[2] One of the two options had to be chosen from the following list: English, French, Français, geography, Greek, history, Latin, mathematics, science, agriculture, biology, chemistry and physics. The second might be one from the same list or from the following: art, commercial, economics, elementary school, geology, guidance, home economics, industrial arts, German, Italian, Russian, Spanish, music (instrumental or vocal), physical and health education, political science, psychology and sociology, school librarianship, and theatre arts. Both options might nevertheless be taken in commercial work. With the approval of the dean or the Council of the College, a student could, as mentioned previously, take a third option or arrange to take a graduate or undergraduate course in another faculty or school.

ARRANGEMENTS FOR TRANSFER BETWEEN ELEMENTARY AND SECONDARY LEVELS

Steps were also taken in 1966 to break down the barriers to the movement of teachers between elementary and secondary schools. The holder of a Permanent Elementary School Teacher's Certificate, Standard 4, might, upon accepting a contract from a board to teach in the grades of a secondary school, be granted an Interim High School Assistant's Certificate, Type B. Under similar conditions, the holder of a Permanent High School Assistant's Certificate might be granted an Interim Elementary School Teacher's Certificate, Standard 4. It was expected that most such transfers would take place in the grades 7 to 10 range. Those proposing to transfer beyond this range might be counselled to take appropriate summer courses.

ADMISSION OF NON-ONTARIO CANDIDATES FOR TEACHING

Measures were also taken to facilitate the entry of suitably qualified people from abroad. It was provided that a Letter of Standing would be issued to a university graduate from any part of the world whose university transcript indicated that he had met the academic requirements applicable to Ontario graduates, whose professional training fulfilled Ontario requirements, and who was a Canadian citizen, or a British subject with landed immigrant status, or had made a declaration of intention to become a Canadian citizen. A special committee in the Department of Education would appraise his qualifications and conduct an interview.

FURTHER CHANGES IN ACADEMIC REQUIREMENTS

After July 1, 1967, candidates for the Type B Certificate were to have two full university courses, equivalent to six credits, in each optional subject selected from the following list: biology, chemistry, English, Français,

French, geography, history, Latin, mathematics, and physics. The change was generally welcomed, although some people on the college staffs asserted that the requirement was still not sufficient to ensure adequate standards.

B ED FOR TEACHER PREPARATION

A development of major importance in recent years has been the trend toward the introduction in the universities of the B Ed or similar degree in recognition of the program for the Type B Certificate, with or without additional requirements. The matter is one for each university to decide for itself. Dean Dadson discussed some of the issues in his section of the report of the president of the University of Toronto for 1965–6.

On its merits the Type B course has a good claim for recognition by a second undergraduate degree – a Bachelor of Education or a Bachelor of Arts in Teaching or a Bachelor of Teaching Arts – after the pattern of the Bachelor of Library Science degree in the University of Toronto and of similar degrees in other universities. The award would have other advantages also. It would leave the University free to set its own standards for the degree which might, conceivably, differ from the Department's standard for the certificate; it would recognize the superiority of the full year of professional training by contrast with the summer courses, thus attracting, perhaps, more good students into the better course; it would open a professional degree course to foreign students who cannot now qualify for the High School Assistants' Certificate because they do not have Canadian citizenship.[3]

The staff of the College of Education at the University of Toronto in 1967 were in favour of granting a degree or a Dip Ed to many, but not necessarily all, students graduating from the college.[4] It would have been difficult, however, for any college to withstand the pressure to award a degree for the minimum achievement recognized in the other colleges. The decision by Queen's University to award the B Ed to graduates of the Type B program, and the University of Ottawa's comparable arrangements, are no doubt indicative of the trend. The college at Toronto fell in line in 1969–70. Beginning in the summer of 1970, the Department of Extension of the University of Toronto offered a program in summer and winter sessions to enable graduates of the Type B program to qualify for the B Ed degree.

SEVEN

The response of the colleges of education to the shortage of secondary school teachers

THE NATURE OF THE CHALLENGE

Compared with later years, the early part of the 1950s was a relatively placid period for the Ontario College of Education. There was reasonable stability of staff and an enrolment that did not change drastically from year to year. The introduction of the special summer courses produced a major transformation. Suddenly there were hordes of students to be dealt with under greatly changed circumstances and often, for the first few years at least, by the staff members who handled the lecturing in the winter. It may be that there were faults in the program that could and should have been remedied, despite the difficulty of dealing with so many students under emergency conditions. But it must also be acknowledged that the staff were blamed for many of the irritations that were traceable to circumstances over which they had no control.

Some of the first of the emergency summer courses were referred to in the *Report of the Minister, 1954*. The emergency training plan for teachers of industrial subjects was said to have been helpful in reducing the shortage in that field. Also, 150 teachers were enrolled in commercial courses qualifying for elementary, intermediate, or specialist certificates. It was pointed out, however, that there was a continuing shortage of teachers with special qualifications in commercial subjects, science, agriculture, home economics, and girls' physical education. In general, the number of secondary school teachers qualifying annually at the Ontario College of Education had become insufficient to meet the needs of the school system.

THE INTRODUCTION OF THE SPECIAL SUMMER COURSE IN 1955

The introduction of the special summer course in 1955 recognized this rapidly developing shortage. School boards were increasingly forced to employ staff on Letters of Permission, to the particular annoyance of the Ontario Secondary School Teachers' Federation, which kept calling attention to the number of these and suggesting such remedies as higher salaries to attract more candidates to the profession. The original hope was that a new pool of potential teachers could be drawn upon, consisting of people who had secured university degrees a number of years earlier, and whose reluctance to transfer from other occupations to teaching was largely explainable in terms of the time and expense required to qualify by the regular method. Men with families could not afford to take the full year off but might be prepared to attend summer courses before and after a first year of experience.

According to the prescribed procedure when the special summer course was in operation, a school board was expected to make every effort to secure the services of a qualified teacher. If it failed to obtain such a teacher by advertising after April 1, it could apply for a Letter of Permission to employ an applicant who undertook to attend the special summer courses. The department tried to make sure that preference was given to qualified applicants by warning that an application for a Letter of Permission made less than three days after the final day of the advertisement would not be considered. If the Letter of Permission was granted, the board entered into a contract, which was valid only on the condition of the applicant's admission to the first summer course. It was the candidate's responsibility to apply for such admission, for which he had to submit a copy of his contract. If he was accepted, the Ontario College of Education notified the board; if not, it notified the Registrar of the Department of Education, and the Letter of Permission was cancelled. After successful completion of the first summer course, the applicant would be granted a Letter of Standing valid for one year. If the applicant did not complete the course successfully, the Letter of Permission was valid for one year, but might not be renewed.[1]

The basic conditions for admission, apart from the contract with a school board, were the same as those for the regular course for the Interim High School Assistant's Certificate, Type B, including a certificate of graduation from a university on completion of a course approved by the minister. The first course originally covered a period of ten weeks and consisted of general professional courses and instruction in methods. Some classes of students desiring special assistance were assembled in local secondary schools to provide a token amount of observation and practice teaching.

A student who was successful in the ten-week course might have his Letter of Standing renewed for an additional year on the recommendation of the principal of the school and the secondary school inspector. The school board could then employ him for the ensuing year on condition that he attend the second summer course. If the principal and inspector did not recommend him, his Letter of Standing was cancelled and could not be renewed. The second summer course, of five weeks' duration, consisted of further professional courses and methodology leading to the award of the Interim High School Assistant's Certificate, Type B. Neither of these summer courses included any of the optional supplementary courses available to students in attendance during the regular session of the Ontario College of Education. Those who attained their basic certificate through summer courses could, however, secure supplementary certificates by attending Department of Education summer courses.

Special supervision within the school was prescribed for a teacher during the year after he completed the initial ten-week course. Particular attention was supposed to be given to his efforts during the first two months. From November on, the principal was supposed to visit his classes in order to observe at least two lessons a month. He was asked to make a careful record of the date, grade, subject, and topic of each lesson observed, as well as a written estimate of its success. His observations were expected to cover a variety of lessons, both formal and informal. He was to make helpful suggestions for the improvement of teaching methods, class management, organization, and other phases of school work. If there was any evidence of difficulty, the assistance of the secondary school inspector was to be requested. Before the first of April of the year in question, the principal was to submit to the department a report on the lessons observed.[2]

The 1958 memorandum concerning principals' supervisory responsibilities recognized that "in nearly all cases" the principals had been living up to their supervisory responsibilities in a most conscientious and effective manner. But it was also indicated that there were a few examples of spasmodic or even negligible supervision. Principals were advised that casual observation could not take the place of the more formal visit accompanied by a considered, constructive criticism conveyed to the teacher soon after the close of the lesson.[3] The fact that this message was sent to all principals in a general memorandum suggests that there was more neglect than the wording indicated.

The almost immediate effect of the summer course was to divert many students who would ordinarily have proceeded from university graduation directly into the regular session the following winter. The prospect of saving a year of study and earning a full year's salary exerted a very strong appeal. From their particular viewpoint, many of the students did not see any overwhelming advantage in the regular session, and some of them reported that their university professors had encouraged them to regard professional preparation as a necessary nuisance to be got over with as soon as possible. Of course, the enrolment in the regular session was maintained to some extent by the fact that it was the only one in which the Type A course was offered. Nevertheless, the number in the regular session declined from 479 in 1955–6 to 347 in 1956–7 or, counting those in academic courses only, from 411 to 264. In quoting these figures in the Legislature, John Wintermeyer said:

> I quite appreciate there is a problem. As we were saying earlier, we are in an emergency period wherein we have to take emergency measures. But my concern in this respect is that herein we are perpetuating the emergency, that

is, fewer and fewer people apparently are going through the regular prescribed course at the Ontario College of Education, and more and more people are taking the subsidiary or part-time summer course ...

In all probability, the time will come when we will lose substantially the enrolment of the Ontario College of Education.[4]

On the whole, the idea of bringing suitable people from other occupations into teaching was a sound one, and many good teachers were added to the profession in this way. But a certain number of the candidates who were thus attracted had rather mediocre prospects in any field. The writer's experience on selection committees during this period involved encounters with some who, after ten or fifteen years, had not yet found any occupation they liked, and thought it was time to "give teaching a whirl." The selection committees developed a suspicion of older candidates and were inclined to question them closely, while putting through the fresh young graduates almost automatically.

Premier Frost speculated in the Legislature in 1959 on various possible methods of dealing with the provision of adequate methods of secondary school teacher preparation. He observed that the summer courses at the Ontario College of Education were taking care of twice as many people as the regular course. His friend, Dean B.C. Diltz, had observed that, while the situation was not desirable, summer courses had come to America to stay. He proceeded to suggest the possibility that a semester system based on a twenty-week cycle might overcome some of the disadvantages of the existing arrangement. A school board might hire two teachers at one year's salary. One would teach and be paid for the first part of the school year, while the second would spend twenty weeks at the college. Then the situation would be reversed.[5]

Another of Frost's suggestions sounded like a kind of modified concurrent plan of teacher preparation. It was that part of the theoretical training be taken in the form of optional subjects in the universities. He thought they might be given after the manner of religious instruction or military training. He recognized that educators, and no doubt also university people, had misgivings about this idea, and he was not prepared to press it.

A few days later, Diltz staged one of his dramatic performances before the Education Committee of the Legislature. He offered some support for Frost's semester scheme, as well as pointing out some of the difficulties. In commenting on his presentation later in the day, D.H. Morrow, member for Ottawa West, expressed preference for a three-semester system as a better means of integrating the existing ten-week summer course.[6] Since this scheme was rather complex and involved more switching of teachers during the year, it had less chance of being introduced. The most serious obstacle to any semester plan was that the school boards generally felt it would be too disruptive of the school program. For them, the existing summer school course was relatively straightforward and simple to operate.

Bascom St John reported Diltz's encounter with the Education Committee and observed that he had dealt effectively with many criticisms of the department, the college, and the teaching profession in general. Diltz made the following points.

1. Full integration of teacher courses in universities is a "fantastic" proposal.
2. Many mature people are returning to the teaching profession, more than 200 in the past few years.
3. There are not enough qualified students to accept the scholarships now available. Scholarships are not the full answer to recruitment of teachers.
4. Summer courses are inevitable.
5. Ontario is not "terribly" short of teachers.
6. Recruitment at the high school level is well advised.
7. Summer school is a facet of the semester system which is already in evidence at the university level.
8. Summer school trained teachers are of very, very good quality. They are more mature, dedicated, interested.[7]

The first statement demolished in a most unceremonious fashion the proposal Frost had made that part of the program be given in the form of university options. As far as the summer school course was concerned, Diltz managed to dampen current criticism for a considerable period of time.

Certain modifications were made in the course series in 1960 and 1961. In the former year, the ten-week and five-week combination was changed to two sessions of eight weeks each. At the same time, the summer courses were offered for the first time, under the supervision of the Ontario College of Education, at London and Kingston. Later, the second course was reduced to seven weeks, and finally to six. Beginning in 1961, a third special course of eight weeks was offered to permit candidates with the required academic qualifications and a High School Assistant's Certificate, Type B, to obtain a High School Assistant's Certificate, Type A, in their special field of scholarship.

MISCELLANEOUS EMERGENCY COURSES

Commercial teachers

An emergency special commercial summer course of five weeks' duration was announced in 1962 as a temporary measure to increase the supply of teachers capable of giving specialized instruction in commercial subjects to meet a growing demand in the schools. The course, leading to a Vocational Certificate, was open to candidates who held acceptable certificates, diplomas, or degrees as chartered accountants, certified public accountants, or certified general accountants in Ontario, or were graduates of the three-year course in secretarial science at an Ontario institute of technology, of a three-year post-secondary school commercial course in the United Kingdom, or of an accredited university. They had also to pass tests in the skills or subjects they would teach, and to have obtained positions in schools where there were no other qualified applicants or applicants willing and able to enrol in the initial summer course with commercial subjects as an option.[8] These latter were able to take commercial work as one of the three required methods options for the first time in 1962.

In 1969 a question was raised as to whether graduates of the secretarial science courses in the colleges of applied arts and technology would be accepted on the same basis as those from Ryerson Polytechnical Institute in this Commercial-Vocational summer program. The College of Education of the University of Toronto declined, however, to accept the qualifications as equivalent. Among the differences noted were the higher standards of professional preparation of the Ryerson faculty and the established record of competence among its graduates.

The first summer session of a three-summer sequence leading to an Interim Vocational Certificate, Type B, Commercial, valid for teaching subjects named on the certificate, was offered for the first time in 1963. Admission was based on an Ontario Secondary School Honour Graduation Diploma or equivalent, with standing in eight or nine papers at a level sufficient to secure university admission. Evidence was also needed of at least five years of successful office experience. The candidate had to secure a contract with a secondary school board or an inspected private school to teach the commercial subjects in which he had passed a trade test. After the three-summer sequence, the candidate received a certificate which was valid for five years. At the end of that time, the certificate was to be made permanent provided the holder had secured at least half the credits required for a university degree. After completing the degree, the teacher could proceed to commercial specialist status.

Retraining for industrial arts teachers

The introduction of the Reorganized Program and the strong financial support for technical-vocational education provided by the federal government in the early 1960s created problems for many industrial arts teachers. In a number of cases, high schools and collegiate institutes were made into composite schools, and existing industrial arts shops were converted to other uses. As a result, teachers of industrial arts in such schools had either to revert to other subjects which they were qualified to teach or seek positions as teachers of industrial arts in other schools where the demand remained. For a holder of a Specialist Certificate in Industrial Arts who lacked the qualifications to teach other subjects, the department tried to ease the situation by offering the following alternatives. 1 / He might teach academic subjects in his school provided that he worked toward a degree, gaining at least two course credits each year. His board would, on request, be granted a Letter of Permission to employ him year by year until he received the degree. 2 / He might qualify for an Interim Vocational Certificate, Type B, in one of drafting, electricity, electronics, carpentry and millwork, machine shop, or welding by taking a practical work course consisting of at least two summer sessions of two hundred hours each to enable him to pass the trade test required of candidates for the Vocational Certificate. The course would be offered only if there were enough candidates in a particular trade subject. 3 / He might qualify as a teacher of diversified occupational trades by taking a practical work course of the same duration as that specified in 2 / and, on passing the trade test, receive an Interim Vocational Certificate, Type B, Occupational Training. This latter was a new variation of the Vocational Certificate made available to grade 12 graduates with adequate practical experience and was awarded after they took three summer courses and passed a trade test.

Teachers of girls' physical education

The shortage of teachers of physical education for girls led to the offering of a special five-week summer course in 1963 for Ontario elementary school teachers who held a Permanent Elementary School Teacher's (or First Class) Certificate and had academic standing satisfactory for admission to the regular first-year degree course at an Ontario university. Each applicant had also to secure a position with a school board to teach in a secondary school the following year. At least half her timetable had to involve physical education. After the summer course, her board would receive a Letter of Permission to rehire her year by year, provided her work was satisfactory, and provided that she secured credit for at least one university credit each year, and two every three years, until she obtained a degree.

Vocational teachers

Beginning in 1964, a two-summer sequence replaced the three-summer sessions formerly required for emergency courses for the Interim Vocational Certificate, Type B, and the Interim Occupational Certificate, Type B, (Practical Subjects). The hours of lectures were lengthened, however, so that there was no reduction in total course content. At the same time, provision was made for a teacher in either of two groups to secure the Interim Occupational Certificate, Type A: 1 / one who held a Permanent High School Assistant's Certificate and a Specialist's Certificate in auxiliary education with the secondary school option, with at least two years of successful teaching experience in the Occupational program and 2 / one who held a Permanent Occupational Certificate (Practical Subjects), had grade 13 standing as required for the Vocational Specialist's Certificate, and had successfully completed the two requisite five-week summer sessions.

Librarianship
Arrangements were made in 1962 for the introduction of a two-part summer course in school librarianship, but over a period of years this course lost some of its emergency characteristics. As of 1968 it was offered in London and Toronto and led to the Intermediate Certificate in School Librarianship. The admission requirements included an Interim High School Assistant's Certificate and at least one year of teaching experience in a secondary school. The Intermediate Certificate was awarded only after a year of successful school library experience subsequent to completion of Part I. After another year of successful experience, holders of this certificate might attend a further session to secure a Specialist Certificate in School Librarianship.

TERMINATION OF THE SPECIAL COURSE

In May 1967 Davis announced the end of the special summer course for recent university graduates.[9] The first summer course would be offered for the last time in 1968 and the second in 1969. In line with ideas advanced by Dadson and others, however, there would be such a course for the lesser numbers of university graduates who had secured their degrees at least five years earlier and had been otherwise occupied after that time. Later there was some modification of the definition of a "mature" student who was eligible for the course. He was to have an acceptable university degree and one of the following additional qualifications: 1 / at least five full years' employment or experience other than as a student before or after a three-year degree beyond grade 13 or equivalent; 2 / at least four full years' employment or experience other than as a student before or after a four-year degree beyond grade 13 or equivalent; 3 / at least three full years' employment or experience other than as a student before or after a master's degree. For the year 1969, admission was granted to the initial summer session to a candidate who held an acceptable university degree and by June 27 of that year had completed at least two years of teaching in a secondary school on a Letter of Permission.

The minister mentioned the widespread consultation that had preceded his decision. The problem had been studied by the staffs of the colleges of education, officials of the department, professional organizations, supervisory staffs, and educational administrators. He referred in particular to an *ad hoc* committee headed by T.D. Boone, Director of Education for Etobicoke, and consisting of representatives of the Association of Directors of Education of Ontario, the Ontario School Trustees' Council, the Ontario Secondary School Superintendents' Association, the Ontario Teachers' Federation, the Ontario Secondary School Headmasters' Council, the Ontario Secondary School Teachers' Federation, the colleges of education, and other interested groups.

The move was taken with some misgivings. There was still a very great demand for teachers, and some difficulties might be caused by the change. But representatives of all the different educational groups concerned made commitments that they would take extraordinary measures to meet the difficulties. As one such measure, an accelerated and concentrated program was undertaken to attract more graduates into the teaching profession. Beginning in 1967 a $500 fellowship was awarded automatically to every full-year student at a college of education. At the time of his announcement, Davis saw some relief being provided by the opening of McArthur College of Education and a new college at the University of Ottawa. He also held out the hope of renovations and extended facilities at the College of Education in Toronto.

The staff of the College of Education, University of Toronto, made some suggestions about how the problems resulting from the abolition of the special summer course might be dealt with. In order to stimulate recruitment, they suggested

a) that the teachers' federations, as well as College staff members, increase substantially their efforts to attract more highly qualified candidates to the profession;
b) that governments, universities and other appropriate agencies provide more substantial financial aid to prospective teachers;
c) that Colleges of Education offer degree courses in education;
d) that the Department of Education should empower school boards to enter into provisional contracts with undergraduates prior to their enrolment in the regular College program and consider some form of financial aid to such graduates.[10]

They also had some ideas about how the immediate problems of greatly increased enrolment in the regular session might be solved. These included

a) a double-shift system with augmented staff and additional accommodation;
b) the establishment of several faculties or colleges of education associated with Ontario universities;
c) the introduction of an internship plan for carefully-selected candidates.

Their suggestions for dealing with the transitional year were

a) a higher than desirable pupil-teacher ratio, where possible;
b) postponed retirement of senior teachers;
c) special provisions to enable retired teachers to return temporarily to full-time teaching;
d) intensified recruitment of qualified teachers from other provinces and countries;

e) engagement of married women who are qualified teachers, on a part-time basis;
f) engagement of university graduates for a one-year period under close supervision with the written condition that the "assisting teacher" will take the regular teacher-education course the following year.

In March 1968 the minister outlined some further steps the department had taken to deal with the situation. 1 / Letters of Standing had been reintroduced at the secondary level for well-prepared secondary school teachers from anywhere in the world provided that they could meet academic, language, and citizenship requirements. 2 / Admission requirements for colleges of education had been redefined to permit a more generous interpretation of the approved degree. 3 / An elementary school teacher with an approved university degree and a permanent teaching certificate could be awarded a High School Assistant's Certificate on being appointed to a secondary school teaching position.[11] Later on, Davis announced that Boone had agreed to serve as chairman of a new committee representing the same organizations as the one that had recommended the termination of the summer course route. This committee was to consider new and additional programs to prepare teachers at the secondary level.[12] Its members included J.B. Callan, Ontario Secondary School Headmasters' Council; D.F. Dadson, Dean, College of Education, University of Toronto; H.B. Henderson, Regional Superintendent, Department of Education, Niagara; N.J. Hill, Ontario Teachers' Federation; J.F. Kinlin, Superintendent, Curriculum Section, Department of Education; R.D. MacDonald, Ontario School Trustees' Council; A.H. McKague, Superintendent, Supervision Section, Department of Education; V.S. Ready, Dean, McArthur College of Education; J.W. Singleton, Ontario Association of Directors of Education; W.S. Turner, Dean, Althouse College of Education; and G.L. Woodruff, Director of Teacher Education, Department of Education.

In the Legislature, Tim Reid took the minister to task for apparently redefining the committee's terms of reference so as to restrict the scope of its activities. At one stage, the minister had announced that it was meeting "to examine existing concepts, standards, methods and facilities for training secondary school teachers." At a later stage, he had said that it was merely recommending ways and means of keeping a flow of teachers moving into the secondary schools at the same time as the summer school program was discontinued. Reid expressed great disappointment at the change. But, noting that the members of the committee were all from administrative and supervisory positions, and did not include a single classroom teacher, he said, "I suppose that we in the Opposition should be thankful that this committee of administrators and technicians is not being asked ... to really look into concepts of teacher training."[13]

Having responded to the strong criticism that had been levelled at the special summer course from various directions over the years, and having been assured by the leaders of the important educational groups that they would endure certain difficulties in the process of readjustment following its abolition, except for "mature" students, the minister nevertheless ran into difficulty when the pinch began to be felt. It was said that there might be a shortage of as many as two thousand secondary school teachers in the fall of 1969. Walter Pitman took issue with him in these terms.

> We have just heard that there is going to be a shortfall – we have not been able to get any exact figures from the Minister – of perhaps 2,000 teachers in the coming fall at the secondary level. Now, this is a serious matter ... when you have 2,000 teachers in your secondary schools who have not had the minimum amount of training which is considered to be adequate by the standards of the Department of Education at the present time. They are on letters of permission, apparently in order to get into the summer courses. Unless we are all willing to accept the limitations of the summer course, we will simply have no course and we will have people in classrooms who have had no training whatsoever.[14]

The supply situation in 1969–70 turned out not to be as serious as some of the more pessimistic forecasts had indicated. The necessity of changing the student-teacher ratio to the teachers' disadvantage did not materialize. The school year was hardly well started before the teachers were planning a campaign for a continuing reduction in this ratio. With larger numbers of graduates emerging from the universities, the prospect of a surplus of candidates began to be imminent.

EIGHT

Ideas about the preparation of secondary school teachers

EARLY VIEWS

Some of the main events in the establishment of institutions and facilities for the preparation of secondary school teachers before 1900 are recounted briefly in chapter v. Among the outstanding characteristics of such programs were the following. 1 / They were not taken very seriously since, until almost the end of the century, it was quite acceptable to teach without certification. 2 / They were very brief and thus of slight effect, although intensive enough while they lasted. 3 / They were not sharply differentiated from programs for elementary school teachers. 4 / They were under the control of practitioners, and scholars were involved only peripherally.

The Ontario Normal College, operating in Hamilton between 1897 and 1907, provided High School Assistant's and Specialist's Certificates along with the First Class Certificate. When the program for the latter was turned back to the normal schools in 1920, the separation of training for the elementary and secondary levels was relatively complete. Only university graduates were accepted into the High School Assistant's program. There was henceforth no alternative to the consecutive pattern of teacher preparation in Ontario. A similar practice was established, although not so quickly or directly, in other provinces. For a time, courses in education were taken during the third and fourth undergraduate years at McGill, but a year of graduate training was subsequently required. When the universities of Nova Scotia first began to offer courses in education for certification, the professional work was taken concurrently with academic work. In 1932, however, the consecutive plan was adopted.[1]

Another characteristic of secondary school teacher preparation in Ontario dating back to before the turn of the century is the provision for the Specialist's Certificate. The honours degree has been the standard requirement for admission to the course for this certificate. Possession of the latter has always meant extra remuneration and it has been an effective requirement for promotion to the position of academic department head. With reference to specialist teachers, Robin Harris wrote: "The influence of such teachers on secondary education in the province cannot be measured or defined, but it can scarcely be exaggerated."[2] No doubt the prevalence of the specialist's qualifications has led to the establishment and maintenance of high standards of achievement and respect for scholarship in individual subjects. Unfortunately, it has also contributed to a fragmentation of the curriculum and a failure of the high school to deal with the student's over-all needs. It must, furthermore, bear much of the responsibility for the long neglect of the interests of vocational students. Harris pointed out that the requirement of the honours degree for specialist standing militated against the concurrent type of training program, since the honours course demanded a high degree of concentration on academic studies. He considered also that the specialist arrangement had a very stimulating effect on the enrolment in honours courses in Ontario universities. Without such an arrangement, he thought it doubtful that the honours course system would have been developed in so many Ontario universities and embraced so many different fields of concentration. With the sudden discovery of serious flaws in this system in Ontario universities in the late 1960s, and the consequent haste to dismantle it, at least in its traditional form, it is interesting to speculate on how the change will interact with all the other changes occurring in the secondary schools.

RECOMMENDATION OF THE ROYAL COMMISSION, 1950

The Royal Commission, reporting in 1950, endorsed the consecutive approach to the preparation of teachers for the post-elementary schools, with all candidates obtaining a bachelor's degree before training. It was claimed that this particular scheme was best suited to the particular conditions and needs of the province. Since the commission's proposed structure for the school system would have ended the elementary school at grade 6, the implementation of their recommendation would have meant degrees for all teachers of grade 7 and beyond.[3]

The commission recommended that a member of the staff of the Ontario College of Education should posses, unless he was appointed to the Department of Educational Research or to that of Graduate Studies, the following:

(i) at least a permanent Secondary School Teaching Certificate or its equivalent;
(ii) at least six years' successive teaching experience approved by the Minister, not less than two of which shall have been in a junior college or its equivalent;
(iii) preferably, the possession of an Elementary and Secondary School Inspector's Certificate and at least two years' successful experience as a principal or inspector of a secondary school or junior college, or similar experience approved by the Minister;
(iv) the passing of a medical examination conducted by a medical examiner appointed by the Minister;
(v) the possession of high personal qualifications.[4]

There is no mention here of scholarship. In fact these recommendations, about at fatuous as any contained in the whole report, would have excluded all but a narrow range of careerists. The commission apparently did not speculate on the possibility that a university might be reluctant to accept a program handled exclusively by former administrators and supervisors.

IMPLICATIONS OF THE SPECIAL SUMMER COURSE

Throughout the period when the special summer course was offered as an alternative to the regular session for recent graduates as well as for "mature" students, that is from 1955 to 1968, it had its defenders. They tended to fall into two main categories: 1 / those who did not feel that it was adequate, but who could see no alternative to it for the time being except to let large numbers of teachers into the schools with no formal preparation at all, and 2 / those who did not really see a great deal of value in professional preparation and preferred to see it reduced to a minimum. Toward the end, voices raised against the course tended to become quite unequivocal in their denunciations. In the early stages, great efforts were sometimes made to show that it was really practically the same as the regular course.

W.J. Dunlop, then Minister of Education, minimized the difference between the quality of the special summer course and that of the regular winter course. In answering criticism from John Wintermeyer, he said on one occasion in the Legislature:

> In this special emergency plan, in those 15 weeks, the students get – and I have been assured of this by a dean who was there for 11 years and by a dean who is there now – the students get everything that is given ordinarily in the year in the College of Education, except one subject which they make [*sic*] take in a third summer course, one optional subject, drama, literary society, music, camera club and that sort of thing.
>
> It is an all-inclusive programme where everything that is required is given, and some people are telling me it should be carried on indefinitely. I do not think we should carry it on indefinitely, because those other things are desirable but not necessary but this is filling the gap in the meantime.[5]

Obviously if he thought that the optional supplementary courses consisted of drama, literary society, camera club, and "that sort of thing," he had been badly misinformed.

There was some very high praise for the teachers who came through the summer course route. In part, their quality was a result of the fairly rigorous selection procedure that was often, although not always, involved in securing a position with a school board. The over-all quality of the regular course group suffered somewhat because some students attended after failing to persuade a board to hire them so that they would be eligible for the summer course. Those who had misgivings about the effects of the summer course based their case on general principles. In essence, they felt that a student who did well after a makeshift program should do better after an adequate period of preparation.

In 1963 D.F. Dadson, newly appointed dean of the college, reviewed the advantages and disadvantages of the summer course.[6] Among the former, he mentioned the financial advantages, including the opportunity to obtain credit for an extra year in the superannuation fund. He also referred to certain educational factors in its favour. Motivation was strong, since an assured position gave the student a very practical objective. Dadson thought that the pattern of the summer courses, beginning with introductory study and practice, followed by real responsibility, and then by further study in the light of genuine experience, provided a good sequence of learning. On the other hand, the number of subjects offered in summer school was restricted, practice teaching was short and slight, and courses for the Type A and most supplementary certificates had to be taken in subsequent summers. He expressed his view of the educational disadvantages as follows.

> These short summer courses are so rushed and crowded that it is difficult for many students to master the material. More important than that perhaps, it is too short a time for a prospective teacher to become imbued with his professional responsibilities. All learning takes time and the acquisition of a good professional attitude takes considerable time. Moreover the summer school staff, good as it is, is not so well qualified as the permanent staff. The general opinion among educationists is that the one-year course is a far superior preparation for teaching.

Dadson went on to note that about 8,000 of the 14,500 secondary school teachers then in service had been trained in summer courses. He felt that this situation represented the dilution of standards on a very large scale, that such a trend was dangerous, and that it should be stopped as soon as possible. He noted the recommendation of the Minister's Committee that emergency summer courses be completely abandoned, but he did not think it necessary to accept this recommendation in its entirety. The number of university graduates turning to secondary school teaching after some years of successful experience in another occupation was markedly on the increase, and there was good reason to allow such people to follow the summer course route if they chose. But he thought that recent graduates should be directed into the regular session. He conceded that the change would be difficult to make. Once a practice had become firmly entrenched in an educational system, it was a very dangerous kind of operation to get it out. Such an operation would require the co-operation of principals, departmental officials, and others.

Dean V.S. Ready delivered a very severe condemnation of the special summer course. He called it "totally inadequate," and observed: "I have talked with many of these young teachers who came to the courses full of idealism and zest for teaching, and left chastened, discouraged and grimly braced for the battle ahead."[7]

Few assessments of the special summer course have been more adversely critical than that formulated at a conference sponsored by the staff of the College of Education, University of Toronto, on November 9, 1966. Resolutions adopted there described the course as "a critical and chronic problem" and urged that it be ended immediately.[8] The staff felt that "no type of summer training can provide genuine experience in practical teaching and observation of schools in action." They declared that, in one day of practice teaching in the regular course, a student usually had more practice than most summer students had in two summers. They thought that, with two-thirds of new secondary school teachers receiving their training in the summer, there must be thousands of students in Ontario high schools "who suffer serious educational deprivation while their ill-prepared teachers grope frantically for a few survival techniques." Because of the sheer futility of the practice teaching component in the summer program, they agreed to discontinue it completely in the summer of 1967.

RECOMMENDATIONS OF THE MINISTER'S COMMITTEE ON THE TRAINING OF SECONDARY SCHOOL TEACHERS

The Minister's Committee, which presented its report in 1962, attempted to assess the relative values of the broad, general type of university course and the specialized type as preparation for high school teaching.

> All university courses have a direct bearing on teaching insofar as they produce an educated person, but such an educated person does require some depth to his studies rather than a surface knowledge of a wide field of studies. The problem is one of degree not of kind. With this kind of background, graduates of the general course can bring to the college of education, and later to the schools in which they teach, a breadth of interest and flexibility which will contribute to the well-being of the teaching profession ...
>
> Graduates of honour and specialized courses should bring to the college of education and later to the schools in which they teach, a sense of scholarship and of achievement which adds immeasurably to the quality of instruction. The danger that honour graduates may become purely subject-centred and fail to see the education of the student as a process on a broad front is real but greatly exaggerated ...[9]

The last assertion, at least, has been widely challenged in recent years.

The committee had a certain amount to say about appropriate methods of instruction for student teachers. One of the suggestions was that the seminar and tutorial systems already being used to some extent in Type A and other small classes be extended to all subjects. For such subjects as psychology and philosophy, large lectures to about 150 students, supplemented by seminars of about fifteen students, were recommended, and for the methods subjects, classes of about thirty, supplemented by tutorials of twelve to fifteen. Dean Dadson judged this pattern rather rigid, and suggested that it was based on a dubious distinction between the theoretical-professional and the practical-method subjects.[10] There were, however, many advantages, particularly in the opportunities for personal contact. In Dadson's words, "personal counselling of students, so often the catalyst in the training of teachers, would be regular and systematic; it would open the way to a mature, personal sort of teacher education which should be attractive to postgraduate students."[11] The possibility of adopting the proposed scheme in the College of Education was remote, mainly because the old-fashioned structure, with its standard-sized classrooms, was completely inappropriate, and because of the impossibility of obtaining enough well-qualified staff, including part-time assistants. It was, however, possible to build Althouse College of Education with this system of instruction in mind.

Robert Nixon, then Liberal education critic, suggested that the report of the committee was already out of date. He thought that it failed to take account of the degree to which the special summer course had become ensconced in the system.[12] It seemed to him that those who wished to go into secondary school teaching felt that they did not need to subject themselves to the full-year course. He pointed out that the report of the committee made only passing reference to the possibility that university graduates might go directly into the schools on an internship basis and take their training as assistant teachers. With the kind of education they had already received, he thought them quite capable of taking part in classroom instruction under the supervision of an experienced teacher. As interns, they would be able to assist with many chores having to do with preparing and marking tests, setting up laboratory apparatus, and performing a variety of other tasks around the classroom and the school. The experience might be spread over a number of types of schools.

For the remainder of the program, he advocated something like the scheme that Premier Frost had mused on a few years before. What he called the topics of educational value might be given at the university level along with the undergraduate program. These might include educational philosophy and psychology. He did not suggest that the full training program should be included at this stage because there would be too great a loss in terms of academic instruction.

APPRAISAL OF COLLEGE OF EDUCATION PROGRAMS

The programs for secondary school teacher preparation have been subject to some very harsh criticism over the years. Since the college at Toronto has until very recently had a monopoly in this field, it has inevitably been the object of most of the criticism. It has sometimes been difficult to determine whether the critics have intended to make one or several of the following points: 1 / that professional preparation for teachers is an unnecessary time-waster and merely an obstacle in the natural progression from formal learning to teaching in the secondary schools; 2 / that the programs, although potentially useful, have been badly organized or cheapened by such concessions to teacher shortages as inadequate emergency programs; 3 / that the staff of the college have been unscholarly, unimaginative, and determined to treat the students as if they were still in high school. If any constructive response is to be forthcoming it is necessary to sort these factors out and to deal with each one appropriately. Except to an insensitive lover of the status quo, it would seem very foolish to assert that the critics have all been stupid, malicious, or misinformed, and that the ostensible causes of dissatisfaction have been purely imaginary. It is not much better to agree that there has been a basis for criticism, and then to insist that the circumstances have made it impossible to take any effective action.

One opinion commonly expressed by students is that the part of the program involving formal study is of little use, and that the only aspect with any value is practice teaching. In a letter to a certain newspaper shortly after Dean Diltz met the Education Committee of the Legislature, a former student wrote: "I doubt if I am the only one who, after spending a regular session at the Ontario College of Education, came to the conclusion that its chief value lay in the opportunity it provided for practice teaching in the schools of Toronto. I came to this conclusion with no lack of respect for the many fine people who make up the faculty of that institution." Defenders of the system have often attempted to counter this low opinion of the internal program by asserting that it has values that a student cannot be expected to recognize immediately but that will eventually become apparent. This is an extremely weak approach and tends to conflict with recent psychological findings about motivation. It is becoming increasingly difficult to excuse a teacher who claims that his message must be delivered by compulsion because it is impossible to persuade the potential learner of its value.

One of the strongest and most comprehensive criticisms ever leveled at the college was delivered in the Legislature in 1964 by Stephen Lewis.[13] Some of his points were reinforced by reference to the *Varsity*, the University of Toronto student newspaper. He made certain general comments.

> Instead of being viewed as an exciting intellectual milieu, it is viewed as an oppressive and much-to-be-avoided tedium.
>
> For a vast number of people, OCE is the last refuge of the undecided. It

does not have the tremendous appeal that an institution of that kind should have. It is considered as a year wasted in the curriculum of students entering the field of secondary teaching.

Among his specific points was a reference to a reputed excess of regulation.

> ... OCE still has a definitely high school atmosphere imbued with some regimentation, what students feel is an excessive degree of classroom discipline. A sort of paternalistic knuckle-rapping has haunted OCE for the last several years.

He observed that the dean (to whom he referred as "the principal") and the staff were making a very real effort to change this atmosphere, a point on which the minister agreed, but he felt that this change was not yet decisive.

The next point was a criticism of the building, one that might equally as well be leveled at a few of the older teachers' college structures:

> ... the very building itself ... is a study in depression ... An institution it is – an impossible environment. It is bleak, it is overcrowded, it is cramped, it is desolate, it is cell-like. The greatest instinct is to flee.

But he regarded the hangover of paternalism and the nature of the physical facilities as much less important than his third point of criticism – that the course structure was obsessed with technique and methodology at the expense of almost everything else.

> What is more it is a methodology of a "how" and "what" kind. It is the ancient type of methodology. It does not probe "why"; it does not ask the goals for approaching certain subjects in the schools.
>
> ... There is psychology and the philosophy of education. But these ... are exceedingly superficial. They are survey courses, not substantive – "Why Will James was a pragmatist" or "What John Dewey believed" – in a sense highly uncritical, as all survey courses tend to be; and leading to undesirable results.

Lewis turned to James Conant for a description of the way these subjects were usually taught in institutions for the preparation of teachers, thus demonstrating that the problem was a universal one, and implying, whether intentionally or not, that whatever fault there was must lie more in the set-up than in the conduct of individual instructors. He proceeded, however, to tell of an incident, recounted to him by some students who witnessed it, that certainly did not reflect well on the instructor.

> In another incident to which some of the students would be willing to attest,

they were asked to check a list on what makes a good teacher. On the form were listed all the various attributes – voice modulation, gestures, etc., etc. One of the students put up his hand and said, "What about knowledge of subject matter?" and the professor said, "Surely that is there." The student said, "No, it is not there." The professor replied, "Well, that is a very good idea – put it down, class."

That, I think, is basic to the fundamental problems in the psychology and philosophy of education courses that they are taught at OCE; that they take second place to the methodology fixation and preoccupation; that they are essentially survey courses; that they often teach too little, and too little knowledge continues to be dangerous, and that they breed – and this is what disturbs me – an anti-intellectual atmosphere.

Lewis's fourth point of criticism was the idea that "only teachers can teach teachers," by which he obviously meant only those who had been through a formal course of preparation. He declared that it was a "fictitious mentality" that only the practical classroom experience gained over a certain period of time was relevant to the Ontario College of Education. He saw evidence of this mentality in the fact that the Minister's Committee on the Training of Secondary School Teachers included only one member of the organized university community, and that even he was an administrator.

The fifth point was that reports of student teachers on their experiences in practice teaching were expected to be non-critical and non-analytical. The sixth was that there was a serious lack of experimentation and exposure to educational cross-currents. Lewis characterized the University of Toronto Schools as "very much an eminent high school, but part of the establishment not generally reflective of community trends and classes." He brought in his special interest in the emotionally disturbed in suggesting that more direct contact with this group would be a desirable experience for student teachers. His final point was that the college was "not a humming centre of research in the meaningful sense." He recognized the surveys being carried out in the Department of Educational Research, but pointed out the lack of contact between these activities and the work of the students: "Clinical research, meaningful teaching pattern research in methodology goals, special experiments, and all the aspects that now come within the ken of modern thinking on education; these things are not being communicated to the students at the regular level." From an insider's point of view, there was certainly no question about the validity of this observation.

Lewis proposed four fundamental revisions in the program. The first was that the college should be a post-graduate university faculty or institute under university control and not under the aegis of the Department of Education. The staff should be "qualified university professors conversant with the theory and practice of education."

A new faculty or institute of education in the Province of Ontario should have the power to invite eminent outsiders to give specialized courses in various aspects of university education. I would say James Conant, Paul Goodman, Eric Fromm, Robert Hutchins – *les eminences grises* in other fields of education – should be brought in and asked to give specialized courses.

Lewis did not offer suggestions about how these worthies might be persuaded to do as expected, however excellent the idea might be. It would perhaps be more practical to pursue his next suggestion: that the proposed institute might draw on agencies with responsibilities in areas like criminology and child study in order to develop a community of learning. He suggested a system of admissions involving the acceptance of people with mature adult experience in various fields, such as businessmen, authors, scientists, and journalists, who could come in, even in the absence of precise academic entrance qualifications, to take extra courses leading to certification.

The second proposal was to de-emphasize methodology, "leaving it only to the bare-bone basic subjects and there apply it intensively with emphasis on the goals of methodology; why we teach the new mathematics, not merely how we teach the new mathematics." The released time would be devoted to the general framework of learning in such disciplines as psychology, sociology, history, philosophy, economics, and anthropology. "Intensive seminars in the behavioural sciences should be given by university professors attached to the faculty of education by virtue of their specialized knowledge." Additionally, Lewis advocated that a much greater proportion of time be spent on practice teaching. This experience would allow the student teachers analytical critiques and evaluation of their experience and criticisms of the people whom they observed.

The third proposal was that there be unrestrained experimentation, with research an integral part of the curriculum. All of the materials of research would be available to students in their course instruction. The students would prepare intensive research papers as part of their program of studies and thus participate in the development of knowledge about the learning process. At their disposal would be specific experimental schools or experimental classes in schools throughout Ontario, for which a certain percentage of practice teaching time would be designated. There the students would have the opportunity to try every single new technique in every area.

Lewis's final suggestion was that the college, as a university faculty, should launch a continuous learning program for its graduate teachers. Such a program would go considerably beyond the existing graduate courses, although the distinction was not altogether clear. As he put it: "There should be some kind of curriculum devised for year-long sabbatical leave, for intensive specialization over summers, or even specially led learning and experiment groups within the staffs of individual schools."

This vision of an ideal faculty or institute is both impressive and inspiring. It is perhaps not entirely unlike the one that Dadson had in mind when he assumed the deanship in 1963. Where circumstances have permitted, he has tended to move in these directions. It will perhaps do the ideal no harm to point out how difficult are some of the obstacles in the way of its realization, not to suggest that they should not be tackled, but to guard against too many unrealistic expectations. 1 / Not only eminent authorities but also professors in other faculties generally are reluctant to engage in lecturing to student teachers. It may of course be agreed that their attitude would change if the atmosphere of the program were more congenial, but even then, the reality must be faced that a professor's set of values is ordinarily tied in closely with specialized work in his own department, and he does his career no good by straying off into neighbouring fields. 2 / The students Lewis talked to were no doubt very thoughtful, alert, and eager for intellectual experiences. But it would be a mistake to assume that the great majority of candidates for teaching come to the college hungering for intensive intellectual challenge. Dean Diltz's comment on the need for a better quality of university graduate was based on many years of perceptive observation. Ten years before Diltz became dean, the writer observed a college professor begin the session with an attempt to teach methods of instruction in French to a class of university graduates, all of whom had studied the subject through high school and into university. So obviously defective was their knowledge of the subject that she had to give up her original plan and put them through the texts used in grades 9 and 10, simply to ensure that they would have something to teach. Many are the stories, no doubt with a solid factual basis, of students being presented with something absurdly below their level of knowledge. But what may be deadly boring for the good students has often been essential for large numbers who have been foisted on the college with inadequate prior preparation.

The advisability of attempting to use any great part of the year of preparation for deeper forays into the basic disciplines is open to question, unless they are slanted toward the needs and interests of teachers. The three or four years of undergraduate work, when properly used, are surely enough to establish an abiding interest in the pursuit of knowledge, if it has any chance of developing. The short year of special preparation, reduced even further in Lewis's scheme by the extension of practice teaching, would leave little time to reverse unfavourable attitudes developed earlier or to establish good ones where none existed. On the other hand, there is much to be said for reinforcing the continuing growth of knowledge in one or more specialized fields by providing some opportunity, however small, for further study.

Certain regulations applying to college of education students' dress and conduct have been defended, particularly in earlier years, on the grounds that the students might as well get used to the kind of regime they will encounter in the high schools when they begin to teach. Such an attitude implies that they will be unable to make an adult response to the demands made on them when the time comes, and that they must be pointed, like automata, in the right direction. It certainly rules out consideration of the possibility that some questioning of the typical high school approach to the regulation of student behaviour might be advantageous to education and to the broader interests of society. The taking of attendance and the direct imposition of penalties for absence have tended to disappear rapidly in recent years. Another recent development, exemplified by the attitude expressed at the Althouse College of Education, is that the college will not interfere with the students' appearance or dress; they must, however, conform to the specifications of the schools where they go for practice teaching.

The writer's discussions with students, particularly at McArthur College, have reinforced the impression that what they really want is evidence of personal interest and concern on the part of the staff. They want to feel that the staff member is prepared to put himself on their level as a human being and to claim superiority only for the knowledge and experience he has gained that may be of some use to them as teachers. They are more gratified that he is willing to join them in a game of hockey in the evening or accommodate one of them in an emergency in a spare cot in his home than that he can display an extraordinary depth of scholarship. One would, of course, hope that he might have genuine intellectual achievements to his credit. These would certainly have a maximum opportunity of influencing the students' development in the atmosphere created by other comradely gestures.

PROGRAM INITIATIVES AT MCARTHUR COLLEGE

The calendar of McArthur College for its first regular session, conducted in 1968–9, gave the views of the staff on how the program should be organized. The statement began with a declaration that what was learned in school or college might often be derived less from formal instruction than from the experience of living and working in the institutional environment. The staff therefore set out to give the preparatory year a student-centred rather than a prescription-centred focus.

> We believe that Administration can set the direction by being open, understanding, and flexible, within the limits imposed by public policy. Faculty also can assist by regarding their role to be more that of resource persons and counsellors than that of dispensers and examiners of skills and information. We would hope that the students in their turn will display the necessary curiosity and concern to profit from the opportunities and choices provided for them.[14]

The implementation of this approach involved a recognition that there was not a single curricular program of equal suitability for all candidates. Account was taken of the great variation in their backgrounds, their needs, and their aspirations. It was assumed that university graduates had some capacity for assessing their own requirements. The use of individualized study plans allowed them "the widest possible latitude of preference and selection."

The approach involved a policy of continuous assessment which entailed a de-emphasis of term examinations and increased attention to all aspects of application and development over the entire year. This policy was said to anticipate the kind of professional assessment that prevailed in the schools, where teacher performance was judged in terms of such factors as dedication, effectiveness, creativity, and interpersonal relations. The objective was to improve motivation by directing it toward the primary task of meaningful achievement, rather than to make the work easier or the professional work less demanding.

To judge by the statement of "commitments" in the calendar, the college was determined to ensure that it gained a reputation for respecting intellectual achievement. The first assumption in its approach to the preparation of teacher candidates was said to be the conviction that teachers must be masters of their subjects. All members of the college, faculty and students alike, were encouraged to persevere with their private studies. Also, in its desire to foster the intellectual outlook, the college would "not allow education for utility to supplant education for wisdom."

The point system for the selection of units of study was designed to implement the policy of providing opportunities for individualized programs. Of the 135 points he needed for graduation, the student ordinarily chose forty from educational foundations, thirty from curriculum and instruction, forty from observation and practice teaching, ten from clinical or field studies, and fifteen from supporting or related studies.

The only course in the whole spectrum that was required of every student in the college was one in the educational foundations area called Professional Issues in Contemporary Education. It was designed to provide a realistic initiation into some of the significant problems of administrative and professional practice. It was described in the calendar as having been developed partly on the case study approach and as an experimental course seeking "to utilize student and faculty contributions in a joint examination of specific educational issues." The other foundations subjects were comparative education, history of education, philosophy, psychology, and sociology. An attempt was made to offer courses at more than one level to accommodate students with varying backgrounds. Those who entered the college with no previous work in psychology or philosophy were required to take these subjects. Those who had a strong background in any of the foundation disciplines, on the other hand, might have their point requirement reduced to twenty-five from the standard forty.

The seminar approach was used in the curriculum and instruction area. The students considered "such general questions as the principles of developing courses of study, the philosophical justification of particular subjects in the school curriculum, and possible interdisciplinary approaches." They also dealt with more mundane matters such as "principles of lesson preparation, methods of classroom presentation, handling of assignments, and evaluation procedures." The calendar proclaimed the intention of paying particular attention to procedures for working with individuals differing markedly in maturity, motivation, and competence. Most of the subject options were dealt with on two levels for the benefit of Type B and Type A candidates. Students had to have a minimum of six university credits or two courses in a particular subject before they might choose it as an option for this part of the program. If they offered only the minimum in their major field, however, they had to take an additional university course as part of their work at the college.

The "supporting" or "related studies" area included university courses in arts and science, techniques of effective communication, measurement and evaluation, student counselling, sensitivity training, a workshop in instructional communications, developmental reading, outdoor education, computers in education, and remedial or other private studies. This part of the program was particularly designed with the students' individual needs and interests in mind. In order to provide extra flexibility, some of the courses were offered more than once a year.

The clinical and field studies area was said, no doubt correctly, to represent a new dimension in teacher training programs in Ontario. The studies were based on the students' need for "a deep personal knowledge of the modern adolescent." They were intended to provide a variety of "direct client-centred experiences" in the hope of cultivating a functional idealism through responsible social service. The activities were expected to occupy the students for about two hours a week for not less than ten weeks.

Those anticipating attendance at the college were expected to apply to the principal of a convenient elementary or secondary school for permission to spend some time in observation at the beginning of the year. Observation and practice teaching took up to eight weeks of the regular session. The college undertook to explore new developments in practice teaching such as "micro-teaching" (involving small-scale encounters with groups of about four pupils), video tape playback, and interaction analysis.

McArthur College was in an extraordinarily good position to carry out the proposals resulting from thoughtful initial planning. Most important was the opportunity for the selection of a group of staff members who were committed to its principles and determined to make a serious effort to put them into practice. Also, during the first year, the college enjoyed an exceptionally favourable student-staff ratio – one that unfortunately was unlikely to last. The writer's impression, after talking near the end of the 1968–9 session with a group of the students, was that the staff had used their opportunities to most unusual advantage. The enthusiasm of these young people for the program was in sharp contrast to the attitudes of many students who go through parallel experiences elsewhere. The impression created was that most of the ills of programs for the preparation of secondary school teachers can be cured by the right approach. But one doubts that these circumstances can be maintained in a large college or faculty. The lesson of McArthur might be to press as quickly as possible for the dispersal of facilities among most or all of the universities of Ontario in the hope of preserving the vital spark of human contact.

NINE

In-service teacher education

DEPARTMENT OF EDUCATION SUMMER COURSES

Content and growth of the program

The Ontario Department of Education has long maintained an extremely varied and comprehensive program of summer courses for the improvement of teachers' skills and qualifications. For the most part, these have tended to supplement rather than duplicate the courses offered through university extension. Some of them have been designed to follow up an area of study begun in the program of initial preparation. Others have offered opportunities for specialized study that are considered best begun after a period of experience. Courses such as those for school principals are obviously intended as preparation for a new type of activity or responsibility.

The year 1955 is a purely arbitrary date at which to delineate the dimensions of the program. The list of departmental courses offered in that year was as follows: 1 / agriculture for the Intermediate and Specialist's Certificates; 2 / art for the Elementary, Intermediate, Supervisor's, and Specialist's Certificate; 3 / audio-visual aids; 4 / auxiliary education for the Elementary, Intermediate, Supervisor's, and Specialist's Certificates; 5 / commercial subjects for the Elementary, Intermediate, and Specialist's Certificates; 6 / grade 13 subjects; 7 / guidance for the Elementary, Intermediate, and Specialist's Certificates; 8 / the High School Assistant's course, Type B; 9 / the High School Principal's course; 10 / home economics for the Elementary Certificate; 11 / industrial arts for the Elementary Type B, the Elementary Type A, and the Specialist's Certificates; 12 / vocal music for elementary and for secondary schools and instrumental music, each leading to the Elementary, Intermediate, and Specialist's Certificates; 13 / physical and health education for the Elementary Types A and B, Intermediate Types A and B, Specialist's, and Supervisor's Certificates; 14 / primary methods; 15 / vocational courses. Refresher courses, to be offered on condition that enrolment was sufficient, were announced as follows: 16 / an Elementary School Principals' refresher course; 17 / a guidance refresher course; and 18 / a music refresher course. The great majority of these courses were offered in Toronto exclusively, although agriculture was given at Guelph; physical and health education at Kingston and Hamilton; primary methods at Hamilton, London, and Ottawa; and grade 13 subjects at Ottawa as well as at Toronto.[1]

The following year, significant additions to the program included courses in school librarianship, junior education, and teaching the deaf, as well as a Vocational School Principals' course. In 1958 courses were provided in intermediate education for grades 7 and 8 and in teaching English as a second language. By this time, Sault Ste Marie, Sudbury, Owen Sound, St Catharines, and Peterborough were being used, as well as the larger cities, for some of the program. In 1960 the names of such places as Fort William, Chatham, and Pembroke also appeared.

The plan for elementary school teacher certification that went into force in 1962 gave the summer courses a new stimulus. A Standard 1 Certificate could be upgraded to Standard 2 solely by means of credits obtained in this way. Between 1961 and 1963 the number of teachers attending the courses rose from 7,079 to 9,970. The new courses added in 1962 were the Elementary School Teacher-Librarians' course, a course for heads of departments in secondary schools, and intermediate science; those added in 1963 were intermediate division mathematics and the teaching of French to English-speaking pupils in elementary schools; those in 1965, language arts and teaching the deaf; those in 1966 elementary mathematics, an Elementary School Principal's course, and French conversation; those in 1967, science (grades 1–6), intermediate history and geography (grades 7 and 8), new techniques in the teaching of modern languages, and updating courses in business and commercial subjects; in 1968, elementary social studies (grades 1–6), art et science du langage, and fundamentals of educational television.

The complete list of courses for 1969, as given in the departmental announcement, with the places where they were offered, was as follows:

ART: Elementary, Intermediate, Supervisor's, Specialist – at Toronto
Elementary, Intermediate Part I – at Lindsay, Owen Sound and Timmins (see Short Courses also)

ART ET SCIENCE DU LANGAGE: at Ottawa

AUDIO-VISUAL METHODS: (see Learning Materials Methodology and Learning Materials Management)

COMPENSATORY EDUCATION: at Toronto

DANCE: at Toronto

ELEMENTARY SCHOOL LIBRARIANS: Elementary, Intermediate Part I and Intermediate Part II – at Toronto
Elementary – at Sudbury (instruction in English and in French)
Intermediate Part I – at London
Elementary and Intermediate Part I – at Ottawa (instruction in French only)

ELEMENTARY SCHOOL PRINCIPALS: at Kingston, London and Waterloo (July 7 to August 1)

ELEMENTARY SCIENCE (Grades 1 to 6): at Pembroke, Port Arthur, St. Catharines, Sault Ste. Marie and Watford (at Hawkesbury instruction in French only). (See Science Field Studies also.)

ELEMENTARY SOCIAL STUDIES (Grades 1 to 6): at Galt and Windsor

FRENCH CONVERSATION INTENSIVE SUMMER COURSE: at Compton, Quebec

FUNDAMENTALS OF EDUCATIONAL TELEVISION: at Toronto

GUIDANCE: Part I (formerly Elementary), Part II (formerly Intermediate), Part III (formerly Specialist) – at London and Toronto
Part II and Part III – at Kingston
Part II – at Sudbury
Part I – at Belleville and Fort Frances
Part IV (formerly Fourth Summer Course) – Kirkland Lake, Toronto, Guelph-Kitchener Area, Brantford, Hamilton, Niagara Falls Region, Sault Ste. Marie, Windsor, Chatham, London-St. Thomas Area, Ottawa

HEADS OF DEPARTMENTS SEMINAR (Secondary School): (see Short Courses)

INTEGRATED STUDIES 1969: (This course replaces Junior Education and Elementary Mathematics for 1969) – at Bancroft, Chatham, Prescott, Toronto and Woodstock

INTERMEDIATE DIVISION GEOGRAPHY AND HISTORY (grades 7 and 8): at Barrie

LANGUAGE ARTS: at Cornwall, Sarnia and Toronto

LEARNING MATERIALS METHODOLOGY (formerly called Audio-Visual Methods): at London, North Bay, Peterborough and Toronto

LEARNING MATERIALS MANAGEMENT: (see Short Courses)

MUSIC: Vocal (for Elementary Schools) Elementary Type B, Intermediate Type B, and Supervisor's – at Toronto
Vocal (for Secondary Schools) Intermediate Type A, Parts I and II, and Specialist – at Toronto
Instrumental (for Elementary Schools) Elementary Type B, Intermediate Type B, and Supervisor's – at Toronto
Instrumental (for Secondary Schools) Intermediate Type A, Parts I and II, and Specialist – at Toronto
(See Short Courses also)
Vocal and General Music Workshop for Teachers of Grades 7, 8 and 9; (see Short Courses)

NEW HORIZONS FOR YOUNG CHILDREN (a pilot updating course): (see Short Courses)

NEW TECHNIQUES IN THE TEACHING OF MODERN LANGUAGES: (see Short Courses)

PHYSICAL AND HEALTH EDUCATION: (see Dance also)
Type B, Combined courses for men and women, Elementary, Intermediate Parts I and II, and Supervisor's (Units 1, 2, 3 and 4) – at Hamilton
Elementary, Intermediate Parts I and II (Units 1, 2, and 3) – at Guelph and Toronto
Elementary, Intermediate Part I (Units 1 and 2 only) – at Ottawa

NB – Intermediate Part II may be taken at Ottawa if Unit 3 has been taken previously.

PRIMARY EDUCATION, SUPERVISOR'S: at Toronto
PRIMARY METHODS: Parts I and II – at Hamilton, St. Thomas, and Toronto (2 locations)
Part II only – at Midland
Parts I and II – at Ottawa (instruction in French only)
PRIMARY METHODS PARTS I AND II PILOT COURSE: at Kitchener and Ottawa
SCIENCE FIELD STUDIES: at Orielton Field Centre, Pembrokeshire, South Wales and Malham Tarn Field Centre, Yorkshire (July 16 to August 20)
SECONDARY SCHOOL PRINCIPALS: Parts I and II – at Kingston and London (July 7 to August 1)
SPECIAL EDUCATION: Elementary, Intermediate, Specialist – at Toronto
Elementary – at Brantford and Seaforth
TEACHING ENGLISH AS A SECOND LANGUAGE: at Hamilton and Toronto
Second Summer Course: at Toronto
TEACHING TRAINABLE RETARDED CHILDREN: Elementary and Intermediate at Toronto
THE TEACHING OF FRENCH TO ENGLISH-SPEAKING PUPILS IN ELEMENTARY SCHOOLS: at Ottawa and Toronto
Second Summer Course: at Toronto
THE TEACHING OF FRENCH TO ENGLISH-SPEAKING PUPILS IN ELEMENTARY SCHOOLS, Special Course: at Toronto
Second Summer Course: at Toronto

SHORT COURSES

ART REFRESHER: at Toronto
HEADS OF DEPARTMENTS SEMINAR (Secondary School): at Waterloo (August 18 to August 22)
LEARNING MATERIALS MANAGEMENT: at Toronto (July 7 to July 25)
MUSIC (Vocal and Instrumental) REFRESHER: at Toronto
MUSIC (Vocal and General Music Workshop for Teachers of Grades 7, 8 and 9): at Geneva Park, Lake Couchiching (June 30 to July 4)
NEW HORIZONS FOR YOUNG CHILDREN (a pilot updating course): at Elliot Lake Centre for Continuing Education (August 10 to August 22). Two three-day follow-up workshops, one in November, 1969, and one in February, 1970, will be conducted at North Bay, Port Arthur and Sudbury
NEW TECHNIQUES IN THE TEACHING OF MODERN LANGUAGES: at London (August 11 to August 15); Ottawa (August 18 to August 22)

Additions to the list in 1970 included a course for teachers of Indian children, designed for those working in reserve communities who wanted to improve their lessons on Indian culture. Among the topics covered were Indian historical and cultural background, the contemporary situation, the role of the teacher in the community, the teaching of English as a second language, and an introduction to the Indian languages of Ontario,

Other new courses were New Directions in Intermediate Science, Junior Environmental Studies and Environmental Field Studies, Local Studies, Child Education, and Physical and Health Education. The last three of these were scheduled to take place in Great Britain, where the participants could combine professional improvement in a stimulating environment with some recreational activity. The fact that teachers were able to bear the travel and other expenses involved was evidence that they were attaining at least a moderate level of prosperity.

Courses for heads of departments

It is possible to present here only a small amount of information about certain courses offered over the years. As an example of the seminar approach, a one-week session was offered for heads of departments of secondary schools at what was then the Ontario Agricultural College at Guelph late in August 1961. While primarily designed to assist those who already held department headships, it was also regarded as helpful for aspirants to these positions. Those who attended were divided into subject groups. General sessions, individual subject seminars, and special demonstrations were included in a concentrated course relating to areas such as the following:

(a) efficient organization and administration of a department;
(b) the duties of a Head as seen by the Superintendent, Principal, Inspector, and other teachers;
(c) effective in-service training for young teachers;
(d) the building of good courses of study for the various grade levels and Branches of the Secondary School Program;
(e) teaching-aid materials;
(f) texts and reference books in a subject field;
(g) testing procedures;
(h) supplementary reading and reference in all subject fields;
(i) any kindred topics in which the subject groups may be interested.[2]

The course was subsequently offered in other locations.

French conversation

The course in French offered at Elliot Lake in and after 1966 was designed to assist those who were engaged in teaching the language to English-speaking pupils in elementary and secondary schools. It was a concentrated six-week "immersion" course intended principally to develop oral fluency. Those who were accepted for it lived in residence where they experienced an intensive program of French conversation and studied culture and customs using a range of modern methods and media, including language laboratories. Their recreational activities included French films and the singing of French songs. Participants were required to give an undertaking to use only French as a medium of communication from the time of arrival until the course was completed.[3] A similar course was offered in the summer of 1968 at Sainte-Thérèse-de-Blainville in Quebec.

In the summer of 1967, the department first offered a special course to assist qualified teachers to become familiar with some of the more recent developments in facilities for the teaching of modern languages. Covering a five-day period, it involved instruction in the operation of language laboratories, overhead projectors, tape recorders, and film projectors. The practical work was combined with classes in theory and methods as they related to the use of audio-visual aids. For this course, the special facilities of the University of Waterloo were made available.

Out-of-doors education

A co-operative five-week program at the Albion Hills Conservation School was sponsored jointly in the summer of 1968 by the department and the College of Education of the University of Toronto. Designed as an interdisciplinary program, it was open to teachers of both elementary and secondary schools. It actually consisted of a series of six-day courses entitled as follows: Science and Conservation, Science and Archaeology, Science and the Arts, and Geography in the Field. The final week was devoted to a conference and practical work on "learning theory in the out-of-doors." Participants attended for varying periods of time, most of those in the early and later periods being elementary and secondary teachers respectively.

Science field studies

A summer course in science field studies was offered for Ontario teachers in Great Britain in 1969. A four-week course, it was given in two parts, the first in Pembrokeshire, South Wales, and the second in Yorkshire. In the week intervening between these two parts, the teachers could, at their own expense, study at any of seven other field centres. Those completing the course successfully were eligible for a certificate in Science Field Studies.

Guidance

Courses for guidance certificates perhaps justify special comment. The first school guidance courses in Canada were offered by the Ontario Department of Education in 1925. In 1945 the department began a four-phase program leading to the Specialist's Certificate. F.J. Clute recently reported the dimensions this program reached in the subsequent twenty-four year period. The enrolment grew from 150 initially to 1,600 in 1968. Each of these school counsellors received the equivalent of six university semester hours of instruction, at least some of which was provided by graduate lecturers from universities. In addition to lectures, these students participated in seminars, workshops, and group discussions. During the school year, nearly all of them tried out in daily practice the theories dealt with during attendance at courses, and many of them worked under the direct supervision of guidance specialists.[4]

In Ontario guidance certificates are awarded at the elementary, intermediate, and specialist levels. Before 1965 entry to the elementary course required two years of successful teaching on a basic teaching certificate or Letter of Standing valid in Ontario. This period was reduced at that time to one year. Advancement to each successive level required the successful completion of an additional summer course. The Specialist's Certificate required, in addition, the submission of an acceptable report of an original study in the field of guidance. In 1965–6, provision was made for an alternative route to the Elementary Certificate through a supplemental course in guidance offered at the Ontario College of Education in conjunction with the regular course leading to the Interim High School Assistant's Certificate, Type B. This route demanded successful teaching experience in an elementary or secondary school in Ontario subsequent to completion of the course. Also beginning in 1965, the Intermediate Certificate might be obtained by taking two specific units of the Master of Education degree program of the University of Toronto. The course requirements for the Specialist's Certificate could also be obtained by completing four units of the same MEd program. The departmental courses leading to the Specialist's Certificate were not offered after the summer of 1966.

Clute, who directed the departmental guidance program for many years, recently examined in considerable detail the courses in guidance and counselling leading to masters' degrees in Canadian, American, and British universities and conferred with counsellor educators at home and abroad. As a result of these investigations, he made a convincing case for the proposition that in time, course content, and qualifications of the instructors, the departmental program compared very favourably with any of them.[5] He acknowledged the criticism that a small proportion of the teachers admitted to the Ontario program lacked undergraduate degrees but did not think this fact seriously affected the soundness of his claim. Unfortunately, universities are very difficult to persuade to recognize the validity of credits for courses offered by government agencies. Clute welcomed the good relationship established between the department and the graduate school of the University of Toronto, whose programs in education were offered by the Ontario Institute for Studies in Education. Despite the best efforts of both, however, there was a prospect of an insufficient number of trained counsellors for many years to come.

Updating course for electrical teachers

Under Program 7 of the Federal-Provincial Technical and Vocational

Training Agreement, the department sponsored a two-week course in electrical theory and test at Central Technical School in Toronto in the summer of 1966. The course was particularly designed for teachers whose certificates were in electricity or electronics, but who found themselves called upon to teach electrical theory and test. Those who had certificates in the latter area were familiarized with the newer styles of laboratory equipment and with recent developments in the electrical field.[6]

Other departmental training activities

The department's in-service activities have of course gone beyond formal courses offered during the summer. Advantage has sometimes been taken of unusual opportunities to arrange for a special program. For example, Miss Edith Biggs, one of Her Majesty's Inspectors from England, joined the Curriculum Section during the last four months of 1967. A recognized expert throughout the world in assisting teachers to develop techniques to encourage learning through inquiry, she conducted six-day workshops in Kitchener, London, Ottawa, Peterborough, Sudbury, and Toronto Township.[7]

Fees

The fees for departmental courses have always been very modest. In 1955 ex-service men and women were admitted free, while others paid $10 for a regular five-week course, $5 for a two-week refresher course, and $2 for a single week. The calendar for 1957 stressed in bold type that this amount was payable in cash at the opening of the course. The fee for the Secondary School Principal's course, as announced in 1959, was $25. In 1961 these rates were raised to $50 for the principal's course, $25 for other regular courses, and $10 and $5 for two-week and one-week refresher courses respectively. There were further increases in 1964 to a rate of approximately $7 a week, although the fee for the principal's course remained unchanged. The entire charge for the French language course initiated at Elliot Lake in 1966 was $100 for the six weeks and covered board and room as well as instruction. Charges for a regular five-week course, a three-week course, a two-week course, a one-week course, the principals' course, and the intensive course in French conversation were respectively $75, $45, $30, $15, $60, and $200 in 1969.

BOARD SPONSORED WINTER COURSES FOR TEACHERS FOR CERTIFICATE CREDIT

In 1964 the Ontario Association of Directors of Education approached the minister with a request that school boards be permitted to conduct winter courses for teachers, leading to the same certificates granted for equivalent departmental summer courses. As a result permission was given to five boards to organize such courses on an experimental basis during the subsequent school year. Etobicoke, North York, and Toronto took advantage of this opportunity by offering courses in guidance, mathematics, and school librarianship. When the experiment was judged successful, a set of conditions was formulated under which other boards might be allowed to follow suit. The substance of these conditions was as follows: 1 / the board had to secure the minister's approval; 2 / only courses for which the department currently offered a certificate and for which the board could provide enough qualified staff were to be offered; 3 / admission requirements, attendance regulations, and hours of instruction were to be the same as those for equivalent summer courses; 4 / course content, assignments, examinations, and qualifications of staff were subject to departmental approval; 5 / the department might exercise such supervision of a course as was considered necessary; 6 / where it was reported to the minister that too few candidates were in attendance, or that a board had failed to supply enough qualified and experienced staff members to conduct a course effectively, or that the regulations of the department were not being observed, certificate credit for the course might be withheld.[8] Evidently, the department was not prepared to let the boards assume any excess of independence or responsibility. They were, however, to bear the entire cost of the courses.

The regulations applying to departmental summer courses were quite strict. For example, "necessary" absence of three days was permitted; absence up to five days was reported to the department for a decision; absence of more than five days for any reason prevented a candidate from receiving a certificate. It was decreed that the same rule should apply to winter courses, with "session" substituted for "day." Winter courses could not offer less than one hundred hours of classroom instruction, with twenty additional hours for reading, study, and assignments.

The department observed in 1966 that the introduction of these courses had made it possible for teachers to acquire advanced qualifications, such as Supervisor's and Specialist's Certificates, in considerably less time than was required by following the departmental summer course sequence. Since it was assumed that successful classroom experience and a certain degree of maturity were necessary before a teacher was competent to assume supervisory duties, changes were made so that the experience requirements for summer and winter courses would be uniform. That meant that a minimum of one year of teaching experience was necessary before a teacher could enrol in certain of the courses at the next level.

UNIVERSITY EXTENSION COURSES

It has been estimated that university extension courses, offered both in winter and summer, involve even more practising teachers than do courses offered by the department. Many of these involve credit toward degrees or toward the upgrading of certificates. University work is not explored to any great extent in the present context. It seems appropriate, however, to indicate briefly the nature of some of the efforts made to provide refresher and informal upgrading courses in certain subject areas.

Early in the 1965–6 school year, the chairmen of chemistry departments in Ontario universities, in co-operation with the Department of Education, made plans for a series of refresher courses in their subject area. During the winter, series of from ten to twelve Saturday morning sessions were offered at McMaster University, the University of Western Ontario, Brock University, and the University of Toronto. Courses of from three to four weeks were also offered during the subsequent summer at Lakehead University, Queen's University, the University of Windsor, Carleton University, Laurentian University, and the University of Waterloo.[9] Similar courses were offered in 1967 in biology, chemistry, and physics at Althouse College of Education; in chemistry at Carleton University; in biology at McMaster University; in biology, chemistry, and physics at the University of Toronto; and in chemistry at the University of Waterloo. The College of Education at Toronto has followed the practice of giving refresher courses in certain subjects, varying from year to year.

During a week in August 1968 an institute was held at Brock University to explore various aspects of Latin teaching. The topics considered included teaching Latin literature, new curriculum trends, course organization, and audio-visual aids. Video tape demonstration lessons were presented for discussion, and opportunities were provided for teachers to practise Latin reading.

COURSES OFFERED BY TEACHERS' FEDERATIONS

The Ontario Secondary School Teachers' Federation initiated two-week summer courses in grade 13 chemistry and physics in the summer of 1955. These courses were originally designed to give assistance to teachers who were about to teach the subjects for the first time. Of the approximately fifty who enrolled, however, a considerable number took the work as a refresher. They were apparently interested in observing different teaching methods and, because of revisions in the course of study, in increasing their knowledge of new material.[10] This motive shaped the program from that time on. The courses were given by outstanding teachers, department heads, and administrators with recent experience in the instructional field. The federation bore the cost of the program, and the participants were liable only for their living expenses.

By 1958 the program included not only physics and chemistry, but mathematics, English, Latin, and French as well, and attracted 160 participants. The latter were said to have gained three outstanding benefits from the courses. 1 / They received a great deal of reference material beyond an exposition of individual texts. 2 / Their knowledge of teaching methods was enlarged by the discussion of problems of presentation engaged in with their instructor and their fellow teachers. 3 / The variety of opinions expressed in the discussion of departmental examination marking methods, supplemented by reports from those who had worked on marking committees, gave them a clearer grasp of the standards required.[11]

The following summer, the program underwent substantial further expansion. It included not only grade 13 English, French, Latin, history, chemistry, physics, biology, algebra, geometry, and trigonometry, but such grade 12 subjects as English, physics, and chemistry as well. Although participants ordinarily registered in only one course, various combinations were possible. In subsequent years, subjects down to grade 9 were offered according to demand.

A great deal of concern was demonstrated during the 1950s over the declining proportion of specialists in various subject areas in the high schools. The OSSTF particularly urged that something be done to enable holders of the High School Assistant's Certificate to upgrade their academic qualifications in order to secure specialist standing. It was simply not practical for most of them to go back to the university for at least a year, and in many cases two years or more, to convert a general or pass degree to an honours degree.

In 1957, Dunlop assembled the heads of the universities to discuss the problem. A committee was set up with Dean Earl of Queen's University as chairman and Dean Lewis of the Ontario College of Education as vice-chairman to work out a plan. The resulting scheme did more to protect traditional requirements than to meet the teachers' practical needs. There was no assurance that the number and variety of courses needed to provide for upgrading through summer courses would actually be available from year to year. A contribution was made, however, in the formulation of the scheme for endorsing certificates. Still unhappy with the results of its efforts, the federation worked out an arrangement whereby the University of Waterloo would guarantee to offer the required courses and the federation would meet any deficit in operating costs that might result from small enrolments. Some irritation was caused in federation circles when other universities then made moves to offer competing courses, thus threatening to undercut Waterloo's program and increasing the financial burden on the federation.

The work of the federation in the field of professional development has covered a wide range of activities. Some consideration of the results of the Annual Professional Development Conference in 1963 may give some idea of the scope of the organization's intentions and aspirations.[12] The group of twenty-three district delegates examined the following areas in which professional development might operate: improvement in teachers' qualifications, deepening and broadening of the teacher's educational background, improvement of teaching techniques, and understanding of correct professional attitudes and behaviour. Projects suggested for the current year included subject councils and weekend conferences; annual one-day teacher conventions; Saturday morning discussions; weekly study groups; publication of teacher aids; interschool visits; subject area conferences; university, industry, and community tours; lecture series; and in-service training programs. The formation of the Ontario Secondary Education Commission and subject councils in 1965 represented a move toward the encouragement of this kind of activity.

Davis has given emphatic encouragement to the federation in its efforts to improve the profession. At a conference sponsored by the commission on December 14, 1965, he told the delegates that there must be a combined attack on the problem of updating the teacher in service. He said that it would be a major blunder for the department itself to try to discharge the entire responsibility. Along with the universities and business and industry, he invited the co-operation of the teachers.[13] The department actually left the responsibility for organizing up-dating courses for secondary school teachers to the federation. In 1968 the former made a substantial financial contribution to the holding of grade 13 conferences.

IN-SERVICE COURSES OFFERED BY OTHER AGENCIES

Industrial and business organizations have occasionally offered summer courses of interest to teachers, particularly those involved in vocational work. An example of this type was a course in automotive mechanics provided by the General Motors Corporation in Oshawa in 1963. It consisted of approximately 160 hours of advanced theory and practice in the various aspects of automotive construction and operation. No credit was granted toward a Department of Education certificate. Nevertheless, the department's official attitude was regarded as favourable. In 1957, S.D. Rendall, Superintendent of Secondary Education, notified principals and teachers of secondary vocational schools that

> ... I am authorized to draw to the attention of those concerned the fact that this Department strongly favours the holding of such refresher courses during the summer vacation period ...
>
> It should be emphasized ... that refresher courses of this type are looked upon by this Department as extremely helpful in enabling teachers to maintain their skills and to keep fully informed as to currently approved trade practice.[14]

The Metropolitan Toronto and Region Conservation Authority is another agency that has responded to an interest demonstrated by teachers, in this case in conservation. In 1965 it offered two concentrated five-day courses consisting of a series of field trips in and near the Albion Hills Conservation Area. The program included a study of various aspects of soils and land use, agriculture, geology, geography, forestry, water conservation, fish and wildlife, and ecology. The course was presented by specialists from universities and government departments and agencies.

TEN

Research and development: definitions and issues

The terms "research" and "development" are usually linked when applied to education, as to so many other fields. This practice has, however, become established rather recently; development is a relatively youthful partner in the team, although the concept behind the label is by no means of recent origin. The two concepts are associated mainly because they are both seen as essential steps in the process of constructive innovation. But they are by no means synonymous, or even very similar.

DEFINITION OF RESEARCH

The term "research" has been employed to cover a great deal of ground, from the vaguest process of seeking information to the most exacting and rigorous procedure. There seems little point in attempting to discard certain associations that have resulted from the inevitable and uncontrollable growth of language. The contemptuous assertion "That's not research!" with reference to some approach that does not satisfy one's idea of the appropriate procedure is a rather futile gesture. About the only practical course of action is to interpret the term according to the context.

A very broad definition tends to be retained for research as applied to the humanities. Desmond Pacey used the term to describe "systematic scholarly enquiry which leads eventually to published results in the form of a thesis, article, lecture, or book."[1] He expressed regret that even this definition had shrunk with the passage of time. In earlier centuries, research had no connection with publication at all. He asserted that a person "may be engaged in research in the humanities if he is earnestly and sensitively reading the great books, whether or not he ever publishes the results of his enquiries, and indeed he may be legitimately engaged in research even if he is only contemplating the processes of his own mind or noting with clarity the nature of his own reactions to artistic expression."

In scientific fields, research has come to be associated with the narrower term "experimentation." Experimental methods have, of course, evolved over a period of centuries as a means of extending scientific knowledge. They were leading to discoveries of enormous importance long before a concerted effort was made to specify their essential criteria. Much early research ignored what are now considered important, if not vital, steps and proceeded without the measurement and statistical tools that have come to be regarded as indispensable. At the present time, most authorities would regard as basic elements of the experimental research approach 1 / the identification of a problem, 2 / problem definition, 3 / hypothesis formation, 4 / hypothesis testing by observation of actual phenomena, 5 / analysis of the data so obtained in order to reach conclusions relating to the hypothesis, and 6 / relating the results of the process to a generalization or theory. Subsequent observation of a phenomenon that does not appear to be in accordance with the theory may be considered to constitute a new problem, and the whole process may be repeated, resulting either in further support for or rejection of the theory. The conduct of experiments of acceptable quality demands an effective means of controlling the circumstances under which a phenomenon manifests itself; it also requires procedures for quantification and accurate measurement of the phenomenon, as well as of related factors.

The extension of scientific research procedures to individual and group phenomena in human affairs rests on the assumption that they bear enough resemblance to phenomena encountered in the natural and physical sciences to justify an application of comparable techniques. To a large extent, the difficulties centre around control and measurement. Obviously human behaviour is not subject to the same kind of direct physical control as is a substance or a specimen handled in a laboratory. Social scientists have thus been forced to seek a number of substitutes for direct control as of course have some other scientists, notably astronomers. As far as psychological and educational measurement are concerned, the development of reliable and valid techniques has almost been limited to the present century. In many areas of human behaviour, the objective of moderately accurate measurement remains elusive. A further problem with social science research is that the units dealt with, particularly if they are human characteristics, are usually extremely variable. Real progress has thus waited for the development of techniques that will make it possible to estimate the extent to which conclusions based on a sample can be validly generalized to the larger group of phenomena or the "population" from which it is drawn. Most of the complex structure of inferential statistics, which is designed essentially for this purpose, is also a creation of the present century.

One of the distinctions of major importance is that between basic or fundamental research on the one hand and applied research on the other. Applied research is undertaken to answer a question or to solve a problem that has immediate, practical implications. It is often a valuable aid to decision-making, provided, of course, that the answer can be obtained before the necessity for making the decision has passed. Basic research, on the other hand, is undertaken to satisfy intellectual curiosity or to add to the fund of human knowledge without regard to the possibility of specific applications. Its results may turn out to have tremendous practical value, but no assurance is demanded beforehand that such will be the outcome. Basic research in education is regarded somewhat differently from that in many other fields in that, although it may begin with a comparable motive, it is not usually considered worthwhile if it fails to produce at least some ultimate effect on practice, whereas an extension of knowledge about some of the natural phenomena of the universe is in itself considered a worthy intellectual objective. Nevertheless, basic research in education, if it is justifiable at all, must be allowed to operate under rules similar to that in other fields, since it is often impossible to foresee what the implications of a particular effort will be. A reasonable risk must be run that the research will not pay dividends.

There are certain ideas about educational research that carry a great deal of weight in the mind of the teacher or other practising educator. He is usually in favour of research into "practical" or immediately relevant problems. He tends to draw a contrast between this type of activity and that devoted to the building of theory, which is "impractical" and therefore useless for the attainment of any immediate objective. In fact, a practical-theoretical dichotomy does not represent a valid distinction. Theorizing is in essence a method of generalizing which may prevent a repeated and wasteful investment of resources to solve the same problem over and over again. A theory may deal either with extremely practical or quite abstruse questions. In real circumstances, a very specific and non-recurring problem may demand a straightforward, specific answer, and any attempt to relate the results of the necessary investigation to a theory may be pretentious or ridiculous. Under other conditions, however, the development of a theory may represent the ultimate in practicality. The real challenge is to determine when theories can profitably be employed and how they rate in terms of valid criteria.

THE CASE FOR RESEARCH

The idea of relying on research for the improvement of education has appealed strongly to those of a certain turn of mind. If it has done so much for science and technology, why should it not make a comparable contribution in human affairs? F.G. Robinson, certainly not a completely uncritical enthusiast, put one aspect of the case as follows:

> ... in the long run, increased educational efficiency will depend upon improvement in our educational technology – i.e., in the means which we use to attain our educational goals. Some economists are of the opinion that, despite external appearances, the technology of education has become stagnant and its unit cost relatively high. Undoubtedly one cause of this stagnation is that there is no *systematic process of invention in education*, so that we must continue to attack new problems with old methods.[2]

The degree to which this point wins support depends on the relative weight one is prepared to place on methodology, particularly technology.

A contribution from an anonymous author of a proposed plan for the expansion of the Ontario Institute for Studies in Education reads:

> Just as research is an obvious means of improving business and industrial production, so also should research be the means of safeguarding our educational investment. Research can save us money, and good research can save us a great deal of money. True, we may never know exactly how much a successful research program will save, since we will have no way of knowing how much we would have wasted without it. When we build our schools in the convenient form in places where they are most needed, as indicated by research, we cannot calculate how much we would have lost had we erected buildings on undesirable sites, although substantial savings may be assumed. When we teach our children the right things by the most effective methods, in the light of research findings, we cannot tell how much it would have cost had they been turned loose without the means of earning their living in a modern economy and without the necessary attitudes for good citizenship, but the savings may very well be tremendous. Our inability to estimate how much we may benefit from spending our educational funds according to the most up-to-date knowledge is surely no excuse for spending carelessly or blindly. As costs continue to rise, the taxpayer who insists on good education for his children is almost certain to demand also a closer accounting of the way in which the money is used toward that end.

Some educators have been impressed by claims that the average human mind possesses a great deal of unused capacity for learning. They have looked to research to show how presumed mental roadblocks can be removed and intellectual potential fully exploited. R.W. Kluge has expressed this viewpoint: "In the next ten years we will have to double or triple the knowledge given to children in the same amount of time used now. Only with basic research in the field of learning are we going to be able to multiply the process by the factor of two or three."[3] The subsequent decade certainly did not witness the realization of Kluge's high hopes, but he might perhaps argue that research was not given an opportunity to show what it could do.

Support for research in education is often based on analogies with other areas of human concern. In this respect, comparisons with industry have been popular. The following comment, although more than a decade old, still typifies many present-day attitudes.

> How much money does industry put into research? The year before last, industry put between four and ten per cent of its gross sales into research ... I am not sure but it seems to me that the petroleum industry has gone up to the ten percent level. What makes them do this? Competition and monopoly!
>
> Let us look at another industry – the industry of education. Is it in the competitive position, or does it have a monopoly?[4]

Robert S. Donaldson has made an excellent case for utilizing the full potential contribution of research.

> The operation of our educational establishment has become one of the biggest, and most important industries in the nation [i.e., The United States], commanding, next to defense, our greatest investment of people and money. Active concern about the well-being of our total economy must involve serious study of the effectiveness of this influential segment. Big questions as to whether we are using our people and money wisely need to be answered. Other industries have seen the expansion of the individual's influence through technology and organization, with people producing more and using higher skills because machines are helping them do the jobs better. Similar use of technology to increase a teacher's influence is more difficult, and has had less attention. These are compelling reasons why major efforts are necessary to assess our progress, and learn what changes may be appropriate to speed up the achievement of our social and economic objectives.[5]

These references to education as an industry have of course been offensive to many people and have tended to associate research with education for strictly utilitarian purposes. Others would argue that education need not be inefficient to meet cultural and spiritual needs.

Much of the support for educational research is coupled with some kind of warning against excessively optimistic expectations. J.C. Morrison made the following statement: "The search for adequate measurement of quality in education may prove as elusive as the current search for the prevention and cure of cancer and in the long run may prove as important."[6] Numerous observers have also insisted that it is futile to expect really important or valuable results without a large investment of funds and human energy.

CRITICAL APPRAISALS

Most of the really serious sceptics or outright opponents fall into two classes. 1 / Those in one group are doubtful that techniques developed in the natural and physical sciences can ever be so extended or adapted as to produce effective results in human affairs. They suggest that the phenomena and environmental circumstances that must be taken into account are practically infinite in their variations. They point to the large number of apparently contradictory findings when attempts have been made to replicate particular studies and claim that the only problems that can be solved unequivocally are those to which the solution was obvious in any case. 2 / The other group of opponents consists of those who see education mainly as the recognition and definition of values, as the cultivation of feelings and emotions, or as the conveying of inspiration. While scientific research may have some peripheral relevance to these intangibles, it can never deal with the matters of real importance. To the adherents of this point of view, researchers are mainly, at their best, dabblers in the inconsequential and, at their worst, perpetrators of absolute fraud.

Researchers are in a particularly well-placed position, in the short run, to perpetrate a fraud on the educational community. The techniques needed to conduct competent studies are acquired with a great deal of effort and involve the use of highly specialized terminology. The initiate is protected by a shell of mystery. Many a would-be critic is intimidated by the fear of showing his ignorance. But the relatively high degree of protection for any specific effort does not extend to an entire program, and ultimately the effects of trivial or irrelevant studies become known. The research movement in education has suffered severely from a widespread awareness of the incompetence of many of its participants.

Some of the strong supporters of the potential value of good educational research have been very critical of the quality of the work actually done. Michael Scriven wrote in the *Review of Educational Research* in 1960: "95 per cent of the work in the field ... that is concerned with causal analysis is, by either theoretical or practical standards, invalid or trivial."[7] Three years later, W.B. Michael expressed similar sentiments: "Probably, on the average, only 10 percent of published papers in educational journals are worthy of being reported in the *Review*."[8] N.V. Scarfe, Dean of the Faculty of Education at the University of British Columbia, made these remarks at a symposium in Toronto in 1964:

> ... the best report on educational research that has been published over the past 10 years was produced by Dr. Smith in my faculty. It is a damming [*sic*] report about research in education. In the past seven years in Canada only four researches have been directly on the problem of what is the purpose of education in Canada. Most of the researches have been quite valueless and in particular there seems to be an avoidance of the really practical research of how learning goes on in the classroom. Then there are so many people doing research for the purpose of getting a degree. Their work is often trifling. It takes an awful lot of work though – they get their degree for effort, not necessarily for what they've produced.[9]

R.L. Ebel defended the thesis that basic research in education can promise very little improvement in the process of education, either at present or in the foreseeable future:

> ... if the primary task of professional educators is to improve the process of education as much as possible, as rapidly as possible, they will do well to direct their efforts, not toward basic research on the conditions of learning or the processes of instruction, but instead toward applied research designed to

yield information immediately useful in the solution of contemporary educational problems.[10]

Ebel explained why he thought basic research could promise very little improvement:

... formal education (i.e., purposeful instruction), which is what we are trying to improve, is not a natural phenomenon. It is a human invention, a cultural institution designed and built by men. It is not so much in need of analysis and understanding as one of the givens in our universe as it is in need of redesign and reconstruction to serve our human purposes better. And we make a grave mistake, I fear, if we believe that the best way to redesign and reconstruct it is to study its current forms scientifically with a view to understanding them. Is the case for a scientific study of education, as a means of improving education, any stronger than the case for a scientific study of poetry as a means of improving poetry?

In casting doubt on the value of basic research into education as a phenomenon, Ebel was obviously not condemning this type of research into those aspects of such disciplines as psychology, sociology, or economics that concerned educational processes and structures. Such activity has produced some very important contributions to the improvement of education. One of the major questions is where or under what auspices research should be conducted. It is common for members of university psychology departments, for example, to complain about the fragmentation resulting from the establishment of special agencies to study psychology as it relates to education. The effective answer has often been that the creation of special agencies is needed because otherwise little or nothing would be done to assist educators. The field offers so many possible areas of specialization that even a large department can concentrate its efforts mainly on other aspects.

Derek Morrell seems not to question the validity of the concept of basic research, but he has emphasized that it cannot be relied upon for much immediate assistance:

... it is clear that the main justification for undertaking an increasing volume of basic research lies less in its relevance to immediate problems than in its likely relevance to the problems which our successors will face in the years to come. It is, in other words, part of our responsibility to future generations of pupils to invest some of our current resources in improving the problem-solving capacities of our successors. But, for our part, we are bound to rely very heavily on the basic knowledge now available as a result of wise investments made by our predecessors.[11]

The suggestion has been made that, because the validity of this assertion is sure to be recognized sooner or later, in a country like Canada only the federal government can be counted on to provide stable support for basic research in education. Only the federal government, it is claimed, is far enough removed from the direct influence of the voters that it can afford an investment with so little prospect of immediate return. The argument runs that provincial or local governments may be persuaded, under false expectations, to establish agencies for basic research. When they realize the true situation, however, financial support will be withdrawn.

Another frequently-voiced criticism of research has also been expressed effectively by Morrell.

> We are no longer at the stage where organisational planning can usefully assume that the lone-wolf researcher is likely to make an important contribution – though one hopes that room will always be left for the occasional, but utterly unpredictable, researcher of the calibre of a Piaget. The large-scale study of systems of interaction requires, by contrast, an ongoing institutional setting large enough to be capable of crossing the boundaries of many different disciplines ...[12]

The ineffectiveness of research inspired, organized, and carried out by a single individual is a reason commonly offered for the failure, pointed out by Scarfe and many others, of degree-seeking students to make any perceptible contribution to educational progress. Much of the work may be inconsequential, not because it is incompetently conceived or carried out, but rather because it represents single fragments inadequately related to any larger whole.

Yet there is a dilemma here that is not easily resolved. C.T. Bissell has presented it in the starkest terms:

> ... research should originate with the scholar; it must be the outcome of his own work, and follow inevitably from what he has already done. Research that is imposed upon him from outside is not really research at all; it is just a form of academic prostitution. A scholar should not confuse the collection of data with research, no matter how worthy the purpose or how benevolent the sponsoring organization.[13]

If this point of view is valid, it leaves no real alternative to the organization and mode of operations developed at the Ontario Institute for Studies in Education, as described in chapter 13. Perhaps the idea that a substantial proportion of the program might be "imposed" by the representatives of the educational community could be sufficiently modified if staff were selected because their previously-developed interests reflected those of the community.

Some adverse criticisms do not make it altogether clear whether the basis for the condemnation lies chiefly in the inadequacy of the approach itself or in the ineptness of its practitioners. The following comments by LaFountaine fall into that category.

My own contact with education "research" is the result of my attempts to document problems which appear to be constantly disturbing the education endeavour; in such areas as teacher education, educational television and adult education, I find "research" doing its utmost to render itself ineffective. I also find it bending over backwards to explain how it accomplishes this. Its contribution to knowledge about classroom television will always be a standing example of a class of verbal gymnastics which defies rational description. The whole question is weighted down with the standard faith in test scores, statistical analysis, control of variables, the assumption of the constant, and all the other elements which make up the grandfather of all myth, the "scientific method." To date, the sum of knowledge we have from over a thousand research "studies" in classroom television equals precisely nothing. The sum of knowledge research has discovered during seventy-odd years of "study" in the area of teacher education is precisely nothing.[14]

DEFINITION OF DEVELOPMENT

The term "development," as it has come to be applied to educational concerns, refers to a kind of engineering process by which some idea or concept is prepared for adoption and use. It may refer to the production of a textbook, a set of equipment for scientific demonstrations, a building of a particular design, or something else equally tangible. Quite commonly, also, it applies to an instructional technique, an organizational approach, or an administrative procedure. The process of development normally involves a demonstration of the article, device, or technique in question in a school, a school system, or some other realistic location. It is modified and perfected through various evaluative procedures. Development stops short of adoption and installation, functions normally assumed by the constituted authorities.

Sound development is reinforced by the contributions of research, but it is sometimes carried out without reference to the latter. Important questions revolve about the extent to which it should await research support. Morrell comments on this issue.

In time, we can no doubt increase the fractions of certainty and fill many of the gaps. But we cannot wait, so we have to make choices in areas of uncertainty or ignorance, using judgement informed by whatever evidence is available. This, in part, is the purpose of development: it involves the organised backing of hunches – informed, carefully formulated, and subsequently evaluated – but still hunches.

The greater danger lies however in viewing development ... as no more than a temporary and rather unsatisfactory substitute for research. On this view, research is the only approach which is wholly satisfactory; we undertake development while awaiting the millennium when all decisions can be taken on the basis of evidence.

This view seems to me to be profoundly mistaken. It supposes that the schools may ultimately be run like computers, capable of producing the right answers when suitably programmed and fed with relevant data. More fundamentally, it supposes that it is legitimate to talk about the properties of human personality in the same way that one can talk about the properties of matter.[15]

What is relatively new about the concept of development is that it has come to be regarded as a conscious, distinct, specially organized process. With the acceptance of this view have come difficult questions about suitable institutional provisions for it. Should it be associated with organized research activities and, if so, what should be the nature of the relationship? What are the implications of attempting to carry it out under independent auspices or, conversely, as a government function? What should be the respective roles of practising educators and of specialists? The attempts to answer these questions within a particular institutional form in the Ontario Institute for Studies in Education are treated in chapter 13. Other countries have offered different solutions with varying degrees of success.

TEACHER INVOLVEMENT IN RESEARCH AND DEVELOPMENT

There is, of course, no question that teachers should be concerned with the results of research and development activities. If they are not, the whole process is obviously futile. There are, however, varying views about the extent and form of their participation. Should they be encouraged to initiate and conduct their own research projects? If so, under what conditions?

To the extent that it is synonymous with mental alertness, intellectual curiosity, and a desire to put matters of opinion, where possible, to an empirical test, the research attitude is highly commendable. It is in close harmony with the Hall-Dennis view that the chief aim of education should be to further the child's search for truth. A teacher who is constantly seeking the same end must surely be the best kind of guide and partner in this quest. It might seem that the only reasonable limitations on the teacher's conduct should be those imposed by time, facilities, and knowledge of suitable techniques.

To pose a question, collect the necessary data, and arrive at an objective answer with no particular implications beyond a single classroom, school, or school system does not require an advanced level of training. In some form, it goes on continuously, and might be encouraged to the great advantage of most school systems. In order to improve its quality, efforts could be made to ensure that teachers become more conscious of measures to control relevant variables, of the importance of precise measurement, and of other aspects of the research process. As F.G.

Robinson has written: "It seems only reasonable to believe that the validity of the decisions made at the school level will be enhanced in proportion to the time and effort spent on systematic study of the various factors and problems involved."[16] Several incidental benefits may also be realized. Active participation in a study arising out of a problem of genuine concern may enhance teachers' feeling of professional responsibility and add zest to their work. Involvement in research also tends to produce a greater receptivity to change. The attempt to apply appropriate techniques or contemplation of the actual findings may help to make teachers aware of their own deficiencies and provide a stimulus for further in-service training. Co-operation with others in a matter of vital interest is also a good way of improving professional esprit de corps.

It is desirable that teachers be impressed with the necessity of restricting their generalizations. There is often a tendency for those who have carried out a study of purely localized validity to proclaim the universal applicability of their findings. They deliver papers at conferences and rush into print in whatever professional journal is available. While they may have learned to utter the conventional warning that their findings must be interpreted "with caution," the impact of their message is otherwise. It is hardly a wonder that a great variety of contradictory findings can be cited for almost any problem.

There is a theory that generalizations of wide applicability can be obtained by combining the findings from large numbers of small-scale projects conducted by individual teachers in their own classrooms. There might be a certain attractiveness in such an idea, but for several reasons it does not hold up under critical examination. 1 / The major problems in education cannot be defined in terms of multitudes of small additive units. They usually demand depth of study and sophistication of technique that puts them in a different qualitative category. 2 / The unsound or erroneous elements in small-scale studies will not be squeezed out by some miraculous process when the results are cumulated. 3 / Unless the process is planned and co-ordinated in a way that has seldom if ever proved possible, what appear to be many similar studies turn out in fact to be quite different.

Research conducted by practitioners as an incidental part of their work must be restricted to certain types and approaches. Generally speaking, it cannot be fundamental or basic and cannot make any great contribution to the more abstract theories. As Robinson has suggested, the realistic view seems to be to regard staff research as a process that complements studies undertaken at other levels in the educational hierarchy.[17]

The case-study approach has had a particular attraction for some teachers. Since they are in close contact with certain individuals, it may be beguiling to think that their observations may turn out to have important scientific value. Confusion apparently arises because the case study as a preparation for some kind of therapeutic action is widely used in various fields. But the case study as a means of adding to the fund of scientific knowledge is a complex technique requiring much more than perception and sensitivity.

A clearer understanding of the distinction between research and development would be of great assistance to teachers in finding a fruitful role in the process of innovation. They are often in an excellent position to assist with development, especially if they have the active encouragement of the administration. Successful development without teacher participation is in fact an impossibility. And teachers can often go beyond co-operation with an outside agency to the actual initiation of their own development projects.

ELEVEN

Structures for educational research and development before 1965

BACKGROUND

The appearance of formal agencies for research and development in education is strictly a phenomenon of recent decades. The concept of research has itself evolved into something that was quite foreign to education before the turn of the century. C.E. Phillips traces the development of systematic, structured inquiry in Canada to a school inspector in Prince Edward Island who, in 1849, introduced a method of testing and recording results that he hoped would provide "instead of uncertain, varying opinions, authentic facts [which] when continued from year to year, become reliable statistics."[1] The method he used was to ask pupils in different schools the same question, to record all correct and incorrect answers, and to compute the percentage of correct answers. On the basis of this objective recording of performance, he was able to rank the schools in order of excellence.

Before there were any permanent structures, committees and commissions of inquiry were established from time to time, as they still are, to investigate various questions of concern to those responsible for the administration of the educational system. A point has occasionally been strained somewhat to trace research activity, like so many other educational developments of importance in Ontario, back to Egerton Ryerson. It is true that Ryerson did use the word "research" once in recounting his experience in Europe in the 1840s during which he picked up so many of the ideas that were to exert a powerful influence on the establishment of the Ontario system. The term was obviously to be applied to careful and accurate personal observation, an activity that is as old as intelligent human behaviour.

The subsequent period reveals examples of issues of importance that were subjected to fairly systematic inquiry before decisions were made and definite policies established. One of these was conducted under the direction of G.W. Ross, Minister of Education from 1883 to 1899, who became concerned about the exclusive use of French and German as languages of instruction in certain schools in Ontario. The situation uncovered by this survey led to the regulation that English be taught in every school in the province. Problems in the same area led to the appointment in 1889 of a commission consisting of A.H. Reynar, J.J. Tilley, and

D.D. McLeod. Their findings were published in a sessional paper in 1890 under the title "Regulations and Correspondence Relating to French and German Schools in the Province of Ontario."[2] On the basis of their recommendations, further regulations were drafted relating to the use of English as a language of instruction. The same commission reviewed the situation in 1893, when it was able to report some improvement in existing conditions. It was as a result of further direct investigation that the famous Regulation 17 was put into force in 1912, limiting the use of French as the language of instruction to the first form of elementary school. Another commission was appointed in 1925 under the chairmanship of F.W. Merchant, then Chief Director of Education. Its detailed examination included no fewer than 330 French language schools. Its recommendations led to the adoption of more conciliatory measures in 1927.

Various other matters of interest were investigated from time to time. In 1906, for example, concern about the availability and cost of textbooks led to the appointment of a commission to collect relevant information. John Seath's famous report on technical education in 1911 was the result of a careful study of the problem, both at home and abroad.

These activities, although the forerunners of organizational structures for the conduct of research, showed little sign of being influenced by the techniques of measurement and experimental design that began to be felt in university and other learned circles. Apart from lively and ingenious speculation on causes and consequences, there was no evidence of an interest in the systematic formulation and testing of abstract hypotheses. Attention was focused strictly on immediate needs and problems and the devising of satisfactory solutions. Until very recent years, educational research in Ontario was conspicuously characterized by this orientation.

THE DEPARTMENT OF EDUCATIONAL RESEARCH OF THE ONTARIO COLLEGE OF EDUCATION

Establishment and early activities

It was chiefly an interest in the educational testing movement that led to the establishment of the Department of Educational Research in the Ontario College of Education in 1931, the first formal organization of its kind in Canada. This interest in testing was demonstrated by a number of articles on the topic in a periodical, *The School*, which was published at the college until 1948. Reference is made in chapter 15 of the present volume to an experiment undertaken to appraise the possibility of using objective tests in the middle school examinations conducted by the Department of Education. The favourable verdict resulting from this effort is evidence of the climate of opinion among the university professors, departmental officials, and secondary school teachers who participated. Considerable concern appeared in the 1920s over the suitability of tests and test norms developed in the United States for application in Canadian schools. In part, this ever-present issue has been based on an awareness of certain differences in content and approach characteristic of Canadian curricula, and in part also on objections to the references to American symbols and the employment of typically American political and social concepts in measures of achievement. Peter Sandiford, then a professor at the Ontario College of Education, exerted a great deal of his famous initiative in arousing the necessary enthusiasm and support for a new organization to be primarily devoted to the construction of tests adapted to meet peculiarly Canadian needs. Although the province, like the rest of the western world, was entering a bleak economic period, and there was little hope for the adoption of new educational programs, Sandiford managed to secure funds from the Carnegie Corporation of New York to launch his venture.

Through most of the 1930s, the efforts of the Department of Educational Research or, to label it more briefly, the Research Department were applied vigorously to its primary purposes. A small nucleus of permanent staff, with a certain number of temporary assistants, laid the foundations for a range of standardized group intelligence and achievement tests that were to dominate the field and exert considerable influence on educational practice in Ontario and in other provinces for many years. Known as the Dominion tests, they had a well-deserved reputation for excellence in concept and construction as compared with their contemporaries. This reputation carried them considerably beyond the period when active developmental work and the application of the latest techniques were keeping them up to date.

A special contribution to early work in test development was made by Miss K. Hobday, whose active career spanned the entire life of the Research Department, from 1931 until its merger into the Ontario Institute for Studies in Education, where she served as editor until her retirement in 1969. Other distinguished figures whose participation dated from the early years include J.A. Long, who served from the beginning and assumed the directorship on Sandiford's death in 1941, a position which he held until his own death in 1957. R.W.B. Jackson assumed a permanent position in 1939, after his return from studies in London. From 1945 to 1950, he served as secretary of the Royal Commission on Education, an activity which also involved E.B. Rideout, whose appointment dated from 1946. Others who went from temporary association with the Research Department to prominent positions elsewhere include Maxwell Cameron and C. Ebblewhite Smith.

In the late 1930s and early 1940s, the program expanded and the department's role began to change. Test development, of course, remained an area of primary emphasis. During the war a contribution was made toward the practical problem of selecting suitable armed forces personnel for special tasks. Investigations into measurement theory began at the same time to add a new dimension to the work. During his productive period of specialized scholarship in statistics, measurement, and research methodology, lasting well into the 1950s, Jackson gained a worldwide reputation. The late 1930s also saw a growing concern with financial studies, a particularly relevent interest considering the economic conditions prevailing at the time and one that was manifested by the establishment of a committee of inquiry under the chairmanship of Duncan McArthur in 1935.

The development of ties with the Department of Education

Jackson, who became director in 1957, developed an early awareness that the future of organized educational research depended to a large extent on the direct contributions of the process to fill governmental needs. His brief association with V.K. Greer, who served first as Chief Inspector of Public and Separate Schools and later as Superintendent of Elementary Education, has received comment in volume II, chapter 8. His work with the Royal Commission gave him opportunities to develop his associations with officials at the highest levels. By recognizing and seizing the opportunity to assume responsibility for the studies required to expand and improve the increasingly complex system of provincial grants, he established a lifeline to the Department of Education that would do much to carry the Research Department through any period of lack of enthusiasm in the Ontario College of Education, of which the Research Department remained organically a part. This element of security indeed proved valuable after the retirement in 1958 of Dean A.C. Lewis, who took an active and encouraging interest in research.

The Royal Commission included in its report several pages in which the importance of educational research was emphasized and the role of the Research Department recognized. The report contains this particularly significant statement: "We suggest that the staff of the Department of Educational Research should, upon request, undertake the supervision and co-ordination of the work of all groups engaged in educational research."[3] A set of formal recommendations was also included.

With reference to the organization of research and experimentation in education in Ontario, we recommend

(a) that the Department of Educational Research in the Ontario College of Education be recognized as the educational research bureau for the province;

(b) that the activities of the Department of Educational Research be financed through provincial grants from the Department of Education;

(c) that the Department of Education provide funds, and solicit additional amounts of money from other sources, to establish scholarships tenable in the College of Education in the University of Toronto for purposes of educational research;

(d) that, through grants-in-aid, the Department of Education encourage research conducted by individuals and educational organizations under the supervision of the Ontario College of Education;

(e) that the Department of Educational Research prepare and distribute widely information relating to the findings of educational research and experimentation;

(f) that the Department of Educational Research and the Vocational Guidance Centre, through the establishment of a Research Clinic, investigate and evaluate developments in instruments and techniques for diagnostic, prognostic, and remedial work in education, and publicize their findings;

(g) that, upon request, the Department of Educational Research co-ordinate, supervise, and assist in research activities in education undertaken by individuals or voluntary organizations.[4]

Most of these recommendations were carried out in some form. The Research Department and what became simply the Guidance Centre never managed to establish a research clinic for the indicated purposes. Nor did the Research Department co-ordinate or supervise the research work of outside organizations. Assistance was, however, abundantly provided. A notable example was the effort devoted to the founding of the Ontario Educational Research Council. On the other hand, such associations as the teachers' federation were at the time rather wary of any close embrace by the Research Department, since its status as the research arm of the Department of Education identified it uncomfortably as an agent of officialdom.

Significance of the Atkinson Study of Utilization of Student Resources

An opportunity came for the Research Department to assume a new and larger role with the launching of the Atkinson Study of Utilization of Student Resources in the mid-fifties. Reference to its origin may be found in chapter 12 of this volume. One of the concerns that gave rise to the study was an interest in new devices for screening candidates for admission to university in order to free grade 13 from the departmental examination restrictions. P.A.C. Ketchum, Headmaster of Trinity College School, was hopeful that the College Entrance Examination Board tests, or a suitable adaptation of them, would provide a satisfactory substitute. There was also considerable concern about the wastage of human talent in the reputed failure of many young people to continue their education to the limit of their potentialities. A small group, including Ketchum, Sidney Smith, then President of the University of Toronto, and Lewis, Long, and Jackson from the Ontario College of Education, approached the Atkinson Charitable Foundation for a grant of $35,000 to pay for the comprehensive testing program that would be required in the initial stages. The need for additional staff in the Research Department was the occasion for the employment of the present writer at the end of 1954. During his period of service as a research assistant the previous year, he drafted the prospectus which, after appropriate additions by Jackson, was submitted to the Atkinson Foundation in support of the appeal for funds. This appeal was successful, and the Research Department accordingly attained a new scale of activities.

The Atkinson Study, to use its abbreviated title, was under the general supervision of a steering committee consisting of the President of the University of Toronto, the Dean of the Ontario College of Education, the Director of the Department of Educational Research, several officials of the Department of Education at the superintendent level, and representatives of the Ontario Teachers' Federation, the independent schools, the Roman Catholic private schools, and other agencies. The meetings of this committee helped to focus attention on the activities of the Research Department and to give it a new importance. A successful appeal for an additional grant of $50,000 from the Atkinson Foundation in 1957, and the consequent continuation and extension of the study, helped to sustain interest and to lead to a new and larger enterprise, the Carnegie Study of Identification and Utilization of Talent in High School and College. This investigation, which initially involved approximately ninety thousand students in grade 9 and, on a subsidiary basis, an additional twenty thousand pupils in grades 7 and 8 in Toronto schools, was begun in 1959 with a grant of $90,000 from the Carnegie Corporation of New York. As compared with the Atkinson Study, it involved a larger-scale analysis, from an earlier stage, of the degree to which high school students were taking advantage of the opportunities open to them. The assumption of the responsibility for carrying it out required the appointment of new recruits to the academic staff, including W. Brehaut, J.F. Flowers, and H. Savage, all of whom were engaged in or just completing doctoral studies.

The Department of Education looked kindly on the Atkinson and Carnegie Studies and in fact provided most of the money required to support them through approved increases in the budget of the Research Department. Thus, in addition to the school grant studies, they constituted a major link with the Department of Education, on which the security of the Research Department rested. A third link developed in 1957 with the first experimental administration of objective aptitude and achievement tests at the grade 12 level. A regular testing program dependent on test scoring machines and other data processing equipment operated in the Research Department became a regular aspect of the provincial examination system the following year. The program was conducted on the basis of an unsigned but clearly understood contract between the two agencies. The fourth major link in terms of regular research and administrative responsibilities was the assumption of an obligation for machine analysis and reporting of the grade 13 departmental examinations after 1960.

These functions were of course supplemented by the increasingly important consultative role played by Jackson and, to a considerably lesser extent, by other members of the staff.

Dunlop's attitude

The status attained by the Research Department in 1959 was indicated by Dunlop in a comprehensive and sympathetic summary of its activities.

> ... the department of educational research of the Ontario College of Education is very properly considered to be the research arm of the provincial Department of Education.
>
> ... it draws, through the Ontario College of Education, a major portion of its financial support from this government ...
>
> ... a very considerable amount of research is being carried on at the Ontario College of Education at the request of my department, and with the active co-operation of its officials ...
>
> Department of Education officials have been intimately associated with the guidance of the Atkinson study of Utilization of student resources and, at present, with the beginnings of an even greater undertaking known as the Carnegie study. This is probably the most comprehensive educational research ever undertaken on this continent.[5]

Procedure for dealing with schools

Relationships with the Department of Education did not always run smoothly, as might be surmised in view of the lack of any formal legal ties between the two entities. Occasional problems arose because the Department of Education itself was a complex organization that spoke with a number of voices, not all of them well harmonized. Also, the Research Department's relationships with local school systems and with school principals evolved gradually in response to specific needs, and it was not always clear what kind of control or supervision the department wished to maintain over these contacts. School officials themselves were by no means always certain that a request for co-operation from the Research Department was not to be understood as an order, even though considerable efforts were made to assure them that participation in certain research activities, apart from Department of Education testing programs, was entirely voluntary.

Some issues came to a head in 1962 when G.A. Pearson, Superintendent of Elementary Education, took exception to the administration of a program of test revision in certain elementary schools, of which he claimed to have received no previous notice. In a letter to H.W. Savage of the Research Department, he asked that no research of any kind be undertaken in the elementary schools without his prior approval. He proceeded to make a further demand: that schools be selected for research purposes, not at random, but on the basis of his opinion of their suitability. Jackson reacted strongly against this proposition on the grounds that the results could be subject to a bias of unknown magnitude and all generalizations rendered invalid. He therefore approached H.E. Elborn, deputy minister with particular responsibility for the elementary school level, to seek a clarification of the situation.

Elborn's reaction was characteristically kindly and conciliatory. The results of the subsequent negotiations were, however, to tie the Research Department somewhat more closely to the structure and operation of the Department of Education. Jackson summarized the understanding in a memorandum for the information of the research staff. He proclaimed the principle that the officials of the Department of Education were to be kept informed "on a current basis, if necessary week by week, of all activities in research which affect schools and involve the participation of pupils and the use of school time." Reports of activities and of proposed studies would be sent to the officials not just once a year according to current practice, for inclusion in the minister's diary, but from time to time as circumstances required. While complete details of any particular study or testing program did not necessarily need to be reported, sufficient information was to be given to enable the officials concerned to understand the scope of the study, its possible implications, and the amount of school time required. The specific procedures governing future relationships were outlined under four headings. 1 / All official studies undertaken at the request of the Minister of Education, other government ministers, or senior Department of Education officials were to be arranged through the chief director. 2 / All large-scale studies undertaken or proposed by the Research Department were to be arranged through and approved by the same official. The latter would arrange for permission, where necessary, to seek participation by schools, teachers, principals, inspectors, and others. He would also be kept fully informed about the progress of each such study. 3 / Minor research studies were to be arranged through the Elementary School, Secondary School, Special Services, or Registrar's Branch, as appropriate. The Research Department would prepare in advance an outline of the testing programs and minor research studies planned for the academic year. The superintendents concerned would be informed of these plans in some detail, including the reason for each study, the anticipated outcomes, the number of schools and pupils involved, and the amount of school time likely to be used. Additional specifications elaborated on the way in which contacts were to be made at various levels of the system, and the information that was to be supplied in each case. The point was clearly made, however, that the initiative for selecting participants was to reside in the Research Department and that the process was not to become a Department of Education function. 4 / Additions to or changes in the approved set of testing programs and minor research studies were to be made only under exceptional or emergency circumstances, and then only with the prior approval of the chief director, deputy minister, or superintendent concerned.

In the writer's opinion, these arrangements constituted a very satisfactory basis for co-operation between the two agencies. They enabled departmental officials to assume their normal responsibilities toward the school system, since they could be reasonably sure of knowing what was going on. Although they were not in a position to bias samples of schools or pupils in any serious manner, they could always make a case for the exclusion of the occasional school from a proposed experiment on the grounds that it was experiencing unusual difficulties and that any exceptional burden during the period of emergency might have deleterious effects on the welfare of the pupils. The arrangement, of course, had to be guarded against evolving in undesirable directions. But in retrospect it seems unfortunate that more account was not taken of precedents established at this time when the status of the Ontario Institute for Studies in Education was being established. No agency devoted to educational research, or especially to educational research and development, can expect to succeed in the long run unless it works out an arrangement to avoid unnecessary interference with the performance of official functions, while at the same time enjoying complete freedom to generate ideas with the most radical implications for ultimate practice.

The mode of operations in the department

Relationship with the rest of the college and the university

The Department of Educational Research remained a structural unit of the Ontario College of Education and thus of the University of Toronto. Its requests for funds were submitted as part of the college budget, which was scrutinized item by item by departmental officials and was subject to arbitrary alteration, although such action was rarely taken. The government grant to the college was separate from that to the rest of the university, but it was administered through the university accounting office. Thus the Research Department's business and employment procedures were carried out according to university practice and, where necessary, with university authorization. The issue of the Research Department's entitlement to control of funds from the sale of tests and publications was settled in its favour. Arrangements were also made to ensure its exclusive management of grants for specific purposes from charitable foundations.

Status of professional staff

The members of the staff with academic appointments enjoyed professional status mainly in terms of those activities in which they participated as members of the graduate Department of Educational Theory of the university, and consequently took part in the conduct of the program of graduate studies. They constituted almost the exclusive resource for lecturing and advising graduate students in educational measurement, statistics, research methodology, and educational finance, and also made contributions in certain other areas. In statistics and design, the reputation Jackson earned in earlier years made him the outstanding resource, even after other activities began to demand almost all his attention and his lecturing activities became sporadic.

Until his retirement as Dean of the College of Education, A.C. Lewis assigned duties in graduate instruction in the same way that he did all other responsibilities. Lecturing was thus, in a sense, mandatory. His successor, B.C. Diltz, managed that part of the operation in a different way. C.E. Phillips was recognized as Director of Graduate Studies and given exclusive charge of the program. Under Phillips it was immediately established that the members of the Department of Educational Research were not subject to assignment except perhaps by their own director, should he choose to exercise the prerogative. Such action was unlikely, since relations between him and Phillips were not regarded as excessively cordial. In fact some of Jackson's staff were given to understand that work undertaken in connection with their participation in the graduate program should be done outside regular office hours, except for actual lecturing. Instruction in summer sessions caused no problem, since it occupied what theoretically constituted vacation time. The Research Department staff were eager to play an active role in graduate work for several reasons: they generally wished to continue teaching, which was for all of them an initial choice of occupation; they felt that the organization of the college gave them a moral obligation to sustain the graduate program; they saw such an activity as necessary if they were to maintain their claim to scholarly status. Considering the low level of salaries prevailing just before and after 1960, the pecuniary interest in the extra stipend for teaching summer school was by no means an insignificant factor. There was, in fact, some temporary friction between the Research Department staff and Phillips about what the staff saw as a tendency to expect them to carry the full burden of instruction in their areas of specialization during the winter, while visiting lecturers were secured for the privilege of giving summer instruction. The fact that research duties were so heavy that the presence of Research Department staff members was required at the college during the summer meant that failure to secure appointment for summer lecturing involved a real financial loss without compensation in time off.

With respect to their research responsibilities, it would be inappropriate to characterize the position of the staff as truly professional. In theory, part of their efforts might be devoted to self-chosen activities resulting from the pursuit of their own particular interests. In fact, the official program of the Research Department was so heavy that it was virtually impossible to put such a theory into practice without neglecting some imposed obligation that seemed vital to the welfare of the organization. Even despite extraordinary efforts, a certain amount of shoddy work was produced among the many contributions of high quality, and some projects were executed so slowly and with so many delays that much of their potential value was lost. Jackson's appetite for new projects was voracious, and it was difficult in the early years of his directorship to persuade him that the resources at his disposal were not inexhaustible.

There were, of course, some factors that seemed conducive to the development of scholarly reputations. There were excellent facilities for publication and extremely competent editorial services. The *Ontario Journal of Educational Research*, established in 1957, was in constant need of high-quality contributions on almost any research topic. But there were at least four serious handicaps to the development of scholarship. First, supervisory duties became so heavy with the increase of projects involving the collection and analysis of masses of routine data that few academic staff members had the physical or mental resources left to devote to writing. Second, many of the routine surveys and straight administrative tasks such as the organization of a testing program did not produce reportable results. Third, some of the reports were confidential or at least not appropriate for general distribution. Fourth, work undertaken on projects initiated by someone else, no matter how conscientiously one accepts one's obligations, can seldom provide the substance on which scholarly reputations are usually built. The policy maintained throughout was that every report should bear the real author's name, and the Department of Education policy of anonymous publication was consciously rejected. Yet the lack of prestige of most members of the staff was such that newspaper reporters and columnists would go through the most extraordinary contortions to comment on the contents of reports of public interest without mentioning the actual writer's name, referring instead to the director's foreword. Despite these circumstances, various members of the staff did manage to make a reasonable name for themselves.

Effect of the Diltz regime

The appointment of B.C. Diltz as Dean of the Ontario College of Education in 1958 cast a chill over the Research Department from which, in its existing form, it never recovered. Such an assertion might astonish the man, who could rightly say that he never took any steps to interfere with its activities. In a sense, his lack of interest was part of the trouble. Many who have known Diltz still classify him as the most dynamic and impressive classroom performer they have ever seen in action. He was also known as a kind and deeply humanitarian, if domineering, man. Furthermore, his service as dean of the college did not, as many feared it would at the time of his appointment, seriously diminish the lustre of his educational contribution. But his attitude was totally and fundamentally opposed to the application of scientific principles for the illumination of any important educational issue. For him, education was of the spirit, and must not be debased by attempts to dissect and tabulate the components of human personality. Research was perhaps more justifiable than guidance or psychology, but it should be confined to the accumulation of the statistics that were obviously needed for the performance of certain mundane administrative tasks.

Diltz did nothing specifically designed to destroy or seriously damage existing structures for the promotion of guidance activities or the facilitation of research projects. He even resignedly lent some occasional assistance. When the writer went to him with a request for his signature on a memorandum designed to elicit the support of school principals for the Carnegie Study testing program, he consented, wondering aloud if people would think "the old boy was getting soft in the head." As the writer learned from later contacts in the schools, this signature had a tremendously favourable effect. It was commonly remarked that an objective testing program that even Diltz approved must be really sound. The writer never felt compelled to correct anyone who mistakenly thought that the passage preceding the signature was a genuine specimen of Diltzian prose.

Yet in the Diltz regime, the Research Department remained somewhat of a holding operation. Budgets were increased mainly because of enlarged obligations assumed in response to requests from the Department of Education. The failure to give any great consideration to academic qualifications in recommending promotions was a source of resentment to the research staff. Moreover, the research operation was almost completely removed from the rest of the college program. The Research Department was moved to a neighbouring building under pressure of student enrolment at the college, and there was no provision for staff contact except for social events. During the five years of Diltz's deanship, the writer recalls only two occasions when all the professional members of the college staff were assembled. One meeting was held to discuss the imposition of parking fees by the university and the other, without the dean's knowledge, to discuss an appropriate gift for him on his retirement.

Diltz expressed the private view that it would be desirable if the Research Department were incorporated into the Department of Education. Since he was not prepared to press actively for such a change, he left matters entirely in Jackson's hands. Such an arrangement provided an almost unheard-of invitation to arbitrary action on the latter's part. He quite probably could have dismissed his entire staff without fear of immediate retaliation, although how he could have replaced them is another question. But his prestige at the highest levels of the government was such that an action of this kind would probably not have been directly questioned. There would have been no effective staff appeal to Diltz, who was so clearly uninterested in the staff as a group. Nor would there have been any prospect of worthwhile support from the main part of the university. University authorities were still smarting from the insulting treatment meted out to them by Dunlop in his appointment of Diltz, and had never, in any case, held the Ontario College of Education in high regard. Nor did the informal status of the Research Department as the research arm of the Department of Education particularly endear it to the university. The point is not so much whether or not arbitrary powers were used, but that they were constantly in the background.

Reputation in scholarly circles

The Research Department did not enjoy high prestige in scholarly circles in other parts of the country. The administrative procedures to which its members were subjected were observed with disapproval. So also was its failure to make any notable contributions in important areas such as curriculum and learning theory. At national conferences, its members were questioned on the extent to which their efforts were devoted to the production of material that was beyond the access of the scholarly community. The familiar scholarly antipathy to the subordination of research efforts to the needs of government decision-making was very much in evidence.

In terms of its understood policy, the Research Department must of course be judged very successful. Jackson was at the elbow of the key decision-makers with many original ideas and had, to outward appearances, a smoothly operating machine that provided him with all kinds of useful information. The valuable services performed had much to do with the provincial government's unique investment in educational research and development after 1965.

The situation was, however, precarious, and in the writer's judgment could not have lasted much longer. The increasing demand for competent researchers, the growing feeling that, even in education, a professional scholar must attain a level where he can select his own areas of investigation, and the developing pressure for more basic research would have made it impossible to continue under existing conditions.

A natural and healthy evolution from the Department of Educational Research as it existed in 1964–5 might have involved such an accretion of staff that each qualified professional researcher, who had earned his position both by obtaining appropriate degrees and by proving his capacities through experience, might have been able to divide his time equitably between the pursuit of self-generated interests and the organization and supervision of studies that reflected the needs and interests of the educational community, a community consisting not only of the government, but also of local education authorities, universities, teachers' organizations, and other agencies. Those who aspired to professional status would be expected to prove themselves by their performance in these latter studies, with sufficient opportunity to demonstrate their capacity for original contributions along the way. The hierarchy of merit would be so structured that the exercise of individual talent, originality, and wisdom would be reconciled with the educational community's need for assistance in solving its very vital and immediate problems.

VOLUNTARY ASSOCIATIONS

The establishment of voluntary research associations and the extension of the responsibilities of others to provide for various aspects of the research function are dealt with in volume VII. Some brief reference to them at this point will demonstrate the increasing interest that was characteristic of the 1950s. In 1954 the efforts of people like Henry Bowers, then Principal of the Stratford Teachers' College, and of various members of the Department of Educational Research led to the establishment of a Research Section in the Ontario Educational Association. Its main function during its relatively brief existence was to encourage and publicize research activities. At one of its early meetings, an opponent of the separate school system urged that a study of achievement in the public and separate schools be undertaken in order to prove the inadequacies of the latter. The section did not, however, become associated with projects of this type. It was a forerunner of the larger and more pretentious Ontario Educational Research Council, founded in 1958, into which it was absorbed. Initiative for the establishment of the council came most strongly from teachers' groups through the Ontario Association for Curriculum Development. Like its predecessor, the council concentrated on publicizing, stimulating, and liaison functions. Somewhat different in emphasis was the research agency established by the Canadian Teachers' Federation in 1953. A substantial stream of reports, mainly concerning the issues of particular concern to the federation as an organized teachers' group, emerged during the next few years. In the late 1950s, a grant of $100,000 to the Canadian Education Association by Imperial Oil Limited made it possible for the latter to establish what was described as a clearing house, a co-ordinating agency, and a repository for educational research findings. This body was not designed to conduct research, but to foster and facilitate research by others.

THE ONTARIO CURRICULUM INSTITUTE

Background

The Ontario Curriculum Institute was a grass-roots manifestation of dissatisfaction with the inadequacy of the school program to meet contemporary needs. It reflected the ferment in the United States and other countries resulting from the realization that the superiority of western science and technology could not be taken for granted. The doubts and questions of the time affected every aspect of educational practice. The Ontario Department of Education, however, retained an air of complacency and self-satisfaction, despite the presence of many officials who proved themselves abundantly capable of enlightened leadership once some of the fetters of tradition and custom had been removed. For the time being, the initiative rested with local school systems, the teachers' federations, and the universities.

The Joint Committee of the Toronto Board of Education and the University of Toronto

The main inspiration for the chain of events that led to the establishment of the Institute came from Roy C. Sharp, trustee of the Toronto Board of Education. This dynamic and impassioned man surely deserves more credit for a vital influence on the course of education in Ontario than he has yet received. His service on the Toronto board did much to make it a chief centre of vital and creative activity radiating far beyond the city itself. In the developments that led to the founding of the Ontario Curriculum Institute, he had the support of Robin Harris, a University of Toronto professor and administrator, who also served a number of years as a Toronto school trustee.

In 1960 five members of the Toronto board and five members of the university's Committee on Policy and Planning were appointed to a joint committee to explore matters of common interest and to report to the chairman of the Toronto board and the president of the university. An immediate area of concern was the co-ordination of the efforts of the two agencies, already linked by the progress of large numbers of students proceeding from Toronto secondary schools to the university. The sharp divisons among levels of the educational system seemed to many of those concerned to be increasingly anomalous. The committee sought to find ways of bringing together those engaged in teaching at all levels, and to take a broad view of the educational process. It was at this time that forward-looking educators were all taking a "synoptic view" of education.

According to Northrop Frye, the committee members talked at random during the summer, hoping to define a central question. Among the problems considered were the number of students not finishing high school, the number of able students not reaching university, the number of secondary school graduates unable to adjust to university methods of work, and the role of grade 13 in the transitional process. They finally defined their central question as follows: "Does teaching in the schools, or at least the secondary schools, reflect contemporary conceptions of the subjects being taught?"[6] Their future course of action was determined by the answer that it did not.

The joint committee appointed five subcommittees in the major areas of the curriculum: English, mathematics, science, social sciences, and foreign languages. Each of these groups included elementary and secondary school teachers and university professors. Consultative service was provided by the Director of Research of the Toronto Board of Education, the Librarian of the Toronto Board's Education Centre, and the University's Department of Psychology. The Atkinson's Charitable Foundation made a grant of $15,000 to enable some of the members of three of the subcommittees to work full time for one month during the summer of 1961 on curriculum reform in their respective areas. They submitted reports to the joint committee in November 1961.

President Bissell expressed his enthusiasm for the venture in these terms.

As far as we know, this particular approach to curricular studies is unique on this continent. Obviously the curriculum must change and develop as knowledge increases and technology provides new tools for learning. Too often, however, changes in the curriculum are made in piecemeal fashion, without sufficient study, without reference to the theory of learning, and – most serious of all – without the direction of active teachers. This project of the Joint Committee may well be the beginning of an important development in educational research.[7]

The reports of the three subcommittees provided the basis for a book, *Design for Learning*, edited and introduced by Frye, who expounded some of his distinctly anti-progressive ideas.

Because the authors are writing as teachers and not as educators, their approach is pragmatic. Nevertheless one can see the reflection in them of a considerable change of emphasis in recent educational theory. This change of emphasis is something very different from what is discussed in newspapers and in popular rumour. The learned have their demonologies no less than the unlearned, and the bogey of the "progressive" educator, with his incessant straw-threshing of "teaching methods," his fanatical hatred of the intellect, and his serene conviction that everyone who is contemptuous of his maunderings must be devoted to the dunce cap and the birch rod, still haunts university classrooms. He does in fact still exist, though educators today pay him little attention and no respect. Never, perhaps, a major threat to Ontario schools, his incompetence elsewhere helped to create the power vacuum which has done much to make education more subject to political interference than the other professions.[8]

Fortunately most of the book was more characterized by reasoned argument than this particular paragraph.

Unlike some of his colleagues, Frye did not give any support to the unrealistic notion that the school years ought to constitute a tooling-up stage devoted to the acquisition of factual knowledge so that real understanding and thought could begin in the university. The guiding influence of the subcommittees' work was to be found in Jerome Bruner's idea that a body of knowledge has a structure, and that its basic concepts can be understood at an early age. With proper teaching, the learner's grasp of the subject becomes more complete as he grows older and advances to higher levels of comprehension. *Design for Learning* attracted widespread attention because of its analysis of the potential role and values of the subject areas dealt with. It also caused considerable concern by revealing the inadequacies of instruction in what were usually considered some of the province's outstanding schools.

The emergence of the institute concept

The success of the joint committee's venture led to the idea of a provincial organization devoted to a more comprehensive program of curriculum research and development. The term "research" received more emphasis at this stage than it did later; the change in emphasis possibly represented an attempt to avoid offending the sensibilities of the Department of Educational Research, although the latter's activites at the time hardly touched on curriculum. Again the outstanding driving force was Roy Sharp. He secured the support of a large number of school boards and of the Ontario Teachers' Federation and its affiliates. The latter promised support amounting to up to $60,000 a year. It was hoped that the bulk of the needed funds would be contributed about equally by the teachers' federation, the school boards, and the provincial government, with additional assistance from universities, business and industry, and charitable foundations. A substantial grant from the Ford Foundation made a vital contribution in the beginning, but the common problem of financing a large operation mainly by voluntary means ultimately proved overwhelming.

As its active participation and financial contribution indicated, the official attitude of the Department of Education, now under Robarts, was favourable. There was, however, a certain amount of uneasiness on the part of various officials. The prospect of an independent agency established to deal with matters so closely related to the department's vital functions could hardly fail to be seen as something of a threat. The drive for decentralization of educational responsibility, which became one of the main planks of the later Davis program, had not got under way. In a sense, also, the move to establish the institute was seen as an implied criticism of the department's failure to arrange for the desired services. A ringing endorsation of the following view expressed by Sharp was hardly to be expected: "It is unreasonable and unfair to expect the Ontario Department of Education to shoulder the entire responsibility for research on curriculum."[9] In the long run, the primary reaction of the department was the constructive one of devoting much more active attention to curriculum development.

It was intended that the work of the proposed institute would be carried out mainly by teams of university scholars, outstanding teachers from different levels, and curriculum experts from the Department of Education. They were to maintain the strength of their roots in actual practice by serving for limited periods of time only. It was felt that the lack of any large group of permanent staff would prevent the development of a particular institutional point of view. Control of the operation would be deliberately kept out of the hands of a new type of specialist or a new vested interest.

Sharp's address on November 2, 1962, gave some specific details about the way the institute might function. He suggested a division of its operations into three stages: design, testing, and dissemination of material to be adopted or adapted. The design phase would be the responsibility of the teams already mentioned. Each team would review the curriculum in its subject area from kindergarten to university and make a written submission on curriculum revision. If necessary, it would prepare material for textbooks and teachers' manuals. In order to avoid any premature judgments or conclusions, however, its submission would be presented as a hypothesis rather than as a recommended curriculum. The second phase, testing, would involve evaluation of the proposals, with appropriate statistical treatment. Where the latter was not possible, the published report of the research team would nevertheless benefit from analysis, suggestions, and criticism from teachers. The final phase would be to translate recommendations into specific improvements in school curicula. When evaluation had justified definite recommendations, the department or local school boards could adopt, adapt, or reject them as each saw fit.

In the same address, Sharp explored the sharing of roles and possible conflicts with three agencies: the Ontario Association for Curriculum Development, the Department of Educational Research of the Ontario College of Education, and the Curriculum Branch of the Department of Education. He concluded immediately that there was no difficulty as far as the first of these bodies was concerned; its major function was to sponsor conferences and meetings at which different aspects of the curriculum were discussed and conclusions formulated that might be submitted to various sponsoring bodies. The new institute need only avoid duplicating this function. Referring to the Department of Educational Research, he rather over-generously acknowledged its active engagement in certain aspects of curriculum research and development, and suggested that there would have to be special efforts made to avoid conflicts of interest. One precaution would be to ensure the representation of the Research Department on the institute's Board of Governors. The greatest danger of conflict would be with the Curriculum Branch of the Department of Education. It was necessary to distinguish between two parallel functions. The first of these, curriculum research and development, was basically theoretical and included the development of learning theory; experimentation with various arrangements of curricula, courses, and teaching methods; and the development and exposition of aims and objectives which the curriculum was designed to attain. The second function, necessarily making use of the first, involved the implementation of suggestions, proposals, and findings into an on-going or working curriculum. This activity included the preparation or authorization of courses of study, the preparation and selection of textbooks, and the determination of teaching methods required to attain accepted aims. This division of functions sounded very reasonable and logical. And there is no question that the department had been concerning itself almost exclusively with the second. The new institute proposed to move into a vacuum.

While these events were occuring, the Ontario Conference on Education gave strong support to the curriculum institute idea in 1961. A discussion group formulated a recommendation that the Ontario Association for Curriculum Development establish a non-political curriculum study council consisting of elementary and secondary school teachers, university personnel, and other interested groups to plan for excellence in the educational program of Ontario. (The term "excellence" was one of the catch-words of the day.) The council was to be financed by grants from the government, industrial foundations, and school boards. Its finding would be widely distributed to teachers, school boards, and others involved in education. The resolution did not indicate any awareness of the Toronto developments, although at least some of the participants must have known about them.

The establishment of the Institute

Once the vision of the new institute had caught on, the question arose as to how to set it up. Sharp later described the possible courses of action. 1 / The University of Toronto and the Toronto Board of Education might establish an institute jointly and invite other boards, universities, and the teachers' federations to join them later. They would not, however, have the benefit of widespread support and advice and would risk the impression that their action was of purely local significance. 2 / They might assemble representatives from all the universities, the Ontario Teachers' Federation, and boards of education and attempt to work out a detailed plan at a single conference. 3 / They might, as they actually did, call a conference of such representatives with the objective of working out an agreement in principle, with details to be filled in later.[10]

The conference passed the following resolution.

> This Conference, recognizing the importance of and need for further systematic research and development of curriculum at all levels, approves in principle the formation of an institute for curriculum study as a continuing body to study all phases of curriculum from the standpoint of content, sequential organization and the nature of the learning process and to suggest planned revisions in the light of the rapid development of knowledge characteristic of our times.

This resolution represented the views of the Ontario Teachers' Federation, the Ontario School Trustees' Council, the Department of Education, the universities, and various other groups such as directors, superintendents, inspectors, researchers, and teachers' college staffs.

The institute's charter, granted in January 1963, established it as a non-profit corporation. Apart from its legal powers, its main objective was stated as follows: "In the interest of the advancement of education, to study and to promote study of all phases of the curriculum in the Schools and Universities of Ontario from the standpoint of content and the nature of the learning process and to disseminate the results of such study." The first full-time director, J.R.H. Morgan, elaborated on his view of the institute's role.

The curriculum will be examined from the points of view of content, of sequential organization, and of the nature of the learning process. From the point of view of content, the Institute will keep abreast, as best it may, of the rapid development of knowledge that is a phenomenon of our day, and will eliminate, or at least reduce, the time lag between the discovery of new knowledge and its incorporation into the school curriculum. From the point of view of sequential organization, it will attempt to eliminate the stops and starts in the present curriculum and the learning of certain items at one level that have to be "unlearned" at another – a state of affairs due largely to the phenomenal expansion of knowledge referred to above. From the standpoint of the nature of the learning process, it will give thought to the synchronization of the concepts being presented with the age and maturation levels of the pupils. In this latter area, it is shocking to compare the very considerable knowledge we have of how children learn with the very feeble attempts that have been made to fashion curriculum in the light of that knowledge.[11]

Morgan's appointment, which took effect at the beginning of 1964, was a very significant development. He left his position as Superintendent of Secondary Schools for the Toronto Board of Education many years before reaching mandatory retirement age. The fact that one of the province's best-known educational leaders was willing to assume the directorship of the new entity was an indication of the significance given to its establishment by the educational community.

Structure

Sharp's initial proposals envisioned a board of governors consisting of three representatives of school board officials, three representatives from the universities, three representatives from the Ontario Teachers' Federation, three trustees, and whatever number of representatives the department chose to send.[12] This group would have been fairly compact in comparison with other similar bodies. However, this feature was lost when, after an initial provisional board carried on during 1963, a regular Board of Governors was established consisting of six representatives of each of five groups: the Ontario Teachers' Federation, the Ontario School Trustees' Council, the universities, organizations of school administrators, and the Department of Education. An executive committee of ten members exercised a good deal of delegated power. In 1963 working committees were also set up to deal with finance, conferences, and program.

The full-time administrative staff consisted of the director, the executive secretary-treasurer, and secretarial and clerical assistants. The main group of staff consisted of members of study committees appointed for temporary periods to carry out specific tasks. An early brochure indicates the "research" procedure. 1 / Specific areas of study were identified by a standing committee of the institute. 2 / Study committees were set up, consisting of members appointed on the basis of their special qualification for the job. Membership might be for periods of a few days to several weeks or months, depending on the nature of the inquiry. Members were chosen from among leading scholars, professional educators, teachers, psychologists, university faculty members, and administrators. Some were paid by the institution lending their services and some by the institute. 3 / A period of inquiry and analysis followed, punctuated by progress reports. 4 / Innovations and changes might be recommended as a result of the inquiry. 5 / Proposals were tested in pilot projects, where possible, in co-operation with local school boards and the Department of Education. 6 / Test results were published and specific recommendations were submitted to the Department of Education. This procedure was of course an ideal one, and one or more of the later stages might fail to be carried out.

The board was clearly no mere caretaker body responsible mainly for ensuring that legal requirements were met and that the staff were protected against undesirable outside pressure. It was not only formally entitled to, but also exercised, definite control over the program. This position was unchallengeable chiefly because there was no group of professional staff capable of taking independent action. The director might sell ideas for programs and activities to the board if he so desired, but his chief function was to carry out its wishes. This role was valued by such groups as the teachers and trustees, and they were justifiably reluctant to give it up only a short time later.

Program

Committee work

One group of study committees covered specific subject areas from grade 1, or wherever the subject became relevant, to grade 13. Two of these were set up immediately in 1963: one for science and the other for French as a second language. Their reports, published at the end of the year, recommended study in depth in several fields. Other committees of the same type were set up in the course of 1963 or in 1964 as part of a three-year program. The subjects covered were mathematics, technical education and trade training, reading, English, and third languages. Brian

Burnham, who played an active role in the institute's affairs for several years, commented on the activities of this type of committee in rather restrained terms: "From these microcosmic studies might result marginal gains in the quality of course content, methods, and learning resources in traditional areas of instruction."[13] Most of them suffered from one common characteristic, a kind of self-centredness that was quite understandable under the circumstances, in that they advocated greater emphasis on the subject under review. They were thus of little help in planning any major restructuring of the curriculum. For those who participated – a limited group, to be sure – there were great benefits from the exchange of points of view.

Although the term "research" was used rather freely, few of the committees actually gave much weight to such activity by any commonly recognized definition. In some cases, they arranged with other agencies such as the Department of Educational Research to conduct surveys of opinion or practice. But their procedures were more properly described as a high-level exchange of points of view. There are, of course, serious limitations on the benefits to be expected from this approach. While it may be true that much that is already known is still waiting to be incorporated into a modern curriculum and new teaching methods, this kind of knowledge requires a certain type of research to assemble, refine, and make it immediately available.

The second area of committee work dealt with the "weaving of the component parts into fabric from which to fashion a total curriculum."[14] The committees dealt with 1 / theories of instruction and cognitive development, 2 / instructional aids and instructional techniques, 3 / implications of social change for educational theories and practices, 4 / continuing education for youth and adults, 5 / development and integration of the creative arts, and 6 / the scope and organization of the curriculum. The results of considerable perceptive thinking were published in the reports of some of these committees. In view of its terms of reference, however, the committee assigned to work on theories of instruction and cognitive development not surprisingly indicated that the field had absorbed and would continue to absorb the efforts of numerous psychologists. Without even attempting to add anything significant to existing knowledge, the committee instead devoted itself to outlining the kind of organizational structure that would make a worthwhile contribution possible. By this time, plans for the establishment of the Ontario Institute for Studies in Education were under way, and some of the ideas and suggestions of the Curriculum Institute committee were taken into account in the formation of its Department of Applied Psychology.

Demonstration centres

A new type of activity was initiated in 1964 with the establishment, in co-operation with the Lakeshore Board of Education, of a pilot demonstration centre in reading. The board's reading supervisor assumed the responsibility of co-ordinating the work of the centre under the direction of an institute committee consisting of a large representative group of specialists in reading and related areas, as well as local administrators, supervisors, and others. The committee's task was to demonstrate how elements in the community could be assembled to effect changes in the teaching of reading. A first grade demonstration class was set up under a teacher with suitable experience and special qualifications. The committee met regularly at the school at which the class was located to plan and evaluate the program and to discharge a responsibility for guiding the teacher and the local authorities with respect to reading activities. Arrangements were made for other teachers to visit the class and observe the program. As a development project, the demonstration centre generally proved to be effective. Other particularly successful efforts involved the use of special science materials in selected classes.

Another activity of a practical type entailed co-operation with the Ontario Mathematics Commission in field-testing the development of geometry concepts in kindergarten through grade 3 and concepts of mapping, charting, and graphing in grades 4 to 6. The work began in 1965–6 and extended into the period when the Curriculum Institute was merged into the Ontario Institute for Studies in Education. Thirty-five school systems were involved in the program in 1966–7.[15]

Financial problems

The founders of the institute did some optimistic arithmetic to show how it could be maintained. Sharp noted that the Ontario Teachers' Federation was prepared to contribute from $50,000 to $60,000 a year. He suggested that, if the school boards represented at the founding conference would pay a membership fee of 10 to 15 cents per pupil, the proceeds would amount to a further $50,000 to $100,000 a year. The universities might also be asked to contribute 10 to 15 cents per student. One foundation he knew of would be prepared to donate $15,000 per year for five years. School boards and universities could be asked to allow their staff leave of absence with pay for brief periods, thus making a contribution in kind that might be equivalent to a quarter of a million dollars annually.[16]

The institute was in financial difficulty from the first. Support from what might be considered normal sources amounted to $142,000 in 1963. The operating budget for the subsequent year was, however, approximately half a million dollars, of which about half had to be obtained from foundations, corporations, and individuals through a fund-raising campaign. It was realized that only short-term assistance could be expected from foundations. Long-term plans involved broadening the base of corporate support and raising the level of giving from existing sources, with the hope of achieving relatively balanced support from the Department of Education, the Ontario Teachers' Federation, the school boards, and private corporations and individuals. After valiant efforts, Morgan, no mean fund-raiser, was forced to conclude that the task was hopeless. The only realistic course of action was to abandon the widely-proclaimed advantages of independence and seek full government support. The shotgun pointed to the waiting arms of the Ontario Institute for Studies in Education.

THE INSTITUTE OF CHILD STUDY OF THE UNIVERSITY OF TORONTO

Origin

The beginning of the movement that led to the founding of the Institute of Child Study may be traced to the establishment of the Child Study Laboratory at the State University of Iowa in 1911 through the efforts of Carl E. Seashore and associates. The experiment was sufficiently successful that similar steps were taken at other leading universities such as California, Minnesota, Harvard, Yale, and Columbia. While studies of child development were curtailed during the First World War, that period saw an intensification of interest in longitudinal psychological studies of individuals throughout life. Valuable findings resulted from attempts to improve rehabilitative treatment of disabled veterans. Among those who became interested in the broader implications of these findings was William E. Blatz. In order to prepare himself for further study of human development, particularly at the earlier stages of life, he undertook advanced studies in the University of Chicago in 1924. He returned to Toronto in time to participate in a study of mental hygiene problems in public school children undertaken with financial assistance from the Rockefeller Foundation, and in a study of pre-school children in the university, which had the support of the Laura Spelman Rockefeller Memorial. Blatz became Director of St George's School for Child Study during the 1925–6 academic year.[17]

At first the school had a Nursery School Division and a Parent Education Division, each with its own staff responsible to the director. It operated on a Rockefeller grant under the sponsorship of the Department of Psychology of the University, with a management committee which included members from several university departments. In 1938, it was taken into the university as an independent unit and officially became the Institute of Child Study. It was managed by a committee of the senate, with representation from the faculties and departments that were mainly concerned.

Organization and purposes

As described in 1951, the institute had four chief functions: to contribute to child study through the maintenance of a research program in child development; to contribute to childhood education and guidance through a demonstration program in nursery education; to provide the community with leadership in parent education; and to conduct a student training program. In actual operation, the divisions were closely interrelated. Students acted as part of the Nursery School assistant staff and were involved as well in parent education.[18]

In 1953 the federal government undertook to finance a five-year program of research into the development of mental health in children. This project resulted in a number of reports, including one entitled *Studies of the Growth of Security*. Until 1958 the emphasis on mental health was predominant. During that year, the institute became fully absorbed into the University of Toronto, a modification in status which was accompanied by a reorganization and a change in emphasis. The new program involved a balance between research and teaching. St George's Nursery School and St George's Elementary School, as well as the clinic for children, were used as laboratories and as demonstration centres for students in the institute diploma course and for those registered in other parts of the university.[19] Instruction was provided for groups of students from the Departments of Psychology, Psychiatry, and Household Economics, the School of Nursing, and the Primary Specialist Course of the Toronto Teachers' College. Non-credit courses were provided for several other groups.

The schools were arranged for a maximum of twenty children at each level from junior nursery to grade 6. Their primary purpose was to serve as a research centre in which children's growth and development from three to twelve years of age might be studied. Older graduates of the school were also available for research. Studies that might distract children unduly from their school life or which might interfere with their mental health were not regarded as suitable. There were facilities for observing children in nursery school, in classrooms, on the playground, and in the dining-room. In general, the facilities were most suitable for small-scale, intensive studies, particularly of the longitudinal type, in contrast to large-scale investigations.

Commitment to the maintenance of schools for research and demonstration purposes played a vital part in shaping the character of the institute. It was intended that the children admitted should be a normal, representative group, but some of the rigidities that usually affect such schools became fairly firm. The fee charged was high enough to exclude children from families with an "average" income, although it fell considerably short of the real cost. Since the demand for places was great, additional selective factors had to be taken into account by those responsible for admission.

In 1967 the diploma course in Child Study was extended from one to two years. There were exceptions, however, for applicants with a number of years of teaching experience and other qualifications, who could still obtain the diploma in one year. Some progress was reported in having the diploma recognized as equivalent to an MA for purposes of salary and promotion.[20]

The institute did not enjoy high favour in the University of Toronto in the late 1960s. M.F. Grapko, who succeeded K.S. Bernhardt on his retirement, retained the title "acting director" for several years after his appointment in 1964. There was some question of the possibility of a merger with the Ontario Institute for Studies in Education when the latter was formed in 1965. Those planning the new organization were definitely cool to the idea, in part because they felt that it would be inadvisable to assume the responsibility for running a demonstration school. All the evidence from relevant experience elsewhere suggested that it would be preferable to maintain flexibility by conducting programs in schools rather than conducting a school. An article in the *Toronto Daily Star* on December 11, 1968, reported that an institute spokesman had said that the education group (the Ontario Institute for Studies in Education) had never been approached. Such an assertion could mean either that the spokesman did not know what had transpired earlier or that no formal negotiations had occurred. The same article reported the assistant director of OISE, J.H.M. Andrews, as saying that there was little duplication between the two organizations and that there was no immediate prospect of their working together.

The article in question was headlined "Girl student, 21 rallied friends saved child study." Apparently President Bissell intended that the institute would be closed down by 1975. He reputedly included two paragraphs indicating this intention in a secret brief to be presented to the Committee on University Affairs as part of a five-year plan for capital construction. The student in question is said to have rallied thirty-four students and twenty-three faculty members to prepare a brief making a case for the continued existence of the institute. According to the report, she confronted the president and induced him, under threat of a student sit-in, to release the brief and to eliminate the fatal paragraphs. There was no assurance at the time that the next capital budget would not deliver the dreaded blow.

A Presidential Advisory Committee on the Role in the University of the Institute of Child Study reported early in 1970. It expressed the view that "the apparent lack of desire to move deliberately beyond the original organization and goals of the Institute has prevented the development and maintenance of a solid international reputation as a centre for child development research." Blatz's emphasis on education, counselling, and parent participation were held responsible for keeping the program unique and also for keeping it outside the mainstream of research in human development. Four major options seemed to offer themselves to the committee: 1 / to leave the institute's position and program as they were; 2 / to recommend internal changes in the institute's program and administrative structure; 3 / to transfer the institute to some other jurisdiction either inside or outside the university; 4 / to recommend the termination of the institute's relationship with the university. The second of these had the greatest appeal.

In the light of this decision, the committee arranged for external appraisals and for consultation with various individuals. Investigation showed that the physical separation of the institute's facilities constituted the most obvious reason for its isolation from the rest of the university. Even more serious was the professional isolation of institute researchers and research programs. The committee felt that a multi-disciplinary approach to child development problems was essential to the future growth of the institute. Its recommendations follow.

(1) *The base upon which the Committee recommends changes in the Institute's program is the establishment or re-establishment of a multi-disciplinary research facility with all other activities taking a lesser place, and the development of a variety of empirical research enterprises to support and complement the applied educational research already taking place.*

(2) *In order to achieve this new and expanded research emphasis, the Committee believes that the teaching and research functions of the Institute should be separated ...*

(3) *The research Institute described here should be administered by a multi-disciplinary council which would be responsible for research policy.*

(4) *The Committee believes that the Institute should become a part of the School of Graduate Studies as in the case of other multi-disciplinary institutes and centres in the University.*

(5) *Membership on this re-constituted Council of the Institute would be drawn from members of the University who are active researchers in the field of child development and who are members of the graduate faculty of one of the School of Graduate Studies' constituent departments.*

(6) *The Committee recommends that a striking committee be selected by the President to establish such a research council for the Institute ...*

(7) *The Committee believes that the diploma in Child Study would have the best opportunity to develop as part of the program of the College of Education.*

(8) *... the Committee recommends the establishment of a Child Study Committee within the College to administer the program under the Council and Dean of the College of Education.*

(9) *All those members of the staff who teach in the diploma course should, therefore, be appointed to the staff of the College for whatever percentage of their time is allocated to this program.*

(10) *The Committee noted above should be largely made up of those engaged in diploma teaching. For the purpose of dealing with problems of utilization of the Institute's research facilities by diploma students, some representation from this Committee, in addition to the Dean of the College*

of Education or his designate, should also have membership in the Council of the Institute ...

(11) *The Committee recommends that the Laboratory School be retained but that its primary function as a research tool be re-emphasized.*

(12) *It also recommends that the new Council of the Institute which would have the responsibility of administering the School give priority in its discussions to the role of the School as part of the research program ...*

(13) *The Committee ... recommends that graduate degrees with major work in child development continue to be granted via traditional discipline departments ...*

(14) *... the Committee recommends that all future appointments to the Institute be joint appointments with one of the constituent graduate departments of the School of Graduate Studies.*

(15) *The Committee recommends that the staff of the Institute with primary responsibility for the co-ordination of the research program and the administration of the Laboratory School remain small.*

(16) *The Director of the Institute should be nominated by the new Council, or by a special committee set up for this purpose, to the Dean of the School of Graduate Studies ...*

(17) *... current financial arrangements should be retained for the short run with negotiations to follow among the appropriate University bodies.*

At a meeting of the President's Council in March 1970 the main recommendations of the report were endorsed. It was agreed that the Laboratory School would be retained until the multi-disciplinary council was formed and had an opportunity to investigate it. Any decision to phase it out would require adequate notice to staff and parents.

RESEARCH EFFORTS BY SCHOOL BOARDS

The organization and contributions of educational research at the school board level are dealt with mostly in volume VI. It should be noted here, however, that these have come to occupy a reasonably important place in the educational system. The movement owes its beginning in considerable measure to Roy Sharp who, as a school trustee for the city of Toronto, succeeded in having a research department established there in 1959. The Toronto department had rather unusual characteristics, at least at the beginning, and did not really set the pattern for other boards. Sharp and others were convinced of the value of basic research and wanted to ensure a substantial place for that type of activity. Early recruitment policies were therefore conducted accordingly. Successive directors, A.R. MacKinnon and E.N. Wright, were eager to examine some of the fundamental issues in education as well as to solve practical problems of the system.

It was soon obvious that strong pressures were to be exerted for the production of tangible results. The inevitable problem of unrealistic expectations was encountered. Some of the initial doubters had their original suspicions confirmed, and some of the supporters of the idea of basic studies fell away. While the department continued its efforts to maintain a balanced program, its example was not one that inspired widespread emulation. Research under the jurisdiction of other school boards is largely a disciplined and controlled process tied in closely with the needs of the system as defined or approved by the administrators. This is not to say that researchers are denied the opportunity to exert initiative, nor is it to suggest that their efforts are not very valuable. The movement is much to be commended, and fills an important need. It is obvious, however, that it should be looked upon as a supplement to the efforts of research agencies that are in a position to operate at a more general level and to work on projects that involve a greater risk of proving unproductive.

THE METROPOLITAN TORONTO EDUCATIONAL RESEARCH COUNCIL

The Metropolitan Toronto Educational Research Council was a phenomenon of a particular period of time and a special set of organizational circumstances. It expressed a need, to a reasonable extent met such a need, and then disappeared when the reorganization of the school boards in the area made it something of an anachronism. It was in a sense representative of the need for voluntary efforts to supplement the rather limited co-ordination existing among the boards under the system established in 1953.

Origin

For some time after its establishment in 1959, the Research Department of the Toronto Board of Education was the only such organization in the Metropolitan area. But research projects of varying degrees of sophistication, many of them shading into administrative operations, were being conducted by teachers, administrators, and school officials. Many of these were at best of strictly local interest, but a good deal was said about the possibility of unnecessary duplication and waste of effort. There were no formal channels of communication about interests, activities, and findings from one municipality to another and no facilities for conducting studies of general interest to the whole area. In order to consider possible means of remedying this situation, a meeting was held in October 1961 at the Department of Educational Research of the Ontario College of Education. In attendance were R.W.B. Jackson, then director of that department, and representatives of the municipalities of Etobicoke, North York, Scarborough, and Toronto. This group agreed on the need for a co-ordinating agency and, with the support of the senior officials of their boards, established the Metro Educational Research Committee. This committee began to hold monthly meetings and to circulate minutes of these meetings to officials of all the boards. By the end of the 1961–2 school year, the Forest Hill, Lakeshore, and York Township boards were represented, and East York, Leaside, and Weston joined during the following year.

Purposes

The declared purposes of the organization, the name of which was changed in 1963 to the Metropolitan Toronto Educational Research Council, had to do with three areas. It proposed 1 / to collect and interpret certain data, to collect information on research work being done in the Metropolitan Toronto area, and to disseminate research information; 2 / to study the extent to which projects being conducted within the area might be coordinated; and 3 / to ascertain the research needs and define the purpose and role of research in the area, to suggest a program of research to meet these needs, and to outline the organization and facilities at the metro level that would be required to sustain and develop such a program.[21] In its first year, the organization set out to identify a limited number of areas of special interest to all or most of the member boards, and fourteen such areas were selected. In order to test the feasibility of Metro-wide research activity, a research assistant was employed to investigate provisions for brighter children in the schools of Metropolitan Toronto and to determine the success of such programs. This investigation was sufficiently promising to encourage further activity along the same lines.

Activities

Toward the end of 1962, the members of the council met the senior administrative officials of the member boards and reviewed their first year's efforts. It was agreed that the council should continue to carry out its proposed program. Approval was given for the employment of an executive-secretary. The council was financed by contributions from the member boards according to the number of pupils they had enrolled: that is, they agreed to assess themselves at so much per pupil. The Department of Educational Research, and later the Ontario Institute for Studies in Education, also made contributions.

The Department of Educational Research and, in the final stages of the council's existence, the Ontario Institute for Studies in Education, also acted as a source of consultants and provided some of the research assistants and the facilities needed to carry out part of the program. R.W.B. Jackson not only generated much of the interest required to establish the council, but continued also to act as a kind of elder statesman after he relinquished the presidency.

Since preliminary exploration had revealed that fears of unnecessary duplication of certain studies were indeed valid, the council undertook to prepare an annotated bibliography of projects in progress or completed in the Metro area between 1961 and 1963. Some of the problems subsequently investigated were 1 / the effects of age of admission to kindergarten and grade 1; 2 / criteria for promotion, with their academic and social concomitants; 3 / the use of reading tests in the schools; 4 / existing and planned activities of member boards in elementary school French; 5 / further educational and career opportunities for graduates of the four-year program in Arts and Science in the secondary schools. Another area of activity involved the publicizing of information about specific studies carried out by member boards. These included 1 / a study of alternative programs for teaching elementary arithmetic conducted in Etobicoke and 2 / a study of failure rates in junior high schools conducted in Forest Hill. The council also made some attempt to familiarize its members with relevant research being done outside the area. On one occasion, they heard a presentation on a study of Hamilton secondary school students who did not complete the courses in which they had enrolled. On another, they were given a report of the findings of a Canadian Education Association study of students transferring from one province to another. On a third, they were presented with a study commissioned by the Ontario Educational Research Council on research departments established by school boards, most of which were in Metropolitan Toronto. Thus for the group who attended the meetings the council became an effective means of keeping up with some of the important research activities of a practical nature being conducted beyond their immediate sphere of responsibility.

Among later activities of the council were certain studies of the applications of data processing and computer technology in the field of education. Arrangements were made for council members to attend a number of workshops and conferences in the United States. A substantial amount of effort was also invested in the compilation of age-grade statistics for the Metropolitan Toronto area. This study represented a response to an earlier discovery that differences among the boards in definitions and methods of tabulation made it impossible to combine statistical material from the different sources. Initiative for the conduct of these studies owed a great deal to the efforts of Miss Dormer Ellis and A.J. Zimmerman.

The council of course had to be careful about circulating information that might have encouraged invidious comparisons among the member areas. The policy followed was to prepare a main report for general circulation describing the results for the area as a whole, but avoiding identification of individual teachers, schools, or boards. Copies of this report were distributed among schools and officials throughout Metro. A representative of a particular board could, in addition, obtain a private report dealing with the situation in his own area. The studies were intended for the information of educators within Metropolitan Toronto, although provision was made for the purchase of some reports by individuals not associated with member boards. In some instances, this outside demand was very great.

Functioning of the council

The functioning of the council was on the whole reasonably harmonious. But, as a few of the larger boards began to follow Toronto's example and employ their own professional researchers, the membership began to fall into an increasingly distinct dichotomy. The professionals were doers, while the other members participated mainly to hear about what others were doing, to encourage them as much as possible, and to assist with the publicity. Those with specialized training in research methodology also tended to be set apart somewhat from their colleagues in terms of the standards they regarded as acceptable for the projects being conducted. There was inevitably talk about a reorganization of the council to enable the professional group to carry more formal weight in decision-making, even though their views were generally deferred to when important matters were under discussion.

Dissolution

When the Royal Commission on Metropolitan Toronto began its investigation of the structure of municipal government in the area, the council appointed a committee to draw up a statement on research needs and the possible ways in which they could be met. The statement recognized the type of activity that was basically an attempt to solve an immediate problem, with an outcome that was mainly of benefit to the class or school where it was conducted. A plea was made for the kind of structure that would facilitate and encourage this type of activity. The council also acknowledged that certain kinds of research could only be carried out by a central agency.

In 1966 the council was faced with urgent questions about its own future existence. A committee was established to review the situation and suggest a suitable course of action. This committee concluded that the studies carried out by the council were of value, but that the latter lacked the financial resources required to meet the need for Metro-wide research projects. After the anticipated municipal reorganization, it would need substantial support from the Metropolitan Toronto School Board if it were to continue to function. It was made clear, however, that the board intended to establish and maintain a research department of its own with functions that would closely parallel those of the council. Bowing to the inevitable, the members of the council passed a motion at their meeting in November 1966, empowering the executive to dissolve the organization as soon as various matters had been adequately attended to.

TWELVE

Contributions of various agencies to educational research in Ontario before 1965

EARLY INITIATIVES

Educational research, according to Barr, Davis, and Johnson, has passed through several stages in its manner of solving problems.[1] The first of these was characterized by an exchange of individual experiences. The papers and addresses of educational leaders presented at meetings and conferences dealt mainly with reports of what they were doing in their own school systems and what they had personally found effective. This personal experience approach was gradually supplemented by what the same writers call the "deliberative" approach. It also involved a discussion of problems, but tended to include committee action. It provided a means of defining significant educational problems and reaching conclusions as a result of group thinking and remains a useful method of obtaining a consensus on problems requiring an immediate solution. Between 1910 and 1920 the measurement movement began to revolutionize appraisal and research techniques and to lay the foundations for a tremendous growth in modern research studies.

Many of the early problems selected for study were of immediate and local interest only, as Barr, Davis, and Johnson have indicated in a list presented by Kohl at a meeting of college teachers of education in 1911.[2] The first half dozen of these illustrate the nature of the current interests: Which is better, one or two sessions a day? What should be the length of sessions for the different grades? Are shorter sessions for six days of the week better than longer ones for five days? Are a number of short vacations better than one or two longer ones? What seasons of the year are most conducive to good school work? What are the best days of the week for good school work?

As was indicated in chapter 11, the early history of Ontario education demonstrates the same resorting to inquiry of one kind or another to resolve some particular problem. There is no reason to suppose that the intelligence or perception of the investigators of those days differed from that of their modern counterparts, but there was an obvious lack of formal or systematic techniques. It was only in the present century that signs of a scientific movement in education became evident. Major influence has been attributed to the periodical, *The School*, which from the time of its appearance in 1912 was supervised by an editorial board composed of staff members of the Ontario College of Education. It published articles showing a strong contemporary interest in measurement devices, then in the early stages of development. In 1925 Peter Sandiford, the founder of the Department of Educational Research, contributed an article dealing with what might be considered for that period reasonably advanced statistics. He showed that, in writing examinations in educational psychology at the Ontario College of Education, the candidate's ability in written English counted more than his knowledge of subject matter. Articles on educational research continued to be devoted to many kinds of tests.

The Department of Educational Research, established at the college through Sandiford's efforts in 1931, was not at first a research agency in the modern sense. Its function, as mentioned in chapter 11, might more properly be described as development in the specific area of testing. That the Department of Education was interested in the same field is shown by its participation in a study committee, also involving the universities and the secondary schools, which was established in 1928 to determine the value of objective tests in the middle school departmental examinations.

STUDIES BY MISCELLANEOUS GROUPS AFTER THE SECOND WORLD WAR

The period beginning near the end of the Second World War witnessed an interest in research activity in general and in various problems that seemed amenable to research. Mention of a few of these will be sufficient to demonstrate the general nature of the trend. The Ontario School Inspectors' Association, for example, established a Research Committee which sent a questionnaire in 1943 to all inspectors in the province designed to find out what research was needed in Ontario schools. The somewhat meagre returns stressed reading and related topics. The committee issued a more detailed report the following year containing listings and compilations of data on eight topics. The association submitted a brief to the Royal Commission on Education, which included detailed recommendations on the future of research in the province. Its own encouragement and reporting of individual projects continued in what was, for the time, a fairly substantial operation.

In 1943 the Ontario Public School Men Teachers' Federation set up an Educational Research Committee to study the curriculum with a view to suggesting improvements in various school subjects. Its report the following year indicated a lack of thoroughness in all subjects, with insufficient drill and review.[3] In 1944 a committee of the Toronto Assistant Masters' Association prepared a thirty-two-page report on juvenile delinquency, which included recommendations on how to attack the problem.[4] The Toronto Vice-Principals' Committee began in 1951 to devise a series of standardized tests in spelling and in arithmetic computation, problems, and reasoning to supplement existing tests in reading. In strict terms, this was a development project; it represented one of the earliest examples of a substantial, tangible contribution resulting from the efforts of a voluntary group.

There were examples of projects, some of which were fairly ambitious, initiated by an outside agency and conducted largely by the Department of Educational Research in accordance with some kind of agreement or contract. The initiating agency sometimes made a financial contribution, which was usually not large enough to cover more than a minor proportion of the real cost of the project. In the mid-1950s, the Ontario Secondary School Headmasters' Association arranged for a survey of English and arithmetic in grades 9 and 10 in Ontario schools. This study involved the administration of thousands of tests, which were scored in the schools as a result of co-operation solicited by the headmasters. It lacked the controls and completeness of the later Carnegie Study of Identification and Utilization of Talent in High School and College, but nevertheless provided some interesting insights into achievement at the indicated levels. Another co-operative study was carried out by the Department of Educational Research at the instigation of the Ontario School Trustees' and Ratepayers' Association. Called the Rural Schools Survey, it dealt with certain aspects of achievement and related factors in small schools in rural areas, tending to point up some of the inequalities that were prevalent in the system at that time.

SURVEYS OF EDUCATIONAL RESEARCH

The first issue of the *Ontario Journal of Educational Research*, published in October 1958, included a retrospective survey of educational research done in Canada between 1953 and 1956. The list included 328 projects for Ontario. The Ontario Educational Research Council subsequently undertook to conduct a series of similar surveys for its own province. The first of these, carried out in the Department of Educational Research, involved the mailing of questionnaires to 393 individuals and agencies. Although the 267 who responded constituted fewer than two-thirds of the total, the results were probably more complete than might appear at first glance, in view of the likelihood that many non-respondents had nothing to report. The results of the survey were reported in September 1959.[5]

Seventy-seven of the respondents reported a total of 397 completed or proposed research projects. The report classified these according to educational authority, location, and subject. The distribution by educational authority was as follows: the Department of Education, 129; secondary schools, 44; elementary schools, 82; teachers' colleges and university departments or colleges of education, 114; other university departments, 10; associations, 9; councils, 6; others, 3. In terms of type of research, the report indicated that basic research was still mainly, although not exclusively, a university-level pursuit. Except for the activities of the Department of Educational Research, however, most educational research studies carried out in university circles were for graduate theses. Counting thesis-type papers submitted for the departmental course for the Specialist's Certificate in Guidance, theses made up about one-half of the total number of projects reported by all agencies. Committees of provincial organizations and *ad hoc* bodies were engaged in fact-finding studies and other similar projects of an applied nature. There was apparently almost no research being done in teachers' colleges or in technical institutes. In local school systems, research activity was usually carried out by departments of guidance, special services, and psychological services, or by administrative officials or teachers on a voluntary basis. Most such studies were of the service or action research type. Among all the agencies covered in the survey, a great number of different areas of interest were included.

GRADUATE THESES

The program of graduate studies in the Department of Educational Theory in the University of Toronto involved only a small number of advanced students during this period. Nevertheless, their efforts constituted a major proportion of the research contributions. In a survey and evaluation of education theses produced between 1935 and 1955 in Canadian graduate schools, Brehaut had some critical things to say about their level of sophistication.[6] The fact that Ontario theses were not characteristically theory-oriented was no serious fault for a person seeking interesting or useful information. While some of them were valuable from this latter point of view, however, they tended to demonstrate the fragmentation that inevitably results from extreme emphasis on the candidate's responsibility for choosing his own problem.

THE WORK OF THE DEPARTMENT OF EDUCATIONAL RESEARCH

The Department of Educational Research of the Ontario College of Education was responsible for a large proportion of the educational research conducted in Ontario until the time of its final disappearance in 1966. The exact proportion would of course be impossible to determine. Quite different results would be obtained depending on what one classified as research, as contrasted with administrative operations or routine data collection. At the First Invitational Conference on Educational Research in Canada in 1959, R.W.B. Jackson reported that about half of the 370 studies and research projects undertaken prior to 1956 in Ontario were sponsored and financed by the Department of Education. Since most of the latter's interests were handled by the Department of Educational Research, and since there was no other comparable agency, this statement provides an indirect indication of the latter's role.

School grant studies

The Research Department's first studies in educational finance date from the 1930s. Their importance tended to increase as the provincial system of school grants, described in volume II, chapter 8, became more complex and sophisticated. The following informal statement by E.B. Rideout, who had a major responsibility for the program, gives an indication of the nature of this activity in 1960.

> The Research Department ... examines each new proposal in detail, determining not only an estimate of what it will cost the province but also what effect it will have on each individual school board. The Research Department not only evaluates proposals of the Special Grants Committee in this way, but also works closely with the Grants Committee of the Department of Education, suggesting refinements in and extensions to the grant regulations, keeping a particular eye out for the equalizing and non-equalizing effects of each proposed change in the regulations.
>
> At any one time a number of special studies are under way to supply basic data for proposals which may be made to the Grants Committees in future years. A special service performed each year for the Department [of Education] is the punching of most of the information contained in the grant forms for each board into IBM cards and the submission to the Chief of Grants and Superintendent of Business Administration of totals for the province, by type of board, of all data so punched. Help is given to the Department also in the drafting of new grant regulations, the revision of existing regulations, the interpretations and applications of the regulations, and the solutions of special problems arising out of peculiar local situations.

This comprehensive program absorbed a fairly substantial part of the resources of the Research Department throughout the year.

Major longitudinal studies

The origin of the Atkinson Study of Utilization of Student Resources and of its more grandiose successor, the Carnegie Study of Identification and Utilization of Talent in High School and College, are dealt with in chapter 11. An attempt is made in that context to show their influence on the developing role and structure of the Research Department. The present treatment is intended to describe and appraise them briefly as contributions to educational research.

The two studies, which effectively began in 1955 and 1958 respectively, although preceded by a considerable period of preliminary negotiation and preparation, were devoted to essentially the same purposes. As their name implies, they attempted to measure various student talents and abilities, to demonstrate how these were being utilized in terms of school retention and educational and occupational objectives, and to provide suggestions for improvement. To a considerable extent, they dealt with the development and appraisal of tests and other devices for the measurement of educational and, to a lesser extent, occupational success. They were both on an unprecedented scale, the Atkinson Study involving the participation of what began as almost a complete grade 13 student group, consisting of 9,573 individuals, and the Carnegie Study including about 90,000 grade 9 students, with a subsidiary group of about 20,000 grade 7 and 8 pupils from Toronto schools. While the Atkinson Study was often compared with studies with similar stated objectives which were begun during the same period in Alberta and in the Atlantic provinces, it carried out a vastly more comprehensive, thorough, and extended program.

During the 1955–6 school year, arrangements were made for the Educational Testing Service of Princeton, New Jersey, to administer the Scholastic Aptitude Test and the School and College Ability Test to the Atkinson Study group in grade 13. As part of the program of initial description and identification, student participants and teachers completed separate questionnaires providing a substantial amount of information about personal characteristics and attitudes, family background, and career intentions. Teachers' estimates of each student's prospects of educational success at later stages were solicited. A reading test was administered to the entire group, and various other tests and inventories were given to selected samples of about 1,500 each. The results of grade 13 departmental examinations were obtained at the end of the year and, for those who failed one or more subjects, for the following year. During the five subsequent years, and for some particular groups even beyond that period, follow-up questionnaires were sent out at intervals to trace the progress of the participants. Achievement records were obtained from universities and other educational institutions which many attended. Ratings were secured from employers for those who proceeded directly from school to remunerative work. Approximately twenty reports in one series or another were produced at intervals for more than a decade, many of them by the present writer, presenting conclusions reached about various groups. For sheer volume of words and figures, no research study carried out in Canada has ever equaled the Atkinson Study. It would be dangerous to make a comparable claim for its influence on the progress of education.

The Carnegie Study, to use the abbreviated term attached to it almost of necessity, resembled the Atkinson Study, which it was designed to complement, in certain important respects. 1 / A complete group was identified and described initially and traced through several years of further progress. 2 / The devices used were principally formal instruments such as tests and inventories along with specially constructed questionnaires. 3 / Both studies had the advantages of complete coverage of a large group, eliminating any problem of sampling error, although not, of course, the possibility of errors in measurement. 4 / The statistical-survey approach excluded in-depth analysis of fundamental social or psychological factors bearing on retention or career choice. It was intended that subsidiary studies would be developed by graduate students and others interested in studying these factors, but such a hope proved unrealistic. Besides the fact that the two studies differed in the grade level at which the participants were selected, the studies were dissimilar in certain fundamental respects. 1 / Aptitude and achievement tests were specially developed as part of the Carnegie Study program for use in grades 9 and 10. Some of these, with suitable modifications, proved of value for a number of subsequent years. Others were rather quickly outmoded by organizational and curricular changes in the secondary schools. 2 / The much larger scale of the Carnegie Study posed entirely different organizational and procedural problems. 3 / When the attempt to follow the careers of students withdrawing from grades 9 and 10 proved unproductive, unlike corresponding efforts to secure information from and about the more mature participants in the Atkinson Study, the investigation became confined essentially to the group remaining in school in successive years. 4 / The Carnegie Study called mainly for the co-operation of the formal school system, while the Atkinson Study did so only at the beginning and later depended on other agencies.

The Atkinson Study achieved most of the objectives, in terms of depth and extent of coverage, that were defined for it in the original prospectus. The Carnegie Study did not. Its tangible products consisted of the tests already mentioned and a number of slim reports presenting census-like data indicating the findings about the group during successive years of testing and questionnaire administration, and explanatory information about the tests. The declared intention of identifying patterns of development through the high school years, requiring the integration of information obtained from one year to another, was never realized. Also disappointing was the failure to obtain information from more than a minor proportion of the withdrawing students, despite the reduction of the follow-up questionnaire to a few simple questions printed on a post-paid returnable card.

There were several reasons for the disappointing nature of these results. As one of the group directly responsible for the operation, it may be expecting too much to suppose that the present writer will place the major blame on the incompetence of the supervisors. There were, however, other factors that can be objectively identified. The project was beyond the resources of the Department of Educational Research in two important ways: the number of staff was inadequate, and data processing techniques and equipment then available were not sufficiently advanced to make possible the collation and analysis of data recorded on as many as thirty separate sets of punch-cards. Since obligations assumed when the study was undertaken were of a general, long-term nature, important aspects were constantly being shelved temporarily in favour of some other project or service activity with a specific deadline. Meanwhile, time was passing and the relevance of any conclusions was rapidly diminishing. By the time the Ontario Institute for Studies in Education was formed, new staff, new interests, and coolness at the administrative level resulted in the effective burial of what might, a few years earlier, have been an immensely productive collection of data.

Two successive grants were provided by the Atkinson Charitable Foundation for the Atkinson Study, the first amounting to $35,000 and the second to $50,000. The Carnegie Corporation of New York made a single grant of $90,000 for the Carnegie Study. These sums, however, defrayed only a small proportion of the cost to the Research Department, the remainder being supplied by the provincial government through annual operating budgets. A very large contribution in kind was made through the efforts of teachers and school administrators. In this writer's view, the intangible values would have to have been very substantial to justify the funds and effort spent on the Carnegie Study.

In reviewing the contributions of the two studies in 1966 at the time the Board of Governors of the Ontario Institute for Studies in Education assumed the responsibility for carrying out any remaining responsibility for them, R.W.B. Jackson suggested that there were a number of useful results, some of them peripheral to the achievement of the objectives originally specified. Particular contributions of the Atkinson Study had, in his view, been as follows. 1 / It had helped to provide a pattern for the Service for Admission to College and University (SACU) program then being developed. 2 / It had demonstrated the value of school marks for the prediction of success in university. 3 / In documenting variations in marks among schools and teachers, it had pointed to the need for scaling, and had also provided data upon which scaling schemes were based. 4 / It had provided the basis for the development of the Scholastic Aptitude Test for Ontario (SATO) and for the program of grade 12 achievement tests, the results of which had assisted Department of Education officials to supervise the work of the secondary schools. 5 / The Atkinson Study reports had influenced university admission procedures. 6 / Data from the same study had influenced the deliberations and recommendations of the Grade 13 Study Committee. 7 / In Jackson's own words: "It was not altogether an accident that in both of these Studies the students were identified by the name of the Study itself; that is, those who participated in the Atkinson Study were known as Atkinson Students; many of them have come to us later, even after graduation from university, and identified themselves as one of our Atkinson Students. The effect on personal lives, quite unanticipated on our part, may have been greater than anyone could have dreamed, but this, of course, we have no means of assessing." 8 / It was a productive experience for teachers and students to be involved in a study of major significance. For the schools, participation in a common study had an integrating effect that may also have affected the relationship between publicly-supported and private schools. 9 / Perhaps one of the greatest values of the Atkinson Study was the attention focused in the newspapers, in parents' meetings, and in meetings of teachers and other groups of educators on the students who went to university and those who did not, and on the possible size of the groups capable of profiting from university studies but who did not attend.

Some of the particular contributions of the Carnegie Study were identified as follows. 1 / It may have had an indirect effect on school retention or on the attitudes of parents and students to dropping out of school. 2 / It had also helped to familiarize educators with the concept of the data bank. It was the prototype of an information system such as each province was trying to set up. 3 / It, as well as the Atkinson Study, led to the development of machine methods and applications, in particular, of test scoring, data processing, and reporting.[7] A number of other claims were made, but space does not permit them to be reported here.

Other projects

In addition to the school grant studies and the Atkinson and Carnegie Studies, the Research Department used a major part of its staff and financial resources on the departmental objective testing program in grade 12 and, increasingly during the 1960s, on processing, scaling, and reporting the results of the departmental examinations in grade 13. These activities are dealt with in chapter 15 in connection with the examination system. There were also large numbers of activities of lesser individual significance, an important group of which had to do with test development and revision. A survey of active studies produced in 1959 included the following titles in this category: 1 / the administration of an experimental edition of a test of learning capacity in grades 3 and 4; 2 / the validation of short-form reading readiness tests; 3 / the administration of an experimental form of a grade 1 reading survey test; 4 / the construction and printing of quick-scoring editions of certain tests in the Dominion series; 5 / an evaluation of Dominion tests of achievement in grade 8; and 6 / developmental work on the Scholastic Aptitude Test for Ontario. At that time, a considerable amount of work was being done on the production of the tests being used in the Carnegie Study.

Some work was still being done on studies, already referred to, being conducted in co-operation with the Ontario Secondary School Headmasters' Association and the Ontario School Trustees' and Ratepayers' Association. In somewhat the same category was a survey designed to assist the School of Dentistry at the University of Toronto in the appraisal of its program. An evaluation of the so-called Newcastle method of teaching reading with the assistance of film strips was being carried out in co-operation with officials of the Toronto Board of Education. A study of achievement growth patterns was also being conducted in association with the same board. A study of socio-economic status at the University of Toronto involved some of the latter's officials. Tests were being scored, the results analysed, and a report prepared for the St Catharines School of Nursing. A questionnaire was being administered for the Ontario Educational Research Council and a report prepared for the members. There were also several minor studies being carried out for or in co-operation with various educators on an individual basis.

The assembly of information and publication were activities of some importance at the time of the survey. An annotated guide to research materials was being prepared. The early issues of the *Ontario Journal of Educational Research* had been completed and material for subsequent issues was being assembled. A report on a commercial spelling study was approaching the publication stage. Abstracts of certain graduate theses, considered to have findings with useful implications, were also being published.

The same major projects continued to dominate the program until 1965 but with a continuous expansion of minor studies, as well as publication and service activities. A list of items prepared for 1964–5 contained over two hundred separable units of activity involving a dozen research-conducting staff, including the librarian and the editor. These individuals were supported by an approximately equal number of part-time and full-time research assistants, and about thirty non-academic staff. The units referred to were not, of course, all different studies, since some of the larger projects were broken down into a number of aspects. They also included many service and advisory activities. Nevertheless, even allowing for these factors, the Research Department was obviously involved in an extraordinary number of educational concerns involving the widest range of individuals and agencies. The capacities of the staff were, of course over-extended, with the result that some responsibilities were carried out superficially, and certain projects were allowed to drag on much too long. A case might, however, be made for the proposition that the best way to get assistance is to demonstrate a desperate need for it. In that sense, the organization was supremely successful.

In discussing the contributions of the Research Department in the Legislature in 1965, the minister singled out two studies for particular comment.[8] One of these was built in part on the Carnegie Study and involved the problems and careers of school youth in Sault Ste Marie. Davis was hopeful that similar studies would be launched in other communities. The other study that he found of special interest concerned the education and employment of women. It encompassed not only what had been done in the past and what was being done currently, but also a preliminary consideration of the demands and needs of the future. Davis's further comments indicated the relevance of the study.

> Many questions are being raised about what the future holds for this half of our population; there is every indication that we will, in the future, require women for service in industry, commerce and the professions as well as in the home. What education should young women then receive to enable them to return to the world of work after they have married and after their family

obligations have, for the most part, been met? This is but one of the many problems which demand our concern and for which answers need to be found.

This expression of views may be regarded as symbolic of Davis's general interest in the possibility of improving the educational process through a realistic investment in research, an interest which he had been demonstrating so dramatically during the previous year.

ACTIVITIES OF THE INSTITUTE OF CHILD STUDY OF THE UNIVERSITY OF TORONTO

Under the direction of W.E. Blatz, who directed the organization until 1960, the Institute of Child Study was known for its extremely permissive approach to the development of mental health. Among other things, Blatz conducted a strong campaign against such repressive measures as the use of the strap. After 1960 a more traditional approach to discipline was noticeable, although the original theme was not renounced. Blatz's contribution to the president's report for 1959 mentioned progress in children's emancipation from parents, social relationships, and longitudinal progress in reading.[9]

The corresponding report for 1962 referred to the wide range of studies in progress dealing with learning, decision-making, and development in cognitive, intellectual, personality, and social areas. These could be pursued, not only in the St George's School, but also in many outside organizations including schools, nurseries, recreation groups, centres for exceptional children, and hospitals. The list of research studies in progress in the calendar for 1965–6 was as follows: a longitudinal study of children from birth to twelve years of age; measurement of infant security; assessment of pre-school children's mental health; measurement of the security of elementary school children (the "Jimmy" and "Tommy" Tests); children's relationships with their peers from four to twelve years of age; change with age of children's preference for adult or child associates (the "Birthday Test"); longitudinal study of children's intelligence related to security; perceptual-motor performance of young children (Kephart and Frostig measures); conceptual development of children four to ten years of age; development of the perceptual verbal aspects of intelligence from two to six years of age; a measure of children's emancipation; the relation of parents' feelings of adequacy to their children's security scores; a study of spontaneous writing in nursery school children; the development of word recognition in nursery school children; a study of pre-school children's sense of time; space orientation of the nursery school child; awareness and use of number in the nursery school child; initial adjustment of children to nursery school; a longitudinal study of a group of deprived children.[10] No information is to be obtained from a mere reading of this list of the scope, depth, or quality of these studies. But they do indicate that the attention of the staff and students was focused on a wide variety of aspects of child development. The impact of the institute's activities on the relevant literature has certainly diminished since the Blatz days. It would, however, be difficult to determine to what extent this situation is a result of the rapid proliferation of similar studies elsewhere, thus giving the institute, relatively static in terms of staff and students, a smaller share of the field.

THIRTEEN

The creation and development of the Ontario Institute for Studies in Education

ORIGIN

As the Davis program for educational reform and expansion got into high gear by early 1964, it began to be known in the Department of Educational Research that the minister wanted to put the organization on a new basis. Why the minister was prepared to make an unprecedented investment in educational research and development is to a considerable degree a matter of speculation. There is, of course, no question that he was thoroughly familiar with the means by which industry and commerce had made tremendous forward strides, and the arguments for parallels in the educational field must have been convincing. Also, as his conviction grew that progress depended to a large extent on the breaking down of structural rigidities in the system and in the decentralization of responsibility, he must have felt that every effort should be made to channel intellectual resources into the production and testing of new ideas. Jackson's influence as a consultant must also have been of vital importance. The efforts of the Department of Educational Research had been carefully directed toward conspicuously useful objectives. To some extent, the proposed new agency was certainly seen as a means of providing more of the same. Whatever the reasons, the believers in the potential value of educational research and development were given a unique opportunity to justify themselves. And, whether the institute succeeded or not, Davis's action would always demand their warmest appreciation.

It should be noted that opposition members in the Legislature were prodding Davis into taking action in the research field. In April 1964 Leo Troy noted that the budget provided $50,000 for research on wages and salaries in the civil service, $733,000 for research in the Department of Lands and Forests, $760,000 for the study of northern Ontario development through the Department of Economics and Development, $1 million in the Ontario Research Foundation, and fairly substantial amounts in other branches of the government. He thought that, since the entire budget for the Ontario College of Education was only $1.9 million, the amount being spent on educational research was small, considering that the Department of Education was the largest in terms of expenditure. There was a sharp contrast with the amount being spent in industry, where the object was simply to produce better products. He thought that, in relation to an annual budget for education that had reached $400 million, a total expenditure of $10 million on research would be reasonable. Some of this amount he thought might be raised from sources other than government.[1] He also referred to criticisms that the Robarts Plan had been put into operation without much research.

Initial proposals

Jackson himself did not seem to have sufficient information in early 1964 to explain just what the minister had in mind. He was sure only that Davis envisioned research activities on a much enlarged scale. When he brought up the point again in September, he said that his staff faced a great challenge and a great opportunity. He himself was not, however, going to pressure them into action; the choice was up to them. The writer's reaction was to initiate discussions among his colleagues, and to request each of them to outline some of his concepts of the structure and functions of an institute of educational research. He also consulted J.R.H. Morgan, who then occupied an office in the same building in his capacity as director of the Ontario Curriculum Institute. Morgan had been thinking about the possibility of a merger of some kind between the Research Department and the institute from the early days of his assumption of the office. When the writer first volunteered a suggestion along these lines, Morgan showed every sign of enthusiasm. Now that the time had come for specific proposals, Morgan advised him to draw up a plan and send it to the minister with an offer to elaborate further on a suitable occasion. The writer proceeded to act on this advice.

The bulk of the discussions about this plan, which was to be submitted to the minister, took place between Morgan and the writer. There were some fundamental differences in point of view, largely centring on the former's relatively negative and the later's positive views about the values of the academic type of research. On the practical side, there was a problem of integrating an agency primarily concerned with research, but also substantially involved in development work (the Research Department) with an agency primarily concerned with development, but with definite research concerns (the Ontario Curriculum Institute).

At this particular time, certain ideas about research structures and functions were being generated by J. Bascom St John, who had recently been appointed chairman of the new Policy and Development Council. In a memorandum to the minister, he commented on the difficulties being experienced by school board research departments. They were encountering a slackening in the degree of enthusiasm felt for them by trustees and seemed to lack sufficient independence to do uniformly impartial work. Another difficulty, which might perhaps have been reduced in time, was that trustees and officials often misunderstood the real nature of educational research. Local research units were often on the defensive when asked to do the impossible and, in the local context, the effectiveness or the actual existence of the research unit might be destroyed as a result of disillusionment. Furthermore, the proliferation of research departments was not seen as desirable, partly because there were too few qualified staff to go around. For these and other reasons, St John recommended the establishment of a special unit in the Department of Educational Research "designed to conduct research in and for local school systems, on their request, or for Department of Education purposes, by agreement with the local school boards concerned."[2] The writer sought out St John for a further discussion of these ideas and incorporated some of them into the proposal for a Field Services Division in the new institute.

The writer's initial scheme, which received Jackson's prior approval, was entitled "Proposals for an Institute of Educational Research in the University of Toronto." As the name implied, it envisioned an agency that would be an integral part of the university. The scheme elicited a prompt response from the minister, who invited the writer to elaborate on the proposals at a meeting on November 2. In addition to the minister and the writer, the ensuing discussion involved C. Westcott, the minister's executive assistant, T. Campbell, then personnel director for the department, and J.F. Flowers, a member of the Research Department. The writer spent a long time presenting the reasons why the new institute should not be structurally linked with the Department of Education. Davis proved, however, not to be thinking along these lines at all, but rather envisioned a truly provincial agency without formal ties either with the department or with any specific university. While Davis expressed approval of the general tenor of the proposals, at least in terms of the objectives to be achieved, he requested a revised plan for an independent institute.

The rather lengthy set of "functions and objectives" listed in the original document are presented here not merely as an indication of the writer's thinking at the time, but more particularly as a distillation of the views of the small group mainly, although not exclusively, in the Research Department to whom the planning initiative fell in the earliest stages.

1. To initiate and conduct educational research activities arising from the capacities and interests of its staff members. These should include both fundamental and applied research, and may deal with any question having to do with education or with educational implications.
2. To co-operate with federal, provincial, and municipal government agencies, with universities, with organizations of teachers, educational administrators, trustees, and others involved in education, and with individuals in the solution of educational problems amenable to research. To undertake, at its own discretion, studies arising out of the needs of these agencies according to either of the following plans: (a) the findings to be the joint property of the Institute and the co-operating agency, both having unrestricted publication rights; (b) the Institute to contribute service only,

according to an explicit or implicit contract, and the findings to be the sole property of the co-operating agency. This second arrangement will make it possible for the Institute to fulfill research needs of the Ontario Department of Education according to present policy and practice of the Department of Educational Research.

3. To focus the interests and competencies of specialists in various university disciplines on the problems and needs of education and to improve the quality and value of educational research by enlisting the co-operation of such individuals in studies and projects.
4. To offer advice, consultation, and guidance, at its own discretion, to public and private agencies and to individuals interested or involved in educational research projects.
5. To develop a knowledge of and stimulate an interest in educational research among educators and the general public throughout the province and, where possible, beyond its borders, by giving addresses, participating in the work of educational organizations, calling educational conferences, and by other appropriate means.
6. To participate in the work of the Department of Educational Theory of the University of Toronto by assisting in the preparation of candidates for post-graduate degrees in education. To assist in the expansion of this programme in order to help meet the needs of education in Canada and abroad. In particular, to take responsibility for the training of professional educational researchers by offering formal course work and practical training in research procedures. To be a particular source of inspiration for leaders in educational thought.
7. To co-operate with institutions such as the Ontario College of Education in the preparation of teachers, according to its capacity and at the request of such institutions.
8. To participate in non-degree in-service teacher education in co-operation with appropriate agencies.
9. To publicize by all appropriate means the contributions of agencies or individuals to educational knowledge and thought.
10. To assist developing countries with the solution of educational problems by offering some measure of expert assistance.
11. To undertake comparative studies in education in co-operation with agencies in other countries, particularly those of the Commonwealth and the United States.
12. To contribute financially, at its own discretion, to the educational research activities of deserving agencies or individuals.
13. To sponsor, at its own discretion, one or more experimental schools as a means of testing various educational hypotheses having to do with learning principles, methods, curriculum, etc.
14. In general, to act as a source of knowledge and ideas to be made freely available to policy makers in all branches of the educational system, particularly, but not exclusively, in Ontario.

15. In general, to stimulate public interest in educational problems and issues.

The structure suggested in the original proposal would have involved an advisory council, including representatives of the minister, branches of the university other than the institute, the Ontario Teachers' Federation, the Ontario School Trustees' Council, and institute faculty members, as well as officials of the institute, the Ontario College of Education, and the university. The Senate and Board of Governors of the university would have had the same authority over the institute as over any other part of the university. Internally, the "divisions" as they were then labeled, were very similar to those incorporated in the structure as it was established in June 1965: Test Development and Administration; Educational Administration; Educational Finance; Educational Planning; Psychology of Learning; Curriculum; Information, Communication, and Data Systems; and Research Field Services.

The concept of an independent institute

The minister's suggestion of an independent institute posed fundamental questions. To most of those involved, participation in graduate studies seemed to be an essential element in the role that professional researchers would wish to assume. Furthermore, their qualifications would be such as to constitute the resources needed for a first-class graduate program in education, something that the University of Toronto did not then have. Such a program would be essential if the results of worthwhile research were to be disseminated among a new generation of educators, and if the educational climate were to be made more favourable to constructive change. But it was difficult to envision a new and independent institute with a good graduate program. What kind of recognition could one expect for degrees from an instant specialized university based on a model unknown in the English-speaking world? And how could a competent faculty be attracted in the initial stages? Jackson was prepared, if absolutely esential, to go ahead without a program of graduate studies at all. The writer could have been persuaded to try the instant degree idea, but not to dispense with the graduate studies function. G.E. Flower, Director of Graduate Studies at the Ontario College of Education, who by that time had been brought into the discussions, felt that any arrangement other than a continued association with the School of Graduate Studies of the University of Toronto would be unworkable. He was in fact most reluctant to see any breach in the organic ties with the Ontario College of Education, until persuaded that the minister's plans ruled out such an arrangement.

The proposal that emerged from discussions among the informal planning group was the one that was finally accepted, that is, that the new institute be chartered as an independent college, but that it be affiliated with the University of Toronto for graduate studies. The university

Graduate Department of Educational Theory would in effect be based largely, although not necessarily exclusively, in the institute, and those of the institute's staff whom the university found acceptable would be appointed to this graduate department. The chairman of the department, who was at that time Director of Graduate Studies at the Ontario College of Education, would simply lose the latter title upon appointment to a corresponding position in the institute. Students enrolled in the graduate program would continue their progress toward Toronto degrees. Conditions for the award of the degrees would continue to be established by the university through its normal procedures.

This proposal was discussed with Vice-President M. St A. Woodside of the University of Toronto. The only obstacle to the idea was that almost the entire graduate program in education would be handled by people who received their salaries from another agency. This arrangement might be opposed on the grounds that the precedent so established could encourage disintegrative tendencies in the University, but Woodside did not appear to be too worried that such a development would occur.

In preparation for a meeting on November 11 the writer sent President Bissell a letter on November 9, outlining how far plans had evolved and offering suggestions for his consideration.

(1) The proposed Ontario Institute of Educational Research should be chartered to grant degrees in education.
(2) For an unspecified period of time, the Institute should suspend its degree granting powers, and work out a form of affiliation with the University of Toronto that would involve having its degrees awarded by the latter.
(3) Presumably, in order to satisfy itself that adequate course content and standards are being met, the University of Toronto might wish to approve course outlines and the instructors appointed to teach courses offered for Toronto degrees.
(4) Affiliation with the University of Toronto should involve as convenient access to the numerous University library collections on the part of the proposed Institute as is now enjoyed by the Department of Educational Research. The present research program of the latter, and correspondingly, that of the proposed Institute, would be crippled if it were forced to rely exclusively on its own library resources.[3]

The delegation that met Bissell and Woodside in the former's office included D.F. Dadson, Dean of the Ontario College of Education, as well as Flower, Morgan, and the writer. Bissell was not very favourably impressed with the proposals. He expressed a strong preference for an organization that would be under the financial control of the university. Any other arrangement, he felt, would involve government domination, with undesirable consequences for the integrity of scholarly studies. In a subsequent contact with Dean Sirluck of the School of Graduate Studies, the writer realized that there were unfavourable reactions to the possibility that affiliation might be regarded as a temporary arrangement, to be terminated as soon as the institute was firmly enough established to begin granting its own degrees. The university was determined to develop a first-class program in all departments, and if that meant beginning afresh in educational studies, it might as well start at once. The writer expressed the opinion that the kind of people the institute would attempt to attract would probably place considerable value on an association with a great university and would be likely to work for the consolidation of that relationship rather than for its dissolution.

Dadson took the opportunity at the meeting with Bissell to mount a vigorous defence of the interests of his college. He felt that the college could afford the loss of the Department of Educational Research, although he did not look forward to its departure with any great degree of enthusiasm. But graduate studies constituted an essential element in his plans for the future development of the institution. By relating these studies more closely with the program of initial teacher preparation, he hoped that both might be strengthened and invigorated. He had intended to use the prospect of participation in the graduate program as an attraction in his campaign to recruit outstanding additions to his staff.

Dadson's efforts were, of course, in vain. The legacy of the Diltz years had been impossible to throw off in the brief period since his appointment in 1963. Those departments of the college not directly involved in initial teacher preparation, including both graduate studies and research, had been for too long allowed to go their own way. The proposed affiliation of the institute with the University of Toronto constituted an extra blow, since there could not be two agencies administering programs for degrees in the same field in the same university. Thus the Ontario College of Education, as it was still called at the time, would be at a disadvantage in comparison with the new colleges of education, which were to be encouraged to develop graduate programs through their parent universities. Dadson was assured that close co-operation between the college and the institute could, despite organic separation, provide for the realization of some of his hopes. As it turned out, these hopes were too optimistic.

Legal arrangements

The active process of drafting legislation got under way in March 1965. A critical stage was passed on the seventeenth of that month when the Treasury Board took action as recorded in the following minute: "Treasury Board approved in principle a proposal to establish a new agency to be known as the Ontario Institute for Studies in Education reporting to the Minister of Education with a budget for 1965–66 of approximately $1,850,000." An early draft of a bill refers to the Ontario Institute for Studies in Education as a "corporation," and the assumption seems to have been that *The Corporation Act* would apply. Another version, which designates the act as an amendment to *The Department of Education Act*, has a notation that certain sections of *The Corporations Act* would not apply. At the time, the prospect of establishing the institute as a crown corporation was certainly being considered. Feeling that such a course of action would be inadvisable, the writer suggested that the word "college" be used in the legislation. This suggestion was adopted, and plans proceeded for the writing of an act paralleling those establishing provincial universities.

In producing a rough draft of those parts of the bill that were intended to establish the essential characteristics of the institute, the writer exerted an influence in favour of giving the board complete legal powers, including the right to establish an academic council. The early draft includes this specific wording: "The Board may establish an Academic Council composed of any class of officers of the Institute to advise the Board on academic and administrative affairs of the Institute." The act, as finally passed, stated that "the Board shall establish an academic council composed of any class of instructional staff and officers of the Institute with such powers and duties as may be prescribed by by-law of the Board."[4] Although there were still no defined powers, two important changes had been made. The establishment of the Academic Council was now mandatory because of the use of the word "shall," and the idea of the council's offering direct advice to the board had been dropped. The by-laws adopted in July gave the council the right only to advise the director.

The lack of legally defined powers for the Academic Council occasioned severe criticism at a later stage from the Ontario Council of University Faculty Associations as well as from the faculty members of the institute. Whether or not these have been justified, the proposals were made for quite specific reasons. 1 / The expected affiliation with the University of Toronto would place the whole of the graduate program under the jurisdiction of the Senate, on which the institute staff would be represented, and thus for that particular aspect of the program it seemed inappropriate to give the Academic Council overlapping responsibilities. 2 / The Board of Governors, which was to consist of representatives of the important educational interests of the province, was not seen as a caretaker body with purely legalistic authority but as the active determinant of general policies and programs. The proposal to include faculty members was to be the means whereby their interests would influence policy. The assignment of independent powers to the Academic Council would involve a risk of neutralizing the board's role. 3 / In the initial stages, it appeared safer to let the Academic Council evolve toward a position of entrenched powers than to attempt to remove such powers should they prove in actual experience to be inappropriate.

The details of an affiliate-type relationship were presented in a paper which G.E. Flower wrote on the subject.

In effect this means that a person appointed in the rank of Assistant Professor or higher in the Institute," ... being engaged in research and in the instruction of students registered in the School of Graduate Studies ... "would be recommended to the Graduate School by the Head of the Department for listing as a member of that Graduate Department. In a sense this might be regarded as a cross-appointment, if you wish, to the School of Graduate Studies. The Department is represented on the Council of the School of Graduate Studies – which is itself subject to the Senate of the University. It is the prerogative of the President of the University, with advice, to appoint the Head of Department. The Dean and Council of the School exercise detailed supervision over the Department of Educational Theory, apart from school-wide regulations and policy, through an annually-appointed M.Ed.-Ed.D. Committee consisting normally of four members of the Department of Educational Theory, plus three members of other graduate departments.[5]

Flower felt that the main interest of the dean of the School of Graduate Studies and the president of the university was to ensure the highest possible level of scholarly work in every graduate department. The proposed concentration of extensive resources, with more specialized staff, more and better research facilities, and more funds to support promising full-time students should have appealed to them. Flower indicated a series of steps that had to be taken to work out a specific arrangement.

There was never any serious support in the small planning group for the idea that graduate studies in education should be a monopoly of the new institute. It was recognized that other Ontario universities would be interested in sharing such a development. There would be substantial local or regional needs to be met and it would be difficult to attract appropriate scholarly staff to a basic program of teacher preparation in the absence of opportunities for graduate study and research. There was also some slight, although at that stage by no means adequate, recognition of the possibility that the number of candidates for graduate study in education might increase so rapidly as to threaten to overwhelm any single institution.

Despite this appraisal of the over-all situation, there was a strong feeling that, for the immediate future, at least, there should be a concentration of resources in the proposed institute. Flower presented the case for this policy in a working paper dated March 2.[6] 1 / Graduate study and research were complementary activities, each reinforcing the other. The best prospect for an outstanding graduate program was that it should be closely associated with the extensive research resources to be concentrated in the institute. 2 / With the rapid expansion of knowledge in all fields, there was an increasing need for specialists among the graduate teaching as well as the research staff. Only a very large institution could hope to assemble such a group of specialists. 3 / The institute would have a concentration of resources of materials and date-processing facilities that would be just as much needed for graduate study as for institutional or staff-initiated research. These could not be made available in a series of centres at economical cost. 4 / A large graduate studies program would make available many part-time research assistants who could make an important contribution to the institutional and service programs. The students would benefit from the resulting financial support and experience. 5 / Only a large organization with extensive graduate resources could be expected to attract the highest quality of academic staff and the most promising graduate students. 6 / Concentration of resources would represent the most economical use of public funds.

A crucial meeting was held in the minister's office on March 16, 1965, attended by Bissell and Sirluck, representing the university, and Jackson, Morgan, Flower, and the writer, representing the interests of the proposed institute. The arrangements agreed upon were essentially those already described. In terms of immediate action, Davis was to proceed with legislative arrangements for the establishment of the institute, Bissell was to seek an agreement on the part of the Board of Governors of the university for the proposed affiliation, and Sirluck was to take any necessary steps involving the Department of Educational Theory.

Interim decisions on structure and staffing

As time went on and it began to look as if the institute might be a reality during the current calendar year, the writer became concerned lest decisive action be taken too late to permit the recruitment of the key people whose contribution would be vitally needed. The minister, however, provided a solution to the problem by authorizing an approach to certain selected individuals, with an informal guarantee of their salaries for the first year, regardless of how the plan worked out.

Since recruitment implied the existence of positions, the writer's designation of institute divisions was accepted with only slight revisions in the original proposals. His putative position as Coordinator of Studies (later "Research") also entailed the prerogative of recommending division heads. In the haste to get the institute established, his definition of the functions of the divisions, of the officials, and even of the Board of Governors itself was accepted virtually without change at the board's first meeting in July.

One of the major difficulties in the immediate establishment of the institute was that operating budgets for the intended components had long since been approved. There seemed no feasible means of terminating the independent existence of the Ontario Curriculum Institute until mid-1966 without a serious loss of committed funds. But Jackson devised an ingenious procedure for a kind of intermediate status for the two departments of the Ontario College of Education – graduate studies and the Research Department – that would form the nucleus of the institute. Assuming the passage of the necessary legislation before the end of June, they would continue in the college for the following year until their approved budgets had been spent, but their staffs would also receive appointments to the new institute and carry out their activities under board policies. At the same time, extra funds would be provided for the employment of new staff who would owe exclusive allegiance to the institute. Thus for the 1965–6 year, Jackson was director of both the Department of Educational Research and the Ontario Institute for Studies in Education, and others had comparable dual titles. It became practice among continuing members of the staff of the Ontario College of Education to look upon this arrangement as a legal fiction, and to consider their colleagues as having departed in 1965.

Discussions with interested groups

For much of the 1964–5 academic year, the discussions and negotiations were conducted in relative secrecy. Of course, a number of individuals were informed of the plans on a confidential basis. Many of these were approached by the writer, who felt that a wide spectrum of opinion should be solicited in order to devise the best possible structure. By late winter, garbled versions of what was going on began to appear in the newspapers. It seemed particularly important that matters be brought into the open, not only to correct mistaken impressions, but also to make it possible to consult such influential associations as the teachers' federations. The writer eventually secured authorization to discuss matters with the Secretary-Treasurer of the Ontario Teachers' Federation, Miss Nora Hodgins, who suggested that the teachers would probably welcome the institute idea in principle, at least, but would understandably be rather chagrined if they were not given the opportunity to express their views before the legislation took final form. In April the Board of Governors of the Ontario Teachers' Federation and the Executive of the Ontario Secondary School Teachers' Federation assembled to hear and discuss the plans. Flower, Morgan, and the writer each made a statement about a particular aspect of the proposed institute's functions. The teachers' groups, after expressing some scepticism about the practical implications of the proposals, went on record as supporting the idea. They registered disapproval, however, of the proposal to include members of the faculty on the institute's Board of Governors. To the planning group, this attitude seemed incomprehensible, since they had hoped the idea would appeal to the teachers' desire to see an expansion of responsibility for professional educators.

The developing plans for the institute had involved continuous consultation between Morgan and the Board of Governors of the Ontario Curriculum Institute. A decisive meeting of this board was held on April 9, 1965. The alternatives by that time were 1 / to enter a period of cautious negotiations with the new institute involving an attempt to employ the remaining resources and prestige of the OCI to secure such concessions as its particular purposes and orientation made appear desirable, or 2 / to make an unequivocally favourable decision and hope to exert maximum influence through the strength of the endorsement. After an eloquent appeal by Morgan, supported by others, the latter course of action was chosen. The decisive motion read as follows: "That the government, conduct, management and control of the Ontario Curriculum Institute, and all personal property under the supervision of or provided for the use of said Institute immediately before the 1st day of July, 1966 be transferred as of that date, to the Board of the Ontario Institute for Studies in Education."[7] Certain suggestions were made at the meeting for changes in the institute bill. One of these was that the principle of staff representation on the Board of Governors not be accepted. The matter was debated at length and the adverse vote was carried by a narrow margin.

Consideration of related experience elsewhere

The opinion was not infrequently expressed then and later that it would be better to proceed more slowly and carefully. Such a view did not seem easy to accept at the time. There was keen awareness that the educational system was under the control of a unique minister who was willing to give educational research and development the kind of opportunity to prove their value that they had never experienced anywhere else in the world. While he seemed deeply committed to a number of fundamental initiatives, it was always well to remember the short tenure of office of the average minister. Changes in the economic climate might also wreak disaster on plans for the more radical innovations such as this. It thus seemed essential to seize the opportunity when it was presented, and to push ahead as quickly as possible. Problems entailed by the rapid absorption of staff and the fuzziness of some of the structural and administrative details might be dealt with later.

The practice developed at an early stage of emphasizing the unusual nature of the institute concept. There was said to be nothing else like it in the world. In a sense this was true. But emphasis on the point tended to obscure certain warnings from experience elsewhere that might have been taken to heart to the institute's advantage. One of these was reiterated in a review of the status of educational research in Canada in 1964 by F.G. Robinson, then director of the Canadian Council for Research in Education.[8] In this report, Robinson observed, as many others had done before, that research studies conducted by members of faculties of education in pursuit of their own individual interests tended to be isolated, fragmentary, and non-cumulative in their effect. For this and other reasons, the impact of such efforts on educational practice was slight. The institute planners were aware of the fact that faculty research had such a reputation, but there seemed to be an assumption that the difficulty would be overcome if enough people with enough financial support were turned loose in the field. Presumably their areas of interest would amount to such complete coverage that a forced coalescence of the fragments would result.

A second warning might have been derived from more careful attention to contemporary developments in the United States. Large amounts of money were being made available in the early years of the Johnson administration for the improvement of various aspects of education. Two types of agencies were receiving a substantial amount of support for research and development: the regional laboratories and the research and development centres. Both attempted to combine and co-ordinate the efforts of public and voluntary agencies for the improvement of educational practice. As an example, the Center for Research and Development in Education established at Harvard University in 1964 had the support of the Massachusetts Department of Education; the public school systems of Boston, Concord, Lexington, and Newton; the New England School Development Council, with 170 member school systems throughout a six-state area; the New England Education Data Systems, a co-operative program of research and service in educational data processing; Educational Services Incorporated, an organization devoted to the development and nationwide application of improved curriculum materials; the National Association of Independent Schools; WGBH-TV, Boston's educational television station; and the Harvard-MIT Joint Center for Urban Studies.[9] The research and development centres tended to direct part of their efforts toward fundamental research on such themes as the individual, social, and cultural factors that influence learning. They were also concerned with the development of teaching methods, curriculum materials, and programs of teacher preparation in order to speed the application of research findings to classroom practice. The regional laboratories placed a stronger emphasis on developmental work.

An observer of these developments would have noticed, and should have pondered carefully, two outstanding features: 1 / each agency selected certain areas of education in which to concentrate its effort, and 2 / every funding agency required evidence of sound planning for specific projects, and an accounting for money spent. The idea that large sums should be made available to a professional group to use according to their own best judgment does not seem to have been thought a practical possibility. American experience with faculty research contributions was apparently similar to that noted in Canada and ruled out any serious consideration of the notion that if enough funds were pumped into an agency organized essentially as a faculty, educational progress would inevitably result.

The strings attached to supported activities by the funding agency were sometimes rightly regarded as more of a harassing device than anything else. There were examples of professional extracters of grants, who specialized in identifying the prejudices of those who distributed the funds. Also, in many cases, sound ideas had to be twisted and distorted in order to make them eligible for assistance. But if American devices for trying to ensure that money was productively spent were regarded as mere foibles, sufficient Canadian examples might have been identified to make the point. There are good reasons why a society does not allow individuals or special groups the privilege of spending large amounts of public funds without substantial restrictions from outside.

The Ontario Institute for Studies in Education Act

As finally passed on June 22, 1965, in the dying days of the Legislative session, the act identified the institute as a college. This title ensured that the institute would be exempt from federal taxation as well as from taxation for provincial, municipal, or school purposes. The institute would have maximum attraction for competent staff and promising students if its status as an institution for higher education were made clear. The term "college" would also enable the institute to qualify for federal grants for students.

The "objects" of the institute were defined as follows: "(a) to study matters and problems relating to or affecting education, and to disseminate the results of and assist in the implementation of the findings of educational studies; (b) to establish and conduct courses leading to certificates of standing and graduate degrees in education." The writer's notes on the act explain that the objects were defined in a comprehensive and general way so as to cover study and investigation of all educational areas including curriculum. While implementation was mainly the responsibility of the Department of Education and the school boards, the institute might assist these agencies by creating greater receptivity to change and by communicating and publishing its findings. It was indicated that the instructional activities of the institute would include short courses, seminars, and other forms of in-service training, as well as formal courses leading to certificates of standing and graduate degrees. They would not, however, include initial teacher preparation.

The Board of Governors was to include the director *ex officio* and the following: 1 / representatives of the teacher-training institutions of Ontario; 2 / representatives of the University of Toronto, nominated by the president; 3 / representatives of the provincially assisted universities of Ontario, nominated by the Committee of Presidents of Provincially Assisted Universities of Ontario; 4 / representatives of the Department of Education; 5 / representatives of the Ontario Teachers' Federation, nominated by its Board of Governors; 6 / representatives of the Ontario School Trustees' Council, nominated by its council; 7 / representatives of provincial associations of directors of education, school superintendents, and inspectors, nominated by the associations; 8 / "persons who are residents of Ontario" (a category to be filled by distinguished educators or other citizens who would not be likely to be nominated, or who would be ineligible for nomination, by any association); and 9 / members of the administrative and instructional staff of the institute, in addition to the director. The relevant regulations, initially drafted by the writer, specified the number of representatives in each category. The explanatory note refers to the senatorial functions to be performed by the board, such as "business arrangements, academic matters, studies and projects."

Perhaps the most significant of the board's powers were to "prescribe ... the powers and duties of the academic council"; to "appoint, promote, transfer or remove such members of the administrative staff, instructional staff and maintenance staff as are necessary for the proper conduct of the affairs of the Institute, and fix their salaries or remuneration and increments and define their duties, qualifications and tenure of office or employment"; and to "appoint a Director, who in the first instance shall be a person recommended by the Minister, and other officers and prescribe their powers and duties and fix their salaries or remuneration and tenure of office or employment." These powers were obviously intended to be very comprehensive. The arrangement for the minister to nominate the first director was intended to ensure Jackson's appointment. The explanatory notes indicate that the director should also be secretary-treasurer of the board so that he could co-ordinate administrative services.

Certain powers that might be exercised with the minister's approval related to the process of implementing the institute's objectives. One of these was to "make arrangements for the use by the institute of any publicly-supported educational institution for demonstration or experimental purposes or for the services of one or more teachers in such educational institution in the conduct of any demonstration or experiment or other research study." The exercise of this power would in actual fact have to have the approval of the deputy minister or some other appropriate official and would thus depend on harmonious relations with the department. A further power, the exercise of which was to be formally subject to the minister's approval, was to "enter into agreements with any association or organization having objects similar to those of the Institute providing for the joint operation of research programmes ..." It was considered likely that, in the period up to July 1, 1966, it would be desirable to operate some research programs jointly with the Ontario Curriculum Institute. Other organizations with which there might be co-operation were the Ontario Educational Research Council, the Metropolitan Toronto Educational Research Council, and the Canadian Council for Research in Education. Another significant power in the same category was to "enter into agreements of affiliation with one or more universities relating to the establishment and conduct of programmes leading to degrees in education." The explanatory notes indicate that, in addition to affiliation with the University of Toronto for degree-granting purposes, it would be possible to extend graduate instructional services by recognizing suitable instructors and courses at universities and colleges of education in various parts of the province. Thus opportunities for graduate work would be provided outside Toronto without the necessity of trying to offer complete programs in a number of centres.

The explanatory notes about the Academic Council read as follows: "The Academic Council will be a device to ensure some cohesion and unity of purpose among academic staff members. It will enable the director to present broad policy matters for general discussion and to make reports to the staff. It will provide the staff with an opportunity to discuss matters relating to their general welfare, their conditions of service, and the nature of their work. It will not, however, have powers comparable to those of a university senate." It was obviously seen as more akin to the type of faculty council described in the Duff-Berdahl report than to any of the regular organs of university government.

THE INSTITUTE IN OPERATION IN ITS EARLY STAGES

Initial issues

The challenges faced by the Institute when it began operations in July 1965 were indeed formidable. The situation bore no resemblance to the establishment of a new university, school, or other institution with numerous successfully functioning models. No one had shown that, let alone how, such disparate functions as graduate studies, fundamental research, "practical" research, development, and educational service could be balanced and enabled to work harmoniously in a single organization. It was ominous, furthermore, that there was disturbingly little evidence that anyone realized how disparate, or even antagonistic, such functions really were. In most countries, educational research ordinarily demonstrates two entirely different types of orientation and structure. On the one hand, those who are devoted to the solution of practical problems arising out of the processes of instruction or administration are usually found in government organizations. Their academic qualifications are normally limited, their tasks to a large extent prescribed, and their liberty to speak and publish freely to some degree circumscribed. They often combine their research activities with administrative responsibilities. In some countries, their contribution is extremely important, providing the basis for a continuous adaptation of the administrative structure to changing conditions. On the other hand, there are researchers whose role is to contribute to knowledge. They are ordinarily located in universities and, like researchers in other fields, they attempt to achieve the highest academic qualifications. They place great value on scholarly writing, which frequently deals with the construction or modification of abstract theories. Immediate applications of their findings are not expected. In a sense they are regarded as contributors to the world fund of knowledge, which may or may not contribute to educational practice in a subsequent generation. The writer has observed manifestations of this dichotomy in countries as far apart as Australia, Japan, and Poland and apparently there has been no serious contemplation of the possibility of reconciling them.

If there are such fundamental differences in types of research, there are also serious problems in reconciling research and development. These concepts have so often been referred to in the same breath that they have mistakenly been treated almost as different aspects of the same thing. Development, as indicated in chapter 10, actually refers to the production, modification, or adaptation of a device, a process, or a technique in order to fit it for immediate application. Although it should ideally be harmonized with conclusions supported by research, there is no necessary relationship between the two. Furthermore, as such American authorities as Egon Guba have pointed out, a successful worker in development needs qualities that differ from those of the ideal researcher. Derek Morrell, Joint Secretary of the Schools Council in England, did not make himself particularly popular with institute officials during his visit to Canada in the summer of 1965 when he expressed the opinion that research and development should be kept separate. This view might have been taken as a constructive warning that the most extraordinary and perceptive efforts would be needed to combine them successfully.

The essence of the challenge was to provide not only a structure but also a mode of operations that would ensure that appropriate value systems, interests, academic and financial rewards, and conditions needed for successful effort would exist for the different groups, and that none would become predominant. The chief threat came from the group with the orientation toward basic or fundamental research. In the institute as it was established, they had all the advantages of university traditions, both real and mythical, to draw upon. Of the group of planners, Morgan, in the writer's opinion, appraised this situation most realistically. Unfortunately, however, ill-health and disillusionment, mingled in some indefinable combination, led him to retire from his position as director of the Ontario Curriculum Institute in the early fall of 1966.

There are some knowledgeable and intelligent people who believe firmly in the "think-tank" concept. In its extreme form, this idea calls for an organization primarily devoted to the individual participant's freedom to think and express himself without restraint. If he observes practices of which he does not approve, he must be allowed or even encouraged to criticize them in whatever manner he considers appropriate. According to this point of view, educational systems can usually benefit from a certain amount of shaking up. Officials, administrators, and teachers are subject to chronic lethargy and traditionalism and need to be confronted with the inadequacies and inconsistencies in their ordinary activities. The process may be painful, but constructive results will finally emerge. Strong proponents of this view abhor authoritarian structures and anything that suggests the exercise of formal power. Since structure is needed, however, they are determined to provide it by complete internal "democracy." Because some kind of leaders are necessary, if for no other reason than to provide buildings, facilities, and supplies, they must be selected by and remain under the constant control of the group. They must at all costs be kept from developing any ideas of grandeur, preferably by being prevented from serving for more than a brief period in office. As far as outsiders are concerned, they are best kept at a distance, although self-protection may demand lip service to the idea of co-operation with practising educators.

Another identifiable view, essentially a variation of the extreme think-tank position, is similar in that it maintains that high quality research can result only where the researcher is at complete liberty to select his own areas of research and to carry them out in his own way. Structure and administration must be designed to facilitate this process in every possible manner. The proponents of this position differ from those just described in that they perceive no particular incentive to act as social irritants. They accept an obligation to pursue their interests and proclaim their findings with a sensitive recognition of social forms. Such an attitude is typical in the traditional university disciplines, and in many areas it seems entirely justified, although there are complaints that it does not provide for a thoroughly co-ordinated attack on a problem too large to be solved by a single inspired genius. Partly for this reason, many research enterprises, particularly in the United States, have grown up outside universities.

If the researcher is to fulfil his role as a potential contributor to the improvement of the educational process, it would seem that he must accept limitations on his choice of topic. Given agreement on that proposition, the question becomes one of whether he can be counted upon to impose limitations upon himself through his own appraisal of the needs of education, or whether he should be at least to some degree subjected to the requirements of the educational community as expressed by its recognized leaders.

The writer's views about a desirable structure have already been presented in his appraisal of the Department of Educational Research in chapter 11, and need not be repeated here. It is sufficient to observe that they represent a compromise between the individually determined and the community-prescribed programs, with individuals enabled to climb a ladder of merit from a predominance of the latter to a predominance of the former. Provided that what has been described as the social-irritant aspect of the think-tank position can be prevented from nulifying the other types of contributions, some element of it should be incorporated. What happened in the Ontario Institute for Studies in Education, almost from the earliest days, was an evolution into a position where the individually selected program became supreme, and where inadequate room was left for a response to community-defined needs.

Acceptance of the structure by the Board of Governors

The early meetings of the Board of Governors were crucial. To some extent, it had to accept a *fait accompli.* Several individuals had been recruited from outside to act as division (later "department") heads (later "chairmen"), and some members of the Department of Educational Research had agreed to act in a similar capacity. Thus it would have been difficult for the board to challenge either the divisional structure or the nominees to key positions. Also, the institute came into being with a full-blown program of graduate studies and a large roster of research activities inherited from the Department of Educational Research. The list of by-laws drawn up by the writer and Derek Horne, who was to be recommended as Comptroller and Assistant Secretary-Treasurer of the board, had received the prior approval of Jackson and Flower. But it was so lengthy, and the meeting time so limited, that the board accepted it without the minute examination that it justified. An interim chairman served until the appointment of the distinguished scholar and jurist, Bora Laskin, near the end of 1965.

The board's mode of operations

Of the greatest significance was the pattern of board activities established at early meetings. Utmost deference was paid to the board's legal right to govern the institute in that all kinds of business arrangements and decisions were submitted for its approval. It was customarily kept busy with such details until well into an afternoon session when various members were eager to leave. At the same time, there was no effort made to establish any committee of the board with a primary responsibility for graduate studies, research, or development programs. A request by members of the teachers' organizations in particular that there be a discussion on "policy," by which they meant the institute's activities, was shelved indefinitely under pressure of ostensibly more urgent business. On certain occasions, a group of board members succeeded in securing an explanation for some aspect of the program, but a demand for such an explanation had negative and critical overtones. Had the explanation not been found acceptable, there was no realistic way in which the dissatisfied members could have ensured that an alternative would have been genuinely accepted and sincerely carried out. There was no vehicle by which the board could exert initiative in defining the specific objectives to be pursued. It became a caretaker, and to some extent a buffer, but not an active interpreter of the needs and desires of the educational community.

The first year's progress

All the academic staff except the director and the coordinators were concentrated in what were then called the studies divisions. Initially these consisted of Educational Administration, Curriculum Research and Instructional Techniques (later simply "Curriculum"), Field Services, Educational Foundations (later History and Philosophy of Education), Information and Data Systems (later Computer Applications), Measurement and Evaluation, Educational Planning, and Educational Psychology. Initial plans included a Division of Adult Education, but its actual establishment was delayed a year so that the recruitment of a suitable head could be undertaken at leisure. The Department of Applied Psychology, at first under the direction of F.G. Robinson, former Director of the Canadian Council for Research in Education, immediately became the largest. Its activities involved research and graduate offerings, not only in the nature of the learning process, but in special education and guidance as well. A major thrust was planned also in educational administration under the direction of J.H.M. Andrews. The development of a program in curriculum awaited the arrival of the world-renowned scholar, Marion Jenkinson, from the University of Alberta.

Co-ordination of the activities of the studies divisions was managed at weekly meetings presided over by the writer in his capacity of Coordinator of Studies. This group was at the time quite informal, although in 1966–7 it was given specific structure and status as the Administrative Council. During the first year, when there were many problems of procedure arising out of the novel and rapid growth of the organization, this group inevitably got into the habit of discussing policy issues and reporting the results of its deliberations to the director. Matters considered of major importance were also customarily passed on to the Academic Council through its chairman.

During the fall of 1965 a great deal of attention was devoted to a fundamental restructuring of the program of graduate studies. Since the regular teaching staff had approximately doubled as compared with the previous year, it became possible to offer a considerable number of new courses. Many of the newcomers had the benefit of experience elsewhere, and were able to contribute valuable new ideas. One of the most important decisions was to discontinue the recommendation of candidates for the Ed D degree. It had become obvious that the requirement of a single year of attendance was no longer adequate and, since there appeared to be no other essential factor to distinguish between the Ed D and the Ph D, the latter became the sole degree actually offered at that level. The M Ed became, under ordinary circumstances, a terminal degree, with emphasis on studies presumed to be of practical value to educational practitioners, and the MA in Education became the usual route to doctoral studies.

The rather restricted quarters occupied by the Department of Educational Research at 344 Bloor Street West, with some additions, constituted the headquarters of the institute for its first year. In December, the writer led his colleagues on a search which culminated in the rental of most of the fourteen-storey building then under construction at 102 Bloor Street West. This structure was to serve for the major part of the institute's activities until a permanent new building was erected. The growth of the institute was, however, so rapid that additional quarters soon had to be found.

As previously mentioned, the year saw the departure of Morgan from the directorship of the Ontario Curriculum Institute, although he subsequently continued to serve as a member of the Board of Governors of the new institute. In his place K.F. Prueter, Superintendent of Public Schools in Etobicoke, was appointed to terminate the affairs of the Ontario Curriculum Institute. He subsequently served as Coordinator of Curriculum Projects and Special Services, then in the same position under the designation "Coordinator of Development" until it was abolished in 1969 when he became Coordinator of Field Development.

Arrangements for dealing with schools

The accession of the Ontario Curriculum Institute posed serious questions about procedures for dealing with schools. As far as OISE was concerned, it seemed essential to exert some kind of control over these contacts. Major problems could be expected from the sheer volume of research and development activities and from the involvement of many newcomers to the system. A meeting was held at the Department of Education in 1966 which included the Coordinator of Curriculum Projects and Special Services and the writer as representatives of the institute. The result was an agreement that projects involving the schools would first receive the approval of the Director of the Program Branch. They would not, however, be subject to unilateral amendment by the department. An attempt to make this arrangement work was not successful, mainly because there was too much delay in securing approval.

In December 1966 a less onerous arrangement was announced by the department. The memorandum read in part as follows.

> For the information of school officials and boards, requests by the Ontario Institute for Studies in Education to undertake research projects in a school will be made directly to the local school board for its decision. It is felt that the principal and board concerned will wish to consider approval of such projects individually in the light of their present program and plans already made for future developments or pilot studies.
>
> With respect to schools outside municipal areas in the province, the Institute personnel may wish to approach the area superintendent, or inspector concerned, for advice before making contact with the school officials.[10]

For the institute, that did not of course end the problem. School officials were understandably reluctant to have pupils and teachers involved in research projects with remote and elusive goals, lacking demonstrable immediate benefits. In the long run, their continued participation in such studies could be expected only if they were offered some compensatory services. It was especially important that requests for assistance be made with the utmost tact and diplomacy. These requests had also to be distributed equitably. There was some danger that particularly agreeable or favourably disposed officials and school boards would be so inundated with appeals for experimental classrooms and subjects that their initial friendliness would turn to hostility.

For 1966–7 the Coordinator of Curriculum Projects and Special Services agreed to be responsible for making initial approaches to school boards or for authorizing persons whom he felt were suitably qualified to make their own contacts. Tentative efforts were made to set up suitable machinery to co-ordinate this function. The effort was not, however, successful, in part because there was not sufficient control over individual members of the institute to prevent them from ignoring official procedures. There were examples of irritation and ill-feeling caused by inept and insensitive actions. One distinguished faculty member undertook to tell officials of a major school board that the institute had the right to insist on their participation in one of his studies; when he discovered his error, he expressed considerable embarrassment.

DEVELOPMENT OF THE POWER AND INFLUENCE OF THE ACADEMIC COUNCIL

As defined in the by-laws of the board, the responsibilities of the Academic Council were as follows:

(a) to suggest to the Director such administrative policies as will facilitate the most effective attainment of the objectives of the Institute;
(b) to suggest to the Director structural or organizational changes in the Institute;
(c) to develop a pattern of professional responsibilities and obligations for academic staff members.
(d) to suggest to the Director measures relating to the welfare of academic staff members.

In drafting this by-law for the board's consideration, the author intended that every matter having anything to do with the structure, role, or activities of the institute should be subject to the full and free discussion of the professional staff members. There was no suggestion, however, that the council should be exclusively entitled, among institute organs, to deal with policy matters.

Toward the end of the 1965–6 academic year, pressures began to develop to give the council a dominant position, in reality if not in form. In 1967 one of the most active members of the council declared that he believed that a very restricted role for that body had been a faulty concept from the beginning and should be corrected. A 1969 committee report refers to the following assumption: "That *the academic staff or faculty should be ensured a determining role in the policy-making process at all levels in the Institute.* This is hardly a new assumption. It is firmly institutionalized in the policy recommending role of the Academic Council at the central level."[11]

A major aspect of the drive for Academic Council domination naturally involved a weakening of the informal group of coordinators and division heads, which had no better name at the beginning than the "Studies Group," although it was later designated the "Administrative Council." It was accused of frustrating the policy recommendations of the Academic Council by discussing the same matters and offering conflicting advice to the director. In early 1967 there was lengthy discussion of a recommendation that the work of the Administrative Council be limited to day-to-day administration, to the co-ordination of administrative activity, and to the devising of administrative procedures for the implementation of policy recommendations approved by the Board of Governors. The proposal also enjoined the Administrative Council to restrict its recommendations to the director to routine administrative matters. It would specifically not be empowered to re-examine policy recommendations which had already been made by the Academic Council and were pending approval by the Board of Governors. To some participants in the discussion, there was something rather absurd in the idea that the director's access to advice from any source he chose should be formally circumscribed. Perhaps for this reason, the matter was not put to a formal vote. But the strong support the recommendation received from many council members had a profoundly restraining effect on future initiatives by the Administrative Council. The latter agreed in June 1967 to distribute the minutes of its meetings to members of the Executive Committee of the Academic Council. It also recommended that a provision be made whereby the Executive Committee would have an opportunity to question or comment on items in the minutes through the director or his representative.

In the fall of 1968, a committee of the Academic Council set up to investigate certain questions about recruitment decisions in departments proposed a reorganization of the Administrative Council. It was reported that the new Administrative Council recognized the Academic Council as the only legitimate channel through which policy recommendations could reach the director, and that the chairman of the Academic Council could decide whether a recommendation was major or not. Probably the real significance of this development was in its curtailment of the director's powers. There appears to be no evidence, however, that he saw it that way, or at least that he made any effective protest.

Status of departmental chairmen and other administrators

In accordance with patterns of university government developing elsewhere at the time, a very significant effort was made to change the status of what became known as departmental chairmen. The underlying concept was that a chairman should be responsible for co-ordinating and focusing the efforts of his department, for performing essential administrative routines, and for ensuring the availability of necessary services. An essential requirement for his selection should be the approval of his colleagues in his own department. In order that he could maintain his scholarly status, his term of office should be limited. This concept was reinforced by appeals to university tradition, where departments are primarily organized to retain conditions necessary for freedom to teach, to pursue independent scholarly research, and to speak and write without fear of restraint within limits prescribed by law. Where these are the exclusive or paramount objectives, the case for such an arrangement seems excellent. But Academic Council members appeared unwilling to concede that the institute's declared responsibility for conducting large-scale programs of research and development, and for making an organized response to the needs of the educational community, called for anything different.

As mentioned earlier, the writer, as Coordinator of Studies (later "Research") had had the prerogative of nominating department heads. While he would have supported a formalization of the advisory procedures used in discharging this responsibility, his resignation from this position, as well as from the assistant directorship, in late October 1966 prepared the way for drastic changes. Earlier that month the council went on record as favouring the principle that the appointment of department heads was in part a matter of faculty concern and responsibility and that, when the headship of a department became vacant, representation on the search committee for a new head should be given to faculty members of that department, as well as to the heads of the related departments. Similarly, the appointment of the director and the coordinators was a concern and responsibility of the Academic Council, and when a vacancy occurred in these positions, the council should have elected representatives on the committee charged with the recruitment and selection of the person recommended to fill the vacancy. Apparently no one thought of including the assistant directorship in this resolution, thus leaving the director a legalistic loophole to recommend a candidate for that position in the summer of 1968 without formal consultation.

There was some hesitation in the Executive Committee of the Board of Governors over the proposed limitation in the term of office for department heads. The director was, however, able to persuade it and the board to agree in the fall of 1967 to an arrangement that defined the normal term of office of heads (now called chairmen) as four years. At least eight months before the end of a departmental chairman's term, a review committee would make a recommendation to the director as to reappointment or otherwise. Such a committee would be appointed on an *ad hoc* basis and would include at least two members of the department concerned. The director's arrangement did not follow the Academic Council's wishes in limiting a departmental chairman's tenure of office to two terms. Neither did it include initial appointees for whom no time limits had been specified. These latter were, however, to be subject to persuasion to accept the new arrangement. Their ranks were diminishing rather quickly by resignations in any case.

These developments had the salutary effect of giving department members an effective means of combatting arbitrary or unfair treatment on the part of an administrative superior. They also provided a device for coping with administrative incompetence. But they dealt a serious blow at any prospect of having commitments accepted by the top levels of the administration carried out effectively unless they were in accord with the wishes of rank-and-file staff members. The department chairmen who desired reappointment could hardly afford to antagonize the latter.

A set of policy guidelines for decision-making in academic departments was approved by the Academic Council in November 1969. The stated purpose of these guidelines was to ensure that both the interests of the institute and the rights and well-being of its members were safeguarded in the operating procedures of the departments. There were two basic assumptions: 1 / that all categories of staff and students were full members of the institute, "having the right to participate and to exercise leadership in the decision-making processes affecting the objectives, policies, staff and programs of their department and of the Institute as a whole," and 2 / that the chairmen should be in a position to exert strong leadership, influencing both their own departments and the institute as a whole. While responsibility was still to be delegated from the top down, it was to be balanced by the flow of influence from the bottom up. The guidelines provided a mechanism for the resolution of conflicts.

The policy of limiting the terms of office for administrative officers received further support at a meeting of the Academic Council on February 11, 1970. At that time, support for the four-year limit for department chairman, with the possibility of renewal, was reaffirmed. At the same meeting, the council voted that the terms of office of the director, the assistant director, and the coordinators be five years, with the possibility of renewal, and that the terms of office of the assistant coordinators and the Academic Services Officer be governed by the policy applying to departmental chairmen.

Salary recommendations

In mid-1966 the council turned its attention toward the question of salary recommendations and proposed that the director appoint a committee of four each year from among the members of the Academic Council to receive recommendations from the division (department) heads with respect to salary increases for members of the respective divisions. Division heads would present their recommendations in person, though otherwise membership on the committee was to be secret. No more than two members of the committee were to be persons with administrative responsibility. After hearing from all division heads, the committee would prepare a comprehensive recommendation for the administrators responsible for forwarding salary recommendations to the board. This motion was carried and subsequently put into force.

Review of appointments, promotions, and tenure

An Academic Council committee was set up to establish criteria for appointment and promotion to the various academic ranks. In May 1967 the director agreed to appoint a committee of five members, no more than two of whom might be members of the Administrative Council or belong to one department, to receive and review recommendations for appointments and promotions to professorial ranks from the chairmen of departments and the coordinators.

The question of a formal tenure arrangement was inevitably raised. In the 1966–7 academic year a number of plans in operation or under discussion in various universities were studied, and a series of proposals formulated. The version considered in early 1967 included extremely complex provisions for the protection of a tenured faculty member under threat of dismissal. In practical terms, they seemed to make the dismissal of such a member virtually impossible should he choose to resort to every weapon at his command. A serious disagreement with the board developed, however, over recognized reasons for dismissal. The majority of the council seemed determined that neither "gross misconduct" nor any comparable expression should be included, for fear it would be used to restrict freedom of expression. Some members were not even persuaded that dismissal should be countenanced for a person imprisoned after conviction for criminal offence, unless a case could be made under the "neglect of duty" clause. The board maintained its point of view, and the proposed tenure agreement was accordingly long delayed.

Standing committees

In May 1967 the Academic Council arranged to establish six standing committees in the following areas: institute research, institute development projects, graduate programs, staff development, staff welfare, and student affairs. Their broad duties, within the scope established by the act and the by-laws of the board were 1 / to review general policy and its implementation within each area of concern; 2 / to study and report to the Academic Council on any matter referred to them by the council or its executive; and 3 / to recommend to the Academic Council new policies or the revision of existing policies that came within their proper area of concern.

In the 1968–9 academic year, the Student Affairs Committee was dropped. Even though it had included student representatives, it seemed to suggest an excessively paternalistic attitude. Instead, the practice was adopted of giving students more direct representation on the other standing committees and an opportunity to participate in the deliberations of the Academic Council itself. It was also concluded that the Standing Committee on Staff Welfare and Development was redundant. The concerns of this committee seemed to fall clearly within the jurisdiction of the Association of the Teaching Staff. On the other hand, it was observed that certain services and facilities did not come within the purview of any Academic Council standing committee. With the changes the five standing committees for 1969–70 dealt respectively with institute research, institute developmental projects, graduate programs, the library, and services and facilities.

In June 1967 the director indicated that he had hoped that the Academic Council would have indicated long before that stage the basic principles underlying the growth and development of the institute. This appeal for guidance in determining what directions the institute should take produced a motion in September of that year establishing a special committee of the chairmen of the standing committees of the council. Their responsibilities were to undertake a study of policy affecting the institute's future work in research, development, and graduate teaching, its rate of growth, optimal size, relationship with other educational institutions in Ontario, and the co-ordination between departments in the main areas of the institute's work.

Assumption of administrative functions

The growing tendency for the council to move into areas of administrative responsibility was shown by a motion that was carried with one dissenter in December 1967 to replace the *Ontario Journal of Educational Research* by a new publication. The motion included a clause to the effect that the Academic Council recommended the election of a publication editor from among the existing staff of the institute. Another clause provided that the council would elect four faculty members to be associate editors of the proposed journal. Still another provided that the council would appoint a search committee immediately from among its members to find a suitable person to serve as publications editor.

A further move into what are normally considered administrative responsibilities involved budgetary matters. A motion was carried at a meeting in October 1967 expressing the view that internal decisions regarding the institute budget were primarily policy-making matters lying within the purview of the council. This action was followed up by arrangements for council involvement in the extremely complex procedure evolved between 1967 and 1969 for producing budgetary estimates.

Desire for greater representation on the board

There were several discussions from 1967 on revolving around the possibility of increasing staff representation on the Board of Governors. While the council overwhelmingly supported the idea, the board was unenthusiastic, and the request failed to produce affirmative results. Coupled with this issue was that of a policy-making rather than a policy-recommending role for the council. During one discussion, a perceptive member observed that in actual fact the council was determining policy and that nothing would be gained, and something might be lost, if the demand for formal powers were pressed too hard. The council's real position was demonstrated by the retiring chairman's comment in December 1967 to the effect that the director had, without exception, presented the council's recommendations to the board or its several committees, and that he had, almost without exception, fully endorsed those recommendations. The director himself pointed out to the council that all questions such as the reorganization of the development function and the establishment of an educational clinic and a Department of Sociology had been referred to the council, and that he had without exception accepted its advice. With the board in little position to reject the director's recommendations, except on what it regarded as major questions of principle, such as the "gross immorality" issue in tenure, or that of additional faculty representation, there indeed seemed to be little to be gained by any structural or legal change.

The criteria for tenure and promotion specified that participation in developmental work, graduate instruction, and other institute functions were to be given full credit. There is no doubt that there was a desire to balance recognition for different kinds of contributions, but the academic hierarchy of values nevertheless remained. An individual with the capacity to win a reputation by scholarly writing knows that, by so doing, he can establish solid credentials that are relatively beyond the personal biases of his immediate colleagues. They have a kind of international currency. It is hardly realistic to expect a person to reject the opportunity of leaving a permanent record of his contributions in scholarly journals in favour of a testimony from his fellows that he has worked conscientiously on an OISE team project. Clearly, equality of incentives means adding something very substantial, probably of a financial nature, to the latter type of activity.

Orientation of the council

The significance of Academic Council domination can be understood only in the light of its composition and orientation. During the first year of the institute's existence, it consisted of all those at the level of assistant professor or higher. With the addition of the Ontario Curriculum Institute structure, provision was made for membership for project directors and others concerned with development, whose status was equated with that of professorial ranks. But those in this category were never numerous, and the tone and orientation of the council remained highly academic. Although good field work could be and was done by conscientious individuals concerned with the improvement of educational practice, neither the atmosphere nor the predominant value system encouraged it.

A second significant characteristic of the council was its highly internationalist and cosmopolitan tone. Ontario's long neglect of higher studies in education had made it inevitable that rapid progress could be made only by drawing upon the trained human resources of other provinces and countries. But the proportion of those with little or no Ontario background or experience became so large that the institute became a self-contained society looking outward on the international arena and inward upon itself rather than around it toward the provincial educational community. A faculty member could function quite successfully without concerning himself particularly with provincial and local needs, and so many did just that that the educational community felt little incentive to adopt the institute as an integral part of itself.

A third notable characteristic was that the Academic Council recognized no hierarchy of status or position, but gave every newly admitted member the same voting and office-holding privileges as the most outstanding world scholar. In this respect, the council was entirely unlike the university senate recommended by the Duff-Berdahl report, where status beyond initial qualifications had to be earned. When a Research Review Board and later a Development Review Board were established with the responsibility of ensuring the quality of projects requiring substantial institute resources, the provision for a majority of the members of these bodies to be elected by the council meant that the plans of highly qualified and experienced experts could be judged by relative amateurs. This is not what the university community usually means when it refers to subjecting one's scholarly work to the judgment of one's peers.

As a final appraising comment, it may be observed that the Academic Council demonstrated a tremendous facility for generating meetings and committee work. One individual, quite high in the administrative hierarchy, was heard to estimate that this type of work demanded about 80 per cent of his working day. There were several categories of response to the opportunities and demands for committee work: 1 / those with "political" proclivities enjoyed the give-and-take and the struggle for influence; 2 / those who feared threats to their opportunities for promotion or their access to the facilities needed to carry out their work attended and participated for the sake of self-protection; 3 / those who found it impossible to reconcile the demands made by participatory democracy on their time and effort with the carrying out of their normal professional obligations ceased to attend. The attendance at some meetings fell off so badly that absentees were chided for lack of commitment.

EFFECTS OF RAPID GROWTH

In 1965–6 the academic staff of the institute numbered 27; in the two succeeding years it rose successively to 66 and 117. During the same three years, there were successively 117, 198, and 318 non-academic staff.

Subsequent growth was much slower; in 1969–70 there were 145 academic and 485 non-academic staff members. Needless to say, the problems of assimilation were very great. In a sense, it would be inappropriate to talk about existing members assimilating the newcomers; it was as much a case of the newcomers assimilating the institute. Each year, drastic changes were made, and decisions made previously were reversed. Naturally, many procedures were given too little opportunity to demonstrate their value. There were also extraordinary incentives and opportunities for individuals to seek to establish their influence in the group.

GRADUATE STUDENTS

Before the establishment of the institute, the enrolment in the Department of Educational Theory at the Ontario College of Education was large. The overwhelming proportion of students, however, attended only winter session afternoon or summer session courses. In 1964–5 there were 598 summer school students, including 168 in the BEd program and 509 students registered in the regular session, of whom more than 80 per cent were taking only after-hours courses. Since somewhat more than 200 were enrolled in both winter and summer courses, the total, excluding duplicates, was a little more than 900. It was a major objective of the institute to swing the balance in favour of full-time winter students. It is perhaps sufficient to observe here that the popularity of the winter courses developed so rapidly that qualified applicants outran resources, and by 1969–70 many had to be refused admission.

Part of the reason was financial. Abundant provision was made for student assistance from the beginning, so that it was possible to provide funds right through the 1968–9 session for nearly every winter student with reasonable prospects of success. In 1967–8 the 208 students who received assistance constituted more than two-thirds of the student group. Only in 1969–70 did it become necessary to leave numbers of good students unassisted. There was a certain amount of unhappiness in the universities over this special provision. It was defended, however, on the grounds that there was a tremendous backlog of need for the graduates of advanced programs in education and that there was a special advantage in attracting mature and experienced people, who were often supporting families and could not be treated on the same basis as those just completing undergraduate programs.

The special characteristics of the institute made it possible to avoid outright scholarships and bursaries, but instead to combine assistance with the requirement of service. Under University of Toronto regulations, service was restricted, as far as full-time students were concerned, to a maximum of ten hours a week throughout the academic year. While his actual contribution to research programs might be small, the assistant did have the opportunity to participate in them and thus gain a certain kind of experience. The normal amounts involved were established at $3,000 a year for a candidate for a master's degree and $4,500 for a PhD candidate. Until 1969 supplements of $1,500 could be added to attract educators in senior positions. For 1969–70, however, these were granted on the basis of demonstrated financial need.

There were complaints from the Ontario educational community about the relatively small proportion of Ontario students in the winter program. In 1967–8 these constituted less than half of those who received assistance. Since the supplemental awards were made on the basis of financial need alone, there was no particular means of giving preference to students from the province. It would have been at odds with university practice to have lower standards of admission for local applicants, and even that might not have made any substantial change in the number. The only satisfactory solution seemed to be to awaken a feeling of need for the courses among highly qualified Ontario educators.

A Graduate Students' Association was established in the institute, with three major objectives defined in the constitution and by-laws, as amended in May 1969:

i) to promote the best interests of the students of The Ontario Institute for Studies in Education, hereinafter referred to as the Institute, and to allow for discussion and resolution on any issues to which they may wish to address themselves.
ii) to coordinate the activities of students among departments of the Institute.
iii) to represent the Members of the Association to the organizations and governing bodies of the Institute and of the University of Toronto.[12]

Perhaps because of the level of maturity of most of the students and the degree of professional commitment they had already made, they showed little sign of defining or pressing points of view that differed drastically from those of the faculty. They did, however, make a strong case for representation on departmental councils, with little prospect of any concerted opposition.

STRUCTURAL CHANGES, 1966–9

The major structural changes that were made after the first year of operations may be summarized under the following headings: the creation of new departments; the temporary acceptance of responsibility for the Regional Data Centre; the creation of review boards for research and development; the creation of advisory committees in the same areas; the extension of supporting structures; the creation of new offices and administrative positions; the evolution of the development function; and the establishment of extension development centres. Some of these have already been mentioned in connection with the activities of the Academic Council.

New departments

Plans for the establishment of the institute called for the early creation of a Department of Adult Education. However, it did not begin formal operation until the fall of 1966 under the direction of the distinguished Canadian and international educator, J.R. Kidd. Its late beginning constituted a rather long-lasting handicap in view of the rapidity with which the relative sizes of departments began to solidify. The next developments of the same nature were the creation of an Educational Clinic and a Department of Sociology in Education. Initial provisions for sociological studies had been scattered among the Foundations, Educational Planning, and Educational Administration Departments. The new development led to the renaming of the Foundations Department as the Department of History and Philosophy of Education. The Department of Sociology in Education had a relatively academic and theoretical orientation as compared with some of the others. The Educational Clinic ultimately became the Department of Special Education in 1969.

The Regional Data Centre

Discussions leading to the establishment of the Regional Data Centre, and its inclusion in the institute structure, occurred in the first year of the institute's existence. This centre was intended to be a prototype of a series of units designed to co-ordinate the collection and processing of data and to provide data-processing services for various parts of the province. Serving as a kind of pilot project, or a development project in the broad sense, it would co-ordinate activities for the Department of Education, local school boards, and certain post-secondary educational institutions, including, of course, the institute. The idea was dealt a serious blow when most of the boards of education in Metropolitan Toronto opted to go their own way. The centre did not fit well into the institute structure, since it required an organized administrative hierarchy quite unlike the institutional democracy that was developing around it. By 1967 it was obvious that the arrangement was not working. The initial reasons for locating outside the Department of Education, chiefly that the existing civil service salaries were too low to attract qualified personnel, were overcome, and the centre was moved into the department, incorporating certain statistical services being provided there.

Advisory committees and review boards

The desirability of having outside advice and suggestions on the type of research and development activities undertaken by the institute led to the establishment of a Research Advisory Committee and of a Development Advisory Committee. These agencies had wide representation from provincial educational groups. In a sense, they appeared to be designed to perform some of the functions originally envisioned for the Board of

Governors. There was a fundamental difference, however, in that they had no power. As a matter of fact, the amount of influence wielded by the review boards, already referred to, was open to question. A report by the Development Review Board in early 1969 complained about the lack of an efficient way of obtaining information from all departments on their development activities. In some cases, it reported, the department chairmen declined to submit a report, while in other cases the report was incomplete and had little bearing on the actual work in progress. It may be noted that by this time there was a Standing Committee on Institute Research Projects, a Research Review Board, and a Research Advisory Committee, as well as a departmental structure, all concerning themselves with some aspect of research. A similar situation existed with respect to development. It would indeed be surprising if there were not considerable confusion about the function of each body.

Supporting services

By 1969 the list of supporting services and facilities included Computer Services, the Editorial Division, the Division of Finance, the Division of External Services, Physical Facilities, the Conference Office, the Funding Office, and Media Services. In May 1969 the board appointed an Academic Services Officer to co-ordinate the services area and relieve certain other high-level officials of the supervisory activities involved. There were suggestions that the library should be included, but the recommendation of an outside consultant in 1969 was that the librarian should report to the assistant director.

Other changes

The growing size of the institute led to a provision for associate chairmen of departments. The position of assistant director, unfilled since the writer's resignation in 1966, was reactivated with the appointment of J.H.M. Andrews in 1968. It was, however, separated from the position of coordinator of research. Lengthy discussion for much of the 1968–9 academic year led to board approval for the establishment of the office of coordinator of research and development to combine the previously separate offices.

Development

The question of how best to accommodate the development function was difficult to solve from the beginning. In 1966 the institute accepted the responsibility of carrying out the existing program of the Ontario Curriculum Institute which was mainly in the hands of the series of committees that had developed as described earlier. OCI supporters had been quite insistent that there be a "curriculum branch" in the new organization and had opposed the idea that development, as well as research, might be a departmental function. The position of this "branch" was anomalous, however, particularly in relation to the Curriculum Department, which was responsible for research related to curriculum and for a program of graduate studies in the same area. Certain adjustments emerged from discussions in the fall of 1966 whereby field services became directly incorporated into the development program. The attitude of the academic departments toward the separate development structure was not, however, favourable. On the one hand, these departments made it difficult to secure highly qualified staff for development functions by insisting on strict academic qualifications before they would agree to cross-appointments. Without such cross-appointments, the development staff felt, in the prevailing academic value-system, like second-class citizens. On the other hand, academic criteria were applied to developmental studies, and many of them were accordingly judged inferior.

Two fatal blows were dealt in 1967–8 at the attempt to maintain a separate developmental staff and program. One emerged from the deliberations and recommendations of the Academic Council Standing Committee on Institute Development Projects. Its proposed solution hinged on what might seem, to the practising educator, to be rather technical terminology. In essence, it provided that the development of educational innovations up to the point of working prototypes of verified promise would be primarily the function of academic departments. Development of innovations beyond the point of inventions or working prototypes, including refinement, further evaluation, and dissemination, was to be primarily the function of the Office of Development. The primary responsibility of the Department of Curriculum was to engage in innovative curriculum development with related research and instructional activities.

In accordance with the recommendations of the committee, the Office of Development went through another of its regular reorganizations. The separate Division of Field Services disappeared, and two divisions emerged, the first to "coordinate diverse projects into thematic programs," and the second to provide design, evaluation, and dissemination services for the projects. It was at this time that the Development Review Board was established.

The second blow was delivered in the budgetary review, when projects were assigned priorities according to their merits. In the light of the criteria used, most of the development activities were placed low on the list, and a drastic reduction in budget was recommended for the 1969–70 financial year. Whether a successful development program could be mounted in the existing organization, considering the mode of operations generally established, was doubtful. The Development Review Board offered some worthwhile comments on this question.

It is generally agreed that future recruiting practices within the Institute must be tailored to the reality that a larger number of large scale development projects will be required and that a majority of staff members cannot usually expect to pursue their own individual development interests. Academic staff will have to be made fully aware that Institute practices in regard to individual research are not the same as are generally practiced in most universities.[13]

This diagnosis of the problem was unexceptionable, but it did not explain how the recommended recruiting practices were to produce the desired results when there was no real way of ensuring that a professional staff member, once appointed, could be controlled. Exhortations to submerge individual efforts in favour of team work are in themselves not very effective.

Extension Development Centres

It seemed possible that the Extension Development Centres would give developmental activities a new lease on life. The idea for these was first proposed in 1968 partly, no doubt, as a means of narrowing the gulf between the institute and the actual practice of education, and partly in order to persuade the Treasury Board that the organization merited a further investment of funds. The latter hope was not realized. The 1969–70 budget provided only for normal salary increases and the implementation of existing commitments. The centres thus had to be financed from the regular budget. It was suggested initially that they might eventually carry out all three of the main functions of the institute: research, development, and graduate studies. For the time being, however, it would seem likely, and certainly advisable, that they provide practical research and informational services for local school systems and agencies. There was a possibility that, considering their removal from the overpowering academic domination of the central body, they might be able to develop a sense of harmony with local needs. Service is not, of course, development, but service is what seemed to many to be most needed.

The first three centres, established in 1969, were the Western Ontario Centre in London, the Trent Valley Centre in Peterborough, and Niagara Centre in St Catharines. In 1970 two others were added: the North-Western Centre in Thunder Bay and the Mid-Northern Centre in Sudbury. Further additions were planned for subsequent years. Each centre was expected to devise a program to suit the needs of its own area. It might establish an advisory committee on which the chief local educational organizations would be represented. Subcommittees might be formed for specific projects. Close co-operation was expected with the Regional Offices of the Department of Education as well as with local school systems.

STUDIES OF THE INSTITUTE'S STRUCTURE AND FUNCTIONS

The Academic Council showed its concern for the future by arranging in 1968 to establish a Task Force Committee to study and prepare recommendations on the mechanism for reformulating and reassessing the objectives of the institute, and the means whereby its functions might be implemented. It was also to concern itself with the desirability and methods of carrying out a restructuring of the institute in terms of its functional structure, departmental organization, and decision-making processess. Some people had difficulty reconciling the existence of this group with that of a Special Committee of the Board of Governors, the terms of reference of which seemed to encompass much of the same ground, although there were also certain differences. The board's committee was to undertake an assessment and the formulation of principles with regard to the role of the Board of Governors, the role of the Academic Council, and the position of the director in furthering the purposes of the institute. Since the Task Force's functions were within the advisory area, no real conflict was identified, unless, of course, contradictory recommendations should emerge.

Report of the Special Committee of the Board of Governors

The Special Committee of the Board met with the institute Task Force and interviewed a considerable number of institute officials and staff members, representatives of outside organizations, and Clark Kerr, former President of the University of California. It also considered fifty documents on university government in general and on institute affairs in particular.

In the introduction to its report, the committee recognized the existence of a considerable number of problems.

Uncertainty about the purposes, activities, and decision-making processes of the Institute had created an atmosphere of considerable tension. This tension was reflected in widespread and increasing dissatisfaction within and outside the Institute over the degree to which the basic objectives of the Institute were being achieved.

A good deal of this criticism was based on lack of accurate information about what the Institute in fact was doing and on unrealistic expectations for the Institute. Many of the critics had tended to make no distinction between basic and applied research and there had been no clear understanding of what was meant by development.

However, even accepting these qualifications, one could not escape the conclusion that the view was widely held that the three prime functions of the Institute had not been carried forward with the emphasis and balance which the founders of the Institute had conceived. Subject to certain reservations, there was general acceptance that the Institute had made satisfactory progress in the development of its graduate teaching. There was recognition, too, that many faculty members had pursued sound basic research studies. In short, the achievements had been solid within those aspects of its function which fall within the university model. The disappointments were felt mainly within the area of applied research and in development activities which would lead to new programs and innovations within the schools. Many had still to be convinced that a single institution could successfully carry out the threefold objectives of graduate teaching, research, and development. Certainly it was clear, that if the unique combination of tasks was viable within one institution, the proper model and structure had not yet been devised to meet its priorities.

There was no doubt that a highly talented faculty had been assembled to undertake the programs of the Institute. Most had been recruited from university appointments or directly from graduate schools, and in the desire to marshal the best available scholarship and research potential, perhaps not enough emphasis had been placed on explaining the uniqueness of the Institute concept from that of the traditional university. As a result, many had come expecting the Institute to grow along the lines of the university model with its departmental power structure, its concepts of promotion and tenure, and its highly individualized notion of academic freedom. These ideas were no doubt reinforced by the affiliation agreement with the University of Toronto and the Institute's clear association with the University's School of Graduate Studies.

It was understandable that tensions would develop in a situation where The Board of Governors held the supremacy which the provincial statute had provided. Many of the faculty were resentful of the fact that its Academic Council was a creature of the Board. *In fact* this Academic Council had over the three years of its life gradually become the chief policy-proposing body within the Institute and the Board had accepted with only minor modifications most of the recommendations of the Council. Nevertheless, as the Academic Council grew in experience, it was restive with a situation where an external Board of Governors theoretically could thwart the wishes of the faculty. At the same time, the Board was becoming apprehensive as it sensed a situation developing where the powers being demanded by the Academic Council could reshape the Institute into something other than its original concept. Clearly, the Institute could not prosper until these basic issues were resolved.[14]

The special committee produced a series of thirty-six recommendations. The first of these was that there should be a bicameral system of government consisting of a Board of Governors and a Senate. The Senate was to consist of six *ex officio* members – the director, assistant director, coordinators, and the chief librarian; ten representatives of the three operating divisions including four from graduate studies, four from research and development, and two from field development (to be increased to four when the number of centres warranted it); fourteen representatives-at-large from the academic staff; eight representatives of the Graduate Students' Association; four members of the Board of Governors; two representatives of the Association of Research Officers; and one member representing the senior professional and professional staff. The Senate would be the main source of policy on the institute's academic programs and would have assigned powers to govern, manage, and carry out the programs of graduate studies, research and development, and field development undertaken by the institute. On major policy decisions, the concurrence of the board would be required. There would be an Executive Committee of the Senate consisting of the director as chairman, the assistant director, the coordinators, four others elected from and by the Senate, and the secretary of the Senate, who would not have a vote. This Executive Committee would perform the functions of the existing Executive Committee of the Academic Council and possibly some functions of the Administrative Council. The director of the institute would keep both the board and the Senate informed of each other's proceedings. His judgment would normally serve as a guide in deciding which matters required the agreement of both governing bodies. The Senate would share with the board the appointment of the senior administrative officers of the institute. Four standing committes of the Senate would deal respectively with the budget and with the programs of graduate study, research and development, and field development. The later two would assume the duties of the existing Research Review Board and the Development Review Board. Additional committees, not necessarily restricted to members of the Senate, might be formed as needed.

The Association of the Teaching Staff would remain the voluntary professional association of all faculty members and would concern itself chiefly with matters of staff welfare and professional development. Its recommendations to the board would be submitted through the director.

The Board of Governors would consist of thirty-two members: the director of the institute; two representatives of the teacher-training institutions of Ontario; two representatives of the University of Toronto; two representatives of the other provincially assisted universities and colleges; three representatives of the Ontario Department of Education; three representatives of the Ontario Teachers' Federation; three representatives of the school trustees' organizations in Ontario; one representative of the Ontario Association of Education Officials; six "persons who are residents of Ontario"; four members of the administrative and instructional staff of the institute; two representatives of the colleges of applied art and technology; two representatives of the OISE student body; and one representative of voluntary educational agencies of Ontario. Whenever the board considered it appropriate, it might make recommendations to the Senate concerning institute programs. The board would hold full powers over 1 / approval of the budget and budget transfers; 2 / provision of physical and financial resources and facilities for the operation of the institute; 3 / determination of salary policy, and the appointment, remuneration, and conditions of employment of all members of the institute, on the recommendation of the director. It would be the board's prerogative to decide which matters involved major policy decisions and therefore required its concurrence.

The director would be appointed by the board on the recommendation of a search committee composed of equal numbers of members from the board and Senate, with the chairman of the board acting as chairman of the committee. The assistant director would be appointed by the board on the recommendation of a search committee appointed by the Senate, subject to the approval of the director. The search committee would be chaired by the director and would include the coordinators. The coordinators would be appointed by the board on the recommendation of a search committee appointed by the Senate, subject to the approval of the director. The search committee would include adequate representatives of the full-time staff of the division concerned and would be chaired by the assistant director.

Recommendations 27 to 36, dealing with the operating structure of the institute, are reproduced here in full.

27. That a new operating structure be adopted within the Institute, to consist of three divisions, one concerned with graduate instruction and the research studies of individual faculty members, the second with research and development projects organized around thematic centres, and the third with field development. Each of these divisions will be funded separately and organized in the way that is best suited to its tasks.
28. That in this proposed tri-divisional structure a formula of "normal support" be developed so that faculty members know what resources in money and staff they can expect to support their research.
29. That the Coordinator of Graduate Studies be given a budget allocation to be used to supplement normal support for individual research, and that the recommendation of the Graduate Studies division's committee or council govern the distribution of this money.
30. That if a faculty member devotes himself primarely to research, or if the research he wishes to undertake requires more substantial support than that provided, the faculty member must find a base for that research in a thematic centre within the Research and Development division.
31. That the thematic centres in the Research and Development division each have a director, who may draw staff from within and outside the Institute, and that these staff members need not be attached to the Institute's academic departments.
32. That thematic centres be established for specific periods of time, be funded for specified terms rather than year to year, and be reviewed periodically.
33. That both the Research and Development and the Field Development divisions establish their own staff designations, distinct from the usual academic ones, with provision for opportunities for advancement.
34. That each of the proposed operating divisions of the Institute be supported by three committees: (1) an advisory committee similar to the existing ones for research and development; (2) a divisional council with sufficient representation of both staff and students to permit broad participation in

debate and decisions on policy; (3) a Senate standing committee for review purposes.

35. That the criteria established for appointment, promotion, and tenure of staff members take into account all the objectives of the Institute, and thereby give consideration to demonstrated competence in the performance of any of the functions or kinds of endeavour required to achieve those objectives.
36. That the comments on the graduate studies program be placed before the appropriate bodies or committee of the Institute in order that they may be given serious study.[15]

The report of the special committee aroused a variety of reactions on the part of board members. Some of the comments, in summary, were as follows. 1 / The specific powers of the board and Senate were not clearly enough defined. 2 / Instead of a Budget Committee of the Senate, there should be an Academic Planning Committee to establish budget guidelines relating to academic matters alone. It should be the board's responsibility to decide on the total budget. 3 / The Ontario Teachers' Federation was concerned about the proposal to reduce its membership on the board from six to three, which would mean that only half its constituent groups would be represented. 4 / If the board's approval was to be required for the establishment of new academic programs, the staff of the institute should have more than four representatives. 5 / The number of members on the Executive Committee of the Senate chosen from and by the Senate should be more than four of the total of nine.

Report of the Task Force

The Task Force produced 112 recommendations under a series of headings. The first groups dealt with the government of the institute. Like the Special Committee of the Board, the Task Force advocated a bicameral system of government with a Board of Governors and a Senate, the former to represent external interests and the latter the "OISE community." Separate areas of jurisdiction would not be specified, but each major proposal would require the approval of both bodies. Where agreement could not be reached, a special joint committee would be established with the power to make binding decisions. The board would have the final authority and responsibility for the provision of physical facilities and financial resources for the operation of the institute. It would also retain final authority in personnel matters, including appointments, salary changes, salary policy, and conditions of employment for all employees.

Recommendations for the composition of the Senate did not differ substantially from those made by the special committee. One interesting difference was that the Task Force proposed to include a representative of the general supporting staff. There were, however, vital differences in the way the two groups felt about the management of the Senate. The Task Force envisioned a lesser role for the institute administration, as indicated by its proposal that an elected speaker, rather than the director, preside over Senate meetings, and that the Executive Committee consist of the director as chairman, the speaker, and four other members elected for and by the Senate. Such a group might be expected to act quite differently from the one proposed by the special committee, consisting of five administrators and four other voting members.

The Task Force advocated procedures for appointments that were similar to those of the special committee, except that the Board of Governors would have representatives on the search committees that recommended candidates for both the directorship and the assistant directorship rather than the former only. The director's powers and duties were defined in a similar way. The chief actual difference would be that the Task Force would give him less support from other appointed administrators if he chose to take a position in opposition to that of a majority of the staff.

The Task Force agreed that an alternative to overwhelming departmental responsibility for research and development programs had to be devised. It proposed that the departments be concerned primarily with the provision of graduate instruction, and that centres be established as separate budgetary and administrative units with major responsibility for general research and development objectives. Projects would be established as independent program units for individual or small team research and development activities. They would be attached administratively to the Office of Research and Development and located in that office, or in departments by arrangements with that office, with their use of facilities provided on a charge-back basis.

There would be five co-ordinating committees: a Graduate Studies Coordinating Committee, a Research and Development Coordinating Committee, a Field Development Coordinating Committee, a Services Coordinating Committee, and an Institute Coordinating Committee. These committees would study and recommend policy matters to the Senate and advise the director or the coordinators, as delegated, in ensuring effective implementation of established policies. Successive recommendations indicated the composition of these committees. The existing Editorial Board would become the Editorial Review Board, to be constituted as a subcommittee of the Services Coordinating Committee. The Educational Clinic Committee, Library Advisory Committee, and Computer Policies Committee would be discontinued, to be reinstated by the Senate only if evidence were provided that they were needed. The Institute Coordinating Committee would have jurisdiction over all areas not of primary concern to other co-ordinating committees. These would include the over-all function and effectiveness of the institute; relationships among graduate studies, research and development, and field development; budgeting; personnel matters, including salary, conditions of employment, and staffing; the external relationships of the institute; and funding. Reports from the following would go through the Institute Coordinating Committee to the Senate if dealing with policy matters, and to the director if dealing with administrative matters: the Budget Review Board, the Academic Appointments and Promotions Committee, the Academic Staff Salary Review Committee, the Supporting Staff Salary Review Committee, the Supporting Staff Continuing Education Committee, and the Academic Study Leave Committee.

Program review boards would be established for graduate studies, research and development, and field development. The co-ordinator of the program area would be chairman of the relevant review board, which would contain at least one other member of the co-ordinating committee and three other members of the institute to be appointed by the co-ordinating committee. Each review board would have authority to make recommendations to the director, within limits of policy and criteria determined by the co-ordinating committee. The Research and Development Review Board would have delegated responsibility and authority to receive, evaluate, and fund all research and development proposals for internal centres, projects, and seed money, and to evaluate current projects subject to the approval of the director. The Graduate Studies Review Board and the Field Development Review Board would have comparable responsibilities in their own areas.

There would also be an advisory committee for each of the three program areas of graduate studies, research and development, and field development. Each advisory committee would be a joint committee of the board and Senate, with the appropriate co-ordinator as chairman. Reports from each advisory committee would be submitted by the chairman to the director and by him, with his recommendations, to the board and Senate. Each advisory committee would consider all aspects of the program in its own area and make recommendations concerning its purpose and extent. A joint committee of the board and Senate would be responsible for determining appropriate advisory committee membership in each of the three program areas.

Under the heading of "institute budgeting," it was recommended that each activity be rigorously scrutinized and, if approved, funded for a period of up to three years. During that period, there would be a need only for indications of satisfactory progress. Seed money for funding the development of proposals would be retained in the hands of the review board as considered appropriate and not committed in advance to approved projects. Program activities would be presented as proposals for funding in sizable, meaningful units: for example, a proposal would be submitted for a centre rather than as separate proposals for activities within the centre. Money allocated to graduate studies, research and development, or field development which was not committed to an approved activity would be retained in the budget of the co-ordinator for distribution during the year as activities were approved and funded by the program review boards. Decisions on priorities and the commitment of funds for major new program activities (centres and programs of graduate studies) would be made initially by the program review board and forwarded for approval, in turn, to the program co-ordinating committee, the director, the Senate, and the Board of Governors. Research and development projects, seed money applications, and mid-year course proposals would, however, require only the approval of the program review board and the director if funds were available in the co-ordinator's budget. Program review boards would undertake annual reviews of activities funded on a long-term basis and, if necessary, recommend modification of the original funding arrangement.

A series of recommendations dealt with program proposals for graduate studies, research and development, and field development. Among those concerning graduate studies, it was proposed that affiliation with the University of Toronto be maintained "for the present," but that OISE should "be active in shaping its own standards rather than accepting unquestioningly the standards of the School of Graduate Studies." These and accompanying recommendations suggested the possibility of conflict with the University of Toronto. Of particular interest was number 69.

> The Graduate Studies Coordinating Committee undertake the task of defining the requirements for residence and an acceptable Ph.D. thesis which are compatible with the purposes and interests of OISE, and with determining whether these requirements conflict with the requirements of the University of Toronto Ph.D.

With respect to academic staff, it was recommended that the prime consideration in recruiting should be professional competence, and a secondary consideration the selection of individuals whose backgrounds differed in significant ways from those of existing staff members. The Senate would review existing policy and propose criteria for judging scholarly achievements in each of the three areas of institute endeavour. It would also study the problem of how to evaluate and reward administrative performance, as well as reviewing policy concerning terms of office and related matters for incumbents of administrative positions.

Establishment and role of the Joint Committee on Institute Structure

The recommendations of the Task Force had dealt with procedures for the implementation of structural and other changes in the institute. Leading members of the Academic Council protested vigorously over the minor role the Task Force seemed to envision for it in this process. Before the end of 1969, however, agreement was reached on the formation of a Joint Committee on Institute Structure, consisting of representatives of the Academic Council, the Board of Governors, the Administrative Council, the Association of Research Officers, the Association of the Teaching Staff, the Graduate Students' Association, the Professional Staff Association, and the general supporting staff. The composition of this body reflected the idea, rapidly growing in university circles, that all those earning their living in, or in any way contributing to the welfare of, an institution were entitled to a voice in its management. The joint committee was expected to formulate proposals for the reorganization of the institute, taking into account the views of the various constituent bodies and of individuals and respecting the reports of the Special Committee of the Board and the Task Force. The Academic Council would have the right to accept or reject the proposals.

Activities of the Special Committee of the Academic Council on Structural Changes in the Institute

A Special Committee of the Academic Council on Structural Changes in the Institute was formed to consider the issues and to crystallize the opinions of the members for submission to the joint committee. By the beginning of 1970, the possibility of adopting a unicameral form of government was being widely discussed. A group of the leading members of the Academic Council took note of this issue and, in presenting it for consideration, made no secret of the fact that they themselves preferred a bicameral system as recommended in the two earlier reports. They wrote that institutions like OISE required, on the one hand, a high degree of internal autonomy in establishing their own objectives, policies, and programs and, on the other, a great deal of responsiveness to the general public in the way they utilized the public resources allocated to them. The question was whether a unicameral or a bicameral system would serve best to reconcile these two needs.

The group noted that the Board of Governors, as then constituted, was largely representative of the educational community, and had very few members from the general public. They speculated that the responsiveness of the institute to the educational community might be better secured through a system of advisory committees like those in actual operation. They did not dwell on the danger that the advice of such committees could be ignored and almost certainly would be unless institute staff members shared substantial common interests with them. There was a suggestion that it might be thought desirable to give the institute the power to elect members to the Board of Governors who were not on its own staff or otherwise connected with it. In the minds of some people on the Academic Council, the members of the board selected to represent various educational associations and organizations did not really express the views of their rank-and-file membership. The only way to get around this problem was for those who controlled internal institute policy to make the selection themselves. It is difficult to see how the institute could claim to be seeking the real views of the educational community or of the general public if it declined to recognize the normal methods by which these interests organized themselves and chose their representatives. For the institute to exercise the right to determine who had the interest, enthusiasm, knowledge, or other qualities needed for service on the board might be to move in the direction of a self-centred oligarchy.

The Academic Council recommended a Board of Governors consisting, in addition to four members from the Senate and the director of the institute, of five "categories of Institute publics": 1 / the Ontario general public, not related directly to the educational system or affiliated with an educational organization; 2 / the Ontario educational system, including Department of Education officials, trustees, administrators, and others not in teaching roles; 3 / Ontario classrooms, that is, teachers and students directly involved in the teaching-learning process; 4 / the Ontario universities, that is, the peers of the institute faculty members competent to evaluate the quality of its work; and 5 / other Ontario publics considered by the institute itself to be crucial for the attainment of its objectives, to be nominated by the institute, with its own staff and students ineligible. Nominations for all categories of membership would be invited publicly by the minister and not restricted to formal organizations or institutions. The powers of the board would be much like those recommended by the Task Force.

The Academic Council proposed to limit the powers of appointed officials to a greater extent than either the special committee or the Task Force had suggested. It advocated a Senate with the director as the only official serving *ex officio*. The presiding officer would be a chairman, who would be followed automatically after a one-year term by the chairman-elect. Instead of the co-ordinating committees recommended by the Task Force, which seemed too likely to be dominated by the administrators, there would be standing committees of the Senate, like those of the Academic Council. These would be chaired by elected members, with the administrators serving as executive officers and bringing before them the business of their offices. Certain over-all co-ordinating functions would be performed by an Institute Executive Committee consisting of the chairman and vice-chairman of the board, the chairman and chairman-elect of the Senate, the director, and three members elected by each of the board and Senate.

The results of the highly complex referendum on the committee's proposals showed that 70 per cent of those voting favoured a bicameral system of government, and that 60 per cent considered it necessary that the two governing bodies have co-equal status. Between 86 and 88 per cent were said to have felt that OISE's main goal should be to serve the Ontario public, that the organization should have maximum autonomy, and that there should be useful interaction between the decision-making and implementing functions within OISE. In general, varying majorities ranging from decisive to very large, supported most of the major recommendations of the committee.

Activities of the ATS *Committee on Institute Structure*
The Association of the Teaching Staff had a Committee on Institute Structure which was at the same time formulating a different set of proposals. It envisioned a unicameral system of government, with the central governing body called the Board of Governors. This board would have sixty voting members, including twenty-four internal members, twelve mixed members (full-time or part-time OISE students), and twenty-four external members. The internal membership would be from the following groups: academic staff, academic supporting staff, non-academic supporting staff, and professional staff. The director and assistant director would be non-voting, non-office-holding members of the board, with the director serving as executive secretary of the board. While all academic staff members except the director and the assistant director would be eligible for election to the Board of Governors, there would be an upper limit on the number of administrators who could serve at any given time. The external members of the board would represent relevant groups or categories such as industry, labour, practising teachers, and school students chosen by the minister on advice from a "blue ribbon" committee.

The Academic Council and the Association of the Teaching Staff of course had a large proportion of their membership in common. It is thus not surprising that, despite some considerable differences in the proposals of their respective committees, there were basic similarities in points of view. 1 / Both wanted to make administrative offices completely responsive to the institute community; 2 / both accepted the idea that all constituencies in the institute, even those that contributed only unskilled support in terms of the defined educational objectives, be represented on the governing body or bodies; and 3 / both agreed that outside interests on the governing body or bodies should not be dominated by representatives of educational associations or institutions.

Recommendations of the joint committee
The joint committee recommended that the governing body of the Institute be a deliberative assembly called the Institute Council, which would be composed of representatives of the external public, representatives of the institute staff, and institute students. The external membership would be as follows: two from the Ontario Department of Education, four from the Ontario School Trustees' Council, five from the Ontario Teachers' Federation, one from the Ontario Association of Education Officials, two from teacher education institutions, three from post-secondary education, one from voluntary adult education associations, one from other voluntary educational agencies, six residents of Ontario, and three students not registered at OISE. Initially seventeen members of the OISE academic staff

and equivalent ranks, three members of the professional and supporting staff, four members of the general and supporting staff, and four members of the academic supporting staff would be appointed to the Institute Council. The most significant aspect of these recommendations was that the external membership would continue to be from organized educational bodies.

The representatives of the external public would be constituted as the Regents of the Institute, a kind of organization within an organization with final authority in financial and personnel matters. Residual powers would be vested in the Institute Council. In many respects, the regents would operate as the Board of Governors had been doing. It would have a personnel committee to conduct negotiations with the staff and student organizations regarding personnel matters. The director would be executive officer of the regents with voice but no vote.

The director would be the official head of the institute, with the responsibility for operating it in keeping with policies established by the Institute Council. In his capacity as executive officer of the council, he would provide leadership, draw important issues to the council's attention, and be responsible for the preparation of meetings and for implementation of the council's decisions. He would have the right to attend meetings of the Institute Council, with full voice. He would not be eligible for election as speaker of the council. The assistant director could attend meetings of the regents with voice but no vote. He and other administrative officials might be invited by the director to attend meetings of the Institute Council, with voice but no vote.

The Institute Council would elect a speaker who might or might not be a council member. His chief function would be to chair the meetings of the council in a non-partisan fashion and to be the arbiter of procedures of debate and decision. He would also ensure that proper procedure was followed in the elections and activity of the Institute Council and its standing and *ad hoc* committees.

The Institute Council would have standing committees, empowered to concern themselves with both the formulation of policy and its implementation, for graduate studies, research and development, field development, media and communications, budget, personnel, administrative services, and academic services. All *ex officio* members of these committees (i.e., administrative officials) would have both voice and vote, but would be ineligible for the chairmanship. Further recommendations of the joint committee suggested that the standing committees would have a very powerful role in the operation of the institute, and that administrative officers would be little more than their agents.

The report of the joint committee was distributed to institute staff members, students, and governors in June. Each constituency was to hold an open meeting to discuss the recommendations and report to the committee by July 1, 1970. The Drafting Committee was to collate the reports and to prepare a revised report to be considered by the joint committee in September.

TRANSFER TO UNIVERSITY AFFAIRS

A probable change in status that was discussed on many occasions was the transfer of the institute from the jurisdiction of the Minister of Education to that of the Minister of University Affairs, who might well be, at some future time, different individuals. Members of the staff appeared to feel that such a transfer would be desirable in that it would tend to reinforce the institute's independence. There seemed to be little concern over the symbolic widening of the distance between the institute and the school system. The main difficulty would be in incorporating the institute's particular budgetary needs. Adherence to the formula for operating grants would remove the existing financial provisions for research and development activities. It seemed unlikely that the university community would look kindly on a special arrangement to accommodate the peculiarities in the institute's status.

RELATIONSHIP WITH THE DEPARTMENT OF EDUCATION

There was little evidence of enthusiasm in the Department of Education for the establishment of the institute. Administrators with heavy practical responsibilities are seldom the strongest admirers of academically oriented individuals who can let their imaginations roam freely without regard to the consequences. They do not relish the disruption in the schools caused by the activities of the experimenters. They are all too aware of the vast difference between abstract theory building and useful application. If new ideas are needed, they tend to think that they themselves can produce all that is necessary. Thus an enterprise such as OISE faces a serious challenge in establishing even an atmosphere of toleration, let alone one of harmony. Of course, if the idea is to maintain an organization designed to irritate the bureaucracy into constructive action, that is another matter. But such an intention seems more than a little unrealistic.

Jackson's long association with practical problems and activities had enabled him to talk to departmental officials in their own language. But he was not a departmental "regular," and his status as consultant to ministers and prime ministers had produced resentments. The creation of "Jackson's empire" seemed to provide a kind of rival to the department.

A far more important source of antagonism was, however, attributable to the actions of individual staff members of the institute. In some cases, their willingness to make pronouncements against a background of obvious ignorance proved annoying. Their former experiences had inculcated in many of them the idea that provincial or state departments of education could safely be assumed to be reactionary obstacles to progress, and that the only reasonable course of action was to work around them. They failed to make the necessary effort to discover that the Ontario department, under the influence of a dynamic and imaginative minister, had seized the educational initiative in a most unusual fashion, and that the best prospect for the achievement of their own objectives was to work closely with it.

On December 8, 1967, J.R. McCarthy, then just completing his first year as deputy minister, gave the banquet address at the Ninth Annual Conference of the Ontario Educational Research Council. He commented with enthusiasm on the remarkable progress made in the attitudes of professional people towards educational research in Ontario during the previous few years. There had been "a developing awareness of the meaning of research in education, of the possibilities for improvement of the instructional program through experimentation in the classroom and of the necessity to have a highly competent staff of professional researchers to give leadership and direction to this most important aspect of the educational enterprise." But he felt that there was no justification for complacency. He referred to the large amounts of money being provided by the federal government in the United States and recognized the possibility of adding significant contributions to the literature. He suggested, however, that the law of diminishing returns was becoming operative, and that some of the work being done could not be justified in terms of the utilization of either human or financial resources. He warned that priorities must be established in educational research, as in all other areas of the educational enterprise. Every research proposal must be subjected to the closest possible scrutiny to make certain that it held promise of making a significant and recognizable contribution to the betterment of education.

McCarthy asserted that, to a large extent, the kind of discipline he was advocating must come from the professors and other leaders in the research field. If they promoted esoteric studies with little prospect of relevance to the educational scene, they would be able to find some school administrators on school boards who would be willing to have them undertaken in their schools. This would happen because of a lack of knowledge on the part of many boards, administrators, principals, and teachers of what was worth undertaking, and possibly because of the aura attached to research and the status which the conduct of it brought to those involved. But McCarthy felt that there were long-range implications which could only be harmful to the future of research because of the development of attitudes of disillusionment and disappointment among those who would find that, after a considerable investment of time and money, they were engaged in a meaningless endeavour.

McCarthy had a few positive suggestions about the emphasis needed in research. He particularly stressed its role in planning. "If there is to be a desirable degree of flexibility, it will have to be exercised within a framework that has been developed with regard for the realities of the times and the knowledge we have about how children grow and develop, how they learn, and the views they hold of themselves ..." McCarthy also pointed out the need to co-ordinate the efforts of specialists in many different fields and with many different points of view if really adequate planning was to be done. He also delivered the customary warning that researchers must learn to communicate with educational practitioners if their work was to be effective. There were also financial reasons for successful communication. It was increasingly necessary to justify the expenditure of funds for educational research when more easily recognizable benefits were competing for the tax dollar.

The address was delivered to a group largely composed of teachers and administrators who had assembled to hear about and discuss studies mainly conducted by practitioners like themselves and primarily designed to throw light on problems of immediate, and localized, concern. McCarthy was assumed, however, to be speaking to the professionals, most of whom were based in the Ontario Institute for Studies in Education. In certain respects, it seemed that he was reacting adversely to some of the things they had been doing. A careful reading of his address, however, can lead to no other conclusion than that he was issuing a friendly and constructive warning about the unfavourable reactions they were producing and of the unpleasant consequences that would ultimately result unless corrective action were taken.

A number of positive contacts were developed between various parts of the institute and individuals and groups in the department. Particularly noticeable to the observer are those involving the Planning Department, the Adult Education Department, the section of the Department of Applied Psychology concerned with graduate programs in guidance and special education, and some interests in the Department of Educational Administration. On the other hand, the practical responsibilities of the Department of Measurement and Evaluation for the administration of testing programs tended to be phased out.

There was a great deal of potential value in the consultative and informational services that individuals in the institute were capable of providing for department officials. Where necessary, the latter could provide the practical component. It should have been made clear from the preceding description, however, that the institute was not so organized as to be able to accept and carry out any large number of contractual agreements, especially those requiring results by a specific date. Even if researchers on the professional level could be induced to agree voluntarily to participate in a project requested from outside, there was no effective way of preventing them from subsequently finding themselves too busy with other obligations to make the necessary contribution. If they lost interest, no effective disciplinary action could be taken.

In his remarks in the Legislature on June 6, 1968, Walter Pitman showed an awareness of certain difficulties.

I wonder if the Minister could indicate whether there has been an integrating function with the department itself. I think the institute is sort of away out here on the edge – at least it gives that impression – and there sometimes does seem to be an impression left that they are operating in different spheres, that sometimes they scarcely touch, and that there is not a great deal of liaison between what goes on in the research function of the OISE and what is going on in the more practical day-to-day activities of education in the department itself.[16]

At a later stage in the debate, he suggested that there was little connection between what was going on at the institute and some of the major legislation that had come into the House.

RELATIONSHIP WITH OTHER AGENCIES

It is perhaps easier and more valid to attempt to identify some of the different reactions to the institute, depending on the specific program and the group involved, than to offer only a sweeping assessment. Some of the areas of most interest are 1 / conferences, 2 / research involving experimentation in schools, 3 / institute development projects, 4 / assistance with development projects undertaken by outside agencies, and 5 / consultative and other services.

Generally speaking, conference-holding has been regarded as one of the most favourably received of the institute's contributions. Naturally those conferences are most successful where there has been a careful matching of program and participants. An audience with primarily broad, general interests will rather readily label a highly technical address "jargon," and it is always possible, of course, that they are right. Arrangers of institute conferences have heard enough adverse reactions to their misjudgments that they have learned to call on appropriate outsiders when the organization itself has lacked the necessary resources.

The report of the Committee on Religious Education contains a particularly strong tribute to the institute for a contribution in this area.

We note that in June 1968, the Departments of Applied Psychology and of History and Philosophy of Education in the Ontario Institute for Studies in Education brought together a number of leading international authorities in several unrelated fields in a conference whose topic was "Moral Education: An Interdisciplinary Discussion of Selected Questions." We commend both the spirit and the vision behind this project, whose reported discussions we ourselves have found most valuable, and we express the hope that the subject will continue to be explored seriously by educationists in such ways as this.[17]

In many cases, efforts to conduct research in the schools have not been well received, and some large school systems are regarded as virtually inaccessible for this purpose. In certain instances, the reasons have been attributable to the selfish lack of consideration demonstrated by the researchers. One class is said to have waited in vain in a suburban school in Metropolitan Toronto for an institute researcher to show up with his tests. Not only did he fail to appear, but no explanation was offered.[18] In other cases, the problem may be blamed on lack of communication. This explanation is often too facile, however, since if the researcher and the practitioner have very different interests and values, the better the latter understands the purpose of the research, the less he may like it.

The large-scale development programs initiated by the Ontario Curriculum Institute, including the demonstration of innovations in the teaching of science and reading, were undertaken in schools where there was a keen interest in participation. These projects attracted the attention of large numbers of observers, who wished to employ similar approaches in their own work. A problem in earlier years was that the projects might become so comprehensive that the department's right to guide the curriculum program seemed in danger of being effectively challenged. With the increasing decentralization of curriculum responsibility, and with the strong encouragement of local experimentation, this particular problem seemed to diminish in importance. So also, apparently, did the institute's desire or capacity to initiate such activities.

The institute has made some of its most favourable impressions in providing assistance with locally-initiated development projects and in offering consultative services at the request of outside groups. In numerous visits around the province in early 1969, the writer heard a number of expressions of gratitude for such contributions. Most of these were attributed to a rather small group of people, including half a dozen individuals in mid-career with a long-standing commitment to Ontario education, two or three conscientious recruits from outside the province who had dedicated themselves from the time of their arrival to serving the needs of the local community, and a few outstanding educators who were devoting their efforts since their retirement from prominent positions to the implementation of the institute's practical objectives. There were, however, expressions of antagonism that any organization concerned with its future should take very seriously. The straightforward director of one of the largest school systems described the evolution of his own feelings about the institute from high hopes to "bitter disappointment." This attitude is to a considerable extent based on what is seen as a striking lack of applicable research fundings. There is scant comfort in the possibility that original expectations may have been entirely unrealistic.

APPRAISAL

The Institute has been appraised by a great many people from a great many points of view. Of particular interest was an article in the March 1968 issue of the *Bulletin* of the Ontario Secondary School Teachers' Federation by J.D. McNabb, a prominent educator and federation member, and a member of the OISE Board of Governors from the beginning.[19] He paid tribute to the objective of bringing together the three activities – research, development, and graduate studies. He pointed out that, by its multi-disciplinary nature, the institute was geared to attack problems in education on many fronts. He expressed some concern, however.

As a member of this Board I realize the tremendous potential for direct contact with the educational community and yet I am often frustrated with the seeming slowness of any remarkable change in classroom procedures ... after more than two years of strenuous meetings and much success in the structuring of this institution we still await a first significant impact on the immediate classroom performance. I remain immensely enthusiastic about the ultimate returns from O.I.S.E., but I must confess to a growing impatience to see some more returns operating directly to the benefit of the classroom teacher.

McNabb saw particular promise for the Ontario Secondary School Teachers' Federation in working with the Office of Development.

It seems to many of us that the relationship between Research and Development activities is capricious. Certainly the output of Research is useless if it remains at the stage of research papers, blueprints, and models. The flux of ideas, information, and prototypes must be followed by innovation and diffusion. Teachers must help identify objectives and assist in the diffusion of results.

He commented on the importance of the recently-formed Development Advisory Committee, on which practising teachers were well represented. He seemed to see some possibility that this committee would exert a real influence on the course of events, a hope that subsequent events hardly supported. In any case, the substance of his message was that the institute retained the good will and support of teachers, despite some impatience.

The Provincial Committee on Aims and Objectives observed that the institute was unique among North American educational institutions in "the breadth of its program, its multi-disciplined personnel, the extent of its financial subsidy, and its high degree of autonomy."[20] The committee found reason to be impressed by its personnel resources for research and for graduate studies. However, it made several "qualifying observations." 1 / Colleges or faculties of education engaged primarily in the pre-service preparation of teachers in other universities should be able (and presumably assisted) to establish masters' degree programs. Such programs would help them attract scholarly applicants for positions on their staffs, would make it possible and economical for a staff member to do all his teaching in the area in which he was best qualified, and would help link the faculty of education with other graduate departments in the university. 2 / Research and training centres should not get involved in the implementation of educational policies (as OISE always disclaimed any intention of doing). 3 / The institute should not be given a provincial monopoly either in educational research or in graduate studies in education. 4 / The developing role of the institute as an official organization giving tests to substitute for the grade 13 examinations was felt to be undesirable. "Such a role clouds the organization's image as a research centre. More seriously, the depersonalized nature of these tests may be inflicting serious harm upon many of the young people subjected to them."[21] 5 / The institute seemed to be functioning in isolation from the remainder of the educational system.

With respect to the last point, the committee elaborated as follows:

> In its examination of OISE, the Committee experienced some concern about the apparently unrelated and unrooted nature of the Institute. In some instances it gave the impression of operating in isolation, almost overburdened by the weight of its yoke of autonomy and freedom. It is obvious that lines of communication seriously need to be established between OISE and various levels of the Department of Education. In many instances the future plans of both are obviously merged in purpose, yet are unshared. Their efforts could easily overlap, create confusion of roles, and eventually hamper the development of the plans of both and arouse unnecessary tensions between them.[22]

Criticism from outside sources was particularly severe during 1969–70. For the first time, the structure and operations of the institute were examined in detail in the Education and University Affairs Standing Committee of the Legislature. Several of the institute's members were present to answer questions. The minister began the discussion with a presentation which sounded, on the whole, favourable but less enthusiastic than some of his statements at earlier stages of the development of the institute. He preceded his observation that the budget of about $10 million represented a very minor increase over the previous year with an assertion that an effort had to be made to ensure that funds went "in the direction where they could have the most useful application." He singled out the graduate program of the institute for special praise, pointing out that there was a greater demand for it than the organization could handle, and that it was considered outside the province and the country to be of high quality. He also spoke well of work in the field with school boards. He offered the view that there should be a greater thrust at the level of the operating school system and expressed confidence that this kind of development was actually occurring.

The first evidence of serious criticism during the discussion was an observation by Walter Pitman that many teachers felt that research being conducted at the institute was too widely dispersed.

The general feeling is that there has to be some kind of concentration of research, that there must be developed some main thrusts, that there has to be some development of priorities, as to what are the really important educational problems in this province, and that the OISE has a responsibility to identify these major problems and perhaps develop a teamwork approach.[23]

He said there had been a feeling on the part of the critics that too much of the research had been of the low-risk type designed to produce a paper for a degree. The institute was being accused of failing to put enough emphasis on the main problems and of neglecting to relate research to development. It was said to be too tied up with the academic world and its obsession with publishing and perishing.

Jackson's response was that this weakness had been recognized nearly two years before, and that since that time the institute had been working toward the development of themes or thematic programs in both research and development. "This means that we will be tackling, not the minute small problems, but devoting a large proportion of our resources to the larger programmes, and in many cases these will be defined or identified in consultation with practitioners through our development committees, or rather our advisory committees."[24] He did not undertake to explain how this reversal of policy was to be made effective despite the autonomy of the individual professional staff members, the steady erosion of the powers of those in administrative positions, and the purely advisory nature of the committees to which he referred. The continued prevalence of faculty autonomy was questioned by S. Apps who asked who determined what social problems developing in the schools would be looked into. D.S. Abbey, Coordinator of Research and Development, replied: "Now the question of social issues – who determines these – I think in large measure the staff member who looks out at the field and picks the most critical problem that he can handle given his particular background."[25]

Abbey explained what was meant by the thematic nature of the program. He had just completed an analysis of the studies, numbering more than three hundred, then being conducted in the institute. He had found that these could be grouped into eight categories: roughly 10 per cent dealt with society, schools, and teachers; roughly 20 per cent were on resource allocation and evaluation of education – typically educational planning studies and computer simulations of the educational system of the province; about 10 per cent were on language learning and thinking; about 10 per cent were on curriculum development; roughly 10 per cent were on the individual and social development of the student; about 15 per cent involved the analysis of student behaviour; somewhat less than 10 per cent were on media and information systems designed to retrieve information about education; and somewhat more than 10 per cent were on OISE program development. Walter Pitman demonstrated concern about the difference between categorizing individually selected and conducted studies in groups and engaging in co-ordinated teamwork planned to discover solutions to major problems by asking: "Are these theme groups developed into teams or are they just working on individual projects with not too much communication with each other?" Abbey responded partly in terms of resolutions for the future: "We will become more integrated than we are now." He also declared:

There are currently many teams under way. I would have to say that the majority of these studies involve individual staff members, but not in isolation because they all are in the same teaching programme. So there may be six curriculum development projects. But they are by curriculum specialists who are in a curriculum department. They do not go on in isolation. They may not involve two men collecting the same piece of data.[26]

Stephen Lewis returned at a later stage in the discussion to the question of co-ordination of projects. After listing a large number of these, he stated

... if a man can divine from this proliferation of subject matters, coherent themes, then he is a well endowed academic indeed. One worries a little whether or not some of the themes have not been imposed on a chaotic array of projects. Many of them are appreciably worthy in themselves. I do not impugn the usefulness of this kind of research, but I question whether or not it is having the relationship to the school system that will both be of value to the system and will reassure the system.[27]

Raising the point of external influence and control, Robert Nixon suggested that, since the funds for the institute came from the government, the institute's program was too directly under the control of the minister.

... I feel that surely we should be contemplating cutting some of the apron strings, if I can use that phrase, which bind the institute so tightly to the Minister ...
Frankly, I am a little suspicious ... that the organization is an emanation of the Minister's office and the direct responsibility of the Minister.[28]

Davis responded with every justification that control by the minister did not in fact exist.

There was some rather sharp discussion about the cost of the new building for the institute. Stephen Lewis had to probe rather persistently before he got a statement to the effect that the yearly cost would be $2 million over a thirty-year period. He concluded that the total cost would be $60 million, which he called an astronomical sum. It was pointed out that this amount covered interest, depreciation, and maintenance, and that the real cost of the building, if it were to be purchased outright immediately, would be only about $17 million. This issue had given the institute unfavourable newspaper publicity during the fall of 1969 which had been tardily and ineffectively counteracted by institute spokesmen despite the essential validity of their case.

Lewis also questioned the need for public relations or information officers. J.H.M. Andrews, the assistant director, explained that the purposes of the institute were widely misunderstood by the public and that this misunderstanding had caused rather serious damage. The intention was to provide factual information. Lewis thought it ironic or odd that an information office was needed to repair the image of OISE "in terms of the general public, or in terms of those in the educational field who are responsive to OISE." He was concerned about a soap-selling type of campaign to try to make the institute palatable to the educated public. On the other hand, he thought it highly desirable to publicize programs such as those developed by Ausubel and Bereiter.

When the discussion turned to the studies of the structure and operations of the institute being conducted by committees of the board and faculty, Davis defended such activities in these terms: "Any post-secondary institution today that is not in trouble as the hon. member for Scarborough West would define it is dead. If he is saying that there is a restructuring needed, or that re-organization or re-definition is an on-going situation and needs to be, then I agree with him completely."[29] No one during the subsequent discussion in the Legislature, raised the objection that there had been so many changes in organization and procedures since the establishment of the institute that there had been too little chance for any scheme to come to fruition.

Lewis brought up the question of undue foreign – particularly American – influence. He referred to a unique panel established the previous year to judge and make recommendations about allocations of the OISE budget. An administrator in the institute had written that, of about forty people who were making recommendations for the use of OISE resources, not more than one-third had had any contact with Ontario education for more than eighteen months, and at least one-third were not citizens. Lewis was not opposed to the idea of having a community of academics from a number of different countries, but did not think there should be a preponderance from one country in any institute which was directly related to the educational future of the children of Ontario. Although he stood to be corrected, he declared that, to the best of his knowledge, fifteen of the twenty-three active people in the Curriculum Department were Americans. He thought there was also an imbalance of a similar type in the Departments of Applied Psychology and Educational Administration. Lewis found it ironic that, despite the large proportion of staff members from foreign countries, there was not a single French-Canadian scholar from any of the universities of Quebec. Jackson said in response that the reason there were no such scholars was that none had applied. He did not seem to feel that it was a source of embarrassment that no active recruiting efforts had been made, or at least none that had been successful.

Near the end of 1969 the *Globe and Mail* indicated that the Toronto school trustees proposed to denounce OISE for failing to meet the research needs of Toronto. They reputedly charged that the institute had failed to act on a request made in June 1968 for research into the problem of the inner-city school. They had made the approach on the grounds that experts from many disciplines were needed, and that the project was thus beyond the capacity of the Toronto Board's Research Department. In a letter to the editor of the *Globe and Mail* on December 5, Jackson declared that the Toronto Board of Education had consistently thwarted repeated attempts by the institute to undertake studies of urban education recommended by researchers, teachers, and officials of the board. He wrote that, unlike other school boards in the province, the Toronto board had been most resistant to the introduction of research studies into its schools. OISE proposals had been bogged down in the board's own red tape and had been rejected by trustees who were unfamiliar with either the procedures necessary for sound research or the type of data which must be collected if a social or educational problem was to be analysed properly. He expressed the hope that the incoming board would be more favourably disposed toward the problems of inner-city education and would be more inclined to co-operate with OISE.

OISE has undoubtedly suffered from unjustifiably antagonistic publicity. On the other hand, observers have noted that any unfavourable criticism, whether from outside or within, tends to be treated as evidence of hostility and to be handled accordingly. Another irritating response to criticism is a recital of some of the more successful, sound, and useful among the multitude of individual projects. It is quite conceivable that activities genuinely deserving praise could be outweighed by trivial or excessively esoteric studies conducted mainly as therapeutic exercises for the benefit of the staff. A franker over-all appraisal might do a good deal to persuade outsiders that there was a real desire to improve the situation.

Criticism reached a kind of crescendo in April 1970 when the *Globe and Mail* in an editorial entitled "A horrible example of waste in education" complained:

> Between 1938 and 1970, in Ontario, the education bill rose from $11.7-million to $1.6-billion. This has created a somewhat edgy attitude on the part of the taxpayers who are paying the bill, which in turn has caused some members of the education establishment to make lofty remarks to the effect that we can't let the red-necks cripple education.
>
> What has hardly at all penetrated the consciousness of the educators, and only here and there – and usually among the opposition – the consciousness of the politicians, is that it isn't the red-necks they ought to fear. It's the sober citizens, who are all for education but are beginning to suspect that the

education *establishment* has been given a free hand to milk them for a multitude of perquisites and empires that do boom-all for education.

Such sober citizens will find some verification of their suspicions in The Globe Magazine today, in an article by Martin O'Malley entitled Just Ask OISE. OISE is the Ontario Institute for Studies in Education, which was established in 1965 to do educational research, has a $10-million budget this year and will move into a new $17-million building next month.

Mr. O'Malley found, as trustees, teachers and some politicians (he is able to quote them) have found before him, that OISE is full of academics conducting all manner of research projects which may or may not relate to education. It's hard to tell, because even when they do find something they seldom communicate their findings either to each other or the world of teachers and students beyond their ivory towers.

It is certainly reasonable to study the learning disabilities of five-year-olds drawn from deprived backgrounds; but what in the name of the English language is "development and construct validation of active-passive and preparatory-participatory scales"? Perhaps a case can be made for spending $100,000 on a study of Blackfoot Indians in Alberta; but couldn't OISE find any Ontario Indians? And while we don't hold with rejecting U.S. academics, it seems a bit excessive for 30 per cent of the staff to be U.S. academics, especially when some of them persist in studying U.S. instead of Canadian education, and especially when OISE hasn't been able to find a single French-Canadian recruit.

Put roughly, by quite a broad assortment of critics, the trouble with OISE is that much of what it is doing is esoteric and that most of what it is doing is so badly communicated that it has no impact on Ontario schools. As Trustee Barry Lowes said of all those brains up at OISE, "I think that every two years they should be made to go out to work to find out what education is all about." If they did, they might come back and tell OISE – and in doing so, rescue it. One thing is certain, the institute's future will be in jeopardy as long as it exists in isolation.[30]

Both the editorial and the article by O'Malley touched on many matters of concern both to the public and to the staff of the institute. Any constructive results were damaged, however, by the rather snide tone of the approach, as exemplified by such statements as: "Something smells at OISE, but the odor is elusive." O'Malley declared that some of the academic alchemy that went on in the "splendid laboratories" was exciting and promising but accused the institute of consistently falling on its face in attempting to describe it. He expressed a feeling of frustration over his unsuccessful efforts to elicit information about some of the studies. He was able, however, to describe an experiment in informational retrieval television being conducted in co-operation with the Ottawa Board of Education, as well as some studies with pre-school children. He poked fun at certain activities that had not been helping the public image of the institute.

> Two delightful innovations developed at OISE are The Box and The Bag. The Box is a ragtag of films, newspaper clippings, tapes and records about the Thirties and the Depression. Just drop it in a classroom and let the children dig into it. "It is one of our notions that disorganization has positive educational values," says Anthony Barton, an OISE researcher.
>
> From The Box, Barton and co-worker David Stansfield came up with The Bag, which contains a delicious collection of sensations for the five senses, including a tape of a group therapy session, a bug's eye view of the world, and the smells of a martini and an outhouse.[31]

O'Malley presented a series of uncomplimentary quotations about the institute, from prominent educators, including Barry Lowes and Ying Hope as well as the education critics in the Legislature. He emphasized the bad impression that had been created in the Toronto system and the lack of co-operative relations between it and the institute. Whatever the motives and tone of the criticism, these matters should have aroused a good deal of concern among those responsible for the future development of the organization.

The annual budget of the institute may or may not grow substantially from the $10 million level where it was hovering in 1970. In one sense, this appears to be a substantial sum of money, but it is only a very small proportion of the total expenditure on education. Such an investment could be easily justified even if the contributions of the organization fell very far short of what critical appraisers believe could ideally be attained. The graduate program, which certainly appears to be a success if judged by the number of interested candidates, might in itself be considered sufficient return for the total budget. If one could begin from that basis, then any useful consequences from the research program, and any smaller contributions in terms of development and service, might be regarded as extra dividends. It might be possible to tolerate a number of studies that could hardly, by their nature, be expected to affect practice in the present generation, as well as others devoted to entirely inconsequential matters with no value except to add to someone's list of publications.

Unfortunately, things are not that simple. The institute must expect to suffer not only from its failure to do the things that are being neglected by deliberate choice or reprehensible ineptness but also for failure to achieve the impossible. Publicity has never claimed that the results of the institute's programs would transform the entire educational enterprise, either initially or eventually. But that impression has nevertheless been widespread, and much disillusionment has resulted. As far as the institute's publicity is concerned, it is not blameless for some present and future difficulties.

Much of it reflects a blurring of what someone would like under ideal conditions with what actually exists.

Perhaps the most unfortunate aspect to the position of OISE in 1970 was the lingering impression in some quarters that it was in a position to meet all the research needs of the province. In every type of institution, and at every level, the system was crying out for practical research assistance. Provincial and local program consultants were encouraging all kinds of innovative activities, but too few resources were available to provide the guidance necessary for effective evaluation of such initiatives. The OISE regional development or extension centres could do a great deal to fill the need provided they could establish and maintain the necessary close working relationships with the departmental Regional Offices, if they could escape the excessively academic orientation of the institute headquarters, and if they were financed and staffed on an adequate scale. It was not at all obvious, however, that it would not be better to have evaluation officers as part of the regular staff complement of the departmental Regional Offices to work hand in hand with the remainder of the team.

FUTURE PROSPECTS

In a paper circulated internally in 1970, Cicely Watson, Chairman of the Department of Educational Planning, wrote with respect to the probable future of the Institute's role:

> Up to now we have enjoyed a monopoly of publicly funded educational research in Ontario. That condition will not last much longer either. It existed because teacher training was lodged in colleges staffed by non-research-oriented faculty, who were heavily loaded with teaching duties and whose whole approach to problems of education might be termed "the craft of classroom practice". Within five years we will have some 14 university faculties of education, staffed to some extent by persons recruited from university colleges and faculties of education elsewhere – as OISE has largely been staffed. Their ambition to undertake graduate teaching and research will fit admirably into the universities' need to earn money through enrollment in the higher funding categories. So within five years we shall have a large number of competitors. Politically it will be impossible to give OISE "protected" research funds. We shall earn only a small portion of our income from enrollment, at present it would be about a third, and it is not at all unlikely that we shall have to earn our research funds by "program" – i.e. that the provincial government would set an annual research expenditure figure and we shall have to bid for all or a substantial part of our research and development income from this pool in competition with the education faculties and the professors of the social science departments of the universities. The history of education project, sociology, psychology, economics, administration projects of professors here will be weighed against the research proposals of professors of the same

disciplines in other institutions. What will persuade them that ours are different, more worthy of funding?[32]

In the writer's view, this line of development seems almost inevitable. Those who plan the future expenditure of millions of dollars of public funds according to the judgment of internally established and controlled OISE committees are somewhat out of touch with reality. The results of a few years of this approach, despite the conduct of some very commendable research and development projects, have amply demonstrated the soundness of the assumption that public expenditure requires public control.

FOURTEEN

Activities in research, development, and graduate studies at the Ontario Institute for Studies in Education

SCOPE OF OPERATIONS

The regional laboratories and the research and development centres in the United States have tended to restrict their areas of concentration to a particular field or group of problems. The Ontario Institute for Studies in Education did not recognize any such limitations. While no one was unrealistic enough to claim that impressive progress would be made in every area, initial publicity made it clear that efforts might be devoted to all types of problems, covering the widest possible range of content and varying from the most abstract to the most immediately practical. This course of action, whether realistic or not, was dictated in part by the intention of creating a very large institute, and in part because it would be the only one of its kind that Ontario, the richest province in Canada, could afford. The hope of doing full justice to the development function was defended, not only because it seemed politically expedient to make comfortable room for the Ontario Curriculum Institute, but also because there seemed to be a compelling logic in the idea of combining all the most important elements required for the process of change.

INITIAL DIVISIONAL RESEARCH OBJECTIVES AND EARLY STUDIES

The early divisional organization was intended to provide for a full range of activities in research and graduate studies. Attention was given to the basic disciplines that are normally assumed to have the most direct bearing on education. Thus there was a Division of Applied Psychology and a Division of Educational Foundations, the latter of which was intended to provide for studies in the relevant aspects of history, philosophy, sociology, and comparative education. This placing of sociology was the result of considerable soul-searching, since research techniques in the discipline involve experimental approaches that are quite at variance with the methods of inquiry employed in history and philosophy. The initial decision was soon reversed by the establishment of a separate Department of Sociology in Education.

A second category of divisions had to do with areas of particular concern to the organization and practice of education but which do not correspond directly to any traditional disciplines. These constituted three of the largest divisions: Educational Administration, Curriculum, and Measurement and Evaluation. Two others reflected a special concern with areas of current interest: Educational Planning and Information and Data Systems (later renamed Computer Applications, suggesting a considerably narrowed field). The plans for a Division of Adult Education, which were implemented in 1966, represented the only departure from the principle that divisions would not correspond to specific levels of the educational system. It was felt that this particular level was characterized by quite special philosophies, approaches, and needs. The Field Services Division was quite unlike the others in that its purpose was to provide for the interpretation of the message from the other divisions to educational practitioners. Shortly after the entry of the Ontario Curriculum Institute, the logical step was taken of transferring this unit to the development area, although of course the interpretation of research to the system is not synonymous with development.

The way in which the educational field was carved up was not entirely determined by anyone's idea of logical analysis. To some extent it reflected the particular areas of emphasis that had characterized the program of the Department of Educational Research. The Division of Measurement and Evaluation, for example, inherited a comprehensive program of test development dating from 1931. The Educational Planning Division could build on the population projections and other related activities for which the Research Department had acquired a creditable reputation. The Division of Information and Data Systems was formed against a background of substantial contributions to education by the development of modern techniques of data processing. The Division of Field Services could hope to expand a wide network of existing contacts with individuals and agencies.

Obligations inherited from the Department of Educational Research

According to comments in the *First Annual Report of the Board of Governors*, the research program for 1965–6 reflected the lack of balance in, and the limitations of, the activities inherited from the Department of Educational Research.[1] An undue past emphasis was identified in the areas of test development, statistical surveys, and service work for official decision-makers. The heads of the Applied Psychology and Curriculum Divisions assumed full-time duties only in January and April 1966, respectively.[2] The hope was expressed that narrow divisional interests would not prevail in the devising of programs of research lest there be unnecessary overlap and concentration on studies of limited scope. In fact these two trends were already in evidence, particularly the latter. Divisional autonomy was such that there was little evidence of genuinely co-operative planning and sharing of effort in studies of major proportions.

Educational Administration

The research and development interests of the Division of Educational Administration were to be focused on the organizational context in which education took place. The general objective was to determine the forms and conditions of organization and the operating styles of people in the organizations that contributed most to the effectiveness of learning. The environment of the school was to be studied in its economic, sociological, political, and legal contexts. Structural arrangements, functional aspects, and internal economic elements of school system organization were to be examined. Studies of the informal organization within school systems would concern students, teachers, and administrators. Further areas of investigation were to involve organizational leadership, including leadership theory, the relationship between leadership style and other organizational factors, and applied leadership theory. Attention might also be given to such abstract fields as communication theory, inter-generation co-ordination, and decision-making theory.

Activities during the first year involved a continuation of the school grant studies. Three projects were also undertaken to solve particular structural problems in school systems. The major theoretical study was designed to throw light on the conditions in schools that fostered or impeded educational change; it dealt mainly with the attitudes and values of teachers in relation to the acceptance or rejection of new ideas in classroom and school practices. A beginning was also made on a project involving co-operation with the Ontario School Trustees' Council on various aspects of school board administration.

Curriculum

It was expected that the results of various individual studies in the Curriculum Division would be brought together to form "a conceptual framework of curriculum components and interactions." This integration, it was hoped, would make it possible to examine the dynamics of teaching and learning within the school system. Research might range from the examination of materials and techniques of presentation through the problems of differentiating motivation to the effectiveness of varying teaching styles. The importance of co-operation with the Divisions of Applied Psychology, Planning, Measurement and Evaluation, and Information and Data Systems was emphasized, as was the necessity of establishing close links with the curriculum committees maintained by the Ontario Curriculum Institute.

Field Services

The Field Services Division, despite its very small staff, soon developed a wide network of outside contacts in pursuit of its objective of providing expert assistance to those conducting studies under other auspices. These included school boards, affiliates of the Ontario Teachers' Federation, and the Department of Education. What was described as possibly the most ambitious study involving the division was an attempt to determine how well several groups of Oshawa students were being prepared for occupational opportunities within the community. Assistance was provided to the Ontario Teachers' Federation and the Scarborough Board of Education for a development project which entailed the introduction of programmed learning materials and their evaluation in selected schools. A particularly important service activity involved the provision of assistance in setting up research workshops and conferences. One of these workshops brought together members of a research committee of the Teachers' College Masters' Association for three days in the spring of 1966 to discuss possible research activities at the teachers' colleges.

Educational Foundations

During its first year the Division of Educational Foundations concentrated on the assembly of information about what had been accomplished in the history of education in Ontario and in other parts of Canada. It also investigated the possibility of using suitable data retrieval equipment. A major event was the institute's first International Seminar in Philosophy and Education.

Information and Data Systems

The central focus of the Division of Information and Data Systems was to determine how the computer and related devices could be applied to the improvement of organizational and administrative procedures and to the learning process itself. Plans were made for the establishment of a computer-based training laboratory for the testing of methods and materials of instruction. There were also studies of the possibility of computer applications in the field of content analysis. Some work was done on information retrieval. All these activities typically involved close association with outside agencies such as the Institute of Computer Science at the University of Toronto. A practical development project, begun by the Department of Educational Research some time earlier, involved the attempt to produce school timetables by computer.

Measurement and Evaluation

The programs of test administration undertaken by the Department of Educational Research continued to absorb a substantial proportion of the efforts of the new Measurement and Evaluation Division. These activities became subordinated to programs for the development and administration of objective tests for admission to colleges and universities, as described in chapter 18. Additional work was also undertaken on the Dominion tests, including the revision of existing forms, the production of up-to-date norms, and the devising of improved answer sheets and explanatory literature. Some initiatives were also taken toward the production of new tests. Considerable attention was given to the organization of workshops and seminars.

Educational Planning
Much of the work of the Educational Planning Division involved a continuation and expansion of activities undertaken previously. Some of this work assisted such entities as the Grade 13 Study Committee and the Minister's Committee on the Training of Elementary School Teachers. Studies of the characteristics and supply of university teachers were continued. A number of the projects involved the analysis of confidential material to assist public bodies or institutions in their planning work. In the more theoretical areas, projects included the development of a planning model of a community college and a model for forecasting requirements for highly trained professional and university-level manpower in Ontario.

Applied Psychology
Two basic objectives were defined for studies in the Division of Applied Psychology: 1 / to develop relevant behavioural theory in order to improve understanding of those kinds of human behaviour considered important in relation to the aims of the school system, and 2 / to bridge the existing gap between behavioural theory and findings on the one hand and, on the other, the educational decisions currently being made. There were said to be serious gaps in knowledge about the features and variables that were unique to education. It was considered desirable to translate, extend, and modify current psychological hypotheses to illuminate educational phenomena. The division proposed to undertake a broad range of studies varying from general psychology at one extreme to specific applied projects at the other.

During the first year, members of the staff of the division were involved in field work, liaison, and public relations functions. Projects were initiated in mathematics learning, concept development and curricular planning, and group counselling procedures. A survey was undertaken to assess the province's needs in special education and trained guidance personnel. But the main research program was not to get under way until the following year, when a basic staff group was assembled.

The list of studies of one kind or another that were considered to be active in 1965–6 was quite a lengthy one. The first annual report listed nine in the office of the Coordinator of Studies, seven in Educational Administration, nine in Applied Psychology, three in Curriculum Research and Instructional Techniques, twelve in Field Services, nine in Educational Foundations, seven in Information and Data Systems, twenty-nine in Measurement and Evaluation, and fifteen in Educational Planning. This list was not in any sense directly comparable to the more than two hundred units for which the Department of Educational Research was responsible in 1964–5, since the latter included many purely advisory and service activities and many individual projects that might properly be grouped under one study title.

SUBSEQUENT EXPANSION OF RESEARCH ACTIVITIES

In late January and early February 1967, the writer analysed the research studies then under way for which formal plans were on record. The results of this personal, non-official review are shown in part in Table 14–1. The

TABLE 14-1
Classification of research studies in OISE according to area of study, February 1967

CATEGORY	NUMBER OF STUDIES
Administration, general	5
Administration, psychological emphasis	1
Administration, sociological emphasis	4
Adult education, provisions and facilities	2
Adult learning, principles	3
Adult learning, techniques	1
Comparative education, purposes and procedures	1
Counselling	1
Curriculum	5
Cybernetics	1
Demography	1
Facilities and opportunities, general	1
Finance	2
Handicapped children, perceptual problems	3
History of education	15
Instructional procedures	4
Learning processes	17
Measurement	35
Methodology of research, statistical procedures, computer techniques	9
Philosophy	5
Prediction, pre-school and elementary	1
Prediction, secondary	3
Prediction, post-secondary	3
Sociology, general	1
Sociological, economic, cultural environment	6
Sociological, cultural factors in learning	2
Sources of information, general	1
Student characteristics	7
Teacher characteristics, training	11
TOTAL	151

figures should give a reasonable indication of the distribution of studies over various content fields. The heavy emphasis on measurement studies is partly attributable to the extent of the program and partly to the practice of listing relatively minor test revision projects as separate studies.

The studies were further analysed in terms of the predominant technique employed. The results, shown in Table 14–2, demonstrate a heavy emphasis on various types of surveys and statistical analyses, with little controlled experimentation. This situation was perhaps to be expected in

TABLE 14-2

Classification of research studies in OISE according to predominant technique, February 1967

PREDOMINANT TECHNIQUE	NUMBER OF STUDIES
Broad survey	3
Intensive survey with heavy reliance on statistical analysis	21
Intensive survey with heavy reliance on qualitative analysis, rational processes	19
Survey of literature, analysis of documents, with tracing of implications	34
Statistical analysis, projections, etc.	18
Statistical analysis balanced by rational processes	27
Field experiment	12
Laboratory experiment	4
Rational processes	7
Devising of applications	2
Unclassified	4
TOTAL	151

a relatively new organization where thorough coverage of the ground might be expected as a preliminary step toward more intensive investigations.

A third stage of the analysis was undertaken to determine roughly where the studies might be located along a continuum from abstract theory building to the solution of problems of purely localized interest. Of the total of 151, there were fifty-five studies showing a predominant emphasis on general theory, seventy-six in a middle position, and twenty demonstrating little or no application beyond the specific group or situation studied. The final step was to estimate the weight of the studies in terms of the amount of time, effort, and resources invested. The four categories defined to assess this factor, and the results of the analysis, were as follow: 1 / major or extended investment involving the participation of several senior staff members – five studies, or roughly 3 per cent of the total; 2 / major or extended investment involving the participation of no more than one or two senior staff members – fourteen studies, or roughly 9 per cent; 3 / moderate investment extending over no more than a year, and involving no more than one or two senior staff members, or short-term intensive effort involving a few weeks' participation on the part of more than two senior staff members – 127 studies, or roughly 84 per cent; 4 / minor investment involving no more than one senior staff member – five studies, or roughly 3 per cent. The tendency toward dispersal of effort and individual initiative is clearly evident from these figures. The paucity of long-term studies suggests a lack of interest in the fundamentals, a lack of confidence in the stability of the institute, or a tendency to regard it as a temporary resting place. Some groups claimed that their individual projects were specially planned to relate to central themes, thus constituting a thematic, if not an organizational, unit. It was difficult to see that this claim could be substantiated except in a few minor instances.

RESEARCH REPORTED IN 1968 AND 1969

An *Annual Review of On-Going and Completed Research Projects* was prepared in the Office of the Coordinator of Research in March 1968. The number of on-going and completed studies by department was as shown in Table 14–3. No further analysis was provided to make possible a direct comparison with the situation as described a little more than a year earlier. Since the 1967 list included recently completed studies, it may be concluded that the total number increased but perhaps not at the same rate as the research-conducting staff. If so, this may be regarded as a healthy trend.

TABLE 14-3
Research activities in OISE, 1968

DEPARTMENT	NUMBER OF RESEARCH PROJECTS	
	Completed	On-going
Adult education	3	4
Applied Psychology	11	27
Computer Applications	5	8
Curriculum	5	10
Educational Administration	15	5
Educational Planning	7	14
History and Philosophy	16	19
Measurement and Evaluation	8	25
Miscellaneous*	11	2
TOTAL	81	114

*Includes Office of the Coordinator of Research, Office of Development, Division of Field Services.

A further report under the same title as that of the previous year was issued in April 1969, the results of which are summarized in Table 14–4.

A few references to specific studies will help to clarify the nature of the program during the two years to which the reports refer. There is to be no great value, in the pursuit of this objective, in distinguishing between completed and on-going projects. The eight-category scheme of classification developed by D.S. Abbey has been used as a frame of reference. Illustrations are given only from the first seven categories since the eighth, covering OISE program development, is mainly of internal interest.

Studies of society, schools, and teachers were scattered over a considerable number of departments. One being conducted in the Department of History and Philosophy of Education was entitled "Nineteenth Century Urban Social Structure: Hamilton, Ontario, as a Case Study, 1850–1880." It was designed to reveal information about the stratification of pre-twentieth-century society, the effects of industrial and urban development

TABLE 14-4
Research activities in OISE, 1969

DEPARTMENT	NUMBER OF RESEARCH PROJECTS	
	Completed	On-going
Adult Education	10	9
Applied Psychology	24	35
Computer Applications	1	11
Curriculum	1	12
Educational Administration	2	10
Educational Clinic	1	1
Educational Planning	3	25
History and Philosophy	0	24
Measurement and Evaluation	12	27
Sociology in Education	0	11
Miscellaneous	2	1
TOTAL	56	166

on social structure, the social composition of various religious dominations, the relation of the family size and school attendance to class, ethnicity, and religion, the relative weight of different factors in promoting social mobility, and the relation of attitudes and values to social structures and changes. Another study falling in the same category, entitled "Students and their Programmes in the Scarborough Secondary Schools," was an attempt to describe students in the five-year, four-year, and two-year programs in Scarborough secondary schools in terms of selected socio-economic background factors, psychological adjustment, attitude toward school, and previous academic aptitude and achievement. Information was gathered by means of questionnaires, psychological tests, and data from Ontario Student Record Cards. An evaluation of the Reorganized Program in the secondary schools was expected to result. This particular study was conducted in the Office of Development. A third study in the same category from the 1969 list, entitled "Canadian Teachers and Educational Policy: Attitudes and Influence," involved an examination of the development, attitudes, and influence of teachers' organizations in Canada, with particular attention to the position of such organizations in relation to educational policy in each province. A study in the Department of Sociology, entitled "The Teacher as Foreman," dealt with the teacher's position in an organizational context with reference to such aspects as vertical and horizontal relations, activity structure, and integrative mechanisms. Some of the studies carried out in the Department of Educational Administration fell into the same category. One of these, reported in 1968, was entitled "Bureaucratic Structure of Schools and Its Relationship to Leader Behaviour." The Department of Adult Education was interested in teaching at the adult level, as shown by a study on the qualifications, experience, and professional attitudes of instructors in the

Ontario Manpower Retraining Program and by another called "Teacher Participation in Continuing Education Activities."

The second of the eight basic categories consisted of studies of resource allocation and evaluation of education, including planning studies and computer simulations of the educational system of the province. One such project, reported by the Department of Educational Planning in 1968, involved the construction of a planning model for a community college for a given region of Ontario. In the same category was a study called "School District Size and Educational Quality" conducted in the Department of Educational Administration. It was designed to isolate factors and add to knowledge about the complex relationships between school district size and educational returns, to establish criteria for judging which combinations of size-related factors were so disadvantageous to a school system that reorganization would be profitable, and to add to information about the Ontario school system. Another study involving evaluation was one entitled "Complementary and Competing Nature of Expenditures for Health, Education, and Recreation and Welfare in Metropolitan Toronto," being conducted in the Department of Educational Planning in 1969. Of somewhat comparable purpose was one called "Research Allocation in Post-Secondary Education in Ontario: The Choice between University and Non-university Training in Selected Fields," also being conducted in the same department.

The third category, consisting of studies in language learning and thinking, would include a study called "Reading, Language, and Cognition (Grade 4)," which involved an investigation of children's understanding of a wide variety of concepts in concrete situations and in verbal and symbolic form; a report was being prepared by a member of the Curriculum Department in March 1968. Studies in this group were commonly found in the Department of Applied Psychology. Examples of these were "Retroactive Interference in Meaningful Verbal Learning" and "Short-term Memory Capacity and the Acquisition of Reading Skills." A number of research activities and test-construction projects in the Department of Measurement and Evaluation had a bearing on language learning. Among these was a revision of the Dominion Group Test of Reading Readiness, involving the standardization of new batteries for Ontario in 1970–1 and the preparation of new manuals. At a different level were a critical review and updating of the Canadian Achievement Tests in English for grades 9 and 10.

Research studies having a bearing on curriculum development were naturally to be found most commonly in the Department of Curriculum. Typifying these was a survey of curriculum diversification in Canadian secondary schools, reported in 1968. A study entitled "Image of Science Scale Development Project" was designed to develop an objective instrument, or several alternative instruments, to assess the student's image of science. Under the title "Investigation of Possibility of Sequencing Geographic Concepts at the Junior High School Level" was an investigation of the possibility of determining the stages in terms of mental concepts and chronological age at which two selected geographic concepts could be most effectively introduced to students in the junior high school. There was also an attempt to establish experimentally the logical and psychological sequence of the selected items. A study of the structure of the curriculum in English at the secondary school level involved collecting, editing, and analysing published and unpublished papers on the structure of knowledge concept as it applied to four aspects of English teaching: language, composition, literature, and communications and media.

Many of the studies in the fifth category, having to do with the individual and social development of the student, were carried out in the Department of Applied Psychology. A comparison of two experimental treatment programs for perceptually handicapped pre-schoolers involved training procedures designed to improve the functioning of children with specific motor-visual difficulties. A study entitled "Conceptual-Level and Value Orientation of Early Adolescents" was expected to determine the relationship between cognitive development and value orientations in judging moral dilemmas. An investigation under the title "The Child's Acquisition of Diagonality and Its Implications for a Theory of Concept Formation and for Education" consisted of a series of experiments with children between the ages of three and six to determine the course of development of the concept of the diagonal and the influence of specific experiences on its acquisition. A study in the fifth category being conducted in the Department of Sociology in Education was called "Education, Occupation, and Adaptability to Change."

The sixth category, analysis of student behaviour, is not altogether easy to distinguish from the fifth. A fairly clearcut example from the Department of Applied Psychology was one called "Group Counselling and Behaviour Modification," which provided an evaluation of the effects of using structured behavioural techniques in group counselling of "problem" students at the secondary school level. Another example was entitled "Effects of Induced Failure on Curiosity." A study of similar purpose, "The Effect of Anxiety upon Meaningful Verbal Learning" was designed to test two hypotheses: 1 / that compared to low- and average-anxiety students, high-anxiety students exhibit a relatively high ratio of immediate retention to delayed retention scores and make relatively high scores on factual and representation items, and 2 / that high-anxiety students benefit more in their retention scores from opportunity to learn the organizer. A study of adult behaviour, conducted in the Department of Adult Education, was called "Why an Adult Begins, Continues, and Stops a Learning Project." Two members of the Department of Sociology in Education were studying social norms and behaviour in the elementary classroom.

Studies in the seventh category, dealing with media and information systems designed to retrieve information about education, were found mainly in the Department of Computer Applications. One of these, called "Design of Computer-Controlled Learning Aids," involved work on a device for selecting large numbers of audio messages under computer control and on the design of slide projectors and similar devices for direct control of the computer. An evaluation of information retrieval television was undertaken in co-operation with the Ottawa Public School and Collegiate Institute Boards before the new administrative arrangements came into force in Ottawa in 1970. In the initial stages, research was undertaken in four areas: publicity, structure, traffic, and instructional change. A study in the same category conducted in the Department of History and Philosophy of Education, was entitled "Preparation of a Classification System for Use in the Retrieval of Information Related to the History of Canadian Education."

It would, of course, be possible to devise other classificatory schemes that would present the total research program in a somewhat different light. Another approach might focus more attention, for example, on historical studies, on studies of educational administration, and on research in educational and psychological measurement, even though these can be classified within the Abbey scheme. Whatever plan is used is certain to reflect the particular background of the person devising it.

There is too little information available to classify recent studies in any systematic fashion on the basis of the amount of human effort invested in them, much less according to their relative quality or their impact on scholarship or educational practice. It might be very desirable to have such information, especially if it were used to influence the future development of the program. The difficulty and the amount of work involved in obtaining it would, however, have to be weighed against the results that might be expected if the resources required were invested in other ways.

APPRAISAL OF RESEARCH PROGRAM

The writer, after studying the entire list of research projects completed and underway, was impressed by several general traits: 1 / researchers constitute a very distinct subgroup with their own special way of looking at education, and with their own special language; 2 / most of the activities in which they engage in the pursuit of their own interests have at least some ultimate, potential value for the improvement of education; 3 / there is a tremendous need for mediators between them and educational practitioners if these values are to have any hope of being realized. The estimate of some authorities that four or five interpreters are needed for every productive researcher does not seem too high. Unless the Ontario government is prepared to balance its investment, it is in danger of losing many of the benefits that might be realized from a large-scale research program.

Unfortunately, the Ontario Institute for Studies in Education has shown a particular talent for making these interpreters or mediators uncomfortable. It might be better to provide for them under other auspices.

The organization of the Schools Council in Great Britain represents a recognition of the problems resulting from the existence of different orientations and subcultures among different agencies and interests concerned with education. It also represents a different type of response. According to its Secretary, D. Morrell,

> For the first, and most important, form of support open to human beings who face anxious problems is to draw closer together, and to pool resources, experience, and perspectives. Unless this is done, it is easy for particular functional groups within the education service to imagine that they alone are the guardians of important educational values, which other groups either do not value so highly, or even wish to destroy. It is virtually impossible for any one group, acting alone, to realise that we are all in the same boat. But this is in fact the position. We are all seeking to respond to change without adequate knowledge of its characteristics, and without adequate means of harmonising our own response with the responses made by others whose perspective is different.[8]

These words point to a fundamental weakness in the institute program. It is not that individual studies show many glaring deficiencies, although the practising educator is entitled to an answer when he expresses scepticism that certain activities have any real chance of exerting an influence. The problem is rather that the program represents a set of prescriptions set down by a group whose status suggests to some a position of intellectual dominance. Their freedom to choose their own topics for investigation clearly implies an over-riding right to determine what is best for the educational system. They express their desire, with unquestionable sincerity, to co-operate with outside individuals and agencies, but co-operation is forthcoming entirely on their own terms. This situation was directly attributable to the relegation of the Board of Governors to the role of approving institute initiatives, occasionally questioning some action in a foot-dragging sort of way, and providing the legal framework for the staff's activities. The board did not ensure the integration of the efforts of the research specialists with the rest of the educational community on the basis of equality, but has rather allowed the researchers to place themselves on a self-erected pedestal.

EXPANSION OF THE PROGRAM OF GRADUATE STUDIES

There were four substantial changes in the program of graduate studies, as developed by the academic staff and approved by successive committees of the School of Graduate Studies and the University of Toronto Senate: 1 / provision for a much greater degree of specialization in graduate programs; 2 / a greater emphasis on full-time study, including two years of post-master's residence for the doctorate; 3 / the assignment of each student, including part-time students, to a faculty adviser; and 4 / the discontinuance of the Bachelor of Education program in its existing form.

Failure to offer specialized programs had been the main reason for the declining prestige of the graduate program in education while it had been based in the Ontario College of Education. The course offerings had simply not kept up with the times. Plans were made during the first year of the institute's operations for specialized programs in thirteen fields: Administration, Adult Education, Applied Psychology, Curriculum and Instructional Techniques, Educational Planning, Guidance, Higher Education, History of Education, Information and Data Systems in Education, Measurement and Evaluation, Philosophy of Education, Sociology in Education, and Special Education. In some cases, staff resources were considered sufficient to provide full programs up to the PhD. In others, only a beginning was possible. The specific courses planned for 1966–7 included thirteen in the Division of Educational Administration, six in Adult Education, twenty-five in Applied Psychology, eleven in Curriculum, twenty-two in Educational Foundations, nine in Measurement and Evaluation, and six designated to serve all fields. Only seventy-six of these courses were actually offered. While a casual observer might feel that this number of offerings should be adequate to cover practically all definable areas of interest in education, the process of proliferation was by no means ended. The same tendency is of course typical of university programs in many areas. There are grounds for suspicion that part of the expansion is a result of academic empire building. How much coverage of the same ground occurs is impossible to say, since there appear to be no reports resulting from an adequate investigation of the problem. Pressure to rationalize budgetary expenditures in the institute led to the submission of a rating form to faculty members in 1968–9 asking them in effect to pass judgment on the importance of courses in terms of a list of their titles. It is absurd to suppose that this kind of exercise can make any real contribution to the avoidance of content duplication, or that it can provide for the filling of important gaps.

The extension of the attendance requirement for doctoral programs to a minimum of two years beyond the master's degree was clearly in line with current practice in other institutions. It was also obvious that a doctoral degree in education could hardly expect to enjoy status in the University of Toronto comparable to that of degrees in other fields without such a requirement. Nevertheless, the decision was questioned by teachers' groups and others on the grounds that the attainment of the degree would become impossible for many candidates who could not afford to take off so much time from their regular duties. Even though a very small proportion of those undertaking doctoral work during earlier years before the founding of OISE had completed their programs without attending more than the minimum period of time, there was pressure to maintain even an extremely unpromising route to the degree. The academic point of view, however, won out, and the subsequent burgeoning enrolment showed that warnings about drying up the source of supply were unfounded.

The decision to cease recommending candidates for the Ed D in favour of the Ph D was made in part in recognition of the lack of prestige enjoyed by the former in American institutions. Since OISE proposed to make the major requirements for the two degrees virtually identical, it seemed advisable to prepare candidates exclusively for the Ph D. This decision implied a desire to relate studies in education more closely to those in other disciplines and to submit degree candidates more formally to the appraisal of faculty members in other departments of the university in the final oral examination. On these grounds, the decision was welcomed in university circles. On the other hand, there was considerable apprehension over the prospects of great floods of Ph Ds in education. Any tendency on the part of institute faculty members to gain more complete control over conditions under which the degree was offered might pose a threat to the university's standards. Quite according to expectations, a desire was soon expressed to eliminate the requirement that a Ph D minor be taken in another university department. Impatience was also expressed with the language requirement on the grounds that it had little relevance to the development of a science of education.

The MA program was designed to follow the regular University of Toronto pattern in that it could be completed in a minimum of one year of full-time resident study by possessors of an undergraduate honours degree in the same field. Those with a general degree, or those seeking a master's degree in another field, had to undertake a more extended program. The MA was relatively research-oriented, demanded a thesis, and provided the normal route to the Ph D. The M Ed program, on the other hand, could be completed on the basis of part-time study and did not require a thesis. It accounted for the overwhelming proportion of students in courses offered in the summer session.

In 1967–8 the number of graduate courses or half-courses offered reached 141, almost double that of the previous year. In addition, there were reading and research courses for individual students. There were now sixteen fields or subfields of concentration within the Department of Educational Theory, in most of which there were programs up to and including the doctorate.[4] In 1968–9 the academic staff, by this time numbering about 130, were able to look after the needs of almost 300 full-time students of whom more than 120 were doctoral candidates.

In 1969–70 the departments offered specialized programs of study as follows: the Department of Educational Administration – the M Ed, MA, and Ph D with specialization in Educational Administration; the Department of Adult Education – the M Ed, MA, and Ph D with specialization in Adult Education and the M Ed with specialization in Adult Education and Counseling; the Department of Computer Applications – the M Ed, MA, and Ph D with specialization in Computer Applications with programs worked out for individual students; the Department of Curriculum – the M Ed, MA, and Ph D with specialization in Curriculum; the Department of History and Philosophy of Education – the MA and Ph D with specialization in History of Education and the same degrees with specialization in Philosophy of Education; the Department of Measurement and Evaluation – the M Ed, MA, and Ph D with specialization in Measurement and Evaluation; the Department of Educational Planning – the M ED, MA, and Ph D with specialization in Educational Planning; and the Department of Applied Psychology – the MA and Ph D with specialization in Applied Psychology, the M Ed with specialization in Guidance and Counseling, the MA with specialization in Applied Psychology (School Consultant Option), the M Ed with specialization in Special Education, and the M Ed for Special Purposes; the Department of Sociology in Education – the M Ed, MA, and Ph D with specialization in Sociology in Education for individual students, while full programs were under development.

There were some changes in the range of offerings in the Department of Applied Psychology in the calendar for 1970–1. The list at that time was as follows: the MA and Ph D with specialization in Applied Psychology (Educational Psychology Option), the M Ed with specialization in Guidance and Counseling, the M Ed with specialization in Adult Education and Counseling, the Ph D with specialization in Applied Psychology (Counseling Psychology Option), the MA and Ph D with specialization in Applied Psychology (School Consultant Option), and the M Ed for Special Purposes. The new Department of Special Education offered the M Ed, MA, and Ph D with specialization in Special Education. Outside OISE it was possible to obtain the M Ed, MA, Phil M, and Ph D in Educational Theory with specialization in Higher Education.

In the annual report of the Board of Governors for 1967–8, the Coordinator of Graduate Studies, G.E. Flower, reflected on some of the problems of rapid growth and on some of the prospects for the future.[5] He noted that there would be an increasing need in the foreseeable future for well-qualified graduate specialists in education and commented that, if the institute's graduate work were to continue expanding at anything like the early rate, its budget and resources would have to grow accordingly. If the annual increments were to be modest, widespread pressures to take in more students and to offer more programs would have to be resisted. Under such circumstances, only a fraction of the total need could be met.

Assuming resources that would be too limited to meet all needs, the question of defensible priorities had to be dealt with. One alternative would be to devote a relatively large proportion of available resources to wide-reaching M Ed programs, including after-hours and summer sessions.

Another would be to concentrate on more expensive doctoral studies. Flower wondered how the development of new graduate programs at other Ontario universities, which the institute was trying to encourage, would affect the situation. There was also the question of giving priorities to programs in some subfields in education over those in others.

DEVELOPMENT ACTIVITIES

Some of the divisional projects belonged from the beginning in the development category. In fact, a major proportion of the program in Measurement and Evaluation could properly be called development. The part of the institute's responsibilities that came directly under the official later designated the Coordinator of Development was inherited in the summer of 1966 from the Ontario Curriculum Institute. The projects that were still being actively pursued at the time involved the following topics: creative arts; education for industry and commerce; social sciences; the problems of transition from secondary school to university; the change process; preparations for an International Curriculum Conference; international understanding; mathematics from kindergarten to grade 13, involving study by three separate committees; science; reading; English; modern languages; and cognitive development and learning theory. The publication of interesting and valuable reports resulting from these projects continued for some time, but the OCI committee approach did not really flourish in the new environment, and much of its inspiration soon faded. Despite their protestations of a sincere desire to work with outsiders, the effect of the full-time professionals generally proved overpowering.

In February 1968 the Office of Development issued a comprehensive report on development projects in progress or in proposal form.[6] Some were being conducted under the auspices of the office itself, and others in various departments. In the former category, there were twenty-two projects and fourteen active committees, most of which had been established originally by the Ontario Curriculum Institute. Of the departments, Adult Education reported nine projects; Applied Psychology, five; Curriculum, eight; Computer Applications, six; Educational Administration, three; Educational Planning, four; and Measurement and Evaluation, two (including the production of six tests). The Curriculum Department was conducting two projects in co-operation with Applied Psychology and one with Computer Applications.

A fairly standard definition of development was provided at the beginning of the report, and most of the activities administered through the office were in reasonable accord with that description. For example, the Language Arts Committee was engaged in a language-reading project designed to develop demonstration centres in which available knowledge of child development and reading could be translated into practice and to test and disseminate such practice. The purpose of another, entitled "The

Use of Video Tapes for Student Teacher Counselling," was described as follows.

> This study is concerned with the uses of audio-visual materials for individual learning experiences with specific focus upon experimental evaluation of "audio-visual feedback-counselling" as a potentially effective aid in the training of student-teachers in the Ontario Teachers' College program. Secondary concerns of the research are directed towards evaluation of innovational effects in the Teachers' College.

The reference to research raises a question about the exact status of the activity. As one further example, a project called "Pictorial Representation and Measurement (Grades 1–3)" was designed "to develop content and methods of presentation with emphasis on activity-centred approaches."

Many, although by no means all, of the projects developed and administered within departments were of lesser dimensions. Some of them appeared to conform quite well to the development definition. For example, the Department of Adult Education was involved in a demonstration of the kind of curriculum that should be offered for manpower teachers in Ontario, with the additional purpose of developing criteria for their certification. Another project was designed to explore possible uses of television in teaching and development work in the same department. A project in the Department of Computer Applications undertook to develop individually prescribed program instructional systems in elementary schools. One in the Department of Curriculum was intended to "develop, teach, and evaluate an approach to the study of literature and film which does not divorce the study of literature from the study of film, but which explores the intersecting and diverging forms of expression in both." In the Department of Educational Administration, some of the studies of long standing in the area of school grants were described as development.

There were other projects designated in the same way which, according to all the usual criteria, appeared to belong to the research category. For example, the Department of Educational Planning was engaged in administering a teachers' college student questionnaire designed to investigate the social characteristics of teachers, the motivation of students for choosing a teaching career, and the academic qualifications and backgrounds of the students. An activity engaged in by the Department of Educational Administration would appear, on the surface at least, to be most properly described as service. It was designed to "assist schools in initiating, creating and sustaining self-renewing change efforts." An evaluation of some aspects of high school teaching by the Department of Curriculum would be rather difficult to classify, but hardly qualifies as development in the usual sense.

The Development Review Board reported the results of some thinking about the concept of development in early 1969.[7] It recognized that the meaning of this concept varied from one department of the institute to another. The close association of development and service functions is shown by the following statement: "In particular, we acknowledge that there are vital and useful service functions (as opposed to product-oriented activity) which may be contributed by some departments." The board proceeded to define certain criteria applicable to any development activity:

1. The existence of an educational need in Canada which the results of the project may contribute to fulfill either in the long term or short term.
2. The suitability of the proposed project to the results it is designed to achieve. The Board considers the suitability of the project in relation to the following criteria:
   (a) the existence of a sound rationale on which the project is based and the relevance of the rationale to the educational need the project is intended to fulfill.
   (b) the adequacy of the project design, including the proposed organization of personnel, to the achievement of the project goals.
3. The adequacy of the means and criteria described in the proposal for evaluating the results of the project.
4. The evidence that the originators of the proposal have given adequate consideration to the existence of alternative means for achieving the goals of the project.
5. The cost of the project in relation to the anticipated educational benefits to be derived from it.

The report distinguished between development and service activities on the basis of whether they were "project-oriented projects" initiated within the institute or a direct response to a specifically expressed external need. Since these definitions of the terms vary from those normally encountered in the relevant literature, one must conclude that they were generated specifically to suit the institute's need. Under ordinary circumstances, it might be supposed that a development project in the strictest sense of the term might be initiated by an outside agency.

In March 1968 the Academic Council set up a development pool of $150,000, to be allocated by the Coordinator of Development on the advice of the Development Review Board. The titles of certain projects which were thus supported give some idea of the projects within departments that were defined as development: 1 / Development and Research Operations of a Demonstration Educational Program in the Canadian Mothercraft Society Infant Day Care Center; 2 / Development of a Model of Coordinated Service by Professional Resource Personnel in the Schools of Ontario; 3 / Development of Auxiliary Material for the Mathematically Gifted Student; 4 / Canadian Studies Program; 5 / Thematic Approach to an Integrated Study of Film and Literature; 6 / Planning for Change in the Organization of the School Divisions.

INVOLVEMENT OF SCHOOL SYSTEMS

In March 1969 the institute published a brief report entitled *School Boards Cooperating in some OISE Research and Development Projects and Studies.* A note on the cover indicated that the listing enclosed "identifies some typical projects in research and development now under way, and many of the places where OISE is working with local teachers and boards of education." The implication was that there were some unspecified places and projects not included. Nevertheless, the participation of fifty-six boards was recorded – an impressive total considering that the county board system was established on January 1 of the same year and that the public systems of Metropolitan Toronto were counted as a single unit. Only one place mentioned, Montreal, was outside the province. Within these local systems there were no fewer than 203 contacts of all kinds, ranging from a single graduate student's collection of data for a thesis to fairly substantial efforts. Of the total, 122 contacts were classified as research and eighty-one as development. There were also five research studies and one development project in private and post-secondary schools.

Space limitations preclude the inclusion of all the titles in the list. The following selection, consisting of every tenth entry, is intended to indicate the general nature of the activities: 1 / development project in grade 12 chemistry (D – for development); 2 / reorientation in educational thinking (D); 3 / counseling procedures and practices (R – for research); 4 / science project D6 (D); 5 / innovation in classroom organization and methods (R); 6 / the same as 1; 7 / language learning project (D); 8 / survey of study habits and attitudes of grade 13 students (R); 9 / use of desk-top computers for learning mathematics (D); 10 / systems analysis for educational management (R); 11 / early childhood education (D); 12 / Canadian studies program (R); 13 / development of curiosity and creativity (R); 14 / creative arts program (D); 15 / the same as 3; 16 / the same as 5; 17 / factors contributing to students' feelings of alienation or isolation (R); 18 / the same as 5; 19 / mathematics K6 project (D); 20 / continuing education of teachers (R). The fact that some of these items occurred two or more times of course indicated a project involving more than one school. It would be interesting to have an appraisal of the size, quality, and effectiveness of these projects according to type and purpose. Although such an appraisal would be expensive, it might be extremely important for the institute's future role, especially if some effective method were devised to act upon the lessons learned.

EXTENSION CENTRE PROGRAMS

As indicated in chapter 13, the programs in the extension centres were expected to develop in different ways in accordance with the special needs of the areas in which they were located. A few references to progress made at the Niagara Centre cannot, therefore, be described as typical but only as an indication of the possibilities. At an early stage, the Advisory Committee decided that the highest priority should be given to the provision of information about OISE activities. It was recognized that there would be no graduate extension courses offered in the foreseeable future.

One of the chief activities approved by the Advisory Committee was the dissemination of mathematics material for gifted students. Some very promising developments had recently been reported from the United States, and researchers at OISE headquarters were making useful contributions. It was also agreed that a communications network among interested mathematics teachers and Department of Education program consultants would be established in the region. Another project that received particular attention was the field testing and dissemination of the conceptual skills program developed by Carl Bereiter and Ellen Regan as a means of assisting culturally disadvantaged and language-handicapped pre-school children. The proposed implementation of the program would involve familiarizing interested people with the materials and methods, determining whether the kind of problem the program was designed to remedy existed in regional schools, and selecting a teacher who would be receptive to the program and capable of carrying it out. At a later stage, the teacher would have opportunities to gain familiarity with the program, in part through visits to OISE. A third area which attracted the interest of the Advisory Committee involved the application of information about exceptional children. The staff of the centre also committed themselves to spending a substantial amount of time on locally initiated studies. Finally, the committee approved a project centring on parental involvement in education. During the year, this project entailed the participation of large numbers of parents from the area. It was expected to involve several phases extending over a number of years.

SUMMER DEVELOPMENT COURSE PROGRAM

During 1969–70 a need was recognized for non-credit courses at the graduate level for administrators, curriculum consultants, principals, teachers, and trustees who wanted opportunities to keep up to date and informed on recent developments in education. Much of the impetus for such courses is said to have come from people who wished for an association with scholars in various areas of educational studies. It was proposed that the courses take between one and two weeks and that they be offered in various parts of the province in the form of workshops. Arrangements were made by the Office of Field Development, with the co-operation of the institute departments.

FIFTEEN

The Ontario grade 13 departmental examination system

THE HISTORICAL BACKGROUND

External examinations in Ontario officially date from 1871, when the high school entrance examination was established. In fact, if the term means external to the school where the child is taught, they were flourishing earlier than that. In the city of Toronto, final examinations were conducted during the 1850s by a committee of "strangers appointed by the board," of which the headmaster of the grammar school became the regular chairman. These examinations, oral except in the senior division, were for three boys and three girls selected from each division in each school, or a total of eighteen per school. The purposes of the examinations were to test the instruction, to compare the standing of the various schools, to stimulate the pupils, and to encourage regular attendance. By 1860 the board had persuaded the city council to use part of its annual grant to the grammar school for scholarships for the seven boys who did best in this contest, such scholarships to give them two years' tuition at the grammar school. These examinations did not, of course, replace rigorous examinations held within each school.[1]

The provincial examination system was introduced with the idea of bringing the grammar schools into line. These schools had obtained nearly all of their financial support from students' fees and government grants, the latter of which were based on student enrolment. In order to increase their grants, the schools had adopted the practice of admitting children who had not yet completed elementary school. Reminiscing in 1969, C.A. Brown, former Registrar of the Department of Education, emphasized the lasting effect of the reprimand implied in the high school entrance examination. He pointed out, presumably with tongue in cheek, that only recently had most secondary schools recovered sufficiently from it that they dared to admit students who had not completed the elementary school course, and that even then these unqualified students were admitted only by a form of translation rather than by promotion.[2]

The next stage in the construction of the external examination machinery occurred in 1876 with the introduction of the intermediate examination to determine promotion from the lower to the upper school, consisting respectively of the first two and last two secondary school years. The examination papers were prepared by a board which took over the examination duties of the defunct Council of Public Instruction. The first intermediate examination produced a disastrous result, with more than half the schools failing to pass a single candidate. During the previous year, the "payment by results" policy had been devised. With the use of the intermediate examination as a criterion, payments made as a result of the first year's program were extremely unbalanced. Seven schools got approximately half of the part of the grant to be distributed according to results.[3] The policy was abandoned after seven years, but subsequent observers are agreed that its evil effects lasted for decades in the inordinate amount of emphasis placed on examinations.

The situation at the upper end of high school long remained confused. By 1890 each of the universities, the Law Society, the Medical Council, and the divinity schools had its own set of entrance examinations. Dentistry, pharmacy, and engineering also had their particular examinations for admission to their respective professional courses of study. The Department of Education provided examinations for admission to normal schools and other institutions for teacher preparation such as county model schools. These examinations were based on different curricula and were held at different periods of the high school term. Candidates often had to bear the expense of going away from home to write.[4] The inspectors responsible for the examinations tended to find the work extremely burdensome as time went on and the number of candidates increased. This feeling led to a movement to combine departmental and matriculation courses and examinations.

As a result of the efforts of John Seath, then a high school inspector, joined by James Loudon, an influential member of the faculty of the University of Toronto, a scheme for a Joint Board was devised. This board consisted of four members of the University of Toronto appointed by the Senate, and four members of the Department of Education appointed by the minister. The first high school leaving and university matriculation examination was held in 1891. There were papers at two levels with provisions for some variation in the questions at each level: 1 / junior high school leaving and university pass matriculation, and 2 / senior high school leaving and university honour matriculation.

In 1896 the Joint Board was replaced by the Educational Council, which was responsible for appointing examiners for all levels, including high school entrance. It was made up of nine representatives from the universities, one from the high school teachers, and one from the public school inspectors. The council continued the practice of appointing fifteen examiners from the universities for the combined leaving and matriculation examinations; these were divided into five equal groups, one each for classics, mathematics, English and history, modern languages, and natural science.

The Educational Council in its turn was replaced in 1906 by the Advisory Council of Education, a larger and more widely representative body.

Its chairman *ex officio* was the President of the University of Toronto. It also had three additional members from the same university; one each from Queen's, McMaster, and Western; representatives of high school, public school, and separate school teachers; inspectors; and school trustees. In 1908 the senates of the four universities represented in the council decided to create the University Matriculation Board to conduct and control their annual matriculation examinations. It consisted of four members from the University of Toronto, two from Queen's, and one each from McMaster and Western. The records in the possession of the Department of Education do not disclose the reason for this change in policy.[5] In any case the department continued to provide the machinery for the examinations and to bear the expense, although the board had the sole responsibility for setting and marking the papers and for authorizing and issuing certificates.

In the meantime, there had been some moves to relax the examination system at earlier stages. In 1904 bookkeeping, reading, spelling, writing, and science were dropped from the list of examinations for teachers, and in 1908 "approved schools" were permitted to deal with geography, grammar, and arithmetic in the same way.[6] These approved schools were so designated by the inspectors after being found properly staffed and equipped, and after their principals had certified that the students had properly covered the prescribed course. This was an early scheme of accreditation which enabled students to enter professional training schools without examination in the subjects mentioned.

From 1909 through 1919 parallel systems were operated during the last three years of secondary school, that is, through middle and upper school. One course of study was issued by the University Matriculation Board for pass and honour matriculation, while the other was issued by the department for normal school and faculty of education entrance. The courses were usually taught by the same teachers at the same time, and candidates for the two examinations wrote simultaneously. The departmental system was regarded as inferior; candidates for its certificate were, however, allowed to take extra work to obtain matriculation standing. Liaison between the two systems was provided at the administrative level by the Registrar of the department, who was both secretary of the University Matriculation Board and chairman of the Board of Examiners.

A single examination system was restored in 1920, after the minister requested that the University Matriculation Board give consideration to such a move. A Joint Committee was set up, consisting of two members of the University Matriculation Board, two members representing the department, and the departmental Registrar. Its reponsibilities were to recommend for the approval of the board and the minister the appointment of the Supervising Board of Examiners, the examiners-in-chief to set the papers, and the associate examiners to read and mark the answers. The University Matriculation Board was joined in 1931 by a representative of the University of Ottawa and subsequently by representatives of other universities. Successive presidents of the University of Toronto continued to act as chairmen. The declining importance of the board was demonstrated by its failure to hold a formal meeting between 1939 and 1944, and between 1945 and 1952, its business during those intervals being conducted by correspondence. With a reorganization in 1952 it resolved to mend its ways and meet at least once a year.

A series of interesting arrangements, many of them long maintained in their original or in a modified form, were made during the early years of the University Matriculation Board.[7] In 1910 rules that were to stand for years with only slight changes were adopted for the dropping of unsatisfactory examiners, mainly based on the number of errors in marking. In 1911 a physically handicapped candidate was authorized to write the examinations at home on payment of the extra costs of supervision. In the same year, examiners-in-chief were required to submit with their papers an outline of the expected answers, and a committee of the board was asked to review the papers before they were printed. Markers were requested to express their opinion of the question papers, and examiners-in-chief were instructed to assemble subject groups to discuss their papers before they presented them to the board. In 1912 blind students were permitted to use typewriters for the examinations, and special provision was made for candidates whose supplemental examinations fell on religious holidays. In 1913 the board began to study statistical information on the examination results, and arrangements were made for the comments of the markers to be sent to the following year's examiners-in-chief. In 1915, at the request of the provincial cabinet, junior matriculation standing was granted to enlisted candidates on the principal's recommendation. In the same year the University of Toronto made a request, often to be repeated in subsequent years, for the earlier release of the junior matriculation results. Preparation of matriculation papers was placed under the supervision of a committee, paralleling the practice with respect to departmental papers. In 1916 a case requiring the adjustment of original marks on one of the papers was dealt with. Scaling has a longer history than many have supposed.

A major change occurred in 1921 after the Joint Committee was established and the matriculation and leaving examinations were combined. Previously the candidate obtained credit only if he wrote and passed all his examinations at one time, subject to the privilege of writing supplementals. This practice placed him under severe strain and created serious timetabling difficulties for the principal. After this date, credit was given for individual subjects regardless of the combination in which they were taken. A student required 50 marks to obtain credit for each paper instead of the former 40 per cent with a minimum over-all average of 60 per cent. For many years, the universities took no decisive action to distinguish between the candidates who completed the program in one year and those who extended it over two or more years, even though it was realized that the latter generally had a poorer chance of success. Steps have been taken during the last decade to put extra obstacles in the way of such individuals: for example, by requiring a higher average for admission to certain courses.

By 1923 it had become excessively difficult to administer the supplemental examinations, to mark the papers, and to issue the certificates in time for use by the universities and other institutions. They were therefore dropped and, as a kind of substitute, the minister established the Special Revising Board. The activities of this body are described more fully later.

A major step was taken in 1923 to reduce the burden of the lower school examinations with the introduction of the recommendation system. Only those whose prospects were too poor to justify recommendation were required to write. The same arrangement was also made during this period with respect to the high school entrance examination. In 1932 it was extended to middle school, and in 1935 to upper school candidates in collegiate institutes and high schools, but not continuation schools, although grade A continuation schools were added in 1938. The entire lower school examination system was abolished in 1937 and the middle school system, as a wartime measure, in 1939. In the latter year, however, the privilege of recommendation was removed from upper school and, with certain exceptions during wartime, candidates again had to write examinations. There were certain rumours of unethical conduct preceding this action, because some schools had no candidates with an average below the minimum of 66 per cent that excused them from writing.

The wartime recommendation scheme for upper school applied to those who had an average of 66 per cent or more on work done up to March 31, along with proof of enlistment for active service or engagement in farm work or essential food production. The University Matriculation Board also adopted a flexible policy with respect to the recognition of various kinds of educational credits received during the war, such as Canadian Legion Educational Services Certificates.

With the other external examination barriers falling, the high school entrance examination lasted for some time longer. The system continued to be administered according to regulations that had an archaic ring, seeming to imply that an elementary school principal could not be trusted to carry out his responsibilities unless they were pointed out to him in minute detail, and unless the threat of a punitive inspector were held constantly over him. Examination requirements outlined in the course of study in 1936 divided subjects prescribed for form IV into two groups: group I – art and constructive work, hygiene and physical culture, and nature study and agriculture; group II – oral reading, writing, spelling, geography, history, grammar, literature, composition, and arithmetic. For admission to high school, it was sufficient for the principal to certify that the courses in the subjects specified in group I had been taken according to the regulations. The pupil either wrote examinations in all the subjects of group II on question papers provided by the department, or was given a recommendation on a basis similar to that mentioned for group I subjects. In the latter case, however, the recommendation "shall be accepted by the Entrance Board only after due investigation" as indicated in the appropriate regulation.

> When ... an Entrance Board decides to consider the expediency of adopting the scheme of admitting candidates from a school on the Principal's certificate in Group II, it shall direct the Inspector concerned to make, as early in each school year as practicable, a report to said Board in the case of each school in his Inspectorate preparing candidates for admission to the High Schools, as to whether the subjects prescribed therefor in Groups I and II respectively are being taken up to his satisfaction in all the forms of the school, having regard to the character of the teaching, the organization, and the management.[8]

The continuation of the high school entrance examination until 1949 was an indication of the gap that remained between the elementary and secondary levels. The division at that point was particularly anomalous after education was made compulsory up to the age of sixteen, with the implication that every pupil capable of making normal progress might be expected to complete at least some work in secondary school. In a sense, the examination reflected the continued strength of certain older European traditions, in contrast to the American trend toward a view of education as continuous progress. The fact that the Ontario Department of Education was organized then, and long after, on the basis of separate elementary and secondary school operations no doubt helps to explain why the system was so slow to change. Many members of the Ontario Secondary School Teachers' Federation were opposed to the abolition of the high school entrance examination, and for years after its abolition kept calling for its reinstatement.

It had been known that the Royal Commission was going to recommend the elimination of the entrance examination. Its thunder was stolen to some extent when the action was taken prior to the publication of the report.

Now that there was only one set of external examinations in the whole system, it might seem that the program should have remained for some time within manageable limits. But problems began to develop in the early 1950s. There were complaints about the difficulty of persuading members of university faculties to act as examiners-in-chief. The remuneration offered was very small, and increased federal grants for summer research were providing a counter-attraction. The Matriculation Board resorted to more active persuasion, including an effort to induce prospective examiners-in-chief to obtain necessary marking experience by applying for appointment as associate examiners. At this stage, problems were still relatively small and hardly foreshadowed the crises of the 1960s when the numbers of candidates and papers began to multiply.

In 1953 there was some discussion of the possibility of reducing the number of examination papers by offering only one paper in the languages instead of two. This idea, later put forward with more enthusiasm when there were stronger incentives for reducing the marking burden, was at this time considered and rejected. So also was the proposal to report a single mark in English and the foreign languages while the use of the two papers in each subject was continued. An innovation introduced in 1952 was a dictation test in French which was administered by means of a phonograph record. This device was often inappropriately referred to as an "oral French test," even though it covered a very limited component of oral language.

An interest in the application of certain kinds of statistical analysis was demonstrated in 1953 when the Department of Educational Research of the Ontario College of Education conducted a study of the 1952 marks in French authors to try to determine why the marks were out of line. The services of this department were subsequently available, at first sporadically and then almost continuously, to attempt to answer questions that arose. A further example was the assistance provided in the assessment of experimental papers in French and mathematics written by a sample of 1,100 candidates in 1957. The proposal for these papers was made by F.C. Asbury, Assistant Superintendent of Secondary Education, who was interested in finding ways of improving the selection of candidates for university. This particular scheme foreshadowed in some respects the later proposals for courses at the ordinary and advanced levels. It would have provided one paper in French on the general level and one on the special level in place of the currently employed papers in authors and composition, and one in mathematics at each level in place of the papers in algebra, geometry, and trigonometry and statics. The results were inconclusive, and nothing came of the scheme, although it indicated a constructive desire to explore new possibilities.

THE OPERATION OF THE EXAMINATION SYSTEM

The machinery

It is desirable at this stage to interrupt the account of successive events in order to observe the departmental examination machinery as it functioned about 1960. At that time the Matriculation Board consisted of eleven members, eight from the universities and three from the department. The university membership was made up of the presidents or principals of Assumption University of Windsor, Carleton University, McMaster University, the University of Ottawa, Queen's University, the

University of Toronto, and the University of Western Ontario. The University of Toronto had one additional member. The department was represented by the Chief Director, the Registrar, and one other member. The university heads and the Chief Director constituted the executive. The President of the University of Toronto had always been elected chairman of the executive, and the Registrar of the department was *ex officio* secretary of the board.

The Joint Committee, appointed by the University Matriculation Board, consisted at this time of three university representatives and three from the department. The latter consisted of one of the deputy ministers, who acted as chairman, the Registrar, who acted as secretary, and the Superintendent of Secondary Education. The Joint Committee played the active role in terms of the conduct of the examinations. After the pattern mentioned with reference to its initial establishment, it recommended the appointment of examiners-in-chief, associate examiners, and members of the Supervising Board. These recommendations were subject to the approval of the board and the minister.

The "Board of Examiners" was said to be a little-used term which served mainly to give the Registrar of the department, officially its chairman, the responsibility of supervising the whole examination system.[9] The board included the Supervising Board, the examiners-in-chief, and the associate examiners. There was also a close implied relationship to the Special Revising Board. The Supervising Board was responsible for setting the papers and for adjudicating any disputed points about the marking schemes. It consisted of eighteen members, equal numbers representing the universities and the department. The objective was to have at least one university and one departmental representative for each of the subject areas of English, history and geography, mathematics, science, and modern languages.

The examiners-in-chief, who were responsible for setting the papers, subject to the approval of the Supervising Board, and for directing the marking, were chosen from among nominations supplied by the universities. They were appointed for annual terms that were nearly always renewed so as to provide a three-year cycle of service. Conditions for appointment included previous service as an associate examiner. Most examiners-in-chief were from university faculties, although a few high school inspectors were also called upon. For the most part, the universities were entrusted with the responsibility of interpreting the secondary school point of view. How desirable this practice was depends on one's opinions about the purpose of secondary education. Those who felt that the interests of the non-university bound were being slighted were by no means happy about the situation. One advantage from the department's point of view was that the universities were in a weak position to complain about the value of the Secondary School Honour Graduation Diploma. It was not, of course, likely to be from those who participated in the examination process, but rather some of their colleagues, that criticisms were likely to come.

The associate examiners, who marked in a drill-hall set-up under the general direction of the examiner-in-chief and the immediate supervision of their own chairman and committee members, were largely drawn from the public secondary schools. Only about 10 per cent came from private schools or universities. Secondary school markers had to have permanent teaching certificates and experience teaching at least one grade 13 class during the year of marking. As the shortage of markers became more severe, there was some relaxation in these requirements. Annual appointments, as for examiners-in-chief, were normally renewable so as to provide a three-year cycle. The experience of marking was considered a desirable form of in-service training for teachers. A departmental memorandum described the advantages as follows:

A marker who participates in discussions with the Examiner-in-Chief and with experienced teachers, who becomes aware of many of the fine points involved in the paper, who has practice in judging the relative merits of different answers, who learns the necessity of having questions clearly worded, and who sees the weaknesses which some pupils exhibit in their answers, cannot fail to become a better teacher.[10]

The Special Revising Board did not actually work under the jurisdiction of the University Matriculation Board. As mentioned earlier, it was established by the minister to act as a kind of substitute for the supplemental examination system. It was intended to ensure that candidates received as favourable treatment as they could have hoped for under previous arrangements. The board consisted of fourteen members, one from each of the universities and seven from the department. The appointments were made by the minister without reference to the executive of the University Matriculation Board. The members reviewed each candidate's marks before the release of the certificates, giving particular attention to candidates who failed in one or more subjects and might be entitled to compensatory marks because of high standing on other papers. They also dealt with claims to aegrotat standing and to suspected cases of cheating or other offences.

Preparing the papers

The examiners-in-chief were notified informally of the coming honour of their appointment more than a year before their paper would actually be written. If they were marking papers in July, they might profit from the experience by thinking about possible questions. Official notice of appointment came in September, with instructions about procedure and a warning of the complete confidentiality of the operation. Material supplied for the appointee's perusal included copies of the examination papers of the previous six years, along with comments of the markers on the previous year's paper and on the candidates' answers. At times, additional items might include the following: directions from the Supervising Board of the previous year, relevant directives sent to the schools from the department, and resolutions of the Ontario Educational Association and other organizations. The examiner-in-chief then proceeded to prepare a draft of the paper and a fairly detailed outline of the answers he expected. The results of these efforts were scrutinized by one or two members of the Supervising Board. The first of these was the Registrar, who might make minor changes in punctuation, wording, or format; the next critic was a specialist in the subject concerned. Suggestions for change at this stage might range from slight to drastic, involving such matters as the apparent difficulty of the questions, the suitability of the topics or sight passages, or the appropriateness of the wording. The examiner-in-chief could either accept these suggestions or carry the issue to the subject committee. This latter consisted of the examiners-in-chief of related subjects, the members of the Supervising Board representing the subjects concerned, the Registrar, and one or two retired teachers of the subject. Lest the absence of the Registrar at some later stage cause a disaster, the Assistant Registrar also attended so that he might be prepared to take up the reins. Before meeting, members of the subject committee were given an opportunity to study the questions and the proposed answers.

The retired teacher co-opted for service on the committee was expected to bring the practitioner's point of view to bear on the process. He had to be retired because of the rule that no practising teacher could see the examination paper before it was taken from the sealed envelope in the examination room by the presiding officer. C.A. Brown, who was Registrar for many years before and after 1960, recalls that some effort was made to relax this rule, but that it was feared that a prior knowledge of the questions would have placed a teacher responsible for a grade 13 class in a very awkward position. It was thought that the most common reaction would be for such a teacher to lean over backward in order to avoid giving the paper away. The students would thus be placed at an unfair disadvantage.

The work of the committee was very thorough. The questions were assessed to ensure that they were at the right level of difficulty; that they were based on the course of study, and made no specific reference to any topic not specifically listed, or to any topic in the supplementary list; that the questions were clearly worded and unambiguous; that there were definite instructions about the length and depth of treatment expected in the answer; that questions dealt only with topics covered in all alternative recommended texts; that the easiest questions appeared in the first part of the paper; that questions considered to have political or religious overtones were avoided; that the weight of the questions corresponded roughly to the amount of time allotted to the various topics in the course of study;

and that the suggested questions would actually be likely to elicit the expected answers. It may be wondered whether all the conscientious people involved in this procedure realized that the more restrictions they imposed, the more predictable they were likely to make the paper, and the greater the premium placed on final cramming.

Two additional problems were singled out in the 1960 report.[11] One was that the paper was supposed to serve for both high school graduation and university admission. The way this objective was to be achieved was to construct most of the questions as a fair test for graduation, with one, two, or three designed to select the best candidates for university. It was easier to agree on objectives than on the appropriate means of attaining them, and there were many arguments about suitable content and emphasis. There were particular disagreements in science, where university people tended to move ahead and leave secondary school teachers and textbooks behind.

The second problem was that there was no provision for a preliminary tryout of the examination questions. The frequency with which papers turned out to be harder or easier than expected, despite the most conscientious efforts to achieve a given standard, provided an excellent confirmation of the research finding that subjectively developed standards cannot be trusted. There was no doubt in the minds of those closely involved that some method of adjusting marks was needed to avoid serious injustice to students. Despite any generalization on this topic, there were always exceptions. The writer recalls the discussions aimed at persuading one examiner-in-chief that adjusting or scaling was needed as a general policy. Events demonstrated that it was, but not in his particular case. In successive years of his cycle of service, he proved to be able to achieve almost exactly the results he aimed at.

After the subject committee's deliberations, there was still another hurdle for the paper to clear in that it had to be considered by the Supervising Board. According to reports, this stage was far from a formality. Specialists in disciplines other than the one to which the paper applied were able to make useful suggestions. Occasionally the examiner-in-chief might even be asked to submit a new question. As a follow-up, the examiner-in-chief and two members of the Supervising Board made a final check to ensure that the changes recommended by the Supervising Board had actually been carried out. Even yet, the examiner-in-chief might wish to object to board decisions, and agreement would have to be reached before the paper was finally printed. The examiner-in-chief checked the final copy from the press run to ensure that nothing had gone amiss in printing. Then the papers were carefully stored until time for distribution and use.

Preparations for the examinations by candidates and schools

The prospective candidate received a form early in March on which he was expected to indicate the papers he intended to write and the name of the intended examination centre. This was normally his own school, since all high schools in the provincial system, and certain private schools as well, were centres under the regulations. The candidate also gave information about his plans for the future, the papers on which he already had standing, and the papers he expected to write. This so-called Candidate's Statement was available for the use of the Special Revising Board in case there was a need to consider some adjustment of his results at a later stage. As a penalty, candidates were for some years charged a fee for late registration. The expense of collecting this fee amounted to a large proportion of the sum collected. The local school boards or private school authorities were responsible for the expenses involved in the actual conduct of the examinations. The department provided only the question papers, the envelopes for their return, name slips, and other materials. However, at university centres, which might be established specially by the minister, mainly for the use of privately-prepared candidates, the department paid all expenses. Centres could be established in universities outside the province with the candidate meeting the full cost.

The principal was responsible for returning to the department such information as the name of the chief presiding officer, his postal address, and the express office to which the papers were to be sent. Before the examinations, each candidate's teacher in each of his respective subjects was expected to supply a "recommended" or "confidential" mark indicating how he was expected to perform. Although these marks were not used to determine actual standing, except in cases considered by the Special Revising Board, they were appraised to determine the extent to which the teacher's verdict did or did not agree with that of the examiners on the basis of the evidence available to them. Under ordinary circumstances, the principal was the chief presiding officer in his own school; arrangements might however be made with the department to delegate this responsibility. There were very rigorous regulations to ensure that the envelope containing the papers was not opened before the examination.

Marking

Great efforts were made to ensure the maximum of objectivity in the marking. For this purpose, very detailed marking schemes were worked out in order to leave the marker with comparatively little opportunity to use his own judgment in assessing the answers, all in the interest of ensuring equitable treatment for the candidates. Marking schemes might run up to forty pages in length. Emphasis was placed on the point system in marking most of the papers, to the exclusion of the subtler and less easily measured objectives. In the latter part of the 1950s, the assignment of 10 per cent of the marks in history for "presentation" was the beginning of what was referred to as "a barely discernible trend toward allowing markers more freedom."[12] The "presentation" mark was not for literary style but for clear expression and logical arrangement of subject matter. One shudders to think of the implication that the candidate, even after this innovation, might have received 90 per cent without showing any evidence whatever of these qualities.

Apparently the presentation mark scheme did not accomplish even its limited purpose, according to the 1962 report of the Social Sciences Study Committee of the Joint Committee of the Toronto Board of Education and the University of Toronto.

> The experience of the Grade 13 matriculation papers in history is relevant to our problem. It has long been felt that the traditional Grade 13 examinations were inadequate as a testing device for students leaving upper school or entering university. A marking-scheme using the point system tested factual information almost exclusively. The good student could organize his material, select the relevant information, answer the question as asked, and still not get a substantially higher mark, or might even get a lower mark, than the student who filled in three pages with scattered information. The scheme did not permit the examiner to exercise any discretion in appraising the paper on its general merits. The use of presentation marks was an attempt to overcome this deficiency, but this too became so stereotyped that the original purpose was defeated and they became simply a bonus to every student who passed. The only discretion left the examiner was that which is involved merely in measuring an answer, sentence by sentence, against the marking-scheme.[13]

The procedure for devising the marking scheme was fairly involved. The examiner-in-chief was expected to prepare the first draft by April 30, after his paper and proposed answers had been finally approved. Copies were prepared for a committee consisting of between four and eight experienced teachers, who gathered with the examiner-in-chief for six to eight days before the main group of markers arrived in order to examine two or three hundred answer papers and test the scheme in practice. For a long period of time, it was the rule not to put the number of marks to be assigned to the questions on the examination paper as a guide to the candidate in allotting his time. This very bad measurement practice was justified as a means of enabling the committee to juggle the value of the questions so as to allow for any that turned out to be unexpectedly easy or hard.

Considerable criticism was voiced over the long period of time spent in producing the marking schemes and over their elaborate nature. The advantage claimed was that the investment in committee work produced faster marking, fewer discussions once the marking started, and the most equitable treatment of the candidates. Although the last objective still appears very creditable, it is to be wondered how much the desired equitable treatment cost in terms of real education, whether it was achieved by the preliminary development of forty-page marking schemes or by highly objective procedures devised by the examiners as they moved through their work.

The associate examiners or markers received a copy of the revised marking scheme on arrival. Every effort was made to ensure that they followed a uniform scheme throughout the period. It was considered undesirable to have them pay too much attention to the number of passes and failures in case they should consciously or unconsciously modify their standards. The department was to retain the responsibility of making any adjustment, and the less the markers knew about it, the better. The atmosphere in the marking room was reminiscent of a penal institution. This is how it was actually described.

> The marking is done under what may be considered reasonably strict discipline. Attendance of the markers is regular, complete, and punctual. A university regulation prohibits smoking in the buildings. [It is a question how many of the faculty ever heard of this rule.] While there is no official statement regarding conversation among markers, it is the exception rather than the rule to see or hear any talking other than that which obviously deals with the work in hand.[14]

This, it will be recalled, was a group of grade 13 teachers! It is little wonder that teachers keep finding it necessary to reassure themselves that they are members of a profession.

The quality of the markers' work was under constant supervision by the committee chairman and a member of the committee. They were especially on the lookout for markers who could not or would not follow the marking scheme. Elaborate arrangements were made to ensure that the marking was done anonymously: that is, that only a number, and not the candidate's name, appeared on the paper. There were carefully devised rules about where marks and subtotals were to be entered. Precautions were taken to see that rough work was considered, and that nothing was omitted because of intervening blank pages. When the examiner completed his efforts, each bundle of papers was placed on the desk of the appropriate committee member, who had a particular responsibility for rereading all papers assigned from 43 to 49 marks. A special check was made later for mechanical errors, such as failure to total the marks correctly or to count parts of questions. That this procedure was as careful as human beings are likely to devise can hardly be doubted, but some of the writer's direct experience with the analysis and reporting of the results indicated that errors could and did occasionally slip through.

The papers written by students who were considered to be of such calibre as to make them eligible for university scholarships were marked in special sections by associate examiners chosen for unusual expertise. These examiners were under the supervision of the same examiner-in-chief as were those who marked the regular papers in the same subject, but differences in location sometimes made contact difficult. The purpose of the special marking was to provide every assurance that those who were on the borderline did not lose their chance to win a scholarship by any carelessness in marking. There was continued speculation as to whether the arrangement achieved the desired result.

Processing the marks

For certain organizational reasons, it was apparently very important that all papers be completed for each examination centre in the order in which the centres started through the process. Thus it was vital that delays for corrections of various types of errors should not interfere with this order. Entering the marks on the permanent record cards, a hand process at the time referred to, had to begin when something like 25 per cent of the papers had been marked in order to ensure that all the necessary steps could be taken before the official release of the results. Thus it was important that any adjustment to the marks be made before that stage. When the entries in question had been made, the examination marks were compared with the teachers' recommendation or confidential marks to determine whether each class had actually done better or worse than the teacher had expected, and by how much. It became the practice to enter on the permanent record of each candidate who failed both the teacher's recommendation mark in the subjects concerned and an entry indicating whether this mark was over or under the actual performance of the class on the examination.

Another type of analysis of the results involved a search for "completers," that is, those who were eligible for a Secondary School Honour Graduation Diploma if they passed in all the papers written during the current session. Certain entries were made on each completer's Candidate's Statement: specifically, 1 / his grade 13 marks from previous years, if any, 2 / his grade 13 marks for the current year, 3/ his teachers' recommendation marks, and 4 / the figure designating the extent to which his teacher's recommendation marks for each paper were over or under his average marks. This information was of particular concern to the Special Revising Board, which tended to look with extra favour on completers in order to help them live up to the term.

The Special Revising Board

The status and basic functions of the Special Revising Board have already been explained. It was in continuous session from the period shortly after the marking began until it had dealt with all the centres, although not all the members were in continuous attendance. It was authorized to grant pass standing to candidates who missed the pass mark by a small margin on one or more papers, but whose record was otherwise satisfactory. The general principle was that marks in excess of the minimum on total performance or on related papers could be taken into account according to a formula in granting credit for failed papers. Although the Special Revising Board was officially authorized only to make recommendations to the minister, its decisions were actually final.

Release of results

In 1960, before modern techniques of data processing had been developed, certificates were individually typed, checked, and mailed to the person designated by the school board to receive them, usually the principal. The latter had to arrange to transfer the results to the school records and then send the certificates to the candidates. The latter had at that time to supply the necessary information to a university to which they might apply for admission. The official date of release was always regarded as very important. The universities had such a short time to process the applications that a delay of two or three days could have serious consequences for them. There were complaints that many good candidates were lost to American colleges because these institutions could give them a much earlier indication of where they stood.

Appeals

A candidate who failed might appeal, not later than the middle of September, to have his paper reread. The resulting obligation fell on the examiner-in-chief, who was expected to deal with the appeal according to his best judgment. In some cases, resort to leniency in handling appeals was the method employed to correct an unexpectedly severe failure rate that had not been compensated for at an earlier stage. The defect in this solution was that marks could be raised only for those who took the trouble to appeal. Candidates for university scholarships did not have the privilege of appealing, since their papers were treated with special attention in any case.

August examinations

After the supplemental examinations were abolished, a special set of August examinations was established in 1924 for teachers only. These were intended to assist elementary school teachers to improve their academic standing and thus up-grade their professional qualifications. The scarcity of teachers led in 1948 to the opening of these examinations to students who required standing in one or more grade 13 papers in order to enter the one-year course in a teachers' college. In order to make sure that only those who were seriously interested in a teaching career took advantage of this provision, and that the examination did not become a restored supplemental examination for all comers, provision was made for cancellation of a certificate earned through credits gained in August if the possessor did not actually attend teachers' college.

The August examinations constituted a somewhat anomalous arrangement in an otherwise highly centralized system. They were customarily held at least in Ottawa, Toronto, London, and North Bay, and at various other centres if sufficient applications were received. Question papers were provided in the main subjects, but not in those that attracted only a small proportion of the total number of grade 13 students. Prospective teachers who needed to write one or more papers to qualify for the one-year teachers' college course often had a problem that did not affect teachers who took them for up-grading in that they had to submit an application to write before they had the results of their June efforts, and thus before they were sure which credits they needed.

The examination postmortem

A kind of postmortem was done on each paper after the marking was completed. The results were then available to be taken into account by the examiners-in-chief, members of the Supervising Board, and others concerned with the next year's proceedings. The following extracts from the chairmen's comments for one particular year in the mid-1960s give some idea of the kind of observations made.

GEOGRAPHY

The ... question paper was considered by the Section to be a very fair paper. The two essay questions required not only knowledge but organization and understanding to answer well ... The main criticism concerned the length of the examination. It was clearly too long. Some students did not finish; many were obviously rushed on the last question ... It was the opinion that Questions 1 and 2 actually needed more time than it appeared at first.

ENGLISH

It was ... felt that instructions about the number of sentences to be used in an answer were useless unless progressive penalties were to be incurred for exceeding the stated number ... Most associate examiners were in favour of not attempting to question on every part of the course, but many examiners felt that more comparison questions involving related topics would have better tested the candidates ... Although it was generally agreed that the candidates' answers were better organized than usual, there is still much room for improvement. For this reason, the use of a style mark based on the examiner's reading of an entire paper was heartily endorsed, but it was also felt that the inclusion of a long essay question to be marked for style, or of an entire section to be marked for style, would aid greatly in equalizing the literature and composition valuations on the paper. The ... English examination frequently got away from factual answers which could be answered by the candidates who memorized the course or whose teachers had merely drilled on facts.

ALGEBRA

The ... Algebra paper was very fair ... The fact that a surprisingly large number failed would seem to raise suspicions regarding the over-all ability of the candidates or the quality of instruction they received.

PHYSICS

To set an examination in Physics, so that the intent of the question is properly interpreted by the candidate, is a most difficult task. Strange as it may seem the process of communication is the factor which causes the most confusion. I feel sure that this condition exists because there is a difference between the vocabulary used by the University professor and the High School teacher.

FRENCH

The three hours available were not sufficient to allow the students to organize and to check good answers to the many different types of questions. This was further aggravated by the fact that the indication of options was not clear enough and that, consequently, many students wrote much more than was required.

There were pages of comments on the handling of specific questions, but several general observations stand out. 1 / It was a matter of luck if the paper turned out not to be too long, even though there is every indication that the candidates wrote under great pressure and at high speed. It seems, incidentally, nothing short of miraculous that those who wrote the English paper could have attained more than the most mediocre level of style on a "long" essay question that constituted only a fraction of a three-hour paper. 2 / Despite all the careful attention devoted to the setting of the paper, there was often considerable uncertainty as to how the candidates would interpret the questions. 3 / The tendency to scold candidates for the way they approached their task seemed to carry the implication that they should have spent more time acquiring skills required for writing examinations. 4 / There was a naïve impression that, if the answers were not up to the chairman's standard, the fault was not necessarily in the paper, but might actually be attributable to a substantial fall in the quality of the thousands of candidates and scores of teachers involved within a period of two successive years.

The beginning of the crisis period

A study conducted in the Department of Educational Research at the end of the 1950s was a kind of stock-taking operation and also revealed certain interesting facts and trends about the system as it had operated from 1927 to 1958. The main findings, from an unpublished reference paper by D.G. MacEachern, were as follows:

1 / Roughly one-fourth of the papers written were judged successful by recommendation between 1935 and 1940, and about one-third under the wartime recommendation plan from 1941 to 1945.

2 / The average number of papers written by each candidate rose sharply

in the years 1941–3, and fell off slightly after 1944. No explanation was offered for this phenomenon.
3 / The total number of papers written in all subjects showed a steep rise in the early 1930s, and again in the 1950s, with a slight dip during the late 1930s, and again in the war years. It was of course the rise in the late 1950s that was the primary cause of the subsequent flurry of studies and of proposals for shortcuts and more efficient procedures.
4 / The percentages of successful papers in all subjects reached a peak of 87 in 1943, and declined to 81 in 1958. This finding was a surprise to those who assumed that a process of continuous relaxation of standards had been in operation. Of course, no definite pronouncement on this subject is justified by the data in the absence of any specific information on the quality and preparation of the candidates or the qualifications, attitudes, and efforts of the teachers. But it would be a safer deduction under the circumstances that standards were rising rather than that they were declining.
5 / Contrary to the general trend, the percentages of successful papers showed a steady upward trend in Latin and English. German produced an unusually high percentage of success. Mathematics, French, and the sciences had not been showing any strong trend in this respect in the years immediately preceding the study.
6 / The percentage of the total number of papers written in each subject remained fairly constant over the thirty-year period, but there was an increase in the sciences and a decrease in Latin and English.

In 1958 the minister, W.J. Dunlop, appointed a Committee on Grade 13 Examinations consisting of C.A. Brown, Registrar of the department, F.C. Asbury (replaced by A.H. McKague on Asbury's retirement), G.J. Westwood, Assistant Registrar, and R.W.B. Jackson, Director of the Department of Educational Research of the Ontario College of Education, to study ways of coping with the increasing number of candidates. It was considered particularly important to maintain the existing date, somewhere in the neighbourhood of August 12, for the release of the examination results. The committee decided that every effort should be made to provide for earlier release.

In announcing the studies being conducted at the time, the department was apprehensive about possible adverse reactions from principals and teachers to the prospects of modifications and expressed no great confidence in their readiness to change. A memo signed by C.W. Booth, Deputy Minister of Education, began as follows.

> The Grade 13 Departmental examinations occupy such a time-honoured place in the Ontario educational system that any suggestion that they be changed in any respect is likely to be looked on with some apprehension by the great majority of secondary school teachers.
>
> Nevertheless, it must be remembered that these examinations, important

as they undoubtedly are, constitute a means to an end and not an end in itself. Hence the possibility of their improvement must not be ignored.[15]

During this period C.A. Brown, who was long the central figure in the departmental examination system, made a number of visits to observe comparable practices in the United States and Great Britain. Some of his observations during these visits help to explain the subsequent train of events in Ontario. What impressed him favourably on his travels was likely to receive serious consideration when he got home, if not to provide the basis for actual experimentation.

One of his early excursions was to Albany, New York, on January 30 and 31, 1958, where he investigated the administration of the Regents' examination system. The fact that those responsible for that operation had about three million answer papers to handle each year, as compared with the Ontario department's 105,000, put the operation on an entirely different scale. Because so much use was made of objective tests and mechanical marking, Brown found many of their procedures inapplicable to his work. There were, however, several points that interested him. 1 / The Regents' examination papers at the end of grade 12 were set by teachers who were not teaching the subject during the current year. A small committee in the department indicated the topics to be covered and, in general, the type of question to be used; it also reviewed the question papers. 2 / The answer papers were marked by the classroom teachers and then sent to Albany, where about 25 per cent were spot-checked. This process often resulted in changes in marks. Thus no results could be released locally until the department's approval had been received. Brown commented with perhaps a touch of pride that the Regents' examinations were not conducted on as careful a basis as were the Ontario grade 13 examinations. They did, however, serve to set a uniform standard of achievement across the state, and thus seemed to provide a measure of support for the departmental testing program for grade 12 that was just in the experimental stage in Ontario. Only in the scholarship examination did Brown find marking conducted with the care that was typical in Ontario. Security measures were so tight that not even the presiding officer saw the question paper. It was handed to the candidate in a sealed envelope, and he sealed up the booklet again after answering the questions. Brown felt that much of the value of the visit would become apparent in more or less minor refinements of the procedures used in the Registrar's branch as time went on. He was quite positive about one conclusion – that they must resort to a judicious use of objective-type items along with essay-type questions.[16]

Another of Brown's tours involved a study of examination practices in England in 1960. He observed that procedures followed in the three centres he visited differed considerably from those in Ontario. To a casual observer, the approach in England seemed to be somewhat more authoritarian. It is a bit difficult to tell exactly what Brown meant by this comment, although it may have been based on the fact that the papers, model answers, and marking schemes were evaluated by more people in Ontario. It certainly appears that individual English markers were given a higher level of responsibility. They received draft marking schemes immediately following the examination, and had them confirmed after two or three days of isolated practice at home and one day's conference with the examiner-in-chief at a central point. There was provision for the markers to bring to the attention of the examiner-in-chief any exceptionally good answers not provided for in the scheme. The markers sent in their first twenty-five papers for review by the examiner-in-chief or one of his assistants, and then adjusted their marking in the light of the comments received. By spot-checking the work subsequently, the examiner-in-chief was able to determine whether the marks for certain examiners should be raised or lowered. Brown observed the contrast between this relaxed procedure and the regimented conditions prevailing in Ontario, with the marking under close and continuous review by committee members. He gained the impression that, by the end of the marking period, the examiner-in-chief was well informed about the proficiency and standards of each marker.[17]

Among other differences that interested Brown was the fact that practising teachers acted jointly with university representatives as examiners-in-chief, particularly at the ordinary level of the General Certificate of Education examination. Teachers, and sometimes even candidates, commonly knew who was marking the papers. In one centre the name of the candidate even appeared on the answer paper. Some safeguard against bias was provided by having an applicant for appointment as associate examiner declare his interest in a particular school or candidate. Brown noted that the absence of some of the security measures employed in Ontario contributed to the prompt handling of the enormous number of papers involved. He was interested in the open acceptance of scaling, which had been used at some centres for many years. The distribution of numbers in the various proficiency grades was determined by a small group headed by the examiner-in-chief in the subject concerned on the basis of past experience and the current year's performance. Official standing was reported by grades rather than by marks. Ontario had recently moved in the opposite direction at the request of the universities by showing actual marks on the certificates rather than proficiency standing. There was no counterpart in England to the Special Revising Board, since credit was awarded entirely on an individual subject basis, and overall achievement could not be taken into account to reverse minor failures.

By May of 1960 Brown was ready to urge a bold approach to the solution of some of Ontario's problems.[18] Some of his observations included specific recommendations. 1 / Because the three agencies he visited used essay questions, he received no help with respect to objective-type items, but he was encouraged to observe that at least one prominent official in London was impressed by the possibility of introducing the latter. 2 / Since the marking was done at home, he received no help in devising time-saving procedures such as having certain examiners mark part of the paper and having clerks add up the marks. 3 / He was persuaded that a good deal of the clerical work might as well be done on the data processing equipment of the Department of Educational Research, which was already playing this role with respect to the grade 12 testing program. 4 / He felt that, with increasing numbers seeking admission to university, a more selective type of test should be developed for that group. 5 / He thought it no longer practicable to invest as much time and money as Ontario was spending in marking papers for graduation only. The latter purpose might be served by decentralizing the marking and having it done in the district inspectorate areas. 6 / He expressed doubt that marks needed to be given for standings on a graduation paper, but felt that it would be sufficient to indicate whether the student had received pass or honours. Such a change would cut down the marking schemes and the time spent in preparing them. 7 / He doubted that the expense of marking was any longer justified as in-service training. 8 / He gathered support for the idea behind the experiment with general and special papers in 1957. It was pointed out to him, however, that the advanced level paper in England was written after two years of study beyond the ordinary level, and that the work was done by a group that had already been carefully screened and received instruction on a tutorial basis. The English authorities doubted the advisability of having one teacher teach both general and special work to the same class at the same time. In any case, Brown saw this approach as a way to change the "graduation" level of the examination into a "school" examination, marked locally under careful supervision, while a more selective examination could be developed for university admission.

University attitudes

As part of the investigation of the grade 13 examination question in the late 1950s, the minister consulted the university authorities about their attitude toward the continuation of the existing system for at least seven to ten years. The essential elements of that system were understood to be the predominance of essay-type questions and central marking under carefully controlled conditions. The response from the universities was overwhelmingly in favour of the existing set-up, with provision for limited modifications and, of course, improvements. That changes might have to be greater than expected was indicated by the projected increase in candidates and papers. Between 1954 and 1960 the number of candidates had risen from 15,466 to 26,638, and the number of papers from 86,460 to 148,485. By 1966 it was estimated that there would be 43,000 candidates and 236,500 papers. These figures turned out to be fairly close to the mark.

Report of the departmental committee

The report of the Committee on Grade 13 Examinations, submitted in November 1960, reflected some of Brown's impressions from his visit to England but in certain respects was more cautious.[19] It began by emphasizing six characteristics of the system that tended to restrict speed in marking. 1 / The dual purpose of the examinations required extra care in setting the papers and demanded more detail in marking than would otherwise have been necessary. 2 / The grade 13 examination was the only external device then in use in the entire system, and thus the only guarantee of a uniform standard of achievement. The results were also highly useful as a predictor of success in university. 3 / The functions of the Special Revising Board, justified because of the "group" character of the examination, meant that the results could not be released until the candidate's marks in all his subjects were available for review. 4 / The feeling that the essay-type question was one of the strong features of the examination made it unlikely that the objective-type question, despite the greater ease and speed of marking, would be an acceptable replacement. 5 / The use of the examination as a device for in-service training, and the resultant practice of passing the work around among eligible teachers, made it impossible to seek out and retain only those teachers with a special facility for efficient and speedy marking. 6 / Marking was necessarily a temporary, seasonal activity of those employed in it. "A casual staff of 26 Examiners-in-Chief, 850 associate examiners, 200 clerks, and 70 typists working in the heat of the summer and at the conclusion of their regular year's duties, is at best a somewhat unwieldy working force."[20] The committee expressed the view that the integrity of the examination must not be sacrificed to mere speed in marking and in issuing the results.

The committee reported a series of measures already taken or contemplated by the department to bring about the earlier release of the results.

1 / The Supervising Board would be asked to take whatever measures it could to facilitate the marking, such as having all sentences for translation of equal value and stating clearly the number of points and the length required in many of the answers.

2 / Candidates were to be urged to concentrate more on learning how to write examinations. It was true that the deputy minister had sent a memorandum during the previous year asking principals to bring this matter to the attention of teachers and candidates, and the warning had

apparently fallen on deaf ears, but a renewed effort was to be made. One wonders whether the teachers and candidates were merely obdurate or whether they might just possibly have been trying to reserve a little time for education.

3 / The Statement of Availability, introduced in 1960, gave the department a better selection of associate examiners and reduced the number of appointees who declined to act. Thus a certain amount of duplication and wasted time was eliminated in the preliminary work. While the new approach produced an adequate number of examiners for most subjects, there were not enough for English and French. It was suggested that the deficit might be made up by recruiting more markers from the private schools and universities. There was also some hope that an increase in the living allowance might attract more of the experienced teachers.

4 / Changes in procedures along the lines indicated depended for success on the provision of adequate departmental staff.

5 / The imposition of a $2 fee was an administrative burden, but seemed inadequate to deter carelessness over the late submission of applications. School principals had been almost unanimous in the view that no injustice would be done if the fee were raised to the point where late applications were practically eliminated. It was therefore recommended that the fee henceforth be $10, and that the marking of papers of late candidates be delayed until all others had been dealt with.

6 / Somewhere between 7 and 9 per cent of the papers marked in 1959 and 1960 had been awarded fewer than 35 marks, representing a waste of marking time and the expenditure of $40,000. It was felt that very weak candidates should be discouraged, although not prohibited, from taking their chances. It was therefore recommended that a candidate who could not secure a recommendation mark of at least 35 per cent from an authorized principal or the Director of the Departmental Correspondence Courses should pay a fee of $5 for each paper written, the fee to be refunded if he passed.

7 / The use of a limited proportion of objective-type items on the basis used in 1960 was commented upon with favour. This topic is developed more fully in subsequent pages.

8 / There was a review of the criticisms of the long period of time required to prepare and test marking schemes. Mention was made of the cost and of the objection of some school boards to releasing key people before the end of the term. The committee nevertheless doubted the wisdom, practicability, and economy of shortening the period of committee discussion. The main objection to such a change was that it would result in a fundamental alteration in the examination system. If consultation among an academic expert representing the universities, the examiner-in-chief, and representatives of practising teachers were reduced, more authority for setting standards and deciding on what material was to receive credit in the candidates' answers would devolve on the examiner-in-chief. Because

most examiners-in-chief had not taught in secondary schools, it was considered undesirable that they should have such authority.

9 / The department was commended for having introduced the practice of retaining the chairmen of the marking sections after their usual three-year term as associate examiners had expired. The delay in promotion of competent examiners to the chairman's position was considered a small price to pay for the advantages in speed and efficiency of making the position semi-permanent.

10 / Some advantage might be gained in changing the format of the examination books.

11 / For the previous two years, some sections had used sectional marking, involving concentration on one or more questions by specific groups. This policy of specialization had resulted in faster marking, and an extension of the approach to other sections was recommended.

12 / Clerks had been provided for some of the sections in 1960 to add up the marks on the different questions. A general adoption of the practice was recommended.

13 / Certain unspecified steps were to be taken to improve and speed up the checking of papers to ensure that all parts of the questions had been marked and that the marks were added correctly. Sectional marking was thought to entail the risk of increased carelessness on the part of individual examiners, who might tend to rely on one another for accurate checking. It would also be more difficult to hold examiners accountable for errors.

14 / The activities of the Special Revising Board delayed the release of the results by several days, but this extra period was considered completely justified in terms of the guarantee of equitable treatment provided for all candidates. Some speeding up of procedures was nevertheless possible, and plans were being made accordingly.

15 / It was the practice to retain the results for almost all centres until the entire set of certificates could be released. There was a promise of continued consideration of the possibility of staggering the process, but it was felt at the time that any change would cause more trouble than it was worth. An investigation showed that very little time elapsed between the release of the certificates from the department and their receipt by the candidates. Applicants for university admission also lost very little time in sending their certificates to the university of their first choice. However, they experienced considerably difficulty if they wished to apply to two or more universities. For this purpose, they usually had to obtain extra statements of standing from the department. Not only were their university applications delayed for a considerable period, but the department was also put to considerable extra work at a busy time when appeals were being dealt with and diplomas were being prepared. The committee simply recognized the problem without making any concrete proposals for dealing with it.

16 / To the proposal that more marking centres be set up in different parts of the province, departmental officials had responded that this type of decentralization would increase rather than decrease the time required for marking the papers and processing the results. Central marking was expected to be facilitated somewhat by the availability of additional space in the University of Toronto. The committee chairmen of 1960 had expressed themselves against any immediate change.
17 / The discontinuance of the August examinations for teachers and prospective teachers was recommended for several reasons. a / Their existence tended to increase pressure for supplementals for all candidates, constituting a demand that could not possibly be met. b / The preparation of the papers made demands on the Supervising Board and the printing office at a very difficult time. c / Expenditure for setting and printing the papers, arranging for examination centres, and providing for presiding officers and markers tended to reduce funds needed to administer the June examinations. d / Responsibility for marking at the end of August kept the examiners-in-chief from dealing as expeditiously as possible with appeals. e / Although some elementary and vocational teachers were taking advantage of the opportunity to improve their qualifications, the original purpose of the examinations had lost most of its urgency. f / Most of the teachers' college applicants did little better in August than they had done in June. g / There were now enough promising applicants for admission to the teachers' colleges that it was no longer necessary to make special provision for weak students.

A consideration of these recommendations as a group leads to the conclusion that they represented a thoughtful approach to specific weaknesses and difficulties within a very restricted framework. It is obvious that the committee was not prepared to sacrifice any fundamental part of the existing system. It appealed constantly to what it identified as the supportive attitudes of educators in schools and universities as well as those of the public. The fresh inspiration and the preparedness for much more radical innovation reflected in Brown's observations during and after his travels seem to have got lost in the deliberations of the group. The evidence suggests that Jackson, McKague, and Westwood must have been fairly well united in favour of minor tinkering with the machinery.

In addition to these matters that came within the area of responsibility of the Department of Education, there were certain other issues which also concerned the universities on which the departmental committee made observations and, to some extent, recommendations.
1 / Dissatisfaction was expressed over the "uncontrolled subject representation" on the Supervising Board, apparently meaning that there was too much bias or special concern with particular subjects. The Joint Committee was said to be planning to draw up a scheme for the rotation of subject representatives to improve the situation.

2 / The continued difficulty of finding and retaining suitable examiners-in-chief was pointed out. The heads of the universities did not seem to be taking their responsibility of nominating suitable candidates any too seriously.
3 / The earlier introduction of formal scaling of the marks was noted with approval. A justification for the regular use of this practice was provided, and a plan for its implementation was offered. This topic is reserved for later elaboration.
4 / It had once been the practice for the examiner-in-chief to mark all the papers of university scholarship candidates in order to ensure uniform treatment. As the number increased, it had become necessary to provide him with the assistance of from two to ten markers. The committee recommended that these scholarship papers henceforth be marked in the regular sections. It offered a number of reasons for this proposal. a / The extra fourteen marking sections constituted an undue administrative burden. b / The segregation of the scholarship papers as they arrived from the schools added to and delayed the work. c / It was difficult to decide on standards because the segregation of the scholarship papers and the unequal rate of marking the two groups of papers made it harder to obtain a representative sample. d / In view of the increasing number of different scholarships based on the grade 13 results, it was difficult to justify special treatment for the university scholarships. e / The necessity of having groups of markers deal with the papers had removed the original advantage of uniformity provided by a single marker. f / There seemed to be no good reason why the marking of the scholarship papers, whether easier or harder, should be different from that applying to the other papers. g / It would be advantageous to the regular sections to return a number of highly competent markers to them. h / The existence of separate scholarship and regular sections, often located in different parts of the building, made it difficult for the examiners-in-chief to keep in contact with them. i / The scholarship group actually included many candidates who were not of scholarship calibre. Although the abolition of separate marking was proposed, it was suggested that papers by scholarship candidates should continue to be identified so that the examiner-in-chief could provide for special checking.
5 / In view of the prospect of faster marking, it seemed advisable to consider the use of modern data processing equipment for the speedier and more accurate processing of many clerical operations. It was noted that equipment of this nature was in use in several of the western provinces and by the three examining bodies that Brown had visited in England. Proposals involved the use of the equipment to assign identification numbers to schools and to candidates before the examination, to tabulate the marks in preparation for scaling, and to prepare permanent record sheets. Particularly promising was the suggestion that a number of copies of

each student's record might be produced so that the schools, students, and provincial universities might all be given the information at the same time.

6 / The privilege of appeals was strongly supported. The growing burden of handling them under the existing procedures was, however, pointed out, and certain suggestions for improvements were made.

7 / The committee raised the possibility of reducing the number of papers by combining the two or more in certain subject areas. Note was taken of unsuccessful efforts in this direction in 1952 and 1956. The first received short shrift from the universities. The second, involving the experiment with general and special papers already referred to, had not led to conclusive rejection, but there was apparently a fear among some secondary school teachers that a reduction in the number of papers might lead to a curtailment of the time allotted to their subject in the timetable. It was suggested that the board consider establishing a committee representing itself, the department, and the secondary schools to deal with the question.

8 / There was speculation from one university on the possibility of establishing two levels somewhat along the lines of the advanced and ordinary levels of the General Certificate of Education in Britain. One system would be for secondary school graduation, and would be marked locally. The second would be for university admission, and would be handled by examination machinery in current use.

9 / The committee emphatically denied that the question papers had ever been made more difficult in order to reduce the number of candidates who were eligible for university. There was a strong recommendation that the Supervising Board continue to be independent of both the minister and the University Matriculation Board with respect to the level of difficulty of the papers.

MAJOR VARIATIONS AND TECHNICAL IMPROVEMENTS INTRODUCED

The use of objective test items

The primary purpose of the introduction of objective items into the grade 13 examinations was to save marking time. This objective was never realized, partly because the procedure did not get beyond the first step of having the associate examiners do the marking. The second step was to have involved clerical markers, and the final one, turning the process over to machines. Those responsible for examination policies could never bring themselves to the point of letting the marking slip out of professional hands. The extra time required to handle the objective section of each paper and to total the results largely cancelled out any gain in the actual marking. A warning that the expected advantages might be illusory was contained in a letter from H.M. Good, Associate Professor of Biology at Queen's University, to C.A. Brown on August 15, 1958.

I believe the advantages of this type of paper are more apparent than real. Questions which could be successfully asked in this form are ones which are marked very rapidly in the regular marking. If 30 or even 50% of a botany paper were in the form of an objective test, I think that there would be little saving in time. Separation of the objective and essay type questions, and then recombination of the marks would increase the clerical work and the remainder of the paper would still absorb nearly the time taken now.

Originally there was a great deal of apprehension about the way in which the proposals for the use of objective items would be received. The attachment of university professors and secondary school teachers to the essay-type question was considered, no doubt rightly, to be very strong. The matter had to be introduced well before definite action was contemplated to ensure that the ground was properly prepared. It was a fitting challenge for the diplomatic skills of Brown, who was always the soul of kindly tact. As he recalls it, things went very smoothly, and the feared cries of outrage never came from any quarter. Many potential opponents were no doubt impressed by the problem of dealing with the rapidly increasing number of papers and accepted the introduction of the objective item as a practical, although somewhat unpleasant, necessity. Others saw considerable potential advantage in its use as a valid examination device. The least enthusiastic were inevitably the specialists in the humanities, and the most enthusiastic, those in the sciences.

F.C. Asbury, Assistant Superintendent of Secondary Education at the time, expressed considerable appreciation of the virtues of the objective item. In an article in the *Bulletin*, he wrote:

... there has, of course, been a tremendous improvement in the calibre of objective-type tests. They have become the product of the work of highly skilled professional people. They have gained widespread recognition as useful and reliable aids in diagnosis of scholastic weakness, in evaluation of achievement, and in the determination of a candidate's fitness to proceed with his formal education ...

That the range of objectives in a Grade 13 subject which can be tested effectively by objective-type questions is much wider than one might at first suppose, is realized only after careful study of items from the best modern tests and a serious effort to make up suitable questions on one's own.[21]

A memorandum from the deputy minister announcing the change in examination policy also expressed conviction about the value of the objective test. "The gradual improvement in recent years in the character of objective-type tests and the mounting evidence of their effectiveness as indicators of scholastic ability and readiness for further education can hardly be ignored."[22]

This memorandum stated that the minister was proposing, with the concurrence of the University Matriculation Board, to incorporate some objective-type questions, with a combined value of not more than 30 per cent of the total, into some of the grade 13 papers for 1960. The department was seeking the assistance of the appropriate district committees of the Ontario Secondary School Teachers' Federation, as well as of the departmental consultative committees in the various subjects, to provide a pool of suitable test items for use in this venture. In a letter to S.G.B. Robinson, General Secretary of the Ontario Secondary School Teachers' Federation, the deputy minister elaborated on the nature of the request. He hoped that the federation would deliver the collected questions to the Registrar of the department by April 30, 1959, after which time they would be under the jurisdiction of that official. The department, with the co-operation of the Department of Educational Research, would then arrange to have the questions checked as to content, wording, format, validity, and reliability. (How the last two qualities were to be verified was not made clear. There were certainly no plans for a preliminary tryout.) The questions on the particular topics chosen for objective-type testing in 1960 were to be made available to the examiners-in-chief concerned. However, the question papers in their entirety would continue to be subject to the review and approval of the Supervising Board. Questions were to be of the matching, completion, or multiple-choice types, but not true-false. They were to cover most of the subjects for which grade 13 papers were set. The department promised to make certain illustrative material available for the use of the federation committees. A later memorandum contained a statement from the Department of Educational Research on the preparation of objective-type test items and a number of illustrations.[28] The latter were by no means received by the teachers with universal plaudits, as the writer's direct experience can attest.

The federation officials were in general gratified at being consulted, and the members in secondary schools attacked the task with vigour. Their approach differed considerably, with some groups producing a substantial list of items, and others devoting all their efforts to the production of a single gem. No fewer than 3,500 items were prepared and sent in from the entire province. As a means of stirring up interest, this project was undoubtedly very successful. In many cases, participation in the process of item construction reduced the propensity to criticize. The item pool, however, never developed as planned. On the whole, the examiners-in-chief preferred to make up their own items. Brown's observation in 1969 was that most of the results of their efforts measured purely factual knowledge, and that there was little effort to get at the more sophisticated objectives. Although no doubt thoroughly acquainted with their subject areas, the examiners-in-chief largely lacked the necessary technical training. For the most part, however, there was support for the continued use of the items over the years, and the examiners-in-chief in a number of subjects chose without constraint to include them. Brown feels that there were two definite gains from the procedure: there was more adequate coverage of the courses, and a new and stimulating variation on traditional practice was provided.

Scaling of marks

The informal adjustment of marks was resorted to long before it became a regular and recognized practice. It was necessitated by the unavoidable variations in the level of difficulty of the papers already commented on. The usual practice involved the raising of marks near the borderline between pass and failure in order to compensate for a paper that had turned out to be too severe. The major disadvantage of this approach was that it did nothing for those further up the scale, who might have been penalized with a second-class mark when they would, under normal circumstances, have got a first.

Steps toward the institution of a formal scaling procedure were taken in 1959. During the early stages of the marking in the summer of that year, it became clear that the failure rate for one or two of the papers was considerably out of line with what was thought desirable. Brown and G.J. Westwood, Assistant Registrar, approached the writer to ask about the possible application of appropriate statistical procedures to make the necessary adjustments. The writer outlined various approaches that might be considered, including transformation of the raw scores to fit the normal curve and a less drastic adjustment designed to produce a specified proportion in each of the five categories: first class, second class, third class, credit, and failure. Brown and Westwood were dubious of the results, partly because they were produced overnight. It did not seem possible that a sound scheme could emerge from anything short of several days of experimental juggling of the figures. They therefore rejected the writer's recommendation and applied their own system. When they made a leisurely study of the situation later, they discovered that it would have been better to use the alternative scheme. The pendulum thereupon swung in the other direction, and the writer was in constant apprehension lest they place more confidence in his calculations than they warranted.

Several factors were making the need for scaling more obvious, and at the same time that it was becoming more feasible. 1 / Statistical information on the performance of candidates during earlier years had shown how erratic the distribution of marks had been in some papers. 2 / The large scholarship and bursary program based mainly on examination standing made it highly undesirable for candidates at a specific level of ability to be able to obtain higher marks, on the average, in some subjects than in others. 3 / The introduction of objective-type items made scaling almost mandatory on at least that part of the paper where they were used. On the basis of these and other considerations, the Committee on Grade 13 Examinations included in a confidential memorandum to the minister a recommendation for the formal introduction of scaling.

Scaling had to be employed in 1960 when objective items were used on five papers. Prior apprehension about the likelihood of opposition proved to be unjustified, since no open objection was registered. The practice was supported by a recommendation from the Special Revising Board. In its report of November 1960 the departmental committee proposed that, until further notice by the University Matriculation Board, the final grade 13 departmental examination marks be assigned on a distribution to be determined each year for each paper by a committee consisting of the members of the Committee on Grade 13 Examinations, the Chairman of the Special Revising Board and one of its members representing the universities, and the examiner-in-chief and the chairman for the paper concerned. This committee would make its decision on the basis of past experience and that of the current year. The proposal received the approval of the Matriculation Board, and the committee was formed accordingly.

The essential preparatory task was to decide on the percentage of marks on each paper to be given first class, second class, third class, credit, and failure standing. The results of the previous eleven years were chosen as a basis for the calculations. When marks on all papers were averaged for this period, it was discovered that the percentages in each category were as follows: first class – 15 per cent; second class – 16 per cent; third class – 17 per cent; credit – 32 per cent; and failure – 20 per cent. During the early discussions, it proved impossible to secure agreement as to whether the distribution in all the major subjects should be the same or whether it should differ from subject to subject. There were special difficulties in deciding how to deal with papers written by comparatively few candidates.

The tentative decision was made at the time to move gradually toward a uniform percentage of marks in each category for all papers. Any gap was to be closed over a three-year period. For example, if the percentage of first-class marks in one particular paper had averaged 21 over the basal eleven-year period, it would be moved to 19 per cent in the first year of formal scaling, to 17 per cent the next year, and to 15 per cent the third year. This plan was never carried out in its entirety because of a later recognition of the strength of the argument that the general quality of the candidates differed considerably from one paper to another. Concrete evidence of this fact was provided by an analysis of data from the Atkinson Study of Utilization of Student Resources. During the first year of the scheme, and indeed in subsequent years, great patience and tolerance were shown by departmental officials in reaching decisions on scaling which would be acceptable to the examiners and the chairmen of the marking sections. When the latter felt strongly about some particular point, their desires were allowed to take precedence to a certain extent over the strict enforcement of the decision. One examiner-in-chief objected to the low percentage of failures proposed under the scheme, as well as to the complex plan to scale the essay and objective parts of the paper separately, and then to scale the total. This latter practice proved too unwieldy and was later simplified.

The process of scaling, which was carried out for a number of years by the writer within the range of objectives set by the committee referred to, and subject to its approval, posed certain rather vexing problems. Perhaps the most serious of these resulted from the fact that the scale had to be produced on the basis of the performance of the first 20 or 25 per cent of the candidates. Since the entering of marks on the permanent records, a laborious manual operation, had to be completed by a certain date, no further delay could be countenanced. Unfortunately for the accuracy of the process, the first papers were not representative of the entire provincial group but, because of certain arrangements to provide for the smooth functioning of the handling and marking machinery, came from selected centres in the Metropolitan Toronto area. Generally speaking, these papers were of better quality than the average, but by an amount that varied from one subject paper to another and from year to year. While scales developed on such a group had to be more "lenient" than the provincial scaling plan in order to ensure against excessively high failure rates in the province as a whole, there was a large element of sheer guesswork in making the necessary allowance. The writer lamented the impossibility of providing anything close to a random sample for the development of the scales, but it was not until after some very bad guesses were made that the machinery was modified to make the necessary change possible.

Another problem was that of allowing for the effect of appeals. If a certain percentage of failures was desired as a final outcome, the scale had to place an excessive number of cases below the pass mark in order to allow for the raising of a certain number on appeal. In a sense, the scaling was designed to cancel the effect of appeals, although it could be pointed out that the decisions made through the appeals process were selective rather than general.

A third and purely mechanical problem sometimes made it impossible to come very close to the scaling objective. It resulted from the fact that, especially in the middle section of the distribution of marks, large numbers of candidates received the same original mark. Thus if the proposed scale called for 16 per cent of the marks in the third class category, changing all the 59s to 60s might raise that percentage to 17, while leaving them at 59 would keep it at 15.

It was always difficult to decide what to do with marks obtained on papers written by very few candidates. The writer continually pointed out the invalidity of the regular scaling procedure where only a few dozen cases were involved. On those occasions when it was tried over his objections, the results were often unsatisfactory. It was eventually found possible to wait until all the papers in this category were marked before any adjustment was made, rather than producing a scale on a preliminary group and then applying it to all the subsequent results, as was done with the major papers.

Information about the scaling process was not secret after Robarts, as Minister of Education, gave it his official approval in 1960. But no steps were taken, to say the least, to publicize what was being done. It was considered best not to stir up unnecessary trouble by discussing a matter that was too complicated to explain fully and completely. Bascom St John seems to have felt that, as a journalist, he encountered a blank wall in his efforts to elicit specific information.

An interesting interchange occurred in the Legislature in April 1964 between Robert Nixon and Davis on the distribution of grade 13 marks and on scaling.

Mr. R.F. Nixon (Brant): Mr. Chairman, I was quite shocked to see in the statistical section of the report of the department that 46.28 per cent of the papers written in 1963 at the Grade 13 level were graded under 60 per cent. And I was quite interested to see that the range of percentage failure from subject to subject at the Grade 13 level was from 7.84 per cent failures in German composition to a high of 32.45 in accountancy practice, and – if you want to get away from that to something better known – to 24.47 in geography.

I wonder if the hon. Minister has any views when he considers the importance of the mark obtained in these various papers as to whether or not more uniformity from subject to subject in the final statistical result might be achieved?

Hon. Mr. Davis: Well, to a degree, Mr. Chairman, this depends on the number of papers written. There are not as many papers written, I think the hon. member will notice, in, say, the geography course. So that actually what would amount to a fewer number of either passes or failures would affect the percentage more substantially than it would, say, in English or history or some of the larger papers.

Mr. Nixon: There would not be many in the German composition?

Hon. Mr. Davis: There are not as a rule too many in the German composition. It is difficult to forecast, of course, from one year to the next what the percentage will be, but there is a greater fluctuation in those subject areas where fewer papers are written. I have not the 1961 and 1962 reports here, but you will not find quite the same fluctuation in the English courses or in the history courses.

Mr. Nixon: Do those in charge of the examinations have the power of some overall adjustment if the results tend to be considerably out of line?

Hon. Mr. Davis: Yes, Mr. Chairman. It is a very complicated procedure but there is a special revising committee. I think it is obvious that if a paper were set, and written by, say, 200 students, and 199 of them failed, that there would be a substantial revision. This has not occurred in these figures, but there is a revising committee, and the marks are revised.[24]

These remarks show that Davis was prepared to be quite forthright in acknowledging the practice of scaling.

The use of modern data processing equipment

The first serious involvement of the Department of Educational Research in a co-operative program with the Department of Education entailing the use of data processing machines developed with respect to the departmental grade 12 testing program. By 1959 services were being extended to include certain aspects of the grade 13 examination system. The fact that a scaling table could be constructed quickly depended entirely on the ability of the machines to produce a frequency distribution of marks already awarded in each subject. This function continued to be an important one up to the time the departmental examination system was abolished. In 1962 the tally lists used by the principals to indicate the papers to be written by each candidate were prepared at the Department of Educational Research and sent to the schools with the candidates' names already entered. The assignment of candidates' identification numbers was carried out at the same time; these numbers did not appear on the schools' tally lists but were reserved for later use.

In 1962, with the use of the IBM 1401 computer, the Department of Educational Research tabulated the marks of all candidates and prepared dummy certificates for about one-third of them on a trial run. A second experiment the following year involved the unofficial preparation of certificates for ten thousand candidates on the actual printed forms designed for official use in 1964. Thanks to the expert and conscientious work of D. Carder and his team in the Department of Educational Research, the experimental run worked almost perfectly the first time, an almost unique event in the history of the use of computers for educational operations. From the latter year on, all the certificates were produced by machine. In 1961 the University Matriculation Board set up a committee of registrars to co-operate with departmental officials in working out a plan for sending computer-produced copies of all examination results to the universities. When the scheme was introduced in 1963, it enabled the university officials to begin checking the grade 13 results of applicants for the current year a few days earlier than previously, since there was no need to wait for the candidate to submit a certificate or a duplicate of it. This development was particularly helpful in eliminating the need for multiple copies of the certificates to meet the requirements of applicants for admission to more than one university.

THE SPECIAL COMMITTEE OF THE MATRICULATION BOARD, 1961

Composition and activities

It was obvious that the problems that led to the establishment of the Committee on Grade 13 Examinations in 1958 were going to call for continuous study. The acceptance of certain improvements recommended by this committee did not for long alleviate the difficulty created by increasing numbers of candidates and the desirability of having the examination results released as early as possible. Thus in 1960 the University Matriculation Board appointed a Special Committee under the chairmanship of C.A. Brown and consisting additionally of J.B. Callan, Principal, Nepean High School, Ottawa; Dean J.A. Gibson, Carleton University; A.H. McKague, Assistant Superintendent of Secondary Education in the department; R. Ross, Registrar of the University of Toronto; and Dean N.J. Ruth, Assumption University of Windsor. The Special Committee had the power to add to these numbers. Its terms of reference were to investigate 1 / the possibility of reducing the number of papers and 2 / the possibility of adapting the examination system to meet the needs of two distinct types of students: a / those who were proceeding to the university, and b / those for whom grade 13 constituted high school leaving.[25]

The committee set out to obtain the opinions of certain professional groups on what it considered the most vital questions. For this purpose, views were solicited from the heads of the universities; the directors of education, as individuals; the Association of Secondary School Superintendents, as a group; the secondary school inspectors, as individuals; the Ontario Secondary School Headmasters' Association, as a group; the Ontario Secondary School Teachers' Federation, as a group; the English Catholic private schools, as a group; the French-speaking private schools, individually; the Canadian Headmasters' Association (Independent Boys' Schools), as individuals; the Association of Headmistresses (Independent Girls' Schools), as individuals; and various additional individuals from the above groups. As a result of the contributions received from these sources, the committee made what it considered to be a report consistent with the majority opinion of those who were in close touch with teaching and administration in the secondary schools and the universities.[26]

Recommendations

The committee's recommendations fell into four categories: 1 / those that might meet with immediate acceptance; 2 / those calling for short-term studies; 3 / those calling for longer-term studies; and 4 / those calling for study by other interested groups. Specific deadlines were suggested in the hope of obviating the delay typical of inquiries of this nature. The committee hoped that a steering committee might be appointed to give immediate direction to the implementation of those recommendations that received approval.

Majority opinion had at last reached the point where a substantial reduction in the number of papers could be recommended. Fear was still being expressed by some secondary school teachers that there might be timetable reductions. This was no doubt the reason why there was a tendency to prefer that, if there was a reduction in any subject, it should apply to all. Most of the secondary school teachers still seemed to prefer to have two papers in English. In accordance with opinions expressed in the survey, the committee's seven recommendations were as follows: 1 / that for 1963, one three-hour paper be provided instead of two 2½-hour papers in Latin, Greek, French, German, Spanish, Italian, Russian, and biology; 2 / that there be two three-hour papers instead of three 2½-hour papers in mathematics, with the problems paper retained as an extra paper; 3 / that each three-hour paper be treated as a unit rather than being divided into parts corresponding to the former two papers; 4 / that, for each of the subjects mentioned in the first two recommendations, the minister be asked to appoint a committee, sympathetic to the proposal, consisting of representatives of the universities, the Department of Education, and the Ontario Secondary School Teachers' Federation, with instructions to prepare a sample three-hour examination paper for the information and guidance of teachers; 5 / that the minister be asked to have the revised combined course of study in biology completed by November 15, 1961, in order that teachers might become familiar with it before September, 1962; 6 / that the minister be asked to take the necessary steps to ensure that the reduction in the number of papers did not result in a reduction of time allotments in secondary school timetables; 7 / that, for the period of transition to a reduced number of papers, the mark on the reduced papers referred to in the first recommendation be given double weight in computing averages for scholarships and bursaries.

The Special Committee recommended that no steps be taken, for the time being at least, to establish a dual system of examinations at the grade 13 level. The members felt that the public would be unwilling to accept a lower level of achievement for those who were not planning to go to university, nor did the members themselves think it desirable. It seemed certain that the university admission standard would still be required for admission to teachers' colleges and various professional and technical organizations under any dual system.

A revision of the elementary and secondary school courses was recommended to reduce the existing thirteen-year program to one of twelve years. It was thought that such a revised course would result in a greater challenge to a larger number of students and would tend to promote desirable habits of study and work. This recommendation was discussed in volume III, applying, as it did, to courses rather than to examinations. A recommendation that a uniform external examination be reintroduced at the end of grade 12, along with a series of supporting proposals, is discussed in chapter 16.

The sixth chapter of the report offered suggestions for a revamped "Senior Matriculation" year, thus preparing the way for the work of subsequent committees. It was recommended that a more restrictive set of examinations confront the student who wished to enter such a course, and that the examinations at the end of it would be a means of determining his mental power and resilience, and his capacity for growth. Regardless of whether or not the view could be justified in the abstract, there is an air of unreality about this statement: "The Committee is strongly of the opinion that if the 'Senior Matriculation' year is to provide a more desirable form of intellectual experience than it does at present, more rigorous screening in the 'Junior Matriculation' years will be necessary ...[27] The 1960s were certainly not a period in which ambitious students and parents would willingly tolerate new or higher barriers to educational opportunity at the upper level, the reintroduction of grade 12 external examinations notwithstanding.

One very specific recommendation, offered to provide secondary school teachers and students the opportunity to make the grade 13 year a richer educational experience, was that the universities be asked to adjust their admission requirements from five subjects to four (or a corresponding reduction from nine papers). A supplementary recommendation was that the Chairman of the University Matriculation Board be asked to appoint a committee to explore this possibility with the universities. The next recommendation was that the dual purpose of the examinations be improved by including on the proposed three-hour papers a sufficient number of questions of a type that would enable the average student to obtain pass standing, as well as some additional questions that, in the opinion of the university people, were valuable in selecting promising university students. According to earlier descriptions of the examination system, this is exactly what the examiners had been trying to do all along and, in the process, encountering a good deal of trouble reconciling the two interests involved. If the committee had any new ideas about how the objective in question could be realized more effectively, there was no evidence of it in the report. The chairman was, however, to be asked to appoint a committee to gather and forward to the department sample questions of the type the universities would like to see on the grade 13 papers, so that they could be used for the guidance of teachers.

A section of the report elaborated on the desirability of close and continuing liaison between the universities and the secondary schools. The committee's observations on this point are relevant here mainly because of the implication that departmental examination results should be supplemented as admissions criteria with evidence of achievement and other relevant factors on record in the schools. The universities were urged to give further favourable consideration to the possibility of granting tentative early admission based to a considerable extent on this kind of information.

In attempting to come to grips with the problem of devising ways of speeding the release of the examination results, the committee recognized that arrangements previously initiated by the department, in addition to the proposed combination of papers, could at best produce gains of only a few days and that whatever advantage was achieved would soon be counteracted by the increasing number of candidates. Further changes would have to be made. To the committee, it seemed an obvious solution to hold the examinations early enough to have the papers marked by June 30. That it would raise new problems was recognized, but these seemed amenable to solution by negotiation with principals and school boards. There seemed to be two strong advantages in addition to earlier availability of the results. 1 / It would be easier to obtain the services of associate examiners, the best of whom were in increasing demand by the school boards, the Department of Education, and the Ontario Secondary School Teachers' Federation as summer school teachers. 2 / It would give students more time for summer employment. In view of the storm of protest that was aroused when the examinations were advanced by a single week in 1963, the committee can only be charged with a serious lack of political perception in its assessment of the situation.

RESULTS OF COMMITTEE RECOMMENDATIONS AND FURTHER EFFORTS TO DEAL WITH THE CRISIS

Much of the presentation thus far has dealt with suggestions and recommendations for the improvement of the examination system. A review of subsequent events shows that a considerable number of these were carried out, some immediately and others after a certain delay. The August examinations were completely and finally abolished after 1961. In 1962 the fee for late registration was raised, not to $10 as recommended, but to $5, and was to be exacted after an April 15 deadline. It was also provided that candidates prepared in secondary school classes, private school classes, and night school classes connected with a secondary school or an inspected private school, and those prepared through the Department of Education correspondence courses, must pay a $5 fee to write any paper on which they had not been assigned a teacher's recommendation mark of at least 35 per cent. Private study candidates for whom no confidential mark was submitted must also pay the same fee for each paper written. The fee was to be refunded for each of the papers in question on which they received at least 50 per cent. The pay and allowances for associate examiners were raised at this time.[28]

It was announced in early 1962 that the recommendation of the special committee of the University Matriculation Board in favour of the use of three-hour papers in place of a larger number of 2½-hour papers would not be implemented in 1963. Departmental officials felt that current revisions of certain courses had not progressed sufficiently to make this change possible for the time being. In the meantime, experimental three-hour papers were being tried out in French and Latin based on the 1961–2 course of study. Work on a sample three-hour paper in biology had been at a standstill because of the difficulty of basing a three-hour paper on the current separate courses in botany and zoology when many of the students had taken only one of the two subjects.[29] By the end of the year, the obstacles had been overcome. It was announced that beginning in June 1965 there would be a single paper in each of the languages other than English; beginning in June 1966 there would be a single paper in biology in place of the existing papers in botany and zoology; beginning in June 1967 there would be two papers in mathematics in place of the existing three papers in algebra, geometry, and trigonometry and statics.[30] Teaching time allotted to the subjects concerned was not to be reduced because of the number of grade 13 examination papers, although it might be affected by significant changes in the content of the course.

Certainly the most controversial change attempted, and one that was not repeated, was the attempt to advance the date of the examinations by one week in 1963. In announcing that they would begin on Monday, June 3, the minister gave an assurance that boards would not lose any attendance grant on behalf of the students because of the change. The scheme required markers of English and French papers to report for duty in Toronto on June 18, and those for the other papers about a week later. Boards and principals were asked to arrange for the release of about one thousand teachers, or one in fifteen of the secondary teaching force, for this purpose. The secondary schools were to close on the usual date despite the change.

The reaction to this proposal is worth examining in some detail, particularly in the light of the storm of complaints over the attempt in 1969, whether or not it could justifiably be called a lengthening of the school year, to keep high school students in school *longer* than they originally expected. Bascom St John expressed most of the objections in very emphatic terms.

> The announcement that the Grade 13 final examination is to begin a week earlier than has been the case recently was made unexpectedly by the Ontario Department of Education last week. Unfortunately, as usual, no consultation was made with the schools, which will have to administer the examination. It already appears that in a large system such as Toronto's, the educational effect, not to mention the administrative confusion, will be destructive.
>
> Admittedly the motive is powerful ... The surge of candidates and the breadth of their effort is overwhelming. To find the time for the marking, the

teachers to do it, and to organize the office procedures to get the results out to the right places, is a monumental job. The temptation to steal a week from the school year must have been irresistible.

However, the consequences to the schools are very extensive. For one thing, the examinations will begin on June 3. (This year, they began on June 11, and concluded on June 29. Time has to be allowed for 30 examinations at the rate of two a day.)

During the week prior to the examination, it has been the practice in some school systems to allow an easy timetable, in which the prospective candidates could study at home, or get special assistance from a teacher. If this were to be done next year, it would mean shoving the preparatory period back into May.

The most unsatisfactory impact which the new policy will make is in connection with the rest of the school. The Grade 13 examination is of such immense importance to the students trying it, that the noise and distraction of the classes in the other grades moving around in their usual rotations is intolerable. In almost all schools, it is the practice to let the others go home when the examination starts ...

In a significant discussion of this problem in the Toronto Board of Education last week, it was noted that the effect of the new regulation will be to create great difficulties in the administration of the year-end examinations in the other forms. There has to be enough time to hold these examinations, and to mark them. In effect, it was said, the moving ahead of the Grade 13 examination by one week will shorten the school year for the rest of the school by possibly a month.

And on top of all this, the Department of Education is going to start withdrawing teachers for marking duty on June 18, further complicating the administrative problem.

... Perhaps, if the universities are unwilling to delay their own opening a week or two in the fall, the secondary schools might be started in the middle of August, to make up.[81]

The last suggestions could hardly be regarded as practical. If a change of the proportions of the one actually announced caused so much disruption, one can well imagine that St John's proposals would hardly do less. Most of the points made about the effect on the schools were valid, although by no means underemphasized.

A very contentious aspect of the issue was that the teachers released for marking continued on full salary for the remainder of June. The remuneration they received from the department for that period thus constituted double pay. School boards and other teachers were unhappy about the inequity of the situation.

One of the most extreme of the adverse reactions came from Thornbury District High School. At a meeting held on April 25, 1963, the following motion was passed by a group of teachers: "Resolved that commencing with 1964 teachers from this school will not accept appointments to mark papers in Toronto during the summer until after the end of the legal school year in June."[32] From the Renfrew and District Collegiate Institute Board came this declaration: "The Board wishes you to be informed ... that in future years, they will not permit teachers to leave before regular closing date for this purpose."[33] An example of a very moderately worded expression of disapproval came from the Kingston Board: "The Board feels that every effort should be made to find some other solution to the problem for 1964 and subsequent years."[34] The Ontario Secondary School Teachers' Federation decided to let the department deal with its self-created problems as best it might. The general secretary, S.G.B. Robinson, expressed the federation's official view.

> In the opinion of the Provincial Executive of OSSTF teachers are employed by a school board until whatever day in June the board considers to be the end of the school year for that school and that teachers who wish to be absent from school prior to this date should seek leave of absence from the school board, which leave may or may not be granted, with or without pay.[35]

The charge by Bascom St John and others that the announcement was made without consultation bears careful examination. Since every decision made and announced by the department can hardly be subjected beforehand to endless discussion by all important educational interests, the question hinges on the relative importance of this particular issue. The writer was present in a relatively passive role when the matter was being discussed before the minister's announcement and does not recall that the officials concerned were in any way prepared for the strength of the adverse reaction. Undoubtedly their concern with the problem of early release of the examination results after the marking was overwhelming. In a sense, there was a good case for the claim that consultation had indeed occurred. The action was taken as a result of the recommendation of a committee that had obtained opinions from over four hundred separate individuals and groups on many aspects of the examination question. If the members of that committee were not able to assess the general situation after such an amount of consultation, one might well wonder on whom the minister could rely for advice.

With the prospect of another sharp rise in numbers, the Registrar was released from most of his regular duties to prepare a series of study papers on various aspects of the problem. The Committee on Grade 13 Examinations, consisting largely, but not exclusively, of departmental members, continued an active review of the situation.[36] Proposals contained in Study Paper No. 13 were of particular interest.[37] Copies were sent to the secretaries of the Association of Directors of Education, the Association of Secondary School Superintendents, the Ontario School Trustees' Council, the Ontario Secondary School Headmasters' Association, and the Ontario

Teachers' Federation. These organizations were requested to express their opinion on the proposals within a reasonable period of time.

The paper stated first that, in view of the problems created for school boards and principals by the early holding of the examinations in 1963, the experiment would not be repeated, except that a special arrangement might possibly be made for English composition.[38] The first specific proposal for change was that two-hour papers be substituted for the traditional 2½-hour papers. There might be a saving of a significant amount of time, although not the 20 per cent that simple arithmetic would suggest. The idea had already received reasonable support from a group of over sixty representatives of the universities and the department, mainly the examiners-in-chief and members of the Supervising Board. It was, of course, too late by this time to make the suggested change in 1964.

Another proposal was that part of each answer paper be marked in the schools. It was stated that, because of the difficulty in having the more searching, subjective-type questions marked uniformly, and because of the admittedly competitive nature of the examination, a significant part of each paper must be marked at a central point. The details of the proposal were as follows: 1 / that where a question paper contained an objective-type part, the items be marked in Toronto by clerks or by mechanical means; 2 / that between 25 and 30 per cent of the essay-type part of each paper be marked by the grade 13 teachers in the schools immediately following the examination in accordance with a marking scheme to be provided, and subject to checking in Toronto; and 3 / that the remainder of the paper be marked in Toronto in the usual way at the usual time. It was suggested that one of the advantages of the scheme was that it would extend to all grade 13 teachers some of the benefits of in-service training claimed for the experience of marking at a central point. The proposal raised the question of whether principals could free the grade 13 teachers from presiding and other duties for two or three days to participate in the local marking. In view of the earlier protests, there was also speculation about possible objections to the teachers' receiving a small amount of extra remuneration for the service provided.

This proposal for partial decentralization of the marking did not produce a very favourable response. The Ontario School Trustees' Council, for example, announced its flat opposition, warning that local marking "would be extremely disrupting to the schools." Other groups were willing, under the circumstances, to have the scheme tried, but they were not at all enthusiastic.

Some of the objections to the idea of having a single three-hour paper for English literature and composition had subsided sufficiently by the latter part of 1963 to make possible the setting of such a paper, and its administration on an experimental basis, in 1964. An additional objective was to find a more valid method of assessing the candidate's writing ability than that used previously. Part of the investigation involved the study of a number of essays written by the participating students during the year. A comparison was made between the results achieved under the relatively leisurely conditions characteristic of regular school sessions and those obtained under the intensive pressures prevailing during the examination. Arrangements were made for thorough consultation with the Ontario Secondary School Teachers' Federation and the Ontario Secondary School Headmasters' Association. The comments received were considered constructive and undoubtedly helped to create a climate that was favourable to a certain amount of change.

THE GRADE 13 STUDY COMMITTEE, 1964

Appointment and terms of reference

The situation was obviously not going to be solved by trying to persuade the educational associations to agree to minor palliatives. On January 31, 1964, Davis took steps to prepare the way for major changes. It is true that his immediate action was to "appoint still another committee," but this one was somewhat different from those that had gone before, both in the range of its membership and in the fundamental nature of its objectives. In the Legislature, Davis outlined the full extent of the problem of numbers. He reviewed the studies that had been made up to that point and indicated the changes that had made it possible to maintain up to that time approximately the same release date in successive years. After assessing the whole situation, he had come to the conclusion that the time was "opportune for a comprehensive study of the nature and function of the grade 13 year in our educational system."[39] He was appointing a committee that would represent the department, the schools, the universities, and the school boards "to look into this question and to recommend for my consideration any changes which appear to be necessary and advisable in the grade 13 year, including the examinations."[40] In view of this undertaking, there would be no effort in 1964 to introduce local marking. Davis hoped that school boards, directors, superintendents, principals, heads of departments, and teachers would feel disposed to do everything they could to make available a sufficient number of markers for the current year.

The specific terms of reference of the committee were as follows.

1. The Committee is asked to inquire into and report upon the nature and function of the Grade 13 year in the Ontario educational system, particularly in the light of opinions expressed frequently by responsible persons that, despite the fact that much can be said in its favour,
(a) Grade 13 is a cram year with too much emphasis upon the memorization of factual information and upon preparation for the final Departmental examinations;
(b) the year should provide a richer educational experience than it does for all students, whether they propose to go either to universities and other

institutions of higher learning or directly to some form of employment; and

(c) the year should be a better liaison between the school programme and the programmes of the universities and other institutions of higher learning.

2. While it is not intended to restrict the Committee's authority to look into any matter which it considers relevant, to the extent permitted by the time available, the members are asked to keep in mind that the following programmes have been initiated, after considerable study in each case:

(a) the Re-organized Programme in the Secondary Schools;

(b) the curriculum revision programme in most subjects in all grades; and

(c) the progressive reduction in the number of Grade 13 papers to be written by each candidate, through the replacement, in several subjects, of two papers by a single paper and of three papers by two in Mathematics.

3. Specifically, if the situation as outlined in section 1 is found to exist, the Committee is asked to recommend for the Minister's consideration,

(a) changes which might be made immediately to improve the situation;

(b) an ideal solution for the problems presented by the situation; and

(c) successive steps which might be taken to implement the ideal solution, including means of determining whether the candidates concerned have met satisfactory standards for (i) graduation from secondary school, and (ii) admission to universities and other institutions of higher learning.[41]

Recommendations

During its short but intensive period of study, the committee examined about 170 briefs from individuals and groups all over the province. A "reassuring consensus" among the views expressed was said to have helped it reach conclusions on general principles. The situation was described thus.

Most frequent were complaints about the over-crowded content of the Grade 13 year, the emphasis on factual information rather than the exploration of ideas, the reliance on one set of examinations as the gauge of a student's ability, and, arising from these examinations, a variety of other problems ranging from emotional strain to administrative burdens. All signs pointed to the need for some immediate relief and for significant and far-reaching reforms ...

With the ever-increasing number of Grade 13 students it would be impossible even if it were desirable, to continue the present system of external examinations.[42]

The last sentence was to prove a fateful one, since it was used to justify the minister's decision to abolish the whole centralized apparatus for administering the departmental examinations after 1967. The committee, it is true, saw that the existing system could not last for long in its existing form and certainly did not think that it should. But it definitely favoured some form of external control over variations in standards and some uniform criteria for university admission. Its long-term proposals for changes in the examinations were linked to a drastic restructuring of the school system, including a reduction of the program from thirteen years to twelve and the establishment of general and advanced levels of study. It recommended that "when proper safeguards are developed external examinations which circumscribe the teaching and encourage the cramming of factual material should be eliminated."[43] It is doubtful that those who were responsible for this recommendation would have felt at the time that the OACU and SACU programs, as they actually developed, could be regarded as "adequate safeguards."

The successor to the 1964 committee which was set up to examine the proposal for general and advanced levels of study in grade 13 did not express a very radical view on the examination question, as indicated by this statement.

> The Committee recognizes that some type of uniform external examination is necessary as part of the assessment of the proficiency of graduating students, in order to ensure some standardized measure of achievement, since admissions to university and other institutions of higher learning depend so directly on standing in Grade 13. It is unfortunate that because of the difficulty in having answers to comprehensive and thought-provoking questions marked in an equitable manner, it has been considered necessary to use question papers which placed undue stress upon the organization and presentation of factual material that can be marked in a reasonably objective manner. The Committee urges strongly that with the introduction of Advanced Level courses, and with less detailed courses of study, care be taken to have examination questions which will emphasize testing of the candidates' study in depth rather than the mere accumulation of factual knowledge. It is noted that a beginning has already been made in this direction on the present Grade 13 examination papers, but further extension of the policy will require concerted effort toward the training of teachers in marking subjective-type questions as part of the updating plans.[44]

It is clear from this passage that the committee anticipated nothing more than reforms of the existing system. It was clearly not thinking of relying for external control on a program of objective testing.

Conscious of the urgency of some of the immediate problems, the Grade 13 Study Committee of 1964 made a series of proposals designed to relieve some of the pressures on the candidates.

1. That, for the purposes of the 1965 Departmental examinations, steps be taken to remove from the Grade 13 course of study in each subject, topics which at present require a total of approximately three weeks of teaching

time, and that announcement of these reductions be made before September 1, 1964.

2. That brochures be prepared for distribution to teachers in September, 1964 as a guide to the most advantageous use of the additional time which will be at their disposal because of the reductions in course content referred to in Recommendation No. 1 ...
3. That for the 1965 Departmental examinations, 25% of the final mark assigned to a candidate in each subject or in each paper, as the case may be, be based upon the recommendation mark which in the opinion of the principal and teacher represent the candidate's proficiency as reflected in his year's work, and 75% of the final mark bc based upon the June Departmental examination.
4. That in the case of English and Français the 25% referred to in Recommendation No. 3 be based upon the candidate's proficiency in writing as indicated by essays which he has written during the year.
5. That for the 1965 Departmental examinations all question papers be relatively shorter than those of past years, with fewer questions and more options, and with the relative values of the questions shown.
6. That for the 1965 Departmental examinations a private-study candidate (a) who has not been in attendance during the school year 1964–65 at the day or evening classes of a secondary school or a private school which is an examination centre, or (b) who has not been studying the subject concerned through the Correspondence Courses Branch of the Department of Education, have his final mark based entirely upon the written June Departmental examinations.
7. That for the 1965 Departmental examinations there be one 3-hour examination in each of English, Français, French, German, Latin, Greek, Spanish, Italian, and Russian in place of the present two 2½-hour examinations ...
8. That for the 1965 Departmental examinations there be a 2-hour examination in place of the present 2½-hour examination in each of History, Algebra, Geometry, Trigonometry and Statics, Physics, Chemistry, Botany, Zoology, Geography, Art, Music, Accountancy Practice, Secretarial Practice, and Mathematics of Investment ...
9. That for the 1965 Departmental examinations there be a 3-hour examination in Problems in place of the present 2½-hour examination.
10. That where suitable and applicable to the subject, greater use be made than in the past of non-essay type questions (short answer, completion, matching, and multiple choice, up to the usual limit of 30% of the marks assigned to the written paper in June.[45]

The committee continued with a series of recommendations to apply to the 1965–6 school year. Those related to the present discussion were as follows.

12. That for the 1966 Departmental examinations, 35% of the final mark assigned to a candidate in each subject or in each paper, as the case may be, be based upon the recommendation mark which in the opinion of the principal and teacher represents the candidate's proficiency as reflected in his year's work, and 65% of the final mark be based upon the June Departmental examination.
13. That as already agreed upon by the Minister and the University Matriculation Board, there be one 3-hour examination in Biology in place of the present separate examinations in Botany and Zoology.
14. That the Secondary School Honour Graduation Diploma be discontinued after the school year 1965–6 ...
16. That in order to encourage the enrichment of high school courses and a more penetrating study; to relieve the pressure of examinations; and to prepare for a year with greater concentration and depth, the universities be requested to review their admission requirements and to consider reducing the number of subjects required for admission, having due regard for the essential preparation for their courses and the general equipment of a university student ...
17. That if a reduction in the number of Grade 13 subjects required for admission to university in September, 1966 has not been announced by the end of February, 1965, the situation with respect to the marking of the Departmental examinations in English and French be reviewed in the light of the 1964 experience in marking the increased number of answer papers in these subjects ...
19. That a study be made by the Department of Education of the problem of securing comparable marks from the various schools under the proposed system of using the recommendations of principals and teachers.[46]

These proposals, applying to the two specified years, were designed to facilitate a smooth transition to more drastic and fundamental reforms.

Response to recommendations

The extraordinary efforts made by the Registrar's Branch in the summer of 1964, with the effective assistance of the data processing staff of the Department of Educational Research, provided some relief from the crisis atmosphere under which the committee made its recommendations. Although the normal date for the beginning of the examinations was restored, and despite an increase of approximately 25,000 answer papers, the results were released to the schools by August 11. Full reliance for the first time an electronic data processing of all clerical operations, along with improved marking procedures, had succeeded in staving off disaster. In fact, because the universities received complete sets of examination results for all candidates at the same time the certificates were mailed to the schools, the situation with respect to university admission was somewhat improved. It was said that many applicants even received notices of acceptance a day or two after the department had delivered the mark lists to the universities.[47]

In response to the committee's recommendations, and in accordance with plans in most cases already formulated, a single three-hour paper was substituted for the traditional arrangement in each of the languages, including English and Français. At the same time, plans were announced for a single paper in biology in 1966. It was first announced that students who were caught with credit in only one of the original pair of papers could obtain credit only by writing the new combined paper. Numerous protests were instrumental in bringing about a change in this ruling. Extra single papers were provided along traditional lines for those who needed them. The announcement of this change was made in a memorandum dated December 10, 1964.[48] It thus appears rather strange to read the following remarks by B. Newman, member from Windsor-Walkerville, in the record of the legislative debates for February 11, 1965.

> I have had at least three different students appeal to me because they have failed one of the two English Departmental exams. As the policy is now, they will have to repeat a subject in which they were successful; they will have to repeat both English composition and literature written as one exam, yet they have passed the literature exam. This is not fair, this is an injustice.
>
> ... Surely the department can provide separate exams for such people in 1965? This is not a difficult administrative problem, yet the department insists it would not be possible to provide separate examinations in 1965.[49]

His concerns were no doubt genuine but somewhat out of date.

Incorporation of teachers' marks

Serious difficulties resulted in 1965 from the attempt to implement the committee's recommendation that marks supplied by the teachers count for 25 per cent of the candidate's final standing, thus reducing the weight of the examination mark to 75 per cent. Sound principles of measurement would have indicated that the teachers' professional contribution would be to place their candidates in the proper rank order, and that a scaling procedure would thereupon be applied to establish a uniform standard from one school to another. Any other procedure had necessarily to result in unfairness to candidates whose teachers marked them severely and would give the advantage to those with lenient markers. The examination results themselves provided an entirely satisfactory means of performing the scaling operation. The decision was to study the variations in standards, but not to adjust the marks unless they differed by as much as five points on either side of the provincial average. The way it actually worked was this. Candidates from school A might have averaged 63 per cent on a given paper. On the basis of provincial figures, the teachers' marks for the candidates in the same school should have averaged 65. But in actual fact, the standard was not adjusted unless the teachers' average sank as low as 60 or rose as hight as 70. A source of uncontrolled variation of this magnitude appears somewhat out of line with the great care employed in other parts of the operation to ensure fairness to the candidates, even though the effect was considerably lessened when the teachers' mark was reduced to carry only 25 per cent of the final weight.

Serious public repercussions arose from the effect on the scaling process of combining the teachers' marks and those obtained on the examination. It was decided that only the latter would be scaled, and that the former, adjusted only if they reached the five-mark limit of acceptable variation, would be added later. The result was to invalidate fundamental assumptions on which the scaling tables, derived from a fraction of the papers from an erratic "sample," were based. Consequently, some of the mark distributions were at serious variance with the scaling objectives. The unusually high rate of failures in English aroused particular criticism, although that was by no means the only paper affected. The unofficial department solution was to adopt an especially lenient policy with respect to appeals.

On February 10, 1966, B. Newman spoke in the Legislature on this question of appeals. Among various sources, he read from a press report by Dell Bell in the *London Free Press* of January 24, 1966.

> One principal says he had a student appeal five papers and got all five. Another school authority says he heard of one youngster who appealed three papers, all under 40, and got them. Veteran London teacher Margaret Falona said 17 students in her school, the G.A. Wheable school, flunked French with marks in the 35 per cent range and all were granted appeal passes.[50]

Another of Newman's quotations was from W.L. Clark in the "As We See It" column in the *Windsor Star*, December 30, 1965.

> Something went dreadfully askew in the marking of Ontario grade 13 examination results this summer. Many young men and women appealed their poor marks. More than half the applicants were successful in having their grades bettered.
>
> If half of those who appealed had been wrongfully marked, about the same average would probably have held for those who did not appeal. These just accepted the markings and let it go at that.
>
> If this is typical of the marking efficiency in Ontario departmental examinations, then something should be done to rule out the incompetence. Many a student's future could be ruined by such incompetence of a marker. From an educational point of view, it is a disgraceful show of inefficiency; worst of all, many a young man or woman is the innocent victim of this affair.

The real significance of the matter was not the injustice done to graduates of that year, however serious and deplorable; it was rather the dramatic demonstration of the inability of the complex examination machinery, despite the efforts of a group of very competent and conscientious people, to ensure a satisfactory result. The system was no longer physically workable.

Some immediate improvements were, of course, possible. Changes were made to ensure that something approximating a random sample of papers from the entire province was available for the production of scaling tables in 1966, and the scaling process was modified in other ways to make it more effective. Perhaps it is significant that the writer's former advisory functions in this area were by now in the hands of Miss Dormer Ellis of the Ontario Institute for Studies in Education. A.W. Bishop, who succeeded Brown as Registrar in early 1966, felt that, considering the complexity of the task and the lack of a trial run, there was no reason to feel discouraged over the result. He thought that at least two years of the same system were needed before adopting any radically different method of testing students at the grade 13 level.

The department issued fairly detailed instructions about how the teachers' contribution to the students' final standing was to be arrived at. Instructions applying to English for 1966 specified that the mark was to be calculated on the basis of 50 per cent for proficiency in the year's work in writing and 50 per cent for English literature. The writing part was to be based on all essays written by the student during the school year. There were to be not fewer than four of these, representing at least two different types, two of which were to be written in the school under supervision, either as part of formal examinations at Christmas and Easter or in the classroom under supervision at any time during the year. The longer critical essay, or literary essay, based on some phase of the literature part of the course, might weigh more heavily than one of the shorter essays. The student's essay notebook or file of essays was expected to be accessible to provincial or municipal school inspectors at any time during the school year.[51] Comparable instructions were issued with respect to Français. Obviously the imposition of an external examination was not the only means by which the schools could be subjected to strict control.

Evaluating performance in grade 13 art offered unusual difficulties because of the inherent problem of measuring creative self-expression and because of the wide range of views about acceptable standards in this area. Of the final mark 35 per cent was to represent the candidate's proficiency in all phases of the course, including history and theory as well as practical work. The remaining 65 per cent was based on 1 / a portfolio to be submitted to the department before the June examination, which would count for approximately 30 per cent of the total of the June examination, and 2 / the departmental examination itself. On the latter, the candidate was to answer questions on the history and theory of art and on reproductions of art which were provided. No actual drawing or painting was expected of him at that time. The portfolio was to contain ten pieces of work distributed over the course according to certain specifications. Elaborate precautions were taken to ensure that the work submitted by each candidate was really his own. For provincial secondary schools or inspected private schools, the signatures of the candidate, the principal, and the art teacher were required on a form provided by the department. A private-study candidate had to submit a legal affidavit to the same effect.[52]

Instructions regarding the evaluation of achievement in history were quite non-prescriptive and helpful. Teachers were advised to consider all aspects of the students' work, including essays, reports, supplementary reading, contributions to panel discussions, projects, and proficiency on term tests and examinations. Within all of these areas, consideration was to be given to the student's ability to analyse historical events, his capacity to marshal relevant facts in order to support a position, his ability to comprehend historical themes and movements, and his ability to develop a historical argument and state a case. Essay topics might encourage the presentation of opposing points of view and the drawing of conclusions. Teachers were advised to judge the quality of the essays on student initiative in research activities as well as on content and comprehension. It was suggested that students' essay notebooks or a classroom file of essays should be readily accessible for perusal by all the students so that they might benefit from the work of others. The departmental memorandum became fairly specific in indicating that 45 per cent of the teacher's mark might be based on research and writing activities, 10 per cent on contributions to class work, and 45 per cent on proficiency on tests and examinations. It was stressed, however, that this was a general indication of possible mark apportionment offered only as a guide.[53]

THE ABOLITION OF THE DEPARTMENTAL EXAMINATIONS

The minister's attitude

The attitude expressed by the minister changed noticeably during the year before his decision to abolish the examinations. On June 3, 1965, he addressed the Legislature as follows.

> I fully appreciate that there are some who feel that we could do this locally, that the individual is quite competent to give the student a grade. I think, statistically that probably they could come fairly close, but we want to be very careful before a departure of this nature is made. We feel there is still some benefit in the principle of external examination. The day may come when we can mark these more readily on a local basis; I don't know, but we have made a fairly major advance in this present year by having 25 per cent of it done on a recommendation of the local people.[54]

An important event contributing to relatively drastic change was the assumption by Z.S. Phimister of the position of deputy minister in early 1965. He was known for his support of the principle of giving teachers a maximum of responsibility in a decentralized educational system. Also Tom Campbell, who enjoyed a strong measure of ministerial confidence, and who became Phimister's executive assistant, was an influential opponent of the departmental examination system.

The minister's announcement

The minister's announcement to the Legislature on March 31, 1966, involved a very comprehensive statement.[55] Characteristically, his approach was low key. He proposed to outline a plan that would eliminate the objectionable features of the grade 13 examination system between then and 1968. He referred to the administrative problem of completing the marking early enough to allow university officials adequate time to handle the admission problem. Despite the fact that the department had been able to hold the line, it was no longer possible on a purely physical basis to continue the existing system. The urgency of solving the practical problems had focussed attention on the implications of external examinations for the educational process, a matter which had received the attention of many groups of educators during the previous two years. There was a growing feeling, as a result, that the student's work throughout the year should carry more weight, and less importance should be attached to the final examination.

Davis quoted the adverse judgments of the Grade 13 Study Committee about the effects of the examinations. He also referred to many of its recommendations, including the one urging a reduction in the number of subjects required for university admission and the development of general and advanced level programs. Steps had been taken to produce suggested outlines for courses for these latter programs, but he was still awaiting the universities' reactions to them. He also mentioned the committee's recommendation for an extended system of post-secondary education. With respect to the proposal to develop a twelve-grade structure, he pointed out that the necessary curriculum revision would take a number of years and must be very carefully and thoughtfully prepared.

Davis mentioned that, in accordance with the committee's proposal for immediate action, 25 per cent of grade 13 students' final standing was based on teachers' marks in 1965, and the percentage was to be raised to 35 in 1966. It had been the committee's opinion that, "subject to the development of adequate controls for a province-wide recommendation system, the proposed emphasis upon the teacher's mark might well lead eventually to the elimination of all external examinations." Reference was made to the development of the Ontario Admission to College and University (OACU) program, which might have the advantage of providing a profile of a student's achievement and potential without requiring the cramming associated with the existing system. Davis hoped that this program would, in due course, extend to all of Canada.

The minister's proposal dealt with successive years beginning with 1966. For the latter year, the system would continue as in the past, with the teacher's mark, as mentioned, counting for 35 per cent of the final standing. In 1967 the students would write the aptitude and achievement tests prepared by the Service for Admission to College and University. (It was, of course, the OACU tests that were actually written.) The departmental examinations would be given in their traditional form for the last time. In 1968 the SACU tests would be repeated, while the department would turn over to the schools the responsibility for conducting the school leaving examinations at the grade 13 level. School records would be made available to the universities and other institutions of further education. It was felt that the combination of information from these two sources would provide a broader and more reliable basis for admission to post-secondary educational institutions. In retrospect, at least, it was surely less valid to make this claim than to assert that the change might free the schools to devote more time to education.

Attitude of the Ontario Teachers' Federation

The minister had consulted the Ontario Teachers' Federation before making his official announcement. On March 18, 1966, Miss Nora Hodgins, secretary-treasurer, wrote to him on behalf of the executive, agreeing that the existing system needed revision and making the following recommendations:

1. that all Grade 13 students write the proposed ability tests and objective achievement tests in the four subjects in their program, since all Grade 13 students will receive the same diploma and since other educational institutions and businesses are just as interested as the universities in the standards achieved by the students;
2. that the ability tests and achievement tests be in terms of Ontario norms and the achievement tests relate to the Grade 13 subject matter;
3. that the achievement tests be *not* given until late May; and
4. that to secure a graduation diploma, as distinct from admission to a university, the students should write the objective achievement tests (as given by the Department) and should also write essay-type examinations set by the Department and marked by the school.

There was nothing in this message that ran fundamentally counter to the minister's plan except the last fifteen words. These certainly represented a substantially different point of view. The proposal was developed more fully in a submission to the minister the following month.[56] The essay-type examinations, set by the department, would be of two hours' duration, and would be marked by the teachers in the schools according to a carefully prepared marking scheme. They would be written not later than mid-May, and students would be allowed to leave school once they were completed. Highly qualified practising teachers would be requested to submit sample questions for use by the department in setting the examinations, which would offer a liberal choice of questions. As a comment on this proposal, it may be suggested that those who advocate local marking and a choice of questions often fail to realize how completely these two factors can destroy the possibility of attaining the desired uniformity of standards.

Critics of the teachers' position made some rather unfavourable comments. It was said that many of the less self-confident teachers expected severe difficulties in managing the freedom of action that would be allowed under the new conditions. The disappearance of the incentive for reviewing old examination papers at the end of the year would force a change in habits on many of those with long experience. Reputations built on success in getting candidates through the examinations would have to be re-established on a new basis. Some would fail to see how standards of achievement could be maintained without the spectre of the examination looming at the end of the year. It was hoped, however, that an awareness of the new possibilities for improved professional status would soon prevail.

Other reactions

Apart from the rather sharply qualified approval of the Ontario Teachers' Federation, reaction to the move was, on the whole, highly favourable. Robert Nixon was generally in agreement, although he was concerned about the maintenance of standards. In a resolution submitted on April 12, the Ontario Secondary School Headmasters' Council endorsed the minister's action. Like the Ontario Teachers' Federation, it was concerned that the Ontario Secondary School Honour Graduation Diploma should be retained. It also favoured a continued departmental supervision of standards. In a particularly enthusiastic letter, A.G. Scott, Headmaster of Trinity College School, wrote as follows: "I think that the cancellation of these external examinations is the most important step that Ontario has made since the introduction of compulsory education in the Province."[57] In the Toronto *Globe and Mail*, David Tough, Superintendent of Secondary Schools for the North York Board of Education, was quoted as saying that grade 13 examinations had been "a millstone around our necks. We always felt we were educating youngsters through grade 12 and then training them in Grade 13 for passing external examinations."[58] In the same article, an equally enthusiastic statement was attributed to Barry Lowes, Chairman of the Toronto Board of Education: "It's the ultimate realization on the part of the Department of Education that these examinations have served no useful function." A strongly opposing point of view was expressed by George Kirk, Professor of Modern Languages at the Ontario College of Education and former Chairman of the Etobicoke Board of Education. He was said to have commented that, if Ontario's education authorities were prepared to accept the standards common in Mississippi, Alabama, and Arkansas, they were heading in the right direction.

Editorial comment in the province's newspapers was supportive of the minister's action. The *London Free Press* summarized its impressions in this way: "It appears that the whole program is aimed at making better use of educational facilities from the elementary to university level. Once tag ends of uncertainty have been removed, the way should be open for a more up-to-date effective system of education in Ontario."[59] In Toronto, the *Telegram* was highly complimentary to the minister: "With his penchant for clarity and decisiveness, Education Minister William Davis made his announcement the other day, lifting burdens from all pupils who haven't yet entered Grade 12."[60] According to the *Globe and Mail*: "The writing has been on the wall for a long time. Grade 13 examinations are an anachronism and should be abolished ... Could be and will be."[61] Many of the editorials proceeded to express the hope that drastic changes would be made in the content and instructional approach used in the final high school year.

The views of C.A. Brown about these events are of particular interest at this point. He was at the very centre of events during the years in which the departmental examination system mushroomed and died. The record shows that he was of a more innovative turn of mind than most of those around him during the search for solutions in the late fifties and early sixties. He saw the basic issues with commendable clarity but could not push too hard lest he endanger the success of the program for which he was administratively responsible. Brown assured the writer at the end of 1969 that he realized for some time before the minister's announcement in 1966 that the end of the system in its existing form was inevitable. He promoted the idea, unsuccessfully, as it turned out, that decentralized marking of centrally-set papers might be the answer. He realized, however, that this solution would have retained some of the most serious disadvantages of the system while failing to ensure the traditional uniformity of standards.

With his intimate knowledge of the complexities of the system, and his appreciation of the herculanean efforts on the part of his collaborators and assistants to make it work, he would have been entirely justified if he chose to feel that some of the attacks launched on the system during the final stages were excessively virulent. Understandably, he was inclined to dwell on some of the more commendable aspects. In an address in 1969, he posed the question: "What conditions have created of the one remaining external examination such a monster that neither the schools nor the general public can countenance its use any longer?"[62] He summarized what he called the alleged reasons:

(a) the hybrid nature of the examination which resulted from the necessity of making it serve a dual purpose, university admission and high school graduation, even though there was but one program;
(b) the fact that at least until quite recent years the absence of practising teachers or at least former teachers from the setting committees sometimes resulted in the use of unsatisfactory questions;
(c) the necessity of emphasizing questions which could be marked by the point system in order that uniformity of marking might be obtained, with consequent evil influence upon teaching practices; and
(d) the pressures which have been permitted to develop around the examination.

Brown mentioned the efforts of the examiners-in-chief to include questions that might have given the candidate an opportunity to show well-organized evidence of the results of wide reading and independent study. But they often let themselves be defeated by the pressure for uniform marking. Brown felt that if all those concerned had been more aggressive in their defence of questions appropriate for study in depth, a different pattern of grade 13 teaching might have been established, and one serious point of criticism removed. The judicious scaling of marks at that stage would have helped them get over the period of difficulty. Brown also had something to say about examination pressures. Among the reasons why these had tended to build up were the development of competition for university places in the 1950s, the restoration of the practice of reporting marks instead of honour classifications, and the introduction of the Ontario Scholarship, with its highly significant distinction between a total of 639 and one of 640. He referred to the influence of parents, students, and teachers in glorifying the examination. Of the latter, he said: "Surely teachers could have prevented this unfortunate situation if they had been able to keep their eyes on educational goals rather than on examinations."

These observations do not of course relate to the threat of excessive numbers of papers, which no system, whether beneficial or harmful in its educational effects, could have withstood for much longer in its existing form. What Brown was saying was essentially that more perceptive and courageous actions on the part of certain individuals and groups might have given the system a more lamented demise. The writer, while respecting this point of view, does not agree with it. He feels that traditional practices had developed such powerful momentum that it was unrealistic to expect any substantial change through voluntary action on the part of the groups mentioned. There seems little use in blaming the teachers, who knew that they and their schools were being judged by the success of their students on the examinations, and that they could depart from a rigid program only at the risk of endangering that success, however spurious the criterion.

THE PERIOD AFTER ABOLITION

New assessment procedures

The department's policy for 1967–8, the first year in which preparation for an external examination could no longer dominate the proceedings, was to continue to provide courses of study but to permit more freedom for the schools to adapt them to what they saw as the students' needs. Assistance with respect to course development and measurement of student programs was provided to teachers by departmental consultants on request. The number of consultants was actually much too small to provide really substantial guidance on any large scale, and the teachers were largely left to work out their own problems. Principals were responsible for issuing a statement of grade 13 standing to each student at the end of the school year. The Ontario Secondary School Honour Graduation Diploma would be issued by the department on the principal's recommendation on the basis of seven credits or more. The departmental officials suggested that a portion of this assessment would normally be based on some type of formal examinations during the year. But, in the true spirit of the reform, it was suggested that the purpose of discontinuing external departmental examinations would be defeated if they were replaced by other types of uniform examinations.[63] In this connection, a warning was given against setting a single examination for two or more schools. Teachers responsible for the education of the students being assessed were said to be the best qualified to evaluate student performance. The new system eliminated any possibility of appeal to the department; the final decision was in the hands of the principal.

The question of how to handle the Ontario Scholarship program under a decentralized examination system had been a difficult one. It was obvious that no large amount of money could be awarded to individual candidates without some uniform criterion. For the time being, at least, it was decided that scholarships in the amount of $150 would be awarded to students with an average of 80 per cent in seven credits required for the diploma.

In order to reduce the emphasis on final examinations, and to combat the temptation to cram, schools were urged to consider a recommendation system whereby students who secured at least 60 per cent on the year's work in any subject might be exempted from writing the final examination. Assurance was given that standing secured by recommendation would be acceptable for credit toward the Ontario Secondary School Honour Graduation Diploma. Although the final decision was in the hands of the principal and staff, it was suggested that, for those who wrote, 50 per cent of the final standing might be based on the year's work and 50 per cent on the final examination.

It was not compulsory for students to take the Ontario Scholastic Aptitude Test and the achievement tests in English, mathematics, and physics administered under the Ontario Tests for Admission to College and University (OACU) program. However, they were urged to avail themselves voluntarily of this opportunity. The provincial government bore the entire cost of the program, and the tests could be written conveniently on school days.

The change created certain problems for the private-study candidate, who must now make arangements as early as possible in the year with the principal of the school where the subject he wished to write was being taught. Schools were urged to help by providing copies of courses of study and other forms of assistance. The candidates had to write the final examinations set for those students who were not recommended on their year's work, and their standing would be based solely on the results of the examination.

The official position of the Ontario Teacher's Federation remained cautious and to some extent sceptical. A brief submitted in January 1967 began with praise for the changes that had been made in the grade 13 course, making possible more study in depth. It urged a corresponding modification beginning much earlier in the school program, with less rigidity in time, content, and requirements in the earlier grades. On the question of assessment, it said: "There can be little quarrel with the ultimate removal of the present method of external examinations even though virtually all systems, outside the United States, still require official proof of competency at the end of secondary education ... Our own misgivings hinge about the stark abruptness of the move. It is not always necessary to kill the patient to cure the ailment."[64] Misgivings were expressed about what was regarded as the department's abandonment of control over standards. The brief claimed that the corresponding lack of control that had existed over grade 12 for many years did not provide a valid analogy. Even there, it had been found desirable a few years earlier to reinstitute external examinations. The fear was expressed that the only alternative to departmental control was an unofficial and undesirable accreditation by the universities.

The federation was doubtful that objective tests of the College Entrance Examination Board type would provide an adequate standard. It was said that "because these will be the only uniform examinations submitted by candidates, universities and other post-secondary school institutions will be strongly tempted to ascribe to the results all the virtues of the absolute."[65] The brief urged that, "from the single criterion we should move to a more broadly based assessment." The stand taken the previous spring was reaffirmed. It was recommended that essay-type examinations, to be written by grade 13 candidates in early May, be set annually by a committee of highly competent practising teachers. They would stress basic or fundamental knowledge and allow an ample choice of questions. In the interests of validity, the results would be compiled by the department, and a method of provincial scaling, acceptable to the teaching profession, would be devised. Final assessment for the Ontario Secondary School Honour Graduation Diploma would be based on three factors: 1 / proficiency on the year's work, 2 / achievement test scores, and 3 / marks on essay-type examinations. The last two factors would carry no more than 50 per cent of the total weight.

A further brief submitted by the federation the following month recommended the establishment of a teacher-centred commission to provide direction to teachers on a consultative basis with respect to course content and examination procedures.[66] Its members would be seconded from classrooms to serve as teacher consultants. The previous month's recommendation with respect to the administration of external examinations was repeated. The brief also urged that the timing of the release of the OACU test results be such that it would not lead to a premature and false assessment of students.

At one stage the minister asserted that teachers' groups were unanimous in their approval of the decision to make grade 13 the responsibility of the schools. While this declaration was in accordance with general statements issued by the OTF, Davis did acknowledge later, in an intriguing display of candour, that there had been a few problems. On May 24 he declared "there was some reaction from the OTF with respect to the grade 13 changes. I was even concerned, as I recall the debate, that the member for York South [Donald MacDonald] was going to turn into a bit of a reactionary and almost agree with the OTF, but I read what he said again and I do not think he really did that."[67] In any case, in March Davis promised to co-operate with the teaching profession in establishing a consultative service utilizing practising teachers for the provision of assistance in course content and evaluation to those requiring it.

Growing teacher enthusiasm

There was evidence of a rapid growth in enthusiasm as teachers realized the advantages of the new freedom they had acquired. In December 1967 G.P. Wilkinson, Principal of Lambton-Kent District High School and Third Vice-President of the Ontario Secondary School Teachers' Federation, wrote:

> We shall protect this power from abuse only if we protect the individual teacher's freedom from incursions by government, by big business and by the professional organization itself ...
>
> We have won a significant victory against the danger inherent in govern-

ment by wresting the control of Grade 13 from the hands of the Department of Education.[68]

This news must have jolted the minister and those of his officials who had lived through the previous few years. They might well have questioned who wrested what from whom. However, they could hardly be other than gratified at the sentiments expressed in the article with respect to teachers' new opportunities for exercising professional responsibility.

Examination practices in schools

Illustrations from one particular school will help to demonstrate how the challenge posed by the elimination of the external examination was met.[69] A meeting of department heads set up a student assessment committee consisting of a group of staff representative in terms of experience and background. This committee was expected to make recommendations to the heads with respect to the following topics: 1 / policy regarding the responsibility for the establishment and control of courses of study, 2 / examinations, 3 / recommendation policy, 4 / relative weighting of term marks and examinations, 5 / the relative credit for each term's assessment, 6 / the amount of uniformity (if any) and the type of flexibility, and 7 / the establishment of school policy and its relationship to policies established by individual departments. A key recommendation of its report was that uniformity among departments was inconsistent with the spirit of Memorandum 28, which outlined Department of Education policy in this area. Another general statement was that there would be a de-emphasis on examinations and an increased emphasis on daily work. Each department of the school was to have these responsibilities:

1. to determine the relative weight of term work and examinations for reporting purposes and for final assessment;
2. to decide whether or not to 'opt out' of an examination schedule;
3. to make provision for sufficient flexibility in the examination of any grade so that no teacher finds it impossible to adapt the course to the potential of the students in a particular class or finds it necessary to structure the course or gear his speed to a 'prescription' of content;
4. to determine at what grade levels students may be recommended and what the terms of recommendation will be;
5. to issue to each student at all grade levels a statement re 'Examinations, grades, and promotions' no later than Nov. 15th of each year.

The policy adopted for the school produced wide variations in procedure from department to department, reflecting different educational points of view. There was, however, an attempt to prevent any serious deterioration in standards. A five-year survey was made of the distribution of standing in the June examinations, and each department was notified of the results. An attempt was made to approximate the same distribution on each set of school examinations throughout the year. The staff were reminded that the Christmas examination might no longer be used as part of a shock treatment, since the first term mark represented one-third of the final standing, and since early university admissions would be affected by the student's assessment at this point.

Reactions

The article did not attempt to report student reaction to the new system in any detail. But it quoted a letter from one student which, it was claimed, reflected the opinions of many. The student had initially disliked the constant pressure of tests and day-to-day evaluation. But by the end of the year he was pleased to discover that he had already learned most of his work and he did not have to face the horror of a final examination. There were other students, of course, who preferred to stake everything on a single cast of the die.

At the end of 1968 marks awarded to grade 13 students by the schools of the province were substantially higher than those achieved on the departmental examinations during the previous year. Although the number of students declined somewhat, twice as many obtained an average of 80 per cent or more to attain the status of Ontario Scholars and receive the accompanying financial award. Failure rates also declined drastically, in some subjects to no more than half the level of the previous year. A strong defender of the new system might assert that the improvement was wholly genuine and attributable to better motivation and instruction resulting from the removal of the examination incubus. He might not feel that any comparison was really valid, since the programs offered in successive years differed in fundamental ways.

The universities might be expected to provide some valid information about the relative quality of the borderline students in the successive academic terms before and after June 1967. The writer discussed this question with a considerable number of university people during the spring of 1969. Some, on the basis of general principles, predicted dire consequences from the move. Others did not think there would be any substantial change in standards. No one was prepared to offer solid evidence that the freshman group was performing in other than the usual fashion, although many suggested that the examinations at the end of the spring term would tell the tale. One might well wonder whether an important difference in attitude or quality of preparation could fail to manifest itself for almost a whole university year.

Robin Ross, Registrar of the University of Toronto, wrote favourably to the Deputy Minister of University Affairs in May 1968: "We have found that the schools in their submissions of interim and final marks have exercised restraint and common sense in the appraisal of their students. We have been greatly helped by the careful and responsible work of the schools." But it must be remembered that, during the first year of the new system, traditional ways of doing things were still strong, and many deeply-ingrained attitudes were still unbroken. Sufficient time had hardly elapsed to enable anyone to discern the patterns that would eventually emerge. G.P. Wilkinson, in a *Bulletin* article, was prepared to make a confident assertion: "An assessment of our experience after one year of decentralization of Grade 13 responsibility is enough to confound the prognostications of those prophets of doom who little more than a year ago forecast that the demise of secondary education would follow swiftly on the heels of this bold venture."[70] It is doubtful that anyone worth listening to believed that the educational field would, after a single year without the external examinations, be strewn with the wreckage of the secondary school system. It will take a much longer period of time before any adequate judgment can be made of the real consequences of the move. No answer is yet available for those who predict that unrestrained teacher initiative will ultimately produce such a chaotic situation that employers, parents, students, teachers, and representatives of institutions of higher education will demand the reimposition of some kind of external control. It is only a matter of faith to hold that the swinging pendulum metaphor does not apply to this situation.

Particularly worthy of note is the rapidly declining interest in objective tests of aptitude and achievement, whether under OACU or SACU auspices, as a means of maintaining uniform standards. When the discontinuation of the departmental examinations was first announced, reliance on such a program was presented as a vital part of the new scheme. But the OTF support, originally very strong, cooled noticeably, and the Ontario Secondary School Headmasters' Council became openly antagonistic. The department's Memorandum 28 outlined principles of evaluation to be followed in the secondary schools in such a way that some teachers interpreted them as incompatible with any form of external testing whatsoever.

One point already made can hardly be emphasized too strongly. If the integrity of the schools' evaluation is to be maintained, it must not be subjected to excessive pressures. To continue to award any kind of scholarship or prize on the basis of interschool competition while using each school's appraisal of its own candidates as the sole criterion would constitute an intolerable strain on all concerned. Few teachers or principals could long resist either a conscious or an unconscious response if it were claimed that the students of the neighbouring school received more scholarships because the marking there was more lenient. It would be quite unfair to expect them to put up with such an unreasonable situation. And yet in the absence of a common criterion, the only alternatives would seem to be to make the awards on the basis of a school quota or abolish them altogether.

SIXTEEN

Departmental essay-type examinations in grade 12

THE UNIVERSITY MATRICULATION BOARD COMMITTEE

The increasing pressure for uniform standards in the secondary schools around 1960 led to the establishment of a special committee of the University Matriculation Board, consisting of two representatives of the Department of Education, one from the Ontario Secondary School Teachers' Federation, and three from the universities, to study the possibility of reintroducing an external examination at the end of grade 12. In March 1961 this committee reported what it regarded as serious consequences resulting from the lack of such an examination. These included a lowering of standards at the grade 12 level, which permitted the entry into grade 13 of many students who were incapable of benefiting from the program; a lack of motivation and of continuity of effort on the part of the students; a stress on cramming in grade 13 to compensate for the apparent lack of preparation in earlier years; and an undue emphasis on grade 13 examination results as a criterion of school achievement. The committee recommended the re-establishment of a uniform examination at the end of grade 12 of the General course, mainly of the essay type and consisting of a two-hour paper in each subject. The examination was to be set under the direction of the department, marked locally by the teachers in the schools with a detailed marking scheme, and subject to spot-checking of the marking by officials of the department before the release of the results.[1]

THE GRADE 12 EXAMINATIONS STUDY COMMITTEE

The minister's response, given in recognition of the fact that the views of most department officials were apparently in agreement with those of the Matriculation Board Committee, was to appoint a Grade 12 Examinations Study Committee. Under the chairmanship of C.A. Brown, Registrar of the department, it consisted of fifteen representatives of the department, the Ontario Secondary School Teachers' Federation, the Ontario Secondary School Headmasters' Association, and the universities whose task it was to consider the advisability of implementing the previous committee's recommendations. Its main contribution was to ascertain the opinions of educational officials, administrators, and teachers or, perhaps, to secure the articulate support of these groups for a policy already largely decided upon.

In the early stages of their deliberations, members of the committee expressed some very definite points of view. 1 / There were comments on the difficulty many teachers experienced in the preparation of suitable examination papers, with suggestions that papers set by groups of experienced teachers would be very helpful. 2 / The committee criticized the grade 12 departmental tests used during the previous three years as limited in scope and at best a temporary expedient for securing minimum standards. 3 / It noted the increasing interest of the universities in the whole school record, and particularly in that of grade 12, as indicated by the consideration being given to the possibility of granting early tentative admission to university before the grade 13 departmental examination results became available. 4 / Although it may be doubted that the view was consistent with other recommendations, the committee was against any type of uniform external examination that would militate against the choice of topics and of texts which was currently permissible or which might lead to undue stress on teaching for examination purposes. 5 / It expressed a belief in the feasibility of having uniform examinations, two hours in length and with suitable options, set by teachers under the direction of the department and written as the school's final examinations in June, with the answer papers marked locally in a uniform manner with the use of supplied marking schemes. 6 / It did not consider spot-checking of papers by the department feasible, since such a procedure would not leave time to decide on the results and issue the diplomas in August, and it would be inconsistent with the current desirable practice of taking the year's record into account in determining the final grade 12 standing. 7 / It believed that, if they were used, uniform examinations should be provided for each of the current courses and in time for each of the three branches: Arts and Science; Business and Commerce; and Engineering (later, Science), Technology, and Trades. 8 / The uniform examination would serve its best purpose as a co-operative effort to assist teachers and schools to achieve and maintain adequate standards rather than as a means of determining the standing of individual students at the end of the school year.[2]

The committee's specific proposals at this stage were 1 / that the grade 12 departmental objective tests be discontinued; 2 / that they be replaced by another type of test, mainly essay-type, prepared by committees of teachers under the direction of the department; 3 / that all schools wishing to recommend students for the Secondary School Graduation Diploma be required to use these tests, where provided, as the June examinations, and that all students be required to write them; 4 / that, in the initial and experimental stages, not more than three subjects be tested in any one year; 5 / that the schools continue to use the year's record for all subjects in deciding final standing, but that, in order to provide a basis for helpful comparisons, all schools be required to use the same ratio of the year's record to the June examination; 6 / that the department provide forms for reporting the marks representing the year's record, the marks obtained on the June examinations, some or all of which would be the grade 12 departmental tests, and the final marks assigned for diploma recommendations, and that the department use this information to help the schools determine standards, although not necessarily in each subject each year; and 7 / that the recommendations, if adopted, become effective in June 1963.[3]

The committee invited comments on its proposals from the directors of education, as individuals; the Association of Secondary School Superintendents, as a group, the Ontario School Inspectors' Association; the Ontario Teachers' College Association; the Ontario Secondary School Teachers' Federation; the Ontario Secondary School Headmasters' Association; the English Catholic private schools, as a group; the French-speaking private schools, as a group; the Canadian Headmasters' Association (Independent Boys' Schools), Ontario members, as a group; the Association of Headmistresses (Independent Girls' Schools), as individuals; and the heads of the universities. A structured response was requested, and the result was quite gratifying.

When the officials of the Ontario Secondary School Teachers' Federation received the invitation to offer an opinion on the proposals, they arranged to canvass their membership by means of a questionnaire. After the members had had reasonable time to answer, approximately nine thousand responses, representing schools with about eleven thousand members, were tabulated. The results showed an overwhelming 79 per cent in favour and only 21 per cent opposed. There was a remarkable degree of uniformity in the balance between these two groups no matter how the teachers were categorized in the survey: that is, it made little difference whether or not they had taught at the grade 11 level or higher or how much experience they had had. Interestingly, in view of the committee's previously declared view that the departmental objective tests should be dropped, 82 per cent of the teachers felt that objective items should be used to a limited extent, 5.5 per cent felt that the tests should be almost entirely objective, and only 12.5 per cent felt that objective items should not be used at all. Nearly 40 per cent thought that the external tests should have equal weight with the year's record, and only about 10 per cent thought they should have less.[4]

The Ontario Secondary School Headmasters' Association mailed comparable questionnaires to 441 of its members and tabulated the 345 that had been returned by January 20, 1962. Support for the external examinations was even more overwhelming, with nearly 88 per cent in favour. Over 71 per cent thought that objective items should be used to a limited extent, and fewer than 8 per cent were completely opposed to their use. The attitude expressed on the amount of weight they should carry was similar to that of the teachers.[5]

In reporting the results of its investigations to the minister on June 18,

1962, the committee recommended the introduction of the examination system. The points the members emphasized in its favour paralleled those that had been mentioned in the memorandum to school officials in the early stages of their work. Advantages not stressed before were the valuable experience the candidates would have in grade 12 as a preparation for writing grade 13 examinations, and the greater weight the grade 12 diploma would carry if it were based on a uniform external examination. Some of the disadvantages were also referred to, with emphasis on administrative problems and expense. J.R. McCarthy, true to his well-known educational philosophy, viewed the move as a retrogressive step that would not accomplish the claims made for it. He agreed, however, to the recommendation that an examination be held in chemistry in 1963 and in two other subjects in 1964, provided they did not include English or history. C.A. Mustard, Superintendent of Teacher Education, also accepted the suggested procedure with some reluctance, feeling that the probable disadvantages of establishing the proposed examinations would outweigh the advantages.

Despite the strong support its case had received, the committee recommended rather cautious moves. Reflecting the favour it had apparently built up among practising educators, nothing was said about abolishing the existing program of departmental objective testing. It was suggested, rather, that an examination in the chemistry part of the science option of grades 11 and 12 of the General course be conducted in June 1963 as part of the established program. In accordance with earlier suggestions, the paper would be prepared by a committee of teachers under the direction of the department and marked in the schools with a prepared marking scheme. The examination would be compulsory as a final test, and weighted equally with the school's term work for all who sought diploma standing in chemistry on the basis of their 1962–3 work. The Superintendent of Secondary Education would be asked to perform the follow-up work on these external examinations in a manner similar to that currently employed with the grade 12 departmental tests. A similar examination in two subjects, not at that time specified, would be conducted in June 1964.[6]

The scheme that was introduced was in accordance with the recommendations of the committee, which disbanded when its task was completed. The examination paper was to be set by a secondary school inspector and four secondary school teachers appointed for the purpose by the minister. The examination was to be administered under a strict system similar to that used for the grade 13 departmental examinations. In view of the possibility of variations in the marking and in the light of the principal's authority and responsibility for making decisions regarding grade 12 graduation, which in effect enabled him to override the results of the examination, there must have been something rather ludicrous in the spectacle of the chief presiding officer opening the sealed envelope containing the question papers in the presence of the candidates, as well as in the rule preventing a teacher from supervising students writing an examination for which he had prepared them.

The answer papers were to be retained by the principal until the Registrar directed that one or more of them be sent to him for checking or until the inspector had completed his inspection. The regulations were worded in such a way that spot-checking was not obligatory in each school, thus ensuring that the burden assumed by the department could be kept from getting out of control. If the spot-checking resulted in a verdict that the papers had not been properly marked, the principal was to receive guidance for the marking of future papers.

That the program was accepted with reasonably good grace is indicated by a letter from Nora Hodgins, Secretary-Treasurer of the Ontario Teachers' Federation, to W.R. Stewart, Deputy Minister of Education, on September 3, 1964. Miss Hodgins conveyed the approval of the Board of Governors of the Federation of a limited program of uniform external examinations at the end of grade 12. The types of examinations they specifically approved were 1 / tests similar to the existing SATO tests (with adequate information about the proper use of results); 2 / the proposed CAU (Canadian Admission to University) tests; 3 / longer examinations in selected subjects to be arranged in an appropriate cycle with not more than two such examinations to be written by any student in any one year.

NATURE OF EXAMINATIONS

Essay-type examinations were administered in the spring of 1964 in geography, Latin, and technical subjects. They were to be based on the course content outlined in appropriate departmental circulars. Whether or not the independence of teachers of these subjects actually declined as compared with previous years, there was little room for initiative, despite the fact that the candidates were presented with options based on different texts. In the preliminary instructions for the Latin paper, candidates were told that part A would consist of two questions, with alternatives according to the text used, one testing the poetry selections and the other the prose; part B would consist of English sentences to be translated into Latin; part C would consist of two Latin prose passages to be translated at sight into English; and part D would consist of objective items to test the student's knowledge of forms, grammar, and other aspects. The exact proportion of the total mark assigned to each part was specified in these instructions.

The essay examinations for 1964–5 were in modern history in the General course and in the shopwork subjects in the Technical course. The first was a two-hour and the second a 2½-hour paper. The preliminary instructions for the former tried to emphasize the leeway permitted for variations in topic choice and treatment.

> Optional questions will be provided so that a teacher should not feel himself obligated to depart from a judicious selection of areas of emphasis or from the

normally good procedures that have proved effective in achieving the aims of the courses. Indeed, the student who reads widely, prepares reports and essays, and enters into the discussions of the classroom or the History Club should be at an advantage over the pupil who attempts to commit to memory a single textbook.[7]

In recognition of the importance of examining for the achievement of some of the more sophisticated objectives, the prospective candidate was advised that part B of the examination would require him to select relevant information, to organize his material, and to present it effectively in order to make a comparison or develop a line of argument. It was pointed out with an air of virtue that the answer would be marked subjectively. The subjectively marked question would be worth about 24 per cent of the total. The memorandum containing this information ended with a warning: "A student should be aware that a mark is not awarded for 'a point' *but only for a clear statement of a fact or idea.* For this reason 'point form' answers must be penalized and sentence and paragraph structure observed."

The examination program for June 1966 included Latin and geography in the five-year programs or the continuing programs, and again in the shopwork subjects in the four-year Science, Technology, and Trades program or the Technical course. This time, control over the Latin course of study was relaxed in that the external paper did not include any translation of prescribed authors but left teachers to measure achievement in this area by means of their own internal examinations or tests. Teachers were urged to weight translation heavily in submitting their own marks as part of the testing program. In other respects, the examination was similar in structure to that provided previously. There were English and French versions of the papers in Latin and geography, with such adaptations in the questions as the difference in language necessitated.

There had thus far been no indication of an intention to expand the program from year to year. As a matter of fact, the way was paved for a reduction in 1966 when it was announced that examinations were being provided by the department until most schools, including those that had opened recently, had prepared students for one or two years. It was expected that, in subsequent years, teachers would be asked to set their own examinations in some of the technical subjects.[8]

External grade 12 examinations were given for the last time in 1967. They covered mathematics in the five-year programs and the continuing programs. In the four-year Science, Technology, and Trades program, the chosen subjects were applied electricity, applied electronics, combined applied electricity and applied electronics, drafting-mechanical, industrial chemistry, and refrigeration, air conditioning, and heating. Part B of the examination in mathematics, counting for 30 per cent of the total, consisted of multiple-choice questions. Each principal was instructed to send ten mathematics answer papers, chosen in a carefully defined manner, to the Registrar of the department for checking. Three answer papers were to be submitted for each technical subject written in each school.

The announcement about grade 12 departmental tests for 1967–8 simply indicated that there would be no departmental examination during that year. It was hardly to be expected that such examinations would continue after they had been permanently discontinued in grade 13. Both the rising sentiment against their constricting effects and the increasing enrolment in grade 12, which tended to make effective spot-checking a more and more expensive and time-consuming process, had had their effect.

SEVENTEEN

Departmental objective testing in grade 12

REASONS FOR THE INTRODUCTION OF THE PROGRAM

The introduction of a regular program of departmental objective tests in grade 12 was a result of two influences: 1 / the desire to reduce discrepancies in standards among secondary schools, and 2 / the search for improved criteria for admission to universities. Perhaps it was inevitable that earlier reliance on the results of the grade 13 departmental examinations would preclude any serious attempt to use test scores for the second of these purposes, especially when available evidence failed to indicate that they possessed any high degree of validity for the prediction of university success. Thus the scores on the grade 12 achievement tests were largely used to compare standards among schools, and those on the aptitude tests to suggest an appropriate level of achievement for the individual student.

EARLY USE OF OBJECTIVE TESTS

An early experiment in the use of objective-type tests for external examination purposes was conducted in 1930.[1] The aim was the highly utilitarian one of trying to find more effective means of dealing with the growing volume and expense of the matriculation examinations. The first steps were taken in December 1928, when a committee consisting of the Supervising Board of Examiners, the deans of the faculties of arts of the universities, and others saw some promise in the new approach. As a result of their discussions, a committee was appointed at the Matriculation Conference held later in the month to go further into the question. In early 1930, the minister agreed to have objective-type middle school papers prepared in algebra, Canadian history, chemistry, French, geometry, Latin, and physics. Twenty-five copies were sent to each secondary school in the province, to be written by students who expected to write the regular middle school papers in the same subjects. Thus it was possible to compare three sets of marks: those on each of the two papers and the regular school marks.

The so-called new-type papers were not standardized in any sense; the items were merely constructed and arranged in order of difficulty according to the best judgment of the examiner. Nevertheless, it was found that they were considerably more reliable than the traditional examination and possessed more value for individual measurement. The scores were almost as closely related to the school marks as were the external essay-type examinations, even though the school marks had largely been determined by traditional examining practices. The saving in cost resulting from the employment of objective tests was judged to be substantial. Despite the favourable conclusion of the experiment, the suggested changes were never accepted. The recommendation system was introduced for the middle school examinations in 1934, and in 1939–40 the examinations themselves were abandoned.

A further attempt was made to assist in reducing disparities in standards when a series of articles was prepared by committees of high school inspectors and the staff of the Ontario College of Education under the sponsorship of the department. These were published under the title "Standards in the Middle School" in *The School* in 1941.[2] In 1956 the Ontario Secondary School Teachers' Federation began the publication of a series of sample papers to assist beginning teachers to set examinations for grade 12.

INFLUENCE OF THE ATKINSON STUDY

In the early 1950s, considerable dissatisfaction with the oppressive effects of the grade 13 departmental examinations on the grade 13 program was being expressed by P.A.C. Ketchum, then Headmaster of Trinity College School, and by others of like mind. Ketchum thought it possible that an acceptable substitute might be found in the Scholastic Aptitude Tests administered for the College Entrance Examination Board in the United States by the Educational Testing Service. While there were no reasonable grounds for hope that scores from such tests would have greater validity for the prediction of university success than the grade 13 examination results, it seemed possible that they might not prove greatly inferior, and that their use might leave the schools with much greater curricular initiative. Others who supported the idea of experimenting with these tests saw them as a possible supplement to the grade 13 marks as a means of improving prediction. A small nucleus of men, including Sidney Smith, then President of the University of Toronto, J.A. Long, Director of the Department of Educational Research of the Ontario College of Education, and R.W.B. Jackson, Assistant Director of the same department, secured an initial grant of $35,000 from the Atkinson Charitable Foundation, and launched the Atkinson Study of Utilization of Student Resources in 1954.

The Atkinson Study, as described in chapter 12, was much more than a study of university admission criteria, but it did make some of its major contributions in that area. Included among the tests administered to almost an entire provincial grade group of 9,573 grade 13 students were the Scholastic Aptitude Test, yielding verbal and mathematical scores, and the School and College Ability Test, yielding verbal, quantitative, and total scores. The results disappointed those who had nourished hope that scores from such tests would prove an acceptable substitute for grade 13 departmental marks as predictors of university success. Among nineteen faculty and course groupings in ten colleges and universities, the median correlation between the verbal scores on the Scholastic Aptitude Test and the first-year average was only 0.32, and the corresponding correlation for the mathematical scores 0.29. The value of the scores on the School and College Ability Test was, in general, somewhat less. In contrast, the median correlation between the average of the grade 13 departmental marks and the first-year average in the same groupings was 0.65. A combination of test scores and examination marks improved prediction by only a small amount over that resulting from the use of the marks alone.[3]

For the benefit of those who are not entirely familiar with the correlation coefficient, it may be explained that an estimate of the weight carried by any single factor among all those, measured or unmeasured, that contribute to the complete explanation of a phenomenon may be obtained by squaring the correlation between the measure of that factor and a corresponding measure of the phenomenon. Thus where the predictive factor was the verbal score on the Scholastic Aptitude Test, and the criterion referred to the phenomenon of first year success, the correlation of 0.32 meant that the former accounted for only a little more than 10 per cent $(0.32)^2$ of the variation in the latter. In fact, admission based solely on such a score would not give substantially better results than completely random selection among the applicants. On the other hand, the coefficient of 0.65 obtained by relating grade 13 departmental examination results to first year results was sufficient to explain a little over 42 per cent $(0.65)^2$ of the variation in the latter. Thus even a correlation that is relatively high under the circumstances demonstrates the basic inaccuracy of the whole predictive process.

When the question was asked in the Atkinson Study about the value of various predictors of success in the students' entire career at university, as compared with first-year success, the correlations were lower, as they usually tend to be under such circumstances. The median correlation for the same nineteen groups between the verbal score on the Scholastic Aptitude Test and the average in third year, the final one for students in general courses in arts and science, was 0.23, and the corresponding correlation for the mathematical score and the same average was 0.20. At this stage, the median correlation between the grade 13 average and the same criterion was down to 0.43.[4] Among the sixteen groups for which a fourth-year average was calculated, the corresponding median correlations for the SAT-Verbal score, the SAT-Mathematical score, and the grade 13 average were 0.37, 0.36, and 0.64 respectively.[5]

EXPERIMENTAL TEST ADMINISTRATION

Experimentation in the use of aptitude tests was undertaken by the department in 1957, when the Scholastic Aptitude Test was administered to about 1,200 grade 13 students in over thirty secondary schools scattered about the province. The main focus of interest in this study was on the experimental essay-type papers in mathematics and French, one at the general, or ordinary level, and one at the special, or advanced level, in each subject. The declared purposes of the experiment have been reviewed in chapter 15. Considerable interest was expressed in the results of a predictive study, based on the experimental data from this test administration, that was conducted by the Department of Educational Research of the Ontario College of Education.

The department, represented particularly by F.C. Asbury, Assistant Superintendent of Secondary Education, devoted considerable attention to testing in grade 12 the following year, with a special administration of the Scholastic Aptitude Test and objective-type achievement tests in the mechanics of English and in chemistry. The experiment was tried in one hundred of the more than two hundred schools, public and private, that volunteered to participate and involved about 2,750 students. The results indicated a wide variation in performance among schools. In reporting to the University Matriculation Board, Asbury listed four reasons for the department's decision to investigate the existing degree of uniformity in the standard of the secondary school principals' recommendations for grade 12 students: 1 / a realization of the natural tendency for standards across the province to become less uniform as time went on, in spite of the restraining influence of the grade 13 examinations; 2 / the increase in the number of schools and teachers and the frequent changes in staff, particularly in the smaller schools; 3 / the fact that certain school systems were questioning whether a standard suited to graduation from grade 12 was necessarily adequate for admission to grade 13; 4 / a desire on the part of the department to investigate the suitability of objective-type tests and related marking procedures for Ontario use.

THE INTRODUCTION OF A REGULAR TESTING PROGRAM

In the following year, 1958–9, the testing program was extended to all General course grade 12 students in all schools, both provincial and private, that presented candidates for the Ontario Secondary School Graduation Diploma. The program was in a sense still experimental, in that future action was based on a study of that year's results. A modified version of the Scholastic Aptitude Test, the Scholastic Aptitude Test, Ontario Edition (SATO), was employed to measure aptitude, and achievement tests were used for English and French. The program was a co-operative one between the Department of Education and the Department of Educational Research of the Ontario College of Education. High School inspectors or assistant superintendents, particularly F.C. Asbury and A.H. McKague, assumed the responsibility for constructing the achievement tests, and the Department of Educational Research provided technical assistance in test construction and also administered the tests, scored the answer sheets or cards, returned the results to the schools, and provided statistical summaries of the results to the schools and to the department. In carrying out its part of the program, the Department of Educational Research pioneered in the use of a number of mechanical and electronic devices for test scoring and analysis.

TESTING PROCEDURES

The test administration of 1959 was judged a reasonable basis for proceeding in the following year. The program was now extended to the Technical and Commercial courses as well as the General course. In addition to the Scholastic Aptitude Test, Ontario Edition, achievement tests in English structure and usage and in chemistry were also provided. The former, referred to as the Canadian English Test, Ontario Edition, or CETO, was designed to measure the relative standing of the candidates in such fields as punctuation, the use of capitals, language usage, organization of material for paragraph or essay structure, and sentence structure and style. It was indicated that neither this test nor the Canadian Chemistry Test, Ontario Edition (CCTO), was intended to measure all the objectives in either course.

In 1961 the Scholastic Aptitude Test, Ontario Edition, was written in its entirety by students in the General and Technical courses, and the verbal part only by those in the Commercial course. Those in the General course who studied world history, algebra, or Latin, took the achievement tests in those subjects; those in the Technical course took the tests, where appropriate, in economics and algebra; and those in the Commercial course, the test in economics. Some advice was offered to the schools with reference to preparation for the tests and use of the results.

> It is expected that the principal and teachers in each school will impress upon the pupils concerned that the tests should be approached with seriousness but not anxiety. The best preparation is steady, consistent work throughout the school year. An undue amount of drill and review before an achievement test invalidates the test, destroys its usefulness to the teachers, and impinges upon other subjects not being tested. The usual review before Easter school examinations should suffice for the purpose.
>
> Since the most important use of the results is (a) to place the class in proper perspective with all classes in the same course throughout the province for purposes of recommendation for diplomas to the Department of Education, and (b) to assist the teachers in determining the readiness of candidates who are border-line pupils on the regular school examinations, these tests must be considered as useful supplements to information and marks normally available to the principal at promotion time.[6]

The schools were promised a statement of the scores of their candidates, with conversion tables for the interpretation of raw scores, in time for promotion and recommendation meetings at the end of the school year. They were warned to be cautious about recommending a student whose achievement test scores were much below average, especially if he was also low in aptitude. Any announcement to the students about diploma awards was to be qualified by a statement that they were subject to review.

Since the tests had to be given several weeks before the end of the school year, the amount of work and the specific topics on which they were to be based had to be specified in advance. The schools were warned, however, that they were expected to cover the rest of the course by the end of the school year. There was an air of paternalism about the whole business that makes one wonder whether the officials concerned did not think of the teachers as just a group of grown-up children. On the other hand, the writer distinctly recalls a departmental official telling about a particular teacher who was given credit, no doubt with reason, for very high standards, and who had the reputation of bringing most of his students up to this level. The question was whether or not he could be permitted to fail two students who, according to the provincial testing program, would have qualified for first-class honours in the average school. A conscientious official was sorely tempted to intervene in order to ensure fair treatment of the students as opposed to the unrestrained idiosyncrasies of a teacher who thought that everyone else was out of line.

ATTITUDES OF TEACHERS AND ADMINISTRATORS

Mention was made in connection with the studies leading to the re-establishment of essay-type examinations in grade 12 of the threat to abolish the objective testing program. The expression of views by principals and teachers at that time showed that there was a substantial degree of support for these tests. This reaction was certainly a surprise to some members of the Grade 12 Examinations Study Committee, who had no doubt been misled by the more vocal critics into thinking that the adverse views were stronger and more widespread than they actually were. In any case, the threat passed, and the new examinations paralleled the objective tests rather than replacing them.

THE PROGRAM IN SUCCESSIVE YEARS

The testing program for 1961–2 was adapted to fit in with that of the Carnegie Study of Identification and Utilization of Student Talent in High School and College. This study, conducted by the Department of Educational Research of the Ontario College of Education, involved a series of tests and questionnaires in which an entire provincial grade group participated as it proceeded through secondary school, beginning in 1959–60. In the spring of 1962 this group was in grade 11, after having taken a series of tests of one kind or another in each of the previous two grades. In that year it was decided that the departmental subjects tested would be geometry and physics, which were taught in grade 12 in some schools and in grade 11 in others. Thus part of the participating group would be regular grade 12 students and part would be "Carnegie" students. The Scholastic Aptitude Test, Ontario Edition, was again administered in grade 12 in the General, Technical, and Commercial courses, including Special Commercial. The schools were told that a few students might justifiably be assigned regular examination marks differing noticeably from their test scores. However, if the average deviation of the students writing the test in the school exceeded 8 per cent, the principal was requested to confer with the teacher, attach a letter of explanation to the summary sheet, and send a copy of the letter to the district or municipal inspector.

The policy of integrating the departmental tests with the Carnegie Study was continued in 1962–3, when those of the students in the latter project who had not failed one or more grades along the way were in grade 12. Co-ordination was an easy matter in view of the fact that the same agency, the Department of Educational Research, administered and scored the tests for both programs, as well as interpreting the scores and reporting the results to the schools. The relevant activities in this department were at that time under the supervision of W. Brehaut, and the computer and machine operations were conducted by a group directed by D. Carder. In addition to the SATO, taken by students in all three of the secondary school courses, those in the General course wrote an achievement test in English, and one of two versions of a French test, one for English-speaking students and the other, still referred to as "Special French," but beginning to be labelled according to Ontario usage "Français," for French-speaking students. Preliminary plans for an objective test in chemistry were abandoned in favour of an experimental essay-type examination in the same subject.

It had become established policy by 1963–4 to administer the SATO in November of each academic year and the achievement tests as late as possible in the spring, leaving sufficient time to report the results to the schools before the promotion examinations. The only achievement test for that year was in algebra, leaving room for essay examinations in geography and Latin. An expression of opinion about the value of the program of departmental tests and examinations was sought in the summer of 1964 from directors, superintendents, principals, and teachers through their respective professional organizations. Although there was some difference in detail, all these groups approved the policy of checking standards by the judicious use of tests and examinations as administered in the existing programs. As a result, it was decided that the policy would continue without substantial change.

In 1964–5, the SATO was administered to those in all courses except Special Commercial, the latter having been dropped the previous year. The achievement tests were given in French or "Français," whichever was appropriate, and in chemistry. Since the test in the former subject, although administered on May 7, covered the entire year's quota of grammar, teachers were advised to concentrate on that and to leave more of the authors work to be dealt with at the end of the year. This kind of instruction gives some indication of the way in which the testing program influenced the curriculum.

END OF THE PROGRAM

No further objective tests of achievement were given after 1964–5. From then on, the responsibilities of the former Department of Educational Research of the Ontario College of Education were assumed by the Department of Measurement and Evaluation of the Ontario Institute for Studies in Education. The departmental testing program for 1965–6 and 1966–7 consisted of the administration of the SATO in November of each of the two years and the essay-type achievement examinations, discussed elsewhere, in the spring. The last administration of the SATO was in the fall of 1968. The demise of the grade 12 departmental testing program was largely a result of the concentration of effort on the development of the Ontario Tests for Admission to College and University (OACU) and the national Service for Admission to College and University (SACU) tests. Although these tests were designed for use in grade 13 and were intended primarily for university admission some people hoped that they would also serve as a means of restraining the wide divergence among secondary school standards. This latter objective seemed less important than it had a few years before in view of the new attitudes sweeping the schools. It was apparent by the late 1960s that those in control of educational policy would not support external testing programs both in grade 12 and in grade 13.

An interesting issue arose in 1967, when increasing attention was being focused on the interests and problems of French-speaking students. As a result of the fact that increasing numbers of these students were continuing their studies in secondary school classes conducted in the French language, the inappropriateness of the SATO as a measure of their developed ability was becoming more and more obvious. The question of producing a French version of the test was raised by the department, but no action was taken, partly because of the difficulty involved, and partly because of the poor life expectancy of the SATO.

EIGHTEEN

Objective testing for university admission

ONTARIO TESTS FOR ADMISSION TO COLLEGE AND UNIVERSITY (OACU)

Origin of the program

The prospect of developing criteria for university admission that would produce comparable results across the country was a subject of discussion long before any direct action was taken and considerably before the decision was made to discontinue the Ontario grade 13 departmental examination. Although the results of external essay examinations conducted by departments of education in each of the provinces were thought to have a high degree of validity for admission to universities in the same province, an assumption that was confirmed for Ontario by the Atkinson Study of Utilization of Student Resources and for Alberta and the Maritime Provinces by concurrent investigations, there were no grounds for believing that these examinations were of equivalent value for those who attended university in a province other than that in which they attended secondary school. Furthermore, there was hope of finding some means of reducing the problem of equating qualifications from one province to another. The universities were also fretting about the short time span between the release of the departmental examination results and the beginning of the university year. Under pressure from increasing numbers of candidates, they were more and more prepared to act on the basis of a criterion that, although possibly somewhat inferior, could be made available sooner.

The United States provided a number of examples of large-scale testing programs for use in college admission. In that country the idea of having a uniform system of external essay-type examinations administered at the end of high school was almost completely foreign. State governments did not think of playing such a role, and any proposal to do so on their part would have been generally regarded as ridiculous. The nearest approach to such a program was the New York Regents' examinations, which were instituted in 1865 to provide a means of assessing the fitness of candidates for admission to the public academies. They later served as a means of evaluating schools and of determining the amount of financial aid to be given to each school. In 1878 the first academic examination for admission to college was administered; it was also used as a basis for granting a certificate to graduates of the public academies. As time went on, the examinations were reserved for the upper high school grades. For decades, they have involved a dependence on objective testing as a means of achieving their purposes.

The College Entrance Examination Board was established in 1900 by a co-operative effort on the part of member high schools and colleges in the United States to try to deal with the great variation in existing standards and bring to an end what was described as educational anarchy. In 1948 the board merged its testing functions with those of the American Council on Education and the Carnegie Foundation for the Advancement of Teaching and formed the Educational Testing Service, a non-profit organization that collected fees from candidates who wrote its tests and used the proceeds for research and the improvement of its programs. Subsequent to the creation of the Educational Testing Service, the new organization contracted with the College Board to administer its testing programs, to construct its tests, and to carry out research, but left the board with administrative control of these activities. The college admission program, which was only one of the numerous activities of the Educational Testing Service, involved the administration of the Scholastic Aptitude Test and a series of subject achievement tests containing questions that were considered sufficiently general to avoid favouring candidates who had followed a particular course of study. A report on each candidate's results was supplied to colleges at their own or the candidate's request for the purposes of admission and the awarding of scholarships. High schools could also obtain results for their own candidates.

The College Entrance Board program, and others of a similar nature developed in the United States, have certain characteristics that tend to be of particular interest to Canadians. 1 / They are a manifestation of a free-enterprise approach that would be difficult to imagine developing in the same form in Canada. For Example, Canadian students are not generally accustomed to paying for the privilege of demonstrating their fitness for university admission, although some have taken the College Board tests in centres in this country under the same conditions as American candidates. Generally speaking, there is considered to be some political disadvantage in any proposal by a provincial government to shift the cost to students. 2 / The College Board and other mass testing programs are committed almost completely to the objective-testing approach, although not without criticism or misgivings. Given the scale of the operation, there is no conceivable substitute. When the writing of a short essay was added to the College Board program a number of years ago, no effort was made to evaluate it; copies were sent to the designated institutions so that they could take it into account as they saw fit. 3 / The concentration of resources in these agencies enables them to devote a great deal of attention to item construction, test validation, and research. As critics have been ready to point out, however, they have by no means been immune from error. 4 / A factor that Canadian enthusiasts have sometimes forgotten or ignored is that American colleges do not normally rely exclusively on the results of the tests for admission purposes. The usual practice is to consider them along with the high school record, recommendations from the school, and other factors. The question of whether or not they could be considered as a substitute for a measure of high school achievement in Ontario, whether obtained from internal or external examinations, is therefore naïve.

The report of the Ontario Grade 13 Study Committee in 1964 dealt a blow to the departmental examination system. It recommended admission to university on the basis of a composite picture obtained from the student's school record at the completion of grade 12, his standing in the suggested matriculation year, and his results on the proposed Council on Admissions to University (CAU) tests, patterned upon, but not identical with, the College Entrance Board tests.[1] Those who envisioned a number of years of negotiations before arrangements for the latter could be completed decided that Ontario should go ahead with an interim program based on the successful departmental testing then being carried on in grade 12. A co-operative arrangement was thus worked out between the department and the Ontario Institute for Studies in Education.

Test development and administration

The Department of Measurement and Evaluation of OISE under the Chairmanship of V.R. D'Oyley, secured the services of Frances Swineford, Head of the Test Analysis Department of the Educational Testing Service, for a short period of time early in 1966. She conducted some valuable studies designed to determine the applicability of the College Board tests to the Canadian student population. Arrangements were also made to use suitable items from those developed by the Educational Testing Service. Plans were pursued for the construction of an Ontario Scholastic Aptitude Test (OSAT), an Ontario Physics Achievement Test (OPAT), an Ontario English Composition Achievement Test (OECAT), and an Ontario Mathematics Achievement Test (OMAT), all to be administered to grade 13 students in the spring of 1967.

The OSAT was largely made up, like the SATO, of Educational Testing Service items selected, and to some extent adapted, to discriminate effectively for the Ontario population. A committee of four was responsible for the construction of this test. For the achievement tests, the corresponding committees consisted of university professors, secondary school teachers, and measurement specialists. The committee for the English test was able to borrow and adapt the American items, and the committee for the physics test made use of some from the same source, but an entirely new mathematics test had to be created to suit the new mathematics curriculum in grade 13.

Student handbooks were supplied to prospective candidates describing the tests and indicating the uses to be made of them. In the OSAT handbook, the reasons for deriving separate verbal and mathematical scores were explained.[2] The verbal questions were said to measure understanding of relationships between words and ideas, extent of vocabulary, and comprehension of reading passages. The mathematical questions were said to measure the ability to undersand and reason with mathematical symbols and the ability to solve problems. Candidates were told that their OSAT scores would help admissions officers in post-secondary institutions to assess their academic ability, although it was also pointed out to them that academic records remained the best evidence of their readiness for further education. While there was no absolutely precise method of predicting an individual's future academic performance, they were assured that a combination of OSAT scores with a variety of other measures would provide a reasonably accurate forecast.

The advice offered by the OSAT handbook with respect to preparation for writing the tests was particularly relevant. It was explained that, since the test was designed to measure abilities that were developed over a long period of time, the bulk of each candidate's preparation was behind him. Special tutoring or intensive study over a short period before the test were not likely to produce significant gains in test scores. Further instructions had to do with taking the test, the correction for guessing, and procedures for dealing with certain types of sample items. Illustrations of these items were supplied, with explanations of the reason why particular responses were designated as correct or preferable to the alternatives.

The handbooks were the only means available to teachers for the evaluation of the tests, since the maintenance of the integrity of the items for future use meant that copies had to be closely guarded and returned to OACU headquarters after the test administration. On the basis of their study of the 1967 handbook, the Association of Heads of English Departments in Toronto Secondary Schools prepared a brief carrying a message that was the more devastating because of the tone of reason and moderation in which it was expressed.[3] Since this document is of interest principally because of its expression of attitudes toward and issues involved in objective testing, it is dealt with more fully in volume III. It is sufficient to note here that the department heads took strong exception to statements that implied that the Ontario English Composition Achievement Test (OECAT) could measure the ingredients for the appreciation of good prose and for the student's ability to write. They feared that such assumptions, if taken seriously by teachers and students, could damage the teaching of composition in the secondary schools. Reflecting criticism of this kind, the corresponding test for 1968 was called the Ontario Standard English Achievement Test.

The 1968 handbook for the OACU achievement tests explained that each test was designed to measure the student's competence in a particular subject and that this competence might consist of a variety of abilities, depending on the subject concerned. The Ontario Physics Achievement Test was designed to measure "(1) the ability to demonstrate an understanding of basic scientific concepts and principles; (2) the ability to apply these concepts and principles to familiar and unfamiliar situations; (3) the ability to handle quantitative relations; (4) the ability to interpret cause-and-effect relationships; (5) the ability to apply laboratory procedures and interpret experimental data."[4] All the handbook claimed for the Ontario Standard English Achievement Test was that it was "to help universities assess a student's ability to write good standard English prose ..."[5] It then proceeded to give illustrations of different types of items. The Ontario Mathematics Achievement Test (OMAT) was designed to assist in the evaluation of the candidate's ability to understand and use what he had learned. The questions were grouped according to the following categories and components: 1 / grade 13, analysis, consisting of function as a mapping, second degree relations in the plane, trigonometry, transformations in the plane, slopes and simple derivatives, and applications of differentiation; 2 / basic principles from earlier grades related to topics such as linear and quadratic functions, exponents and logarithms, circles, and sequences and series; and 3 / miscellaneous topics. The weights assigned to these three categories were respectively 60, 20, and 20.[6] Generally speaking, the 1968 tests were developed with no borrowing from American sources.

By 1968–9 the Service for Admission to College and University (SACU) was ready to begin operations, and a combined program was worked out with the Ontario Institute for Studies in Education for the administration of the SACU and OACU tests in Ontario. The part sponsored by SACU consisted of the Canadian Scholastic Aptitude Test (CSAT) and the Canadian English Language Achievement Test (CELAT), respectively patterned after and similar to the Ontario Scholastic Aptitude Test and the Ontario Standard English Achievement Test. The tests sponsored by OACU were the Ontario Physics Achievement Test (OPAT) and the Ontario Mathematics Achievement Test (OMAT). All the tests were constructed by the Department of Measurement and Evaluation in OISE, although the manual and supporting material for the SACU tests were prepared by officials of that organization. OISE was responsible for sending out to participating schools all OACU test materials and communications relating to them or to the administration of the test, while SACU had corresponding responsibilities with respect to its own operations. The scheme did not work well, and there were a great many criticisms from participating schools.

The last OACU tests consisted again of OPAT and OMAT, which were written respectively on April 7 and May 5, 1970. Ontario students were, as before, given an opportunity to write free of charge. The fact that administrative difficulties had not been overcome seemed to be rather unimportant because there was no need to perfect the machinery for future use. The item patterns for the tests were similar to those of the previous year.

All the tests were designed for machine scoring. Results were reported to the Department of Education, the schools, and the universities. Students received results from their schools, which were also supplied with information to enable them to offer further assistance in interpretation. Performance was reported by standard score and by percentile rank. The range of the standard scores was from 200 to 800, according to a scheme resembling that established for the College Entrance Examination Board tests.

OACU *advisory committees*

An OACU Advisory Group was established at an early stage to "offer expert advice and suggestions in matters relating to the testing program and to research."[7] It was formed from representatives of four interests: 1 / secondary school groups, including directors of education, superintendents of secondary schools, secondary school principals, and secondary school teachers; 2 / school trustees; 3 / admissions officers from the universities; and 4 / the Ontario Institute for Studies in Education. Membership of Department of Education officials was originally provided for, but the plan did not work out because of the implicit conflict of roles. Although the Advisory Group was quite active, it was reined in by the department, which was forced to point out that the responsibility for policy-making resided elsewhere. The Ontario Teachers' Federation asked in 1967, with respect to directions sent out from the OACU office, whether the Measurement Department or the Department of Education had the responsibility for issuing instructions to teachers. The Measurement Department appeared to be following the patterns employed in the Registrar's Branch of the Department of Education. After this point was raised, steps were taken to ensure that the appropriate officials of the department approved all proposed actions having to do with the school system. In 1968–9 decision-making shifted from the Department of Education to the Department of University Affairs.

The OACU Advisory Group established a Research Advisory Committee consisting of representatives from 1 / the Ontario Universities' Council on Admissions, 2 / the Ontario University Registrars' Association, 3 / the Ontario Secondary School Headmasters' Council, 4 / the Ontario Teachers' Federation, and 5 / the Department of Measurement and Evaluation of OISE. It was supposed to meet twice yearly "to review the research conducted on the most recent test administrations and to raise questions about plans for research into various aspects of the testing program."

Research

Evaluation of the OACU program was begun shortly after it was first administered in 1967. An early study was designed to determine the reliability of the tests and to validate them in terms of the following criteria: 1 / marks assigned by teachers at Easter to students taking each grade 13 subject for the first time; 2 / average marks on the grade 13 departmental examination; and 3 / marks on individual papers in the grade 13 departmentals. The first of these criteria was derived from the performance of students in three large schools in Metropolitan Toronto and the second and third from that of a representative sample of all students taking the tests.

Test reliability coefficients were computed by using Kuder-Richardson formula 20. The coefficients for the OSAT and the OECAT were based on a representative sample, and those for the OPAT and the OMAT on the total number of students taking each test. The respective coefficients were as follows: OSAT-Verbal, 0.90; OSAT-Mathematical, 0.88; OPAT, 0.82; OMAT, 0.81; OECAT, 0.95. These results were reported as indicating that the tests were highly reliable.[8] Although it would generally be agreed that a correlation as high as 0.95 under the circumstances does justify such a verdict, it might have been better to identify the OPAT and the OMAT as moderately reliable. A reasonable explanation offered for the difference between the reliability coefficients for the achievement tests and the aptitude tests was that the former had a much smaller number of items.

A first step in the validation procedure itself was to correlate the test scores and, in the case of the OSAT the subtest scores, with one another. It is difficult to say what real value there was in such an activity. Quite according to expectation, the intercorrelations were generally modest, ranging from 0.40 to 0.71. The OSAT-Verbal subtest correlated most highly with the achievement test with the highest verbal component, that is, with the OECAT, and the OSAT-Mathematical subtest with the tests with the highest mathematical component, the OPAT and the OMAT. Further steps involved correlating the test scores with the three categories of teachers' marks. Again, the highest correlations were found between predictors and criteria with emphasis on similar components, whether verbal or mathematical. Of the forty-six correlation coefficients based on the five OACU scores as predictors and teachers' Easter marks on nine papers plus the grade 13 average as criteria, the range was from 0.17 to 0.71, and the median approximately 0.42. When the criteria were grade 13 departmental marks on eleven papers, the range for fifty coefficients was from 0.17 to 0.78, and the median approximately 0.43.

These results are inevitably open to a variety of possible interpretations. A low correlation indicates that the tests measure relatively different things, and a high correlation that they measure similar things or the same thing in imperfect ways. Thus the more distinct one assumes the measures to be, the lower the expected correlation. If tests designed to measure entirely different things are highly correlated, one or other or both must be ineffective, although a low correlation between them does not necessarily mean that either is effective. On the other hand, if they are supposed to measure related or similar things, they should show a high correlation, and a low correlation indicates that one or other or both are ineffective. To apply some of these principles more specifically, if the scores on the OPAT were highly correlated with marks on a physics examination, it might have meant that both were good measures of achievement in that subject, or that neither was. If they were not highly correlated, the possible explanations would be that one or the other was a good measure, or that neither was, or that each was a good predictor of a different and not closely related set of objectives in physics. It is often difficult or impossible to choose correctly among these explanations, and the OACU study was not unlike many others in that it left some important questions unanswered.

Of considerably more potential value was a longer-term validity study completed in 1969.[9] Its purpose was to determine the extent to which scores on the OACU tests, marks on the grade 13 departmental examinations, and teachers' Christmas marks in grades 12 and 13 predicted first-year university achievement. The OACU tests were those of the 1966–7 administration, and first-year performance was that registered in 1967–8 by those students who proceeded to any one of ten universities: Brock, Carleton, Lakehead, McMaster, Queen's, Toronto, Trent, Waterloo, Western Ontario, and York. The criteria were the final averages and individual subjects where available. A separate analysis was performed for each university and in some cases for various programs and for the sex groups. The study was apparently done in a kind of vacuum, since it made the preposterous claim that it "has been perhaps the first attempt to evaluate both school averages and standardized aptitude and achievement scores for predicting first-year performance in the majority of Ontario universities."[10] The writers had apparently never heard of the Atkinson Study of Utilization of Student Resources, which had extended over more than a decade after 1955, and had done exactly that. It was thus of no use to look for comparisons with previous findings.

It would be impossible to review any significant proportion of the hundreds of measures given in the dozens of tables resulting from the study. Some of the summary findings were, however, revealing. Table

66 indicated the median averages between the various test scores and the first year average for each of the participating universities. The results were as follows: OSAT-V, 0.24; OSAT-M, 0.19; OPAT, 0.37; OMAT, 0.40; and OSEAT (OECAT), 0.30. Since these median values were the midpoints of widely varying coefficients, an allowance must be made for possible exceptions to any general statement. Subject to this proviso, it is difficult to avoid the conclusion that the OSAT scores, both verbal and mathematical, were of little value as over-all predictors of the first-year university average. It must be noted that the square of the coefficient represents the proportion of the criterion variance, that is, of the first-year university average, explained by the predictor. The proportion explained by the OSAT verbal score was only $(0.24)^2$, or less than 6 per cent, and by the mathematical score less than 4 per cent. An analysis of the tables shows that the median correlations between the grade 12 and grade 13 (final) averages and the first-year average for all the reported university groups and subgroups in the various tables were respectively approximately 0.46 and 0.58. The grade 13 final examination mark was of course not available in the same form after 1967. The median correlation for all groups where the grade 13 Christmas examination was reported was only about 0.43. How good a predictor the teacher's final estimate might be was not indicated. In the Atkinson Study, however, the final examination mark and the teacher's estimate proved to be about equally effective.

The OACU achievement tests were obviously considerably better predictors than the OSAT. The percentage of the criterion variance explained by the OPAT was $(0.37)^2$, or 13.7; the corresponding figure for the OMAT was $(0.40)^2$, or 16.0 per cent, and for the OSEAT, $(0.30)^2$, or 9 per cent. These figures emphasize the uncertainty of the predictive process and the relatively small contribution made to it by even the better of the objective tests.

Prediction of university achievement in individual subjects from the OACU achievement tests was in some cases fairly good. Unfortunately, the study did not make it possible to compare the relevant correlations with those between individual subject marks in grade 13 and those in university, since these were apparently not computed. Some rather strange results should be examined critically. For example, why were the OSAT verbal scores just as good predictors of achievement in the Faculty of *Mathematics* at Waterloo as were the OSAT mathematical scores? Neither one was of course very good, with correlations of only 0.36.

An examination of the data in this study suggests that, unless there is a radical change in the aptitude tests under the SACU program, the universities will make a gross error if they place any great amount of reliance on the scores as predictors of success. In a combination of predictors the study suggests, just as the Atkinson Study did earlier, that much the greatest emphasis should be placed on the school record, although the changing form and value of that record should be subjected to continuous examination. It is possible that the aptitude scores may in some cases make a worthwhile additional contribution, but this is by no means true for every faculty, course, or program. As far as the achievement tests are concerned, they appear to be of considerably more value than the aptitude tests for general prediction, but even so, they have in general less predictive power than either the grade 12 or the grade 13 average. Here again it must be emphasized that there are apparent exceptions to this general assessment. Particularly if an achievement test in a certain subject is used to predict university success in the same or a related subject, a cautious use of the scores may be justified. But if universities fail to insist on a continuous and critical study of the whole program, and if they do not ensure that competent statisticians interpret the results as they apply to their own institution, students are certain to be subjected to injustices and valuable talent will be lost.

In April 1970 John R. Hills, Director of the Office of Evaluation Services of the Florida State University, completed an appraisal of the Ontario college admissions testing program, which he delivered to the staff member in charge of the validity studies as well as to the chairman of the department. During his visit, he examined a series of reports on the validity of the tests, including the one already referred to. He declared that the studies were basically sound and competently done and that they appeared to be internally consistent. Among his specific comments was the speculation that achievement tests combined with the high school record would yield higher predictions than would aptitude tests and the high school record; that is, that the aptitude tests were redundant. He thought that, ignoring the political considerations, it would be well to discontinue the aptitude tests and require the English and mathematics tests for admission prediction purposes. Hills wrote that he would have liked to have seen what would happen if a high school record that covered several years were used as a predictor in combination with test scores; unfortunately he met no one who was able to tell him that this approach had been tried in the Atkinson Study a few years earlier. Another of his many contributions was his expression of scepticism that the current battery could be dependably used for differential prediction, despite suggestions to the contrary in the report.

Reaction to the OACU *program*

Neither the Ontario Teachers' Federation nor the Ontario Secondary School Headmasters' Council was very enthusiastic about the OACU program. In a submission from the former organization to the minister in January 1967, objection was taken to the possible uses to which the tests might be put.

> An official statement has been made to the effect that these tests, now under preparation, will become the main examination in 1968 and thereafter. We are being asked, then to pin absolute faith on multiple choice tests while relegating subjective examinations, which allow some measure of literate composition and co-ordination of ideas, to a position of minor significance.
>
> In spite of the welter of criticism levelled at the College Entrance Examination Board type of examinations, few will argue against their usefulness *in combination with other factors*. However, because these will be the only uniform examinations submitted by candidates, universities and other post-secondary school institutions will be strongly tempted to ascribe to the results all the virtues of the absolute.
>
> Surely, one of the main criticisms of Grade 13 has been that the student's fate was placed on the balance of a single examination. It would appear logical, therefore, that from the single criterion we should move to a more broadly based assessment.[11]

These comments were of course quite in line with the conclusions of the Atkinson Study.

A more fundamental type of opposition was offered by members of the Ontario Secondary School Headmasters' Council. They pointed to the increasingly valued freedom resulting from the transfer to the schools of the responsibility for the conduct of the school leaving examinations, and indicated that they did not want a privilege ostensibly granted by one policy move snatched away by another. In January 1969 the Board of Directors of the OSSHC reiterated that the organization did not in principle approve of an external standardized program of achievement tests. It was, however, prepared to accept such a program on an experimental basis provided that it was reviewed annually, that no more than four tests were given in any one year, and that serious consideration was given to the possibility of holding the tests at an earlier grade level and at a time of year when test results would be more useful to the schools.[12]

A more favourable reaction has been demonstrated by university registrars. One of these wrote in the spring of 1968 that the Office of Admissions and the Faculty of Arts in his institution had co-operated in evaluating the worth of the tests administered in 1967. They found that the scores stood up well in comparison with the grade 13 examination results and proved to be good predictors of the Christmas examination marks in first year. This particular registrar said that he and his colleagues felt that, if the new grade 13 system were combined with the sophisticated kind of testing program that could be developed, great strides would be made in the achievement of a satisfactory transition from school to university.

THE SERVICE FOR ADMISSION TO COLLEGE AND UNIVERSITY

Purposes

As stated in the letters patent prepared at the time the Secretary of State approved the incorporation of SACU in August 1966 the purposes of the organization were as follows.

(a) To arrange for the development and administration of suitable scholastic aptitude and academic achievement tests through not less than two (2) test service centers: at least one located in the Province of Quebec for French-speaking candidates and at least one located in a province or provinces other than Quebec for English-speaking candidates.
(b) To assist in the further development and improvement of selection and admission procedures and to aid, on request, in the awarding of scholarships and bursaries.
(c) To assist member institutions of the Corporation in the interpretation of the academic record of applicants for admission from other provinces in Canada or from other countries.
(d) To conduct and support research on problems related to the admission of students to universities and other institutions of post-secondary education.
(e) To gather and distribute information about entrance requirements, selection of students, admission procedures, scholarships and bursaries, and related matters.
(f) To provide a medium for the co-operation of secondary schools, universities, other institutions of post-secondary education, provincial departments of education, and other groups and organizations concerned with the transition of students from secondary to post-secondary institutions, and for the discussion of their common problem and other related matters.[13]

Establishment

A brief history of SACU was provided in the 1970 guidance manual for test administration, a review of which will be sufficient to indicate how the organization originated. The first significant step occurred in 1962 when a committee reported to the National Conference of Canadian Universities and Colleges, later renamed the Association of Universities and Colleges of Canada, on the results of its study of the operations of the College Entrance Examination Board and the Educational Testing Service. This committee recommended the formation of a nation-wide Canadian university and college examination board. As a preliminary to possible action, the Executive Committee of the NCCUC initiated a study of the feasibility of establishing an organization which would concern itself with all aspects of the transition of students from secondary school to university. The investigation revealed a strong demand in many universities for such an organization. According to early proposals, this entity would first undertake testing programs and later assume research and information functions. It would become a self-supporting, non-profit corporation.

The next step after the acceptance of the report was the establishment of a planning committee consisting of representatives of the CEA and of the Fédération des collèges classiques as well as of the NCCUC. This committee prepared proposals for the establishment of the organization. While it was engaged in these activities in 1964, the Standing Committee of Ministers of Education appointed an *ad hoc* committee to investigate the matter from the point of view of the provincial departments of education. This *ad hoc* committee worked with the NCCUC planning committee to prepare for a founding conference the following year.

In August 1965 the joint committee thus formed recommended the establishment of a Canadian admissions service. The proposal received the approval of the Board of Directors of the AUCC during the following month, and the board invited the Standing Committee of Ministers to co-operate in implementing it. With the ministers' approval in principle, arrangements were duly made for a founding conference in Ottawa in April 1966, where the proposals were adopted. After the Secretary of State took the appropriate action leading to incorporation, the organization began operations as a non-profit national body consisting of colleges and universities, the departments of education of all of the provinces, and several other national agencies interested in education. There was provision for an interprovincial and interuniversity General Assembly and Board of Directors and an Executive Committee. The permanent headquarters of the organization were in Ottawa. The first director, L. Lamontagne, and the first assistant director, H.A. Elliott, assumed full-time duties in the summer of 1967.

First test administrations

Planning began in April 1968 for the first administration of scholastic aptitude and English and French language achievement tests the following year. Although there was considered to be no time to spare, available funds were exhausted by October, and the work was halted until early December when further fee payments were made. The delay was blamed for difficulties in delivering the tests by the scheduled dates. In February 1969 over 45,000 candidates were tested in Canada and abroad. With the addition of about five thousand English-speaking students in Quebec and 45,000 French-speaking students, the total approached 100,000 by May. A single testing session was arranged for 1970 involving tests in the same areas as in 1969.

Test development

In its early stages, the organization contemplated the administration of tests in a variety of areas. Its plans were reflected in the number of committees set up during its first active year. There were standing committees for guidance, admission, membership, and examinations; test development committees for the Scholastic Aptitude Test, the test de scolaptitudes, the Achievement Test in English, and the test de connaissance en français; and test design committees for English and French achievement tests in mathematics, physics, chemistry, and social sciences, as well as for English as a working language, français langue de travail, English as a second language, and français langue seconde. The practical realities of finance and administration curtailed some of the earlier ambitions.

Rather than undertake to produce the tests itself, at least for the time being, SACU made arrangements with the Ontario Institute for Studies in Education and l'Institut de recherche pédagogique to do the work for it. The contract with the former came into force on May 1, 1969. Under its terms, OISE was to produce only the Canadian Scholastic Aptitude Test and the Canadian English Language Achievement Test but not the presiding officer's manual, the special instructions to candidates, or any other related material. The tests were to comply with SACU specifications, which were to be delivered on or before dates specified in the contract. These specifications were to indicate 1 / the type of test required, 2 / the general subject matter of the test, 3 / the number of versions needed, and 4 / such other information as would be required by OISE to estimate the cost of the test and to construct it. The dates of delivery which OISE undertook to meet were designated in the contract. SACU had a specified period of time in which to indicate its disapproval of the test, and OISE time to make appropriate revisions. Payments to OISE were to be made according to agreed upon conditions. Responsibility for security was spelled out in some detail, along with appropriate procedures if security measures failed. The agreement was to remain in force at least until after the administration in the 1973–4 academic year or until terminated by either party after at least twenty-four months' notice.

The test development committees were representative of each province and were set up in such a way as to maintain a balance among high school, department of education, and university experts, as well as providing a voice for the contracting agencies. Their responsibilities were defined in the guidance manual:

1. To advise and assist SACU and the test development agency in the design and preparation of a test which will have country-wide validity, which, together with examination results and school recommendations, will be sources of information for decisions on college and university admission.
2. To review items written for the test, and, if necessary, suggest changes to make the items acceptable, recommending to the test development agency

acceptance or rejection of such items prior to their inclusion in the item bank.

3. To recommend to SACU the methods, standards and criteria for use by the test development agency.
4. Having been informed of the results of item analyses obtained from sample testing across Canada, to make any appropriate recommendations to the test development agency as to the suitability of the items for future tests.
5. To review the proposed final test forms submitted by the test development agency and, if necessary, suggest rearrangement, deletion or substitution of items until agreement on a final test form is reached. Aproval of the final form must be confirmed by the Standing Committee on Examinations.
6. Having been informed of the item analyses obtained from the final test, to recommend to the test development agency the continued inclusion or rejection of any item in the item bank.
7. To recommend to the Standing Committee on Examinations any changes in test design or construction which appear desirable in the light of the analyses obtained from the results of the final test. Changes confirmed by the Standing Committee on Examinations shall be communicated to the test development agency for implementation.[14]

Administration

Test centres were established, with the co-operation of schools and departments of education, in most cities and districts of Canada. Arrangements might be made to set up new ones as the need arose, either in the country or abroad. All secondary students in their final year in Canada, or those with equivalent standing elsewhere who wished admittance to Canadian universities, were eligible to write the tests. Where they took them as part of a provincial program, the department of education determined their eligibility. For candidates who had to pay their own fees, the charge was $6.50 for CSAT and $3.50 for CELAT. Fees were not applicable in 1969–70 to Ontario students studying one or more grade 13 subjects in a publicly supported or inspected private school or those taking the equivalent in a Department of Education correspondence course. Considerable pressure was placed on candidates for university admission to take the tests by the growing practice of universities to require them for admission. In 1970 all Ontario universities except Trent either required the scores or used them, when available, among other criteria for admission and guidance.

The scores were supposed to be ready for distribution five or six weeks after the date of administration. Each candidate received an official score report of his own results and extra copies on request at $2 a copy. An official transcript was sent to all member universities in his own province and to any two other institutions designated on the application form. Additional copies were also available to such institutions on the candidate's request at the same price. Each provincial department of education and each school received a record of the scores of its candidates.

Validity

In 1970 SACU was following the practice of contracting with OISE on a yearly basis to conduct validity studies. This arrangement appeared likely to continue. The organization should certainly examine its position carefully if the results of these studies do not demonstrate that its tests have substantial predictive value or, if the situation does not look promising at any particular stage, that they are subject to substantial improvement.

In 1968 H.A. Elliott observed in the *SACU Bulletin* that the predictive validity of the tests would have to be checked continuously against the performance of students at university. If validity were to be based on successful graduation from a university, a period of four or five years would be required before results could be obtained. He had a certain amount of confidence in the SACU tests at the initial stage because they had been based on the College Entrance Examination Board Admission tests, and because the individual items had been analysed for suitability in College Board tests and in Canadian classes in all provinces. He referred to the first SACU and the College Board tests as equivalent forms of the same test design and he proceeded to make a case for the similarity between Canadian and American students, high schools, and universities. Such similarities had permitted the successful use of College Board tests for Canadian students going to American universities, for American students coming to Canadian universities, and for Canadians going to their own universities.[15] He failed to note that, or explain why, the Atkinson Study of Utilization of Student Resources had shown that the College Board tests had shown much less ability to predict success in Ontario universities than in American colleges and universities.

NINETEEN

Radio and television

RADIO

General role

Radio has always been seen as a medium with a major educative role in the broadest sense. Since its creation in 1936, the Canadian Broadcasting Corporation has offered public affairs programs, interviews, news analysis and commentary, musical and dramtic productions, coverage of political conventions and national and provincial elections, and many special features. Its more specific efforts in the educational field have involved 1 / broadcasts designed for use in schools, 2 / programs to serve the needs of students in colleges and universities, and 3 / broadcasts for general adult education.

Initiatives of the CBC *and other agencies*

In the years immediately preceding the Second World War, and during the early war years, the CBC offered to provide network facilities for school broadcasting to the department of education in any province that was willing to experiment with programs. At that time, the attitude of the Ontario department was negative. Duncan McArthur, Minister of Education in the Hepburn government, expressed the opinion that the expenditure of public money on school broadcasting was unjustified.[1] The initiative was thus left to local school boards and unofficial agencies. Among the former, a conspicuous contribution was made by London Central Collegiate Institute, which established its own studios and produced programs for broadcasting.

In 1943 the CBC secured the co-operation of the nine provincial departments of education in launching the first in a series of National School Broadcasts. The corporation also combined efforts with the Canadian Educational Association to set up a National Advisory Council on School Broadcasting, with representatives of the departments of education, the National Conference of Canadian Universities, the Canadian Teachers' Federation, the Canadian Trustees' Association, and the Canadian Federation of Home and School. Within the organization itself, a School Broadcasts Department was established in the Program Division, which was for many years under the supervision of Fred Rainsberry. The National Advisory Council maintained a close working relationship with this department, contributing an evaluation of each year's broadcasts and assistance in planning future programs.

In the mid-1950s the Supervisor of School Broadcasts of the CBC defined two general purposes of the National School Broadcasts: 1 / to help teachers make classroom work more effective by enlarging the scope of teaching materials, and 2 / to provide experiences for students that would contribute to their education by enriching their social and cultural background. He also mentioned more specific purposes: 1 / to supply students with supplementary information and illustrative material that they could not easily obtain in any other way; 2 / to supply imaginative enrichment for the study of certain subjects, especially social studies and literature, thereby strengthening students' motives to study, sharpening their capacity to take in information, and stimulating them to the further pursuit of knowledge; 3 / to promote an awareness of Canada and an appreciation of Canadian citizenship among the younger generation, and to strengthen their sense of national unity; 4 / to provide programs of a cultural character that required the full production resources of a national broadcasting system; and 5 / to foster wider international contacts through the exchange of school broadcasts with other countries, particularly members of the Commonwealth.[2]

The CBC school broadcasts have been regarded as an example of successful co-operation between federal and provincial agencies. The basis for this co-operation has been that educators have had the responsibility for planning the educational content of the programs, while the broadcasters have determined the radio or television form and have been responsible for distribution. Provincial authorities have had control over school use.

Contributions by the Department of Education

A rapid growth in provincial school broadcasting paralleled the CBC's efforts in the national field. In 1944 the Ontario Department of Education produced an experimental series in music, social studies, English, and guidance. Ten years later, there were ninety of these broadcasts covering fourteen school subjects. The program had been extended to include twenty-six contributions from the British School Broadcasting system.[3] A few were subsequently added from the Australian Broadcasting Commission. By 1963, a peak year for the early 1960s, Ontario productions numbered 173, with an additional fourteen from the BBC and five from the Australian Commission.

Departmental instructions to the schools indicated that the programs were intended mainly for enrichment. It was also suggested that they could be used "to review facts taught earlier, to teach a specific area of a subject, or to introduce a topic that will be dealt with in future weeks."[4] Teachers were advised to be selective and to attempt to use only the programs that could contribute effectively to their regular work. Radio manuals were distributed widely by school inspectors in order to ensure effective utilization.

The Department of Education made considerable efforts to co-operate with the CBC Schools and Youth Programming Department in order to ensure maximunm effectiveness in programming. Consultants had the responsibility of indicating the points that a teacher was likely to emphasize in teaching the subject, and of suggesting aspects of the subject that would supplement the teacher's work and would be suitable for treatment by radio. Other responsibilities assumed by the department included securing an assessment of the value of each series from personal listening and from the opinions of classroom teachers.

It was the practice for a different consultant or team of consultants to be appointed for each separate series of Ontario school radio broadcasts. These were recommended by a departmental official or by a superintendent for one of the Metropolitan Toronto boards of education. The responsibility for choosing script writers rested with the Schools and Youth Programming Branch of the CBC. When chosen, each writer entered into a contract with the Department of Education involving a commission to write one or more scripts. Drafts of these were submitted to the producer for checking from the point of view of broadcasting. The consultant was responsible for checking them from the educational point of view, with attention to accuracy of information, vocabulary, and suitability for a specific grade level. The approval of both the producer and the consultant was required before a script could be accepted from the writer. The department determined the budget within which the producer had to work. A similar consultative procedure was used in producing in CBC's national series.

The extent of the effort to produce and distribute television programs has tended to eclipse the department's efforts in the radio field. On June 5, 1968, Davis expressed the opinion in the Legislature that by 1970 this particular area of endeavour might well be abandoned. He identified a decreasing amount of interest on the part of the school boards and among the broadcasting stations.[5] In a sense, television and radio must be regarded as competitors for the attention of the teachers and pupils. The problems of adapting the timetable are similar in both cases. Where the comparison is to the advantage of one over the other, the more effective must be expected to prevail. This over-all appraisal is not, of course, to suggest that the advantages are all with television. A convincing case can be made for the superiority of radio for certain purposes, apart from the lesser expense involved. But in view of the difficulty in securing the complete acceptance of either as an integral part of the school program, the department seems well advised to concentrate its efforts on a single medium.

Appraisal

In 1956 a Radio Research Project Committee of the Canadian Teachers' Federation publicized the results of a survey of broadcast usage and of user opinion.[6] Of the 31,018 Ontario teachers approached, 38 per cent identified themselves as users, 5 per cent had no equipment available, and 57 per cent had equipment but did not take advantage of the broadcasts. The two main reasons offered for non-usage were that the programs were unrelated to the curriculum and that they were unsuitable for the grade taught. The first of these reasons was offered by 20 per cent of the teachers and the second by 13 per cent. The report pointed out that the National School Broadcasts could hardly be expected to meet the first of these objections, since they could never be related to all provincial curricula. Neither could provincial school broadcasts be totally related to the teaching program of every school.

The summary of availability and usage showed Ontario in a considerably more favourable light than it did the country as a whole. In that province, 65 per cent of the 7,274 schools involved in the survey reported using the broadcasts; 25 per cent had no available equipment; and 10 per cent did not make use of existing equipment for the purpose.

Despite the fact that considerably less use was made of the programs than might have been desired, they were judged as successful in achieving their primary general objectives. They were said to have been particularly effective in arousing the interests of pupils in the subjects being broadcast and in supplying new ideas and types of information. They seemingly did a good job in presenting current events, in broadening pupils' understanding of different groups of Canadians, in promoting better understanding of people in other lands, and in encouraging tolerant attitudes toward new ideas. They were considered less successful in securing the retention of factual information. The report suggested that negligence in following up the broadcasts on the part of the teachers might have helped to explain this result. The broadcasts also failed to reach their full potential in presenting points of view differing from those of the teacher or textbook and in portraying prominent people. Nor were they particularly effective in encouraging pupils to gather information for work on problems related to broadcast subjects.

Appraisals of radio usage since 1956 have tended to show some expansion, but no very drastic or fundamental change. Perhaps this fact is not altogether surprising in view of the lack of any effort comparable to that being made for television to secure the acceptance of radio programs as a normal and integral part of the instructional process. Radio seems to have had its day before the fundamental significance of the communications revolution was fully realized.

TELEVISION

Early impact of television on education

The introduction of television programs, first through American stations, and then somewhat belatedly by the Canadian Broadcasting Corporation, was greeted with enthusiasm by the general public in Ontario. Innumerable families that were thought to be barely able to afford the necessities of life soon equipped themselves with sets, and antennas seemed to spring from every roof. Children planted themselves in front of the screen and remained there for hours on end. There was no doubt about the appeal of television for them. Their elders were by no means sure, however, that the new medium was a salutary influence. On March 12, 1952, the *Globe and Mail* reported some of the views expressed by Toronto school trustees. One of them said that the development of television up to that point had been the greatest stumbling block to child education they had ever had. It gave the children bad eyes and made them unable to sleep or study. Another commented that it spoiled their reading. A third had had the set removed from his house because of the bad effect it had on his child. Hope was expressed that there would be an improvement when the Canadian Broadcasting Corporation went into production. This agency had already indicated that it planned to experiment with education programs during class time.

In the United States the reaction to the opportunity to use television for specifically educational purposes was prompt and enthusiastic. In 1952 the Federal Communications Commission took the kind of action that corresponding agencies in Canada were still considering near the end of the 1960s. It reserved for educational television about three hundred of the total of 2,200 channels available for use in the entire country. By mid-1966, approximately half of the reserved channels were in actual operation, or licences had been requested. During the 1950s, philanthropic agencies, particularly the Ford Foundation, granted very large sums of money to equip and finance educational television stations and to conduct research into the uses of television as an educational instrument.

In December 1963 a summary of the extent to which educational television was being utilized in the United States was given by Fred Hechinger, Education Editor of the *New York Times*.[7] In that year, it was available to almost 100 million Americans through eighty-four non-commercial ETV channels. If full advantage had been taken of all types of equipment and facilities, including kinescopes and closed-circuit systems, it could have been at the disposal of almost every school. Over ten million American pupils of all ages were enrolled in educational classes in 1962–3. Out of a total of 229,857 classes taught by television during that year, general science, the most popular subject, accounted for 48,188. There were about half as many classes in social science and a third as many in art and music. Other courses covered a wide range of content. Kindergarten through the eighth grade accounted for 79 per cent of the enrolment, high school, 6.6 per cent, and higher education, 5.5 per cent.

Although the number of educational television stations had grown by only fifteen over the previous year, increasing numbers of commercial stations were scheduling instructional programs for classroom use. Closed circuit television was growing rapidly in popularity, with 182 systems already in operation, some of them linking over one hundred schools. The total library content of video tapes was increasing by leaps and bounds, offering material for practically every field and for every level of education. There were 290 taped series and 45 kinescope series produced by colleges and universities.

Although Hechinger declared that educational television had had a greater impact than most people realized, he felt that it was less successful than it should be. It still reached a minority of viewers and claimed "only an occasional scrap" of most students' time. For its "failure" he put a considerable part of the blame on educators. Some of them regarded television with outright contempt, and many more used it in an entirely inadequate fashion as an audio-visual aid, useful mainly to fill a gap in a course outline. Hechinger suggested that ETV might fully come into its own only when teachers were trained to handle the screen as naturally as they were currently expected to handle books.

The initiatives in educational television that eventually influenced education in Ontario came from five main sources: 1 / the Canadian Broadcasting Corporation, 2 / the provincial Department of Education, 3 / local school systems, 4 / the universities, and 5 / independent or semi-independent associations. Where there has been substantial activity in a local system, certain benefits are claimed. 1 / Teachers, especially those who participate in the initiation and production of programs, are constantly challenged to examine their material in a new and original light. 2 / Students who take an active part in the same process have a powerful stimulus to creative activity and an extremely effective influence on motivation. 3 / Different schools and sometimes different levels of the system have important reasons for co-ordinating their efforts for the attainment of common goals. The major emphasis placed at this particular point on developments in the Department of Education is not intended in any way to slight the significance of local contributions.

The Metropolitan Educational Television Association

The Metropolitan Educational Television Association of Toronto, which was established in 1959 and incorporated as a non-profit organization in 1961, consisted of a number of educational and cultural agencies united in pursuit of the following objectives:

To serve as an information and co-ordinating centre for the development of educational television in the Metropolitan Toronto broadcast area. This co-ordination involves relations with the CBC, CFTO, educational and cultural institutions, in the planning, organizing and production of ETV programs at all levels.

To create a climate of opinion which will make possible the adequate and appropriate use of the medium of television by educational and cultural institutions.

To develop in the Metropolitan Toronto broadcast area an understanding of the role of educational television and to encourage the appropriate and adequate use of television in formal education by schools and universities and in the field of adult education generally.[8]

In addition to the school boards in Metropolitan Toronto, some of which have since disappeared, the association included school boards from surrounding areas, the University of Toronto and York University, the Royal Ontario Museum, the Art Gallery of Toronto, the Toronto and Scarborough Public Libraries, the local branches of the teachers' federations, and other organizations. School boards paid fees in relation to their pupil enrolment, while other organizations were assessed according to their character and size.

The following projects were listed for 1964–5: 1 / production and presentation of elementary and secondary school programs, and children's and adult education TV programs on CBLT and CFTO; 2 / ETV program planning and production at all levels of education in co-operation with CBC, CFTO, and member educational institutions; 3 / training teachers, librarians, and other educators in the basic characteristics of ETV production; 4 / researching and reporting on the activities in ETV by educational institutions; 5 / developing standards for classroom television receivers and other technical services; 6 / co-ordinating the television interests of educational institutions in the Metropolitan Toronto area; 7 / study of the potential of channel 19 (UHF) for educational broadcasting in the Metro Toronto community; 8 / promotion and information about ETV – speakers, newsletters, etc.[9]

The 1964–5 edition of *ETV Across Canada* discussed the programming activities of META during that year. In the secondary school area, there had been a series of half-hour productions: *Great Debates: the Factory Act of 1833* (history, grade 11); *The Symbolic Structure of Two Novels:* A Tale of Two Cities *and* Cry the Beloved Country (English, grades 10 and 12); and *The Shape of Drama: From* Henry IV *to* Death of a Salesman (English, grades 11 and 12), all produced in co-operation with the CBC. Three others, produced in co-operation with CFTO, were entitled *The Scientific Method* (science, grades 9 and 10); *A Study of Isms: Nationalism* (history, grades 9 to 13); and *The New Math* (mathematics, grades 9, 10, and 11). There were plans for sixty-two half-hour telecasts for the secondary school level during 1965–6.

The same period saw a substantial expansion of activities at the elementary school level. The report claimed that there had been a marked increase in the utilization of educational television in Metro schools. During 1964–5 META presented 130 programs for elementary schools: forty-five involving new original productions, fifty-nine replays of earlier META productions, thirteen from the National Educational Television Network, and thirteen film programs from other sources. The programs dealt with geography, social studies, language arts, English, French, art, science, music, safety, and guidance; there were also special programs on the United Nations, Remembrance Day, Christmas, and other themes. Particular mention was made of a series entitled *Aventures en Français* for grades 7 and 8. Written by experienced French language specialists, it introduced carefully controlled vocabulary in dramatized contexts.

At this stage, to a considerable extent as a result of comments from teachers using school telecasts, META recognized the need for more adequate explanatory materials. Thus for the 1965–6 school year, a *Teachers' Guide* booklet was prepared containing the schedule of telecasts and all program notes under a single cover. The notes presented the objectives for each telecast, suggestions for preparation and follow-up discussion, directive questions, and a synopsis of the content of each program.

Although it operated under the severe handicap of having access to viewers mainly during the morning and late at night, META undertook to offer the adult viewer a wide variety of enriching educational programs. Among the series given particular mention in the report was one entitled *Metropolis—Creator or Destroyer?* which explored the problems of urbanism by presenting outstanding films, along with an expression of views by Toronto experts in architecture, planning, building, and politics. In co-operation with CFTO-TV and the Ontario Department of Economics and Development, META produced two half-hour programs on regional development and economic change, which received province-wide coverage. Other programs listed among the highlights for the year were *Conversations with Eric Hoffer, The Face of Sweden, World Theatre, Pathfinders, The Fuller World, This is Opera, Focus Canada,* and *Challenge and Change: New Developments in Social Work.*

In 1968–9 META had a board of thirteen directors, a regular staff of fifteen, and a budget of $350,000 per annum. In ten years of development, the organization had increased its annual quota of educational broadcast time from sixty to 796 half-hours. Although concentrating on the particular needs of the people of the area, it was making a contribution, according to the 1968 report, *Educational Television Across Canada*, to the education of no fewer than two million school children.

The report referred both to the achievements of the association and to the soul-searching that was going on with respect to the effectiveness of some of its approaches. In planning its operations, 150 teachers and subject co-ordinators from the Metro Toronto regional community met to organize programs along curricular lines. The teams, covering sixteen curriculum areas, attempted to determine those needs within their schools which the technology and psychology of television would best serve. The META staff faced the perennial problem of relating production expertise and pedagogical planning to give the script material the maximum of television worthiness. There had also been serious discussions about the appropriateness of the horizontal type of structure, which involved separate teacher teams for program planning and production at the primary-junior and the intermediate-senior level.

The report commented on the pronounced community orientation and flavour of the programs, which were designed to deal with problems and to reinforce curricula followed within a specific, densely populated, highly urbanized region. META was said to be faced with the problem of developing productions that related school curricula to the physical, social, and psychological environment of the metropolis. Some of the conditions that had to be taken into account were the existence of inner-city slums and large ethnic blocks, sections of pronounced middle-class values, areas of high affluence, and zones of rapid population expansion around the perimeter. Among recent programs particularly demonstrating community flavour were *Screen Education*, *Our Metropolis*, and a two-part series in mathematics entitled *The Fourth Dimension*, which "was designed for that peculiar breed of sophistication known as the 'urban mind.' "

A META survey of usage of television in the fall of 1968 revealed a very discouraging situation. The programs were viewed much too infrequently and sporadically to be considered an integral part of instruction in the schools of the area. Although it seemed unreasonable to base any decisively adverse judgments on a system that had thus far been forced to limp along using an insignificant amount of time made available by the CBC and private broadcasters, the results of the survey created a rather serious crisis for META. The Toronto Board of Education considered a reduction in its intended per pupil contribution, which would undoubtedly have precipitated similar action on the part of other boards. META's executive director, Elwy Yost, made an effective plea against the threat, but there was no guarantee that there would not be similar problems in the future. META had long participated vigorously in the campaign to have UHF channel 19 made available for educational television. Before means were provided to broadcast the programs at times more convenient to the teacher, educational television had to face criticism for the things it was not given a fair chance to do.

A.F. Knowles, who served as executive director in the early stages of the association, gave an account of some of the difficulties META was encountering in 1962 in getting opportunities for broadcasting.[10] The time available for educational purposes was restricted to a few weekday morning periods, restricted Saturday morning periods, and restricted Sunday morning and late evening periods. There was growing commercial pressure on the three Canadian channels accessible to Metropolitan Toronto viewers, since they had to compete with each other and with the American channels. This pressure threatened to force some non-revenue producing programs, such as those for educational purposes, off the air. During the previous season, it was not possible for the CBC to provide as much help as formerly. Although school program activity had remained stable, the time available to the association for adult education programming had been reduced to twenty-six hours a week. The fact that, during the previous fiscal year, $33 million of the CBC's total income of $107 million was derived from advertising revenue showed that the agency had to be very cautious about extending educational programming.

In the light of these conditions, META proposed that educational groups should become less dependent on both the CBC and private stations by creating a separate educational broadcasting facility.[11] The main recommendations were as follows.

1. An organization, to include outstanding representatives of Toronto's industrial and business community, philanthropy, labour, education, and professions, cultural and religious groups be formed with the objective of applying for the government licence to broadcast television programs of a non-commercial, educational character on Channel 19 (UHF) for the Toronto broadcast area. (Such an organization should include representatives of M.E.T.A., the Ryerson Institute, and the private and public broadcasting industry). Tentative name for the proposed organization; "Metropolitan Educational Television Council of Toronto."
2. An outstanding citizen and leading Canadian educator be approached to act as the chairman of the organization.
3. The initial function and tasks of the organization would be to secure (a) the necessary legal agreement regarding licencing, (b) an agreement on the use of production and studio facilities at the Ryerson Institute of Technology, and (c) to obtain the financial support necessary to acquire a transmitter and antenna, (and related sites) and (d) to be responsible for raising the funds required for the initial three years of broadcasting.

The proposed organization would develop a programming policy designed to satisfy the needs of the educational and cultural institutions in the community. Certain types of programs were suggested: 1 / in-school telecasts, 2 / children's out-of-school programs, 3 / formal adult education courses, 4 / university level credit courses, 5 / informal adult education courses, 6 / public affairs and information programs, and 7 / cultural presentations in the arts.

The brief contained some very optimistic appraisals of the financial situation. It was thought possible to maintain a program service, including some programs of the highest educational quality, on a budget of $100,000 for the entire first year. This amount would include $65,000 for direct program costs and $35,000 for administration and staff purposes. During the initial months of operation, and until the number of UHF-adapted receivers indicated that a sizable audience existed, it was suggested that the more expensive live productions be avoided. The educational institutions wishing to make use of the station for programming purposes would be expected to bear a proportionate share of the costs. Contributions were also to be solicited from business, industry, foundations, and government. The viewing public was considered to be another source of financial support, although the brief did not make clear what procedure was to be used to obtain these contributions. In retrospect, certainly, the hope of establishing and maintaining a really successful operation with the proposed resources seems totally unrealistic.

In 1968–9 META was operating on a budget of $360,000. Contributions were received from the six Metro school boards, the Metro Separate School Board, and the Mississauga School Board. The organization produced 40 per cent of the ETV programs used in Toronto elementary schools and 50 per cent of those used in secondary schools.

In 1969, as the result of a study undertaken by META, the Educational Television Branch of the Department of Education, and H.K. Davis and Associate, Limited, the directors of META approved a plan whereby a ten-channel cable system would be leased from Bell Canada for a period of ten years to meet the needs of the schools of Metropolitan Toronto. There would also be provision for a separate four-channel high frequency system for the schools of Peel County. According to some estimates, the cost would be between $5 and $6 per pupil, as compared with the current school board contribution of 69 cents per pupil. As the scheme was reported in April 1969, four of the channels would be programmed directly from META and six could be used by teachers on a request basis or by universities or community colleges.[12] The scheme was not supposed to be competitive with that involving the use of channel 19. It was under consideration during the 1969–70 school year.

Use of television in local school systems

The school boards in Ottawa have shown an unusual interest in utilizing television to assist with the educational program and in exploring new approaches to the effective employment of the medium. The following brief summaries will give some idea of the kind of programs offered during the 1968–9 school year.

A program entitled *Money Power* was designed to produce in grade 12 home economics students a greater interest in consumer economics. It emphasized the importance of the teenager as a present-day consumer. Through the results of a survey taken in Ottawa schools, it reported the amount of money teenagers had to spend and demonstrated how, with this money power, they could actually influence market trends. The program posed four questions: 1 / Where do teenagers get their money? 2 / How do they spend their money? 3 / Why do they spend their money? 4 / What are the results of this spending? In answering these questions, the program showed briefly the indirect influence of advertising, and tried to impress on the viewers the importance of being selective buyers. Examples were used to illustrate the saving of a considerable amount of money by considering such factors as quality, brand name, and packaging. As part of the program, the head fashion co-ordinator of a large department store spoke of the great interest of the firm in teenage customers.

A program for senior French students dealt with problems of communication, with special emphasis on Canada. These problems were illustrated by a skit involving three live actors: a French Canadian from Quebec City, a French Canadian from the outskirts of an Ontario city, and an English Canadian. The value of keeping abreast of the development and evolution of modern languages was illustrated by a second skit using the same actors. In this case, the three were bilingual or, in a sense, trilingual, since each knew the two national languages and at least one local dialect. As pre-viewing activities, students were encouraged to discuss dialects they had heard in their own area of the country, as well as those in other areas where they had lived or visited. It was suggested also that they explore the reasons for the existence of these dialects, or perhaps the origins of some of them. Post-viewing activities involved a discussion of situations that illustrated the same problems of communication dealt with in the program.

A program written by two grade 13 students entitled *Out of Sight and Near Forgotten* attempted to give a perspective on the Canadian Indian problem. Presenting a student viewpoint, it was used to stimulate discussion in the history classroom and to encourage further student research on the Canadian Indian and other minority groups. The program began with a historical look at the Indian culture and the way in which the white man's coming influenced it. Passages were quoted from the *Indian Act*, and the problems of the Indian in today's society were outlined.

A thirty-minute production for Senior English and Theatre Arts was designed to show the way in which students could prepare a scene from a play for presentation on stage. It also dealt with the techniques of pantomine and improvisation. Its actual content included a reading by student actors of the scene to be presented; a discussion of the uses of pantomine and improvisation and demonstrations of these techniques by student actors; a discussion of the way in which an actor should approach his role; an illustration of the technique of blocking a play prior to performance; and the actual presentation of the scene.

The Ottawa Collegiate Institute Board made provision for the evaluation of its programs by having teachers fill in a form. They were asked to give an over-all rating by selecting one of the following: very good, good, adequate, rather poor, or worthless. The contents were assessed on a five-point scale ranging from too advanced to too elementary. The following questions were posed: Were you able to integrate this program with your regular course lessons? If not, why not? What did you like most about the program? Would you use it again? There was also provision for teachers' and students' comments.

In terms of accessibility of programs, Ottawa was a leader among Ontario cities. In 1969–70 it had a twelve-channel experimental system which delivered programs to a video tape receiver and a telephone in each of four high schools. Provided one of the channels was available, a teacher could order an item from the video tape library and have it in use within minutes. During the same year, London was employing a four-channel system relaying programs to schools from a central transmitter. Windsor had provision for the duplication of programs at a central point; tapes could be delivered for use on video tape playback machines in each high school and in some junior high schools.[13]

The Canadian Broadcasting Corporation

When television service began to expand very rapidly in the United States immediately after the Second World War, the Canadian Broadcasting Corporation undertook a series of engineering and technical studies designed to prepare the way for a Canadian service. These activities led to the formulation of a tentative fifteen-year plan which shaped the policy adopted by the Canadian government in 1949. At that time, the corporation was authorized to set up stations and production centres at Toronto and Montreal and was also requested to provide a basic program service for public and private stations that would be established subsequently. In September 1952 CBFT began operations in Montreal and CBLT in Toronto, each offering about eighteen hours of programming a week.

Services expanded rapidly during the next few months and years. By January 1953 thirty hours of programming were being offered per week, and later in the same year stations were opened in Ottawa and Vancouver. In 1954 a second station in Montreal and new ones in Winnipeg and Halifax extended coverage to about 60 per cent of the total population of the country, and the number of Canadian set owners increased to nearly a million.

A series of changes in the provisions for broadcasting began with the appointment of the Royal Commission on Broadcasting, chaired by R.M. Fowler, in 1955. The report of this body, which was tabled in Parliament two years later, recommended a separation of the two basic functions hitherto performed by the CBC: general regulation of broadcasting, and operational control of the national networks. Legislation in 1958 established the Board of Broadcast Governors to carry out the first of these two responsibilities, leaving the second to the CBC. During the subsequent period, the policy of having a single station in major centres of population was abandoned, and private stations were licensed. Approval was given soon afterward for the establishment of a private network linking independent stations, leading to the organization of the CTV network in 1961.

From 1954 on, the National Advisory Council on School Broadcasting extended its role to include advising the CBC about developments in classroom television. Experimental nation-wide series of telecasts were offered in 1954 and 1956, and the results were appraised by the council. Later broadcasting was put on a regular basis, with a schedule of thirteen weekly half-hour programs.

A description and appraisal of CBC broadcasting in the field of education were given by the Metropolitan Educational Television Association in 1965.[14] During 1964–5 high schools had the opportunity of comparing two quite different interpretations and productions of *Hamlet*. There was a repeat broadcast of a series prepared by two members of the faculty of the University of Toronto, T.N.P. Hume and D.G. Ivey, on *The Ideas of Physics*. A series of poetry, a new type of venture, was called *Exploring with Poetry*. Planned for junior high school grades, it attempted to deal with movement, action, and order in poetry through carefully selected visual material. In the extensive schedule for elementary schools, there was a series entitled *The Depths Beneath* which introduced concepts in meteorology, physical science, natural science, oceanography, history, and geography. A series called *On the Shoulders of Our Ancestors* aimed at making young viewers aware of the debt that the present world owes to past generations. The continuation of the series *Visite au Québec* gave students a chance to hear French spoken in lively fashion in situations geared to their interests. It was also designed to increase their acquaintance with the province of Quebec.

In 1967–8 approximately 2,500 national, regional, provincial, and local school television programs were carried on the CBC networks, along with about 1,500 radio programs. National programs on the English networks included series on Canadian writing; history, geography, and transportation; current affairs; the physical sciences; careers; the everyday use of French; human communications; and the background and values of English literature. The French networks offered programs in geography, forestry, biology, the history of civilizations, the plastic arts, drafting, physical education, and art appreciation. The schedule for 1968–9 included series of programs lasting half an hour or longer on Tuesdays, Thursdays, and Fridays for various age groups from six to eighteen on topics such as the following:

Title of Series	*Title of Programs*
Macbeth	
Frontiers in Science	DNA
	Lasers
	Upper Atmosphere Research
A Place for Everything	Waterfowl (of our inland waterways)
	The Prairies
	The Mountains (on the west coast)

Title of Series	*Title of Programs*
	The Land Arctic
	Sea Islands (on 3 coasts)
Music—From Bach to Rock	All Things Considered
	Musically Speaking
	Mainly Because of the Beat
	Pigments of Imagination
	A Form of Freedom
Introduction to the Theatre	What is Theatre (Part I)
	What is Theatre (Part II)
	The Changing Stage
	The Show Must Go On
Children of the World	Brazil
	Guatemala
	Thailand
	Nepal (Katmandu)
	Dahomey (West Africa)
Young Canadian Poets	
Towards Good Citizenship	Working Together and Leadership
	Respect for Others and Acceptance
	Respect for the Property of Others
	Responsibility

Educational programs for children have by no means been confined to school broadcasts. For the pre-school age group, programming has recently included stories and fantasy, musical training, kindergarten projects, comedy, adventures series, and film cartoons. English network programming has also offered French for pre-schoolers. Programs for teenagers have included popular music and variety, student quiz programs, debates and discussions, drama classics, magazine programs reflecting the youthful viewpoint on current issues, and special documentaries on the problems and achievements of young Canadians.[15]

The META report in 1965 commented on the educational value for adults of programs produced by the Public Affairs Department of the CBC. A number of courses were offered in the Montreal region, for which credit was granted by Sir George Williams and Laval Universities and the Universities of Sherbrooke, Ottawa, and Montreal. Thirty-two programs were produced as non-credit courses under the title *Live and Learn.* A series of six programs produced in Toronto under the title *Challenge and Change* included studies of such diverse problems as those of the chronic petty offender and "automation and non-work." *Of Light, of Liberty, of Learning*, produced in Ottawa, considered the academic disciplines and professional training in the modern university. *Lyrics and Legends*, shown in Ottawa, Montreal, Edmonton, Winnipeg, and Toronto, presented a history of folk music. There was a showing of the 1965

Couchiching Conference on Concepts of Federalism, where the participants examined problems such as dualism, equal partnership, co-operative federalism, associate statehood, bilingualism, and federal-provincial relations. The contributions of the three men who have held the position of Secretary-General of the United Nations, and the work of the organization, were shown under the title *Three Men*. A program called *Bernard Shaw: Who the Devil Was He?* presented a view of the man, as opposed to the playwright. A four-part series, *Ferment*, examined the changing role of the Christian churches. A science series included the following programs: *Viruses*; *Survival*; *Eureka* (presenting facts and fables associated with the scientist's moment of discovery); *Flight*; *Photography*; *Bird Strikes Aircraft*; *Lies, Damn Lies and Statistics*; and *Einstein*. Another science unit series called *A Place for Everything* was similar to the series of that name shown in 1968–9.

Among long-standing CBC efforts in the adult education field have been English language courses for new Canadians. A series of these was developed in co-operation with the Metropolitan Educational Television Association and other organizations interested in the development of adult education facilities for immigrants in the Toronto area and was first offered in the 1961–2 season. The approach was rather a novel one, since the variety of languages used by the participants made it necessary to offer explanations solely in English. A large number of people in the target audience watched at least some of the programs, and a substantial proportion were fairly regular viewers. In subsequent years, the programs have been subjected to research and analysis, and an effort has been made to improve their effectiveness. They have been carried by CBC and affiliated stations outside the Toronto area.

An example of a specialized type of broadcast for a limited audience was referred to in the CBC *Annual Report* for 1967–8. It was a six-part series of refresher courses for Quebec medical practitioners produced by the CBC and the University of Montreal Faculty of Medicine and offered once a month between 11:35 pm and 12:15 am. The programs dealt successively with the early detection of cancer, psychiatry in current medical practice, stress diseases, obstetrics, clinical anatomy, and arthritis. An appraisal of the effectiveness of the series by the CBC showed that an average of about 20 per cent of all doctors in the target area watched the programs, and over 60 per cent watched at least one of the six.

In his preface to the META publication *Educational Television Across Canada*, dated April 1969, Earl Rosen was not very complimentary about recent CBC efforts in the adult education field.

> The CBC and commercial broadcasters, on whom educators have depended for years for whatever broadcast ETV there has been in the country, if anything, have slackened their involvement in ETV. Since adult educational tele-

vision became the direct responsibility of the CBC Public Affairs Department, there has been a significant decline in CBC programs which can be called educational. This year, the only adult ETV series reported by CBC was a local Toronto series telecast on Saturday mornings at 10:30 a.m. While, undoubtedly, there were a great many more CBC public affairs and cultural programs of significant educational value, very few, if any at all, were planned and developed with the cooperation of educators or with educational television in mind.[16]

The Department of Education

The Department of Education made no contribution of any consequence until well into the 1960s. The *Report of the Minister, 1962* stated that, while no television programs were produced, schools were encouraged to make use of the National School Telecasts wherever possible. About the only positive contribution was the provision of some assistance to the Metropolitan Educational Television Association, including a small financial grant and arrangements for the use of facilities at Ryerson Institute of Technology for further experimentation in providing television programs in the Metro Toronto area. Nor was there any willingness to encourage initiatives from any other direction. A joint committee of the Ontario School Trustees' Council and the Ontario Teachers' Federation had attracted representatives of some other agencies, as well as interested individuals, to participate in the formation of the Ontario Educational Television Association. This organization sponsored an evaluation of the of the CBC telecasts, and engaged in a certain amount of discussion and planning. In early 1961, under the presidency of S.H. Deeks, it adopted a laboriously formulated constitution. After a period of complete inactivity lasting until the fall of 1962, there was a serious attempt to revive the organization. During the subsequent brief flurry of activity, a plan was worked out to provide the association with a more substantial structure and a small permanent staff. It would undertake to arouse interest in educational television and to encourage its development and use in Ontario schools. Although it was hoped that funds would be provided from a variety of voluntary sources, it was clear that the Department of Education would have to make a substantial contribution and bestow its blessing on the enterprise. The writer was delegated to present the case to the chief director. In the extremely brief meeting that ensued, Rivers demolished any prospect of approval on the grounds that the plan would simply duplicate current departmental activities. With this clearcut verdict, the association promptly dispersed.

The *Report of the Minister, 1963* had little more to report, except that there had been investigations into developments in Great Britain, the United States, and other provinces. Mention was made of the summer educational television workshop held since 1961 at the Ryerson Institute under the sponsorship of the Ontario Teachers' Federation. Some positive action began to appear in 1964, with the appointment of an Ontario Advisory Council on Educational Television. Although the council's status was different from that of the Ontario Educational Television Association, it consisted of representatives of the same interests, including the Ontario School Trustees' Council, the Ontario Teachers' Federation, the Ontario Federation of Home and School Associations Inc., the department, and the broadcasting agencies. Its purpose, as defined by Davis in the Legislature, was "to advise the department on the development of educational television in the provincial school system, and to suggest specific telecasts in this connection, and also to encourage teacher education in the production, presentation, and utilization of ETV programmes."[17] During the same year, a television adviser, "responsible for organizing television programmes for Ontario Schools,"[18] was added to the staff of the Audio-visual Education Branch.

A really substantial departmental thrust began in 1965. Structural adaptations were made in the department by the creation of an ETV section in the Curriculum Division. In announcing the arrangement, Davis was somewhat more positive about its permanence than the circumstances warranted. He declared that ultimate control of program content would be in the hands of the Assistant Superintendent (Television) of Curriculum, and that this responsibility would always be held by a person who was attached to the Curriculum Division of the department, as would the position of Administrator of Educational Television.[19] His real point was not to try to guarantee the continued dominance of the Curriculum Division as such, but rather to provide assurance that educational interests would remain in control.

Davis expressed keen appreciation for the contribution of public and private broadcasting agencies in the field of educational television. In Toronto particularly, both CBLT and CFTO-TV had, on their own initiative as well as in co-operation with the Metropolitan Educational Television Association, produced many good educational programs. The stage had now been reached, however, when the curricular needs of all levels of education were much too great for the independent programming bodies to meet. Davis mentioned a few of the difficulties that had been encountered. In some cases there had not been a satisfactory relationship between the program producers and the responsible educational authorities. Some of the programs had consequently not met with full approval.

Davis announced on the same occasion that the department intended to apply to the Board of Broadcast Governors for a licence to establish a television broadcasting station for the purpose of producing and transmitting educational programs. Assuming the successful completion of feasibility studies and other projects then under way, he anticipated making a formal application some time during the following twelve months, that is, by June 1966. If the application were approved and construction permits granted, he expected that, within a year of the date of approval, transmission would begin in Metropolitan Toronto and the surrounding area on the ultra high frequency (UHF) channel 19. Service to educational institutions would begin soon after. The Board of Broadcast Governors was also to be advised of the department's intention to seek further licences for broadcasting facilities at other locations throughout Ontario. Plans were to be outlined for setting up a network of stations to serve educational needs exclusively. The minister gave no indication during his remarks that he expected any difficulty in securing the approval of the BBG. The long period of frustration that was to follow was certainly quite unanticipated.

Pending arrangements for the use of its own production and transmission facilities, the department began limited production in 1965. The first two series involved eighteen half-hour programs in grade 7 mathematics and seventeen broadcasts of the same length in grade 13 physics. Production was achieved with the co-operation of the CBC and television station CFTO-TV in Toronto. The telecasts were carried throughout the province in 1966 by these agencies and by all the private television stations in Ontario. The latter were, of course, reimbursed for the time used.

The department's application for the use of channel 19 was made to the federal Department of Transport in March 1966. The latter agency, which had the authority to make recommendations on feasibility to the federal government and to the BBG, declined to forward the application to the board pending the federal government's approval of the principle of granting licences to provincial governments. It was concerned about a possible threat to the federal government's presumably exclusive right, under the British North America Act, to control communications. A lengthy series of negotiations followed this deadlock, with no positive result.

In July 1966 the federal government tabled a White Paper on Broadcasting. In some respects, it appeared to be propitious for the implementation of Davis's plans. A co-operative attitude seemed to be demonstrated in the following paragraphs.

> Federal policies in the field of communications must not work to impede but must facilitate the proper discharge of provincial responsibilities for education. For this purpose, it will be necessary to work directly with the provinces to study the technical facilities required, and to plan and carry out the installation of educational broadcasting facilities throughout Canada.
>
> The Government is prepared to give immediate consideration to the creation of a new federal organization licensed to operate public service broadcasting facilities. This organization would be empowered to enter into an agreement with any province to make such facilities available for the broadcasting within the province, during appropriate periods of the day, of programs designed to meet the needs of the provincial educational system as determined by the responsible provincial authorities.[20]

The Canadian Broadcasting Corporation, despite its nation-wide facilities for production and broadcasting, was not to have any role in educational television. Thus the distinction between federal and provincial jurisdictions was to be respected.

Davis reacted to the White Paper with the statement that he was "more than prepared to discuss with the Federal Government any suggestion which may be proposed to make available television channels or facilities for educational purpose."[21] On August 27 the Board of Broadcast Governors announced special hearings on the opening up of the ultra high frequency broadcasting band, and the department responded with a submission on October 25. This submission pointed out the substantial progress being made in the United States and Great Britain in providing for the transmission of educational television programs. A strong case was presented for the contribution television could make to the effectiveness of the curricular program of the elementary and secondary schools. It could help to improve educational opportunities in smaller schools and in the isolated areas of the province. It could meet some of the increasing needs for in-service teacher education. It could provide more and better instruction to such special groups as handicapped children and advanced learners. The benefits of higher education could be extended through television credit courses for off-campus use. Pre-school children could have their curiosity aroused, their interests broadened, and the disadvantages of unfavourable environment to some extent counteracted by favourable viewing experiences. But it was, perhaps, somewhat injudicious to include the statement: "No one can doubt the necessity for an informed and intelligent public."[22] There was considerable suspicion in federal circles of any provincial proposal to go beyond the bounds of formal school education.

The submission stated the belief that "education, having a place of priority in our present day society, should also have that priority in any allotment of channels, whether VHF or UHF."

> It is understandable, and in principle supported, that public and private interests should be allowed to expand their facilities. However, we cannot emphasize too strongly that such expansion should in no way inhibit the most logical and expeditious establishment of educational television throughout Canada. We see no other safeguard but the reservation of the two most desirable television allocations in all areas for educational purposes, and a freeze on the third most desirable channel pending establishment of the "new federal organization" and a full investigation by the Provincial and Federal Governments. This recommendation implies that the educational television network so established will cover all populated areas.[23]

As a means of providing for the long-term potential broadcasting channel requirements for educational television, it was suggested that the federal government undertake the immediate development of a space communications satellite system. For the interim period, the brief recommended that existing stations in all areas not serviced by ETV stations should be required to carry ETV offerings on a partially paid basis during school hours. In order to encourage the use of ultra high frequency broadcasting the federal government was urged to require that all receivers manufactured should be capable of receiving transmissions from such stations.

The submission had widespread support from educational associations and agencies. It was approved by the Ontario School Trustees' Council, the Ontario Teachers' Federation, the Ryerson Polytechnical Institute, the Sub-Committee on Television of the Committee of Presidents of Universities of Ontario, and leading members of the Ontario Federation of Home and School Associations.

On November 25 the Board of Broadcast Governors announced that it was recommending to the federal government that UHF channel 19 in Toronto be reserved for educational television. It also requested the government to require manufacturers to make all future sets capable of receiving both very high frequency and ultra high frequency transmission. Taking the view that educational television should not be restricted to UHF channels, it recommended that VHF channel 11 be reserved for educational use in Edmonton. It noted also that, while a VHF channel was not readily available in central Ontario, channels might be rearranged to correct this situation. It rejected the Ontario department's request for prior rights for education on the two best unassigned channels, but announced that it would hear new applications in Toronto.

With respect to the consideration given by the Board of Broadcast Governors to applications for the operation of the extra VHF channel in Toronto, A.F. Knowles, then Directer of Instructional Aid Resources at York University, wrote as follows in a letter to the *Globe and Mail* on June 23, 1967.

> Surely a fundamental issue in Canadian broadcasting is, not whether a TV station can be commercially viable, but whether its programming makes a significant contribution to the cultural and educational life of a community.
>
> Does anyone really believe that another Toronto commercial TV station can provide such unique and worthwhile entertainment programming in an already glutted area? What Toronto does need is an educational and cultural TV station on the VHF band, co-operatively run by leading educational institutions, and designed to provide the widest range of educational fare into homes and schools. Just for once, let's put education before profit.

The federal government took no action even on the positive recommendations by the board. The issue became thoroughly entangled in arguments and disagreements over federal-provincial jurisdiction. In the

House of Commons, a broadcasting committee under the chairmanship of Robert Stanbury engaged in a long and detailed examination of educational television and its future. Douglas Fisher and Harry Crowe, in their column in the Toronto *Telegram*, took a very critical view of the deliberations of this committee. They pointed out that Stanbury had expressed strong views about the dangers of letting any provincial government establish a comprehensive program service for ETV which would be available to the general public. Their assessment of the situation was as follows.

> The key point is the jealousy and suspicion of federal politicians over provincial entry into television programming. This feeling hardened immensely a few months ago when Premier Daniel Johnson returned triumphantly from France with plans to bring a lot of French TV programming to Quebec through a provincial ETV network.
>
> The federal politicians won't say it publicly but this Johnson plan is anathema. Bad enough the prospect of Ontario and Alberta developing large-scale TV plans. Consequently there's been immobility and the firming up of a determination to structure the technical processes for ETV so that it will only be available for "in school" viewing and not to the general public using their sets at home.
>
> This can be achieved by refusing to give ETV any VHF channels, by not requiring manufacturers to install UHF channels and by delays and stalling. A number of excuses are at hand, including the possibilities of satellite transmission services in the future and the argument that provincial ETV can use cable systems and 25 megacycle short-distance transmissions.[24]

As far as these accusations were concerned, the delays were obvious. Also, on April 12, 1967, the Honourable Judy LaMarsh, Secretary of State, delivered an address in Sherbrooke in which she indicated that VHF channels would not be assigned for educational television purposes, and that the federal government was not likely to require manufacturers to make all sets capable of UHF reception.

Fisher and Crowe had more to say on another occasion about the effects of the limitations the federal government appeared intent on imposing on educational television.

> So we have ETV bound into a school-time deal.
>
> Look what this does. No propaganda possibilities for self-aggrandizing provincial governments or departments. No public discussion, furore, viewing, or participation in ETV. Daniel Johnson and John Robarts and their menacing minions can't get to the people, only to the kids in school, and there in a fashion watched by the BBG. Old Auntie CBC is excised before the fact of ETV from any future hassles. Quebec autonomists cannot cry foul ...
>
> Are there any losses in the deal? Yes. Adult education and programming for minority cultural interests are out of luck.[25]

On October 17, 1967, Miss LaMarsh announced in the House of Commons that the government was seeking permission to introduce legislation which would declare that facilities for educational broadcasting were to be provided within the framework of the single broadcasting system. She said:

... the bill will not make specific reference to the provision of these facilities. I think most hon. members will understand it is our intention to bring forward a separate bill for this purpose, which will be drafted in its final form only after the subject has been thoroughly considered and carefully examined by the standing committee whose recommendations, needless to say, will be taken into full and careful consideration after the committee has heard witnesses and has reported to the house.[26]

On November 17, the House of Commons passed a resolution referring the question of educational television to the Standing Committee on Broadcasting, Films and Assistance to the Arts.

In order to assist the committee in its deliberations, government officials prepared a document in draft statutory form covering the chief matters that seemed to require legislative action. The definition of "educational programs" provided in this document is of some interest:

"educational programs" means programs that are designed to be presented on a regular and progressive basis, to provide a continuity of program content aimed at the systematic acquisition or improvement of knowledge by members of the audience to whom such programs are directed, and under circumstances such that the acquisition or improvement of such knowledge is subject to supervision by means such as

(i) the registration or enrolment of members of such audience in a course of instruction that includes the presentation of such programs,

(ii) the granting to members of such audience of credit towards the attainment of a particular educational level or degree, or

(iii) the examination of members of such audience on the content of such programs or on material of which that content forms a part.[27]

This kind of definition made it clear that the attempt to establish a sharp line of demarcation between federal and provincial jurisdiction entailed a serious danger that retrogressive concepts could be fastened on education as transmitted by television just when they were being discarded in other areas of the educational enterprise. The broader view of education, whether in school or out, recognized that it involved much more than the acquisition of knowledge. Also, the idea of learning primarily for credit, to be obtained through a process of formal examination, was being downgraded in progressive circles.

Most of the draft legislation was concerned with the establishment of a Canadian Educational Broadcasting Agency. Its purposes would be to facilitate educational broadcasting in Canada, and "the extension of educational broadcasting to all parts of Canada as the need arises and as funds become available to the Agency for such purpose, by providing and operating facilities for the broadcasting of educational programs for or on behalf of provincial educational authorities and educational organizations and institutions."

Commenting on the draft bill in the Legislature in February 1968, Davis indicated that he found it generally satisfactory. He would, however, have some suggestions to make about definitions, particularly as to what constituted educational television programming. His initial reaction was that the definition provided in the draft might be too confining for the needs that the provincial authorities might have to meet. There might also be questions about the propriety of a federal statute setting limits in an area of responsibility that was constitutionally within the jurisdiction of each province.[28]

Davis's presentation to the committee on the following day referred to the earlier submission to the Board of Broadcast Governors. The recommendations contained in that document remained the position of the province of Ontario with respect to the need for transmission facilities for educational purposes. The Ontario government persisted in the request that in all areas of the province, *"the responsible authority assign the most favourable technical allocation, reserve indefinitely the second most favourable allocation and consider freezing the third where demands for a great diversity of programming exist."* The request respecting the second and third most favourable allocations was based both on the need to protect channels for anticipated future growth in programming requirements and on the desirability of providing educational programs in English and French where both languages were commonly spoken. An attempt was made to impress on the committee the urgency of taking some action to increase available facilities. Capacity for the production of programs, which was growing at a rapid rate, had outstripped the capacity to get them before the potential viewers.

With reference to his government's request for the reservation of existing VHF channels where they were available, Davis used some uncharacteristically strong language. He called it ridiculous to deny to the people of northern Ontario, where such channels were available, the best possible means of reception. In addition, the cost of transmission and reception of UHF signals was considerably higher than for VHF signals. Davis asked why the people of Ontario, and indeed of the whole country, should have to pay in taxes the extra cost of UHF transmission in areas where it was not necessary.

As he had previously warned in the Legislature, Davis did raise, in a very low-keyed and disarming manner, the question of definitions. He suggested that any attempt to define educational programs was not really within the prerogative of the committee, but that the matter was one that should be discussed at the federal-provincial level. Such definitions were directly related to the constitution of the country and the division of authority as laid down by it. A closely related question had to do with the proposed powers of the federal agency. Davis expressed the view that the relevant sections should not be construed as giving the federal agency the power of ultimate decision over the programming on the various educational television networks or stations. This power must be retained by the provincial educational authority.

The committee concluded its hearings, but was dissolved without submitting a report when the federal election was called for the latter part of June. When the new Parliament assembled on September 12, 1968, the Speech from the Throne indicated that legislation relating to educational television would be introduced. The formation of the new government involved the appointment of the Honourable Gérard Pelletier as Secretary of State, succeeding Miss LaMarsh.

On October 24 Pelletier reiterated the government's intention of introducing legislation "as early as possible in the current session" to establish a Canadian Educational Broadcasting Agency to provide for the development of educational broadcasting facilities. He also announced the immediate formation of a task force to advise the government on a number of important aspects of the problem, including the details of the proposed legislation and the method of financing the new agency. It would "ascertain provincial requirements and priorities for the provision of facilities" and would "carry out research and planning to ensure the most rational development of these facilities in relation to the country's broadcasting and other communications systems, with particular attention to the rapid pace of technological developments." The task force was to include representatives of the Privy Council office; the Canadian Radio-Television Commission (the successor to the Board of Broadcast Governors); the post office, which included the core of the proposed Department of Communications; the Department of the Secretary of State; and others.[29]

Pelletier offered some hope that there would not be excessive delay by indicating that the task force would also consider and advise on the most practical means of satisfying the most urgent provincial requirements pending the enactment of new legislation. The government would be prepared, if necessary, to consider issuing a formal direction to the CBC to provide required educational broadcasting facilities on an interim basis. Ed Schreyer, then member for Selkirk, indicated the New Democratic party's general approval of the action, but expressed some feeling of disappointment that the government considered it necessary to set up a task force. He thought that, in view of all the briefs heard during the previous year by the Standing Committee on Broadcasting, Films and Assistance to the Arts, the minister might have been confident enough to proceed a little more quickly.

In the summer of 1968 the Educational Television and Radio Association of Canada was formed to represent the interests of educational broadcasters across the country. Its Ottawa office was expected to become the national co-ordinating centre of all Canadian ETV groups. Its functions were to include assistance to school systems in determining what equipment they should buy, how they could produce their own programs, where they could hire personnel, and how teachers could best be introduced to the uses of the medium.[30] The organization was also expected to try to prod the Canadian Radio-Television Commission into action.

Despite earlier indications to the contrary, the Department of Transport did take initial steps in 1968 requiring that all television broadcast receivers offered for sale for use in Canada after May 31, 1969, be capable of receiving both VHF and UHF broadcast channels. It would, of course, take a number of years before UHF receivers would constitute a high percentage of the total. Thus the initial audience for educational UHF television would be largely in schools and specially equipped institutions and among the public who were served by cable television.

In an article in the Toronto *Globe and Mail* in January 1969,[31] Ross Munro made a rather pessimistic assessment of the prospects of a complete federal-provincial working agreement. He speculated that an Ottawa-Quebec constitutional wrangle might dominate the ETV picture and create a long impasse. He referred to a statement of Quebec's Premier Bertrand the previous November that Ottawa did not have the right to set up an ETV agency, quoting him as follows: "Education being one of our exclusive competences ... the entire field of educational radio and television must be controlled by Quebec." He suggested that Ottawa was entering the ETV field for the sole purpose of protecting its constitutional prerogative, and cited Robert Stanbury as half admitting such a contention.

Despite this pessimistic forecast, progress of a kind was made during the months that followed. On February 6 three members of the task force, led by Gilles Bergeron, Assistant Deputy Minister in the Department of Communications, conducted discussions with Davis, Ide, Director of the Educational Television Branch of the Department of Education, and various officials of the branch in order to ascertain Ontario's requirements and priorities and to review the proposed definition of educational television. For the time being, the positions of the two sides on the latter issue remained unreconciled. In Bill C-179, which the federal government introduced on March 10, the disputed definition remained as it had been in the abortive bill of the previous year.

Bill C-179, which turned out to be another false start since it was not debated before the session prorogued, was to have set up the Canadian Educational Broadcasting Agency. It was to consist of a president and six other directors to be appointed by the Governor-in-Council and to hold office during pleasure. Among key clauses of the bill were these.

7. (1) The objects of the Agency are to facilitate educational broadcasting in Canada, and the extension of educational broadcasting to all parts of Canada as the need arises and as funds become available to the agency for such purpose, by providing and operating facilities for the broadcasting of educational programs on behalf of provincial authorities and, subject to subsection (2), educational organizations and institutions in Canada. (2) Subject to subsection (2) of section 18 of the Broadcasting Act, the Agency shall give priority in the use of the facilities provided, and operated by it to the broadcasting of educational programs on behalf of provincial authorities, and in order to ensure such priority, no agreement providing for the broadcasting by the Agency of educational programs shall be entered into between the Agency and any educational organizations or institution without the approval of the provincial authority of the province in which the broadcast would originate, and any agreement entered into in contravention of this subsection is of no force or effect.

Toward the end of April, a member of the task force recommended that, as an interim measure, the Secretary of State direct the CBC to meet the requirements of the Ontario Department of Education for transmission facilities in Toronto. This proposal elicited the approval of the department, and was subsequently implemented. The two agencies co-operated in developing a plan whereby channel 19 became available for the broadcasting of educational television programs.

At its meeting in September, the Council of Ministers of Education gave further attention to the contentious question of the definition of educational broadcasting. It was decided that the executive of the council would seek a meeting with the Secretary of State to present its views on this matter as well as to make representations regarding the financial role the federal government might play in educational broadcasting. The proposed meeting, which was held on October 20, resulted in an agreement to explore the two topics further. A working party, consisting of representatives of both sides, met on a number of occasions and formulated a definition which they presented to the Secretary of State and to the ministers of education at a special meeting in Toronto on December 2. This definition was duly approved:

1. programming designed to be presented in such a context as to provide a continuity of learning opportunity aimed at the acquisition or improvement of knowledge or the enlargement of understanding of members of the audience to whom such programming is directed and under circumstances such that the acquisition or improvement of such knowledge or the enlargement of such understanding is subject to supervision or assessment by the provincial authority by any appropriate means;
2. programming providing information on the available courses of instruc-

tion or involving the broadcasting of special educational events within the educational system.

In the meantime, the federal government had dropped its plan to establish the Canadian Educational Broadcasting Agency, as Pelletier explained on November 5. A factor in the decision was the impossibility of formulating an approach that was satisfactory to all the provinces. Continuing federal interest was shown, however, in the requirement that all existing and future cable TV licencees set aside at least one channel for educational programming and in the arrangement for the CBC to provide transmission facilities for educational broadcasting where the provinces wanted it and were willing to pay for it. The federal government continued its policy of not granting broadcasting licences to provincial governments.

In accordance with the new arrangements, the CBC applied to the Canadian Radio-Television Commission for a licence to operate channel 19 on behalf of the Department of Education or the proposed Educational Television Authority which was expected to succeed it. On the basis of the memorandum of agreement previously reached by the CBC and the Educational Television Branch, the former would build and operate the transmitter and the latter would program it from its own headquarters. Both Davis and Pelletier assured the chairman of the Canadian Radio-Television Commission that agreement would be reached on the financing of the proposed station and, in anticipation of a successful outcome of the December 2 meeting, on a definition of educational broadcasting.

At the time the application was made, Davis took pains to contradict the widespread impression that broadcast television was practically obsolete. He declared that it was the most practical and economical method of making educational programs available to most of the homes and schools in Ontario. Elaborating on the point, he added that "while we are aware of the constantly changing technology of communications and are ever striving to utilize the most appropriate means of communication in all areas of the Province, the very extensive studies we have undertaken make it clear that the channel 19 facilities for which Application has been made by the Canadian Broadcasting Corporation will, if authorized by the commission, represent a major step forward in the development of education in the Province of Ontario."[32]

The Liberal opposition in the Legislature took exception to the action of the minister in pressing for the application without first establishing the proposed independent authority, without knowing for certain who would pay the construction costs of the station, without completing the process of formulating an acceptable definition of educational television broadcasting, and without providing an opportunity for a proper debate in the Legislature. Davis answered the last criticism by declaring that he had been prepared to answer questions, but that none had been asked.

Whether this response was acceptable would depend on one's views on the extent of the government's obligation to take the initiative in offering information. Later developments indicated that most of the unsettled business was well in hand. In February 1970 the Canadian Radio-Television Commission announced its approval of the application.

The creation, growth, and activities of the Educational Television Branch

The Educational Television Branch was established as an entity separate from the Curriculum Division on July 1, 1966, under the direction of T.R. Ide. In speaking of this development later, Davis said that the decision had been the result of much research and thought, as a result of which it had been decided that the appropriate amount of time, energy, and resources could best be provided in a separate branch. Davis felt that educational television might become one of the most significant and far-reaching programs for the extension of educational opportunities in Ontario.[33]

The self-defined purposes of the branch, as they appear in a departmental brochure entitled *Educational Television*, were to

> Search out those areas of education where the unique qualities of the audio-visual media, television in particular, can make a special contribution, and to seek out the views and opinions of teachers and educators concerning ways in which they consider the television medium can assist them.
>
> Provide programs which stimulate and challenge the curiosity and intellect of the students, bring the outside world and the classroom closer together, assist teachers to keep in touch with the constantly growing body of educational research findings and with new developments in pedagogy.
>
> Study the educational uses of the medium, based on continuing evaluation by students and teachers of educational television programs, and on the knowledge of developments elsewhere.
>
> Provide guidance to the television industry and to school boards so that equipment and technical installations in schools are of the highest quality in terms of educational needs.
>
> Initiate a dialogue with the colleges, universities, adult education groups and other organizations concerned with the continuing education of citizens of this province, thus ensuring that the educational interests and needs of all are properly represented in the educational television system which will eventually be established.
>
> Ensure that the most effective methods of production and distribution of educational television programs are used, keeping in mind the need for utmost efficiency and economy.

At the time the branch was established, it was staffed by a handful of people. Their numbers grew from fourteen in July 1966 to about one hundred by the end of the 1967–8 school year, and to 163 in late 1969. The budget rose from $1.8 million in 1966–7 to $3.2 million in 1967–8, to $5.8 million in 1968–9, and to $7.5 million in 1969–70.

Realizing from the beginning that familiarization and training were of vital importance in winning acceptance of educational television, the branch organized a system of utilization vans to carry needed information to educators across the province.[34] Five of these, each operated by a two-man team, began operations in 1967–8. Their headquarters were in the following locations: an area centred in Kenora, extending from the Manitoba border to Thunder Bay; an area centred in Sudbury, covering North Bay and points to the north; an area centred in London, extending from Windsor to Kitchener; an area centred in Ottawa, also covering Kingston, and responsible for bilingual schools; an area centred in Toronto, and extending as far as the Niagara Peninsula. The vans contained miniature ETV systems, including a Sony EV200 remote control video tape recorder and a Sony monitor; a full line of audio-visual equipment, including such items as an overhead projector and a slide projector; and four television sets for demonstration in schools lacking equipment. The two men in each team included an educator and a driver-operator-technician. Each of them made a presentation to the groups of teachers or trustees to whom they carried their message. In some cases, demonstration lessons were provided. The team not only supplied information but also assessed the reactions of teachers and identified particular problems in each area. Their objective was to reach all the teachers in the province as well as the students in the teachers' colleges, in each of which they spent a week.

In 1969 an additional van was added, with appropriate personnel, operating from Kingston. Provision was also made for a conference van carrying equipment for presentation to larger specialized groups. Among other field activities, camera and video taping equipment were supplied to teachers' colleges for experiments in the improvement in student teaching through self-observation. Utilization sessions were held at each of the colleges to introduce student-teachers to educational television in the classroom. During the summer, courses were initiated in utilization, communication, and production techniques leading to an elementary certificate in educational television. These courses were well attended and received favourable comment.

The scale of program production increased very quickly after 1965. The department announced the following series for 1966–7: 1 / for the primary and junior divisions, a series of eleven programs in mathematics, eleven in social studies in English, and twelve in social studies for bilingual schools; 2 / for the intermediate division, a series of twenty-two programs in grade 8 mathematics and a series of ten on local and Ontario history to be produced by the CBC for the Department of Education; 3 / for the senior division, a series of twelve programs in English for four-year program students, eleven on topics related to technical subject of the Science,

Technology, and Trades Branch, and twenty-five in physics for grade 13. There were also Saturday programs to inform teachers, administrators, and parents of curriculum changes as follows: twelve programs on kindergarten to grade 6, five on bilingual schools, and six on science in the senior division.[35]

By the end of the first year of the branch's existence, over two hundred new programs were in production for use during the 1967–8 school year. Along with those repeated from previous showings, and some from other sources, approximately four hundred units were placed on broadcast schedules. Production continued at an accelerated pace, so that in 1968–9, 522 programs, 95 per cent of which were produced by the branch, were transmitted. It would be unrealistic to try to list the areas covered during the year, much less give any thorough description of all the methods of treatment employed. But a small amount of detail on a few arbitrarily selected areas may give some idea of the nature of the enterprise.

During the school year, arrangements were made to broadcast three music series, each consisting of ten programs. Each series was designed for a particular group of grades between kindergarten and grade 9. The series, *A Search for Sounds*, was specifically intended for grades 7, 8, and 9. Topics for the series were selected for their appeal to young teenagers, with each topic being explored in a variety of ways using the best musicians available. Some examples were from current commercial music, but most were derived from serious music from the Middle Ages to the present. Programs on percussion instruments, strings, woodwinds, brasses, and recorders gave brief descriptions of their origin and physical characteristics, along with some discussion of acoustics, where appropriate. Short ensembles emphasized the roles of particular instruments. The content of each of the ten programs was as follows: 1 / *Guitar*. Plucked and strummed instruments from antiquity to the present, e.g., sitar, koto, balalaika, banjo, and classical guitar. 2 / *Percussion*. Definite, indefinite pitched, and Latin American percussion; unusual ensemble grouping; contemporary works. 3 / *Strings*. Hart House Orchestra under Boyd Neel demonstrates each string section and offers music from Purcell to Shostakovich. 4 / *Woodwinds*. Toronto Woodwind Quintet introduces each instrument and plays a variety of ensemble music. 5 / *Brasses*. Toronto Brass Ensemble demonstrates the harmonic series on each instrument and offers a variety of ensemble material. 6 / *Folk Songs*. The Travellers sing a number of Canadian folk songs including Indian, French-Canadian, and contemporary songs. 7 / *Sing Out*. Milneford Junior High School, under the direction of June Tyack, sings a variety of four-part songs. Lloyd Bradshaw discusses and demonstrates choral techniques for changing voices. 8 / *The Orchestra*. Boris Brott conducts a CBC Symphony Orchestra in numerous orchestral excerpts and describes the development of the orchestra. 9 / *Recorder*. Hugh Orr introduces soprano, alto, tenor, bass recorders, and directs an ensemble of recorders, harpsichords, gamba, and crumhorn. 10 / *Electronic Music.* Murray Schafer creates electronic music with simple sounds and describes equipment used in an electronic music studio. A series of this kind would surely appear to offer the student an excellent set of educational experiences.

A series designed to assist with remedial reading in the primary and junior divisions consisted of thirteen programs, each of ten minutes' duration. They attempted to promote vocabulary development and to stimulate reading for enjoyment. Exciting episodes from books were dramatized, and programs featuring an airport, a television studio, and police work presented visual experiences, together with associated vocabulary, for later development by the classroom teacher. Suspense was used in specially written stories to try to develop the pupils' imagination.

A series called *Business as a System*, for use in the intermediate and senior divisions, was developed in response to concern expressed by teachers that students in business and commerce often failed to understand the importance of the individual in the smooth operation of business. The series attempted to show that any business organization is composed of smaller systems. Some of the programs dealt with the languages required for communication between man and man, man and machine, and machine and machine. Against a background of understanding of these languages and of the necessity for efficient use of the appropriate kind of language, the programs outlined the activities of the various systems such as sales, billing, purchasing, shipping and warehousing, promotion and public relations, management planning, and the personnel function. Each was placed in its appropriate relationship to the larger system of business.

A series called *Settings in Geometry*, intended primarily for the intermediate division, related geometry to other subject areas such as science, geography, art, and others. Mathematical models and animation were included where possible. In some programs, an attempt was made to present practical applications of mathematics in industry and science. Four programs dealt specifically with the occurrence of geometry in art, motion, nature, and science. Another group of programs dealt with the mathematical topics of relations, symmetry, and congruence.

A contribution to guidance in the intermediate and senior divisions was offered in a series entitled *Six Careers*. Each program examined a career requiring several years of formal education beyond high school graduation. The focus was largely on the work and the conditions of work involved in the career itself, but attention was also given to the college course taken as a prerequisite to employment. Each program followed a particular graduate of a college of applied arts and technology in an attempt to portray the type of life associated with the career under study.

By 1969–70 production had risen to 810 programs, of which 546 were in English, and 143 were in French for schools where that language was used for instructional purposes. There were also 121 professional development programs for teachers.

One of the most ambitious of the activities undertaken by the branch was the so-called Multi-Media Project on the Thirties: Age of the Great Depression, which was planned, executed, and evaluated over an extended period between 1967 and 1969 in co-operation with the Ontario Institute for Studies in Education. This project combined a television series and a kit of resource materials students could use to recreate the period of the depression in harmony with their own interests. According to an evaluation report: "It was designed to activate the students, allow them to pursue interests which normal classroom procedures could not cater for, and give them an exercise in selecting, organizing and analyzing materials from the wide spectrum in the 'Box'."[36] Many favourable comments were received from student participants, along with a certain number of dissenting views.

Facilities

The department undertook a study of necessary production and transmission facilities prior to the release of the White Paper on Broadcasting in July 1966. The objective was to make a television signal available to every home and school in Ontario. The investigation revealed that many integrated systems and channels would be needed to meet the requirements of the great variety of educational institutions and homes.

The plan that was devised involved the construction of thirty-three television transmitters. Modular developments allowed for the investigation of new and more economical techniques as they became available. The first requests from the proposed federal agency would be for five originating stations to serve regional needs. It was hoped that these would be in operation within two years of the passage of the necessary legislation. The remaining transmitters would be rebroadcasting units designed to make the signals generally available. If improved terrestrial or satellite systems became available, the federal agency might use these as a substitute for the rebroadcast units provided for in the original plans.

Because of the complexity of administration and scheduling within educational institutions, a further need for channels was recognized. Preliminary plans were made to use cable systems or the 2500 megahertz band as a supplementary but integral part of the over-all provincial system. These means of distribution were considered particularly suitable for small, compact areas. Cable transmission offers unique advantages in its ability to provide multi-channel facilities and in its immunity to interference in urban and suburban areas. Cable systems can convert UHF signals to VHF channels for sets equipped only for the latter. The great disadvantage in the use of cable is that it is economical only in areas of high population density. According to estimates provided by the department's Educational Television Branch, a medium power broadcast television station, providing a signal of good quality for a radius of thirty miles, would cost $600,000. It would cost approximately $11,600,000 to serve the same area by cable. The installation charge for cable was said to average $30 in smaller communities, and the monthly rate was about $3.95. In metropolitan areas, there was usually no installation charge, and the monthly rate was about $4.60. The maintenance and operating costs of the cable system were said to be somewhat higher than those for the broadcast transmitter. The 2500 megahertz system had a transmitting range of about fifteen or twenty miles and was considered suitable for the redistribution of programs to schools at reasonable cost. The system was unsuitable for homes, however, since the cost of the receiving equipment was approximately $2,000. A combination of cable systems in highly populated areas and 2500 megahertz systems in those with lower densities was intended to provide for programs originating locally, for information retrieval systems, and for video tape replays to overcome scheduling problems.

The department's plan recognized that the use of video tape offered significant economies over the use of active circuits such as microwave, provided the number of terminals was not too great. It was intended that video tape distribution would be used, at least in the early years, to feed the five regional transmitters. Succeeding stations might be supplied in the same way. Also, individual schools and central schools in a particular district would record programs "off-air" for later distribution by way of cable, 2500 megahertz, or tape. As a general alternative to broadcast television, the department found "visual recordings" uneconomic because of the large number of schools, teaching areas, and individual viewers. The cost of recording and playback machines and the operating costs became very great as the number of terminals increased.

There was an interchange between Robert Nixon and the minister in the Legislature in June 1968 about the possible future cost of the operation. Davis estimated that the fees to the private broadcasters during the subsequent year would be about $250,000. He hoped that the federal government would assume the entire cost of building the anticipated transmission facilities. As to the subsequent costs, he said: "Our own estimate for capital expenditure, say in the first full year after transmission facilities are available to us, would be in the neighbourhood of $45 million. There will be a like sum, I think, for two years thereafter to build up the basic core facility."[37] There were suggestions that the hope that the federal government would pay for the transmission facilities was illusory. The article by Ross Munro in the *Globe and Mail*, previously cited, attributed this statement to Robert Stanbury: "There's nothing the federal Government has said that would prevent this from being a pure business deal ... The federal Government could get back some or all of its investment in use fees."

Part of the department's efforts after 1966 to encourage the utilization of television programs in the schools involved the payment of special grants on the purchase of television receiving sets. The grant specifically referred to receivers that were manufactured, designed, and marketed by a manufacturer for educational television use. These had to conform to certain standards specified by the department. The latter has also provided substantial technical assistance on the utilization of equipment. Instructions were issued as early as 1966 in anticipation of the development of the network based on ultra high frequency transmission. Schools were advised to make provision to receive the UHF signals. In a school with only one receiver, this meant feeding the signal from the UHF antenna directly to the set; where there were a number of sets, the use of a crystal controlled converter was advised in conjunction with a previously installed master antenna system.[38]

Walter Pitman suggested in May 1968 that, in view of the expanded use of educational television, the department's provision for assistance was less than adequate.[39] He asked the minister whether any or all of the following items could qualify for grants if purchased by individual school boards: video tape recorders, accompanying TV tuners and monitors; a master antenna; equipment to permit more than one lesson to be put into a coaxial cable at one time; coaxial cables linking video tape recorders and antenna to the classroom. The minister replied that, under existing grant regulations, the television receivers were the only items of equipment for which grants were made. All the other items were under study, and a decision about possible changes was to be expected within the next few months.

Subsequently master antenna TV distribution systems (MATV) were added to the grant structure, providing $500 per school plus $65 for each eligible area equipped according to specifications. Also, school boards were supplied with technical advice in the reception, distribution, and display of educational television. For example, specialized engineering studies on distribution were undertaken for META and for a number of urban and county school boards.

In an interview with Blaik Kirby reported in the *Globe and Mail* on February 21, 1970, Ide gave some indication of the kind of service that would be available on channel 9, beginning in September, for the 17 per cent of viewers who would have UHF sets and the additional 20 per cent who were on a cable-TV system. It would be possible to watch about 150 hours a week of educational television instead of the twenty-five hours of school programs currently available on channels 6, 9, and 11. Looking forward a few years, he foresaw the time when the third generation of satellites would be in use. Television sets would be able to pick up a signal directly from a satellite. By putting a card in a slot in Sudbury, a person would be able to get what he wanted from a video library in Toronto.

Formation of the Ontario Educational Communications Authority

From the time the government began its large-scale efforts in educational television, there was pressure to have the enterprise removed from the direct control of the Department of Education. In June 1965 Robert Nixon pointed out that the minister had taken steps to set up boards with responsibility for educational research and for the proposed colleges of applied arts and technology. He recommended strongly that a similar board undertake responsibility for the development of educational television. He felt that the minister should get advice from a great many professionals in the field. He thought that the controlling board should be constituted by the Legislature of the province on the minister's recommendation.[40] At that stage Davis was not willing to commit himself to a specific course of action. He did not seem overly concerned about any disadvantages of departmental control and drew a parallel between the approval and issuance of textbooks and the material transmitted by television. People from the Metropolitan Educational Television Association had in fact recommended that any program that was transmitted should be approved by the department.[41]

On February 26, 1968, Davis announced the government's intention of establishing an Authority for Educational Broadcasting in Ontario.[42] This authority would be a board responsible to the minister, and through him to the Legislature. Its members, appointed by the Lieutenant-Governor-in-Council, would be representative of "groups such as school boards, our trustees, universities, teachers, adult education, the public, and, of course, associations linking schools to parents and to the home." It would have power to appoint advisory groups to assist it in developing policy and programs. It would receive funds for any services and programs used by individuals or groups apart from the recognized educational institutions in Ontario. It would also be able to enter into contracts with individuals, private organizations, and public agencies.

Davis offered two reasons for choosing this form of control for educational broadcasting. "First, television is a powerful medium which engenders apprehension about its fair use and control; second, educational broadcasting has a wide range of responsibility beyond the formal school organization." He did not mention the important factor that the universities wanted some voice in the control of the medium but did not want their television activities to be under the supervision of the Department of Education. As to his first point, he was inclined to feel that some of the apprehension was exaggerated. Since television was the most public of all media, he thought that the obviousness of any abuse or misuse of its facilities gave the public protection. Also the days had passed when television had a captive audience. Opportunities for alternative channel viewing were so extensive that ETV would not have any body of captive viewers among the general public. As far as school viewing was concerned, he suggested that it was an injustice to the integrity and ethics of the teaching profession of Ontario to think that it would tolerate programs that did not meet criteria that were fair to the pupils and the public at large.

There were some who felt that Davis was much too complacent about the dangers that might develop under a less benevolent regime. It is entirely too much to expect that viewers, especially children, would have the capacity to reject the subtler forms of propaganda that a government with dictatorial tendencies might care to devise. Furthermore, it is too facile an assumption that, even where bias is recognized, it will necessarily be rejected or lose its capacity to influence the viewer. The "hidden persuaders" know that even a message delivered in an irritating form may effectively accomplish its purposes. One can also take issue with the assertion that Ontario viewers are not a captive audience. Of course no one has proposed to eliminate the option of turning off the receiver, but since the Ontario development in educational television envisions a system under the control of a single directing agency, it is not realistic to talk about alternatives unless one regards the CBC and privately-controlled television as such.

A.F. Knowles, writing in 1966, asked rhetorically how the broad interests and concerns of Canadians could be protected from the potentially parochial and restrictive interests of a provincial department.[43] He suggested that the question was of particular concern to adult and continuing education, university interests, public affairs, political discussions, and other controversial areas. His recommendation was that provincial ETV authorities be established as counterparts to a federal ETV organization, authority, or council to represent the interests, concerns, and needs at the provincial level. In form and functions, the agencies he proposed appeared to resemble closely the authority that Davis actually announced. Whatever the formula used, Knowles thought it imperative to guarantee that all legitimate educational interests in the community would have access to the limited ETV frequencies. Universities should be able to arrange programs and courses of their own choosing because, he asserted, they had the recognized function of acting as leader, critic, and conscience of society. It was their business, and that of a number of other agencies in society, to think, investigate, and announce their findings. It was their function "to be independent, scientific, and objective, to be able to stand aside from the pressures of opposing government or public opinion, or of special pleaders, or of the pressures of nationalism or patriotism, in order to consider the validity of the things our society is doing." It seemed especially important that academic and other kinds of freedom of expression be guaranteed in educational television.

During the provincial election of 1967, Tim Reid, running under the Liberal banner in Scarborough East, injected the issue into the campaign. Scott Young reported his arguments with approval in the *Globe and Mail*.[44] Reid had said: "There is not a home in this province where television has not done its share of shaping all of us by its power alone, *without* the authority of education. Television has the power to present to you an image that has every appearance of truth, but the authority of education can *insist* that it is true. Who assumes this power? Who commands this authority?" Young referred to the opposing argument that there was no particular reason to be specially concerned about the new educational medium because all other education was under the minister's control in any case. His answer lay in the difference between the printed word and the television image. Textbooks could be taken home, read by parents, examined by school boards, and rejected if found to be propagandist or otherwise objectionable. But educational television programs were not subjected to such public scrutiny. The images flashed on the screen and were gone, leaving their impact where it could not be examined or repudiated. Although dismissing the idea that the current minister had anything but honourable intentions, Young saw the danger that a future minister might abuse the power at his disposal.

A short time later, John Bassett, publisher of the *Telegram*, presented a case for ministerial control.[45] He asserted that political responsibility was the cornerstone of our democratic system, and that appointed boards at whatever level of government must be responsible to elected ministers, or control was drastically diluted. An appointed board, with members holding their positions for a specified period, and not having to answer to the minister, could not be effectively hauled before the court of public opinion. Such a board could presumably "go its own sweet way" without answering to anybody until its term of office ran out. Bassett found a cabinet minister, known to press and public alike, who had to defend his actions in legislature or parliament, vastly preferable as a controlling agent to a nameless and faceless board.

The Provincial Committee on Aims and Objectives reinforced the minister's decision, already announced by the time *Living and Learning* appeared. It recommended the establishment of a provincial ETV council, independent of the Department of Education, and composed of Department of Education officials, teachers, trustees, and representatives of regional ETV authorities, universities, colleges of applied arts and technology, and adult education groups. The functions of such a body would be:

1. Encourage and assist in the development of regional, and eventually local, programming under the direction of regional ETV authorities;
2. Provide production facilities to the Departmental ETV branch, to regional ETV authorities, and to other educational agencies;
3. Recommend the grants for production by ETV authorities and the ETV branch of the Department of Education;
4. Co-ordinate the activities of all ETV authorities;
5. Develop the competence of teachers and other persons to assist in educational television by seconding, for limited periods of time, capable persons from the Department, school boards, and local ETV authorities to assist in the development of qualified persons who will assume leadership with other ETV authorities as they develop;

6. Assume responsibility for encouraging and directing research and evaluation of educational television at all levels.[46]

A particularly conspicuous difference between these recommendations and the minister's plans was the assumption that the departmental Educational Television Branch would continue under existing auspices rather than coming under the control of the new agency.

T.R. Ide appeared before the Ontario Universities' Television Council on June 11, 1968, to participate in a discussion about the proposed provincial authority. The minutes of the meeting record the event. "The discussion centred around the possibilities of the Council's involvement in co-operation with the new ETV Authority. Mr. Ide's suggestions regarding the new ETV Authority were most enthusiastically received." There was subsequent discussion in the council about possible programming by the universities in co-operation with the provincial authority. At the meeting of August 6, it was reported that "the Council agreed to work closely with the proposed authority with the hope of furthering the development of the programming."

The legislation was introduced in the third session of the twenty-eighth Legislature on March 19, 1970, to establish the Ontario Educational Communications Authority.[47] This body was to consist of thirteen members, including the chairman, with three or four of the others being civil servants. All were to be appointed by the Lieutenant-Governor-in-Council to serve for three-year renewable terms. For the time being, the members were to constitute the authority's Board of Directors. The objects of the authority, as amended in committee, were

(a) to initiate, acquire, produce, distribute, exhibit or otherwise deal in programs and materials in the educational broadcasting and communications fields;
(b) to engage in research in those fields of activity consistent with the objects of the Authority under clause *a*; and
(c) to discharge such other duties relating to educational broadcasting and communications as the Authority may consider as necessary to the objects, with the approval of the Lieutenant Governor in Council.

The authority also had the following powers, described as "incidental and ancillary to its objects":

(a) to enter into operating agreements with the appropriate agency or agencies of the Government of Canada and with broadcasting stations or networks for the broadcasting of educational programs;
(b) to enter into contracts with any person in connection with the production, presentation or distribution of the programs and materials of the Authority;

(c) to acquire, publish, distribute and preserve, whether for a consideration or otherwise, such audio-visual materials, papers, periodicals and other literary matter as relate to any of the objects of the Authority;
(d) to make arrangements or enter into agreements with any person for the use of any rights, privileges or concessions that the Authority may consider necessary for the purposes of carrying out its objects.

The authority was to appoint regional advisory councils and such other advisory committees as it considered necessary to assist it to develop its policy and operations. The act came into force in September 1970.

Appraisal

Mention was made earlier of the Metropolitan Educational Television Association's survey of educational television viewing in the schools of Metropolitan Toronto in late 1968. It showed that the average elementary school pupil saw only 1.26 educational television programs a month, while the average secondary school student saw an average of only one every four months. Various explanations were offered for this state of affairs. 1 / There were not nearly enough receiving sets; the existing supply fell far short of one for every classroom. 2 / Scheduling was much too inflexible and inconvenient. 3 / Teachers were not sufficiently trained in the use of the medium. 4 / Teachers were indifferent or even hostile toward the medium. 5 / The programs were inappropriate or of inferior quality.

The article by Ross Munro in the *Globe and Mail*, to which previous reference was made, constituted a rather severe criticism of many aspects of the efforts of the Department of Education in the area of educational television. Munro's case was of considerable concern to T.R. Ide, who wrote a rebuttal to the article, which was circulated but never published. A comparison of some of Munro's main charges and Ide's responses may be useful in clarifying matters of substantial public concern.

Munro had a series of points to make about the inconvenience and cost of the equipment needed to implement the plans of the departmental branch. The primary reason for what he called ETV's failure was that it was broadcast on a rigid schedule which could not be adapted to students' and teachers' needs. Teachers were usually unwilling to interrupt their lessons to turn on the television set, and their reluctance was multiplied by their inability to preview a program before letting their students watch it.

Munro noted that the branch was currently co-sponsoring a study of other distribution systems such as cable and the 2500 megahertz system. He seemed to feel that it was regrettable that such approaches were being viewed as backups and not as alternatives to the projected broadcast network. He described the attitude toward the use of video tape recorders as follows:

> ETV spokesmen are reluctant to confront the technological-administrative

> reality of how impractical broadcasting is for schools. But when pressed, they usually come up with the videotape solution.
>
> Put a videotape recorder in every school, they say, and the problem will be solved. Programs can be broadcast, viewed by a modest audience and recorded for later viewing by a much larger audience.

What he found wrong with the video tape system was the cost, which one authority had estimated at more than $10,000 for a single school, to say nothing of the trained technician required to operate it.

Munro declared that the danger was clear. If a broadcast ETV network were to be established in Ontario, it would fail to reach a significant audience because it was not using the appropriate broadcasting medium. Avoiding point-blank condemnation, he wrote: "Because of this, one suggestion is that Education Minister William Davis re-examine and then scrap the broadcast network envisioned by his ETV branch on Bayview. If he doesn't do so, perhaps the taxpayers can hope that Quebec's recalcitrance will be to their benefit." Since he felt that educational television had a profound contribution to make to education, he suggested that a search be made for alternatives to a broadcast network. He considered some of these. 1 / Proposed backup systems such as the 2500 megahertz system and cable might be considered as separate systems. Promising experiments along this line were being conducted in London and Sarnia. 2 / Schools in Ottawa were experimenting with information retrieval television, which allowed teachers to get programs piped into their classrooms on demand. The current drawback of the system was its cost, but new developments promised to make it more economical. 3 / One of these developments was electronic video recording. Its briefcase-sized player units, which used self-threading film cartridges, had wires that connected to the antenna terminals of ordinary television sets. Film laboratories could transfer any image to the seventeen-inch cartridges for as little as $15. The resulting film could deliver an hour's viewing and could be stopped and watched, or read, frame by frame.

Ide responded that there was no justification whatever for the claim that broadcast ETV, or broadcast television for that matter, was obsolete. He wrote that the Ontario plan was modular, designed to make the best use of the most modern distribution techniques. Careful and thorough studies by the branch showed conclusively that broadcasting was by far the cheapest method of distributing television signals and was likely to remain so during the technological life of whatever transmitters were installed. Ide accused Munro of failing to take account of the declared intention of the province to build initially only those transmitters required to ensure that the regional needs of Ontario were met. Should cable or satellite transmission or new electronic recordings eventually prove to be more economical, they would be substituted for the relay stations originally planned a number of years before. The full potential of video tape recorders had not thus far been realized because of the lack of compatibility of the various machines, together with rapidly changing standards and price structures. But branch engineers had been working with representatives of the electronics industry to develop an acceptable set of standards, and prices had been dropping. As far as the widely publicized electronic video recorder was concerned, it was yet untested.

Ide dealt a serious blow at the whole basis of Munro's expressed concern about the cost of transmission by pointing out that production always took by far the largest share of any ETV organization's budget. He said that it was a familiar misconception that transmission was the expensive part of television. During the previous year, transmission costs amounted to only 5 per cent of the total budget of the branch. (This was, of course, during a time when facilities rented from the CBC and private stations were regarded as wholly inadequate.) In 1967–8 the cost of programs had been only four dollars per viewing student and might be expected to drop as the number of viewers rose.

Although Munro conceded that everyone agreed that the potential of educational television was immense, he raised the question: "Is broadcast ETV consistent with trends in education which place more emphasis on individual learning and development?" Ide approved of the latter trends, but asserted strongly that there was no reason to think that ETV, broadcast or otherwise, was inconsistent with this development. There had been an attempt to increase the variety of experiences available to the learner, to give him a surer view of the world, and to encourage his natural curiosity. Good educational television could provide a variety of experiences hitherto beyond the reach of all but a privileged few.

Munro referred to the survey of educational television usage by the Metropolitan Educational Television Association. He claimed that the Educational Television Branch had released the results of a survey showing that, although the number of viewers in Toronto was low, it was the highest in the province. The rate of viewing elsewhere was, at the most generous estimate, 10 per cent lower. Thus it might be assumed that the average elementary school pupil in Ontario watched about four hours of educational television during an entire school year, while a secondary school student watched much less. Munro estimated, on the basis of American children's reported viewing habits, that a six-year-old in Ontario would watch more regular television in the week before he entered school than all the educational television he would see during his thirteen years in school.

Ide replied that, contrary to Munro's assertion, educational television programs were being watched and were warmly received on the whole by the teaching profession. During the branch's second year of operation, 1967–8, it was estimated that over 800,000 pupils saw at least some ETV. The Bureau of Broadcast Measurement projected an audience of over 90,000 viewers per program. While this was not a mass audience, it had to be remembered that the objective of ETV was to educate, and to educate programs had to be directed at specific groups. The critical question for those who evaluated educational television was not how many people watched any given program, but the cumulative total that benefited over a day, a week, a month, or a year. For the time being, the most serious restriction was the lack of broadcast time. In 1967–8 only about six hours a week were available to cater to the needs of 80,000 teachers and two million students. It does indeed seem unfair to condemn a program for the large-scale development of educational television on the grounds that it lacks viewers before any of the regular apparatus for transmission has been provided.

Munro gave an oblique criticism of the quality of the films produced by the branch in this fashion: "Some suggest that the quality of ETVO's programs is not very good and has driven away teachers and students accustomed to viewing hours of polished commercial productions each day." He referred to two film-makers, receiving nearly all their income from the branch, who had talked about the frustration of producing quality films for the organization. They were said to have complained that the educational supervisor usually acted as a damper on the organization. He was often a man with little background in film-making who was prone to impose unsuitable classroom and textbook concepts on filming. He chose too often to show a teacher at a blackboard in preference to many more exciting ways to convey the information.

To judge from Ide's rejoinder, this part of the article must have been largely fantasy. He declared that Munro's two film-makers were a mystery, since the branch produced practically all its own programs. The statement regarding "the frustrating influence of educational supervisors ... and their tendency to show teachers at blackboards" was particularly hard to understand, since practically no programs produced by the branch had taken this approach.

As to the quality of the programs, the Educational Television Branch had some impressive evidence that it had attained a high level of excellence. In February 1969 it received two awards in the Ohio State Award competition, sponsored by Ohio State University, for public service, or non-entertainment, television and radio programs. One of the winning programs, *Histoire du Canada: Vers la Conquête*, was a dramatic presentation in French interpreting the French-English position leading up to the conquest in 1760. The other, *Biology: Enzymes and Digestion*, was one of a nineteen-program biology series in which some of the leading world experts graphically presented aspects of the science which are difficult to illustrate in the classroom. The citation for the first of these two programs called it a "unique supplement to classroom instruction which succeeds in the difficult assignment of providing historical interpretation and perspective." It was said to have used a "well-conceived script presented in simple, dramatic format, achieving its purpose by stimulating attention and interest." The citation for the second program mentioned its exceptional colour photography, and called its presentation "carefully sequenced and timed for optimum learning and reflection." Since the awards were made in competition with commercial as well as educational television procedures throughout North America, including the leading networks in Canada and the United States, it is difficult to make a convincing case for the claim that educational television can excel only in terms of its own limited criteria.

The branch continued its record in the same competition in 1970 by winning two further awards. This achievement gave it recognition as being in the first rank among television production agencies on the North American content. The winning programs were *Richard II—How to Kill a King* and *Symmetry*. The first of these, one of a series of Shakespearean plays produced for secondary school students, won in the Performing Arts and Humanities Division. According to the citation: "For artistic and cogent presentation of an historical event to articulate contrasting political views and for exemplary use of television to recreate human reactions and rhetoric to historical change, this program is an excellent example of television that provokes probing, stimulates discussion and inquiry and one that lives beyond the time it takes to view it." The citation for *Symmetry* read as follows: "For an engaging presentation of the varieties and complexities of a 'simple' concept, for a unique maximizing of the visual while blending in only the most necessary verbal assists, SYMMETRY exemplifies instructional television at its best. This program demonstrates an ideal integration of subject-matter and television technique and is a deft use of television to assist learning and to provoke further experimentation and study."

The branch won further honours at an international competition in Munich in 1970 when it received a commendatory award for the program *What Makes Tommy Run*. World-wide renown has been accompanied by requests for the use of programs produced by the branch from many different countries. These might be considered among the best possible testimonials.

Patrick Scott, writing in the *Toronto Daily Star*, criticized provincial efforts in educational television in much more drastic terms than did Munro.[48] His first point was that ETV was not watched. A *Toronto Daily Star* survey had shown that the first telecast scheduled during the current school year by the Ontario Department of Education, an excellent full-colour introduction to the paintings of Bruegel, was not seen by anyone in any Metro school. He claimed that many, perhaps the majority, of Metro Toronto students were not even aware that there were television sets in their schools, and that many, perhaps the majority, of their teachers wanted to keep it that way. He wrote: "Regularly scheduled school telecasts disrupt the already staggered and precariously overloaded school-day; hit-and-miss programming serves little, if any, purpose. And there are indications that the teachers resent TV's intrusion – with its implications that they need the assistance – for reasons more personal." This particular line could be interpreted as a criticism of school organization and of the unimaginative attitudes of teachers rather than of the medium, of educators' approach to the production of programs, or of the department's efforts in the area. The department had of course been urging most strenuously that it be allowed to develop its own transmitting facilities so that the inflexibilities so often complained of could be overcome. Teachers who boast that they deliberately keep out the influences of the modern world are obsolete.

Scott had a far more serious charge having to do with the quality of the programs. He asserted that the quality of the one which the survey revealed no one had seen was exceptional, but that most ETV programs were not worth seeing in the first place. He charged that, although the existing networks may have had a duty to educate as well as to entertain, they had no obligation to carry "hand-me-down, mediocre material produced by amateurs." He went on to express his idea of what constituted educational television.

When you put it in initials like that it implies a separate, bureaucratic entity; but when you flesh out those initials all they really stand for is educational television, and by my definition this does not have to be bureaucratic.

By my definition it is educational television when we see the Apollo 7 takeoff or splashdown; it is educational television when we see a political convention and its election-night aftermath; it is educational to watch a TV documentary like this week's And We Were Young; it is educational to watch the TV news and such news-oriented programs as The Way It Is and The Day It Is and W5; Pierre Berton's five-part series this week on our penal inadequacies is educational television at its best; Captain Kangaroo has far more to offer for children in the way of educational television than all the dull META and official ETV fare I have seen so far this season.

When it comes to a specific subject – be it music, drama, art or sex – it is simply a question of basic purpose: Do you actually attempt to teach by TV, or do you attempt to instill a desire to learn?

The professional organizations can be just as critical as individuals, judging by the view expressed by an Ontario Teachers' Federation group.

So-called educational television, on the other hand, devised according to the broadcasts that have been observed, suffers from almost every one of the contagions that derive from the assumption that transmission of knowledge is education – uniformity, conformity, verbalization, the presumption of receptive learning and, above all, the timing – on January 10, at 11:00 a.m., "How to Divide by Long Division" is on the air, whether anybody in the province is ready for it or not. One is reminded of those superintendents of schools of the 1920's who used to boast that at any time of the day, in every classroom in the municipality, they knew exactly what was being taught, by whom and how.[49]

It is very difficult to reconcile a report of this kind with statements such as the following from a letter by R.G. Dixon, Administrative Assistant in the Ontario Teachers' Federation, to Vera Good, Assistant Supervisor in the Educational Television Branch.[50] "You may be interested to know that teachers frequently mention the high quality of programs provided by the ETV Branch. In fact, now that I think about it, I have never heard a negative comment about quality." He went on to mention the availability problem, which has received so much attention. As to quality, the very comprehensive surveys of user opinion conducted by the branch have shown the overwhelming proportion of programs receiving an average rating of 4 on a scale ranging from 1 (poor) to 5 (excellent), with only an occasional program being rated 3. Thus it is very hard to make a case for teacher dissatisfaction on this count. This kind of observation is not, of course, a complete answer to such a television critic as Scott. It may be that teachers are much less aware of the undesirable effects of the didactic tone that characterizes certain programs than are others who do not share the particular orientation of the profession.

Although it is undoubtedly part of the preliminary phase that will soon pass, inflexibility of timetabling can hardly be exaggerated as a reason for under-use or non-use of many of the programs. Appraisals of the quality of the programs may very well be even better when they become available at the complete convenience of the teacher. T.A. Burr quoted a letter in the Legislature which he had received from a Toronto teacher indicating the reasons why television was of little use to her.[51] She derided the suggestion by audio-visual experts in Scarborough that the solution was to educate the teachers in the use of the programs. She asserted that most teachers would like to make more use of them, since they were of excellent quality, but they did not fit either subject or period in a school's timetable. She had recently had the good fortune to use a program that had a bearing on her current classroom work. To do so, however, she had to withdraw each of her two classes from one-half of two periods, thus taking half a period from four other teachers. She declared that, if she and every other teacher did this once a month, the school would cease to function.

Ontario's efforts in educational television are imaginative and inspiring. They show a breadth of vision for which it would be difficult to find a counterpart. Against such a background, it is only realistic to recognize that the production of programs that meet the noblest educational purposes, as opposed to complementing the typical current practices, will require continuous study, experimentation, and critical appraisal. It is also highly important to face the problems in securing adequate utilization. A constructive approach to these tasks does not leave room for condemning an energetic and talented group of people in the Educational Television Branch for failure at things they did not have a chance to do, such as making their programs available at fully convenient times and places.

The Provincial Committee on Aims and Objectives did not offer a very favourable verdict on the role of the Educational Television Branch. It noted first that the development of an educational television service had rapidly become one of the department's major activities. It called the production and dissemination of programs bearing the endorsement of the department a good example of an educational innovation. But in its overall assessment it stated that "it is ... the opinion of the Committee that the present predominant role of the Department in educational television may affect adversely the implementation of educational aims and the operating roles of various levels of the educational system in the province."[52] It would no doubt be entirely possible for the provincial effort to be so organized and administered as to overwhelm and suppress regional and local initiatives. But such a course of action would be completely contrary to the orientation of the department in the 1960s when so much was being done to decentralize educational responsibility. What the committee seems to have overlooked is the value of models of excellence. If these cannot be produced by a central agency with the most competent educators, the most expert performers, and the most skilful technicians at its disposal, they are not going to be created by relatively amateur local groups. To suggest that the branch, or its successor, should be curtailed is like suggesting that the movie industry be suppressed lest it interfere with the creative experiences involved in making home movies.

The use of television in universities

Some of the universities have shown a keen interest in exploiting the possibilities of closed-circuit television. With the degree of control they have retained over the internal disposal of their financial resources, they have been able to invest in the necessary equipment and staff where they have seen fit to do so. Their use of the medium has involved demonstration of specimens and processes, the presentation of live and filmed lectures, and more elaborate productions involving advanced techniques.

Some of the same questions that have concerned the elementary and secondary schools about the most productive uses of television have been debated in the universities. Where large classes tend to preclude a useful interchange between instructor and student in any case, it is not too difficult to argue that the televised lecture loses nothing in comparison with the live lecture and may well produce a greater sense of intimacy if the set is strategically placed. The critics maintain that the concept of the large lecture is itself faulty, and that the main effort should be directed at finding methods of humanizing the teaching process. Most university people tend to agree, however, that there are fruitful roles for television, and a great deal of experimentation is being conducted to determine what these are. The examples that follow are intended only to give an indication of the kind of development that has occurred in the universities. No attempt is made to provide complete coverage.

The Instructional Aids Department at Carleton University established a section responsible for educational television with a number of studios at its disposal. Most of the programs were produced by part-time technical staff, students, and faculty members. There were experimental transmissions of lessons in science, social science, and English courses, many designed to explore the possibilities of the medium. Training staff and students in the use of the equipment was also a major objective. According to the 1968 META report:

> The Carleton experience seems to point not to a single major value of television in education, but to a constellation of values whose basic pattern is not yet clearly defined. ETV can provide scholarship in depth as well as real economies through the use of videotaped courses. It can also liberate professors from extremely large groups for face-to-face meetings with small groups and individuals. The appropriate question would seem to be "What is the most effective mix of taped programs, live presentations, direct contact and individual study and practice for a given situation?"[53]

McMaster University decided to teach a number of first-year classes by television as well as to supplement instruction in other courses in the same way. A Department of Medical Learning Resources was given the responsibility of developing the medium for use in medical education. The university has been conspicuously involved in broadcast television, offering programs both for the general viewer and for specialized groups. The format of a weekly program, *For Physicians*, begun in 1968, usually consisted of a prepared educational presentation, a short interview or news item of interest to doctors, and a brief period in which doctors might phone in their questions to receive answers from a recognized expert.

Some very grandiose plans for the development of educational television were discussed at the time Scarborough College was established. Not only were the buildings designed for the convenient use of television, but the college was also provided with a series of well-equipped studios and facilities for closed circuit transmission to laboratories and lecture rooms. As construction continued, more of the same type of amenities were to be added. Ultimately, it was thought that the college might become the centre of production for the whole university complex and perhaps even for the elementary and secondary school system. Some of these hopes have proved excessively ambitious, especially in view of the entry of the Department of Education into large-scale production for the schools.

Within the college, a very substantial effort was made to realize the full potentialities of television. Members of the faculty worked together in the studios to prepare video tape recordings of lectures. These were edited until they were judged satisfactory for release to the students. The program could then be transmitted by closed circuit to any number of laboratories or classrooms, according to need. Discussions following the lectures were led by instructors. The approach was found particularly useful in classes with an exceptionally large enrolment. In 1966–7 something over 40 per cent of the total number of student-teaching hours offered by the college were carried over television.[54] During that year, four complete first-year courses were offered on television: in English, in sociology, in zoology, and in botany. The medium was also used for laboratory instruction in botany, chemistry, physics, and zoology in both first and second years.

Uses of television at the University of Waterloo included the presentation of programs in tutorial groups to stimulate discussion led by graduate students. Introductions to laboratory experiments in the physical and biological sciences were played several times a week to small groups. A feature of particular interest was a 120-seat teaching laboratory in which an eleven-inch television receiver was provided for each pair of students. There were also twenty large monitors providing for two separate video feeds to the students. It was possible for a professor seated at a teaching console to have pictures of himself or of illustrative material transmitted on one channel while the second presented an over-the-shoulder view of the paper on which he was writing or drawing.

In 1966–7 an *ad hoc* Committee on University Television, established by the Advisory Committee to the Board of Governors at the University of Western Ontario, was given the task of determining the feasibility and desirability of establishing a television centre for the university. It brought in an emphatically favourable recommendation, and plans were subsequently made to proceed with the establishment of such a centre. This development offered the prospect of highly competent production and technological assistance for the employment of closed circuit television.[55]

During the year 1966–7 closed circuit television instruction was provided at the University of Windsor for two thousand students enrolled in courses in English, mathematics, and psychology. Most of these were accommodated in classrooms varying in size from twenty-eight to a hundred seats. Near the end of the year, an effort was made through a questionnaire to determine the reaction of both staff and students to their experience with television instruction. Of eight faculty members who compared examination results for students in the television classes with those in conventional classes involving the same course, six found no difference, one thought the television students did better, and one that they did worse. Fourteen out of fifteen faculty members expressed an interest in further experimentation with television teaching, while only one lacked such an interest. Two-thirds of the students stated that they found television instruction either as good as or better than instruction in the conventional classroom.[56]

An Instructional Aids Resources Department was established at York University in 1967, with a major interest in developing the uses of television as a medium of instruction. The facilities were used for the production of both closed circuit and broadcast television programs, some of the latter of which achieved a high degree of sophistication. According to the META report, the emphasis at York was placed on television as "a reinforcement to instruction, a means of providing students with experiences, materials, and ideas that are new or that otherwise would not be available in the classroom."[57]

At the time of writing, a much more ambitious venture was being undertaken in Great Britain than anything yet contemplated seriously in Canada. The launching of the University of the Air was scheduled for the autumn of 1970 to bring a university degree within the reach of anyone who had the necessary ability, interest, and determination. Relying mainly on television and radio programs provided through the British Broadcasting Corporation's BBC-2 channel, it was also expected to use correspondence, movies, tutorials, short residential courses, and local audio-visual centres. Modest fees were to be charged those who took the courses for credit, although a large part of the estimated annual operating cost of £3 to £4 million was to be met by grants from the Department of Education and Science. The White Paper that originally presented the proposal in 1966 mentioned three purposes of the university: 1 / to contribute to the improvement of educational and professional standards in general by making scholarship of a high order available to all who care to look and listen; 2 / to offer those who will accept the full disciplines of study the possibility of gaining first class degrees; and 3 / to provide a valuable service for developing countries in recognition of their urgent need for a highly trained corps of men and women equipped to provide leadership in national life.

The use of television in colleges of applied arts and technology

The colleges of applied arts and technology have had a particular interest in television, since their area of responsibility covers training in all aspects of the uses and applications of the equipment. Those that offer courses in radio and television arts train students and then give them opportunities to practise their skills in producing instructional material for other departments. Like the universities, they rely heavily on closed circuit distribution.

The 1969 META report reviewed some of the most interesting developments in specific colleges. It mentioned that Humber College had produced programs covering such topics as student-teacher relationships, faculty selection committee techniques, and employer-student job interviews. Sheridan College, like many others, made a practice of video taping guest lectures, particularly in the business division and in the field of teacher education. It was a common practice to use television as a means of self-evaluation for teachers. Niagara College produced subject review tapes which were shown to students at the end of each term "to help them see the total concept behind the facts they have been learning in class." The sociology students at Centennial College went out with portable recording systems to shoot scenes of city life, dubbed the tapes at the college, and played them back over twenty monitors in lecture rooms that held 450 people.

A number of the colleges saw a great deal of value for the personal development of the students in participating in live productions. As an instructional medium, however, there was much to be done before the average faculty member developed a full appreciation of the potentialities of the medium.

TWENTY

The provincial library system

THE EDUCATIONAL ROLE OF LIBRARIES

The most basic function of a library is to accumulate and protect information, and to make it accessible under defined conditions to one or more categories of users. Its existence dates from the time when human beings first developed the capacity to record information in forms that were independent of memory. The invention of writing, and later of the printing press, meant that libraries came to be thought of as collections of scrolls, books, papers, and other documentary forms that could be tapped only by those with the capacity to read. Although this stereotype remains, the library is increasingly being regarded as a repository for information stored by means of a variety of devices such as film, slides, records, pictures, and tapes.

The library is the foundation of civilization itself. Only by the accumulation of information, apart from the resources of his own memory, could man acquire the power to master the forces of nature and refine his capacity for expression and appreciation in the arts. Before he gained the means to his liberation, he accomplished mental feats that astonish his modern descendants. But the limits were inescapable, and he himself was too uncertain and perishable an instrument to ensure the survival even of what his own mind could encompass. Every human effort to rise above the bondage of nature had to begin practically afresh.

Libraries enabled successive cultures and civilizations to rise one upon the other by steps of increasing complexity. That is not to say, of course, that each one has gone further than its predecessor. There have been many instances of loss of momentum and backsliding. However, as long as each new culture has had access to the libraries of the preceding era – and libraries, despite disastrous and regrettable losses, have been very successful in avoiding complete eradication – there has been a possibility of moving forward. And not only does accumulated knowledge offer the means of advancement, it has also become the essential means of maintaining progress already made. Knowledge in vast quantities, only tiny fragments of which can be encompassed by a single mind, has become the mainstay of modern society. A full realization of the importance of libraries should place them on a unique pedestal among social institutions. Unfortunately they have been too often taken for granted.

An ability to use, enjoy, and profit from the library represents the fruition of much of the school's effort. The library is the supreme device for continuing education. Unless its resources are successfully employed, much of what is taught in formal classes is certain to deteriorate or disappear. Reliance upon the library not only reinforces learning, but also extends it far beyond the original stimulus. A competent library user is free from dependence on the fallible and restricted capacities of his fellows.

One of the most obvious implications of the "knowledge explosion" is the need for more and better libraries and for increasing skill in their use. Although education must provide a fundamental core of knowledge stored in the mind, if for no other reason than that the individual must be able to identify his own need for further knowledge, there is a rapidly developing recognition of the inadequacy of this core as a means of enabling its possessor to cope with the problems of life. It is more and more important that he understand the nature of stored knowledge and of the means of retrieving it.

Modern librarians stress the movement of their institutions away from the passive functions of accumulation, storage, and protection toward more active educational activities. It is not enough to leave the potential user to identify his own needs and to ferret out the desired material. Various types of individual guidance and group programs are offered, not only to promote more efficient use but also to develop a deeper appreciation of the value of the library's contents.

Libraries have often suffered from a bad image. Some people associate them with a bookish approach to education, as contrasted with education for "real life," by which is meant social activity and involvement in "practical" affairs. Resort to the library seems to stand for a choice of vicarious over direct experience. The confirmed library user is a bespectacled, owlish introvert – to be treated with a mixture of respect and ridicule. A major factor in changing this attitude in recent years has been an increasing awareness of the extent to which the machinery of civilization runs on information.

Librarians have also had to escape from an unfavourable image, which Frank MacKinnon delineated.

No one can more quickly kill the service of a library or students' interest in using it than the bossy, chatty, patronizing librarian who treats the books as if they were her private treasure and the students as if they were her pupils while they are in the library or visitors upon whom she is conferring a great favor. Many librarians are excellent, helpful and encouraging people; many, alas! are tragic liabilities in their jobs, not because they cannot stamp cards or catalogue books, but because they cannot deal with people. I believe, therefore, that the librarian should be located as unostentatiously as possible near the door for convenience of checking books in and out; above all she should not be near the reading room. It is the students' library, not hers, and they should feel it. If she is a knowledgeable person whom they like, they will continuously avail themselves of her services; if she is not, she will do them the most good by keeping out of their way and sight. Use of the library and order in it are always greatest under such an arrangement. I stress this because I have been involved with many libraries and have known gracious librarians who effortlessly make their premises a joy to visit and to use, and whose services are constantly sought, as well as others who with watchful, gimlet eye, or the manner of a warden or proprietor, discourage even the most valiant attempts to enjoy the library and explore its treasures.[1]

Libraries will not stand or fall with society's reliance on the printed word. If other methods of communication become so effective that the traditional ones are outmoded, the necessity for storing and making information available will certainly not be diminished. But there is a danger in overestimating the rate at which print is being superseded. It would be extremely shortsighted to curtail the support provided for traditional methods of storage in anticipation of the conquest of the book by some more modern medium. In other words, we should not starve our libraries on the assumption that the book will soon be obsolete.

BACKGROUND

As in the great civilizations of the world, so also in Canada, libraries in some form preceded the establishment of schools. According to Bascom St John, whose columns in the *Globe and Mail* indicated a particular interest in the subject, one of the first in Ontario was established at Niagara in 1800.[2] Operated by a local association which charged its members an annual fee, it lasted for more than thirty years until it was replaced by a mechanics' institute. The mechanics' institutes were developed in the United Kingdom from the 1820s on as a means of providing adult education and library services. For decades they made a substantial contribution to social betterment in various countries, although early hopes that the ordinary working man might be persuaded to develop an interest in science and technology and to rise to new heights of intellectual achievement proved much too optimistic. The idea of the institutes caught on quickly in Canada, and from about 1835 those in Ontario, although privately owned and operated, received government grants. In 1880 they were placed under the supervision of the Department of Education.

Centennial Story contains a reference to a mechanics' institute, established in 1830 by James Lesslie in the interests of employees. In mid-century it was housed in a handsome new building, and for many years it provided adult education through courses, lectures, and elementary night school. The building, located at the corner of Church and Adelaide Streets, later became the central branch of the Toronto public library.[3]

In the same column in which he traced the roots of public libraries in Ontario, St John commented on the interest shown by Egerton Ryerson in ensuring that schools had libraries. He was said to have made certain that no one was allowed to forget that the chief purpose of literacy was the ability to read books, and perhaps also newspapers. In elaborating on the theme in a later article, St John indicated some of Ryerson's specific contributions.[4] He persuaded the Legislature in 1850 to make a grant of $3,000 for school library books. He also began the mass purchase of books from publishers in England, in the absence of any in Canada, and distributed these at cost through an agency called the Depository. The books were available, not only to schools, but also to other libraries. Ryerson also launched a scheme for awarding books to children as prizes for academic achievement. By the time the Depository was closed down in 1881, it is said to have distributed over a million books as school prizes, another 300,000 to school libraries, and another 35,000 to mechanics' institutes and lending libraries.

The first library legislation in Ontario, the Library Association and Mechanics Institute Act, was passed in 1851, followed by the Free Libraries Act in 1882. Two forms of libraries flourished under the terms of these acts: the private association libraries and tax-supported public libraries. As described in the St John report, the association libraries were begun in the days when libraries were not considered a public necessity, and little public support was available.[5] Funds were raised by subscription or by donations from prosperous members of the community. In later years, when private philanthropy diminished, support came in part from cake sales, book sales, dinners, and other such community efforts. Book donations, often of doubtful value, were sometimes the major source of new additions to collections. Subscribers were the only ones allowed to use the libraries.

Under legislation in force in the early decades of the twentieth century, a public library might be established on the passing of a by-law submitted to the electorate on the initiative of the municipal council. It was also mandatory for the council to put such a by-law to a vote upon receipt of a petition signed by at least sixty qualified municipal voters in a city or town, and by at least thirty in a village. The library was under the control of a public library board, to which the municipal council and the board of education each appointed three members to serve three-year terms, and the separate school board, if any, appointed two to serve two-year terms. The mayor or reeve was an *ex officio* member. Funds were raised by the council at a minimum rate, fixed by the legislation, of fifty cents per capita.

In the larger cities, the municipal libraries consisted of the main library and one or more branches. The use of bookmobiles made it possible to provide service in suburban areas and, before the development of adequate school libraries, in schools as well. County public libraries were established by by-law of the county council and, like municipal public libraries, operated through branches and bookmobiles. They faced greater problems, however, in terms of the larger areas and greater population which they had to serve. County library co-operatives were formed as a means of enlarging service while recognizing the autonomy of the smaller libraries. They attempted to supplement the efforts of the latter, in most cases operating bookmobiles. Association and public libraries in municipalities had the option of belonging to them or not as they saw fit.

In 1900 there were 118 public and 253 association libraries operating throughout the province. The one at Toronto had more than 100,000 volumes, and those at Brantford, Guelph, Hamilton, and London each had between ten and thirty thousand.[6] While according to some views, the expansion of the library system during the early part of the twentieth century was rapid, the fact that library legislation made the establishment of publicly supported libraries a matter of local option meant that a considerable part of the province remained without service. In 1945 the Ontario Library Association in its submission to the Royal Commission on Education reported that 33 per cent of the population fell into this category, as compared with 1 per cent in England and 25 per cent in the United States.[7]

ONTARIO LIBRARY ASSOCIATION BRIEF, 1945

In assessing the situation in its brief to the Royal Commission on Education in 1945, the Ontario Library Association found considerable grounds for dissatisfaction. Of approximately 480 libraries operating under provincial legislation, about 250 were association libraries, the great majority of which were operating on annual budgets of from $100 to $200 or even less. The association pointed out the obvious fact that such institutions could not provide the book stock or trained librarians required to meet the educational needs of the communities in which they were located.[8]

The brief claimed that a population of at least 25,000 was necessary for the economical development of reasonable library service. This fact pointed toward the desirability of organization on a regional, district, or county basis, a type of organization which was said to have solved the problem in the United States, Great Britain, British Columbia, and Prince Edward Island. While a start had been made in Ontario with the setting up of voluntary, co-operative county associations, which had demonstrated the value of larger units, the association regretted that, under existing legislation, county councils lacked the power to establish them.[9]

The financial situation in which the public libraries found themselves was deplored in strong terms. It was said that the fifty cents per capita which *The Public Libraries Act* set as the minimum that boards could demand was commonly taken as the maximum. There had been no material increase in the level of support in twenty-five years. With notable exceptions, the libraries operated at starvation levels and were often unable to employ trained librarians or produce a representative supply of books, much less audio-visual and other materials currently considered part of the educational process. "In general, the libraries of the province are in a deplorable state. They are starved for both moral support and financial aid. As a result they are, in much greater numbers than we care to admit, moribund."[10]

The association made groups of recommendations under a number of headings, the first of which was "provincial administrative organization."[11] 1 / The existing Public Libraries Branch of the Department of Education would be converted into a strong library directorate with a director and the inspectors and staff needed to carry out such duties as preparing a complete revision of *The Public Libraries Act*; establishing a province-wide system of efficient areas of public library service; establishing and maintaining certification standards for library personnel; conducting research into library problems and the provision of advisory service to local libraries; and securing adequate funds from the provincial legislature to ensure adequate support for libraries. 2 / There would be a provincial library, of which the Legislative Library would be a functioning unit, under the direction of trained and experienced librarians. 3 / A supervisor of public libraries would be appointed by the Department of Education, with status comparable to that of other school inspectors, who would be responsible for the organization of libraries in primary and secondary schools, and for setting up and maintaining service and personnel standards in them.

The second group of recommendations, under the heading "library organization in the province," involved the development of a province-wide system of co-ordinated libraries that would 1 / continue and expand municipal public libraries already established in cities and towns of sufficient population to provide efficient service; 2 / provide for the establishment of metropolitan areas to enable libraries of larger towns and cities to extend their services beyond their municipal boundaries where such a procedure appeared to be the best way of looking after the needs of the whole district; 3 / provide larger areas of library service on a county, regional, or district basis, which would strengthen municipal libraries for smaller towns and rural districts and establish new libraries where they were needed; 4 / encourage association libraries to become public libraries and to be local units in their regional, district, or county libraries; and 5 / encourage existing trends among some library boards to provide audio-visual materials and equipment, lectures, exhibitions, discussion groups, and adult classes.

The association asserted that it was essential to the development of library service as an educational force that it be under the direction of properly trained personnel, including specialists in various fields. Its specific recommendations with respect to this theme were 1 / that the

University of Toronto Library School be expanded, and that it be set up as an independent school of the university; 2 / that professional training of librarians be defined and guaranteed by certification regulations for graduates of recognized library schools, with regulations approved by the Ontario members of the profession put into force to cover cases of those currently in service; 3 / that salaries be increased and definite scales of increments established so that recruits could be attracted and academic and training standards maintained in competition with other professions; and 4 / that a satisfactory system of pensions be set up.

The fourth group of recommendations had to do with finances. These recommendations were preceded by a statement that only a modest sum would be required from the Legislature to implement all recommendations for financial assistance. Comparisons with legislative grants to schools in 1943 showed that the latter amounted to $3.76 per capita, while those to libraries were only $.0117 per capita, or 0.31 per cent of total educational grants. Current annual provincial grants to libraries ranged from $9 to $209 for a single library, sums which were too small to be effective in improving library service. The first recommendation with respect to provincial assistance was that grants made to libraries be comparable to those made to schools. These would be made on the basis of the local per capita expenditures and the maintenance of professional standards. Special grants would be available for the encouragement of adult educational and cultural programs such as lectures, classes, audio-visual programs, and exhibitions. There would also be special grants to extend the use of the resources of larger libraries and their services in surrounding regions. Additional funds would also be needed to finance the operations of the proposed Public Libraries Directorate, of the University of Toronto Library School, and of the office of the supervisor of school libraries in the Department of Education. The association recommended priority for library building in any future government-subsidized building program.

The association also recommended a larger contribution on the part of municipal authorities. While it called for an increase in the existing per capita rate of fifty cents, which had been in effect for twenty-five years, it did not suggest a specific alternative.

The association's recommendations dealt with most of the key issues that were to remain important for many years to come. Some of the objectives were met, others were abandoned, and still others were attained only in a limited and unsatisfactory fashion.

THE WALLACE REPORT

W. Stewart Wallace, who had served as librarian at the University of Toronto, was appointed by order-in-council on May 9, 1956, to conduct a study with the following terms of reference:

(a) to study the need for a Provincial Library Service in Ontario;
(b) to survey the probable requirements of such a Service;
(c) to study the present operation of similar Library Services in other provinces of Canada and certain states in the United States;
(d) to determine what assistance and co-operation for such a Service would be available from the National Library at Ottawa, from existing municipal and university libraries within the province, and from other sources;
(e) to report findings and make recommendations to the Honourable the Minister of Education before the close of the fiscal year.[12]

In his report, which was published in 1957, Wallace reviewed the history of the existing Public Libraries Branch from its origin in 1880. It was originally under the supervision of an Inspector of Public Libraries, whose title was changed in 1947 to that of Director of Public Library Service. In 1905 the branch was made responsible for the system of travelling libraries which had been organized a few years earlier. During 1955, fifteen hundred boxes of books containing about seventy thousand volumes had been sent to schools and community centres throughout Ontario, and nearly 1,250 books had been lent to teachers. Wallace commented favourably on the *Ontario Library Review*, which had been published since 1916, but lamented that its true value had not always been appreciated by librarians and library trustees in Ontario possibly, he thought, because its subscription price was only 25¢ a year.[13]

Wallace made the following recommendations:

(1) That the Public Libraries Branch of the Department of Education be re-named the Provincial Library Service of the Department, and that the Director of Public Library Service be designated the Director of Provincial Library Service.
(2) That the proposed Director of Provincial Library Service should inaugurate in his department an interlibrary loan service to the smaller libraries in the province, and an "Open Shelf" system of loans to people in areas without public library service.
(3) That the staff of the proposed Provincial Library Service be enlarged by the addition of an inspector of public and regional libraries, a provincial children's librarian, and at least three additional assistants to meet the initial demands of an interlibrary loan service and an "Open Shelf" service.
(4) That the quarters in the building at 206 Huron Street (the old Grace Hospital) which the Public Libraries Branch now occupies should be enlarged and refitted, and that eventually the whole of this building should be re-constructed and made available to the proposed Provincial Library Service.[14]

Wallace rejected the idea that it would be desirable to bring the Legislative Library into any kind of union with the Provincial Library Service. He found that the functions of this library were to serve the needs of the members of the cabinet, the Legislature, and the Civil Service – an essential and specialized task – while the Public Libraries Branch existed to serve the needs of the general public. Thus the two had little in common. While the Legislative Library might give assistance to a Provincial Library Service, this contribution should be strictly secondary.[15]

As a result of Wallace's report, Angus Mowat, then Director of Public Library Service, recommended the following actions:

I. That permissive legislation be provided for the establishment of county public libraries based upon the principles under which municipal public libraries are established and financed, and with the expectation that such county public libraries, working where possible in close co-operation with the larger city and town public libraries, would supersede and replace the present library co-operatives.

II. That an Assistant Director of Public Library Service be appointed who would assume the task of promoting and supervising county and regional library work, and who would assist the Director of Public Library Service in the administration of The Public Libraries Act and Regulations and in the promotion of public library service generally.

III. That a Supervisor of Children's Library Service be appointed to the Public Libraries Branch. The duties of this librarian would be to select children's books for the Travelling Libraries, and to go among the smaller libraries of the Province to assist and advise the local librarians in bringing their children's book collections and organization of service to a higher level.

IV. That a regional library demonstration be made in an area in Northern Ontario in which, because of the vast distances and scattered population centres, municipal library service cannot function effectively. This demonstration would be financed wholly by the Department of Education for at least 3 years, at the end of which time local authorities would be expected to take over a fair share of the financial responsibilities.

V. That a system of interlibrary lending of books be established, with the Public Libraries Branch acting as a clearing house for requests and shipments. For the operation of such a system, the co-operation of city and university libraries with large holdings would need to be obtained, and compensation would need to be made to these libraries for the service and material provided for them. In addition, the provincial service itself, through the Travelling Libraries, would need to build up a stock of books with which to fill requests that cannot be met by borrowing.

VI. That by making the necessary addition to the stock of the Travelling Libraries, and by providing additional accommodation, a system of lending books to individual residents within the Province be instituted after the pattern generally known elsewhere as "Open Shelf."[16]

The name of the Public Libraries Branch was duly changed to the Provincial Library Service, and small additions were gradually made to its staff complement. Yet it is doubtful that much happened as a result of the report that would not have occurred in any case. Any disappointment with it might perhaps be most justifiably blamed on the very limited terms of reference within which Wallace worked. That he had no intention of breaking through these is shown by his assertion that he did not propose to enter into the whole question of the establishment of regional libraries, by which he meant county and district co-operatives. He did proceed to make a few comments that were not quite consistent with that resolution. Beginning with the statement that he found it difficult to make up his mind on the subject, he wondered whether the efforts made by those who had struggled to get regional libraries started had always produced commensurate results. He did not doubt, however, that co-operation between a regional library and smaller dependent libraries produced vastly better service than the smaller libraries could offer if left to their own devices. He suggested that it might be highly desirable to have an officer of the Provincial Library Service responsible for the growth and development of regional libraries.[17]

PRESSURE FOR IMPROVED STATUS FOR LIBRARIES

Bascom St John repeatedly drew attention to what he referred to as the "subordinate position that libraries have in the educational structure." In the column in which he used that expression, he put a large part of the blame on the failure of Department of Education officials "to recognize an institution outside the formal organization of elementary and secondary schools as educational in the real sense of the word."[18] He proceeded to point out that it was within the public's power to determine in a broad sense the policies that the government followed. Responsible citizens should take an interest in who was appointed to the local library board, since it was this body that largely determined the amount and quality of the library service in a community. St John suggested that, judging by the lack of vigour shown by most library boards, municipal councils were picking the mildest and most unaggressive individuals they could find to serve on them. These often seemed to be retired people whose zeal for reform was not at a high pitch. As far as librarians were concerned, they seemed to feel that professional ethics required them to remain virtually inaudible:

> ... what librarians need more than anything else is a new concept of dignity. Dignity is not submission; it is pride. It is not a masterful withdrawal, it is an absolute determination to be heard and respected. That is going to take some learning, here and there, but it is from the librarians that leadership should come, if we are to have an adequate library service in Canada.[19]

DEVELOPMENT OF REGIONAL LIBRARY SYSTEMS

The development of regional library systems, at first in the form of co-operatives, occurred as a response to the need for larger units of service. Their initial impetus is said to have come from a fact-finding commission established by the newly-formed Canadian Library Association in 1929. Under the leadership of G.H. Locke, Chief Librarian of the Toronto Public Library, this commission toured Canada and made an extremely thorough study of the amount and quality of the service being offered. It found that libraries were receiving an unduly low proportion of public grants as compared with other educational institutions, and made a case for the expenditure of at least $1.00 per capita. Believing that an expenditure of less than $3,000 a year could not provide a community with adequate public library service, it suggested the large library unit as a solution to the problems faced by small towns and villages.[20] Influenced, apparently, by the commission's report, Lambton County organized the first regional service in Ontario in 1932.

According to legislation passed in 1963, regional co-operatives could be established in one of two ways. In the districts, the minister might approve a petition from two district co-operatives to form a regional library co-operative. The district co-operatives were thereupon dissolved, and their assets and liabilities assumed by the new entity. In a county, the petition had to be supported by a minimum of three public library boards, each from a municipality having a population of fifteen thousand or more. The minister determined which counties, cities, and towns would be included, within the restriction that the region must include at least three counties and have a minimum population of 100,000. Eventually the whole of Ontario was organized into fourteen regional systems. The regions were not coterminous with any other provincial divisions, although they corresponded in a rough way to the ten economic regions.

The first regional system according to the modern pattern was the Southwestern Regional System, centred at Windsor, which was established in 1963. In 1966 *The Public Libraries Act* outlined the constitution and powers of regional library boards. By 1968 the other thirteen, which blanketed the province, were as follows, with the location of their headquarters indicated in parentheses: Metropolitan Toronto (Toronto), Eastern Ontario (Ottawa), South Central (Hamilton), Central Ontario (Richmond Hill), Lake Erie (London), Lake Ontario (Kingston), Mid-western (Kitchener), Niagara (St Catharines), Georgian Bay (Barrie), North Central (Sudbury), Northwestern (Fort William), Northeastern (Kirkland Lake), and Algonquin (Parry Sound). The boundaries of these regions are shown in volume I of the present series.

Roedde commented on the variations in the way the regional library boards have operated in recent years as a result of differences in the size and population of the regions and in the strength of library resources and library expenditure.[21] Some have employed bookmobiles, while others have left this form of direct service to county libraries. Some have selected a regional and resource centre, while others, in the absence of an obvious natural centre, have strengthened service in several public libraries. Some maintain headquarters in the largest public library, while others operate from a separate headquarters.

Among the services performed by regional boards, according to Roedde, are planning and strengthening reference service and establishing regional resource centres; promoting inter-library loans of books, films, and special materials, and introducing co-operative plans for the retention and use of periodicals; establishing a Telex and telephone communications network; establishing a regional circulation system and borrower's card; developing co-ordinated services in co-operation with school, college, and university libraries and with adult education agencies; establishing an advisory service to assist in library development and improved methods; publishing regional newsletters; sponsoring conferences and courses; introducing co-operative book selection; arranging for a central deposit of little-used books; establishing central cataloguing and processing; establishing bookmobile service; and administering central or branch libraries.[22] Most of the services are organized on the basis of contracts and agreements with municipal and county library boards. Funds come from provincial grants, fees paid by library boards, and in some cases from municipal councils.

THE ST JOHN REPORT

A report on the results of a comprehensive study of all aspects of libraries in Ontario by Francis R. St John Library Consultants of New York was published in 1965. The study was commissioned by the Ontario Library Association and financed by the Department of Education. It contained a good many sharp criticisms of the existing situation, both in the schools and in the public libraries.

Central organization and facilities

In the report, unfavourable comment was made on the fact that there was little co-ordination among the departmental libraries of the government. Within the Department of Education, co-ordination of public, secondary school, and elementary school libraries was split among three different divisions. Furthermore, there was no adequate library for the staff of the Department of Education, and the immediate creation of such a facility was proposed. It was also recommended that all library functions and duties of the department be combined in a single Library Division, and that its capacity for service be strengthened.[23] The latter objective would be attained in part by the creation of a Provincial Library Council, which would serve as the Board of Trustees of the Library Division and would advise the minister on co-ordinated library development.[24]

Considerable detail was offered on the composition and operations of the proposed council. It would have a total of twenty-three members. Each of the fourteen Regional Library Co-operatives would nominate three candidates, from among whom the minister would select one from each region to serve for a term of six years. Betraying some uncertainty about the status of various organizations, the report suggested that "The Ontario Teachers [*sic*] Federation, the Home and School Association or some other appropriate Provincial group representing the elementary and the secondary schools" nominate twelve suitable candidates, from among whom the minister would again choose one-third for a term of the same length. By a corresponding procedure, the "Committee of College Presidents" would nominate six candidates with a knowledge of the problems of libraries in institutions of higher learning, with two being chosen. There would also be three members at large chosen by the minister to serve for terms of three years.[25]

The Legislative Library of Ontario, which had been transferred in 1964 from the Department of Education to the Department of the Provincial Secretary and Citizenship, was identified as one of the backstops to a total provincial library plan, with its unique collections in history, newspapers, and government documents. This library, dating from 1867, had been set up to serve the members of the Legislature and civil servants. At the time of the St John study, although the needs of these groups remained its primary concern, it provided reference service to the general public and made loans to other libraries and individuals by special arrangement. Students at the University of Toronto had access to material that was not found in the University Library. Co-operation with the University Library involved an effort to divide fields of collection. The report commented favourably on the renovation program undertaken in 1965.

Local library service

The report was extremely critical of the association library, which was called an anachronism militating against the development of a public library in the same area adequately supported by public funds. The trustees were often involved in a struggle, usually looked upon as a social obligation, to keep the library going for another year. It seemed obvious that no community, whatever its size, could be adequately served at an average cost of $543 per year, a sum which, at current prices, would provide fewer than one hundred books, with nothing left for staff, supplies, or maintenance and housing costs. Alternatively, the funds would supply less than one-tenth the annual salary of a trained librarian but no books, supplies, housing, or maintenance.

The report's specific recommendations with respect to association libraries were 1 / that legislation or regulations be formulated to prevent them from receiving public grants; 2 / that they be encouraged to contract either with county public libraries or regional library co-operatives to provide service at a mutually agreeable price; and 3 / that all current assets, including title to land, buildings, book stock, and equipment should be turned over to the larger unit as part of the contract.[26]

In 1964 there were found to be twelve county library co-operatives, with 393,961 volumes and only nine qualified librarians, eight with Class B Certificates and one Class D. Of their total expenditure of slightly over half a million dollars, 38 per cent was provided by provincial grants. Certain organizational complexities made it difficult to estimate the extent of their services. The quality of service depended to a very large extent on the effectiveness of the librarian. The county co-operative was appraised as having substantial weaknesses in that it lacked a sound method of financing and failed to provide complete coverage, since any area or library board that voted against joining the system was under no obligation to do so. Even where the co-operative was reasonably successful, there was still a great inequity of service within the county. The practice of providing service to schools was regarded as having been a major factor in delaying school library development.

The report recommended that county library co-operatives be encouraged to change to county libraries, with a single tax base and the responsibility of providing service to all parts of the county. In the legislation that would be required for such a change, it was urged that there be no prohibition against any municipality wishing to tax itself above the county rate for library purposes.[27] No details were offered with respect to the mechanics of operating such a scheme.

The regional library co-operatives were identified as the true key to a total provincial library plan. The report noted that, although *The Public Libraries Act* gave them broad powers, these were not generally being fully utilized. Reasons offered for this state of affairs were 1 / that before 1963, they were given responsibility only to help member libraries by distributing books, 2 / that many of them were new and not fully organized, and 3 / that there had not been enough funds available for them to perform the full range of services. It was recommended that they be given the financial means to provide, not only basic services, but also field experts in various areas of librarianship such as children's specialists, adult specialists, specialists in work with young people, and liaison specialists to work with schools. It was considered particularly important that funds be available to assist in the development of top-level reference and interlibrary loan service.[28]

The report envisioned field workers from the regional co-operatives working with and training the staffs of individual libraries. They would help to weed out unwanted or useless items, help build up the collections, and develop staff skills in providing service to the reader, in book selection, in story telling, and in reference service. It was suggested that small communities with a population of less than one thousand would be well advised to contract with the regional co-operative for service rather than trying to supply it themselves. The co-operative would be responsible for book selection, weeding, and supervision of service in the local reading centre. As a means of encouraging the development and successful operation of this system, it was recommended that provincial grants be made only to regional library co-operatives, except for those to regional reference centres and to the provincial reference centre.

Provincial co-ordination and service

The report referred to a memorandum prepared in August 1965 by the staff of the Toronto Public Library proposing the establishment, through the co-operation of the major libraries of the province, of a computerized catalogue or bank of bibliographic data which would be available to any library on line to the computer. This machine catalogue would supply information instantaneously about any book or other item previously recorded in the computer. According to the report, this scheme would complement proposals for centralized ordering and cataloguing of all books added to public and school libraries. A parallel recommendation was made that a centralized cataloguing operation be established at the University of Toronto to serve the needs of institutions of higher education in general. The report suggested that the Toronto Public Library proposal should be carried further. The rapid development of magnetic tapes was making it possible to furnish detailed bibliographic information, including abstracts of many of the journal articles which were difficult to locate through normal bibliographic channels.[29]

It was recommended that each regional library co-operative establish a regional reference centre, which would usually be the library that currently had the strongest non-fiction collection. It would be supplied with Telex and some form of quick copy equipment. By adding to its non-fiction and periodical collections, it would eventually have all titles listed in the basic periodical indexes and a minimum of 100,000 volumes of adult non-fiction. According to the relevant recommendation, the regional reference centre would serve the needs of all types of libraries, including public, school, college, and special libraries.[30]

The Toronto Public Library would be a kind of super reference resource, supplying requests received by Telex for items that the regional reference centres did not have. In some cases, the actual book would be mailed, while in others, a photocopy of the required material would be sent. If the Toronto Public Library did not have the desired item, it would check the holdings of the University of Toronto, the Legislative Library, the Toronto Education Centre Library, the National Union Catalogue, or the Union Catalogue of the Library of Congress, and advise the inquirer where it could be obtained. Provincial funds would ensure that the burden of such service did not fall entirely on the citizens of Toronto.

If the scheme were implemented, Ontario would not need a provincial library.[31]

School libraries

Although it is not the intention to deal at any length in the present chapter with recommendations having to do with school libraries, certain observations of the St John report may be noted. In general, the development of libraries in both elementary and secondary schools had been very slow. Only 1.13 per cent of 6,496 schools surveyed reported collections of five thousand or more volumes, and over 75 per cent had fewer than one thousand volumes. A large part of the reference material was out of date. In the 1964–5 school year, 4.62 per cent of elementary schools spent nothing for library materials, 50 per cent spent between $1 and $99, and only 4.71 per cent spent over $1,000. Only 83 per cent of Ontario secondary schools had centralized libraries; the only province with a poorer record was Quebec, with 80 per cent.

There were ten professional librarians serving fifty elementary schools, two serving three intermediate or junior high schools, and forty-three serving forty-five secondary schools. A survey by the Dominion Bureau of Statistics had shown that, instead of the recommended standard of one professional school librarian for each three hundred pupils, the Ontario ratio was one in 7,653, a figure that was less favourable than that for Canada as a whole. Furthermore, there were not enough library school graduates entering the schools to offset losses.

The deplorable state of the libraries existed despite a number of measures taken by the Department of Education. It paid grants for library books and approved the expenditure of up to $20,000 for the construction of a library room in a school with twelve or more classrooms. Summer courses were offered to train teacher-librarians. Guides had been issued indicating minimum desirable standards of school library service. Secondary school libraries were supposed to be supervised by the holder of a High School Assistant's Certificate and a degree in library science or a certificate in school librarianship. A school with an enrolment of one thousand was to have a professionally trained full-time teacher-librarian. A desirable number of books was suggested for schools of different sizes, and an annual expenditure of $2.50 per pupil was recommended for books, periodicals, pamphlets, supplies, and repairs.

Recommendations relating to school libraries were as follows:

It is *recommended* that legislation be prepared to require that each elementary and secondary school with a daily average attendance of 150 or more students be required to maintain a school library.

It is *recommended* that the elementary school library collection should contain not less than 3,000 books for schools with up to 300 pupils and ten books per pupil above this figure.

It is *recommended* that in the secondary school the minimum collection should be 5,000 volumes and an additional ten books per capita for each pupil above 250.

It is *recommended* that the school library should be staffed by a school librarian preferably on a full time basis, but not less than half-time for schools with less than 250 students. Any school with more than 250 pupils should have at least one full time librarian.

It is *recommended* that when enabling legislation is passed that Minister's Regulations be prepared which will state minimum requirements which will be acceptable. Standards being prepared by the Ontario Teachers Federation and the Ontario Library Association should be used as the base in preparing the official minimum requirements.[82]

These recommendations were made at a time when the situation in the schools was changing rapidly for the better. The continuous closing down of small schools, already noted in volume I, was an important influence in ensuring that children at the elementary level had access to better service. At the same time, increased provincial grants for school libraries were having a cumulative effect.

The supply of librarians

The report indicated that, if even minimum standards for personnel established by associations in Canada and the United States were to be met, several thousand trained librarians would be needed for the various types of libraries in the province. There seemed to be no shortage of recruits, to judge by the fact that the School of Library Science at the University of Toronto had three times as many applicants as it could admit in 1965–6. Yet even a rapid expansion of facilities could not obviate the necessity of compromising with the ideal.

It was considered important to have secondary school libraries operated by holders of the BLS degree. Their efforts could, however, be stretched if recommendations for centralized cataloguing, classification, and printing of cards and labels were accepted and if clerical assistance were provided. It was said to be unrealistic to expect that any but the largest elementary schools would be staffed by graduates with the BLS. A solution would have to be found through area supervisors working with teacher-librarians who had completed the minimum number of courses offered for them at the Ontario College of Education. Similarly, the smaller public libraries would not, for the most part, be able to get fully trained professionals, and would have to depend on a small core of specialists or co-ordinators working from regional co-operatives.

THE PUBLIC LIBRARIES ACT, 1966

Main provisions

It was said that, minutes after receiving the St John report, the minister announced, not only that there would be a new grant structure to enable school boards to increase spending on school libraries, but also that there would be a new public libraries act. The latter, as passed in 1966, superseded *The Public Libraries Act*, Revised Statutes of Ontario, 1960, chapter 325, as amended by 1961–2, chapter 118 and 1962–3, chapter 115.

Section 2 of the act provided for the continuation of existing public libraries, except that those established for school sections and police villages were to be dissolved and their assets and liabilities transferred to public library boards to be set up by the municipal councils for the municipalities in which they were located. In territory without municipal organization, however, libraries operated for school sections were to continue until disestablished by a petition signed by a majority of the public and separate school supporters in the section. If and when this action was taken, the assets of the library board were to be distributed as the minister directed.

The qualifications of a member of a board and the composition and provisions for appointment of a board were specified in sections 4 and 5. A board member had to be a Canadian citizen at least twenty-one years of age and a resident of the municipality in which the board was established. Except for the mayor or reeve, who continued, as under previous legislation, to serve *ex officio*, no one could qualify who was a member of one of the bodies entitled to make an appointment. The board of an urban municipality with a population of ten thousand or more was to consist, in addition to the mayor or reeve, of three members appointed by the council, three by the public school board or board of education having jurisdiction in the municipality, and two by the separate school board, if any. The provisions applying to a township in the same population category were similar, except that mention was made only of a reeve, since a mayor was strictly an urban official. Where there was more than one board qualified to deal with public school affairs, or more than one separate school board, the appointments were made by the one with the largest assessment. As before, members appointed by municipal councils and school boards served for three-year terms, and those appointed by separate school boards for two-year terms. In a municipality having a population under ten thousand, the library board was to be composed of the mayor or reeve and four members appointed annually by the council.

Provision was made in section 7 for the councils of two or more municipalities to establish a union public library. Such municipalities would enter into an agreement which would apportion the cost of the establishment, operation, and maintenance of the library among them. They would also make arrangements for the composition of the library boards.

Section 15 authorized any public library board or regional or county library board to enter into an agreement with any other such board or with a municipal council, school board, council of an Indian band, or individual to provide library service. Other powers involved the right to acquire land, including the right of expropriation, and the right to erect or make alterations to buildings. Sale of property had to have the approval of the municipal council or the majority of the councils where there were more than one.

According to section 18, the board in a municipality or municipalities with a population of ten thousand or more was to employ a librarian holding a certificate of librarianship issued by the minister and, where the population was less than ten thousand, a certificate of librarianship or a certificate of library service issued by the minister. Where a properly qualified person was not available, the board was to apply to the minister for permission to appoint an uncertificated substitute. The chief librarian was to be the executive officer of the board.

Section 23 dealt with procedures for raising operating funds. The library board was to submit its estimates according to prescribed form to the municipal council, which had the right to amend them before raising the necessary funds. Where there were two or more municipalities involved, approval of the budget had to be secured by the councils representing more than half the population for which the board was established. The decision was binding on all the municipalities. Municipal debentures could be issued, with the approval of the Ontario Municipal Board, for the acquisition of a site or building, for the erection or alteration of a building, or for the acquisition in the first instance of a supply of books or other necessities. A proposal to issue debentures had to be submitted to the municipal council or the majority of councils where there were more than one. If rejected, the board could ensure that the proposal was put to a vote of the qualified electors.

Section 27 specified that all public libraries operated by boards were to be open to the public free of charge. Fees could, however, be exacted from those not residing in the area of the board's jurisdiction. Section 28 stated: "Every board shall permit the public to have free use of the circulating and reference books and such other services of the library as it deems practicable, but the board may charge fees for such other services as it deems necessary." It would take an ingenious board indeed to figure out, without supplementary information, just what services it could charge for.

Provision was made in section 32 for the government to appoint a Director of Provincial Library Service who was to supervise the implementation of the act and promote and encourage the extension of library service throughout Ontario. Section 33 established an Ontario Provincial Library Council consisting of nine members appointed by the minister and one by the board of each regional library system. Thus the elaborate appointment procedure recommended by the St John report was rejected. The Director of Provincial Library Service was to be the secretary of the council. The function of the new body was to make recommendations to the minister with respect to the development and co-ordination of library service in Ontario.

Sections 37 to 46 inclusive dealt with regional library service. On receipt of a request from five or more public library boards, at least one of which had jurisdiction in a municipality with a population of fifteen thousand or more, the minister might establish a regional library system and determine the boundaries of the region, subject to the restriction that it include at least two territorial districts or counties. Each regional system was to be under the "management, regulation, and control" of a board composed of 1 / one member appointed by the public library board in each municipality with a population of at least fifteen thousand, 2 / one member appointed by each county library board having jurisdiction in the region, and 3 / enough members appointed by the minister or by other public library boards in the region to bring the total up to nine if that figure was not otherwise attained.

Each regional board was to provide a plan for co-ordinating and developing library service within the region and to submit a summary of it each year to the Ontario Provincial Library Council. Municipal councils in the region might, at the request of the regional board and with the approval of the Ontario Municipal Board, raise the sums needed for the acquisition of sites or the purchase, erection, or alteration of buildings. In accordance with the terms of the agreement between the board and a municipal council, the latter could, at the board's request, raise funds by levies on ratable property for the maintenance of library service.

According to the list of its powers given in section 44, the regional board might

(a) establish, separately or within one or more of the public libraries established in the region in which the board has jurisdiction, a collection of reference books and other items as the basis of a reference service for the region;

(b) promote inter-library loan of books and other means of furthering the efficiency and co-ordination of library service;

(c) establish a central service, and determine services that may be provided by one or more public library boards for other public library boards in the region, for

(i) selecting, ordering, cataloguing, processing, circulating, storing and disposing of books, films and other materials,

(ii) providing an advisory service for the purpose of improving public library standards,

(iii) providing programmes of an educational nature for adults,

(iv) providing programmes of an educational nature for librarians and library assistants, and

(v) providing other similar services;

(d) charge fees for supplying any library service, and determine the unit cost of supplying each service;
(e) with the approval of the Minister, undertake responsibilities for providing inter-library loan of books and other services throughout Ontario; and
(f) appoint a regional director of library services, who,
(i) shall hold a Class A, B or C certificate of librarianship,
(ii) may be an employee of a public library board having jurisdiction in the region if that board agrees to the appointment, and
(iii) shall not be an employee of any other public library board. 1962–63, c. 115, s. 3, *part, amended.*[33]

Section 45 provided for the dissolution of the library associations. As of January 1967 all their assets and liabilities were transferred to the boards of the regional library systems having jurisdiction in the area.

Part IV, consisting of sections 47 to 52 inclusive, dealt with county library service. Section 47 provided for the establishment of a county library by the county council where requested to do so by at least 75 per cent of the municipalities forming part of the county for municipal purposes, or by at least half of such municipalities provided that they had a combined population of at least 25,000. The county library served only those municipalities requesting its formation. Unless otherwise provided by by-law, it took over all the assets and liabilities of public library boards and county library co-operatives within the relevant area. According to section 48, the county library board consisted of the warden of the county and six members appointed by the county council, three of whom were members of the council representing municipalities involved in the formation of the library, and three residents of these municipalities who were not council members.

Section 50 required every county library board to operate and maintain a library as a branch in each local municipality that operated a public library before it became part of the county library system. The board had also to appoint a librarian with a class A, B, or C Certificate of Librarianship issued by the minister to act as its chief executive officer. Funds for the operation of the library were to be raised in accordance with a by-law of the county council from the equalized assessment in the municipalities in the area of the board's jurisdiction. Accommodation for branch libraries might be rented from a municipality by the county board.

Regulations made under the act specified the conditions under which the minister granted the class A, B, and C Certificates of Librarianship and different classes of Certificates of Library Service. There was also a rather complex series of regulations indicating the conditions governing the payment of provincial grants.

Appraisal

Francis R. St John's reactions to the act were published in the December

1966 issue of the *Ontario Library Review*. His general comment was that a surveyor was seldom able to see such a rapid implementation of so many of his recommendations. Although there were no seriously harmful provisions in the act, there were, in his view, some obvious compromises. He was unenthusiastic, for example, about the provision that three of the members of a county library board, in addition to the warden, were to continue, in accordance with previous legislation, to be members of the council. His study had indicated that county council members were unable to give proper attention to growing library needs and could not put them in proper perspective. Also, the additional three members were former members of the council, and not necessarily interested in library development. By contrast, the members of a public library board could not be members of any of the bodies entitled to make an appointment.

St John was critical of the fact that county libraries would provide service only to those municipalities that requested it. His group had been appalled during their survey to realize how many citizens had no direct access to public library service. Despite the emphasis on this point in the report, the new act was in substance the same as the old. St John was concerned that a county council appeared to be entitled to refuse the request of the specified number of municipalities to set up a library. He was even more worried that a community supporting a strong library service might not want to become part of a county public library, even though it might thereby save through centralized ordering and processing. The small communities which could not afford library service seemed to be overlooked. Since they had not known what they were missing, they might not ask to be included in a county system.

There was some cause for concern in the fact that the regional library boards were to take over the assets and liabilities of the association libraries. Few of the latter had any assets to speak of, and the regional boards would have to carry them on inadequate funds while at the same time trying to build a real service to member libraries. St John felt that the association libraries should become part of the county libraries as rapidly as these were formed.

The point of view of the Ontario Library Trustees' Association was expressed in the same issue of the *Ontario Library Review* by the Chairman, Helen S. Edwards. She declared that the trustees agreed that a good beginning had been made in a major overhaul of library legislation and administration. While those responsible for the association libraries might feel shocked, there seemed to be an acceptance of the fact that their dissolution would lead to the provision of more adequate service. It was thought that many public libraries were too small to be effective, and there was a desire to see the authority and responsibilities of the regional libraries increased. It was also felt that a county library should include the whole county. Edwards suggested that the formation of the Ontario Provincial Library Council might, as far as the trustees were concerned, be the most important part of the whole act in that it would enable them to make known the varied requirements in their own areas and avoid an excessively standardized service.

REFERENCES TO LIBRARIES BY THE ONTARIO COMMITTEE ON TAXATION

The Ontario Committee on Taxation made some observations and recommendations about libraries that drew a protest from the Ontario Library Association. Among the points at issue were references to libraries as "amenities"; a recommendation that the library regions correspond to those the committee recommended for other purposes; certain recommendations that the system of grants to libraries be simplified; and a recommendation that books purchased for libraries be subject to a sales tax. The association registered its objections in a brief to the Prime Minister.[84]

While there was no dispute that libraries were social and recreational amenities, the association emphasized that they were much more than that. They were actually a service directly related to the educational needs of the people of the province. The Ontario Committee on Taxation had, according to the brief, over-simplified their role in society. The proposition was advanced that everything possible must be done in the current phase of library development to integrate library services, and particularly to establish effective communication among all types of libraries in the province. With respect to the regional proposals, the association claimed that the divisions recommended by the committee were definitely not practical or acceptable for library development purposes. There had been no recognition of the existence of certain strong book collections around which current library development was taking place. The association believed that the need was for larger rather than smaller regional units.

On the question of grants to libraries, the brief merely stated that the improvement of services rather than simplification should be the objective. No specific proposals for a grant scheme were advanced. The association's most strongly stated point was its objection to the recommendation that a sales tax be imposed on books purchased for libraries. This recommendation was said to be the one that best exemplified the apparent lack of awareness shown by the members of the committee of the complexities of library operations in Ontario, of the national and international ramifications of book procurement machinery, and of the probable effect on Ontario-based firms involved in the publication and sale of books. Foreign dealers with whom many libraries did business would improve their existing advantage.

FINANCIAL SUPPORT

Provincial appropriations for the support of public libraries crept up gradually during the 1960s. The impact of the St John report was quite favourable in that the amount of the grants approximately doubled between 1965–6 and 1967–8. In the latter year, however, the total was still only about $6.6 million, a sum that seemed to many of those who were directly concerned to be inconsequential in comparison with the amounts being spent on other aspects of the educational system. Particular concern was expressed over the fact that the appropriation did not increase in 1968–9.

On December 7, 1968, the Ontario Provincial Library Council passed the following resolution:

whereas the increased costs of library resources, employees' salaries, and other factors in public library operation; and
whereas there is a continuing growth in the numbers of library users and use of library resources; and
whereas continuing education programmes and formation of Colleges of Applied Arts and Technology and growth and increase in number of universities across the Province have placed all additional and substantial burden on public libraries; and
whereas the vote for public libraries' grants for the past two years has remained static; and
whereas the change in equalizing factors will result in decreases in grants to many public libraries ...;
The Ontario Provincial Library Council, in an effort to move toward the standards which have been stated in a brief of the Council which was forwarded on October 24, 1968 and cognizant of the various situations outlined above, recommends that:

1. Every effort be made to increase by at least 25% the public library vote in 1969;
2. Grants to public libraries in any one year be not less than those of the previous year unless such a decrease is a result of lower local support;
3. In the future provisions be made to increase financial aid to public libraries in line with increased costs and use.[35]

The council noted that the total expenditure for public library service increased in 1967 by 20 per cent over 1966, and that the average increase for several preceding years had been 15 per cent. The adequacy of service appeared to be threatened by the size of the 1968–9 appropriation.

PROPOSALS TO COMBINE SCHOOL AND PUBLIC LIBRARIES

The St John report was unequivocally opposed to the idea of combining the functions of the public and school libraries in the latter. Where such a scheme had been tried, the results were said to have been disastrous to the interests of adults. It was suggested rather that both types of institutions be strengthened, and that they should work co-operatively and complement one another.[36]

The matter has come up on a number of occasions in the Legislature, with the positive case usually being put in terms of economy and maximum use of resources. On May 29, 1967, V.M. Singer, member for Downsview, spoke on the subject.

It seems to me in this day when we are so concerned about the number of dollars we spend in our educational process, we must be concerned about wasting dollars. It would seem to me we must be concerned about the possibility of coordinating school library services with public library services, particularly since such a large portion of our educational expenditure goes into the provision of space. That space, by and large, certainly on the primary level and in my municipality on the junior high level, and again on the secondary level, goes into a repetition of services, a repetition of the use of space, a repetition by taking trained people away from the educational process, a repetition of the expenditure for books; and further a substantial portion of the community is cut off from these services.[37]

In reply, the minister said that he felt there was an area for joint service, and that some of the school boards had taken this attitude. A number of these boards were making their library facilities available after school hours. The recommendation of the St John report that school and public libraries be developed separately had come as a surprise and, as a result, the situation was currently somewhat obscure.[38]

On June 6, 1968, D.M. Deacon, member for York Centre, asked a question similar to that of Singer a year earlier.

I would like to ask the Minister ... if there is thought of combining libraries to a greater degree with schools, so that we do not have duplication of quite extensive school libraries, and nearby libraries on their own, which the department is assisting, through this provincial library service? What is being done to avoid this duplication and make available, at the same time to pupils, readily available, comprehensive library facilities?[39]

Davis again referred to the St John recommendation, which he said he did not necessarily share, although he obviously thought it should be given very careful consideration. There had been no attempt to inhibit the development of a combined library resource, which had occurred in a number of communities.

Davis's rather hesitant leaning at this stage toward some form of common use of facilities, or at least of co-ordination, was in considerable contrast to views he expressed in 1964.

The problem of using joint facilities is one that has been explored. But there are many problems. I think they are obvious. We have been spending greater funds for the development of libraries in the elementary schools but such libraries are really not suited, perhaps, for use by the general public. They could not be used, of course, during the school hours and if open after school, the books themselves are not very useful. There are not many adults who would want to go in and use the facilities. At least the books that are made available to Grades 3, 4, 5, 6 and even 7 and 8 would not be too suitable. At the secondary level the problem is not quite as difficult, except once again in connection with the timing. A lot of people like to use the public libraries, it has been my experience, that people like to use the public libraries not just during the evenings but during the daytime period, and for this reason it is difficult to use joint facilities.[40]

Miss Ida Reddy, Assistant Director of the South Central Regional Library System at Hamilton, presented the arguments against the combination library in an article in the June 1968 issue of the *Ontario Library Review* under the title "The school-housed public library: an evaluation."[41] She supported her position with references to experiences in the United States, where volunteer groups, in search of rent free premises for a public library, had sometimes made arrangements with schools by which they received space in return for service. In other cases, classroom collections offered by public libraries to schools had grown into central libraries. Reddy identified ill effects from the provision by public libraries of books and service to schools when the latter lacked their own libraries. While the service had been beneficial to the school program from the short-term point of view, the development of school libraries had been delayed, and the interests of the general public had been slighted because of the diversion of funds.

The essence of the case against combining the two types of libraries, both educational institutions, was that their aims and objectives were different. The school library existed to serve the needs of a special segment of the population – students and teachers. It had to be used in close relationship to various aspects of the learning process. The collections reflected the priority of the school curriculum, and duplication of materials depended on the size of the school enrolment. The school library often served as a classroom, and in any case had to have maximum seating capacity, with the floor space taken up with tables, chairs, and equipment. Since attendance was mandatory, the school had no need to entice users to take advantage of the library's services, and it could be located away from busy traffic arteries. Playgrounds could be built without regard to the library's accessibility.

These factors generally conflicted with the capacity of a library to serve the public. On the question of accessibility, Reddy wrote:

Because of the voluntary and informal nature of public library use, the building itself must be visible and accessible to the user. Therefore the public library is located in the densest population area, easily approachable on foot, roller skates, wheelchair, automobile, helicopter or public transport to serve the informational, cultural, recreational and research needs and interests of all citizens. The book collections must be broad in scope, covering a wide range of subjects as well as providing material in depth for the specialist or informed layman. The public library staff is concerned with the individual and his needs. In reality, the public library is two people, the librarian and the user. Only in the public library can the individual pursue his own interests or inclinations at the pace he chooses, to browse, to study, to enjoy.[42]

One type of administrative problem in operating a combined library arose from the differences in outlook and preparation between school and public librarians. The former had specialized knowledge of school problems and of teaching aids and materials while the latter were oriented toward another type of service. In addition to problems arising from the need to co-ordinate these diverse interests, conflict might arise if the school principal tended to regard the public librarian as a member of the school staff, subject to the same rules and regulations as members of the teaching staff.

Other difficulties in the administrative area revolved around hours of service. During school hours, adults were inhibited from browsing and selecting books by the presence of large numbers of students, by corridor noise, by crowding of furniture, and by a general sense of confusion. Class visits to the library would take precedence over other uses. If the public were excluded until after school hours, numbers of potential users would be deprived of service. Beyond the obvious inconveniences, Reddy pointed to the generally recognized psychological barrier to the use of a school library by adults. Children from private schools also tended to be reluctant to go into a library in a public school.

THE IMPACT OF *Living and Learning*

The Provincial Committee on Aims and Objectives expressed the view in its report, *Living and Learning*, that library services should be developed as a single integrated force for the total community. In order to achieve this purpose, it made the following recommendations:

37. Enact enabling legislation which will place all libraries under the jurisdiction of a board of education in areas where the board of education and existing library boards mutually agree that this action should take place.
38. Where no county or regional library exists in an area which is under the educational jurisdiction of a board of education, place the power to develop a regional library program with the board of education.
39. Integrate the development of school libraries with community library services.
40. Create local school policies which will provide greater access to school libraries in other than school hours.

41. Remove restrictions which link grant reimbursements for the construction of libraries to schools of specific size, and place all decisions regarding the need for and location of libraries with the school board concerned.[43]

C.D. Kent, Director of the Lake Erie Regional Library System, wrote a paper in which he took serious issue both with the approach employed by the Provincial Committee on Aims and Objectives in regard to library issues and with its recommendations on the same subject.[44] The main themes he developed were presented in his foreword.

> The librarians of Ontario are appalled that such far-reaching library recommendations as are given in the Report should be presented with such little research and background information ...
>
> Libraries in the Report seem to have been oriented towards academic education completely when they should have been oriented towards culture, of which education is a part ...
>
> It is the belief of many librarians that information centres will play an increasing role in any new learning scheme, and that adequate organization for these must be investigated now. Making public libraries responsible to boards of education is not even part of the answer.[45]

Kent was critical of the committee's neglect of the field of continuing education in general, and of the fact that the recommendations applying to public libraries were offered without any exploration of the background. "The book is basically and fundamentally unrelated to continuing education and therein, despite its terms of reference, lies its great flaw. It stresses almost entirely K-13 education, blowing these years out of all perspective in the living and learning process."[46] The alleged lack of balance was attributed, in part at least, to the lack of representation of library and other adult education interests on the committee. Furthermore, there was said to be no evidence that any committee member had paid an official visit to a public library. None of the listed research papers was devoted to public libraries. It appeared that little of the relevant bibliographical material had been taken into account. No extensive consultations had been carried out with the Ontario Library Association, the Ontario Library Trustees' Association, the Ontario Provincial Library Council, or the Institute of Professional Librarians of Ontario.

With specific reference to recommendation 37 of the report, Kent found a contradiction in an attempt to develop library service as a single, integrated force for the whole community by placing public libraries under the control of boards of education. There appeared to be no recognition of the role of university, college of applied arts and technology, and separate school libraries. Kent suggested alternatively that

> It would be desirable to relate *all* libraries in a community together, but not

under a board of education or under any authority except a *total* community authority, such as a reconstituted public library board. The preferable way would be to develop regional library service and have *all* the libraries in a region part of a regional library board.[47]

The report was said to give no indication of a recognition that public libraries serve special groups such as business, social service workers, leisure-time readers, and leaders in the fields of religion, music, and art.

In view of the fact that all of Ontario had been organized into regional library systems, Kent questioned the validity of recommendation 38, which specified the initiative to be taken by a board of education where no such system existed. He asked further, how a regional system covering several counties could come under a board of education with jurisdiction in one municipality or county.

The paper continued with a review of successive recommendations made by the Provincial Committee. While Kent found most of them basically acceptable as far as they went, he kept pointing out that they said little about continuing education, particularly of the informal type. Recognition of the potential educational contribution of librarians seemed to be lacking. With reference to recommendation no. 109, which urged school boards sponsoring adult education to provide counselling services to adults, he wrote:

Experience in public libraries leads librarians to believe that many adults fear the formal situation. If such people are to enter the school system it needs to be by easy achievement stages. Sometimes through informal methods. Some may be thrust into formal areas by retraining programs. Still more who can get by with what they have will never make it back because their one successful contact with education is the public library where often there isn't the very person who is badly needed – a professional counsellor. This counsellor might send the individual to the Board of Education, to a Community College, to a University, or to an informal course at the YM-YWCA or to the Library. But they would be referred to the right institution at this time in the individual's continuing maturity so that past drop-outs might have a better chance of being future drop-ins. There is always the very large possibility that the adult individual needs no formal course at all, only an introduction to the materials of his public library – a chance to achieve on his own and to put it to work in his adult world without any sort of teacher grading and no one bugging him if he loses interest for a time.[48]

A number of the Provincial Committee's recommendations referred to school libraries and librarians. No. 163, for example, urged that pre-service teacher education involve practice in a number of "unique environments," including libraries. No. 171 advocated training programs for school library assistants, along with school assistants, school secretaries, and audio-visual technicians. Kent felt both these recommendations had a tendency to downgrade public libraries, as did other parts of the report which emphasized the importance of school libraries, without any reference to public libraries.

Kent wondered why, if libraries were to be controlled by boards of education as recommended, nothing was said about libraries or librarians under such topics as "professional organization," "recruitment," "teacher educational programs," "educational TV," "buildings," "research," and "financing." It appeared that libraries were being grouped with schools for administrative reasons and then forgotten. In a sense, Kent seems to have been doing much more than protesting the neglectful attitude of the Provincial Committee; he was expressing the general irritation and frustration of librarians over the persistent failure of society to recognize the value of their actual and potential educational contribution.

Kent concluded with eight conditions which he thought should be adhered to if the recommendation of the Provincial Committee to place libraries under the control of boards of education were carried out.

1. Community library boards would continue as buffers for the legitimate desires of public libraries with their own budgets and responsibilities. The same organization, with boards having corporate powers, would continue. In this case, library boards would simply exchange their requests for funds from city councils to boards of education.
2. Library boards would report not to the Minister of Education as now, but to the Minister of University Affairs. By so doing, greater liaison between university libraries and public libraries might result. In time a network of libraries in Ontario would result.
3. Librarians, in the event public libraries became departments of boards of education, would have the same right as anyone in the hierarchy of the Board of Education to become top administrators, such as directors of education. Otherwise first class people will cease to train as librarians.
4. Regional library boards, encompassing a number of Counties, would be responsible for specific responsibilities such as technical services, reference and resource centres, film services, museum services, planetariums, zoos, and any other service best done regionally with provincial funds.
5. Safeguards would have to be built in which would guarantee that library service did not become solely school library service and that community library service would continue to expand with larger budgets, more staff, materials and buildings (outlets). A per capita expenditure floor for public library service would have to be established.
6. Mandatory legislation for the establishment of community public library service including county public library service would be essential.
7. Provision would have to be for a full and complete integration in time of

all library services in the province including University, Community college, school and public, etc. Perhaps government libraries would be included in this network.

8. Eventually museums and other related continuing education agencies would be included in the planning of additional services.[49]

The apprehensions of spokesmen for the public libraries over the possibility of the implementation of the Provincial Committee's recommendations registered among members of the provincial Legislature. F.A. Burr, member for Sandwich-Riverside, asked on May 1, 1969:

Can the Minister assure the House that he will not introduce legislation enabling boards of education to take over public libraries without consulting representatives of organizations such as the Ontario Library Association, the Ontario Public Library Council and directors of the Ontario Regional Library?

The minister responded:

I have already had a number of discussions with the various groups related to the library service. Nothing concrete or specific is emerging, related to what might be the structure for library development here in this province.

Certainly there will be no significant change made without consultation with the various organizations.[50]

On July 8, 1968, Susan Anderson wrote in an article in the Toronto *Globe and Mail*, under the headline "The lesson on libraries in the Hall-Dennis report," that the recommendation that public libraries be placed under school boards fell with all the impact of a bombshell on the library profession. She noted that the regional directors had formed a committee to prepare a critique of the idea for the minister, and that individual librarians and library boards had "bombarded the Department of Education with protests."[51] John Parkhill, Metro Toronto Regional Director, was quoted as saying that school boards in the province did not have a very good record of setting up school libraries, and that entrusting public libraries to them might add to their difficulty. Yet most librarians were said to agree that the Provincial Committee on Aims and Objectives had tackled the legitimate issue of how library services could be developed as a co-ordinated community service.

In illustrating the need for integration, Anderson claimed that it cost each library, whether school, university, community college, or public, about $3.50 to order, catalogue, and process each new volume. There thus appeared to be great prospective savings in having one or several central processing points. Furthermore, such technological services as the transmission of facsimile reproductions by telephone wires or microwave could not be implemented unless the links between major resource libraries and smaller libraries were greatly strengthened.

Anderson traced support for the idea of putting public libraries under school boards to those who felt that such an arrangement would make it easier to tap for library purposes the very large amount of funds available to the school system. W.A. Roedde was quoted as one of those who were sceptical that things would work out that way. He and others were said to feel that the department was strongly oriented toward the formal system, and that informal education, such as that provided by libraries, was constantly in financial difficulty. H.C. Campbell, Toronto's Chief Librarian, felt that the abolition of the public library board would be a retrograde step in that such boards were more broadly based than were school boards.

Barrie Zwicker quoted Leonard Freiser, just after the latter's resignation from the position of Chief Librarian of the Toronto Board of Education, as saying that the taking over of the public libraries by the schools would be a "catastrophic blow to civil liberties."[52] He reputedly expressed the view that the structures of education were not generally free, and that basic liberty depended on a free library system as much as on a free press. It is not altogether clear from the *Globe and Mail* article whether he thought that school boards would impose censorship on the libraries, or whether he had other apprehensions.

In the January 1969 issue of the *CORL* (Central Ontario Regional Library) *Courier*, the Editor, John R. Adams, referred to a rumour that the minister, having dramatically reorganized the school boards, was going to apply equally drastic treatment to the library boards.[53] There seemed to be some question as to whether the latter would be completely wiped out or reorganized into regional boards. Adams expressed the view that the "dismal" record of the majority of boards directing small libraries, and some of the larger ones, would ensure them a sharp appraisal.

The editor's remarks were offered as an introduction to a critical article in the same issue by David Karry, Chairman of the Ajax Public Library Board, entitled "The Public Library Trustee—Here To-Day, Gone To-morrow?" Karry began with the flat assertion that library boards would soon be a thing of the past. He deduced that the Provincial Committee on Aims and Objectives must have got its idea for the takeover of the public libraries from high officials, since no support could have been obtained from the grassroots. He identified two reasons for the seemingly imminent demise of the public library boards: 1 / the failure of such boards to exercise the authority given to them by legislation to increase their service to the community, and 2 / the failure of the Provincial Library Service to use its authority to insist that the boards adhere to the act.

Karry pointed out that, once appointed, a trustee had no obligation or responsibility to the appointing group, whether it was the municipal council or the public or separate school board. His sole responsibility was to the library. At times, an appointee's capacity for service was reduced by his use of his position on the board as a stepping stone to elected office. In other cases, a subservient attitude seemed to stem from ignorance of the provisions of the act and a failure to realize the extent of the powers it conferred. A board had the authority to buy land, expropriate, and build libraries. If the municipal council refused to give the necessary approval, it could always demand a vote of the people. Yet some boards allowed the council to tell them where and how to build, or even to do the whole job themselves. In such cases, Karry thought the Provincial Library Service should force the boards to accept their responsibilities, if necessary by cutting their grants.

Karry felt that trustees had an obligation to give their community the best service they could fight for. As a member of the Ajax board, he had had "fun" jousting with the council, and thought that some of the members of the council had enjoyed their encounters as well. They had obviously not held his aggressiveness too much against him, since he had been reappointed three times.

He outlined a procedure by which a board could bring pressure to bear on a penny-pinching council in order to ensure that the interests of the public were served. A council had no moral right to slash a library budget which could be intelligently justified on the basis of its provision for reasonable expansion and better facilities. It had only the right to ask the board to re-examine its proposals. Given mutual respect, a reasonably satisfactory compromise could be worked out. There were always certain items, such as salary increases and the hiring of new staff, that could not be changed. If an outright impasse developed, the board could resort to keeping enough money in reserve for salaries and threaten to close the library at whatever time of the year the operating funds ran out, or else reduce service throughout the year. Public pressure might be expected to ensure that such action did not have to be taken.

Karry offered a few pertinent comments on the relationship between the librarian and the board. He felt that the librarian should be allowed to maintain and build the service without interference. He also believed that the board should have an active role in certain areas, such as the approval of all expenditures. He felt that it was highly undesirable for it to allow itself to be run by the librarian to the point of meeting once a month to rubber stamp the latter's decisions. Such a relationship would lead ultimately to the librarian's becoming an employee of the council.

Among the functions the board could usefully perform, according to Karry, was to promote the library. If the need for extra space was foreseen, the campaign to win public support for it could begin a long time in advance. One suggested method was to create the need by conducting activities that crowded existing facilities.

LIBRARY SERVICES IN METROPOLITAN TORONTO

The city of Toronto has traditionally maintained a high standard of public library service. Since the establishment of the Toronto Public Library Board in 1883, many improvements in national and international public library work are said to have been pioneered.

In *18 to 80: Continuing Education in Metropolitan Toronto*, J.R. Kidd described the range of services offered by the board at the beginning of the 1960s.[54] There was a city-wide system, including the Central Library, which housed the Reference Library, the Central Circulating Library, and the Metropolitan Bibliographic Centre, as well as central services for boys and girls next door. There were also twenty-one branch libraries, and library services provided in eight hospitals, eleven homes for the aged, thirty schools, and five other institutions. The services of the Central and branch libraries were used to a considerable extent by residents of other municipalities in Metropolitan Toronto. The Reference Library included general reference; the Hallam Room of Business and Technology; the Baldwin Room of manuscripts and rare Canadiana; a fine art section and gallery; a picture loan collection; the John Ross Robertson and other historical picture collections; a theatre section; and the Toronto Room, where pictures, newspapers, clippings, official documents, films, and other materials illustrating the growth and development of Toronto from early times were available. The Metropolitan Bibliographic Centre was also located in the Reference Library. The Music Library, located in Howard Ferguson House, had a large collection of books on music and musicians, scores, sheet music, and records. A grant was made by the Metropolitan Toronto Council for the Reference Library's service to the whole Metropolitan Toronto area.

The Toronto Public Library premises were available for exhibitions and for meetings of outside groups and organizations under certain conditions. Exhibitions might consist of books, paintings, prints, or other materials of general cultural value, and must be open to the public free of charge. They might be presented by any responsible individual or organization with the approval of the board. Individual artists usually exhibited their work in order to make it better known. Organizations renting the auditorium, and the meetings they held, had to be non-political, non-partisan, and non-sectarian. The library also offered a number of its own programs in the auditorium. Public groups and study circles meeting in the branch libraries had to be under the control of the branch librarian, to be open to the general public, and to be part of the library's own extension work.

Special events taking place in the Toronto Public Libraries in 1959 included book exhibits, art exhibits, a large stamp exhibit, chamber music concerts, French conversational classes, several plays, several photographic exhibits, and a series of play-reading evenings at one branch. The French conversation classes were held in two branches under the auspices, in one case of the North Toronto YWCA and in the other of L'Alliance Canadienne. The Circulation Division reported eighty-four book talks to new Canadian classes, thirty-seven general book talks, and twenty-one play-reading evenings. In the Young People's Department, there were 261 talks to classes visiting the library, fourteen book talks to outside groups, and fifty book lists prepared on request.

When Kidd made his report, there were library boards in operation in East York, Etobicoke, Forest Hill, Leaside, Long Branch, Mimico, New Toronto, North York, Scarborough, Swansea, York Township, and Weston, in addition to Toronto. In 1960 R.R. Shaw, in a study for the Library Trustees' Council of Toronto and District, commented on the wide disparity in the support of library services, in the amount of reading material made available to the public, and in the amount of use made of such material among the municipalities.[55]

A step forward in inter-municipality co-operation was taken in 1958 when arrangements for reciprocal borrowing were instituted for members of the Toronto and the North York Public Libraries. Similar arrangements soon followed between Toronto on the one hand and East York, Forest Hill, Swansea, and York Township on the other.

Among Shaw's recommendations was that, in addition to a central library for the metropolitan area, there should be regional branch libraries, each serving a population of over 100,000 living in an area with a radius of approximately two miles. These regional libraries would supplement the neighbourhood libraries, which would keep small collections to serve the immediate vicinity. The Central Library collections would supplement those of the regional branches, obviating any need for the latter to retain materials such as extensive collections of foreign language books and older periodicals.

In 1963 the Toronto Public Library Board submitted proposals for standards for such regional branch libraries to a special committee of the Metropolitan Council set up to review the Shaw recommendations. The board also proceeded to designate regions within the city of Toronto for the establishment of regional branch libraries. One of these was set up in the City Hall with approximately sixty thousand volumes, about half of which were reference works. Attempts to extend the scheme to other parts of the city were, however, blocked by the Toronto City Council, which refused to approve the necessary expenditure.

The Municipality of Metropolitan Toronto Amendment Act, 1966, established a regional library board – the Metropolitan Toronto Library Board – with extensive powers.[56] It consisted of one appointee of each area municipality, who must be a resident of that municipality, and might be a member of a public library board; the chairman of the Metropolitan Council; one appointee of the Metropolitan Toronto School Board; and one appointee of the Metropolitan Separate School Board. Each appointed member was to serve for a three-year term.

At the request of the Metropolitan Toronto Library Board, the Metropolitan Council could, after January 1, 1967, pass by-laws taking over land or buildings used by the area boards for library purposes and transfer them to the Metropolitan Board. Until the latter was organized, and thereafter without its consent, the area boards could not dispose of or encumber such real property. Similarly, the Metropolitan Board could acquire from the area boards without compensation all books, periodicals, newspapers, manuscripts, pictures, films, recordings, and other material provided for purposes similar to those for which it was established.

Under the terms of the legislation, an agreement was signed in December 1967 whereby the Metropolitan Board took over all the central collections of the Toronto Public Library and agreed to pay the Toronto Library Board $500,000 to maintain, operate, and expand them and to provide service to the metropolitan area in 1968. A crisis occurred, however, when the Toronto City Council failed to approve the $250,000 that would have been needed for full operation. Consideration was given to the possibility of distributing the collections among the area boards. A brief was thereupon presented by the Mayor and Board of Control and the Toronto Public Library Board to the provincial cabinet pointing out the unique value of the collections, and urging that the government ensure that the Metropolitan Council provided enough funds in 1968 and thereafter for the maintenance of the Central Library in keeping with its earlier standards. If evidence of deterioration in services were to become apparent, the petitioners asked that management and control of the Central Library collections be returned to the city of Toronto and that funds be provided by the Metropolitan Council to perform the necessary services.

A solution to the problem was sought in the implementation of the provision in the act which enabled the Metropolitan Library Board to take over the buildings and staff of the Central Library Division. This action was completed on October 1, 1968, and the promised payment to the Toronto Public Library Board was reduced by one-fourth in view of the early termination of the agreement that was to have covered the whole year. By the end of 1968 the Metropolitan Board had assumed complete control and financial responsibility. The Toronto Board thereupon directed its efforts toward the development of larger district libraries in various parts of the city.

AN EXAMPLE OF LIBRARY BOARD AND LIBRARY ACTIVITIES

This section is an attempt to indicate some of the matters that concern the board and the staff in a single library system – that of the city of London. There is perhaps more value in providing such information about one of the most vigorous systems in the province than about an "average" system, since it is possible in this way to suggest the range of potential services. The material, which constitutes only fragmentary coverage, is taken from the 1968 *Annual Report of the London Public Library and Art Museum.*

The year 1968 was one of unusual importance because of the formal opening of an extension to the Central Building of the London Public Library and Art Museum, an event at which Prime Minister Robarts officiated. During the year, book circulation rose by 4.28 per cent to a total of 1,574,795, which constituted a record. Almost all the branch libraries reported a circulation of over 100,000. Service charges had been abandoned on records and films as a result of the insistence of the Retail Sales Tax Office that such charges were rentals and therefore taxable. It was considered likely that it would cost more to collect the taxes than the amounts warranted. As a result of the removal of charges, the circulation of records increased by 11,299, and of films, by 3,466. There was also a growth in demand for projectors and slides. A total of 471,143 people reputedly saw films from the film library. Reference and advisory questions increased by 5,443, or by 6.25 per cent.

An organizational change that took place during the year was the formation of a Library Services Division consisting of Children's Services, the Humanities Department, the Arts and Sciences Department, and the Circulation Department. The move to relate the work of Adult Services more closely with that of Children's Services was said to be in line with a trend that was generally becoming acceptable in most public libraries and had been strongly emphasized at the 1968 Ontario Library Association Conference.

The functions of planning and development were performed by a Property, Buildings and Equipment Committee. With the work on the Central Building having been completed, this committee was turning its attention more to the development of branch services. In connection with the establishment of two new branch locations, there had been suggestions for combining operations with those of the Board of Education and the Separate School Board.

The responsibilities of the London Public Library and Art Museum in its role as reference and resource centre for the Lake Erie Regional Library System continued to expand. The use of Telex and inter-library loan services had increased considerably over the previous year. Agreement had been reached to begin a regional film services program in January 1969 and a regional technical services program in July 1969.

The community relations staff, in their concern for determining how people learn, from what teachers, and with what resources, and in particular what part the London Public Library and Art Museum might play, had developed a pre-program checklist and evaluation sheet. Although their first efforts produced results that were not completely satisfactory, there had been some revisions, and more useful findings were anticipated. Library staff had been sent to take a new course at Fanshawe College entitled "Teaching Adults." A number of tours had been conducted, one of the most important of which was that on opening day. Others had been arranged for the first-year class of the Library School at the University of Western Ontario, the recreation class from Fanshawe College, and a class of adults learning English. Series programs included "The Citizen and the Law," four series of reading improvement courses, spring and fall series of Friday noon hour programs, a fall series on "Efficient Report Writing," "Great Books" programs in the spring and fall, a special discussion of Erich Fromm's *The Art of Loving*, and various "special event" programs.

Library Services reported pioneering liaison work with Central Secondary School's history classes. There had been the usual co-operation with community groups such as the University Women's Club, the Ontario Film Association, the Historic Sites Advisory Committee, the chartered accountants, and many others. This co-operation had taken the form of book talks, film programs, demonstrations, book lists, provision of materials for study, displays, and tours.

Substantial service was provided for children, despite the expansion of school libraries. Staff members assisted teachers and others working with young people in selecting books, locating reference material, and giving advice on professional matters, including story telling and the use of films. A total of 7,720 reference questions were answered. Seventy-five regular story hours were held at the Central Building. Stories for pre-school children had been revived and were proving very popular. Special film programs, held every two weeks, were judged very successful. The seventy-two classes visiting the library represented a drop of fifty-seven from the previous year. Seventeen talks had been given outside the library. The Summer Incentive Reading Program and Young Canada's Book Week were important contributions.

THE FUTURE

In *Canadian Libraries*, published in 1969, H.C. Campbell speculated on the future of library service in Canada.[57] He professed to see signs of a Canadian style in the strengthening of the national role of the federal government library services and in the joint federal-provincial sponsorship of cultural and social services. As a second trend, he claimed that provincial, university, and municipal library services were emerging from subservience to administration domination. Thirdly, he commented on the growth in the quality of library service in urban metropolitan areas and the development of urban regional systems. He singled out Toronto and Ottawa as conspicuous among Canadian cities in this regard.

He wrote hopefully of the possibility of federal financial aid to libraries, claiming that there was no constitutional barrier to such aid, since the federal government could use the device of the conditional grant to finance activities that fell outside its own stated powers. Even if such assistance were forthcoming, however, he foresaw a continuing struggle to secure the financial resources needed for libraries and information services. He prophesied an end to the position of the local public library trustee in urban areas with populations under 100,000. Despite the increasing emphasis on the role of documentation and information services, he believed that the production of books and periodicals would flourish in Canada. He suggested that the spread of the French language as a vehicle of daily communication in all parts of Canada would involve English-Canadian libraries in "all of the complexities of multilingual collections." There would also be a growing need for materials in languages other than English or French.

TWENTY-ONE

Miscellaneous educative institutions

THE ROYAL ONTARIO MUSEUM

The educational role of museums

Museums as educational institutions have certain unique strengths and values. They can make a maximum appeal to the imagination by stimulating the senses through a variety of objects, materials, and substances. They can create a sense of reality to supplement the verbal abstractions that are and will remain a major aspect of the educational process. They can recreate in microcosm a society or a civilization which distance in time or place removes from ordinary experience. Of increasing importance in an era in which the material accoutrements of civilization change so rapidly, they offer a hope that the essential elements of the environment can be observed and to some extent grasped by the ordinary citizen.

Museums have a major responsibility for the preservation of the artifacts of man's developing culture. Where these, unlike samples of substances from the terrestrial or extra-terrestrial environment or of products of current technology, are irreplaceable, care must obviously be exercised to ensure that they are not damaged or destroyed. There has been an increasing realization, however, that the wise use of museum resources of every kind demands that they be made conveniently accessible to observation, study, and appreciation. Furthermore, passive display has given way to active efforts to ensure that the attention of children and adults is drawn to them, and that their potentialities are realized in close association with other educative influences.

There are scores of museums in various parts of Ontario, some with a wide range of collections and others concentrating on some aspect of local history or culture. Many of them are poorly housed and inadequately promoted, and their educational potentialities fall far short of being fully realized. Others play an important part in the cultural life of their communities or of the province as a whole. In the absence of space, and in view of certain other factors, it is not possible to give these individual attention in the present context. It is to be hoped, however, that a review of some of the educational contributions of the Royal Ontario Museum will help to promote an understanding of the actual and potential role of museums in general.

Origin and early development

The Royal Ontario Museum traces the first initiative that led to the establishment of its predecessor institution to Charles Fothergill, a member of the Legislative Assembly of Upper Canada, who in 1833 proposed the creation of a Lyceum of Natural History and Fine Arts. In 1851, after his death, a provincial museum was set up in the Normal Model School on the site of the present-day Ryerson Polytechnical Institute. The legislation which brought the Royal Ontario Museum into being was passed in 1912. Originally there were actually five museums with separate directors, administrations, and budgets: the Royal Ontario Museums of Art & Archaeology, Geology, Mineralogy, Palaeontology, and Zoology, sharing the same building. Toward the end of the 1920s, the collections from the provincial museum were moved into the building, a new wing of which was opened in 1933. Much of the subsequent growth of the institution resulted from donations. A gallery was built and endowed in 1951 by Sigmund Samuel to hold a collection of Canadiana to which he himself made a major contribution. A gift from R.S. McLaughlin in 1964 made possible the opening four years later of the McLaughlin Planetarium.

Control

Early support from the University of Toronto involved the sharing of operating costs with the government, the transfer to the museum of some university collections, and the provision of senior staff. In 1947 legislative arrangements made the museum a part of the university. Uncertainties about the proper role and functions of the institution led to the establishment of a committee which reported to the Board of Governors of the university in 1954. Reviewing the events of that time ten years later, President Bissell recalled the chief of its recommendations: an orientation toward science rather than the arts and a virtually complete separation from the university. Bissell's opinion of these recommendations came out clearly in the way he reported them.

> These recommendations ran counter to both history and tradition. The real creator of the Museum, Dr. C.T. Currelly, was a university man with archaeological and artistic interests, and his idea of the Museum was built into the very fabric of the institution. Under Currelly's guidance it had grown up to embody a union of the artistic and the scientific, the scholarly and the popular. This concept – whatever the difficulties its ambivalence might involve – seemed too inherently valuable to be destroyed in the interests of greater efficiency ...[1]

Although the board did not act on the recommendations, it merged the separate museums into one and appointed the first director of the whole institution in 1955.

A further study was made in 1964 by a committee appointed for the purpose by the Board of Governors. According to the President's report for 1964, its terms of reference were to examine the relationship between the museum and other divisions of the university, with particular reference to 1 / the relative emphasis that should be placed on scholarship, public display, and teaching, 2 / the quality and status in the university of curatorial appointments in the museum, and 3 / internal administration.[2] The committee was said to have had a freely acknowledged prejudice in favour of emphasizing and strengthening the scholarly aspects of the museum's work. The members found their views confirmed in discussions with the senior staff of the museum, with members of academic departments who were closely associated with it, and with well-known authorities in the field. They asserted that any conflict between the museum's functions as a public agency and a scholarly institution was largely attributable to outsiders who lacked any real understanding either of the museum or of the university.

Public display was all the more effective and popular when it was based upon exact scholarship, in the same way that an Extension Department of a university relies upon the fundamental scholarship of the parent institution. The good curator must be no less a scholar than the teacher in an academic department, but he must be able to communicate his scholarship by the display and arrangement of objects as well as by written and oral communication.[3]

The committee's recommendations fell into four groups. 1 / In order to simplify and streamline the museum's administrative structure, there would be an academic head with the responsibility for curatorial appointments and for the maintenance of the museum's scientific and cultural reputation. The details of administration would be largely handled by an associate director. All curators would have access to the director in somewhat the same way as department heads had to university deans. The intermediate level of division heads seemed to make for costly duplication and to impede the development of separate departments. 2 / The second category of recommendations consisted of measures to strengthen the organizational and procedural ties between the museum and other divisions of the university. There would be a council, chaired by the director, and consisting of all curators and cross-appointed members of teaching departments concerned with museum affairs, which would perform functions similar to those of faculty councils. Also, the director and museum staff members who were cross-appointed to university departments would be members of the appropriate policy-making academic bodies of the university. 3 / In order to emphasize and strengthen the scholarly activities of the museum, the curatorial staff would have more time to engage in research, their salary scale would be improved, the relationship with the School of Graduate Studies would be emphasized, arrangements would be made for the publication of scholarly works by the University of Toronto

Press, and the museum library would be related more closely to the main university library. 4 / As a means of improving public service, the existing museum board would be drastically changed. It would be relieved of responsibility for the routine details of museum management and reconstituted as a Museum Advisory Board which would study the needs, opportunities, and future development of the museum and give guidance to the director. It would concentrate much of its energy on the enlistment of popular support and on the promotion of projects such as acquisitions, publications, the renovation and refurbishing of galleries, the provision of graduate fellowships, and assistance for expeditions in Canada and overseas. The members of the advisory board would be exclusively people who were prepared to devote serious efforts to the museum's welfare. The recommendations of the 1964 committee provided the basis for a reorganization.

The staff of the museum continued to express appreciation for the advantages of the association with the university. But there were vociferous complaints about the inadequacy of the financial support that was forthcoming under the arrangement. In his contribution to the President's report for 1967, the director of the museum described conditions as follows.

> It has long been recognized throughout the museum world that the equipment of the R.O.M. is hopelessly inadequate, that it is grossly overcrowded and financially under-supported. The inspiration of men like Currelly and his backers who gave Toronto this great cultural resource seems to have faded. The effect has been cumulative. Galleries have grown antiquated, shoddy and require renewal. The educational services which introduce our rapidly growing population of children to the wonders of nature and man are badly over-worked and under-staffed. Study/storage and offices have been created only at the cost of closing prime exhibition areas. Proper storage for valuable collections, which though vital for research have been squeezed out or are not required for actual exhibition, hardly exists. Some departments like Entomology have no galleries at all. The whole museum needs atmosphere control – an absolute essential in the North American continent and without which, in a humid atmosphere and one of increasing pollution, valuable objects cannot be preserved and museum staff cannot even work. The library cannot keep up with the minimum needs of a self-respecting museum library. Research and expeditions, if they survive at all, do so only on a hand-to-mouth basis. Publications, which carry the flag of Canadian scholarship across the world, are held up for want of finance. The purchase grant to be shared among twenty-one departments works out at less than $1,000 per department per year. Exhibitions must be turned away for want of funds to allow the province to enjoy them. The guardian staff is reduced to dangerous levels as vandalism increases. The decoration of the Museum theatre is a source of shame, the restaurant facilities would daunt even the most tolerant

visitor. An incoming director is driven to the conclusion that the survival of the institution is little more than a triumph of faith and loyalty on the part of its staff over frustrations, parsimony and total lack of appreciation.[4]

The university might theoretically have adjusted its priorities somewhat to support the museum more adequately. In view of its overwhelming dependence on government funds, however, there was general recognition that it had to move within very narrow limits. The government, for its part, could have found ways of channeling more assistance to the museum, even as an integral part of the university. But the easiest way to justify public expenditure on the institution was to remove it from the control of a university which, despite its traditional status as "the provincial university," was gradually losing its predominance and becoming only one of many. It was assumed that the views of the committee of 1964 were not widely shared, and that there was popular appeal in the idea of making the museum a more truly provincial possession.

In 1968 the Ontario government passed legislation establishing the museum and the R.S. McLaughlin Planetarium as an independent corporation under the control of a twenty-one member board of trustees. Links were maintained with the University of Toronto in that the membership included the chairman of the university Board of Governors and the president, as well as the director of the museum, fifteen appointees of the provincial government, and three elected by the museum's subscription members. Under the new arrangement, the museum could seek financial assistance from the general public and the business community. It could also borrow money or issue debentures up to a value of $100,000 without cabinet approval. The first of these two rights was not, of course, new, but there was a feeling that it would be better understood and would produce a more generous response under conditions of independence.

The Toronto *Telegram* reported the new development on June 13, 1968, under the headline "ROM goes back to the public." It attributed to Davis a statement that, in view of the increasing interest in art and culture in the province, the museum clearly needed to be independent and run by people who were fully devoted to its objectives. The article gave the following reasons for dissatisfaction with the former arrangement.

> One criticism of the existing setup is that it makes the museum appear a preserve of the university and a "highbrow" organization, which its supporters claim it isn't.
>
> Another is that people have been reluctant to give money to the museum because they felt – wrongly – it would go instead for general university use.[5]

Naturally the change did not meet with universal approval among the staff of the museum or of the university. Many of the former felt reluctant to lose the status of formal membership in the university, and there was also some apprehension that the museum's efforts in the field of scholarship would ultimately be weakened. The director, Peter Swan, was, however, said to feel that the change would open up new avenues of service, including the ability to provide travelling exhibitions and lectures in other parts of the province.

Educational contributions

Services to school children

The practice of allowing school children to visit the museum under the supervision of their teachers was authorized in 1914, shortly after the formal opening. Although these children might be of any age, it was considered that those from grade 7 and up would benefit most. In 1918 a staff member was appointed to conduct groups through any one of the five component museums. Staff members were also frequently required to give group instruction. About ten years later, the Toronto Board of Education secured approval for the appointment of its own museum teacher on the understanding that her deportment, methods, and instruction would be approved by the director in whose gallery she was teaching. In 1946 the Department of Education appointed two museum teachers to assist with increased numbers.

By 1950 the museum's Division of Education consisted of five regular teachers, a number which remained constant for many years, although increasing numbers of occasional teachers were employed. With the reorganization of 1955, the Division of Education became one of four component divisions of the museum, and in 1964 became a department. The extent of internal instruction in 1957–8 is indicated by the fact that it involved 51,231 children in 1,777 class groups.

The University of Toronto President's report for 1967–8 mentioned influences that had tended to increase the number of visits from school children over the years. One was the creation of the metropolitan form of government in 1954. Another was the construction of highways 400 and 401, which made it easier for outside groups to travel to the city. A more recent event was the celebration of Canada's Centennial, which had given momentum to the development of the concept of the whole world as a classroom. Many of the children who visited Expo were expected to continue to explore the country. Also, the abolition of the grade 13 departmental examinations was given credit for increasing secondary school visits through May and well into June.[6]

Recent approaches to museum instruction have involved a recognition of the visit as a planned learning experience, with classroom preparation and some type of follow-up. Museum teachers have developed the practice of preparing information sheets for Toronto classes indicating what will be covered in the lesson and containing a bibliography of related books and films. Some types of lessons have involved consultation with classroom teachers beforehand, and at times the preparation of questionnaires. Curators check the information sheets and questionnaires for accuracy.

The Education Department reported a new instructional technique in 1969. Classes were assembled in the theatre at three specific hours to view slides of objects they would see as they moved from one gallery to another. Skilled teachers made commentaries designed to prepare the pupils for perceptive looking. The results were regarded as gratifying in a number of ways.

The activities of the Division of Education have by no means been confined to instruction for visitors to the museum. The report of the President of the University of Toronto for 1957–8 mentioned that a winter service, involving teaching with case exhibitions, had brought nearly nine thousand children in the Lower St Lawrence and Muskoka districts into direct contact with the museum. Twelve unaccompanied travelling cases went into about fifty additional secondary schools, and about twelve hundred elementary schools used material circulated by the Division of Education. As well as co-ordinating all the teaching by institutions, other than the university, which used the museum, and collaborating in the preparation of extension courses held there, the museum organized the experimental Camp Museum at the international Centenary World Camp for Girl Guides held at Emsdale, Ontario. A major contribution was also made to the annual workshop sessions conducted by the Ontario Historical Association to aid the volunteer staffs of local museums.[7]

What was called the distant-schools program reached the shores of James Bay in 1959–60, when one of the museum's teachers transported her exhibit cases, films, and projector to Cochrane, Island Falls, Smoky Falls, Otter Rapids, Fraserdale-Abitibi Canyon, Moosonee, and Moose Factory, where she reached 2,771 children and adults. Another teacher visited the secondary schools of Fort William, Port Arthur, Dryden, and Kenora. Some of the more remote settlements to the east and north of Lake Superior which were visited for the first time had relatively little communication with the outside.[8]

The Saturday Morning Club

An outstanding aspect of the museum's contribution to children's education has been the Saturday Morning Club, which has been conducted for many years by a small group of paid leaders assisted by a larger group of volunteers. The members of the club meet for two-hour sessions for twenty weeks extending through the fall, winter, and early spring. The number of children that could be handled grew from two hundred in the latter part of the 1950s to three hundred by the end of the next decade.

Limitations of staff and facilities have consistently meant that many applicants have had to be turned away.

The report of the President of the University of Toronto for 1960–1 mentioned some of the activities of the Saturday Morning Club. An exchange program had been worked out with a school in Ghana which had encouraged the club members to make a special study of that country, to contribute money for art supplies for use in the exchange school, and to send an exhibition of their work to the school. A return exhibition was expected for the following year. Among other club activities, particularly striking work was said to have been done by the group studying the origins and development of writing.[9]

The museum's report on the club's activities in 1968–9 mentioned a morning's program in which the participants found out about the displays and workshops by means of slides and a lecture in the Star Theatre. Another Saturday morning was devoted to free-choice activities preceded by an illustrated talk based on two inscriptions on the outside of the museum. Outside visitors included an Egyptian dancer and musician. There was a demonstration of Chinese music on old instruments which the children were allowed to use. The study of reptiles was given a sense of reality by the opportunity to touch a live snake. The Children's Council initiated the production of a club magazine, which was sold and the proceeds retained to support a similar project the following year. Objects produced for two displays held in the lower rotunda included designs for stamps, Chinese lanterns, headdresses, kites, and cut-out pictures.

Programs for the handicapped

The museum has shown a particular interest in providing educational experiences for the handicapped. The report of the president for 1960–1 mentioned a program for the blind, which involved sessions every two weeks through the autumn and winter, and elicited contributions of time and effort on the part of curators, teachers, volunteer helpers, and volunteer drivers. Ordinarily about thirty blind participants attended; these were divided into two groups, one participating in a general course on museum treasures and the other in a series of three-session lectures on special subjects chosen at the first meeting.[10]

Another project of the same year involved the Ontario School for the Deaf at Belleville. A member of the museum staff spent three days with the intermediate and senior students at the school, contributing to the social studies program with the aid of museum objects and films. The students paid a subsequent visit to the museum.

Services to hospitals have included visits by the teachers of the Education Department. The museum's report for 1967–8 referred to work among children in the primary grades at the Clarke Institute of Psychiatry and to programs in the Occupational Therapy Department of the Ontario

Hospital on Queen Street in Toronto. Patients were allowed to handle artifacts and specimens and to view short films on museum subjects. Visits of museum staff were part of the regular school program at the Hospital for Sick Children, and an after-school event at the Ontario Hospital for Crippled Children.[11]

Adult education

Museum extension courses have been given in collaboration with the university Extension Division. In 1958–9 over 2,500 students attended classes entitled Preserving Ontario History, So You're Going Travelling, Aspects of Archaeology, and Talking of Textiles. The offerings for adults the following year included a course called English Pottery and Porcelain. Other aspects of the adult program consisted of a series of Saturday afternoon gallery talks and Sunday films built around the theme "Peoples in a Changing World." Extension courses given in 1968–9 included Continuous Learning, Digging into the Past, City of the Future, and Chinese Art. The practice was begun of presenting a course in another part of Metropolitan Toronto.

Various university and professional groups have been given a special reception, sometimes including lectures as well as conducted tours. In 1962–3 these included University College freshmen and a class from the School of Physical and Health Education; and in 1966–7 the history specialists from the College of Education and, again, students in Physical and Health Education, who were given two series of six lectures emphasizing the place of athletics in other civilizations.

Work with teachers

The Education Department has recognized the particular importance and value of working with teachers. The hope was expressed in the annual report for 1969 that museum education would, in the future, be given as much attention in the teachers' colleges as educational television was currently receiving.[12] Since the colleges had been given freedom to develop their own programs, many of their students had been visiting the museum to investigate its potential teaching facilities. A program had been organized with the Toronto Teachers' College in connection with an experiment in the Nuffield approach to learning. After an introduction, with slides, to the scope of the museum's collections, about two hundred students had visited the museum to research the topic "Man in his Environment."

Teachers of history from North York participated in a two-day seminar during which they had had an opportunity to observe teaching techniques in the galleries and to discover the work that went on behind the scenes. Two open nights for teachers were also conducted, one in the museum and another in the planetarium, both designed to acquaint teachers with the institution's contents. Seminars were also held for a group of history teachers from Sarnia and for another group under the auspices of the Ontario Secondary School Teachers' Federation.

THE ONTARIO SCIENCE CENTRE

The Centennial Centre of Science and Technology is an institution of considerable appeal and promise as an educational influence on adults and children alike. The concept is one that has evolved and changed considerably over the extended period required to achieve full operation. Before plans for the project were officially formulated, and before the government decided on the procedure for carrying it out, Davis foreshadowed what was to come in a statement to the Legislature in early 1964, at a time when a feasibility study was being made.

As Canada's leading industrial province, and as an area that has provided world leadership in many aspects of science, medicine, engineering, agriculture and transportation, Ontario has a proud technological story to tell – not only to those in the province, but to the hundreds of thousands who visit the province each year. It has a story that is a natural inspiration to its young people and a revelation even to the most sophisticated observer. The story is being told partly through small scattered museums, and annual fairs and exhibitions held throughout the province ...

But such messages are necessarily of a temporary nature and lack the effectiveness of continuity. As well, such displays are not designed for thoughtful research or exploration by students or the advanced scholar, and they cannot in their present form give the general public, including the 1.5 million school pupils in Ontario, a cohesive picture of the accomplishments of industry and science in this vast and varied province ...

Nowhere in Ontario and indeed nowhere in Canada is there a central point of reference on topics of contemporary science and industry. There is no show-window of Canadian technological accomplishments. The genius that went into developing and producing the Alouette satellite and such things as the cobalt bomb immediately come to mind.

With all this in mind, some months ago, I, on behalf of The Department of Education and the province, appointed a special committee to give active study to the feasibility of establishing in Ontario a permanent museum devoted to the display of industrial, scientific and technological accomplishments here in this province and here in Canada. This group is made up of representatives of industry, education, science and other interested citizens prominent in their own fields who are generously devoting their time to this study. It is my earnest hope that out of this will come the establishment of a permanent museum of science and industry in this province.[18]

A short time later, Prime Minister Robarts announced that such a development would constitute Ontario's Centennial project. It would thus be eligible for a Centennial grant from the federal government. The centre was organized as a crown corporation, reporting to the Legislature through the Minister of Tourism and Information, the Honourable J.A.C. Auld, who became chairman of the cabinet Centennial Committee. J.G. Crean, Toronto industrialist and a past president of the Canadian Chamber of Commerce, was named Chairman of the Board of Trustees, and the Minister of Education was the vice-chairman. Total membership on the board was twenty-four "outstanding citizens from across Ontario," as Auld described them.[14] The chairman set up an industry committee whose primary function was to enlist the support of the business and industrial community. Named as director of the centre, George MacBeath proceeded to assemble a large staff.

Davis arranged to have a special committee set up to provide liaison with Department of Education officials, to act as an advisory body, and to carry out some studies. The members of the committee visited relevant institutions in Canada and abroad for first-hand information and ideas. Plans were revised to incorporate more educational features than were at first contemplated. A Department of Education memo was distributed to school board and teachers' college officials in 1964 explaining the project as it was then envisioned, and inviting the submission of ideas and suggestions concerning the potential educational use of the centre.[15] The memo offered a view of the centre's purposes: "The Centre will be designed to inform, to educate, to entertain, and to inspire. It will help us to appreciate and to understand our province, our country, and the world in which we live." It pointed out that the centre might make a great contribution to the educational system at all levels by demonstrating the impact of science and technology in our daily lives. The request for ideas illustrates the policy of wide consultation that was pursued with respect to most of the major developments in the formal educational system during the Davis years.

The following year, Davis elaborated on the educational implications of the centre in a further statement to the Legislature:

> The department sees the science centre as an essential and integral part of the education of the child, the adult, the pupil, the teacher, the specialist, the layman and, of course, the resident and the tourist. In a word the centre, although separated from the classroom, is envisaged, not as an extension of the school, but as a part of it. It should be as important as the science laboratory and the school library.
>
> Class visits to the centre should not be interpreted as enrichment fringes to the science courses but rather as essential and interwoven threads within the pattern of the courses.[16]

This concept may be compared with the view of educational television as an extension of experience and thus an integral part of the educational process rather than as something extra designed to make it easier to swallow the pill of learning.

In the same address, Davis attempted to dispel the impression that the centre was a Toronto project, even though it was located in that city. He expressed the intention of devising means of utilizing modern methods of transportation in order to make its services widely accessible. There was some consideration of the possibility of building dormitories eventually for student visitors from communities beyond convenient driving distance.

A site was designated consisting of 180 acres running south from Eglinton Avenue between Don Mills Road and the Don River. Over twenty acres of this rugged, ravine land were to be used for the initial cluster of three large, interconnected buildings and for the projected expansion in the future. The remainder was assigned for development by the Metro Toronto Parks Department.

While plans were unfolding, a building was leased for the storage and restoration of articles for display, for the design and preparation of exhibits, for a woodworking and metalworking shop, and for administrative offices. In an address to the Legislature in 1966, Auld listed and described some of the outstanding items being donated or loaned.[17] These included the first Cobalt-60 beam therapy unit to be put to work against cancer in a Canadian hospital; a rare, early Jacquard loom; *Miss Supertest*, world champion powerboat; steam locomotives CNR 6167 and CPR 1057; and models of steam engines of historical and scientific importance. The centre had purchased the Matthews collection of thousands of items significant to Canada's earlier years, including steam traction engines, stage coaches, hearses, locomotives, high-wheeled cycles, and early sewing machines. Activities at the time involved researching, designing, and producing exhibit units. An advisory committee for exhibits was formed, with members drawn from industry and the academic world, to review exhibit proposals for accuracy and suitability. An industry committee encouraged individual corporations and groups of companies to sponsor specific exhibits.

The development of the centre did not proceed without criticism. Opposition members in the Legislature attacked the government for lack of proper planning on the basis of two main factors: 1 / the purposes, and consequently the provision of facilities and contents, were substantially modified as the plan unfolded, and 2 / the cost estimates multiplied within a very short time, at one stage being presented as $5 million and later as $30 million. As a response to the first point, an excellent case could be made for the desirability of a flexible approach with opportunities for incorporating the best ideas up to the last possible moment. With respect to the cost, the critics did not generally express opposition to substantial expenditures to promote lofty educational and cultural causes as opposed to undue emphasis on the utilitarian and the material.

Their quarrel was with the apparently erratic way in which the sum had been reached. There were also critical comments when it became obvious that the centre would not be ready until after Centennial year had passed. R.F. Nixon, member for Brant, made this point: "In my view, this is a matter in which the government has showed up in a worse light than in almost anything else that has come before us in this session, because it means that we in Ontario are going to be in the singular position of not having a provincial centennial project to emphasize the importance of this event next year."[18] In view of the great difficulties in planning and implementing such a complex and novel project, this judgment appeared to some people to be rather harsh.

As it finally developed, the centre attempted to combine many functions of museum, school, university, and exhibition. Some of the promotional literature circulated before the official opening provides a useful supplement to the objectives defined earlier by Davis.

> The Science Centre of Ontario – officially the Centennial Centre of Science and Technology – is an institution for public education in the broadest sense.
>
> Although increasingly dependent on technology and the basic science from which it flows, the general public often fails to comprehend the nature of the changes in which they are caught up and hence is apprehensive. Until this understanding becomes more general, we cannot expect to tap the magnificent benefits of modern technology.
>
> It is therefore vital that we grasp the nature and meaning of science and technology; its past accomplishments and if wisely directed its future promise.
>
> We can no longer drift, with passive mistrust, into the new technology. We must direct the evolution of the new technology, to help solve the problems facing us and exploit its potential for extending our prosperity and to share it with more of the world's people.
>
> ... It [the Centre] is a vital link in a series of steps that include a reorganized school system, expansion of universities, and establishment of Colleges of Applied Arts and Technology.[19]

The buildings themselves, designed by the architect Ray Moriyama, were original and impressive. The three-storey core structure had three circular wings buttressing the triangular central section to give the impression of a castle. The buildings included waiting rooms, cloakrooms, washrooms, information desks, a bookstore and science shop, a cafeteria, a heating plant, and other services. The core contained an auditorium with the latest electronic and other visual aids, an education centre with demonstration rooms, and two rotating theatres where man's origins and explorations, and his achievements and potential in science and technology were dramatized. The largest section of the complex contained three exhibit halls, with adjoining workshops, collection and conservation areas, research facilities, and a library.

One exhibit hall was devoted mainly to a junior museum and educational exhibits related to school science curricula. A second hall contained exhibits on pure science, dealing with such aspects as theory and method, mathematics, and the structure of matter. There were also displays on health sciences and man's biological environment. The third hall presented technological exhibits, emphasizing Canadian contributions. The exhibits were subject to frequent change to keep up with scientific and technological developments and to persuade visitors to return. The following description applied at the time the centre was opened in the fall of 1969.

The exhibits in the junior museum were intended primarily, although not exclusively, for children. They were based on such topics as mathematics, simple mechanics, fluid behaviour, heat, electricity, wave behaviour, sound, light, physiology, perception, and animal behaviour. It was intended that the intellectual curiosity of the children should be aroused, and that questions should be raised in their minds without necessarily being answered. Emphasis was on participational exhibits that produced enjoyment and provided a constructive outlet for surplus energy. To paraphrase the promotional literature, the children could manipulate ropes and pulleys, play a pulley-puzzle game, and gain by direct sensation a feeling for the centre of gravity, inertia, friction, gyro action, and mechanical resonance. Some machine components such as transmissions, differentials, bearings, gears, and cams were provided. Mechanical themes were illustrated by fluid behaviour with an exhibit on simple hydraulics involving water pumps, water wheels, chainlifts, and Archimedean screws. The child could generate electricity by sitting on a bicycle seat and pedalling vigorously in order to produce illumination, play music on a tape recorder, and project his own image on a television screen. In another section, he could observe wave phenomena in general, as well as standing waves, torsion waves, waves in ripple tanks, in coil springs, and in a glowing wire tube. The basic principles of sound were explained, with examples of applications of principles from primitive to modern times. Visitors could experiment with different sound-producing techniques. They could hear novel sounds produced on original instruments created for the centre by the well-known musical sculptor, François Baschet. They could manipulate a low-power laser, produce a spectrum, experiment with primary lights and shadows, demonstrate the difference between reflection and refraction, and observe the interrelationship between technology and the arts. A series of exhibits dealt with perception and involuntary self-deception. Visitors could experience dynamic visual illusions that showed how easy it was to reach false conclusions about what was happening in an unfamiliar or distorted frame of reference. Illustrations were provided by distorted rooms, a revolving trapezoid, light pistons, and delayed visual feedback. In the animal behaviour area, there was a cage of pigeons trained by Skinnerian methods to perform a complex series of actions in response to a triggering stimulus. The biological area contained a theatre housing life-size mannequins of a transparent man and woman, with illuminated internal organs, accompanied by a taped commentary explaining their functions. These and a great many other marvels that space forbids mention in this context awaited the youthful visitor to the centre.

Exhibits in the north tower of the core building showed how science probes the molecular and atomic worlds. Models of cyclotrons and linear accelerators were exhibited and their significance explained. A pair of large diffusion cloud-chambers operated continuously, enabling visitors to observe tracks made by subatomic particles, either from cosmic radiation or from radioactive sources mounted in the apparatus. Models showed the shape of electron orbitals involved in chemical bonding, as revealed by quantum mechanical studies. The ways in which they overlapped to create chemical bonds was shown. A group of exhibits displayed sophisticated instruments that illustrated the contribution that modern technology is making to the solution of basic scientific problems. These included infra-red and ultra-violet spectrophotometers, a nuclear magnetic resonance spectroscopy apparatus, a mass spectrograph, a fully computerized and automated x-ray diffractometer, a preparative gas chromatograph, and an automatic carbon-hydrogen analyzer. The idea that the general purpose of such mysterious devices can be made comprehensible to the layman is an intriguing prospect. Other exhibits illustrated various chemical reactions produced by heat and light and by electricity. Visitors could control production of some of the industrial processes used to produce such materials as formica, foam plastics, rayon, and nylon. Certain exhibits illustrated purification techniques used by modern chemists.

The earth sciences exhibits featured a large group of maps, atlases, and globes illustrating the extension of man's understanding of the earth's geography. A historical series was offered in an attempt to recreate the stages of comprehension attained in various periods. Associated with the same display was an exhibit demonstrating progressive steps in the solution of the problem of time-keeping. The central focus of the earth science area was a ten-foot, rotating globe. An exhibit related to the work of Canadian geophysicist Tuzo Wilson, now Principal of Erindale College, described the theory of continental drift and other related phenomena. Another exhibit dealt with reversals of the earth's magnetic field. Still others explained the formation of sedimentary rock, sedimentation off the continental shelves, turbidity currents in the ocean, and other phenomena. Theories of the origin of life were presented, accompanied by illustrative supporting evidence. A great deal of attention was focused on the mineral resources of the earth's crust, with demonstrations of techniques for identifying and extracting them.

Exhibits of particular timeliness dealt with the exploration of space.

Models of the Apollo command module, the Saturn v launch, and the lunar excursion modules used in man's first visits to the moon were on display, with accompanying equipment. Visitors could simulate some of the space manoeuvres performed in the early exploratory flights. Other exhibits demonstrated some of the characteristics of the solar system with its various components.

In the Hall of Life, the biological exhibits illustrated eight major topics: hormones and chemical control of the organism, genetics and inheritance, nutrition, magnification, the physics and biology of radiation, human physiology, biomedical engineering, and dentistry. The discovery of insulin and its functions in the body were given particular attention. The functions and malfunctions of the thyroid gland, the pituitary gland, and others were demonstrated. Other exhibits explained the inheritance of sex-linked characteristics, extending into the mechanism of heredity. Nutrition exhibits dealt with physical and chemical processes in plants, animal nutrition generally, and human nutrition in particular. The role of carbohydrates, proteins, fats, minerals, and vitamins was demonstrated, and principles of diet were explained. Attention was given to the use of the microscope and other instruments in the laboratory. The biological applications of radiation were shown, as well as some industrial uses. The visitor could learn a great deal about the nature and functions of the sensory organs and other parts of the body.

The Hall of Engineering demonstrated important and representative aspects of technology, concentrating particularly on the uses of energy. Exhibits explained the nature and importance of the Great Lakes system, including the St Lawrence Seaway. Motive principles of various types of engines were described and compared. Mechanical principles, such as that of leverage, were explained. There were demonstrations of industrial processes such as the machining of metal, riveting, glass blowing, and the production of plastics. The history, principles, and techniques of automation were thoroughly dealt with, including a variety of illustrations of automated processes. Ontario Hydro had a large exhibit, one aspect of which was a diorama in a theatre-like setting illustrating the rain cycle. Further exhibits showed how energy originating from the sun was transformed into usable power, and how it was controlled by means of circuit breakers, control switches, and transformers. There were also exhibits on the technology of nuclear reactors and their use in electric power generation.

Exhibits on Canadian resources dealt with 1 / renewable resources based on living things, forestry, fisheries, and agriculture, 2 / non-renewable mineral resources, 3 / energy resources based on water and fossil fuels, and 4 / the north. A historical treatment of the development of resources was provided. Improvements in crops, domesticated animals, and fish were dealt with. Various exhibits demonstrated the processes used in extracting fossil fuels and other minerals. Man's efforts to conquer the north through the years were dramatized with historical detail and with explanations of various techniques used in exploration.

Some of the exhibits with the best prospect of impressing the visitor with man's recent technological progress were those dealing with communication. Early devices were demonstrated and contrasted with the highly sophisticated techniques of the modern era. Large exhibits demonstrated the principles of radio and television. The cathode ray tube was shown, with an explanation of the way it evolved into the television tube. There were exhibits on the principles and applications of radar and on the control system used to guide vehicles through space. The applications and potentialities of computers were explained, along with some of the mathematical concepts on which they operate. A centrepiece of the Hall of Communications attempted to present the significance of modern communications, showing them as an enhancement of immediacy and breadth of experience and as a means of coming to terms more effectively with reality.

The exhibits on transportation placed particular stress on Canadian development. Attention was devoted to early locomotives and rail lines. The use of waterways in the exploration and early life of Canada was demonstrated. Models of early ships were contrasted with those of present-day supertankers and submarines. Exhibits showed early automobiles as well as the processes of designing, building, and testing those produced at the present time. The history of air travel was also thoroughly dealt with up to the development of jet aircraft, hovercraft, helicopters, and supersonic transports.

The centre was intended not only to provide a wide range of educative experiences, but also to be closely related to the educational system, in accordance with Davis's original vision. D.A. Penny, an Assistant Superintendent of Curriculum in the Department of Education, agreed to act as Director of Education at the centre and to provide liaison between the centre and the department. It was expected that as many as fifty-six busloads of children would eventually arrive daily. Special facilities for classes included separate entrances, eating areas, and lecture rooms. Staff members were available to offer assistance and guidance. A program of public lectures, courses, seminars, youth clubs, and mobile exhibits was planned as an eventual part of the centre's functions.

THE ART GALLERY OF ONTARIO

What was at one time the Art Gallery of Toronto has had a substantial educational program extending back over a period of many years. Arthur Lismer wrote of it in 1936:

> By its example and growth it has stimulated the development of art education in schools, in art colleges and in universities. It has formed a fertile field for the growth and sustenance of people, explaining and demonstrating the need

of art in daily life. Thousands of citizens have come to recognize its place in the community, many thousands of children crowd its halls and galleries during the year. The Art Gallery is more to them than sticks, metal girders and concrete. It is a living manifestation of the expression that life is not all depression and material possessions, that there are still things in life that we need to see more and more, still new experiences in adventuring into new lands and into the hearts of people everywhere, through an understanding of their arts, which is the most universal voice to-day in an age when international understanding also means collaborating in the experience of music, poetry, architecture and painting in all lands.[20]

Lismer identified two sides in the active life of an art gallery: the provision and housing of the contents and the interpretation of these to the public. The second, the educational function, consisted of establishing entertaining and instructive contacts with users, a task that had to be carried out in the face of competition from the radio, moving pictures, and performances in stadiums and arenas. Lismer declared that the public taste was mainly inclined toward the pleasing and the pictorial, without regard to the more important values of sound technique, expressive symbolism, and compositional values. It was the concern of education, he felt, to help people understand and appreciate these qualities.

The interpretation of works of art has advanced in recent years far beyond the stage of dependence on likes and dislikes, into the realm of study where the background, the social conditions, the form, design, colour and composition become a lively unfoldment of the aims and purpose of the age and the artist who produced it. Analysis and philosophy, history and psychology are all part of the process of elucidation on the part of the interpreter and the spectator.[21]

During the period in which Lismer wrote, the Art Gallery of Toronto was not in a position to compete with the art galleries of Europe in acquiring examples of the art of great periods of painting. The growth of what was identified as the permanent collection was thus comparatively slow. The gallery, however, maintained interest and created opportunities for instruction by holding a new exhibition each month. These exhibitions involved the showing of examples from many countries, representing a variety of schools and styles. The active educational program, begun in the late 1920s, consisted of public lectures and gallery talks, study groups, and musical displays.

Public addresses, often involving distinguished authorities from abroad who spoke on such topics as the etchings of Rembrandt, the art of Renoir, town planning, or interior decoration, were offered regularly on Monday evenings during the winter. Informal gallery talks were given by artists or guides as groups of forty or fifty people moved from one exhibit to another. Groups participating in such talks included students from art schools, technical schools, the University of Toronto, and high schools; teachers from all kinds of educational institutions; visitors from other cities; and members of associations such as women's clubs and church groups. Series of lectures on the work of particular periods or of individual artists were given from time to time, with no charge for admission. Musical evenings gave the public an opportunity to hear quartets, distinguished pianists, groups of folk singers, violinists, singers, and interpreters of the dance form. The musical themes were often chosen from the work of masters who were contemporary with the painters whose work was being displayed.

Formally organized Saturday morning classes for children were initiated in 1929. The program was apparently very attractive, drawing far more children than could be handled. They spent three hours each Saturday engaging in creative self-expression, using paper, wood, metal, printed textiles, and other materials. They were given a maximum of freedom to experiment, while the staff tried to encourage latent talent. Lismer described the purpose of the work as follows.

> It is much more than art lessons, skills, accomplishments and professional careers in the making, it is an effort to release valuable human capacities and provide in some measure for the establishment of a future population wherein the art idea, appreciation and practice, will be encouraged to find exercise in the understanding of a higher responsibility towards art in the home, in industry, in civic life, and what is more important in the happiness and creative energy of the individual himself.[22]

Part of the policy of the gallery in conducting the Saturday morning classes was to detect special talent and help children who were old enough to profit by further study. About thirty-six children were recommended each year for further study at the Ontario College of Art. Many of those who participated in the Saturday morning classes also went on to study in the art departments in secondary schools in Toronto.

Another aspect of the gallery's contribution to the education of children under the jurisdiction of the Toronto Board of Education involved visits by four classes of children each day. They were given an instructive tour by a specialist in both art and children. The number accommodated in this way during the 1930s approached thirty thousand a year.

In the mid-1930s, a Children's Art Centre was established on Grange Road to act as a "laboratory" where more intensive child art activities were carried on than those in the gallery itself on Saturdays and during the week. The centre had studios and workshops, library and museum collections, reception rooms, and a nursery room. The original idea was to provide a place where young people could go after school hours to draw and make things from different kinds of material. The centre extended its coverage to include children of all age levels, including nursery groups of from three to five years of age. Young people engaged in social activities such as the production of plays or the creation of murals. Lismer's progressive educational orientation is shown in his statement about the Art Centre's purpose.

> The aim of the Art Centre is not to train artists, or teach art, or instruct in drawing, but to lead *out* from the child, encouraging every spark of feeling and originality and to aid in the extension and co-ordination of hand, eye and mind toward the development of a more emotionally active and alive little personality.[23]

In 1967–8, about thirty years after Lismer told of the gallery's educational program, many similar activities and a variety of new ones were being conducted. According to the annual report for that year, what was now the Art Gallery of Ontario provided tours through the exhibitions for 47,091 people in 1,780 groups. Sixty-one seminars were held for members of the staff responsible for conducting tours, bringing their number up to thirty-three. The Wednesday night program consisted of eight gallery talks, fourteen special lectures, and other special events. A Thursday morning lecture series was held on the theme "Sculpture of the 20th Century." During International Museums' Week, the Education and Extension Branch organized the Sixth International Film Festival and held free noon-hour concerts.

Junior art classes were offered for four age groups from five to nineteen years, as well as a scholarship course for gifted secondary school students. Space for these classes was made available by the Ontario College of Art. Also, an extension series was held in Don Mills, and senior classes were given in the gallery studio on Tuesdays and Wednesdays.

Either directly or in co-operation with the Art Institute of Ontario and the National Gallery of Canada, the Ontario gallery circulated eleven exhibitions for over ninety bookings. Among the titles of these exhibitions were "Posters by Painters," "Nineteenth Century European Prints," "Early Ontario Architecture," and "Homage to the Square." An archival set of slides was photographed and duplicates were made for circulation around the province. Efforts were being made to build up a film library.

The program for the early part of 1969 included exhibitions entitled respectively "Three by Noland – Three by Stella," "John McCracken," and "Rembrandt and His Pupils." The third of these, organized by the Montreal Museum of Fine Arts to commemorate the three hundredth anniversary of Rembrandt's death, consisted of about twenty paintings by the artist himself and ninety by his pupils. Every Saturday afternoon at 2:30, Sydney Wax, Toronto collector of contemporary art, gave a talk on the gallery's collection or on the exhibition currently on view. Between January 15 and April 24, the gallery offered the Wednesday evening lecture series "The Inter-related Arts," as well as gallery talks and demonstrations. A Thursday evening lecture series in March and April complemented the exhibition "Rembrandt and His Pupils." These and other activities indicated that the gallery was putting up a vigorous fight for the continued attention of the public, despite the increased number of alternative attractions as compared with the 1930s.

THE ONTARIO COUNCIL FOR THE ARTS

The Ontario Council for the Arts was established by an act of the provincial Legislature in 1963. A nine-member body, it was headed for its first five years of existence by former Lieutenant-Governor Keiller Mackay. In some respects, the council was seen as a provincial counterpart to the Canada Council. Its original purpose was to support work in the creative arts, with particular emphasis on assisting major music and theatre organizations to perform in smaller communities. It was also authorized to award scholarships, grants, and loans to individuals wishing to study or do research in the arts. It has been supported by grants from the Department of Education.

The minister reported its achievements during its first four months of activity in a statement to the Legislature in April 1964.[24] Grants had been made to the National Ballet Guild, the Canadian Opera Company, Canadian Players, the Stratford Shakespearean Festival, the Crest Theatre, Toronto Workshop Productions, the Canadian Music Centre, the Art Institute of Ontario, the Toronto Symphony Orchestra, symphony orchestras in Windsor, London, the Lakehead, Brantford, Kitchener-Waterloo, St Catharines, Richmond Hill, and Deep River, the International Symphony Orchestra of Sarnia and Port Huron, the York Concert Society, the Toronto Chamber Orchestra, the Pro Arte Orchestra, the Dominion Drama Festival, the St Catharines and District Arts Council, the Quetico Conference and Training Centre, the Canadian Guild of Potters, and the Hawkesbury Valley School. A student aid program had been inaugurated to provide bursaries for Ontario students to attend the National Theatre School. A study had been launched, in co-operation with the Community Programs Branch of the department, to determine the state of the arts throughout the province.

In a brief to the Prime Minister of Ontario in 1967, the council identified what it called two interrelated axioms underlying the artistic and cultural needs of the province. One was that the role of the spectator in the arts was of far less significance than that of the participant, and the other was that participation in the arts must be made an integral part of the early education and life of young people. Grants made during the previous four years were said to have reflected an increasing awareness of these two factors. Assistance to arts centres at Quetico, the Lakehead, Hockley Valley, Sudbury, Brantford, St Catharines, and elsewhere had been designed to improve the calibre of teaching in music, painting, drama, ballet, literature, and crafts. During the four-year period, bursary assistance to students at the National Ballet School and the National Theatre School had almost doubled. A summer scholarship training program had been undertaken in co-operation with the Ontario Federation of Symphony Orchestras at Camp Manitouwabing near Parry Sound.

Activities for the ensuing year were designed to follow the same principles. The Dr Heinz Unger Scholarship was being awarded for the first time. A favourable view was being taken of a proposal by the York Concert Society that the council supplement its fund-raising activities to assist young people studying conducting. Other examples were given of worthy causes of a similar nature which the council considered worth supporting.

The council proposed to use its appropriation for the year in question for grants to artistic organizations for operating purposes, facilities, assistance programs, and the development of a program of co-ordinated administrative and technical services for artistic organizations. The first of these purposes had been established during the previous four years, while the second would represent a new venture. Often the organization needing assistance required only the means to acquire a converted town hall, church, school, or workshop area. The council saw an obligation on its own part to ensure minimum architectural and technical standards if facilities were to prove adequate for future forms of artistic expression. For this reason, it proposed to assemble a team of architectural, technical, and artistic experts to assist in defining such architectural needs and standards.

The council pointed out that there was a rapid increase in the production and administrative costs of the organizations being supported. It was determined to provide relief at the source, rather than insisting that additional funds be sought at the box office, in order to ensure that performances did not become the preserve of an economic elite. In accordance with this objective, a conference was held in conjunction with the Canada Council, at which representatives of the Toronto Symphony, the Stratford Shakespearean Festival, the Canadian Opera Company, the National Ballet Guild of Canada, and Theatre Toronto attempted to develop a program to minimize administrative and technical costs and to reduce areas of duplication while maximizing the efficiency of operations. The conference recommended the establishment of a Co-ordinated Arts Service to provide for united fund raising, co-ordinated promotion, publicity, booking, touring, subscriptions, and joint planning for audience development, administration, and future expansion. Such services might be extended to other artistic organizations.

The council referred in its brief to the proposal to establish an Ontario Institute for the Arts which it had made to the Provincial Committee on Aims and Objectives. Such an institute, operating under the administration of the council, would co-ordinate its efforts with those of the universities, the colleges of applied arts and technology, the Ontario Institute for Studies in Education, and local school boards in various educational projects. It would respond to the numerous requests being received from the presidents of the colleges of applied arts and technology for assistance in developing courses in applied arts, and from university presidents, who were attempting to enlarge the scope of their arts offerings. It would be concerned with artistic methodology, course content and enrichment, and the facilitation of artists' tours and the work of artistic organizations throughout the school system. Its activities might eventually extend into artistic experimentation with new media, psychological and sociological research in the arts, interrelated arts programs and curricula, and interdisciplinary artistic activity.

The brief suggested that the proposed institute could be established with a minimal financial outlay, since a network of artistic organizations and a fund of artistic and educational talent already existed. The role of the institute would be to cement these organizations together and to commission the best available people to carry out the necessary functions. The main needs were for co-ordination and leadership.

In its fifth annual report for 1968–9, the council unfolded a five-year plan for the future discharge of its functions. As a reason for devising this long-term approach, it referred to its disenchantment with parcelling out money to arts groups. The problem was that there were so many worthy groups that available funds, if apportioned among all of them, would not give any one of them a useful sum. Further, operating grants were described as demeaning to the suppliant, as well as being self-escalating. A more rewarding alternative seemed to be to provide a climate in which the arts could flourish, an objective that might be attained through program grants.

The first program was the Co-ordinated Arts Service, which was established along the lines suggested in the brief to the Prime Minister. A single staff was trying to handle the marketing, accounting, and publicity for all groups instead of having each one operate independently. There were plans for a cost control system, to be implemented with computers. Revenue was to be increased through fund raising, audience development, and a multiple box office network. It would ultimately be possible to phone in requests for tickets for a performance by any of the participating agencies, and to obtain immediate booking or a statement of the options.

The second major program was the Regional Arts Service, an attempt to develop cultural and educational activities in various parts of the province and to de-magnetize in some degree the cultural power centre of Metropolitan Toronto. The service was expected to bring personal expression back to the villages and towns, to encourage fledgling groups as they cropped up, and to buttress those already there. The program was designed in phases. During the first, in 1969–70, two pilot regions, one in the northern part of the province and one in the south, were to be studied intensively as a means of revealing their resources, potential, and problems. In the next phase, to be reached in 1970–1, regional conferences would be held to work out programs based on the analysis of the pilot studies. At the same time, surveys in accordance with techniques learned from the first two would be launched in three other regions, to be followed by similar efforts in the other five in 1972–4. Every effort would be made to devise a unique service for each region based on its own characteristic style.

The third program was a revised form of the Institute for Art Education, a name which had been dropped in favour of the Centre for Arts Research, from which the acronym CARE was derived. It would bring together specialists from the agencies mentioned in the brief to the Prime Minister, in addition to world ranking professional artists and educational television personnel, to develop a systematic approach to art education. It would devise a series of creative programs in music, drama, dance, film, and other fields, to be carried on in the classroom. It would supervise the distribution to the schools of media packages consisting of films, tapes, kinescopes, and records produced by poets, film-makers, actors, and composers. Talented students would assist in the recording, using the media equipment currently being acquired in many Ontario schools.

Additional aspects of CARE are described in the report.

> The centre would provide an overhead theatrical grid system. There are hook-ups for lighting, sound recording, cameras. When needed, the centre beams light and sound film outdoors; in effect, it turns itself inside out. It would be connected by closed circuit TV to activity centres in other regions. Cross-regional seminars, rehearsals and productions would be common ...
>
> The centre would be both an entertainment and a locus for a new kind of art education. It would stress the composite nature of art. It would stress personal enjoyment. It would join the classical arts with the new art vehicle, the electronic media.
>
> It would ... reflect the interbreeding of forms, the cracking of icons, the immediacy, the mobility, the involvement.

Like many other worthy enterprises, the programs of the council have been restricted by lack of all the funds its members believe they could spend productively. Their enthusiasm is, however, impressive, and should ensure that the organization fills a useful role in the future.

Notes

CHAPTER 1

1 J.M. McCutcheon, *Public Education in Ontario* (Toronto: T.H. Best, 1941), p. 213.
2 Ontario, Department of Education, *Report of the Minister's Committee on the Training of Elementary School Teachers, 1966*, C.R. MacLeod, chairman, p. 6.
3 *Report of the Royal Commission on Education in Ontario, 1950*, J.A. Hope, chairman (Toronto, King's Printer, 1950), p. 185.
4 R.S. Harris, *Quiet Evolution: A Study of the Educational System of Ontario* (Toronto: University of Toronto Press, 1967), pp. 73–4.
5 C.E. Phillips, *The Development of Education in Canada* (Toronto: W.J. Gage, 1957), p. 577.
6 McCutcheon, *Public Education in Ontario*, pp. 216–17.
7 *Ibid.*, pp. 217–18.
8 Harris, *Quiet Evolution*, pp. 73–4.
9 J.G. Althouse, *The Ontario Teacher, 1800–1910* (Toronto: W.J. Gage, 1967), p. 86.
10 McCutcheon, *Public Education in Ontario*, p. 223.
11 *Ibid.*, p. 221.
12 *Ibid.*, p. 224.
13 *Report of the Royal Commission on Education in Ontario, 1950*, p. 453.
14 Phillips, *The Development of Education in Canada*, p. 583.
15 Ontario, Legislative Assembly, *Debates*, 24th leg., 5th sess., 16 March 1955, p. 809.
16 *Ibid.*, 14 March 1956, p. 1035.
17 *Ibid.*, 25th leg., 4th sess., 12 March 1958, p. 775.
18 *Ibid.*
19 Ontario, Department of Education, Memorandum re Admission to Teachers' Colleges in September 1957, Circular 611, Toronto, 6 August 1956, C.F. Cannon, Deputy Minister of Education.
20 Ontario, Department of Education, Memorandum to Principals of Secondary Schools re Academic Requirements for Admission to the Pre-Teachers' College Summer Course, First Year, 1959, 1958–59:28, Toronto, 5 January 1959, F.S. Rivers, Deputy Minister of Education.
21 Ontario, Legislative Assembly, *Debates*, 27th leg., 4th sess., 29 March 1966, p. 2009.
22 *Ibid.*, 28th leg., 1st sess., 6 June 1968, p. 4050.

23 Ontario, Department of Education, Memorandum to School Officials re Acceptance of Graduates from the Ontario College of Art for Teacher Education, 1967–68:46, 31 January 1968, G.L. Duffin, Assistant Deputy Minister.
24 Ontario, Department of Education, *Report of the Minister, 1939*, p. 29.
25 *Ibid.*, *Report of the Minister, 1965*, p. 20.
26 R.E. Jones, "The Tradition of Special Education," *Toronto Education Quarterly*, IV, 2, Winter 1964–65, pp. 3–4.
27 Ontario, Legislative Assembly, *Debates*, 24th leg., 4th sess., 23 March 1954, p. 733.
28 *Ibid.*, 26th leg., 3rd sess., 10 April 1962, p. 2205.

CHAPTER 2

1 J.M. McCutcheon, *Public Education in Ontario* (Toronto: T.H. Best, 1941), p. 223.
2 A Report on the Normal Schools of the Province of Ontario by a Committee of the Ontario Normal School Teachers' Association, H. Bowers, chairman, 15 December 1960.
3 *Ibid.*, pp. 4–5.
4 *Ibid.*, p. 11.
5 *Ibid.*, p. 6.
6 *Ibid.*, p. 12.
7 *Ibid.*, pp. 14–15.
8 *Ibid.*, p. 19.
9 *Ibid.*, p. 27.
10 *Ibid.*, p. 59.
11 John Rogers, "Ottawa Teachers' College: Past, Present and Future," *Ontario Education News*, II, 2, February 1966, pp. 2–3.
12 Report of Teachers' Colleges Final Examination Committee to Mr. G.L. Woodruff, Director, Teacher Education Branch, p. 2.
13 Louise Rachlis, "Teacher Education & Professional Development," *New Dimensions in Education*, IV, 3, pp. 3–6.
14 Elizabeth A. Thorn, "The Implications of Language Experience Programs for Teachers' Colleges," paper presented to the Teacher Education Section of the Ontario Educational Association, March 1969, p. 7.

CHAPTER 3

1 *Report of the Royal Commission on Education in Ontario, 1950*, J.A. Hope, chairman (Toronto: King's Printer, 1950), p. 577.
2 *Ibid.*, p. 575.
3 *Ibid.*, p. 579.
4 Ontario, Legislative Assembly, *Debates*, 25th leg., 5th sess., 10 March 1959, p. 1002.
5 *Report of the Royal Commission on Education in Manitoba*, R.O. MacFarlane, chairman (Winnipeg: Queen's Printer, 1959), pp. 93–5.
6 Frank MacKinnon, *The Politics of Education: A Study of the Political Administration of the Public Schools* (Toronto: University of Toronto Press, 1960), p. 165.
7 *Ibid.*, p. 166.
8 Ontario, Department of Education, *Report of the Minister's Committee on the Training of*

Elementary School Teachers, 1966, C.R. MacLeod, chairman, p. 13.

9 *Ibid.*, p. 16.

10 J. Bascom St John, "The World of Learning," *Globe and Mail*, 20 December 1963.

11 Ontario, Department of Education, *Report of the Minister's Committee on the Training of Secondary School Teachers, 1962*, F.G. Patten, chairman.

12 *Report of the Minister's Committee on the Training of Elementary School Teachers, 1966*, p. 15.

13 R.M. Stamp, "Wanted: A Total Commitment to Teacher Preparation," *Bulletin*, XLVIII, 4, October 1968, pp. 245–7.

14 V.S. Ready, "Always There Stands the Teacher," *Bulletin*, XLVII, 2, March 1967, p. 58.

15 *Report of the Minister's Committee on the Training of Elementary School Teachers, 1966*, p. 16.

16 Ontario Association for Curriculum Development, Report of the Ontario Conference on Education, "Education of Elementary Teachers," Windsor, November 1961, p. 59.

17 Northrop Frye, ed., *Design for Learning*, Reports submitted to the Joint Committee of the Toronto Board of Education and the University of Toronto (Toronto: University of Toronto Press, 1962), p. 61.

18 *Ibid.*, p. 100.

19 McMaster University, Senate Committee on the Training of Elementary School Teachers, "Report to the Senate," F.R. Smith, chairman, 19 September 1967, p. 6. (Mimeographed.)

20 MacKinnon, *Politics of Education*, pp. 100–1.

21 Harold J. Uhlman, "Teacher Training at the Crossroads," paper prepared for presentation at the annual meeting of the Canadian Association of Professors of Education, Charlottetown, Prince Edward Island, 9 June 1964, p. 2.

22 F. Henry Johnson, "The Education of Canadian Teachers: Retrospect and Prospect," presidential address to the Canadian Association of Professors of Education Annual Conference, University of British Columbia, June 1965, p. 6.

23 Seymour Metzner, "The Teacher Preparation Myth: A Phoenix Too Frequent," *Phi Delta Kappan*, L, 2, October 1968, pp. 105–6.

CHAPTER 4

1 Ontario, Legislative Assembly, *Debates*, 27th leg., 4th sess., 29 March 1966, p. 2009.

2 Ontario, Department of Education, *Report of the Minister's Committee on the Training of Elementary School Teachers, 1966*, C.R. MacLeod, chairman, p. 1.

3 *Ibid.*, p. 53.

4 Ontario, Legislative Assembly, *Debates*, 27th leg., 4th sess., 29 March 1966, p. 2009.

5 Ontario, Provincial Committee on Aims and Objectives of Education in the Schools of Ontario, *Living and Learning* (Toronto: Newton Publishing Company,

1968), p. 129.

6 Ontario, Department of Education, Memorandum to School Officials re Internship Plan for the Training of Elementary School Teachers, 1965–66:49, 4 February 1966, H.E. Elborn, Assistant Deputy Minister of Education.

7 V.S. Ready, "Always There Stands the Teacher," *Bulletin*, XLVII, 2, March 1967, p. 59.

8 *Report of the Minister's Committee on the Training of Elementary School Teachers, 1966*, p. 52.

9 Ontario, Legislative Assembly, *Debates*, 27th leg., 5th sess., 25 May 1967, pp. 3842–5.

10 *Ibid.*

11 Committee of Presidents of Universities of Ontario, *Collective Autonomy: Second Annual Review 1967/68* (Toronto, 1968), p. 21.

12 Ontario, Legislative Assembly, *Debates*, 28th leg., 1st sess., 6 June 1968, p. 4054.

13 A.B. Hodgetts, *What Culture? What Heritage?: A Study of Civic Education in Canada* (Toronto: Ontario Institute for Studies in Education, 1968), p. 103.

CHAPTER 5

1 Ontario, Department of Education, *Report of the Minister's Committee on the Training of Secondary School Teachers, 1962*, F.G. Patten, chairman, p. 36.

2 J.M. McCutcheon, *Public Education in Ontario* (Toronto: T.H. Best, 1941), pp. 226–7.

3 *Report of the Minister's Committee on the Training of Secondary School Teachers, 1962*, p. 36.

4 *Ibid.*, p. 37.

5 McCutcheon, *Public Education in Ontario*, p. 36.

6 Edwin C. Guillet, *In the Cause of Education: Centennial History of the Ontario Educational Association, 1861–1960* (Toronto: University of Toronto Press, 1960), p. 224.

7 *Report of the Royal Commission on Education in Ontario, 1950*, J.A. Hope, chairman (Toronto: King's Printer, 1950), p. 757.

8 University of Toronto, *President's Report for the Year Ended June 1961* (Toronto: University of Toronto Press, 1961), p. 7.

9 *Ibid.*, p. 52.

10 *Report of the Minister's Committee on the Training of Secondary School Teachers, 1962*, p. 5.

11 J. Bascom St John, "The World of Learning," *Globe and Mail*, 2 February 1963.

12 *Report of the Minister's Committee on the Training of Secondary School Teachers, 1962*, pp. 31–2.

13 St John, "The World of Learning," *Globe and Mail*, 2 February 1963.

14 University of Toronto, *President's Report for the Year Ended June 1963* (Toronto: University of Toronto Press, 1964), p. 74.

15 J. Bascom St John, "The World of Learning," *Globe and Mail*,

18 March 1963.
16 Ontario, Legislative Assembly, *Debates*, 26th leg., 1st sess., 28 March 1960, p. 1829.
17 University of Western Ontario, Althouse College of Education, *President's Report for the Academic Year Ending June 30, 1966*, "Report of the Dean" (London), p. 123.
18 University of Western Ontario, College of Education, *Calendar, 1965–66* (London), pp. 15–16.
19 University of Toronto, *President's Report for the Year Ended June 1966: Part One* (Toronto: University of Toronto Press, 1967), p. 88.
20 *Prospect*, Initial Faculty Report on the Role of the College of Education, University of Toronto, March 1967, p. 4.
21 University of Toronto, *President's Report for the Year Ended June 1964* (Toronto: University of Toronto Press, 1965), p. 69.
22 D.F. Dadson, "What's Ahead for OCE?" *Toronto Education Quarterly*, III, 1, Autumn 1963, p. 21.
23 University of Toronto, *President's Report for the Year Ended June 1967: Part One*, "Report of the Dean of the Ontario College of Education" (Toronto: University of Toronto Press, 1968), p. 84.
24 Letter from Maurice Chagnon, Vice-Rector (Academic), University of Ottawa, to "Leslie Woodruff, Superintendent, Teacher Education Branch, Department of Education," 27 January 1967.
25 Letter from W.G. Tamblyn, President, Lakehead University, to the Honourable William G. Davis, Minister of University Affairs, 21 December 1966.
26 Accompanying letter by T.A. Walter, Secretary-Treasurer, Nipigon-Red Rock District High School, Red Rock, Ontario, 20 November 1968.
27 Ontario, Legislative Assembly, *Debates*, 28th leg., 2nd sess., 20 December 1968, pp. 953–4.
28 Ontario, Legislative Assembly, *Debates*, 28th leg., 2nd sess., 25 November 1969, p. 8893.

CHAPTER 6

1 University of Toronto, *President's Report for the Year Ended June 1965* (Toronto: University of Toronto Press, 1966), p. 77.
2 Ontario, Department of Education, Memorandum to School Officials re (1) number of options required at Ontario Colleges of Education, (2) extension of jurisdiction of Ontario Basic Teaching Certificates (Elementary and Secondary), (3) Letters of Standing (Secondary), (4) Letters of Permission; 1965–66:44, 21 January 1966, H.E. Elborn.
3 University of Toronto, *President's Report for the Year Ended June 1966: Part One* (Toronto: University of Toronto Press, 1967), p. 89.
4 *Prospect*, Initial Faculty Report on the Role of the College of Education, University of Toronto, March 1967, pp. 8–9.

CHAPTER 7

1 Ontario, Department of Education, Memorandum to Secondary School Principals and Secretaries of Secondary School Boards, "Steps Required re Applicant Taking Special Summer Courses," 1956–57:26, 5 March 1957, S.D. Rendall, Superintendent of Secondary Education.

2 Ontario, Department of Education, Memorandum to Principals of Secondary Schools re Supervision of Teachers-in-Training Who Attended the Special Ten-week Summer Course in 1957, 1957–58:5, 3 September 1957, S.D. Rendall, Superintendent of Secondary Education.

3 Ontario, Department of Education, Memorandum to Principals of Secondary Schools re Supervision of Teachers-in-Training Who Attended the Special Ten-week Summer Course in 1958, 1958–59:6, 2 September 1958, S.D. Rendall, Superintendent of Secondary Education.

4 Ontario, Legislative Assembly, *Debates*, 25th leg., 3rd sess., 12 March 1957, p. 993.

5 *Ibid.*, 5th sess., 4 February 1959, p. 136.

6 *Ibid.*, 11 February 1959, p. 308.

7 J. Bascom St John, "Dean Forecasts Teacher Surplus in Two Years," *Globe and Mail*, 12 February 1959.

8 Ontario, Department of Education, Memorandum to School Officials re Training of Commercial Teachers, 1962, 1961–62:33, S.D. Rendall, Superintendent of Secondary Education, 15 January 1962.

9 Ontario, Legislative Assembly, *Debates*, 27th leg., 5th sess., 25 May 1967, p. 3784.

10 *Prospect*, Initial Faculty Report on the Role of the College of Education, University of Toronto, March 1967, pp. 11–12.

11 Ontario, Legislative Assembly, *Debates*, 28th leg., 1st sess., 26 March 1968, p. 1226.

12 *Ibid.*, 4 June 1968, p. 3892.

13 *Ibid.*, 2nd sess., 16 December 1968, p. 712.

14 *Ibid.*, 3 March 1969, p. 1758.

CHAPTER 8

1 Charles E. Phillips, *The Development of Education in Canada* (Toronto: W.J. Gage, 1957), p. 591.

2 Robin S. Harris, *Quiet Evolution: A Study of the Educational System of Ontario* (Toronto: University of Toronto Press, 1967), p. 82.

3 *Report of the Royal Commission on Education in Ontario, 1950*, J.A. Hope, chairman (Toronto: King's Printer, 1950), p. 584.

4 *Ibid.*, p. 587.

5 Ontario, Legislative Assembly, *Debates*, 25th leg., 3rd sess., 12 March 1957, p. 993.

6 D.F. Dadson, "What's Ahead for OCE?" *Toronto Education Quarterly*, III, 1, Autumn 1963, pp. 19–23.

7 V.S. Ready, "Always There Stands the Teacher," *Bulletin*, XLVII, 2, March 1967, p. 57.

8 *Prospect*, Initial Faculty Report on the Role of the College of Education, University of To-

ronto, March 1967, p. 10.

9 Ontario, Department of Education, *Report of the Minister's Committee on the Training of Secondary School Teachers, 1962*, F.G. Patten, chairman, pp. 20–1.

10 University of Toronto, *President's Report for the Year Ended June 1963* (Toronto: University of Toronto Press, 1964), p. 75.

11 *Ibid.*

12 Ontario, Legislative Assembly, *Debates*, 27th leg., 2nd sess., 28 April 1964, p. 2555.

13 *Ibid.*, 30 April 1964, pp. 2639–45.

14 Queen's University, *McArthur College of Education Calendar, 1968/69*, First Session, p. 8.

CHAPTER 9

1 Ontario, Department of Education, Summer Courses, 1955, *General Announcement*, pp. 7–8.

2 Ontario, Department of Education, Memorandum to School Officials re Proposed Summer Course for Heads of Departments, 1961–62:24, 11 December 1961, S.D. Rendall, Superintendent of Secondary Education.

3 Ontario, Department of Education, Memorandum to School Officials re Special Intensive Course for Developing French Fluency of Teachers of French (Elementary and Secondary) to be Offered during the Summer of 1966, 1965–66:12, 1 October 1965, H.E. Elborn, Assistant Deputy Minister.

4 F.J. Clute, "Comment: On Counsellor Education," *Canadian Counsellor*, III, April 1969, pp. 61–2.

5 *Ibid.*

6 Ontario, Department of Education, Memorandum to School Officials re 1. Updating Course for Electrical Teachers; 2. Continuing Programs of Study in the Secondary Schools, 1965–66:78, 17 May 1966, H.E. Elborn, Assistant Deputy Minister.

7 Ontario, Department of Education, *Report of the Minister, 1967*, p. 5.

8 Ontario, Department of Education, Memorandum to School Officials re Board-Sponsored Winter Courses for Teachers, for Certificate Credit, 1964–65:32, 2 December 1964, F.S. Rivers, Chief Director.

9 Ontario, Department of Education, Memorandum to School Officials re University Refresher Courses in Chemistry, 1965–66:36, 8 December 1965, H.E. Elborn, Assistant Deputy Minister.

10 "O.S.S.T.F. Conducts Successful Summer Courses in Physics and Chemistry at Harbord C.I." *Bulletin*, XXXV, 6, 30 November 1955, p. 298.

11 "Many Teachers Attend O.S.S.T.F. Refresher Courses," *Bulletin*, XXXVIII, 4, 30 September 1958, p. 205.

12 J.D. McNabb, "Professional Development Committee Serves Profession Well," *Bulletin*, XLIII, 1, 31 January 1963, p. 17.

13 "Conference on Updating Held

at Toronto Education Centre," *Bulletin*, XLVI, 1, 31 January 1966, pp. 17–21.

14 Ontario, Department of Education, Memorandum for Principals and Teachers of Secondary Vocational Schools re Refresher Trade Courses, 20 February 1957, S.D. Rendall, Superintendent of Secondary Education.

CHAPTER 10

1 Desmond Pacey, "Research in the Humanities," Association of Universities and Colleges of Canada, *Proceedings of Annual Meeting* (Montreal, Quebec, 1967), p. 133.

2 *Educational Research: A Parent's Concern* (Ottawa: Canadian Council for Research in Education, 1965), p. 15.

3 R.W. Kluge, "What Research Methods from Industry are Applicable in Educational Research?" *Meeting the Challenge of Tomorrow through Research Today*. Report to the Western New York School Board Institute, 1956, p. 9.

4 John Strickler, Jr, "How Does Industry Justify the Expenditure of Large Sums of Money for Research?" *Meeting the Challenge of Tomorrow through Research Today*. Report to the Western New York School Board Institute, 1956, p. 3.

5 Robert S. Donaldson, *Fortifying Higher Education: A Story of College Self Studies* (New York: Fund for the Advancement of Education, 1959), pp. 5–6.

6 J.C. Morrison, "Pressing Needs in Research," *Current Educational Research Activities, New York State 1961–62* (Albany: University of the State of New York, 1962), p. 178.

7 Michael Scriven, "The Philosophy of Science in Educational Research," *Review of Educational Research*, XXX, 5, December 1960, p. 426.

8 William B. Michael, "Teacher Personnel: A Brief Evaluation of the Research Reviewed," *Review of Educational Research*, XXXIII, 4, October 1963, p. 443.

9 From an edited version of an interrogation on "Education: A Question of Excellence," *Toronto Education Quarterly*, IV, 1, Autumn 1964, pp. 15–16.

10 Robert L. Ebel, "Some Limitations of Basic Research in Education," *Phi Delta Kappan*, XLIX, 2, October 1967, pp. 81–4.

11 Derek H. Morrell, *Education and Change*, Annual Joseph Payne Memorial Lectures 1965–66 of the College of Preceptors (London, WC1, May 1966), p. 19.

12 *Ibid.*

13 University of Toronto, *President's Report for the Year Ended 1962* (Toronto: University of Toronto Press, 1962), p. 3.

14 M. LaFountaine, "Too Many Masters," address delivered at a Conference of the Canadian Council for Research in Education, June 1964, reported in the *Toronto Education Quarterly*, IV, 1, Autumn 1964, p. 29.

15 Morrell, *Education and Change*, p. 16.
16 F.G. Robinson, "Research in Education. Encouraging Staff Research: A Challenge for Principals and Inspectors," *School Progress*, xxxiv, 2, February 1965, p. 11.
17 *Ibid.*

CHAPTER 11

1 Charles E. Phillips, *The Development of Education in Canada* (Toronto: W.J. Gage, 1957), p. 427.
2 J.M. McCutcheon, *Public Education in Ontario* (Toronto: T.H. Best, 1941), p. 87.
3 *Report of the Royal Commission on Education in Ontario, 1950*, J.A. Hope, chairman (Toronto: King's Printer, 1950), pp. 159–60.
4 *Ibid.*, p. 161.
5 Ontario, Legislative Assembly, *Debates*, 25th leg., 5th sess., 18 February 1959, pp. 427–8.
6 Northrop Frye, ed., *Design for Learning*, Reports submitted to the Joint Committee of the Toronto Board of Education and the University of Toronto (Toronto: University of Toronto Press, 1962), p. 3.
7 University of Toronto, *President's Report for the Year Ended June 1961* (Toronto: University of Toronto Press, 1961), p. 8.
8 Frye, ed., *Design for Learning*, pp. 6–7.
9 Roy C. Sharp, "The Curriculum Institute: A Proposal," keynote address at the Curriculum Conference held on November 2, 1962, Education Centre, Toronto, cited in *Toronto Education Quarterly*, II, 2, Winter 1962–63, p. 2.
10 *Ibid.*, p. 4.
11 J.R.H. Morgan, "The Ontario Curriculum Institute," *Education: A Collection of Essays on Canadian Education*, v, 1962–1964 (Toronto: W.J. Gage, 1965), p. 79.
12 Sharp, "Curriculum Institute: A Proposal," *Toronto Education Quarterly*, II, 2, Winter 1962–63, p. 5.
13 Brian Burnham, ed., *New Designs for Learning: Highlights of the Reports of the Ontario Curriculum Institute, 1963–1966* (Toronto: University of Toronto Press for Ontario Institute for Studies in Education, 1967), p. vi.
14 J.R.H. Morgan, "We Need Curriculum Study," *Bulletin*, XLIV, 6, December 1964, p. 546.
15 Burnham, ed., *New Designs for Learning*, p. 97.
16 Sharp, "Curriculum Institute: A Proposal," p. 5.
17 Karl S. Bernhardt, Margaret L. Fletcher, Frances L. Johnson, Dorothy A. Millichamp, Mary L. Northway, eds., *Twenty-five Years of Child Study* (Toronto: University of Toronto Press, 1951), pp. 15–17.
18 *Ibid.*, pp. 19–20.
19 University of Toronto, *President's Report for the Year Ended June 1959* (Toronto: University of Toronto Press, 1959), p. 75.
20 University of Toronto, *President's Report for the Year*

Ended June 1967: Part One (Toronto: University of Toronto Press, 1968), p. 202.

21 Dormer Ellis, *The M.T.E.R.C.: An Account of Its Activities and Accomplishments*, Research Publication 7 (Metropolitan Toronto Educational Research Council), p. 3. (All of the present section is heavily dependent on this report.)

CHAPTER 12

1 A.S. Barr, R.A. Davis, and P.O. Johnson, *Educational Research and Appraisal* (Chicago: J.B. Lippincott, 1953), p. 3.

2 C.C. Kohl, "Needed Research on the Programme of Studies," *Journal of Educational Psychology*, III, 1, January 1912, pp. 160–1, in *ibid.*, p. 5.

3 Ontario Public School Men Teachers' Federation, Educational Research Committee, Sam Steele, chairman, "Teachers' Committee Makes Statement on Curriculum and Methods," *School*, Elementary Edition, XXXII, 10, June 1944, p. 854.

4 Toronto Assistant Masters' Association, "A Statement on Juvenile Delinquency," *School*, Elementary Edition, XXXII, 10, June 1944, p. 875.

5 K.A. McRobbie, "Educational Research in Ontario: A Preliminary Survey of Experimental and Research Projects in Ontario (a) Completed during the Period July 1958–June 1959, and (b) Planned for the Future," Ontario Educational Research Council, Report No. I, September 1959. (Mimeographed.)

6 Willard Brehaut, "A Quarter Century of Educational Research in Canada: An Analysis of Dissertations (English) in Education Accepted by Canadian Universities, 1930–1955" (Ed D thesis; University of Toronto, 1958).

7 R.W.B. Jackson, "An Appraisal of the Effects of the Atkinson and Carnegie Studies on Educational Progress in Ontario," July 1966. (Mimeographed.)

8 Ontario, Legislative Assembly, *Debates*, 27th leg., 3rd sess., 2 June 1965, p. 3582.

9 University of Toronto, *President's Report for the Year Ended June 1959* (Toronto: University of Toronto Press, 1959), p. 75.

10 University of Toronto, *Institute of Child Study Calendar, 1965–66*, p. 19.

CHAPTER 13

1 Ontario, Legislative Assembly, *Debates*, 27th leg., 2nd sess., 29 April 1964, p. 2587.

2 Memorandum to W.G. Davis, Minister, Department of Education from J. Bascom St John, Director, Policy and Development Council, "A Proposal Concerning Educational Research," 8 October 1964.

3 W.G. Fleming, Assistant Director, Department of Educational Research, to C.T. Bissell, President, University of Toronto, 9 November 1964.

4 13–14 Eliz. 2, Bill 127, 3rd sess., 27th leg., Ontario, "An Act to Establish The Ontario Institute

for Studies in Education," p. 4.

5 George E. Flower, "Points re Relationship with University of Toronto," paper presented for use in planning the establishment of the Ontario Institute for Studies in Education, 26 January 1965.

6 George E. Flower, "The Case for Concentrating Graduate Studies in Education in the Proposed Ontario Institute for Studies in Education," working paper, 2 March 1965.

7 J.R.H. Morgan, Director, Ontario Curriculum Institute, to the Honourable William Davis, Minister of Education, 12 April 1965.

8 F.G. Robinson, "Educational Research in Canada: An Analysis of Potential, Current Status, and Needed Development," 18 January 1965. (Mimeographed.)

9 "Center for Education," *Harvard Alumni Bulletin*, October 1964, pp. 60–1.

10 Ontario, Department of Education, Memorandum to School Officials re Procedure with Regard to the Approval of Research Projects in Schools, 1966–67:50, 5 December 1966, G.L. Duffin, Assistant Deputy Minister.

11 In this section, it has been the usual practice to avoid quoting from minutes or other non-public documents. In the interests of absolute accuracy, that practice has been departed from here, although the anonymity of the source is preserved.

12 Ontario Institute for Studies in Education, Graduate Students' Association, Constitution and By-Laws, article 1, section 2, amended, 23 May 1969.

13 Ontario Institute for Studies in Education, "Report of the Development Review Board, 15 January 1969." (Mimeographed.)

14 Ontario Institute for Studies in Education, Board of Governors, *Report of the Special Committee*, V.S. Ready, chairman, October 1969, pp. 1–2.

15 *Ibid.*, pp. 26–7.

16 Ontario, Legislative Assembly, *Debates*, 28th leg., 1st sess., 6 June 1968, pp. 4092–3.

17 Committee on Religious Education in the Public Schools of the Province of Ontario, Report of the Committee, *Religious Information and Moral Development*, J. Keiller Mackay, chairman (Toronto: Ontario Department of Education, 1969), p. 41.

18 The writer was given only an oral statement about this occurrence from a local official. The evidence must therefore be described as "hearsay," although there are no particular grounds for suspecting its accuracy.

19 J.D. McNabb, "A Functional Approach to O.I.S.E.," *Bulletin*, XLVIII, 2, March 1968, pp. 71–2.

20 Ontario, Provincial Committee on Aims and Objectives of Education in the Schools of Ontario, *Living and Learning* (Toronto: Newton Publishing, 1968), p. 164.

21 *Ibid.*, p. 165.

22 *Ibid.*, p. 166.
23 Ontario, Legislative Assembly, *Debates*, 28th leg., 2nd sess., 6 November 1969, p. S-125.
24 *Ibid.*, p. S-126.
25 *Ibid.*, p. S-132.
26 *Ibid.*, p. S-127.
27 *Ibid.*, p. S-138.
28 *Ibid.*, pp. S-129–S-130.
29 *Ibid.*, p. S-140.
30 "A Horrible Example of Waste in Education," *Globe and Mail*, 11 April 1970.
31 Martin O'Malley, "Just Ask OISE," *Globe and Mail*, 11 April 1970.
32 Cicely Watson, "Future Directions for the Office of R & D Studies," 10 February 1970, pp. 33–4.

CHAPTER 14

1 Ontario Institute for Studies in Education, *First Annual Report of the Board of Governors, 1965–66* (Toronto: Ontario Institute for Studies in Education, 1966).
2 Curriculum Division is an abbreviated name which emerged later.
3 Derek H. Morrell, *Education and Change*, Annual Joseph Payne Memorial Lectures, 1965–66 of the College of Preceptors (London, W.C. 1, May 1966), p. 12.
4 Ontario Institute for Studies in Education, *Annual Report of the Board of Governors, 1966–67* (Toronto: Ontario Institute for Studies in Education, 1968), p. 17.
5 Ontario Institute for Studies in Education, *Annual Report of the Board of Governors, 1967–68* (Toronto: Ontario Institute for Studies in Education, 1968), pp. 36–8.
6 Ontario Institute for Studies in Education, Office of Development, "The Development Program of OISE 1967–8," Toronto, 6 February 1968. (Mimeographed.)
7 Ontario Institute for Studies in Education, "Report of the Development Review Board, 15 January 1969," p. 8 (Mimeographed.)

CHAPTER 15

1 Honora M. Cochrane, ed., *Centennial Story: The Board of Education for the City of Toronto, 1850–1950* (Toronto: Thomas Nelson & Sons, 1950), pp. 44–5.
2 C.A. Brown, "Ontario's Grade 13: Guidelines from the Past," lecture delivered at the Ontario College of Education as part of the Centennial Series, "Between High School and University in 1967," Toronto, February 1969, p. 7.
3 J.M. McCutcheon, *Public Education in Ontario* (Toronto: T.H. Best, 1941), p. 160.
4 Ontario, Department of Education, "The Grade 13 Departmental Examinations," February 1960, p. 1. (Mimeographed.)
5 *Ibid.*, p. 2.
6 McCutcheon, *Public Education in Ontario*, p. 169.
7 These are summarized from Board minutes in "The Grade 13 Departmental Examinations," p. 5.

8 Ontario, Department of Education, *Courses of Study for the Public and Separate Schools, 1936*, p. 34.
9 Department of Education, "Grade 13 Departmental Examinations," p. 10.
10 Ontario, Department of Education, Memorandum to Principals of Secondary Schools, Principals of Inspected Private Schools, Members of Secondary School Boards and Boards of Education re the Marking of Grade 13 Departmental Examination Papers, 1959–60:23, 15 November 1959.
11 Department of Education, "Grade 13 Departmental Examinations," p. 15.
12 *Ibid.*, p. 17.
13 Northrop Frye, ed., *Design for Learning*. Reports submitted to the Joint Committee of the Toronto Board of Education and the University of Toronto (Toronto: University of Toronto Press, 1962), p. 109.
14 Department of Education, "Grade 13 Departmental Examinations," p. 26.
15 Ontario, Department of Education, Memorandum to Principals and Teachers of Secondary Schools, and Secretaries of Secondary School Boards re Grade 13 Departmental Examinations, 1960, 1958–59:32, 21 January 1959.
16 Information from this entire paragraph is from an unsigned Memorandum for the Deputy Ministers and the Chief Director for the Information of the Minister, 12 March 1958.
17 Ontario, Department of Education, "The Grade 13 Departmental Examinations: Report and Suggestions," November 1960, Foreword. (This report ends with the names of the members of the Committee on Grade 13 Examinations: C.A. Brown, R.W.B. Jackson, A.H. McKague, and G.J. Westwood.) (Mimeographed.)
18 Memorandum to the Chief Director, and the Deputy Ministers for the Information of the Minister re the Grade 13 Examinations, C.A. Brown, 5 May 1960.
19 Department of Education, "The Grade 13 Departmental Examinations: Report and Suggestions," chapter 2, pp. 2–3.
20 *Ibid.*, p. 3.
21 F.C. Asbury, "Objectives for 1960," *Bulletin*, XXXIX, 1, 31 January 1959, pp. 23–4.
22 Ontario, Department of Education, Memorandum to Principals and Teachers of Secondary Schools, and Secretaries of Secondary School Boards re Grade 13 Departmental Examinations, 1960, 1958–59:32, 21 January 1959.
23 Ontario, Department of Education, Memorandum to Secondary School Principals re Preparation of Objective-type Test Items for Grade 13 Departmental Examinations, 1958–59:38, 16 February 1959.
24 Ontario, Legislative Assembly, *Debates*, 27th leg., 2nd sess., 30 April 1964, p. 2666.
25 Ontario, Department of Education, Memorandum to School

Officials re Study of the Grade 13 Departmental Examinations, 1960–61:37, 30 December, 1960.

26 Report of the Special Committee of the University Matriculation Board on the Grade 13 Examination System, March 1961.

27 *Ibid.*, p. 7.

28 Ontario, Department of Education, Memorandum to School Officials re Changes in the Regulations for the Grade 13 Departmental Examinations, 1961–62:44, 16 February 1962.

29 Ontario, Department of Education, Memorandum to Directors and Superintendents, Principals of Secondary Schools, and Principals of Private Schools re the Proposal for a Reduction in the Number of Papers on the Grade 13 Departmental Examinations, 1961–62:45, 15 February 1962.

30 Ontario, Department of Education, Memorandum to School Officials re Reduction in the Number of Papers in Certain Grade 13 Subjects, 1962–63:26, 10 December 1962.

31 J. Bascom St John, "Examinations: Grade 13," *Globe and Mail*, 17 December 1962.

32 Letters from Mrs. M.C. Harvey, Secretary, Thornbury District High School, to Registrar, Department of Education, 29 April 1963.

33 Bruce L. Scott, Secretary-Treasurer, Renfrew and District Collegiate Institute Board, to C.W. Booth, Deputy Minister of Education, 25 April 1963.

34 A.C. Ritter, Director of Education, Board of Education for the City of Kingston, to C.W. Booth, 1 February 1963.

35 S.G.B. Robinson, General Secretary, Ontario Secondary School Teachers' Federation, to C.A. Brown, Registrar, Department of Education, 24 April 1963.

36 This Committee consisted at the time of C.A. Brown, Registrar; A.W. Bishop, Assistant Superintendent, Registrar's Branch; A.H. McKague, Assistant Superintendent, Secondary Education Branch; G.J. Westwood, Assistant Registrar; R.W.B. Jackson, Director, Department of Educational Research; and W.G. Fleming, Assistant Director, Department of Educational Research.

37 Ontario, Department of Education, *The Study of the Grade 13 Departmental Examinations with particular reference to marking procedures*, Study Paper No. 13, 12 November 1963.

38 The experiment was in one sense a success, in that it made possible the release of the results on 1 August, about ten days earlier than usual.

39 Ontario, Legislative Assembly, *Debates*, 27th leg., 2nd sess., 31 January 1964, p. 346.

40 *Ibid.*

41 *Report of the Grade 13 Study Committee, 1964*, F.A. Hamilton, chairman (Toronto: Ontario Department of Education, 26 June 1964), terms of reference.

42 *Ibid.*, pp. 4–5.
43 *Ibid.*, p. 5.
44 *Report on the Proposal for General and Advanced Levels of Instruction in Grade 13*, A.H. Dalzell and J.R. Thompson, co-chairmen (Toronto: Ontario Department of Education, 18 March 1965), p. 15.
45 *Report of the Grade 13 Study Committee, 1964*, pp. 22–5.
46 *Ibid.*, pp. 26–7.
47 Ontario, Department of Education, *Report of the Minister, 1964*, pp. 7–8.
48 Ontario, Department of Education, Memorandum to Officials Concerned with Secondary Education, 1964–65:39, 10 December 1964.
49 Ontario, Legislative Assembly, *Debates*, 27th leg., 3rd sess., 11 February 1965, p. 461.
50 *Ibid.*, 4th sess., 10 February 1966, p. 426.
51 Ontario, Department of Education, Memorandum to School Officials Concerned with Secondary Education re the Grade 13 Departmental Examination in English, 1966, 1965–66:19, 28 October 1965.
52 Ontario, Department of Education, Memorandum to School Officials re Grade 13 Departmental Examinations in Art, 1966, 1965–66:33, 4 January 1966.
53 Ontario, Department of Education, Memorandum to School Officials re the Grade 13 Departmental Examination in History, 1966, 1965–66:42, 5 January 1966.
54 Ontario, Legislative Assembly, *Debates*, 27th leg., 3rd sess., 3 June 1965, p. 3659.
55 *Ibid.*, 4th sess., 31 March 1966, p. 2102.
56 Ontario Teachers' Federation, "A Submission to the Minister of Education re Grade 13 Examinations," April 1966, p. 2. (Mimeographed.)
57 A.G. Scott, Headmaster, Trinity College School, to William G. Davis, 5 April 1966.
58 *Globe and Mail*, 1 April 1966.
59 *London Free Press*, 2 April 1966.
60 *Telegram*, 4 April 1966.
61 *Globe and Mail*, 4 April 1966.
62 Corbin A. Brown, "Ontario's Grade 13: Guidelines from the Past," lecture delivered at the Ontario College of Education as part of the Centennial Series, "Between High School and University in 1967," February 1969, pp. 19–22. (Mimeographed.)
63 Ontario, Department of Education, Memorandum to School Officials re Student Assessment in Grade 13, 1967–1968, 1966–67:98, 18 May 1967.
64 Ontario Teachers' Federation, "A Submission to the Minister of Education re Grade 13, January 1967," p. 2. (Mimeographed.)
65 *Ibid.*, p. 5.
66 Ontario Teachers' Federation, "A Submission to the Minister of Education re Grade 13," February 1967. (Mimeographed.)
67 Ontario, Legislative Assembly, *Debates*, 27th leg., 5th sess., 24 May 1967, p. 3768.

68 G.P. Wilkinson, "For Good or Ill," *Bulletin*, XLVII, 6, December 1967, p. 448.
69 H.H. Mosey, "The Philosophy and Operation of the Grade 13 Year," address given before Grade 13 workshop, *Headmaster*, Spring 1968, pp. 6–8.
70 G.P. Wilkinson, "The Old Order Changeth," *Bulletin*, XLVIII, 4, October 1968, p. 211.

CHAPTER 16

1 Report of the Special Committee of the University Matriculation Board on the Grade 13 Examination System, March 1961.
2 Ontario, Department of Education, Memorandum to School Officials, 1961–62:25, 1 December 1961.
3 *Ibid.*
4 Ontario Secondary School Teachers' Federation, "Report on the Survey Regarding Grade 12 Departmental Tests," sheet 1. (Mimeographed.)
5 Ontario Secondary School Headmasters' Association, "Results of O.S.S.H.A. Questionnaire re Advisability of a Uniform External Examination for Grade XII," sheet 5, p. 1. (Mimeographed.)
6 Memorandum for the Minister of Education, Report of the Committee Appointed to Consider the Advisability of Re-establishing a Uniform External Examination at the End of Grade 12 of the General Course, 18 June 1962.
7 Ontario, Department of Education, Memorandum to Officials Concerned with Secondary Education re The Grade 12 Departmental Examination in World History – Part II, 1965, 1964–65:23, 13 October 1964.
8 Ontario, Department of Education, Memorandum to School Officials re Final Examinations in Subjects of Grade 12, Four-Year Program, 1965–66:63, 16 March 1966, H.E. Elborn, Assistant Deputy Minister.

CHAPTER 17

1 Reported by Morris Sniderman, "Standardized Tests for Grade XII Pupils of the General Course," *Bulletin*, XXXVIII, 6, 10 December 1958, pp. 349–50.
2 "Standards in the Middle School," *School*, Secondary Edition, XXIX, 7, March 1941, pp. 619–45.
3 W.G. Fleming, *Personal and Academic Factors as Predictors of First Year Success in Ontario Universities*, Report No. 5, Atkinson Study of Utilization of Student Resources (Toronto: Department of Educational Research, Ontario College of Education, University of Toronto, 1959), Table IV.c.1.
4 W.G. Fleming, *Characteristics and Achievement of Students in Ontario Universities*, Report No. 11, Atkinson Study of Utilization of Student Resources (Toronto: Ontario Institute for Studies in Education, 1965), p. 181.
5 *Ibid.*, p. 183.
6 Ontario, Department of Education, Memorandum to School Officials re Grade 12 Departmental Tests 1960–61, 1960–

61:29, 28 October 1960, A.H. McKague for S.D. Rendall, Superintendent of Secondary Education.

CHAPTER 18

1 Ontario, *Report of the Grade 13 Study Committee, 1964*, F.A. Hamilton, chairman (Toronto, 5 February 1964), p. 29.
2 *OSAT Student Handbook: A Description of the Ontario Scholastic Aptitude Test* (Toronto: Ontario Institute for Studies in Education, 1967), p. 3.
3 Brief Submitted by the Association of Heads of English Departments in Toronto Secondary Schools on "The Testing of Composition" as presented to students of Grade 13, 1967 in the *Student Handbook* (Ontario Tests for Admission to College and University), July 1967. (Mimeographed.)
4 OACU, Ontario Tests for Admission to College and University, *1968 Student Handbook*, A Description of the Achievement Tests: Ontario Physics Achievement Test, Ontario Standard English Achievement Test, Ontario Mathematics Achievement Test (Toronto: Ontario Institute for Studies in Education, 1968), p. 4.
5 *Ibid.*, p. 5.
6 *Ibid.*, p. 20.
7 Ontario Institute for Studies in Education, Department of Measurement and Evaluation, *1968–69 Reference Manual and General Instructions for the Administration of the Tests for Admission to College and University in Ontario, Including the Tests of the Service for Admission to College and University* (Toronto: Ontario Institute for Studies in Education, 1968), p. 1.
8 S.B. Khan, with the assistance of Martin Herbert, *Validation Studies of the Ontario Tests for Admission to College and University*, OACU Research Report No. 1 (Toronto: Department of Measurement and Evaluation, Ontario Institute for Studies in Education, 1967), p. 6.
9 S.B. Khan, Pat Ransom, and Martin Herbert, *Prediction of First-Year Achievement in Ontario Universities* (Toronto: Department of Measurement and Evaluation, Ontario Institute for Studies in Education, 1969).
10 *Ibid.*, p. 17.
11 Ontario Teachers' Federation, "A Submission to the Minister of Education re Grade 13," January 1967, p. 5. (Mimeographed.)
12 C.W. Perry, Executive Secretary, Ontario Secondary School Headmasters' Council, to V.R. D'Oyley, chairman, Department of Measurement and Evaluation, Ontario Institute for Studies in Education, 27 January 1969.
13 Service for Admission to College and University, *The SACU Guidance Manual, 1970 Test Administration*, p. 3.
14 *Ibid.*, p. 6.
15 H. Andrew Elliott, "The Validity of SACU Tests," *SACU Bul-*

letin, 2–1968 (Ottawa: Service for Admission to College and University).

CHAPTER 19

1 Richard S. Lambert, *School Broadcasting in Canada* (Toronto: University of Toronto Press, 1963), p. 82.

2 Canadian Teachers' Federation, Radio Research Project Committee, *Summary Report of a Survey of Radio in Canadian Schools* (Ottawa, July 1956), pp. 48–9.

3 Ontario, Department of Education, *Report of the Minister, 1954*, p. 16.

4 Ontario, Department of Education, Memorandum to School Officials re Ontario School Radio Broadcasts, 1965–66:4, 23 August 1965, H.E. Elborn, Assistant Deputy Minister.

5 Ontario, Legislative Assembly, *Debates*, 28th leg., 1st sess., 5 June 1968, p. 4003.

6 Canadian Teachers' Federation, *Summary Report of a Survey of Radio in Canadian Schools.*

7 J. Bascom St John, *Globe and Mail*, 4 December 1963.

8 *ETV Across Canada, 1964–65* (Metropolitan Educational Television Association of Toronto, 1965), p. 29.

9 *Ibid.*, p. 30.

10 *Ibid.*, p. 42.

11 A.F. Knowles, "A Brief Concerning the Establishment of a Community Educational Television Station to Serve the Metropolitan Toronto Area." (Toronto: META, 1962).

12 "Multi-channel ETV System Proposed for Metro Toronto," *School Progress*, XXXVIII, 4, April 1969, p. 53.

13 Blaik Kirby, "Educational TV: The Birth of a New Channel Is Only the Iceberg's Tip," *Globe and Mail*, 21 February 1970.

14 *ETV across Canada, 1964–65.*

15 "Educational Functions of the CBC, 1967–68."

16 Earl Rosen and Elizabeth Whelpdale, eds., *Educational Television Across Canada: The Development and State of ETV, 1968* (Metropolitan Educational Television Association of Toronto, 1969), preface.

17 Ontario, Legislative Assembly, *Debates*, 27th leg., 2nd sess., 28 April 1964, p. 2546.

18 Ontario, Department of Education, *Report of the Minister, 1964*, p. 15.

19 Ontario, Legislative Assembly, *Debates*, 27th leg., 3rd sess., 2 June 1965, p. 3584.

20 *White Paper on Broadcasting, 1966* (Ottawa: Queen's Printer, 1966), p. 13.

21 Ontario, Department of Education, Educational Television Branch, "Ontario Educational Television." (Mimeographed. [n.d.])

22 Ontario, Department of Education, "Submission Regarding Allocation and Use of the UHF Broadcasting Band," 25 October 1966, p. 1. (Mimeographed.)

23 *Ibid.*, p. 4.

24 Douglas Fisher and Harry Crowe, "How to Get ETV into the Air," *Telegram*, 3 August 1967.

25 Douglas Fisher and Harry

Crowe, "The Uneven Path of ETV," *Telegram*, 25 April 1967.

26 House of Commons, *Debates*, 16 Eliz. 2, 27th parliament, 2nd sess., 17 October 1967, p. 3174.

27 "Educational Broadcasting: Outline of Some Points for Possible Federal Legislation," Submission to the Standing Committee on Broadcasting, Films and Assistance to the Arts, 8 February 1968, p. 1.

28 Ontario, Legislative Assembly, *Debates*, 28th leg., 1st sess., 26 February 1968, p. 204.

29 House of Commons, *Debates*, 17 Eliz. 2, 28th parliament, 1st sess., 24 October 1968, p. 1968.

30 Robert Webb, "Current Obstacles to ETV Development in Canada," *School Administration*, October 1968, pp. 22–3.

31 Ross H. Munro, "The Fuzzy Educational TV Picture," *Globe and Mail*, 25 January 1969.

32 William G. Davis, Address to the Canadian Radio-Television Commission, Ottawa, 25 November 1969, p. 11.

33 Ontario, Legislative Assembly, *Debates*, 27th leg., 5th sess., 17 May 1967, p. 3538.

34 "Television Takes to Wheels to Get Feedback from Teachers," *School Progress*, XXXVII, 4, April 1968, pp. 44–5.

35 Ontario, Department of Education, Memorandum to School Officials re Educational Television Programs for the School Year 1966–67, 1965–66:79, 9 June 1966, H.E. Elborn, Assistant Deputy Minister.

36 Multi-Media Project Committee, "Evaluation Report on the Multi-Media Project on The Thirties: Age of the Great Depression," p. 8. (Mimeographed.)

37 Ontario, Legislative Assembly, *Debates*, 28th leg., 1st sess., 6 June 1968, p. 4047.

38 Ontario, Department of Education, Memorandum to School Officials re Technical Advice for Educational Television, 1966–67:32, 21 October 1966, G.L. Duffin, Assistant Deputy Minister.

39 Ontario, Legislative Assembly, *Debates*, 28th leg., 1st sess., 2 May 1968, p. 2421.

40 *Ibid.*, 27th leg., 3rd sess., 3 June 1965, p. 3613.

41 *Ibid.*, p. 3632.

42 *Ibid.*, 28th leg., 1st sess., 26 February 1968, p. 205.

43 Earl Rosen, ed., *Educational Television, Canada: The Development and State of ETV, 1966* (Toronto: Burns & MacEachern, 1967), pp. 79–80.

44 Scott Young, "Why the Power of Television Should Not Be Controlled by a Politician," *Globe and Mail*, 5 October 1967.

45 *Telegram*, 7 October 1967.

46 Ontario, Report of the Provincial Committee on Aims and Objectives of Education in the Schools of Ontario, *Living and Learning* (Toronto: Newton Publishing, 1968), p. 160.

47 Ontario, Legislative Assembly, *Debates*, 28th leg., 3rd sess., 19 March 1970, p. 845.

48 Patrick Scott, "The Com-

mercial Networks are More Educational than ETV," *Toronto Daily Star*, 19 November 1968.

49 *Pattern for Professionalism*, Report of the O.T.F. Commission to the Board of Governors of the Ontario Teachers' Federation, August 1968, p. A.18.

50 Dixon to Good, 5 December 1968.

51 Ontario, Legislative Assembly, *Debates*, 28th leg., 2nd sess., 17 December 1968, p. 817.

52 *Living and Learning*, p. 159.

53 Rosen and Whelpdale, eds., *Educational Television across Canada*, pp. 51–2.

54 University of Toronto, *President's Report for the Year Ended June 30, 1967* (Toronto: University of Toronto Press, 1968), p. 182.

55 University of Western Ontario, *The President's Report for the Year Ending June 30, 1967*, Report of the Dean of the Faculty of Dentistry, p. 88.

56 University of Windsor, *Report of the President for the Academic Year of 1966–1967*, p. iii.

57 Rosen and Whelpdale, eds., *Educational Television across Canada*, p. 55.

CHAPTER 20

1 Frank MacKinnon, *Relevance and Responsibility in Education*, Quance Lectures in Canadian Education, 1968 (Toronto: W.J. Gage, 1968), pp. 47–8.

2 J. Bascom St John, *Globe and Mail*, 8 April 1963.

3 Honora M. Cochrane, ed., *Centennial Story: The Board of Education for the City of Toronto, 1850–1950* (Toronto: Thomas Nelson & Sons, 1950), p. 29.

4 J. Bascom St John, *Globe and Mail*, 9 April 1963.

5 Francis R. St John Library Consultants, *A Survey of Libraries in the Province of Ontario, 1965* (Toronto: Ontario Library Association through the co-operation of the Ontario Department of Education, 1965), pp. 31–2.

6 W.A. Roedde, *Public Libraries in Ontario* (Toronto: Ontario Department of Education), p. 1.

7 W. Stewart Wallace, *Report on Provincial Library Service in Ontario* (Toronto: Ontario Department of Education, 1957), p. 38.

8 Ontario Library Association, Brief on Libraries in Ontario presented to the Royal Commission on Education, *Report on Provincial Library Service in Ontario* (Toronto: Ontario Department of Education, 1957), appendix B, p. 39.

9 *Ibid.*

10 *Ibid.*, p. 40.

11 *Ibid.*, pp. 41–6.

12 Wallace, *Report on Provincial Library Service in Ontario*, p. 7.

13 *Ibid.*, p. 8.

14 *Ibid.*, p. 26.

15 *Ibid.*, pp. 15–16.

16 *Ibid.*, Recommendations Made by the Director of Public Library Service.

17 *Ibid.*, p. 17.

18 J. Bascom St John, "How to Get Better Libraries," *Globe and Mail*, 10 April 1962.

19 *Ibid.*
20 H.C. Campbell, *Canadian Libraries* (Hamden, Connecticut: Clive Bingley, 1969), p. 13.
21 Roedde, *Public Libraries in Ontario*, p. 2.
22 *Ibid.*, pp. 2–3.
23 Francis R. St John Library Consultants, *Survey of Libraries in the Province of Ontario, 1965*, p. 20.
24 *Ibid.*, p. 22.
25 *Ibid.*, pp. 22–3.
26 *Ibid.*, pp. 33–4.
27 *Ibid.*, p. 37.
28 *Ibid.*, p. 39.
29 *Ibid.*, pp. 52–3.
30 *Ibid.*, p. 57.
31 *Ibid.*, pp. 58–9.
32 *Ibid.*, p. 97.
33 *Statutes of Ontario*, 14–15 Eliz., 2, 1966, "The Public Libraries Act, 1966," chap. 128.
34 Ontario Library Association, "A Brief Presented to the Honourable John P. Robarts, Prime Minister of the Province of Ontario with Respect to the Report of the Ontario Committee on Taxation," 1967.
35 K.G. Booth to William G. Davis, 19 December 1968.
36 Francis R. St John Library Consultants, *Survey of Libraries in the Province of Ontario, 1965*, p. 98.
37 Ontario, Legislative Assembly, *Debates*, 27th leg., 5th sess., 29 May 1967, p. 3941.
38 *Ibid.*, p. 3942.
39 *Ibid.*, 28th leg., 1st sess., 6 June 1968, p. 4085.
40 *Ibid.*, 27th leg., 2nd sess., 30 April 1964, p. 2676.
41 Ida Reddy, "The School-housed Public Library: An Evaluation," *Ontario Library Review*, June 1968.
42 *Ibid.*
43 Ontario, Provincial Committee on Aims and Objectives of Education in the Schools of Ontario, *Living and Learning* (Toronto: Newton Publishing, 1968), p. 183.
44 Charles Deane Kent, "Ryerson Cake with Dewey Icing: Some Reflections on *Living and Learning*: The Report of the Provincial Committee on Aims and Objectives of Education in the Schools of Ontario (The Hall-Dennis Report)," Occasional Paper No. 8, London Public Library and Art Museum (London, Ontario, 1969). (Mimeographed.)
45 *Ibid.*, foreword.
46 *Ibid.*, p. 1.
47 *Ibid.*, p. 8.
48 *Ibid.*, pp. 12–13.
49 *Ibid.*, p. 22.
50 Ontario, Legislative Assembly, *Debates*, 28th leg., 2nd sess., 1 May 1969, p. 3826.
51 Susan Anderson, "The Lesson on Libraries in the Hall-Dennis Report," *Globe and Mail*, 8 July 1968.
52 Barrie Zwicker, "Are Ontario's Educators Schooled in Public Information Services?" *Globe and Mail*, 8 July 1968.
53 John R. Adams, ed., *CORL Courier*, II, 2, January 1969, p. 1.
54 J.R. Kidd, *18 to 80: Continuing Education in Metropolitan Toronto*. Report of an Enquiry Concerning the Education of

Adults in Metropolitan Toronto (Toronto: Board of Education for the City of Toronto, 1961), pp. 52–4.
55 R.R. Shaw, *Libraries of Metropolitan Toronto: A Study of Library Service* (Toronto, 1960).
56 *Statutes of Ontario*, 14–15 Eliz. 2, 1966, "An Act to Amend the Municipality of Metropolitan Toronto Act," chap. 96.
57 Campbell, *Canadian Libraries*.

CHAPTER 21

1 University of Toronto, *President's Report for the Year Ended June 1963* (Toronto: University of Toronto Press, 1964), p. 10.
2 *Ibid.*, pp. 9–10.
3 *Ibid.*, p. 11.
4 University of Toronto, *President's Report for the Year Ended June 1967* (Toronto: University of Toronto Press, 1968), p. 253.
5 "ROM Goes Back to the Public," *Telegram*, 13 June 1968.
6 *ROM Annual Report (18), July 1967–June 1968* (Toronto: University of Toronto Press, 1968), p. 48.
7 University of Toronto, *President's Report for the Year Ended June 1958* (Toronto: University of Toronto Press, 1959), p. 87.
8 University of Toronto, *President's Report for the Year Ended June 1960* (Toronto: University of Toronto Press, 1960), p. 108.
9 University of Toronto, *President's Report for the Year Ended June 1961* (Toronto: University of Toronto Press, 1961), p. 121.
10 *Ibid.*, p. 122.
11 *ROM 19th Annual Report, July 1968–June 1969* (Toronto: Hunter Rose, 1970), p. 42.
12 *Ibid.*
13 Ontario, Legislative Assembly, *Debates*, 27th leg., 2nd sess., 28 April 1964, p. 2546.
14 *Ibid.*, 4th sess., 10 March 1966, p. 1411.
15 Ontario, Department of Education, Memorandum to all Superintendents, Assistant Superintendents, Inspectors of Schools, and Principals of Teachers' Colleges re the Ontario Centennial Project, 22 September 1964.
16 Ontario, Legislative Assembly, *Debates*, 27th leg., 3rd sess., 2 June 1965, p. 3578.
17 *Ibid.*, 4th sess., 10 March 1966, pp. 1411–12.
18 *Ibid.*, 15 March 1966, p. 1545.
19 Douglas A. Penny, *Science Centre of Ontario: Outline of Exhibits* (Don Mills: Centennial Centre of Science and Technology, 1969).
20 Arthur Lismer, *Education Through Art for Children and Adults at the Art Gallery of Toronto* (Art Gallery of Toronto, 1936), p. 7.
21 *Ibid.*, p. 8.
22 *Ibid.*, p. 15.
23 *Ibid.*, p. 20.
24 Ontario, Legislative Assembly, *Debates*, 27th leg., 2nd sess., 28 April 1964, p. 2545.

Contents of volumes in
ONTARIO'S EDUCATIVE SOCIETY

General index

Index of persons

www.ingramcontent.com/pod-product-compliance
Lightning Source LLC
LaVergne TN
LVHW090757070826
844660LV00022B/1005

* 9 7 8 1 4 8 7 5 9 8 6 4 8 *